Communication

Principles for a Lifetime

Sixth Edition

Steven A. Beebe
Texas State University

Susan J. Beebe
Texas State University

Diana K. Ivy
Texas A&M University–Corpus Christi

PEARSON

Boston Columbus Indianapolis New York San Francisco Amsterdam Cape Town Dubai
London Madrid Milan Munich Paris Montreal Toronto Delhi
Mexico City São Paulo Sydney Hong Kong Seoul Singapore Taipei Tokyo

Publisher, Communication: Karon Bowers
Director of Development: Sharon Geary
Editorial Assistant: Kieran Fleming
Senior Field Marketing Manager: Blair Zoe Tuckman
Product Marketing Manager: Becky Rowland
Senior Managing Editor: Linda Behrens
Procurement Manager: Mary Fischer
Senior Procurement Specialist: Mary Ann Gloriande
Program Manager: Anne Ricigliano
Project Manager: Maria Piper
Associate Creative Director: Blair Brown
Senior Art Director: Maria Lange
Cover Design: Pentagram
Cover Illustration: successo images/Shutterstock
Digital Media Specialist: Sean Silver
Full-Service Project Management and Composition: Cenveo® Publisher Services
Printer/Binder: Courier/Kendallville
Cover Printer: Courier/Kendallville

Acknowledgments of third party content appear on page 431, which constitute an extension of this copyright page

Library of Congress Cataloging-in-Publication Data

Beebe, Steven A., Date-
Communication : principles for a lifetime / Steven A. Beebe, Texas State University, Susan J. Beebe, Texas State University, Diana K. Ivy, Texas A&M University Corpus Christi. -- Sixth Edition.
pages cm
ISBN 978-0-13-375382-0
1. Communication. I. Beebe, Susan J. II. Ivy, Diana K. III. Title.
HM1206.B44 2015
302.2--dc23

2015000019

Student Edition:
ISBN 10: 0-13-375382-4
ISBN 13: 978-0-13-375382-0

Books à la Carte:
ISBN 10: 0-13-388248-9
ISBN 13: 978-0-13-388248-3

For our teachers . . . and our students

Brief Contents

Contents

UNIT III COMMUNICATING IN GROUPS AND TEAMS

UNIT IV PUBLIC SPEAKING

Preface

Communication is essential for life. The purpose of this book is to document this claim by presenting fundamental principles of human communication that enhance the quality of our communication with others as well as the quality of our own lives. Most students who read this book will take only one course in communication during their entire college career. We want students to view this course on communication as a vital, life-enriching one that will help them enhance their communication with others—not just as another course in a string of curricular requirements. Because communication is an essential element of living, we want students to remember essential communication principles and skills for the rest of their lives. To remember and apply these essential communication principles, we believe students need a digest of classic and contemporary research and practice that will help them with both the mundane and the magnificent, the everyday and the ever-important communication experiences that constitute the fabric of their lives.

In this edition, as in the five that preceded it, we strive to create a highly appealing, easy-to-use text that is more effective than ever in helping students understand and use five vital principles of communication.

What's New to the Sixth Edition?

REVEL™

Educational technology designed for the way today's students read, think, and learn

When students are engaged deeply, they learn more effectively and perform better in their courses. This simple fact inspired the creation of REVEL: an immersive learning experience designed for the way today's students read, think, and learn. Built in collaboration with educators and students nationwide, REVEL is the newest, fully digital way to deliver respected Pearson content.

REVEL enlivens course content with media interactives and assessments — integrated directly within the authors' narrative — that provide opportunities for students to read about and practice course material in tandem. This immersive educational technology boosts student engagement, which leads to better understanding of concepts and improved performance throughout the course.

Learn more about REVEL
http://www.pearsonhighered.com/revel/

Rather than simply offering opportunities to read about and study communication, REVEL facilitates deep, engaging interactions with the concepts that matter most. For example, as they are introduced to the concept of communication competence in Chapter 1, students are prompted to complete a self-assessment of their own self-perceived communication competence. By providing opportunities to read about and practice communication concepts and techniques in tandem, REVEL engages students directly and immediately, which leads to a better understanding of course material. A wealth of student and instructor resources and interactive materials can be found within REVEL. Some of our favorites include:

- **Audio Examples**
  Students can listen to audio recordings of interpersonal conversations, typical and useful phrases for group discussions, and public speech excerpts while they read, bringing examples and communication tips to life in a way that a printed text cannot.
- **Videos & Video Quizzes**
  Video examples of sample speeches, interpersonal role plays, expert advice, and more throughout the narrative boost mastery, and many videos are bundled with correlating self-checks, enabling students to test their knowledge.
- **Animated Figures**
  Animations show processes in action and provide active visualizations of the relationships among components in models in a way that makes whole concepts suddenly easier to understand and lastingly easier to remember than textual descriptions can.
- **Integrated Writing Opportunities**
  To help students connect chapter content with personal meaning, each chapter offers two varieties of writing prompts: the journal prompt, eliciting free-form topic-specific responses addressing topics at the module level, and the shared writing prompt, which encourages students to share and respond to each other's brief response to high-interest topics in the chapter.

For more information about all of the tools and resources in REVEL and access to your own REVEL account for the *Communication: Principles for a Lifetime*, Sixth Edition, go to www.pearsonhighered.com/REVEL

Reviewers, instructors, and our students have given us feedback about the five previous editions. This feedback has helped us make this new edition the best possible teaching and learning resource. We listened and responded (Principle Four) to their suggestions. Our commitment to providing a digest of essentials that does not overwhelm students has also led us to make some changes. One immediate change you'll see in this edition is a fresh new design with many new photos and cartoons to help draw today's visually oriented learners into the text.

We have also included the following new features in *every* chapter:

- Updated *Learning Objectives* appear at the start of each chapter to provide student with advance organizers and reading goals for approaching the chapter. New in this edition, objectives reappear at key points in the chapter to help students gauge their progress and monitor their learning.
- An updated chapter-end Study Guide reviews the learning objectives and key terms, helping students master chapter content, prepare for exams, and apply chapter concepts to their own lives.
- Significantly updated and expanded research incorporates the latest research findings about human communication principles and skills.
- Fresh, contemporary examples and illustrations to which students can relate.
- New cartoons and other illustrations to amplify the content of our message.

We've also updated popular continuing features that appear throughout the book, including these:

- Revised "Communication & Diversity" features complement and expand discussions of new applications of research about diversity throughout the book.
- Revised "Communication & Technology" features include an expanded discussion of the role of online communication in relationships.
- Revised "Communication & Ethics" features reinforce the importance of being an ethical communicator and may spark discussion of ethical questions.
- Revised "Developing Your Speech Step by Step" features in the public speaking chapters walk students through the process of designing and delivering a speech.
- Two new speeches in Appendix B model best practices in public speaking.

We've made many other specific changes to chapter content throughout the book. Here's a brief list of selected major revisions, changes, and additions that we've made to specific chapters:

Chapter 1: Foundations of Human Communication

- Revised and streamlined chapter organization quickly introduces students to key concepts.
- Updated coverage summarizes recent research on the global value of communication skills, and online communication topics, including social media use and the potential for deceit.

Chapter 2: Self-Awareness and Communication

- New examples, and discussions of new research on topics such as the effects of difficult job searches on self-esteem of recent college graduates, engage students in the chapter.
- Revised "Communication & Technology" feature explores the relationship between Facebook and self-esteem, and new research in the "Communication & Ethics" feature discusses Facebook and narcissism.
- Updated and new coverage summarizes research on the development of self-concept, gender differences and media influences on self-esteem development, and the self-esteem benefits of honest relationships.

Chapter 3: Understanding Verbal Messages

- New "Communication & Technology" feature discusses the communication implications when our words are changed by autocorrect features on mobile devices.
- New "Communication & Diversity" feature updates readers on expanded language options to identify genders.
- New discussion of humblebrags raises awareness and engages readers' interest.

Chapter 4: Understanding Nonverbal Messages

- New "Communication & Ethics" feature contemplates the ethics of intentionally seeking interactive synchrony or mimicry of nonverbal communication.
- Engaging new "Communication & Diversity" feature explores how nonverbal communication and cultural sensitivity contribute to the success of Olympic games.
- New "Communication & Technology" feature emphasizes the risks of texting or talking on a mobile device while walking.
- New examples throughout the chapter and discussions of trends such as the popularity of using "second screen" technology maintain students' interest while enhancing understanding.

Chapter 5: Listening and Responding

- Updated discussions summarize new research on people's preference for talking with good listeners, the importance of listening in medical careers and in group communication, cultural differences in listening and responding, listening styles, gender and listening, increases in listening instruction, characteristics of good listeners, the importance of motivation in listening, and paraphrasing when responding.
- New tables summarize advice for providing social support in an easier to read and understand format.

Chapter 6: Adapting to Others: Diversity and Communication

- Updated discussion of gender identities and sexual orientations raises students' awareness.
- Chapter summarizes newest diversity statistics, as well as new research on millennial generation, globalization, the importance of studying culture, using social media to adapt to new cultures, individualistic and collectivistic cultures, culture and worldview, and adaption of communication.

Chapter 7: Understanding Interpersonal Communication

- New "Communication & Diversity" feature explores research on friendships between straight women and gay men.
- New "Communication & Technology" feature debates the implications of Invisible Boyfriend and Invisible Girlfriend, online services that help users deceive people into believing the users are in a romantic relationship.
- New "Communication & Ethics" feature considers the ethics of uncensored honesty or blurting out unfiltered opinions or responses to others' messages.

Chapter 8: Enhancing Relationships

- New section of the chapter offers research-based advice for relationship breakups, and discusses on-again/off-again relationships and continued friendship after a romantic breakup.
- New "Communication & Technology" feature discusses the role of video chat technology in maintaining relationships.
- Updated coverage summarizes recent research on family relationships, development of friendships, workplace relationships, cyberinfidelity, relational dialectic theory, and conflict.

Chapter 9: Understanding Group and Team Performance

- Updated coverage summarizes recent research on virtual groups, roles of group members, communication patterns in groups, power, stages of group development, group cohesion, and conflict in groups.
- Streamlined discussion of types of groups and teams allows students to focus on learning about the nature, development, interaction and leadership of groups and teams.

Chapter 10: Enhancing Group and Team Performance

- New "Communication & Ethics" feature encourages students to develop their own potential solutions to the common group problem of a member who judges others' ideas during brainstorming sessions.
- Updated coverage summarizes recent research on sharing information in virtual and in-person groups, competent group member behaviour, creativity in group problem solving, avoiding groupthink, leadership, and effective meetings.

Chapter 11: Developing Your Speech

- Updated coverage summarizes recent research on public speaking anxiety.
- Two new figures help students visualize processes involved in selecting a speech topic.
- A new student speech for the "Developing Your Presentation Step by Step" feature focuses on the effects of poverty on the brain, a topic of current interest.
- New advice throughout the chapter helps students prepare speeches to be delivered online or via video.
- Updated examples throughout the chapter model exemplary speeches and help students relate to chapter material.

Chapter 12: Organizing and Outlining Your Speech

- New sample preparation outline and speaking notes provide continuity by showing the development of the same speech in the "Developing Your Presentation Step by Step" feature.
- Updated examples from both student presentations and some of the most acclaimed presentations of the day model techniques students can apply in their own presentations.

Chapter 13: Delivering Your Speech

- New tables offer practical, usable advice for manuscript, memorized, impromptu and extemporaneous speaking in an easy-to-access and review format.
- New and updated figures help today's visual learners understand effective language and presentation aids for speeches.
- Many new examples throughout the chapter model techniques used by exemplary speechmakers.

Chapter 14: Speaking to Inform

- New figure provides a visual advance organizer to help students understand the process of teaching new information.
- Techniques of informative speaking are modeled in the chapter construction and via many well-chosen new examples.
- A new sample informative speech is annotated to model for students how one student speaker effectively used techniques discussed in the chapter.

Chapter 15: Speaking to Persuade

- Streamlined chapter organization and coverage more efficiently introduces students to key concepts of persuasive speaking.
- New figures provide easily accessible practical advice on using fear appeals and on establishing initial, derived, and terminal credibility.
- New figures provide approachable visual reviews of propositions of fact, value, and policy and steps of Monroe's motivated sequence organization for persuasive speaking.
- Carefully chosen new examples throughout the chapter model techniques of persuasive speaking.
- A new sample persuasive speech is annotated to model for students how one student speaker effectively used techniques discussed in the chapter.

Appendix A: Interviewing

- New material on electronic submission of resumes and portfolios reflects current practice.

Appendix B: Sample Speeches for Discussion and Evaluation

- New sample informative and persuasive speeches showcase presentation techniques discussed in Chapters 11–15.

What Stays the Same in This Edition?

In our sixth edition of *Communication: Principles for a Lifetime,* our goal remains the same as in the first edition: to provide a cogent presentation of what is essential about human communication by organizing the study of communication around five fundamental communication principles that are inherent in the process of communicating with others.

Our Integrated Approach Remains Unchanged

To help students remember and integrate essential communication principles, we've organized the study of human communication around five fundamental communication principles:

Principle One: Be aware of your communication with yourself and others.

Principle Two: Effectively use and interpret verbal messages.

Principle Three: Effectively use and interpret nonverbal messages.

Principle Four: Listen and respond thoughtfully to others.

Principle Five: Appropriately adapt messages to others.

We don't claim that everything you need to know about communication is embedded in our five communication principles. These principles do, however, synthesize essential research and wisdom about communication. They are designed to help students in an introductory communication course see the "big picture" of the role and importance of communication, both as they sit in the classroom and as they live their lives.

The problem with many introduction to communication courses is there is often too much of a good thing. An introductory course covers a vast terrain of communication concepts, principles, and skills. Besides learning about several theories of communication, students are also presented with what may appear to them to be miniature courses in interpersonal communication, group communication, and public speaking. At the end of a typical hybrid or introductory communication fundamentals course, both students and instructors have made a breathless dash through an astounding amount of information and number of skills. The barrage of ideas, contexts, and theories can leave students and instructors feeling overwhelmed by a seemingly unrelated hodgepodge of information. Students may end up viewing communication as a fragmented area of study that includes a bushel basket full of concepts and applications, but have little understanding of what is truly fundamental about how we make sense out of the world and share that sense with others. Rather than seeing communication as a crazy quilt of unrelated ideas and skills, we want students to see a unified fabric of common principles that they will remember long after the course is over. The five fundamental principles provide a framework for understanding the importance of communication in our lives.

Our pentagon model illustrates the relationships among the five communication principles that are the overarching structure of the book. As a principle is being introduced or discussed, the appropriate part of the model is highlighted. In most texts, communication principles are typically presented in the first third of the book and then abandoned, as material about interpersonal, group, and public communication is presented. We don't use a "hit-and-run" approach. Instead, using examples and illustrations to which students can relate, we carefully discuss each principle early in the book. Through-

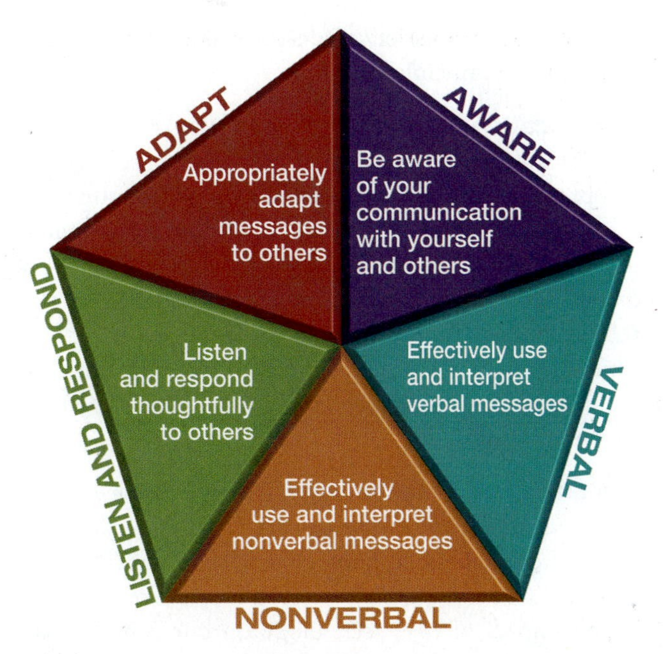

Communication Principles for a Lifetime

out the latter two-thirds of the book we gently remind students of how these principles relate to interpersonal relationships, group and team discussions, and public presentations.

We link the five communication principles with specific content by using a margin icon to indicate that a discussion in the text of a skill, concept, or idea is related to one or more of the five communication principles. The icons, described in Chapter 1 and illustrated here, first appear in the margin in Chapter 7, "Understanding Interpersonal Communication," which is the first context chapter of the book. The icons help students see the many applications our five communication principles have to their lives as they read about interpersonal communication, group and team communication, and presentational speaking.

A subtext for these five principles is the importance of communicating ethically with others. Throughout the book we invite students to consider the ethical implications of how they communicate with others, through the use of probes and questions. As we discuss in Chapter 1, we believe that in order to be effective, a communication message must achieve three goals: (1) it must be understood; (2) it must achieve its intended effect; and (3) it must be ethical. Our five Communication Principles for a Lifetime are designed to help students achieve these three goals.

The Successful Structure of the Book Stays the Same

This sixth edition retains the overall structure of the five previous editions and is organized into four units. Unit I introduces the five principles (Chapter 1), and then each principle is explained in a separate chapter (Chapters 2 through 6). Each communication principle is discussed and illustrated to help students see its value and centrality in their lives. Chapter 2 discusses the principle of being self-aware. Chapter 3 focuses on using and interpreting verbal messages, and Chapter 4 focuses on using and interpreting nonverbal messages. Chapter 5 includes a discussion of the interrelated processes of listening and responding, giving special attention to the importance of being other-oriented and empathic. The final principle, appropriately adapting to others, is presented in Chapter 6; we use this principle to illustrate the importance of adapting one's behavior to culture and gender differences among people.

Unit II applies the five communication principles to interpersonal relationships. Unlike many treatments of interpersonal communication, our discussion links the concepts and strategies for understanding interpersonal communication with our five Communication Principles for a Lifetime. Chapter 7 presents information to help students better understand the nature and function of communication in relationships. Chapter 8 identifies strategies that can enhance the quality of interpersonal relationships with others.

Unit III discusses how the five communication principles can help students understand and enhance communication in small groups and teams. Chapter 9 explains how groups and teams work. We offer practical strategies for collaboratively solving problems, leading groups and teams, and running and participating in meetings in Chapter 10.

Finally, Unit IV presents classic content to help students design and deliver a speech, referring to contemporary research and using the latest tools of technology. Based on our popular audience-centered approach to developing a speech, we emphasize the importance of adapting to listeners while also being an ethically vigilant communicator. Chapters 11 through 15 offer information and tips for developing speech ideas, organizing and outlining speeches, delivering a speech (including using presentational and multimedia aids), crafting effective informative speeches, and developing ethical persuasive messages.

We conclude the book with two appendixes designed to supplement our instruction about communication fundamentals. Appendix A includes practical strategies for being interviewed and for interviewing others. We relate our discussion of interviewing to the five Communication Principles for a Lifetime. Appendix B includes examples of recent presentations to illustrate what effective, well-planned speeches look like.

Our Partnership with Students to Help Them Learn Stays the Same

A textbook is essentially a "distance learning" tool. As we write each chapter, we are separated from the learner by both time and space. To help lessen the distance between author and reader, we've incorporated a variety of learning resources and pedagogical features to engage students in the learning process. This engagement is heightened significantly in REVEL, but you'll also find many features designed to engage students in the traditional print text as well. As we note in the text, information alone is not communication. Communication occurs when the receiver of information responds to it. Our special features help turn information into a responsive communication message that has an effect on students' lives.

Principles Model and Icons Our pentagon model and margin icons help students see connections between the various communication concepts and skills we present. Throughout the text we provide an integrated framework to reinforce what's fundamental about human communication. Long after students may have forgotten the lists they memorized for an exam, we want them to remember the five fundamental principles we highlight throughout the book. Remembering these principles can also help them remember strategies and concepts to enhance their interpersonal relationships, improve group and team meetings, and design and deliver effective presentations.

Chapter-End Summary of Communication Principles for a Lifetime In addition to using the margin icons to highlight material in the text related to one or more communication principles, we conclude each chapter with a summary of the chapter content organized around the communication principles. Our chapter summaries at the ends of the first six chapters distill essential information about the specific communication principle presented in the chapter. Starting in Chapter 7, we review and summarize the chapter content using all five Communication Principles for a Lifetime as a framework. Miniature versions of our principles icons appear with headings to highlight the five fundamental principles. The purpose of this chapter-end feature is to help students synthesize the material related to the context discussed (e.g., interpersonal communication) and the five principles that undergird the descriptive and prescriptive information presented in the chapter. This feature will help students connect the variety of ideas and skills with the five communication principles.

Communication & Ethics To help students consider the ethical dimensions of human communication, in each chapter we provide a special boxed feature called "Communication & Ethics." Students are asked to consider a case study or to ponder their responses to questions of ethics. The cases and questions we pose are designed to be thought-provoking, to spark insightful class discussion, or to be used in combination with a journal assignment or other learning method to help students see connections between ethics and communication.

Communication & Technology Because of the importance of technology in our lives, in each chapter we include special material about technology and communication to help students become sensitive to the sometimes mind-boggling impact of new technology on our communication with others. We also discuss the importance and role of technology in several chapters throughout the book. The prevalence of technology in students' lives offers powerful teachable moments to help students learn and apply communication principles.

Communication & Diversity Each chapter includes a "Communication & Diversity" feature designed to help students see the importance of diversity in their lives. Yet we don't relegate discussions of diversity only to a boxed feature. Because we believe diversity is such an important communication topic in contemporary society, we discuss diversity in the text, not only in relation to our fifth principle of communication (appropriately adapt messages to others) in Chapter 6, but throughout the book.

Comprehensive Pedagogical Learning Tools To help students master the material, we've built in a wealth of study aids:

- Learning objectives provide a compass to help students know where they are headed, which they can check at key points throughout each chapter.
- Chapter outlines preview key concepts.
- Concise and highly praised Recap boxes distill essential content.
- Key terms in boldface with marginal glossary help students master essential terms.
- Chapter-end Study Guides offer narrative summaries and key terms lists.
- The Principle Points, chapter-end summaries of the five Communication Principles, recap applications of the principles to students' real-life communication.
- Chapter-end Apply Your Skill questions guide students to think critically about how they can apply chapter concepts to their lives and relationships.

- Many chapter-end skills assessment and collaborative learning activities have been revised and updated for this edition.

Our Partnership with Instructors Stays Strong

As authors, we view our job as providing resources that instructors can use to bring communication principles and skills to life. A textbook is only one tool to help teachers teach and learners learn. As part of our partnership with instructors to facilitate learning, we offer an array of print and electronic resources to help teachers do what they do best: teach. In addition to the vast array of learning resources we've built into the text, we offer a dazzling package of additional resources to help instructors generate both intellectual and emotional connections with their students.

Key instructor resources include an Instructor's Manual (ISBN 0-13-388244-6), TestBank, (ISBN 0-13-388237-3), and PowerPoint Presentation Package (ISBN 0-13-388241-1). These supplements are available at www.pearsonhighered.com/irc (instructor login required). MyTest online test-generating software (ISBN 0-13-388236-5) is available at www.pearsonmytest.com (instructor login required). For a complete list of the instructor and student resources available with the text, please visit the Pearson Communication catalog, at www.pearsonhighered.com/communication.

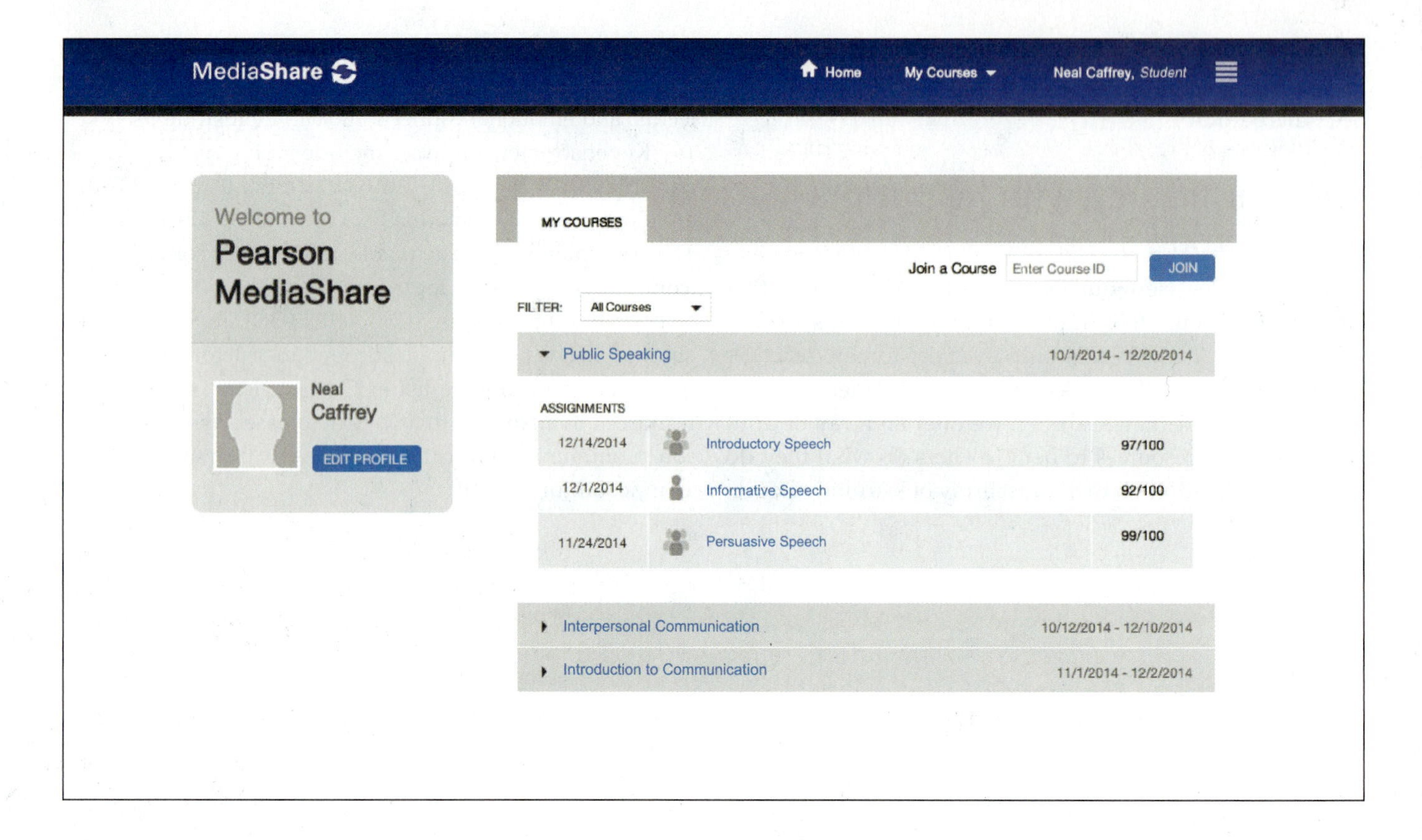

Pearson MediaShare

Pearson's comprehensive media upload tool allows students to post video, images, audio, or documents for instructor and peer viewing, time-stamped commenting, and assessment. MediaShare is an easy, mobile way for students and professors to interact and engage with speeches, presentation aids, group projects, and other files. MediaShare gives professors the tools to provide contextual feedback to demonstrate how students can improve their skills.

Structured like a social networking site, MediaShare helps promote a sense of community among students. In face-to-face and online course settings, MediaShare saves instructors valuable time and enriches the student learning experience by providing contextual feedback.

- Use MediaShare to assign or view speeches, outlines, presentation aids, video-based assignments, role plays, group projects, and more in a variety of formats, including video, Word, PowerPoint, and Excel.
- Assess students using customizable, Pearson-provided rubrics or create your own around classroom goals, learning outcomes, or department initiatives.
- Set up assignments for students with options for full-class viewing and commenting, private comments between you and the student, peer groups for reviewing, or as collaborative group assignments.
- Record video directly from a tablet, phone, or other webcam (including a batch upload option for instructors) and tag submissions to a specific student or assignment.
- Embed video from YouTube via assignments to incorporate current events into the classroom experience.
- Set up quiz questions on video assignments to ensure students master concepts and interact and engage with the media.
- Import grades into most learning management systems.
- Ensure a secure learning environment for instructors and students through robust privacy settings.
- Upload videos, comment on submissions, and grade directly from our new MediaShare app, available free from the iTunes store and GooglePlay; search for Pearson MediaShare.

Pearson MediaShare is available as a standalone product, as part of MyCommunicationLab, or in a package with REVEL.

Acknowledgments

Although our three names appear on the cover as authors of the book you are holding in your hands, in reality hundreds of people have been instrumental in making this book possible. Communication scholars who have dedicated their lives to researching the importance of communication principles, theories, and skills provide the fuel for this book. We thank each author we reference in our voluminous endnotes for the research conclusions that bring us to our contemporary understanding of communication principles. We thank our students who have trusted us to be their guides in a study of human communication. They continue to enrich our lives with their enthusiasm and curiosity. They have inspired us to be more creative by their honest quizzical looks and challenged us to go beyond "textbook" answers with their thought-provoking questions.

We are most appreciative of the outstanding editorial support we continue to receive from our colleagues and friends at Pearson. We thank Joe Opiela for helping us keep this project moving forward when we wondered if the world needed another communication book. Karon Bowers, Pearson Publisher, has continued to provide valued support and encouragement. Our exceptionally thoughtful and talented development editor, Sheralee Connors, helped us polish and prune our words and gave us a wealth of ideas and suggestions. We acknowledge and appreciate the ideas and suggestions from Mark Redmond, a valued friend, gifted teacher, and skilled writer at Iowa State University. His coauthorship with us on *Interpersonal Communication: Relating to Others* significantly influenced our ideas about communication, especially interpersonal communication.

We are grateful to the many educators who read the manuscript and both encouraged and challenged us. We thank the following people for drawing on their teaching skill, expertise, and vast experience to make this a much better book:

Reviewers of the First Edition: Michael Bruner, University of North Texas; Diana O. Cassagrande, West Chester University; Dan B. Curtis, Central Missouri State University; Terrence A. Doyle, Northern Virginia Community College; Julia F. Fennell, Community College of Allegheny County, South Campus; Phil Hoke, The University of Texas at San Antonio; Stephen Hunt, Illinois State University; Carol L. Hunter, Brookdale Community College; Dorothy W. Ige, Indiana University Northwest; A. Elizabeth Lindsey, The New Mexico State University; Robert E. Mild, Jr., Fairmont State College; Timothy P. Mottet, Texas State University–San Marcos; Alfred G. Mueller II, Pennsylvania State University, Mont Alto Campus; Kay Neal, University of Wisconsin–Oshkosh; Kathleen Perri, Valencia Community College; Beth M. Waggenspack, Virginia Tech University; Gretchen Aggert Weber, Horry-Georgetown Technical College; Kathy Werking, Eastern Kentucky University; Andrew F. Wood, San Jose State University

Reviewers of the Second Edition: Lawrence Albert, Morehead State University; Leonard Assante, Volunteer State Community College; Dennis Dufer, St. Louis Community College; Annette Folwell, University of Idaho; Mike Hemphill, University of Arkansas at Little Rock; Teri Higginbotham, University of Central Arkansas; Lawrence Hugenberg, Youngstown State University; Timothy P. Mottet, Texas State University–San Marcos; Penny O'Connor, University of Northern Iowa; Evelyn Plummer, Seton Hall University; Charlotte C. Toguchi, Kapi'olani Community College; Debra Sue Wyatt, South Texas Community College

Reviewers of the Third Edition: Dom Bongiorni, Kingwood College; Jo Anne Bryant, Troy University; Cherie Cannon, Miami–Dade College; Thomas Green, Cape Fear Community College; Gretchen Harries, Austin Community College; Xin-An Lu, Shippensburg University of Pennsylvania; Sara L. Nalley, Columbia College; Kristi Schaller, University of Hawaii; David Shuhy, Salisbury University; John Tapia, Missouri Western State College

Reviewers of the Fourth Edition: Ellen B. Bremen, Highline Community College; Patricia A. Cutspec, East Tennessee State University; Edgar D. Johnson III, Augusta State University; Peter S. Lee, California State University, Fullerton; Kelly Aikin Petcus, Austin Community College; Natalia Rybas, Bowling Green State University; Sarah Stout, Kellogg Community College

Reviewers of the Fifth Edition: Leonard Assante, Volunteer State Community College; Sandra Bein, South Suburban College; Robert Dixon, St. Louis Community College; Glynis Holm Strause, Coastal Bend College; Linda Kalfayan, Westchester Community College; Barbara Maxwell, Linn State Technical College; Kay Neal, University of Wisconsin Oshkosh; Jeff Pomeroy, Southwest Texas Junior College

Reviewers of the Sixth Edition: Kevin Clark, Austin Community College; Cynthia Brown El, Macomb Community College; Diane Ferrero-Paluzzi, Iona College; Gary Kuhn, Chemeketa Community College; Travice Obas, Georgia Highlands College; John Parrish, Tarrant County College; Daniel Paulnock, Saint Paul College; Shannon Proctor, Highline Community College; Kimberly Schaefer, Baker University; Katie Stevens, Austin Community College; Jayne Violette, Eastern Kentucky University.

We have each been influenced by colleagues, friends, and teachers who have offered support and inspiration for this project. Happily, colleagues, friends, and teachers are virtually indistinguishable for us. We are each blessed with people with whom we work who offer strong support.

Steve and Sue thank their colleagues at Texas State University for their insights and ideas that helped shape key concepts in this book. Cathy Fleuriet and Tom Burkholder, who served as basic course directors at Texas State, influenced our work. Tim Mottet, also a former basic course director at Texas State and now Provost at Northwest Missouri State University, is a valued, inspirational friend, coauthor, and colleague who is always there to listen and freely share his ideas and experience. Marian Houser, a former basic course director at Texas State, is a wonderful friend and provides important insight and support. Michael Burns, current basic course director at Texas State is a valued friend and continues to offer his generous support, as does Kristen LeBlanc Farris, Associate Director of Texas State's award-winning basic communication course. Long time friend Kosta Tovstiadi, University of Colorado, provided skilled research assistance to help us draw upon the most contemporary interpersonal communication research. Michael Hennessy, Patricia Margerison, and Daniel Lochman are Texas State English faculty who have been especially supportive of Sue's work. Finally, Steve thanks his skilled and dedicated administrative support team at Texas State. Administrative assistant Sue Hall, a cherished friend and colleague. Bob Hanna provided exceptional support and assistance for this project and many others.

Ivy is grateful to her students, colleagues, and friends at Texas A&M University–Corpus Christi, for their patience and unwavering support for her continued involvement in this book project. In particular, Dean Kelly Quintanilla and Chair Amy Aldridge Sanford constantly reaffirm the value of a well-written, carefully crafted book—one that speaks to students' lives. Their support of Ivy's research efforts, along with constant fueling from her wonderful students, always make this project a joy. Special thanks go to research assistant Roe Cantu, for her help with the sixth edition. Ivy's deepest thanks also go to Steve and Sue Beebe for their generosity in bringing her into this project, and for their extraordinary friendship.

Finally we express our appreciation to our families. Ivy thanks her ever-supportive sister Karen Black, and nephew, niece, and grandnieces Brian, Sumitra, Mackenzie, and Sidney Black. They have been constant and generous with their praise for her writing accomplishments. Ivy will always be especially grateful to her late parents, Carol and Herschel Ivy, for lovingly offering many lessons about living the highly ethical life.

Sue and Steve especially thank their parents, Herb and Jane Dye and Russell and Muriel Beebe, who taught them much about communication and ethics that truly are principles for a lifetime. They also thank their sons, Mark and Matthew Beebe, and their daughter-in-law, Brittany Beebe, for teaching them life lessons about giving and receiving love that will remain with them forever.

Steven A. Beebe and Susan J. Beebe

Diana K. Ivy

Communication

Principles for a Lifetime

Chapter 1
Identifying Foundations of Human Communication

There is no pleasure to me without communication. —MICHELE DE MONTAIGNE

Monkey Business Images/Shutterstock

Chapter Outline

- Why Study Communication?
- The Communication Process
- Communication Models
- Communication Competence
- Communication in the 21st Century
- Communication Contexts
- Communication Principles for a Lifetime
- Study Guide: Review, Apply, and Assess Your Knowledge and Skill

Chapter Objectives

After studying this chapter, you should be able to

1.1 Explain why it is important to study communication.

1.2 Define communication and describe five characteristics of the communication process.

1.3 Explain three communication models.

1.4 Describe three criteria that can be used to determine whether communication is competent.

1.5 Describe the nature of communication in the 21st century.

1.6 Identify and explain three communication contexts.

1.7 List and explain five fundamental principles of communication.

Like life-sustaining breath, communication is ever-present in our lives. That makes understanding and improving how we communicate with others a basic life skill.

Communication is an inescapable and fundamental aspect of being human. Consider the number of times you have purposefully communicated with someone today as you worked, ate, studied, shopped, or went about your daily duties. Most people spend between 80 and 90 percent of their waking hours communicating with others.[1] Even if you live in isolation from other people, you talk to yourself through your thoughts. It is through the process of communication that we convey who we are, both to ourselves and to others; it is our primary tool for making our way in the world.

In the course of our study of human communication, we will discuss myriad skills, ideas, concepts, and contexts. To help you stitch together the barrage of ideas and information, we will organize our study around five fundamental communication principles:

Principle One:	Be aware of your communication with yourself and others.
Principle Two:	Effectively use and interpret verbal messages.
Principle Three:	Effectively use and interpret nonverbal messages.
Principle Four:	Listen and respond thoughtfully to others.
Principle Five:	Appropriately adapt messages to others.

We don't claim that everything you need to know about communication is covered by these five principles. They do, however, summarize decades of research, as well as the wisdom of those who have taught communication over the years, about what constitutes effective and ethical communication.

Before we elaborate on the five fundamental communication principles, it is helpful in this first chapter to provide some background for our study of communication. We will discuss why it is important to study communication, define communication, examine various models of or perspectives on communication, and identify characteristics of human communication. Having offered this prelude, we will then discuss the five foundational principles of human communication that we will use throughout the book to help you organize the concepts, skills, and ideas we present in our discussion of interpersonal, group, and presentational speaking situations.

Why Study Communication?

1.1 Explain why it is important to study communication.

Why are you here? No, we don't mean "Why do you exist?" or "Why do you live where you do?" What we mean is "Why are you taking a college course about communication?" Perhaps the short answer is "It's required." Or maybe your advisor, parent, or friend encouraged you to take the course. But required or not, what can a systematic study of human communication do for you?

Communication touches every aspect of our lives. To be able to express yourself to other people is a basic requirement for living in a modern society. From a practical standpoint, it's very likely that you will make your living with your mind rather than your hands.[2] Even if you do physical labor, you will need communication skills to work with others. When you study communication, you are also developing leadership skills. "The art of communication," says author James Humes, "is the language of leadership."[3]

Although the value of being a competent communicator is virtually undisputed, there is evidence that many people struggle to express themselves clearly or to accurately understand messages from others. One study estimated that one-fifth of the students in the United States were not successful with even elementary communication tasks; in addition, more than 60 percent of the students could not give clear oral directions for someone else to follow.[4] When leaders in major corporations were asked to specify the most important skills for workers to have, 80 percent said listening was the most important work skill; 78 percent identified interpersonal communication skill as the next most important. However, the same leaders said only 28 percent of their employees had good listening skills and only 27 percent possessed effective interpersonal communication skills.[5] In support of these leaders' observations, another national study found that adults listen with 25 percent accuracy.[6] There is also evidence that the majority of adults are fearful of speaking in public and that about 20 percent of the population is highly apprehensive of presentational speaking.[7]

Aren't some people just born to be better communicators than others? If so, why should you work to develop your communication skill? Just as some people have more innate musical talent than others, there is evidence that some people may have an inborn biological ability to communicate with others.[8] This does not mean you should not work to develop your communication ability. Throughout the book, we will offer ample evidence that if you work to improve your skill, you will be rewarded by enjoying the benefits of enhanced communication competence. What are these benefits? Read on.

Warren Buffett, whose savvy investing has made him one of the richest people on the planet, agrees with many other leaders about the importance of communication skills at work. In one televised interview, Buffet declared, "If you improve your communication skills I guarantee you that you will earn 50 percent more money over your lifetime!"[10]
Rick Wilking/Reuters/Corbis

To Improve Your Employability

Regardless of your specific title or job description, the essence of what you do when working at any job is to communicate; you talk, listen, relate, read, and write. People who can communicate effectively with others are in high demand. As noted by John H. McConnell, CEO of Worthington Industries, "Take all the speech and communication courses you can because the world turns on communication."[9] McConnell's advice is supported by research as well as by personal observations.

Based on a survey of personnel managers—those people who are in charge of hiring you for a job—here's a ranking of the top factors in obtaining employment immediately after college:[11]

1. Oral communication (speaking) skills
2. Written communication skills
3. Listening ability
4. Enthusiasm
5. Technical competence
6. Work experience
7. Appearance
8. Poise
9. Resumé
10. Part-time or summer work experience

We're sure you know why we cited this survey. Communication skills were the number one *and* number two factors; note that listening ability was also highly valued. And this survey isn't the only one that reached the same conclusion; several other research studies have shown that communication skills are the most sought-after skills in the workplace.[12] Specifically, new research has found that communication skills, including interpersonal and teamwork skills, continue to be the most valued skills on the planet.[13]

To Improve Your Relationships

We don't choose our biological families, but we do choose our friends. For unmarried people, developing friendships and falling in love are the top-rated sources of satisfaction and happiness in life.[14] Conversely, losing a relationship is among life's most stressful events. Most people between the ages of 19 and 24 report that they have had from five to six romantic relationships and have been "in love" once or twice.[15] Understanding the role and function of communication can help unravel some of the mysteries of human relationships. At the heart of a good relationship is good communication.[16]

Virginia Satir, a pioneer in family enrichment, described family communication as "the largest single factor determining the kinds of relationships [we make] with others."[17] Learning principles and skills of communication can give us insight into why we relate to other family members as we do. Our early communication with our parents had a profound effect on our self-concept and self-worth. According to Satir, people are "made" in families. Our communication with family members has shaped how we interact with others today.

Many of us will spend as much or more time interacting with people in our places of work as we do at home. And although we choose our friends and lovers, we don't always have the same flexibility in choosing those with whom or for whom we work. Increasing our understanding of the role and importance of human communication with our colleagues can help us better manage stress on the job as well as enhance our work success.

To Improve Your Health

Life is stressful. Research has clearly documented that the lack or loss of close relationships can lead to ill health and even death. Having a social support system—good friends and supportive family members—seems to make a difference in our overall health and quality of life. Good friends and intimate relationships with others help us manage stress and contribute to both physical and emotional health. For example, physicians have noted that patients who are widowed or divorced experience more medical problems, such as heart disease, cancer, pneumonia, and diabetes, than do married people.[18] Grief-stricken spouses are more likely than others to die prematurely, especially around the time of the departed spouse's birthday or near their wedding anniversary.[19] Terminally ill patients with a limited number of friends or social support die sooner than those with stronger ties.[20] Without companions and

close friends, our opportunities for intimacy and stress-managing communication are diminished. Studying how to enrich the quality of our communication with others can make life more enjoyable and enhance our overall well-being. Because of Facebook and other social networking software, we are increasingly involved in relationships with others even when we are not interacting face to face. Relating to others, whether online or in person, occurs through communication.[21]

So again, we ask the question: Why are you here? We think the evidence is clear: People who are effective communicators are more likely to get the jobs they want; have better-quality relationships with friends, family, and colleagues; and even enjoy a healthier quality of life.

The Communication Process

1.2 Define communication and describe five characteristics of the communication process.

Communication is one of those words that seem so basic you may wonder why they need to be formally defined. Yet scholars who devote their lives to studying communication don't always agree on the definition of the term. One research team counted more than 126 published definitions.[22] In this section, we'll examine our definition of communication, the characteristics shared by all communication, major models that researchers and theorist have used to explain and study communication, and the three general contexts in which communication happens.

Communication Defined

In its broadest sense, **communication** is the process of acting on information.[23] Someone does or says something, and others think or do something in response to the action or the words as they understand them. Communication is not unique to humans; researchers study communication in other species, as well as between species. For example, you communicate with your pet dog if the dog sits in response to your spoken command, or if you respond to your dog's begging gaze by giving him a treat. However, the focus of this text is **human communication**, *the process of making sense out of the world and sharing that sense with others by creating meaning through the use of verbal and nonverbal messages.*[24] Let's look at the key components of this definition.

communication
The process of acting on information.

human communication
The process of making sense out of the world and sharing that sense with others by creating meaning through verbal and nonverbal messages.

- *Communication is about making sense.* We make sense out of what we experience when we begin to interpret what we see, hear, touch, smell, and taste with sensations, feelings, thoughts, and words. Identifying patterns and structure in what we experience is key to making sense out of what happens to us. Although we often think that "making sense out of something" means rationally and logically interpreting what we experience, we also make sense through intuition, feelings, and emotions.[25]
- *Communication is about sharing sense.* We share what we experience by expressing to others and to ourselves what we experience. We typically use words to express our thoughts, but we also use music, art, clothing, and a host of other means to convey what we are thinking and feeling to others.
- *Communication is about creating meaning.* As we will see again later in this chapter, it's more appropriate to say that meaning is *created* through communication rather than sent or transmitted. To say that we send or transmit messages is to imply that what we send is what is received. However, presenting information to others does not mean communication has occurred: "But I told you what to do!" "It's there in the memo. Why didn't you do what I asked?" "It's in the syllabus." These exasperated communicators assumed that if they sent a message, someone would receive it. However, communication does not operate in a simple, linear, what-you-send-is-what-is-received process. *Information is not communication.* In fact, what is expressed by one person is rarely interpreted by another person precisely as intended.
- *Communication is about verbal and nonverbal messages.* We communicate by using **symbols,** words, sounds, gestures, or visual images that represent thoughts, concepts, objects, or experiences. The words on this page are symbols you use to derive meaning that makes sense to you. Not all symbols are verbal; some are nonverbal. You use gestures, posture, facial expression, tone of voice, clothing, and jewelry to express ideas, attitudes, and feelings. Nonverbal messages primarily communicate emotions, such as our likes and dislikes, whether we're interested or uninterested, and our feelings of power or lack of power.

symbol
A word, sound, gesture, or visual image that represents a thought, concept, object, or experience.

Some scholars assert that *all* human behavior is really communication. When you cross your arms while listening to your friend describe her day, she may conclude that you're not interested in what she's talking about. But it could just be that you're chilly. While all human expression has the potential to communicate a message (someone may act or respond to the information they receive from you), it does not mean that you *intentionally* are expressing an idea or emotion. People don't always accurately interpret the messages we express—and this unprofound observation has profound implications.

Because of the ever-present potential for misunderstanding, communication should be *other-oriented*—it should acknowledge the perspective of others, not just that of the creator of the message. Communication that does not consider the needs, background, and culture of the receiver is more likely to be misunderstood than other-oriented communication. We'll emphasize the importance of considering others or considering your audience throughout the book. Knowing something about the experiences of the person or persons you're speaking to can help you communicate more effectively and appropriately.

Signs are usually carefully crafted examples of symbolic communication. What are the creators of this sign trying to communicate?
© Patrick Strattner/AGEfotostock

Communication Characteristics

The following characteristics are evident any time communication occurs: Communication is inescapable, irreversible, and complicated; it emphasizes content and relationships; and it is governed by rules.

COMMUNICATION IS INESCAPABLE Opportunities to communicate are everywhere. We spend most of our waking hours sending messages to others or interpreting messages from others.[26] Many of our messages are not verbalized. As you silently stand in a supermarket checkout line, for example, your lack of eye contact with others waiting in line suggests you're not interested in striking up a conversation. Your unspoken messages may provide cues to which others respond. As was noted earlier, some communication scholars question whether it is possible to communicate with someone unintentionally. However, even when you don't intend to express a particular idea or feeling, others may try to make sense out of what you are doing—or not doing. Remember: People judge you by your behavior, not your intent.

Figure 1.1 Helical Model of Communication

Interpersonal communication is irreversible. Like the spiral shown here, communication never loops back on itself. Once it begins, it expands infinitely as the communication partners contribute their thoughts and experiences to the exchange.
Nishi 55/Fotolia

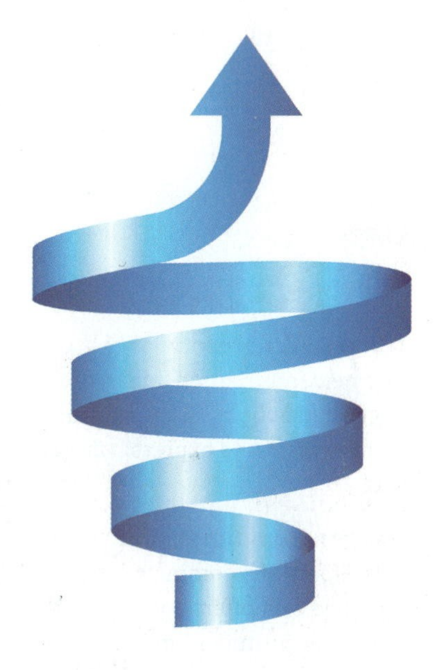

COMMUNICATION IS IRREVERSIBLE "Disregard that last statement made by the witness," instructs the judge. Yet the clever lawyer knows that, once the witness has said something, he or she cannot really "take back" the message. In conversation, we may try to modify the meaning of a spoken message by saying something like "Oh, I really didn't mean it." But in most cases, the damage has been done. Once created, communication has the physical property of matter; it can't be uncreated. As the spiral shown in Figure 1.1 suggests, once communication begins, it never loops back on itself. Instead, it continues to be shaped by the events, experiences, and thoughts of the communication partners. A Russian proverb nicely summarizes the point: "Once a word goes out of your mouth, you can never swallow it again."

COMMUNICATION IS COMPLICATED Communicating with others is not simple. If it were, we would know how to reduce dramatically the number of misunderstandings and conflicts in our world. This book could also offer you a list of simple techniques and strategies for blissful management of communication hassles in your relationships. But you won't find that list in this book or any other credible book, because human communication is complicated by the number of variables and unknown factors involved when people interact.

To illustrate the complexity of the process, communication scholar Dean Barnlund has suggested that whenever we communicate with another person, at least six "people" are really involved:

1. Who you think you are
2. Who you think the other person is
3. Who you think the other person thinks you are
4. Who the other person thinks he or she is
5. Who the other person thinks you are
6. Who the other person thinks you think he or she is.[27]

Whew! And when you add more people to the conversation, it becomes even more complicated.

Life is not only complicated but also uncertain. There are many things we do not know. We seek information about such everyday things as the weather or about such questions as what others think about us. Several communication theorists suggest that we attempt to manage our uncertainty through communication.[28] In times of high uncertainty (when there are many things we do not know), we will communicate more actively and purposefully so as to manage our uncertainty. For example, we are likely to ask more questions, seek information, and listen intently when we are uncertain.

Adding to the complexity of communication and the problem of our own uncertainty is that messages are not always interpreted as we intend them. Osmo Wiio, a

Scandinavian communication scholar, points out the challenges of communicating with others when he suggests the following maxims:

1. If communication can fail, it will.
2. If a message can be understood in different ways, it will be understood in just the way that does the most harm.
3. There is always somebody who knows better than you what you meant by your message.
4. The more communication there is, the more difficult it is for communication to succeed.[29]

Although we are not as pessimistic as Wiio, we do suggest that the task of understanding each other is challenging.

COMMUNICATION EMPHASIZES CONTENT AND RELATIONSHIPS What you say—your words—and how you say it—your tone of voice, amount of eye contact, facial expression, and posture—can reveal much about the true meaning of your message. The **content dimension** of communication messages refers to the new information, ideas, or suggested actions the speaker wishes to express. When you tell your roommate you want the room cleaned, you convey an intentional message that you want a tidier room.

content dimension
The new information, ideas, or suggested actions that a communicator wishes to express; *what* is said.

relationship dimension
The aspect of a communication message that offers cues about the emotions, attitudes, and amount of power and control the speaker directs toward others; *how* something is said.

rule
A followable prescription that indicates what behavior is required or preferred and what behavior is prohibited in a specific situation.

The **relationship dimension** of a communication message is usually less explicit; it offers cues about the emotions, attitudes, and amount of power and control the speaker directs toward others.[30] If one of your roommates loudly and abruptly bellows, "HEY, DORK! CLEAN THIS ROOM!" and another roommate uses the same verbal message but more gently and playfully suggests, with a smile, "Hey, dork. Clean this room," both are communicating the same message content, aimed at achieving the same outcome. But the two messages have very different relationship cues.

Another way to distinguish between the content and relationship dimensions of communication is to consider that the content of a message refers to *what* is said. The relationship cues are provided in *how* the message is communicated. For example, when you read a transcript of what someone says, you can get a different meaning than you would if you actually heard the person's words.

COMMUNICATION IS GOVERNED BY RULES When you play Monopoly, you know there are rules about how to get out of jail, buy Boardwalk, or pass "Go" and get $200. According to communication researcher Susan Shimanoff, a **rule** is a "followable

What are the implicit rules for waiting in a medical waiting room?
Robert Kneschke/Shutterstock

prescription that indicates what behavior is obligated, preferred, or prohibited in certain contexts."[31] The rules that help define appropriate and inappropriate communication in any given situation may be explicit or implicit. The rules of Monopoly are explicit; they are even written down. For a class, explicit rules are probably spelled out in your syllabus.

However, your instructor has other rules that are more implicit. They are not written or verbalized because you learned them long ago: Only one person speaks at a time; you raise your hand to be called on; you do not send text messages. Similarly, you may follow implicit rules when you play Monopoly with certain friends or family members, such as "always let Grandpa buy Boardwalk." Communication rules are developed by those involved in the interaction and by the culture in which the individuals are communicating. Most people learn communication rules from experience, by observing and interacting with others.

Communication Models

1.3 Explain three communication models.

Communication researchers have spent considerable time trying to understand precisely how communication takes place. In the course of their study, they have developed visual models that graphically illustrate the communication process. By reviewing the development of communication models, you can see how our understanding of communication has evolved over the past century.

Communication as Action: Message Transfer

"Did you get my message?" This simple question summarizes the earliest, communication-as-action approach to human communication. These early models viewed communication as a transfer or exchange of information; communication takes place when a message is sent and received. Period. Communication is a way of transferring meaning from sender to receiver. In 1948, Harold Lasswell described the process as follows:

Who (sender)
Says what (message)
In what channel
To whom (receiver)
With what effect[32]

Figure 1.2 shows a simplified representation of the communication process developed by communication pioneers Claude Shannon and Warren Weaver, who viewed communication as a linear input/output process. Today, although researchers view

Figure 1.2 A Model of Communication as Action

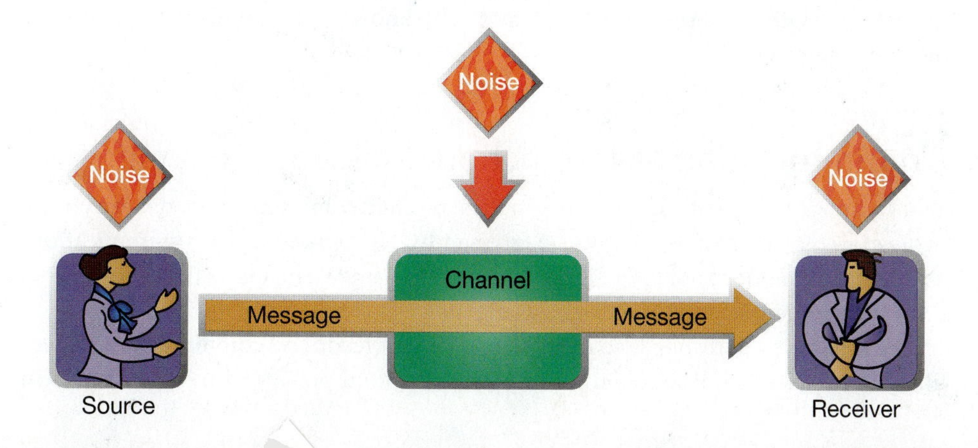

the process as more complex, they still define most of the key components in this model in basically the same way that Shannon and Weaver did.

SOURCE The **source** of communication is the originator of a thought or an emotion. As the developer of that thought or emotion, the source puts a message into a code that can be understood by a receiver.

- **Encoding** is the process of translating ideas, feelings, and thoughts into a code. Vocalizing a word, gesturing, and establishing eye contact are means of encoding our thoughts into a message that can be decoded by someone.
- **Decoding**, the process that is the opposite of encoding, occurs when the words or unspoken signals are interpreted by the receiver.

RECEIVER The **receiver** is the person who decodes the signal and attempts to make sense of what the source encoded. Think of a TV station as a source broadcasting to a receiver (your TV) that picks up the station's signal. In human communication, however, there is something between the source and the receiver: We filter messages through past experiences, attitudes, beliefs, values, prejudices, and biases.

MESSAGE **Messages** are the written, spoken, and unspoken elements of communication to which we assign meaning. As we have noted, you can send a message intentionally (talking to a friend before class) or unintentionally (falling asleep during class); verbally ("Hi. What's up?"), nonverbally (a smile and a handshake), or in written form (this book); or through any number of electronic channels.

CHANNEL A message is communicated from sender to receiver via some pathway called a **channel**. With today's technological advances, we receive messages through a variety of channels, including print, airwave, and wireless channels. Ultimately, however, communication channels correspond to your senses. When you call your mother, the message is conveyed via an electronic channel that activates auditory cues. When you talk with your mother face to face, the channels are many. You see her: the visual channel. You hear her: the auditory channel. You may smell her perfume: the olfactory channel. You may hug her: the tactile channel.

NOISE **Noise** is interference. Noise keeps a message from being understood and achieving its intended effect. Without noise, all our messages would be communicated with considerable accuracy. But noise is always present. It can be literal—the obnoxious roar of a power lawn mower—or it can be psychological, such as competing thoughts, worries, and feelings that capture our attention. Instead of concentrating on your teacher's lecture, you may start thinking about the chores you need to finish before the end of the day. Whichever kind it is, noise gets in the way of the message and may even distort it. Communicating accurate messages involves minimizing both literal and psychological noise.

The communication-as-action approach was simple and straightforward, but human communication rarely, if ever, is as simple a matter as "what we put in is what we get out." Other people cannot automatically know what you mean, even if your meaning seems very clear to *you*.

source
The originator of a thought or emotion who puts it into a code that can be understood by a receiver.

encoding
The process of translating ideas, feelings, and thoughts into a code.

decoding
The process of interpreting ideas, feelings, and thoughts that have been translated into a code.

receiver
The person who decodes a message and attempts to make sense of what the source has encoded.

message
Written, spoken, and unspoken elements of communication to which people assign meaning.

channel
The pathway through which messages are sent.

noise
Interference, either literal or psychological, that hinders the accurate encoding or decoding of a message.

feedback
The response to a message.

Communication as Interaction: Message Exchange

To take into account some of the complexities of actual communication, the early view evolved to include a more interactive, give-and-take approach. The communication-as-interaction model, shown in Figure 1.3, uses the same elements as the action model but adds two new ones: feedback and context.

Feedback is the response to a message. Without feedback, communication is less likely to be effective. When you order your pepperoni pizza and the server asks in

Figure 1.3 A Model of Communication as Interaction

Interaction models of communication include feedback as a response to a message sent by a communication source and place the process in a context.

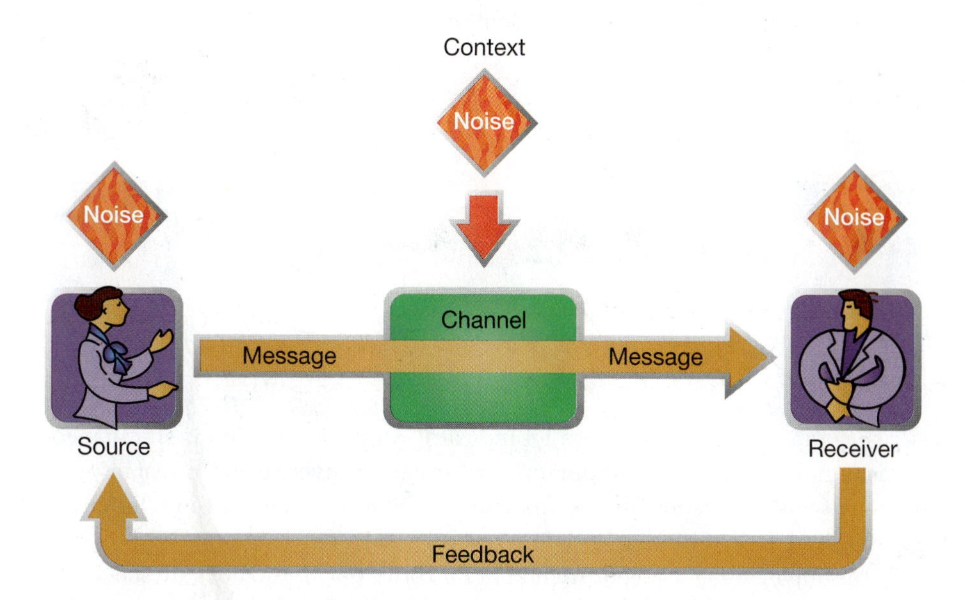

response, "That's a pepperoni pizza, right?" he has provided feedback to ensure that he decoded the message correctly.

Feedback can be intentional (applause at the conclusion of a symphony) or unintentional (a yawn as you listen to your uncle tell his story about bears again); or it can be verbal ("That's two burgers and fries, right?") or nonverbal (blushing after being asked for a date).

As the cliché goes, "Everyone has to be somewhere." All communication takes place in some **context**, the physical, historical, and psychological communication environment. A conversation with your good friend on the beach would likely differ from one the two of you might have in a funeral home. Context encompasses not only the physical environment but also the number of people present, their past relationship with the communicators, the communication goal, and the culture in which the communicators are steeped. The psychological context includes the effect of what is going on in the minds of the communicators; the speaker's and listener's personalities and styles of interacting with others influence how messages are understood.

context
The physical, historical, and psychological communication environment.

Communication as Transaction: Message Creation

Although it emphasizes feedback and context, the interaction model of communication still views communication as a linear, step-by-step process. But in many communication situations, both the source and the receiver send and receive messages at the same time. The communication-as-transaction perspective, which evolved in the 1960s, acknowledges that when we communicate with another, we are constantly reacting to what our partner is saying and expressing. Most scholars today view this perspective as the most realistic model of communication. Although this model uses such concepts as action and interaction to

RECAP

Components of the Human Communication Process

Term	Definition
Source	Originator of an idea or emotion
Receiver	Person or group toward whom a source directs messages and who decodes the message
Message	Written, spoken, and unspoken elements of communication to which we assign meaning
Channel	Pathway through which messages pass between source and receiver
Noise	Any literal or psychological interference with the clear encoding or decoding of a message
Encoding	Translation of ideas, feelings, and thoughts into a code
Decoding	Interpretation of ideas, feelings, and thoughts that have been translated into a code
Context	Physical, historical, and psychological communication environment
Feedback	Verbal and nonverbal responses to a message

Figure 1.4 A Model of Communication as Transaction

The source and the receiver of a message experience communication simultaneously.

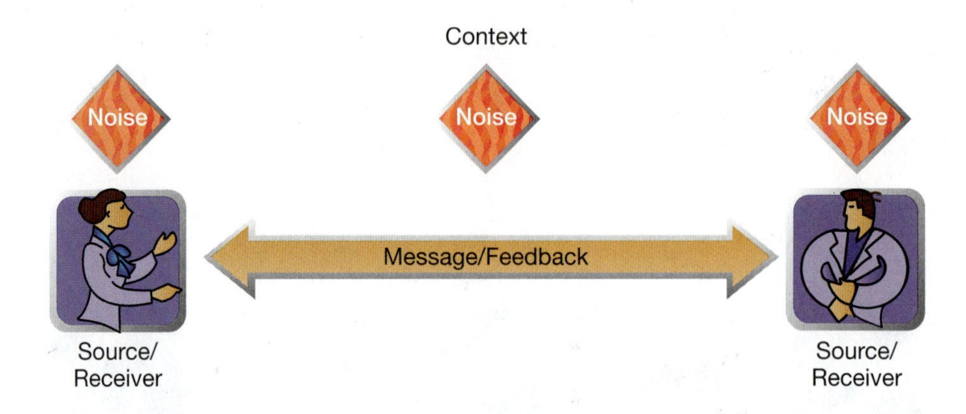

describe communication, as Figure 1.4 indicates, all the interaction is simultaneous. Even as we talk, we are also interpreting our partner's nonverbal and verbal responses. Transactive communication also occurs within a context, and noise can interfere with the quality and accuracy of our encoding and decoding of messages.

For example, if you ask your friend out for coffee but you're not sure she'd like to go with you, even as you're talking to her, you carefully observe her reactions to determine whether she's really interested in your invitation. If you'd really like her company and you sense she'd rather not go with you, you may try harder, using your best persuasive pitch to get your friend to join you. During each communication transaction you have with another person, you look for information about how your message is being received even before you finish talking.

In a communication transaction, the meaning of a message is *co-created* by the individuals who are involved in the communication process. Meaning is created in the hearts and minds of both the message source and the message receiver, based on such things as the characteristics of the message, the situation, and the perceptions and background of the communicators. By drawing on our own experiences while attempting to make sense of a message, we actually shape the meaning of that message. As one research team puts it, communication is "the coordinated management of meaning" through episodes during which the message of one person influences the message of another.[33] Technically, only the sender and receiver of those messages can determine where one episode ends and another begins. We make sense out of our world in ways that are unique to each of us.

RECAP

An Evolving Model of Human Communication

Human Communication as Action
Human communication is linear, with meaning sent or transferred from source to receiver.

Human Communication as Interaction
Human communication occurs as the receiver of the message responds to the source through feedback. This interactive model views communication as a linear sequence of actions and reactions.

Human Communication as Transaction
Human communication is simultaneously interactive. Meaning is created on the basis of mutual, concurrent sharing of ideas and feelings. This transactive model most accurately describes human communication.

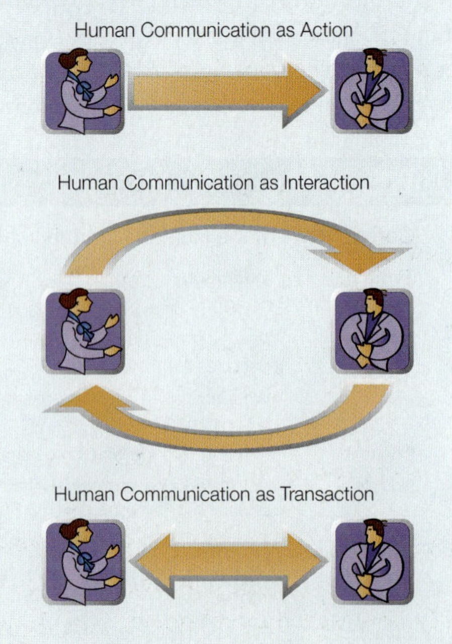

Communication Competence

1.4 Describe three criteria that can be used to determine whether communication is competent.

What does it mean to communicate competently? Does it mean that you are able to present a well-delivered speech? Or does it mean that you are able to carry on a brilliant conversation with someone? Is it evidence of communication competence if you often are asked to chair committee meetings because you are so organized? Being a competent communicator is more than just being well liked, glib, able to give polished presentations, or able to interact smoothly with individual people or in groups and teams. Although it is difficult to identify core criteria that define competent communication in all situations, we believe that certain goals of communication serve as measures of **communication competence**, or the ability to communicate successfully, regardless of the setting. We suggest the following three criteria:[34]

- The message should be understood as the communicator intended it to be understood.
- The message should achieve the communicator's intended effect.
- The message should be ethical.

The Message Should Be Understood

A primary goal of any effective communication transaction is to develop a common understanding of the message from both the sender's and the receiver's perspectives. You'll note how the words *common* and *communication* resemble each other. One of the aims of the principles we discuss in this book is to create clarity of expression and a common understanding.

Message clarity is missing in the following headlines, which have appeared in local U.S. newspapers:

Panda Mating Fails: Veterinarian Takes Over
Drunks Get Nine Months in Violin Case
Include Your Children When Baking Cookies
Police Begin Campaign to Run Down Jaywalkers
Local High School Dropouts Cut in Half

We acknowledge the challenge of communicating with others; differences in culture, language, experience, gender, education, and background all are sources of misunderstanding. Meanings are fragile, and messages can be misunderstood. An effective message is one that the receiver understands.

The Message Should Achieve Its Intended Effect

Another criterion for judging the effectiveness of communication is whether the intent of the message is achieved. When you communicate intentionally with others, you do so for a specific purpose: to achieve a goal or to accomplish something. Because different purposes require different strategies for success, being aware of your purpose can enhance your probability of achieving it.

We often use specific types of communication to achieve typical goals:

- The goal of *public speaking* may be to inform, to persuade, or to entertain.
- In *small groups*, our goals are often to solve problems and make decisions.
- In our *interpersonal relationships*, our goals may be to build trust, develop intimacy, or just enjoy someone's company.

The Message Should Be Ethical

A message that is understood and achieves its intended effect but that manipulates listeners, unfairly restricts their choices, or uses false information may be effective, but it is not appropriate or ethical. **Ethics** are the beliefs, values, and moral principles by which we determine what is right or wrong. Ethics and ethical behavior have long been considered critical components of human behavior in a given culture.

communication competence
The ability to communicate successfuly.

ethics
The beliefs, values, and moral principles by which we determine what is right or wrong.

Communication & ETHICS

Is There a Universal Ethical Code?

Most religions of the world emphasize a common spiritual theme, which is known in Christianity as the Golden Rule: Do unto others what you would have others do unto you.[35] This "rule" is also perceived as the basis for most ethical codes throughout the world.

Hinduism	Do nothing to others which would cause pain if done to you.
Buddhism	One should seek for others the happiness one desires for oneself.
Taoism	Regard your neighbor's gain as your own gain, and your neighbor's loss as your loss.
Confucianism	Is there one principle which ought to be acted upon throughout one's whole life? Surely it is the principle of loving-kindness: do not unto others what you would not have them do unto you.
Zoroastrianism	The nature alone is good which refrains from doing unto another whatsoever is not good for itself.
Judaism	What is hateful to you, do not do to others. That is the entire law: all the rest is but commentary.
Islam	No one of you is a believer until he desires for his brother that which he desires for himself.
Christianity	Do unto others what you would have others do unto you.

Does the fact that virtually all religions appear to have a common theme of valuing others as yourself provide evidence that there are universal human ethical standards?

Philosophers have debated for centuries whether there is such a thing as a universal moral and ethical code.[36] British author and scholar C. S. Lewis argued that the teachings of cultures throughout the world and through time support the existence of a shared ethical code that serves as the basis for interpreting the "goodness" or "badness" of human behavior.[37] In their book *Communication Ethics and Universal Values*, communication scholars Clifford Christians and Michael Traber claim that "Every culture depends for its existence on norms that order human relationships and social institutions."[38] They suggest there are three universal cultural norms: (1) the value of truth, (2) respect for another person's dignity, and (3) the expectation that innocent people should not suffer harm.[39] As represented in the Communication & Ethics box, there appears to be a moral code for how people should treat others that can be seen across most of the world's major religions.[40]

Our purpose is not to prescribe a specific religious or philosophical ethical code, but rather to suggest that humans from a variety of cultures and traditions have sought to develop ethical principles that guide their interactions with others. Having an ethical code does not always mean that people follow the code, however. Scholars and philosophers who suggest that a universal code of ethics exists do not claim that people always behave in ways that are true to these universal standards.

Philosophy and religion are not the only realms that focus on ethical behavior. Most professions, such as medicine, law, and journalism, have explicit codes of ethics that identify appropriate and inappropriate behavior. The National Communication Association has developed a Credo for Communication Ethics to emphasize the importance of being an ethical communicator:

> Ethical communication is fundamental to responsible thinking, decision making, and the development of relationships and communities within and across contexts, cultures, channels, and media. Moreover, ethical communication enhances human worth and dignity by fostering truthfulness, fairness, responsibility, personal integrity, and respect for self and others.[41]

For most people, being ethical means being sensitive to others' needs, giving people choices rather than forcing them to behave in a certain way, respecting others' privacy, not intentionally decreasing others' feelings of self-worth, and being honest in presenting information. Unethical communication does just the opposite: It forces views on others and demeans their integrity. Echoing the wisdom offered by others, we suggest that competent communication is grounded in an ethical perspective that is respectful to others.

Communication in the 21st Century

1.5 Describe the nature of communication in the 21st century.

It is increasingly important to use technology competently when communicating in the 21st century. When you use a medium such as a cell phone or the Internet to carry your message, you are using **mediated communication**, any communication expressed via some channel other than those used when we communicate in person. Some physical media, such as a wire, a cable, a phone line, a cell phone, a TV set, a computer, or some other technology, carry the messages between sender and receiver. The channel of communication is not only physical but also electronic, in the form of the signal coming into your TV set, your phone, or your computer. **Mass communication** occurs when a mediated message is sent to many people at the same time. A TV or radio broadcast is an example of mass communication. Although mass communication is important, our focus in this book is primarily on unmediated and mediated interpersonal, group, and presentational communication.

Facebook and other contemporary methods of communicating with others are relatively recent inventions when we consider the entire spectrum of human history, but people have been communicating with others without being face to face for centuries; sending letters and other written messages to others is a long-standing human practice. A printed textbook provides a form of mediated "distance learning." Even in an electronic textbook, the words were written some time before students read them. What's new today is that there are so many different ways of *immediately* connecting with someone.

Today's technology makes it as easy to communicate with someone either across the street or across the globe. And we can time shift when we communicate. Face to face, we communicate with *synchronous* communication, in real time when we receive immediate feedback. But using e-mail or text messages, we interact with *asynchronous* communication, or out of sync; that is, there may be a time delay between when you send a message and when it is received.

Switching between face-to-face and mediated communication is a normal, seamless way of communicating with others, especially if you are using computers or mobile devices, technological tools that have probably always seemed to be part of your life. If you're under age 25, you are much more likely to text friends than to phone them, for example.[42] But, can you really communicate *interpersonally* with someone on the Internet? Yes, of course. You probably do so every day.

We use the Internet to share both dramatic and routine information, as well as to enrich relationships.[43] Research has found, for example, that immediately after the terrorist attacks on September 11, 2001, both the telephone and the Internet were prime

mediated communication
Any communication that is carried out using some channel other than those used in face-to-face communication.

mass communication
Communication accomplished through a mediated message that is sent to many people at the same time.

ZITS © Zits Partnership, King Features Syndicate

means of spreading news of the attacks. People used text and e-mail messages not only to share the shocking news but also to seek interpersonal support and reassurance from friends that their loved ones were safe. We increasingly rely on the Internet to help us form and maintain interpersonal relationships.

If you are attending a college or university away from family, friends, and loved ones, you may have found that sending text messages or connecting on Facebook can help you stay in touch with others who are important to you. The evidence summarized in the Communication & Technology box suggests that Facebook is especially helpful in maintaining relationships.[44] College freshmen and their parents also report that e-mail and text connections reduce students' homesickness and the sadness parents often feel when their son or daughter leaves home.

Although some research has found that mediated communication can be as satisfying as face-to-face conversation,[45] some observers still express concerns about overreliance on mediated communication. The title of communication researcher Sherry Turkle's book, *Alone Together*, suggests that even though we may be "connected" electronically, we are nonetheless literally alone, separated from others. As Turkle notes, "Our networked life allows us to hide from each other, even as we are tethered to each other. We'd rather text than talk."[46]

Other researchers have also wondered whether spending a lot of time online reduces people's face-to-face interactions. A team of researchers led by Robert Kraut and Sara Kiesler made headlines when they published the results of their study, which concluded

Communication & TECHNOLOGY

Got Facebook? How We Connect on Facebook

Facebook is the predominant social networking site of the second decade of the 21st century. Facebook (FB), now more popular than Google as the most popular website in the United States, is the primary way many people stay connected. Although recent evidence suggests that FB use among teens between the ages of 13 and 17 has dropped by 3 million users during the last three years, the number of people age 55 and older using FB grew by 80 percent during the same period.[47] Overall, FB use continues to grow during the second decade of the 21st century. But what precisely are we using FB to do? Researchers have identified several patterns that provide clues to the way we communicate today.

- *You check FB often.* Almost 80 percent of students surveyed log on to FB every day, and more than 60 percent said they sign in several times a day.[48] And 44 percent of FB users "like" their friends' content or comment on their friends' posts at least once a day.[49]
- *You have a lot of friends.* Teens have an average number of 300 friends (and 70 percent of teens are FB friends with their parents); millennials, those born between 1982 and 2002, have an average of 250 friends (and 62 percent of millennials post what they are doing, where they are, and who they are with); members of Generation X have an average of 200 friends; baby boomers (born between 1943 and 1960) have fewer friends—between 50 and about 100.[50]
- *You're an active communicator.* There are a total of more than 1.26 FB users with more than 150 billion FB connections.[51] Forty percent of FB users check FB more than once a day.[52] About two-thirds of users post status updates to their profile and add comments and likes to their own and others' statuses.[53]
- *You're most likely to share pictures.* More than 85 percent of students surveyed share photos. Eighty percent share their relationship status, and 70 percent share their favorite media, such as movies or TV shows. Fewer share their religious views (46 percent) or political views (40 percent), although college graduates are more likely to share their political and religious views than are current college students.[54]
- Most checked-in location in 2014: Disneyland.[55]
- *Women and men use FB differently.* Men are more likely to share their political and religious views on FB than are women. Men are also more likely to post current events and news-related topics. Women are more likely to post comments and likes.[56] Women share and see photos and videos more than men.[57]
- What you like least about FB is people who share too much information about themselves or post your information or photos of you without your permission.[58]

Got Facebook? Apparently you do. Although not everyone finds FB a vital method of communication, for many it's an important means of communicating with others.

Jeff Stahler/Cartoon Stock

©Jeff Stahler/Distributed by Universal Uclick for UFS via CartoonStock.com

that the more people use the Internet, the less they interact with people in person.[59] These researchers also found a relationship between people who said they were lonely and those who used the Internet. Yet three follow-up studies found that people who use the Internet are *more* likely to have a large number of friends; they are more involved with community activities and overall have greater levels of trust in other people.[60]

The follow-up research suggests that for some people—those who are already prone to being shy or introverted—there may be a link between Internet use and loneliness or feelings of social isolation. This link might exist, however, because shy and introverted people are simply less likely to make contact with others in any way, not because they use the Internet a lot. For people who are generally outgoing and who like to interact with others, in contrast, the Internet is another tool with which to reach out to others.

A link may also exist between general apprehension about communicating with others face to face and using the Internet. Cyberspace can be a more comfortable place to communicate with others if you are apprehensive about talking in face-to-face situations or even on the phone. People who spend a lot of time online may not be more lonely; rather, they may just feel more comfortable having the ability to control the timing of how they interact with others. An ever-increasing number of people are meeting via social media and eventually developing in-person relationships, for example. One study suggests that many of us may prefer to use a less immediate communication channel when we are feeling some apprehension or relationship uncertainty. The researchers found that you are more likely to call a romantic partner on your cell phone when the relationship is going well than when the relationship isn't as positive.[61]

Another concern is dishonest communication. In a digital world, it is easy to send messages and provide feedback anonymously. Because of anonymity, it's easier to be deceitful. For example, in 2014, there were reported to be up to 140 million fake Facebook accounts.[62] Personal appearance plays less of a role in shaping initial impressions when using only text messages, unless we add photos or video. Even then, especially with photos, we can more easily manipulate our image (for example, by sharing a photo of us when we were younger or thinner).

Our recommendation? Your method of communication should fit well with your communication goal. Although connecting to others via the Internet seems to be a normal way to communicate for a significant and growing percentage of the world's population, at times relating to someone live and in person is best—especially for expressing feelings and emotions. In other situations, the ease and speed of mediated communication make it preferable to face-to-face communication.

Communication Contexts

1.6 Identify and explain three communication contexts.

Communication takes place in a variety of situations. As we've discussed, a great deal of the communication in our lives today is mediated. In this section, we'll describe the three classic, face-to-face contexts to which communication researchers study human communication: interpersonal communication, group communication, and presentational communication. All three contexts are part of communication in organizational and health settings.

interpersonal communication Communication that occurs simultaneously between two people who attempt to mutually influence each other, usually for the purpose of managing relationships.

impersonal communication Communication that treats people as objects or that responds only to their roles rather than to who they are as unique people.

small group communication The transactive process of creating meaning among three to about fifteen people who share a common purpose, feel a sense of belonging to the group, and exert influence on one another.

Interpersonal Communication

Interpersonal communication is a special form of human communication that occurs when we interact simultaneously with another person and attempt to mutually influence each other, usually for the purpose of managing relationships. At the heart of this definition is the role of communication in developing unique relationships with other people.[63]

When we treat people as objects, or when we respond to their roles rather than to who they are as unique people, we are engaging in **impersonal communication**. Based on this definition, asking a server for a glass of water at a restaurant is impersonal rather than interpersonal communication. If you strike up a conversation with the server—say you discover that it's her birthday or that you both know the same people—your conversation moves from impersonal to interpersonal. We're not suggesting that impersonal communication is unimportant or necessarily inferior or bad. Competent communicators are able to interact with others in a variety of situations.

We engage in interpersonal communication when we interact with another person.
Golden Pixels LLC/Shutterstock

Interpersonal communication reflects the characteristics of the transactional model of communication discussed earlier. It is a dialogue in the sense that all communicators are influenced and meaning is created simultaneously.[64]

Interpersonal communication is the fundamental means we use to manage our relationships, the ongoing connections we make with others. To relate to someone is to give and take, listen and respond, act and react. When we talk about a good or positive relationship with someone, we often mean that we are "together" or "in sync." In an effective relationship, the individuals involved believe that their verbal and nonverbal messages are understood and that there is a relational harmony based on a common understanding between the communicators. We will discuss interpersonal communication in more detail in Chapters 7 and 8.

Group Communication

Human beings are social, collaborative creatures. We do most of our work and play in groups. One focus of this book is the communication that occurs in groups—how we make sense of our participation in groups and share that sense with others. We define **small group communication** as the verbal and nonverbal message transactions that occur among three to about fifteen people who share a common goal, who feel a sense of belonging to the group, and who exert influence on one another.[65] Today's globe-shrinking technology makes it possible for people to be linked with others in *virtual groups* even when they are in different physical locations.[66] In Chapters 9 and 10, we will discuss groups and teams, both in-person and virtual, more thoroughly.

Presentational Communication

For many people, speaking in public is a major source of anxiety. **Presentational communication** occurs when a speaker addresses a gathering of people to inform, persuade, or entertain. In this book, we will focus on applying the principles of communication when informing and persuading listeners. In Chapters 11 through 15 we present basic strategies for designing and delivering a speech to others. Effective public speakers are aware of their communication and how they interact with their audience. They also effectively use, interpret, and understand verbal and nonverbal messages; listen and respond to their audience; and adapt their message to their listeners.

Of the three contexts in which the principles we present in this book are applied, public speaking has the distinction of being the one that has been formally studied the longest. In 333 BCE, Aristotle wrote his famous *Rhetoric*, the first fully developed treatment of the study of speech to convince an audience. He defined **rhetoric** as the process of discovering the available means of persuasion in a given situation. In essence, persuasion is the process of using symbols to persuade others. Although we have certainly advanced in our understanding of informing and persuading others in the past two millennia, much of what Aristotle taught has withstood the tests of both time and scholarly research.

Applying Communication in Organizational and Health Contexts

Many researchers study the communication that occurs in organizations such as businesses, government agencies, and nonprofits such as the American Cancer Society and other charities. **Organizational communication** is the study of human communication as it occurs within organizations. Although organizational communication includes applications of interpersonal, group, and presentational communication, there are unique ways in which communication functions in contemporary organizations.

Health communication, a growing area of communication study, examines the role and importance of communication that has an effect on our health. Health communication researchers study the interaction between health care workers (such as physicians, physician's assistants, and nurses) and patients. They also study how to best design campaigns to encourage healthy habits (such as messages about getting fit, losing weight, avoiding sexually transmitted diseases, or quitting smoking).

Communication Principles for a Lifetime

1.7 List and explain five fundamental principles of communication.

As you saw at the beginning of this chapter, underlying our description of human communication are five principles that provide the foundation for all effective communication, whether we are communicating with others one on one, in groups or teams, or by presenting a public speech to an audience. Throughout this book, we will emphasize how these principles are woven into the fabric of each communication context.

presentational communication
Communication that occurs when a speaker addresses a gathering of people to inform, persuade, or entertain them.

rhetoric
The process of using symbols to influence or persuade others.

organizational communication
The study of human communication as it occurs within organizations.

health communication
The study of communication that has an effect on human health.

Communication & DIVERSITY

Communication Principles for a Lifetime: Principles for All Cultures?

Are the five Principles for a Lifetime applicable to all human communication, across a variety of cultures? Culture is the learned system of knowledge, behavior, attitudes, beliefs, values, and norms that is shared by a group of people. Is it true that people of all cultures should be aware of their communication, use and interpret verbal and nonverbal messages, listen and respond thoughtfully, and appropriately adapt their messages to others?

We suggest that these five fundamental principles may provide a common framework for talking about communication in a variety of cultures. We're not suggesting that all cultures use each principle the same way. There are obvious differences from one culture to another in language and use of nonverbal cues (Principles Two and Three), for example. But in all cultures, the use and interpretation of verbal and nonverbal messages are important in determining whether communication is effective. There are also clear cultural differences in the way people choose to adapt messages to others (Principle Five), but people in all cultures may adapt messages to others in some way, even though adaptations vary from culture to culture.

Do you agree or disagree with our position? In your communication class, there are undoubtedly people from a variety of cultural backgrounds. Respond to the following questions, and then compare your answers with those of your fellow students.

1. How applicable are the five communication principles to your cultural experience?
2. Do any of the communication principles *not* apply in your culture?
3. Can you think of another fundamental communication principle that you believe should be added to our list of five? If so, what is it?
4. Do you agree that these communication principles apply to all people?

We will expand on the discussion here with a brief introduction and then provide a more comprehensive discussion in the following five chapters to describe and illustrate the scope and power of these five Communication Principles for a Lifetime:

Principle One:	Be aware of your communication with yourself and others.
Principle Two:	Effectively use and interpret verbal messages.
Principle Three:	Effectively use and interpret nonverbal messages.
Principle Four:	Listen and respond thoughtfully to others.
Principle Five:	Appropriately adapt messages to others.

Figure 1.5 Communication Principles for a Lifetime

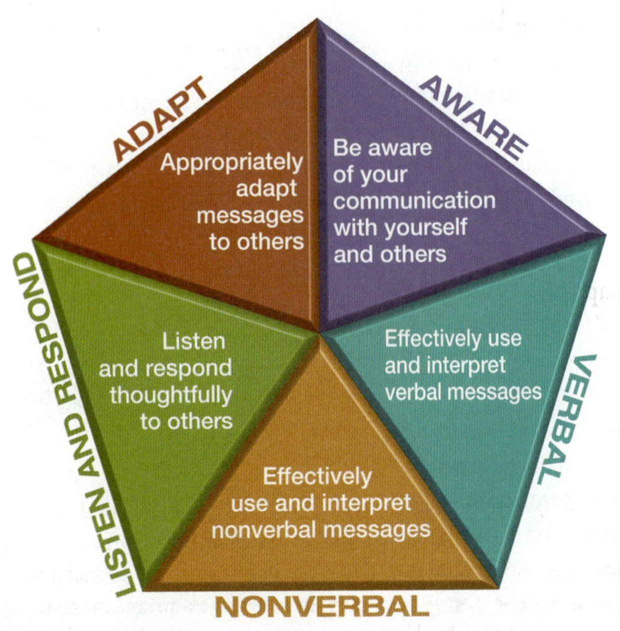

These five principles operate together rather than independently to form the basis of the fundamental processes that enhance communication effectiveness. The model in Figure 1.5 illustrates how the principles interrelate. Moving around the model clockwise, the first principle, being aware of your communication with yourself and others, is followed by the two principles that focus on communication messages, verbal messages (Principle Two) and nonverbal messages (Principle Three). The fourth principle, listening and responding, is followed by appropriately adapting messages to others (Principle Five). Together, these five principles can help explain why communication can be either effective or ineffective. A violation of any one principle can result in inappropriate or poor communication.

Throughout this book, we will remind you of how these principles can be used to organize the theory, concepts, and skills we offer as fundamental to human communication. Chapters 2 through 6 will each be devoted to a single principle. Chapters 7 through 15 will apply these principles to the most prevalent communication situations we experience each day: communicating with others interpersonally, in groups and teams, and when giving a talk or presentation.

To help you see relationships among the five communication principles and the various skills and content we will present in Chapters 7 through 15, we will place in the margin a small version of the model presented in Figure 1.5, like the one that appears in the margin here. We will also label which principle or principles we are discussing. Refer to the principles pentagon in Figure 1.5 as we introduce the principles.

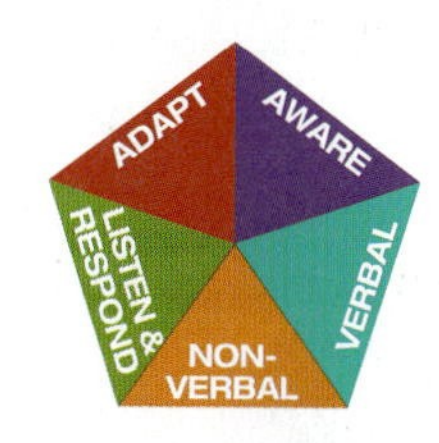

Principle One: Be Aware of Your Communication with Yourself and Others

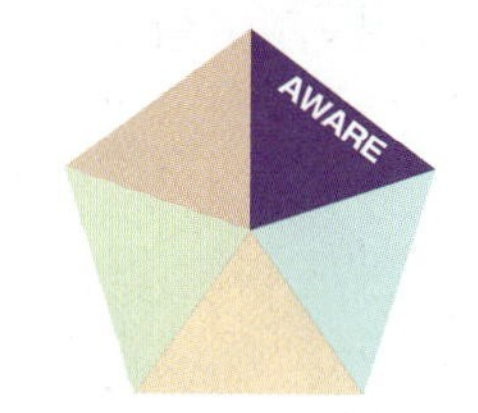

The first foundation principle is to be aware of your communication with yourself and others. Effective communicators are conscious, or "present," when communicating. Ineffective communicators mindlessly or thoughtlessly say and do things that they may later regret. Being aware of your communication includes being conscious not only of the present moment but also of who you are, your self-concept, your self-worth, and your perceptions of yourself and others. Being aware of your typical communication style is also part of this foundation principle. For example, some people realize that their communication style is to be emotional when interacting with others. Others may be shy.

As has been noted, self-awareness includes being conscious of your intrapersonal communication messages. By **intrapersonal communication**, we mean the communication that occurs within yourself, including your thoughts, your emotions, and your perceptions of yourself and others. Talking to yourself is an example of intrapersonal communication. Although our intrapersonal communication is often the focus of psychologists, our intrapersonal messages also form the basis of our communication with others.[67]

Competent communicators are aware of the choices they make when they communicate both intrapersonally and with others; incompetent communicators react to others' messages with thoughtless, quick, knee-jerk responses. Because they do not mindfully censor themselves, they may blurt out obscene, offensive, or profane words. Ineffective communicators operate in an unthinking "default" mode. Being aware of our communication is a foundation principle because all the choices we make when communicating rest on our ability to make conscious choices when we respond to others.

Earlier in this chapter, we noted that human communication is the process of making sense out of the world and sharing that sense with others. Being aware of who we are and how we perceive, or "make sense of," what we observe is a fundamental principle that helps explain both effective and ineffective communication. In the next chapter, we develop this principle and foreshadow how it relates to a variety of communication situations.

Principle Two: Effectively Use and Interpret Verbal Messages

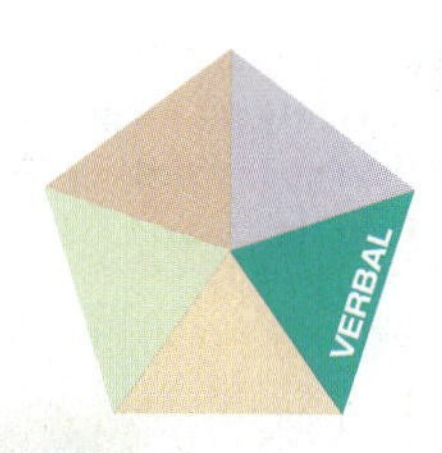

The second principle we introduce here and elaborate on in Chapter 3 is to use and interpret verbal messages effectively. Verbal messages are created with language. A **language** consists of symbols and a system of rules (grammar) that make it possible for people to understand one another.

As we noted earlier, a symbol is a word, sound, gesture, or visual image that represents a thought, concept, object, or experience. When you read the words on this page, you are looking at symbols that trigger meaning. The word is not the thing it represents; it simply symbolizes the thing or idea.

Your reading skill permits you to make sense out of symbols. The word *tree*, for example, may trigger a thought of the tree you may be reading under now, a tree in

intrapersonal communication
Communication that occurs within yourself, including your thoughts and emotions.

language
The system of symbols (words or vocabulary) structured by rules (grammar) that makes it possible for people to understand one another.

your own yard or a nearby park, or a great sequoia you saw on your family vacation in Yosemite National Park. Effective communicators use appropriate symbols to create accurate meaning. Author Daniel Quinn once commented, "No story is devoid of meaning, if you know how to look for it. This is as true of nursery rhymes and daydreams as it is of epic poems."[68] Meaning is created when people have a common or shared understanding.

The effective communicator both encodes and decodes messages accurately; he or she selects appropriate symbols to form a message and interprets carefully the messages of others. The process of using and interpreting symbols is the essence of how we make sense out of the world and share that sense with others. Some people feared that greater use of texting would lead to lower skills in language use and overall literacy. Research doesn't support that supposition, however: People who send and receive numerous text messages show no deterioration of language and literacy skills.[69]

Words have power. The words we use to describe ourselves and our world have considerable influence on how we perceive what we experience. Any good advertising copywriter knows how to use words to create a need or desire for a product. Political consultants tell politicians how to craft sound bites that will create just the right audience response. And words can hurt us. As Robert Fulghum wisely noted, "Sticks and stones may break our bones, but words break our hearts."[70] Words have the ability to offend and create stress. For example, derogatory words about someone's gender or ethnicity can do considerable harm. Throughout this book, we will present strategies and suggestions for selecting the best word or symbol to enhance your listeners' understanding.

Principle Three: Effectively Use and Interpret Nonverbal Messages

Messages are also nonverbal. **Nonverbal communication** is communication by means other than written or spoken language that creates meaning for someone. Nonverbal messages can communicate powerful ideas or express emotions with greater impact than mere words alone. An optimistic hitchhiker's extended thumb and an irate driver's extended finger are nonverbal symbols with clear and intentional meanings. But not all nonverbal symbols are clearly interpreted or even consciously expressed. You may not be aware of your frown when someone asks whether he or she may sit next to you in a vacant seat in a restaurant. Or your son may excitedly be telling you about his field trip to the fire station while you stare into the screen of your phone. You have no intention of telling your son he is not important, but your lack of nonverbal responsiveness speaks volumes. Our nonverbal messages communicate how we feel toward others.

nonverbal communication
Communication by means other than written or spoken language that creates meaning for someone.

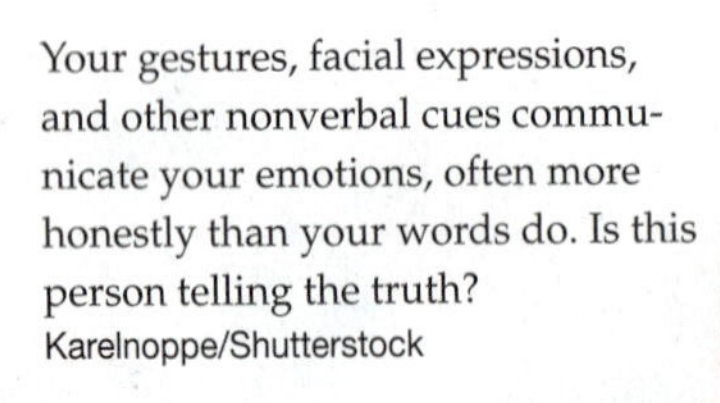
Your gestures, facial expressions, and other nonverbal cues communicate your emotions, often more honestly than your words do. Is this person telling the truth?
Karelnoppe/Shutterstock

When there is a contradiction between what you say and what you do, your nonverbal message is more believable than your verbal message. When asked how your meal is, you may tell your server that the meal is "great," but your nonverbal message—facial expression and flat tone of voice—clearly communicates your unhappiness with the cuisine. As was noted earlier in this chapter, when we discussed the concept of content and relationship messages, our nonverbal cues often tell people how to interpret what we are saying.

Effective communicators develop skill in interpreting the nonverbal messages of others. They also monitor their own messages to avoid unintentionally sending contradictory verbal and nonverbal messages. It's sometimes hard to interpret nonverbal messages because they don't have a neat beginning and ending point—the flow of information is continuous. It might not be clear where one gesture stops and another begins. Cultural differences, combined with the fact that so many different nonverbal channels (such as eye contact, facial expression, gestures, posture) can be used at the same time, make it tricky to "read" someone's nonverbal message accurately. We amplify our discussion of the power of nonverbal messages in Chapter 4

Principle Four: Listen and Respond Thoughtfully to Others

So far, our list of principles may appear to place much of the burden of achieving communication success on the person sending the message. But effective communication with others also places considerable responsibility on the listener. As we explained earlier in the chapter, because communication is a transactional process—both senders and receivers are mutually and usually simultaneously expressing and responding to symbols—listening to words with sensitivity and "listening between the lines" to nonverbal messages join our list of fundamental principles.

Listening can be hard because it looks easy. You spend more time listening than you do performing any other communication activity—probably more than any other thing you do except sleep.[71] But research suggests that many, if not most, of us do not always listen effectively. Both psychological, or internal, noise (our own thoughts, needs, and emotions) and external distractions (noise in the surroundings in which we listen) can create barriers to effective listening.

A widespread perception that listening is a passive rather than an active task also makes listening and accurately interpreting information a challenge. Effective listening is *not* a passive task at all; the effective and sensitive listener works hard to stay on task and focus mindfully on a sender's message. Effective listening requires you to develop an orientation or sensitivity to others when you listen and respond. When you are **other-oriented**, you consider the needs, motives, desires, and goals of your communication partners while still maintaining your own integrity. The choices you make in both forming the message and selecting when to share it should take into consideration your partner's thoughts and feelings. People who are skilled communicators both listen and respond with sensitivity; they are other-oriented, rather than self-focused.

Principle Five: Appropriately Adapt Messages to Others

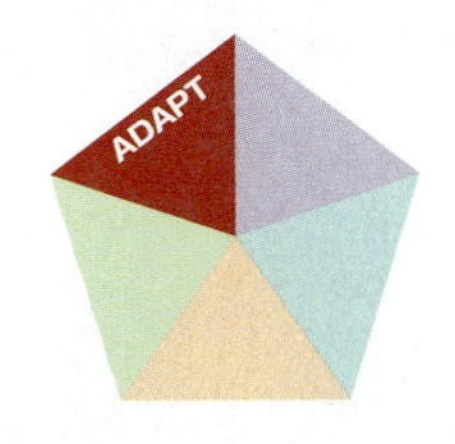

It is not enough to be sensitive and to accurately understand others; you must use the information you gather to modify the messages you construct. It is important to **adapt** your response appropriately to your listener. When you adapt a message, you make choices about how best to formulate both your message content and delivery, and how to respond to someone, in order to achieve your communication goals. Regardless of whether you are giving a speech, talking with a friend, or participating in a small group meeting, as an effective communicator you consider who the listeners are when deciding what to say and how best to say it. Adapting to a listener does *not* mean that you tell a listener only what he or she wants to hear. That would be unethical. Adapting involves appropriately editing and shaping your responses so that others accurately understand your messages and so that you achieve your goal without coercing or using false information or other unethical methods.

other-oriented
Being focused on the needs and concerns of others while maintaining one's personal integrity.

adapt
To adjust both what is communicated and how a message is communicated; to make choices about how best to formulate a message and respond to others to achieve your communication goals.

One of the elements of a message that you adapt when communicating with others is the structure or organization of what you say. Informal interpersonal conversations typically do not follow a rigid, outlined structure. Our conversation freely bounces from one topic to another. Formal speeches delivered in North America, however, are usually expected to have a more explicit structure—an introduction, a body, and a conclusion—with clearly identified major ideas. Other cultures, such as those in the Middle East, expect a greater use of stories, examples, and illustrations, rather than a clearly structured, outlined presentation. Knowing your audience's expectations can help you adapt your message so that it will be listened to and understood.

In Chapter 6, we will discuss this principle in greater detail by discussing the diverse nature of potential listeners and how to adapt to them. Adapting to differences in culture and gender, for example, may mean the difference between a message that is well received and one that creates hostility. Effective communicators not only listen and respond with sensitivity; they use the information they gather to shape the message and delivery of their responses to others.

STUDY GUIDE:
Review, Apply, and Assess Your Knowledge and Skill

Review Your Knowledge

Why Study Communication?

1.1 Explain why it is important to study communication.

Communication is essential for life. It is important to learn about communication, because being a skilled communicator can help you

- Obtain a good job.
- Enhance the quality of your relationships.
- Improve your physical and emotional health.

The Communication Process

1.2 Define communication and describe five characteristics of the communication process.

At its most basic level, communication is the process of acting on information. Human communication is the process of making sense out of the world and sharing that sense with others by creating meaning through verbal and nonverbal messages. Communication is inescapable, irreversible, complicated, and governed by rules, and it emphasizes content and relationships.

Communication Models

1.3 Explain three communication models.

Early models viewed human communication as a simple message-transfer process. Later models evolved to view communication as interaction and then as simultaneous transaction. Key components of communication include source, receiver, message, channel, noise, context, and feedback.

Communication Competence

1.4 Describe three criteria that can be used to determine whether communication is competent.

To be both effective and appropriate, a communication message should:

- Be understood as the communicator intended it to be understood.
- Achieve the communicator's intended effect.
- Be ethical.

Communication in the 21st Century

1.5 Describe the nature of communication in the 21st century.

Today, we commonly use various forms of media to communicate, either asynchronously or synchronously. Mediated communication is usually more anonymous than in-person communication and places less emphasis on a person's physical appearance. Shy or introverted people may prefer online to in-person communication, as do people who are feeling temporary uncertainty about their relationships.

Communication Contexts

1.6 Identify and explain three communication contexts.

Three classic contexts of unmediated communication that researchers have studied are (1) interpersonal communication, in which two people interact simultaneously and mutually influence each other, usually for the purpose of managing relationships; (2) small group communication, interaction among a small group of people who share a common purpose or goal, who feel a sense of belonging to the group, and who exert influence on the others in the group; and (3) presentational communication, in which a speaker addresses an audience for the purpose of informing, persuading, or entertaining. Communication in organizational and healthcare settings involves all three contexts.

Communication Principles for a Lifetime

1.7 List and explain five fundamental principles of communication.

Five principles are fundamental to good communication.

1. Be aware of your communication with yourself and others. Being mindful of your communication is important to help you improve your communication.
2. Effectively use and interpret verbal messages. Words are powerful and influence our thoughts, actions, and relationships with others.
3. Effectively use and interpret nonverbal messages. Unspoken cues provide important information about our emotions, feelings, and attitudes.
4. Listen and respond thoughtfully to others. Being able to interpret the messages of others accurately enhances comprehension and relational empathy.
5. Appropriately adapt messages to others. It is important to adapt messages to others to enhance both understanding and empathy.

Key Terms

Communication, p. 5
Human Communication, p. 5
Symbol, p. 6
Content Dimension, p. 8
Relationship Dimension, p. 8
Rule, p. 8
Source, p. 10
Encoding, p. 10
Decoding, p. 10
Receiver, p. 10
Message, p. 10
Channel, p. 10
Noise, p. 10
Feedback, p. 10
Context, p. 11
Communication Competence, p. 13
Ethics, p. 13
Mediated Communication, p. 15
Mass Communication, p. 15
Interpersonal Communication, p. 18
Impersonal Communication, p. 18
Small Group Communication, p. 18
Presentational Communication, p. 19
Rhetoric, p. 19
Organizational Communication, p. 19
Health Communication, p. 19
Intrapersonal Communication, p. 21
Language, p. 21
Nonverbal Communication, p. 22
Other-Oriented, p. 23
Adapt, p. 23

The Principle Points

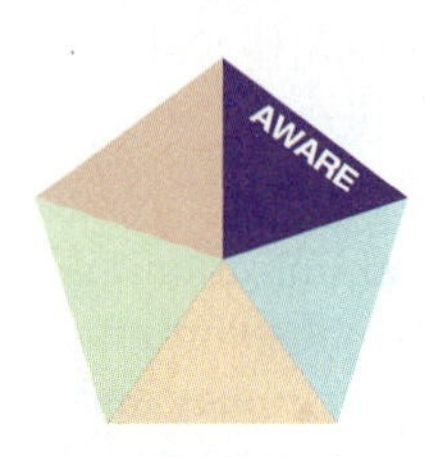

Principle One:

Be aware of your communication with yourself and others.

- Be aware of your intrapersonal communication.
- Be conscious of how your intrapersonal communication or self-talk has an effect on your communication with others and your overall communication behavior.
- Be aware of the communication behavior of others.

Principle Two:

Effectively use and interpret verbal messages.

- Use clear and precise words to explain ideas and concepts to others.
- Make a concerted effort to accurately interpret the words of others.

Principle Three:

Effectively use and interpret nonverbal messages.

- Use nonverbal, unspoken cues to express feelings and emotions to others or to modify the explicit verbal message you are communicating to others.
- Make a conscious effort to accurately decode the nonverbal messages of others.

Principle Four:

Listen and respond thoughtfully to others.

- Be other-oriented by taking special care to listen to both the verbal and the nonverbal messages of others.
- Be deliberate in how you provide feedback to those to whom you are listening.

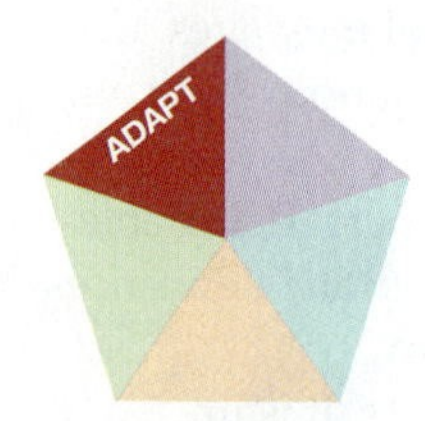

Principle Five:

Appropriately adapt messages to others.

- Use your listening and nonverbal communication skills to help you appropriately adjust both your message and how you communicate it to others.
- Make ethical choices about how to best formulate a message and respond to others to achieve your communication goals.

Apply Your Skill

Consider the following questions. Write your answers and/or share them with your classmates:

1. Recall that early in this chapter we asked why you are here. We're asking one more time, and this time, we hope you'll answer. Why are you here? What benefits do you hope to gain or what questions do you hope to answer through your study of human communication?
2. List the communication rules for a situation you are in regularly, such as a particular class, a regular group or team meeting, or in line at a deli or coffee shop on campus.
3. Describe in your own words an example of a communication transaction in which all parties are sending and receiving information at the same time.
4. Based on your own experiences, do you think that people who do a lot of their communication by text or online are lonely or uncomfortable communicating in person? Explain.
5. In which of the three contexts of in-person communication do you have the strongest skills? Which area(s) do you want to improve, and what skills would you like to develop?
6. As we noted at the beginning of this chapter, the five principles described in Figure 1.5 and throughout this text may not tell you everything you need to know about communication. What additional communication principle(s) would you suggest adding to the list?
7. Is every bit of our behavior really communication? Do we have to intend to communicate a message for it to be communication? Why or why not?

Assess Your Skill

Assessing Your Willingness to Communicate (WTC)

As you begin your study of communication, complete the following assessment measure to determine your willingness to communicate in several communication situations.

Directions: Below are twenty situations in which a person might choose to communicate or not to communicate. Presume that you have completely free choice. Indicate in the space at the left what percent of the time you would choose to communicate in each situation (0 = never, 100 = always).

1. ____ Talk with a service station attendant.
2. ____ Talk with a physician.
3. ____ Present a talk to a group of strangers.
4. ____ Talk with an acquaintance while standing in line.
5. ____ Talk with a salesperson in a store.
6. ____ Talk in a large meeting of friends.
7. ____ Talk with a police officer.
8. ____ Talk in a small group of strangers.
9. ____ Talk with a friend while standing in line.
10. ____ Talk with a waiter/waitress in a restaurant.
11. ____ Talk in a large meeting of acquaintances.
12. ____ Talk with a stranger while standing in line.
13. ____ Talk with a secretary.
14. ____ Present a talk to a group of friends.
15. ____ Talk in a small group of acquaintances.
16. ____ Talk with a garbage collector.
17. ____ Talk in a large meeting of strangers.
18. ____ Talk with a spouse (or girlfriend/boyfriend).
19. ____ Talk in a small group of friends.
20. ____ Present a talk to a group of acquaintances.

Scoring Instructions

The WTC score is designed to indicate how willing you are to communicate in a variety of contexts with different types of receivers. The higher your overall WTC score, the more willing you are to communicate in general. Similarly, the higher your subscore for a type of context or audience, the more willing you are to communicate in that type of context or with that type of audience. The WTC assessment permits computation of one total score and seven subscores. The subscores relate to willingness to communicate in four common communication contexts and with three types of audiences.

Subscore for Communication Context	*Scoring Formula*
Group discussions	Add scores for items 8, 15, 19; then divide by 3.
Meetings	Add scores for items 6, 11, 17; then divide by 3.
Interpersonal conversations	Add scores for items 4, 9, 12; then divide by 3.
Public speaking	Add scores for items 3, 14, 20; then divide by 3.
Subscore for Audience Type	
Stranger	Add scores for items 3, 8, 12, 17; then divide by 4.
Acquaintance	Add scores for items 4, 11, 15, 20; then divide by 4.
Friend	Add scores for items 6, 9, 14, 19; then divide by 4.

To compute your total WTC score, add the subscores for Stranger, Acquaintance, and Friend. Then divide by 3.

Norms for WTC scores

Group discussions	> 89, high WTC; < 57, low WTC
Meetings	> 80, high WTC; < 39, low WTC
Interpersonal conversations	> 94, high WTC; < 64, low WTC
Public speaking	> 78, high WTC; < 33, low WTC
Stranger	> 63, high WTC; < 18, low WTC
Acquaintance	> 92, high WTC; < 57, low WTC
Friend	> 99, high WTC; < 71, low WTC
Total WTC	> 82, high overall WTC; < 52, low overall WTC

Chapter 2

Exploring Self-Awareness and Communication

A person who buries his head in the sand offers an engaging target. —MABEL A. KEENAN

Patricia Malina/Shutterstock

Chapter Outline

- Self-Awareness: How Well Do You Know Yourself?
- Self-Concept: Who Are You?
- Self-Esteem: What's Your Value?
- Communication and the Enhancement of Self-Esteem
- The Perception Process
- Communicate to Enhance Your Powers of Perception
- Study Guide: Review, Apply, and Assess Your Knowledge and Skill

Chapter Objectives

After studying this chapter, you should be able to

2.1 Discuss the importance of self-awareness in the process of improving one's communication skills.

2.2 Describe the components of our self-concepts and major influences on the development of self-concept.

2.3 Describe how gender, social comparisons, self-expectations, and self-fulfilling prophecies affect one's self-esteem.

2.4 Practice six communication strategies for enhancing one's self-esteem.

2.5 Explain the three stages of perception and why people differ in their perceptions of people and events.

2.6 Summarize three communication strategies that can improve your powers of perception.

It's a safe bet that you have some sort of online presence, whether it's your own website, a Facebook profile, or some other means of expressing yourself online. Most college students now have multiple outlets for online expression. Think for a moment about the choices you make when creating and revising your online persona. What factors go into your decision making? For example, if you use a photo in your Facebook profile, do you regularly change that photo or do you leave the same one up most of the time? Is it a photo of you as you currently are, or is the photo of you at a younger age? Some people select photos of their pets, cartoon characters, celebrities, or even food to represent them online. What messages are sent by such choices? Consider your privacy options. Do you share your age, where you're currently living, or your relationship status? Whom do you allow to see what information? Is your profile or website an accurate representation of who you are as a person, or does it reflect just a part of who you perceive yourself to be? Developing a personal website or Facebook profile is an activity that relies on a central, important element: awareness.

Figure 2.1 Communication Principles for a Lifetime

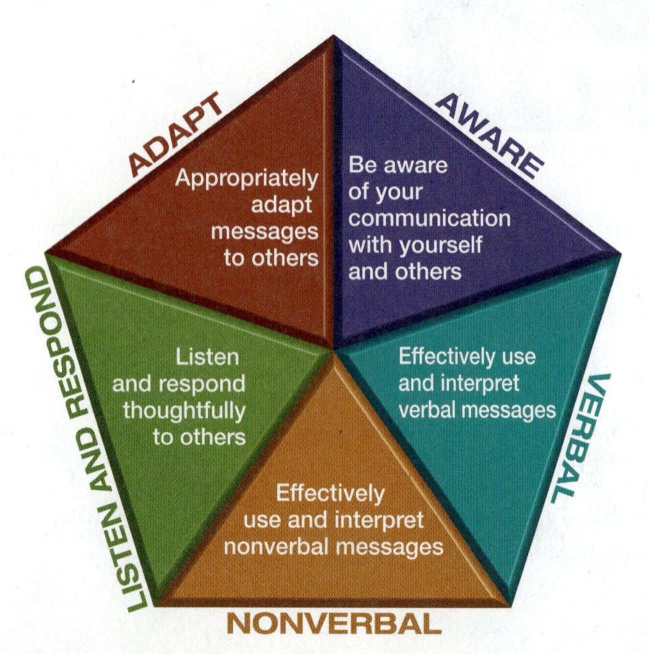

Stephen Covey, author of *The Seven Habits of Highly Effective People,* describes self-awareness as a characteristic that "enables us to stand apart and examine even the way we 'see' ourselves."[1] Interpersonal communication scholar David Johnson points out the importance of self-awareness: "Self-awareness is the key to self-knowledge, self-understanding, and self-disclosure. Being open with another person begins with being aware of who you are and what you are like. To disclose your feelings and reactions, you must be aware of them.[2]

Figure 2.1 presents the Communication Principles for a Lifetime model introduced in Chapter 1. The five principles provide the foundation for effective communication in various contexts you may encounter throughout your life. In this chapter, we explore the first principle: *Be aware of your communication with yourself and others.* Developing self-awareness involves being conscious not only of the present moment, but also of who you are, your values, and your perception of yourself and others.

Self-Awareness: How Well Do You Know Yourself?

2.1 Discuss the importance of self-awareness in the process of improving one's communication skills.

Many of us experience moments in our lives when we're acutely aware that we're learning something important—something that will change us in some profound way. (College years are typically full of these moments.) While a great deal of self-awareness comes gradually and simply, some is thrust upon us in dramatic fashion, and we take leaps in our maturity and understanding of ourselves. In this chapter, we deal with all forms of awareness—the simple and the profound, the casual and the dramatic—because any kind of awareness influences how we communicate and respond to communication from others. Becoming more self-aware is a never-ending process in life. You don't reach a point at which you've maxed out your self-awareness.

By one definition, **self-awareness** is "the capacity to observe and reflect upon one's own mental states."[3] A related view holds that self-awareness, sometimes referred to as **symbolic self-awareness**, is the unique human ability to develop a representation of oneself and communicate that representation to others through language.[4]

The better we understand the complex, multilayered nature of the self, the more aware we will become of our own being; this awareness is critical in becoming an effective communicator. A framework attributed to Abraham Maslow helps explain the process of becoming self-aware. The same framework has also been used to explain our attainment of communication skill. The framework suggests that people operate at one of four levels:

1. *Unconscious incompetence.* We are unaware of our own incompetence. We don't know what we don't know.
2. *Conscious incompetence.* At this level, we become aware or conscious that we are not competent; we know what we don't know.
3. *Conscious competence.* We are aware that we know or can do something, but it has not yet become an integrated skill or habit.
4. *Unconscious competence.* At this level, skills become second nature. We know or can do something but don't have to concentrate to be able to act on that knowledge or draw on that skill.

To illustrate this framework, let's look at an example. Your coworker Stella sometimes says inappropriate things; she just doesn't seem to know how to talk to people in a way that doesn't make her come across like she was raised by wolves. Stella is at Maslow's level 1 when it comes to communication: She doesn't know that she communicates poorly. Eventually, customers and coworkers complain to Stella's supervisor. The supervisor calls Stella into the office, reprimands her for her poor communication skills, and requires her to enroll in communication training so that she can improve. Now Stella is at level 2 because she has become conscious of her own incompetence as a communicator. Stella embraces her communication training and, once back on the job, actively works to improve how she relates to coworkers, bosses, and customers. Her hard work pays off when her colleagues notice the changes she's making and provide positive feedback. Stella achieves level 3, in which she is conscious of her own competence as a communicator. If Stella continues to progress over time, at some point

self-awareness
The capacity to observe and reflect on one's own mental states.

symbolic self-awareness
A unique human ability to develop and communicate a representation of oneself to others through language.

she may reach level 4, in which communication effectiveness is incorporated into her style and self-concept and is no longer something she must make a conscious effort to achieve.

Almost any communication skill can be described in terms of these four levels. It's also possible to be at one level with one skill and at another level with another skill. For instance, you may skillfully meet new people but poorly manage conflict with a close personal friend. Someone may be very engaging when conversing with friends, but she or he would rather have a spinal tap than give a presentation.

Reading a book like this one and taking a communication course like the one you're enrolled in can spark moments of heightened self-awareness. You'll no doubt be challenged to think long and hard about who you are, inventorying what you believe about yourself and how such aspects of identity as gender, ethnicity, nationality, sexual orientation, and social class contribute to your view of self. You'll be encouraged

Communication & DIVERSITY

Self-Concept from East and West

The view of a relatively stable self-concept is culturally rooted in a Western perspective. Communication scholar Gabriel Bukobza has found that people from Eastern cultures tend to view the self-concept as "malleable, contextual, inconsistent, relational, interdependent, and oriented to group hierarchy."[5] According to this view, your self-concept could be quite open to change.

Different cultures have different views of the *sources* from which we get our self-concepts. In Asian countries, the self-concept is constructed around significant social groups—such as one's immediate family, extended family, or community—with each member wanting to fit in and feeling a strong commitment to group identity. In contrast, Westerners first use personal reflection and investigation to form the self-concept and then pursue feedback from others to validate the view of self.[6] We like it when others' views correspond with our own view of self, and we tend to reject messages (and people) who negate our self-concept.

In this global village in which we live, where access to members of other cultural groups is only a mouse click away, it's important to remember that even the most basic element—the self-concept—can vary interculturally. Americans tend to hold independence and individuality as core positive qualities within our self-concepts but let's refrain from judging someone from another culture whose self-concept stems from strong ties to others and an emphasis on community over individual.[7]

The self-concept that we develop through communication with our family stays with us throughout our life.
Wong Yu Liang/Fotolia

to go a step further to consider how you communicate that view of self to others. But the key beginning point is awareness. As Phil McGraw (a.k.a. Dr. Phil) says, "Can't fix what you don't acknowledge."

Self-Concept: Who Are You?

2.2 Describe the components of our self-concepts and major influences on the development of self-concept.

If someone were to ask you, "Who are you?" how would you respond? You might start with basic demographic information such as your age and where you're from. Perhaps you'd describe yourself in relation to groups and organizations to which you belong. Or you might talk about various roles you assume, such as "I'm a student at State" or "I'm so-and-so's daughter (or son)." Whatever answer you give will be incomplete because you can't really convey the totality of who you are to others.

Psychologist Karen Horney defines **self** as "that central inner force, common to all human beings and yet unique in each which is the deep source of growth."[8] Your "Who are you?" responses are also part of your **self-concept**—your interior identity or subjective description of who you think you are, which remains relatively stable despite the changing world in which you live.[9] Some people use the term *self-image* synonymously with self-concept, but we want to avoid confusion over these terms. We subscribe to a narrower meaning for the term self-image, in that **self-image** is your view of yourself *in a particular situation.*[10] That view changes from situation to situation. For example, you may be extroverted in chemistry class but not at a party where you don't know many people. You may become very nervous when talking to an authority figure but be quite comfortable communicating with people your own age. You have several self-images, because they change as the situation changes, but they are part of the larger component we call self-concept. The self-concept is the way we *consistently* describe ourselves to others; it is deeply rooted and slow to change.[11]

self
The sum of who you are as a person; your central inner force.

self-concept
Your interior identity or subjective description of who you think you are.

self-image
Your view of yourself in a particular situation or circumstance.

Self-Concept Components

The self-concept contains many components, but three critical ones are your **attitudes**, **beliefs**, and **values**. Table 2.1 describes each in more detail. Of these three aspects, attitudes are the most superficial and likely to change; values are more at the core of a person and least likely to change.

attitudes
Learned predispositions to respond to a person, object, or idea in a favorable or unfavorable way.

beliefs
Ways in which you structure your understanding of reality—what is true and what is false.

values
Enduring concepts of good and bad or right and wrong.

One or Many Selves?

"I'm just not myself this morning," sighs Sandy, as she drags herself out the door to head to class. If she is not herself, *who is she?* Does each of us have just one self? Or is there a more "real" self buried somewhere within?

Table 2.1 Self-Concept Components

Component	Definition	Dimensions	Example
Attitudes	Learned predispositions to respond favorably or unfavorably toward something	Likes–Dislikes	You like ice cream, video games, and free music downloads.
Beliefs	Ways in which you structure reality	True–False	You believe your parents love you.
Values	Enduring concepts of right and wrong	Good–Bad	You value honesty and truth.

One of the most enduring and widely accepted frameworks for understanding the self was developed by philosopher William James. He identified three components of the self: the material self, the social self, and the spiritual self.[12]

THE MATERIAL SELF Perhaps you've heard the statement "You are what you eat." The material self goes a step further by suggesting that "You are what you have." The **material self** is a total of all the tangible things you own: your body, your possessions, your home.

One element of the material self receives considerable attention in our culture: the body. Do you like the way you look? Most of us would like to change something about our appearance. Research has determined that in the United States, women experience more negative feelings about their bodies than men, which affects how women view themselves.[13] Many women hold images of very thin women, such as supermodels and other media personalities, as ideals and develop dissatisfaction with their own bodies in comparison. Women's dissatisfaction with their bodies has markedly increased over recent decades. Research from the National Institute on Media and the Family finds that, by age 13, 53 percent of American girls report being unhappy with their bodies. That statistic grows to 78 percent by the time girls reach age 17.[14] However, research also shows that men and boys increasingly experience weight problems and are not immune to body dissatisfaction, in that they compare their own bodies with ideal muscular male bodies displayed in the media and are concerned about what others want and expect them to look like.[15] When there is a discrepancy between our desired material self and our self-concept, we may respond to eliminate the discrepancy. We may try to lose weight, have a nose job, or get another tattoo.

We also attempt to keep up with the proverbial Joneses by wanting more expensive clothes, cars, and homes. By extension, what we own becomes who we are. The bigger, better, more high-tech, and more luxurious our material possessions, we may subconsciously conclude, the better *we* are.

material self
The element of the self reflected in all the tangible things you own.

social self
Your concept of self as developed through your personal, social interactions with others.

spiritual self
Your concept of self based on your beliefs and your sense of who you are in relationship to other forces in the universe; also includes your thoughts and introspections about your values and moral standards.

THE SOCIAL SELF Your **social self** is that part of you that interacts with others. William James believed that you have as many social selves as you have people who recognize you and that you change who you are depending on the friend, family member, colleague, or acquaintance with whom you are interacting. For example, when you talk to your best friend, you're willing to "let your hair down" and reveal more thoughts and feelings than you might in a conversation with a professor, your parents, or your boss. Each relationship that you have with another person is unique because you bring to it a unique social self. This means that you are multifaceted, not false with people, because you have different selves in relation to different people.

THE SPIRITUAL SELF Your **spiritual self** is a mixture of your beliefs and your sense of who you are in relationship to other forces in the universe. Notice that this aspect of the self is termed "spiritual," not "religious." The term *religious* implies adherence to a specific religion or faith, typically accompanied by a belief in a supreme being or creator. However, people who see themselves as spiritual often do not subscribe to any one religion, preferring to develop their views from an array of philosophies and belief systems. From William James's perspective, the spiritual self contains all your internal thoughts and introspections about your values and moral standards. It is not dependent on what you own or with whom you talk; it is the essence of who you *think* you are and how you *feel* about yourself. It is your attempt to understand your inner essence,

RECAP

William James's Dimensions of Self

Dimension	Definition	Examples
Material Self	The component of self derived from physical elements that reflect who you are	The self you reveal through your body, clothes, car, phone
Social Self	The variety of selves that appear in different situations and roles, reflected in interactions with others	Your informal self interacting with friends; your formal self interacting with your professors
Spiritual Self	The component of self based on introspection about values, morals, and beliefs	Belief or disbelief in a supreme being or force; regard for life in all its forms

whether you view that essence as consciousness, spirit, or soul. Your spiritual self is the part of you that attempts to answer the question "Why am I here?"

How the Self-Concept Develops

Research suggests we address the question "Who am I?" through four basic means: (1) our communication with other individuals, (2) our association with groups, (3) roles we assume, and (4) our self-labels.

COMMUNICATION WITH OTHERS A valued colleague of ours often says, when he teaches communication courses, that every time you lose a relationship you lose an opportunity to see yourself. What he means is that we don't come to know and understand ourselves in a vacuum. We learn who we are by communicating with others, receiving their feedback, making sense out of it, and internalizing or rejecting all or part of it, such that we are altered by the experience. For example, let's say you like to think of yourself as a real comedian. Now think about it for a moment: How would you know you were funny if not for others' laughing at humorous things you say or do? Sure, you can crack yourself up, but the real test of whether you're funny or not is how others react to you.

avowed identity
An identity you assign to yourself and portray.

ascribed identity
An identity assigned to you by others.

In 1902, scholar Charles Horton Cooley first advanced the notion that we form our self-concepts by seeing ourselves in a figurative looking glass: We learn who we are by interacting with others, much as we look into a mirror and see our reflection.[16] Like Cooley, George Herbert Mead, author of *Mind, Self, and Society* and creator of symbolic interactionism theory, also believed that our sense of who we are is a consequence of our relationships with others.[17] Recent research confirms this idea. Results from a study of self-concept development in adolescents reinforced the important role parents play in developing a strong sense of self in their children. When parents, both generally and through daily conversations, confirmed their adolescents' sense of self and challenged them to realize their greater potential, this form of communication had a powerful effect on the adolescents' self-concept development.[18]

Communication and psychology scholars have explored four characteristics of the self-concept, or one's identity, that reinforce the importance of our interactions with other people:[19]

- *Identity is multidimensional and changing.* Some aspects of identity are stable, such as genetic profile or ethnicity, but most aspects of the self are constructed and therefore fluid, meaning that your identity may change because of circumstances and relationships with others.
- *Identity involves responsiveness to others,* meaning that the self isn't formed in a vacuum but is negotiated, co-created, reinforced, and challenged through communication with others.[20]
- *Identity develops through both past and present relationships.*[21] Who you are today is greatly a function of your family background and relationships. Early messages you received, nicknames you were given, and the ways family members related to you significantly influenced your view of self. Current relationships with family, friends, romantic partners, and coworkers continue to shape your self-concept and identity.
- *We each have two components of our identity:* Your **avowed identity** is one you personally assign to yourself and portray, such as student, athlete, or friend. Your **ascribed identity** involves characteristics others attribute or assign to you, and you may or may not agree with the assignment. For example, you think you have a great sense of humor (avowed identity), but others perceive your

Although identities change along with our circumstances and relationships, messages we receive early in life can have a long-lasting influence on our identities. How might an experience like this one shape these girls' later views of themselves?
Monkey Business Images/Shutterstock

humor to be corny (ascribed identity). When contradictions emerge, you could simply dismiss others' views, but you'll enhance your self-awareness if you instead process the ascribed identity. Take it in, contemplate why people see you the way they do, and consider whether any changes are necessary in the way you relate to others. Avowed and ascribed identities aren't static; they shift and are negotiated through interactions with others.[22]

ASSOCIATION WITH GROUPS I'm a native New Yorker. I'm a soccer player. I'm a rabbi. I'm a real estate agent. I'm a member of the Tea Party. Each of these self-descriptive statements answers the "Who am I?" question by citing identification with a group or organization. Our awareness of who we are is often linked to those with whom we associate. Some groups we are born into; others we choose on our own. Either way, group associations are significant parts of our identities.[23]

ASSUMED ROLES A large part of most people's answers to the "Who am I?" question reflects roles they assume in their lives. Mother, aunt, brother, uncle, manager, salesperson, teacher, spouse, and student are labels that imply certain expectations for behavior, and they are important in shaping the self-concept.

Gender asserts a powerful influence on the self-concept from birth on. As soon as they know the sex of their child, many parents begin associating their child with a gender group by adhering to cultural roles. They give the child sex-stereotypical toys, such as catcher's mitts, train sets, or guns for boys and dolls, tea sets, and dress-up kits for girls. These cultural expectations play a major role in shaping our self-concept and our behavior.[24] By the time we reach adulthood, our self-concepts are quite distinguishable by sex, with men describing themselves more in terms of giftedness, power, and invulnerability and women viewing themselves in terms of likability and morality.[25]

SELF-LABELS Although our self-concept is deeply affected by others, we are not blank slates for them to write on. The labels we use to describe our own attitudes, beliefs, values, and actions also play a role in shaping our self-concept.[26] Where do our labels come from? We interpret what we experience; we are self-reflexive. **Self-reflexiveness** is the human ability to think about what we're doing while we're doing it. We talk to ourselves about ourselves. We are both participants and observers in all that we do.[27] This dual role encourages us to use labels to describe who we are.

RECAP

How the Self-Concept Develops

Communication with Others	The self-concept develops as we communicate with others, receive their feedback, make sense out of it, and internalize or reject all or part of it.
Association with Groups	We develop our self-concept partly because of and through our identification with groups or organizations.
Assumed Roles	The self-concept is affected by roles we assume, such as son or daughter, employee, parent, spouse, or student.
Self-Labels	The terms we use to describe our attitudes, beliefs, values, and actions play a role in shaping the self-concept.

Self-Esteem: What's Your Value?

2.3 Describe how gender, social comparisons, self-expectations, and self-fulfilling prophecies affect one's self-esteem.

It may sound crass to consider your *value,* but you do this every day. Your assessment of your value is termed **self-esteem**. This *evaluation* of who you are is closely related to your self-concept, or your *description* of who you are. Feminist author Gloria Steinem explains that "It's a feeling of 'clicking in' when that self is recognized, valued, discovered, *esteemed*—as if we literally plug into an inner energy that is ours alone, yet connects us to everything else."[28]

While the self-concept pertains to one's enduring identity, self-esteem pertains more to one's current state of mind or view of self. But are the two aspects of the self related? Research continues to explore that very question, focusing on the notion of

self-reflexiveness
The human ability to think about what you are doing while you are doing it.

self-esteem
Your assessment of your worth or value as reflected in your perception of such things as your skills, abilities, talents, and appearance.

self-concept clarity
The extent to which beliefs about oneself are clearly and confidently identified and stable over time.

Theresa McCracken/CartoonStock

self-concept clarity, which Canadian psychologist Jennifer Campbell defines as the extent to which beliefs about oneself are clearly and confidently identified and stable over time.[29] It doesn't mean that you don't change as a person or that your view of yourself doesn't change; we know that people evolve as they mature and experience new things. But self-concept clarity relates to the stability associated with having a clear sense of who you are and being confident in your identity. One of the things Campbell and various colleagues have determined is that people who suffer from low self-esteem also tend to have a less clearly defined sense of self; in other words, they tend to have more questions about their identity.[30]

Self-esteem can fluctuate because of relatively minor events, such as getting a high grade on a paper, or major upheavals, such as the breakup of an important relationship.[31] For example, recent college grads who struggle to land a job related to their field of study may suffer a downturn in self-esteem.[32] Self-esteem can rise or fall within the course of a day; sometimes just a look from someone (or someone's failure to notice you) can send you into a tailspin and make you feel devalued. Or a certain level of self-esteem can last for a while—you may have a series of months or even years that you look back on thinking, "I felt pretty lousy about myself in those days. Glad that period is over." Four factors provide clues about the nature of self-esteem: gender, social comparisons, self-expectations, and the self-fulfilling prophecy.

Gender

Your **gender** is a complex cultural construction that includes your biological sex (male or female); psychological and emotional characteristics that cause you to be masculine, feminine, or androgynous (a combination of feminine and masculine traits); your attitudes about appropriate roles and behavior for the sexes in society; and your sexual orientation (to whom you are sexually attracted).[33] All these elements affect your self-esteem.

Research documents ways that boys' self-esteem develops differently from girls' self-esteem during childhood and adolescence. In a patriarchal (or male-dominated) culture, such as that of the United States, women and girls suffer loss of self-esteem to a much greater degree than men and boys.[34] The trend continues into adulthood, and it has prompted several prominent women to write books addressing the problem of women's general lack of self-esteem and confidence in American culture. Books like Katty Kay and Claire Shipman's *The Confidence Code*, Sheryl Sandberg's *Lean In*, and

gender
A cultural construction that includes one's biological sex (male or female), psychological characteristics (femininity, masculinity, androgyny), attitudes about the sexes, and sexual orientation.

Mika Brzezinski's *Knowing Your Value* all speak to women's general lack of belief in their own worth and how such a deficit impedes their progress, both professionally and personally. These very accomplished female authors encourage women of all ages to think about ways—large and small—that their lack of self-esteem holds them back, and they offer strategies for enhancing self-esteem and confidence.[35]

Social Comparisons

One way we become more aware of ourselves and derive our sense of self-worth is by measuring ourselves against others, a process called **social comparison**.[36] I'm good at playing basketball (because I'm part of a winning team); I can't cook (because others cook better than I do); I'm good at meeting people (whereas most people seem to be uncomfortable interacting with new people); I'm not handy (but my dad can fix anything). Each of these statements implies a judgment about how well or badly you can perform certain tasks in comparison to how well others perform the same tasks.

social comparison
Process of comparing oneself to others to measure one's worth.

self-expectations
Goals you set for yourself; how you believe you ought to behave and what you ought to accomplish.

One powerful social comparison that contributes to self-esteem loss is fueled by images of physical attractiveness in the media. Mass media create and reinforce for consumers notions of what is physically attractive, and achieving that media-driven standard is next to impossible for most people.[37] One line of research has found that females of a wide range of ages—from preadolescents through college students—compare their own physical attractiveness to that of models in ads. When they perceive that they don't measure up, they often experience the "model trap." This trap is a continual cycle of viewing physically "perfect" models, hating them, then growing to like and even love them, followed by failed efforts to be like them, inevitable resentment, and then a repeat of the cycle.[38]

It can be self-defeating to take social comparisons too far, to cause your self-esteem to suffer because you compare yourself unfairly or unrealistically to others. If you're going to do any comparing at all, compare yourself to friends and neighbors, people you know and who are similar to you in many ways, rather than to people who are obviously not like you.

High-school student Galia Slayen built this life-size Barbie doll to show how unrealistic standards for physical attractiveness can damage the self-esteem of girls and women. According to Slayen, if Barbie were a real woman, she would stand six feet tall and have an 18-inch waist.
CB2/ZOB/WENN.com/Newscom

Self-Expectations

Another factor that affects your self-esteem is your estimation of how well you accomplish your goals. **Self-expectations** are goals we set for ourselves, such as losing weight, developing a "buff" body, making better grades, being appointed or elected to an important office in an organization, graduating by a certain time, or acquiring wealth by a certain age. Self-esteem is affected when you evaluate how well you measure up to your own expectations. For instance, if you expect to receive all A's this semester and you don't, it's likely your self-esteem will be affected negatively. You may have to readjust your goals and expectations or just become more determined to achieve the straight-A goal next semester.

Some people place enormous expectations on themselves, probably because their parents had enormous expectations for them when they were growing up. We wish people who are stressed out all the time could give themselves a break, because they place such unrealistic, high demands on themselves. The popular achievement gurus will tell you that you won't accomplish much if you set easily attainable goals. But we're suspicious of that advice; we see too many people whose self-esteem is low because they place such pressure and unrealistic demands on themselves. When they can't live up to those demands, they feel guilty and begin to see themselves as failures. A downward trend involving expectation, failure, guilt, and low self-esteem takes a lot of work to reverse.

Communication & TECHNOLOGY

Got Low Self-Esteem? Can Social Media Help?

Can communicating through social media help if you struggle with low self-esteem? Research says: Yes and No.

We're all probably well aware of the statistics regarding the growth of online social media use. Research done in 2013 by the Pew Institute indicates that while Facebook is still the dominant online platform in the United States (71% of online adults are Facebook users), other social networking sites such as Twitter, LinkedIn, Pinterest, and Instagram are catching up.[39] But research results on how social media involvement makes you *feel* about yourself are mixed.

Some studies have found that the social opportunities online outlets provide can enhance people's self-esteem. Simply reflecting on oneself and editing one's profile as well as receiving positive feedback from Facebook friends can enhance people's views of themselves in terms of physical attractiveness, romantic appeal, and success in maintaining close relationships.[40]

Other research, however, has found that online social comparisons can hurt your self-esteem. For example, comparing your physical attractiveness to profile pictures of beautiful people can lower your self-esteem. Some research has shown that men who viewed profiles of highly successful men saw themselves and their current career status in a more negative light as a result.[41]

One slightly odd effect social media use may produce is that it can diminish your ability to do math! Research has found that people's ability to perform well in cognitively challenging tasks is hampered by exposure to social media sites. So if your math skills are connected to your self-esteem, social media use can harm your view of your own worth. It's probably not a good idea to post on Facebook right before studying for a tough test.[42]

Because online activities take up an increasing part of our daily lives, it's important to consider the effect they have on our view of self and how we communicate that view to others. Is your offline self-esteem different from the self-esteem level you project online? Does social media use make you feel better or worse about yourself?

Self-Fulfilling Prophecy

A concept related to the creation of self-expectations is the **self-fulfilling prophecy**, the idea that what you believe about yourself often comes true because you expect it to come true.[43] If you think you'll fail a math quiz because you have labeled yourself inept at math, then you must overcome not only your math deficiency but also your low expectations of yourself when it comes to math. If you hold the self-perception that you're pretty good at conversation, then you're likely to act on that assumption when you approach a conversation with someone. Your conversations, true to form, will go well, thus reinforcing your belief in yourself as a good conversationalist.

RECAP

Factors Affecting Self-Esteem

Gender	In male-dominated cultures, girls and women suffer self-esteem loss to a much greater degree than boys and men, primarily as a result of males' feeling better able to do things than females.
Social Comparisons	Judgments about how well or poorly you can perform certain tasks compared to others can be self-defeating and can cause self-esteem to suffer.
Self-Expectations	Your estimation of how well you perform in comparison to your own goals or self-expectations has a profound effect on self-esteem.
Self-Fulfilling Prophecies	What you believe about yourself often comes true because you expect it to come true.

Communication and the Enhancement of Self-Esteem

2.4 Practice six communication strategies for enhancing one's self-esteem.

We know the damage low self-esteem can do to us: It can limit our ability to develop and maintain satisfying relationships, to experience career successes and advancement, and to create a generally happy and contented life. Teachers, psychologists, self-help gurus, clergy members, social workers, and even politicians suggest that many of our societal problems stem from our collective feelings of low self-esteem. Our feelings of low self-worth may contribute to our choosing the wrong partners; becoming addicted to drugs, alcohol, sex, online activities, or gambling; experiencing problems

self-fulfilling prophecy
The notion that predictions about one's future are likely to come true because one believes that they will come true.

Communication & ETHICS

Can You Have TOO Much Self-Esteem?

For decades, scholars, teachers, counselors, and others in helping roles in American culture have agreed that many people suffer from debilitatingly low levels of self-esteem. However, growing evidence suggests that the efforts of self-help gurus, psychologists, and parents to build children's self-confidence may have paid off in a big way, perhaps too big of a way.

Although every day in our classes we still witness countless numbers of students whose self-esteem could use a shot of caffeine, we are also beginning to see the fruits of a "be all that you can be" generation. Some children have now grown into adults whose self-esteem is so healthy that, in some instances, it has led to self-centeredness. We, along with some experts, are wondering, "How much self-esteem is too much?"

Jean Twenge, author of *Generation Me: Why Today's Young Americans Are More Confident, Assertive, Entitled—and More Miserable Than Ever Before,* is a leading researcher of college students and **narcissism**, a personality attribute that carries as its primary characteristic a positive but inflated view of self, especially regarding areas of one's own power, importance, and physical attractiveness.[44] In a study of more than 16,000 college students, Twenge and colleagues found that student narcissism had sharply risen since the 1980s.[45]

Increased narcissism isn't being detected only in the United States. International studies also have found rising levels of self-involvement among young people in such countries as China and New Zealand.[46]

Some of today's most popular means of communicating are increasingly used by narcissistic people. People who score high on narcissism scales tend to check Facebook multiple times a day and spend more time in Facebook sessions than those who are low or moderate in narcissism, for example.[47] Narcissists are also drawn to social networking sites that allow them to self-select information for their profiles (possibly inflating their positive qualities), post photos that reveal their lives to the public, update their status to show others what they're doing or thinking about, and provide positive self-descriptions.[48]

While some positive outcomes are related to narcissism, such as enhanced self-esteem and levels of life satisfaction, the downsides include distorted judgment of one's abilities, risky decision making, and potential addictive disorders and compulsions (e.g., alcohol abuse, compulsive shopping, and gambling).[49]

with eating and other vital activities; and opting, in too many cases, for death over life. So we owe it to society, as well as ourselves, to develop and work to maintain a healthy sense of self-esteem, as an integral part of the process of becoming more self-aware.

One team of researchers followed a group of approximately 4,000 Americans for sixteen years, assessing changes in these people's self-esteem during that time. Participants ranged from 25 to 104 years old, allowing the researchers to track the trajectory of self-esteem as we age. The results suggest that self-esteem increases during young and middle adulthood, peaks around age 60, and then declines in old age.[50] This research doesn't seal your fate. Your own self-esteem trajectory may differ from the results of the study for many reasons. But if there's one take-home message from this study, it's this: Now is *prime time* to develop a healthy self-esteem! Although no simple list of tricks can easily transform low self-esteem into feelings of being valued and appreciated, you can improve how you think about yourself. One thing is clear from research about self-esteem: Communication is essential in the process of building and maintaining self-esteem.[51]

narcissism
An inflated view of self, especially about one's own power and importance.

Engage in Positive Self-Talk

intrapersonal communication
How you take in stimuli in the environment or information and make sense of it; also, thoughts and ideas that you say to yourself.

self-talk
Inner speech; communication with the self.

Intrapersonal communication refers to how you take in information or stimuli in your environment and make sense of them.[52] It also involves communication within yourself—**self-talk**, or what some scholars term "inner speech."[53] Your self-concept and level of self-esteem influence the way you talk to yourself about your abilities and skills. The reverse is also true, in that your inner dialogue has an effect on both your self-concept and your level of self-esteem. Athletes use positive self-talk to motivate themselves to play better, especially if they're struggling on the court or field of play. Some also talk to themselves negatively when they perform poorly. Research shows, however, that athletes who engage in negative inner dialogue usually do nothing to improve their performance.[54]

Positive self-talk can motivate us to do our best in challenging situations. Are there situations in which you could make your own self-talk more encouraging?
Anna Jurkovska/Shutterstock

Visualize

Visualization—imagining oneself behaving in a certain way—takes the notion of self-talk one step further. Besides just telling yourself that you can achieve your goal, you can actually try to "see" yourself conversing effectively with others, performing well on a project, or exhibiting some other desirable behavior. Because the United States is such a visual culture, most of us have no trouble visualizing elaborate scenarios in our heads.

Research suggests that an apprehensive public speaker can manage her or his fears by visualizing positive results.[55] In fact, visualization reduces anxiety as well as negative self-talk or the number of debilitating thoughts that enter a speaker's consciousness.[56] If you're one of the many people who fear making presentations, try visualizing yourself walking to the front of the room, taking out your well-prepared notes, delivering a well-rehearsed and interesting presentation, and returning to your seat to the sound of applause from your audience. This visualization of positive results enhances confidence and speaking skill. The same technique can be used to boost your sense of self-worth about other tasks or skills. If you're nervous about a date, for example, visualize each step of the date (as realistically as you can). Think through what you might talk about on the date and how the night will progress. This mental rehearsal will help reduce your anxiety. In addition, visualizing yourself interacting or performing well can help you change long-standing feelings of inadequacy.

Reframe

The process of redefining events and experiences, of looking at something from a different point of view, is termed **reframing**. When a movie director gets different "takes" or shots of the same scene, she or he is striving to get the best work possible. The director alters small details, like camera angles or actor movements, to get yet another look or vision for a scene. Just like that movie director, you can reframe your "take" on events or circumstances that cause you to lose self-esteem.

Here's an example. You get a report from your supervisor that says you should improve one area of your performance, but instead of engaging in self-talk that says you're terrible at your job, you reframe the event within a larger context. You tell yourself that one negative comment doesn't mean you are a bad employee.

Of course, you shouldn't leave negative experiences unexamined, because you can learn and profit from your mistakes. But it's important to remember that our worth as human beings is not contingent on a single *anything*—a single grade, a single relationship, a single response from a prospective employer, or a single play in a football game. Looking at the big picture—at the effect this one event will have on your whole life, on society, on history—places negative experiences we all have in realistic contexts.

visualization
The technique of imagining that you are performing a particular task in a certain way; a method of enhancing self-esteem.

reframing
The process of redefining events and experiences from a different point of view.

Develop Honest Relationships

The suggestion that you develop honest relationships may sound like the latest advice from some self-help website, but it's actually harder to accomplish than it sounds. Think about it: How many people in your life really give you the straight scoop about yourself? How many people are so solid in their relationship with you that they can tell you the things that are the hardest to hear, things that no one else would dare tell you? Most of us can count the number of those people on one hand. That doesn't mean we aren't honest with the many friends and acquaintances we have in our lives, but most of us really trust only a select few enough to deal with the tough stuff.

Having at least one other person who will give you honest feedback and help you objectively reflect on your virtues and vices can be extremely beneficial in fostering healthy, positive self-esteem. As we noted earlier, other people play a major role in shaping our self-concept and self-esteem. You don't want to find yourself at a point where you're oblivious to the feedback of others. That kind of attitude can make you narcissistic, unrealistic, and rigid, unable to adjust to life's changing circumstances. Most people who reject or overlook significant others' feedback end up isolated and with low self-esteem.

Here's one other benefit of having honest relationships: The people in these relationships are the ones you can tell about your feelings of low self-esteem. Some people have learned bravado, an ability to communicate a strong, confident air and work their way through challenges or situations in which their self-esteem may suffer.[57] But *everyone,* at some time or another, suffers a lack of self-esteem about *something.* Whether you reveal that fact and to whom you reveal it are important decisions. But in trusting, honest relationships, sometimes revealing that you don't feel completely confident about something can produce enhanced closeness; it's likely that the person you reveal your qualms to has equally debilitating fears, anxieties, and moments of lost self-esteem. Conversations in which people can divulge their weaknesses or share which circumstances in their lives cause their self-esteem to decrease can be very affirming. Sometimes, knowing that you're not alone in the "low self-esteem boat" can turn even that low self-esteem around.

Surround Yourself with Positive People

Related to the development of honest relationships is a suggestion about the people you choose to associate with the most in your life. If you want to improve your self-esteem and to develop a more positive outlook, it's better to surround yourself with people who tend to have higher levels of self-esteem than with people who are "Debbie Downers." Granted, sometimes you don't have a choice; you get assigned a roommate in college, you end up with an instructor's choice of lab or study partner, and you rarely get to choose the people you work with. So we're not suggesting that you disassociate yourself from people who have low self-esteem, because that's unrealistic. Besides, we all suffer from bouts of low self-esteem at some time or another. People with low self-esteem need to be around uplifting people—those whose positive self-regard will rub off on them.

Dave Coverly/The Cartoonist Group

As an example, we know an elderly woman, Hazel, who was in good enough health to be able to help the Meals on Wheels organization deliver food to shut-ins in her town. Hazel often talked about how sour many of the people on her route were, how their attitudes had "gone south" because of poor health, limited options, and fading hope. She believed that her main purpose wasn't to deliver a hot meal but to extend the gift of her positive outlook. She often told us about how many complaints she heard in the course of one day, but she was determined to stay optimistic and to offer hope to those she visited. One time Hazel described what she viewed as a personal triumph. The most sour person on her route—a woman with very low self-esteem and a cranky disposition, one who never did anything but gripe to Hazel when she visited—began to "thaw." One day when Hazel delivered her meal, the woman actually greeted her at the front door and seemed genuinely glad to see Hazel. She complained less often as she slowly began to enjoy the warm glow of Hazel's sunny disposition and empathic responses. Hazel felt that the woman's self-esteem had begun to improve, that her outlook on life had begun to change.

RECAP

Strategies for Enhancing Self-Esteem

Engage in Positive Self-Talk	If you want positive results, talk positively to yourself. If you are self-critical and negative, you may set yourself up for failure. Rephrase doubts and negative thoughts into positive, uplifting encouragement.
Visualize	In anticipation of a significant event, picture how you want the event to go, as a mental rehearsal. If you feel anxious or nervous, visualize success instead of failure.
Reframe	Try to look at experiences and events, especially those that can cause you to lose self-esteem, from a different point of view. Keep the larger picture in mind rather than focusing on one isolated negative incident.
Develop Honest Relationships	Cultivate friends whom you can confide in and who will give you honest feedback for improving your skills and abilities. Accept that feedback in the spirit of enhancing your self-esteem and making yourself a wiser, better person.
Surround Yourself with Positive People	Associating with people with high self-esteem can help you enhance your own self-esteem and develop a more positive outlook.
Lose Your Baggage	Dump your psychological and experiential baggage: Work to move beyond the negatives of your past so that you focus on the present and relieve your self-esteem of the burden of things you cannot change.

Lose Your Baggage

Not making the team. Getting passed over for a key promotion at work. Seeing a long-term relationship end. Feeling like a failure. We've all had experiences we would like to undo or get a second chance at, so that we could do them differently or so that we would *be* different. We all carry around experiential or psychological baggage, but the key question is, how much space does that baggage take up within your self-concept? To phrase this another way, how negatively is your self-esteem affected by your baggage?

Individuals with low self-esteem tend to lock onto events and experiences that happened years ago and tenaciously refuse to let go of or move past them. Looking back at what we can't change only reinforces a sense of helplessness. Constantly replaying negative experiences only serves to make our sense of self-worth more difficult to repair. A traumatic or defining experience in the past has a serious effect on your self-concept; it will probably always remain a part of you. But it doesn't have to affect your current level of self-esteem. It's important to take mental inventory of experiences in your past and then decide to let go of your baggage and move past those experiences that cause your present-day self-esteem to suffer.[58]

The Perception Process

2.5 Explain the three stages of perception and why people differ in their perceptions of people and events.

This chapter focuses on Principle One of our Communication Principles for a Lifetime: Be aware of your communication with yourself and others. Awareness involves developing greater understanding and skill by becoming more cognizant of yourself, others, and communication. Awareness includes exploring how we perceive ourselves and our communication with others, as well as the many ways in which we perceive other people and their communication. But just what is perception?

On the most basic level, **perception** is the arousal of any of our senses. A sound travels through the air, vibrates in the eardrum, activates the nerves, and sends a signal to the brain. A similar sequence of events takes place when we see, smell, feel, or taste something. So perception begins with the process of attending to stimuli in the environment. The process of perception also includes structuring and making sense of information provided by the senses. You come out of a building and see wet pavement

perception
The arousal of any of your senses.

and puddles of water, hear thunder, smell a fresh odor in the air, and feel a few drops of water on your head. You integrate all those bits of information and conclude that it's raining and has been for a while.

Perceiving people, however, goes beyond the simple processing of sensory information. We try to decide what people are like, making judgments about their personalities, and we give meaning to their actions by drawing inferences from what we observe.[59] When you meet someone new, you notice certain basic attributes, like the person's sex, general aspects of physical appearance, the sound of her or his voice, and whether or not he or she smiles, uses a friendly tone of voice, has an accent, and so forth. You also attend to specific details that the person communicates, verbally and nonverbally. Once you've chosen these stimuli to pay attention to, you then categorize the information into some sort of structure that works for you. Finally, you attempt to make sense of your structured perceptions; you assign meaning to what you have perceived. Let's examine more closely each of these three stages in the perception process.

Stage One: Attention and Selection

attention
The act of perceiving stimuli in your environment.

selection
The act of choosing specific stimuli in your environment to focus on.

organization
Converting information into convenient, understandable, and efficient patterns that allow us to make sense of what we have observed.

You're watching a group of parents at a playground with their children. The kids are playing, running around, laughing, and squealing, as children will do. You view the activity, hear the noise, feel the heat of the day on your skin, and smell hot dogs cooking on a grill. They smell so good you can almost taste them. After a moment, a parent jumps up and runs over to comfort a child who has fallen down and is crying. You were watching the action but didn't see the particular incident and didn't register the child's cry amidst all the noise. But the child's parent did. How did this happen?

The ability of parents to discern their own child's voice from a chorus of voices is one of the mysteries of human nature, but it also exemplifies the first stage of perception. Our human senses simply cannot process all the stimuli that are available at any given moment, so we select which sensations make it through to the level of awareness and ignore or filter out the rest. The activities of **attention** and **selection** constitute the first stage of the perception process. Have you ever listened to music in the dark so that you could eliminate visual sensations and focus only on what you were hearing? Have you ever watched TV with the sound turned off, just so you could enjoy the visual images without the "static" of sound? What we're doing in these instances is selecting what we will and will not attend to.

Selectivity can also cause us to fail to perceive information that is important.[60] A professor may be so focused on lecture material that she or he fails to realize that students are lost and not tracking the information. By selecting certain stimuli, we sometimes miss other clues that might be important, that might help us better understand what is happening and how to respond.

Because we cannot process every stimulus in our environment, we need to select which ones will get our attention. When you communicate in a noisy, distracting setting, how can you focus your attention to improve your powers of perception?
People Images/Getty Images

Stage Two: Organization

After we select stimuli to attend to and process, we start to convert the information into convenient, understandable, and efficient patterns that allow us to make sense of what we've observed. This activity, termed **organization**, makes it easier for us to process complex information because it allows us to impose the familiar onto the unfamiliar and because we can easily store and recall simple patterns.

Figure 2.2 What Do You See?

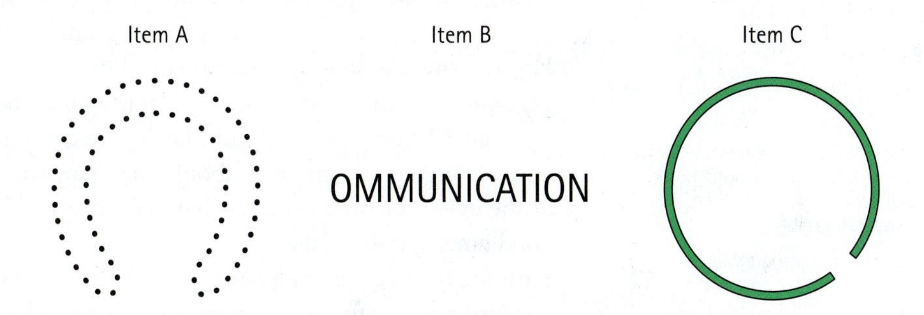

Look at the three items in Figure 2.2. What does each of them mean to you? If you're like most people, you'll perceive item A as a horseshoe, item B as the word *communication,* and item C as a circle. Strictly speaking, none of those perceptions is correct. For item A, you see a pattern of dots that you label a horseshoe because a horseshoe is a concept you know and to which you attach various meanings. Rather than processing a set of dots, it's much easier to organize the dots in a way that refers to something familiar. For some people, a more familiar pattern than a horseshoe might be an inverted U. For similar reasons, we organize patterns of stars in the sky into various constellations with shapes, like the Big and Little Dippers.

In Figure 2.2, items B and C also reveal our inclination to superimpose structure and consistency on what we observe. This tendency leads us to create a familiar word from the meaningless assemblage of letters in item B and to label the figure in item C a circle, even though a circle is a continuous line without any gaps. The process of filling in missing information is called **closure**, and it applies to our perceptions of people as well. When we have an incomplete picture of another human being, we impose a pattern or structure, classify the person on the basis of the information we do have, and fill in the gaps.

Perhaps you've sat in an airport or busy shopping mall watching people and tried to guess what they did for a living, what their personalities were like, or what their backgrounds were. Maybe you saw people you guessed were wealthy, hotheads, teachers, losers, athletes, loners, or surfer dudes. As you looked at people's clothing and saw how they walked or behaved, you made inferences about them. You superimposed some structure by using a general label and filling in the gaps in your information. This activity can get you into trouble, of course, but we'll save that discussion until the end of the chapter, when we focus on the problem of stereotyping.

Stage Three: Interpretation

Once we've organized stimuli, we're ready to assign meaning, a process termed **interpretation**. We attach meaning to all that we observe. In some cases, the meanings are fairly standardized, as they are for language, for example. But others are much more personalized. If you meet someone whose cologne is too heavy and has a scent you don't like, what's your impression of that person? How do you make sense of the perception that the person is wearing enough cologne to flood a whole building? What if the person also has a great handshake and warm smile? Does that change your interpretation of events and your impression of the person? This example illustrates how we impose meaning on what we observe to complete the perceptual process.

Of course, our interpretations can be off-base; we may perceive a situation one way when in fact something entirely different is occurring.[61] Maybe you've been in a social situation and thought someone was flirting with you, only to find the person was focused on someone behind or near you. Embarrassing? Yes, but inaccurate interpretations of our perceptions are commonplace.

closure
The perceptual process of filling in missing information.

interpretation
Attaching meaning to what is attended to, selected, and organized.

RECAP

The Perception Process

Term	Explanation	Example
Perception	The arousal of any of our senses	Hearing the sound of laughter
Attention and Selection	The first stage in the perception process, in which we perceive stimuli and choose which ones to focus our awareness on	Watching TV in your room while hearing giggling and laughter and ignoring the TV show to eavesdrop on the giggler
Organization	The second stage in the perception process, in which we structure stimuli into convenient and efficient patterns	Realizing that the laughter is coming from your younger sister, who's on the phone
Interpretation	The final stage in the perception process, in which we assign meaning to what we have perceived	Deciding that your sister is talking on the phone to her boyfriend because she laughs like that only when she talks to him

When Perceptions Vary

George and Martha have been married for, well, forever. They know each other very well, and each knows how the other thinks. So you'd think their perceptions of things, events, and people would line up, right? Wrong. George and Martha are driving home from a party, chatting about what happened at the event. George believes that everyone had a good time; that the house was filled with interesting, pleasant, relatively good-looking people; and that he received positive responses from everyone he talked to. Martha saw the party differently. She tells George that the reason people looked good was that most of them either had had plastic surgery to "hold back Father Time"; were Botoxed beyond all recognition; or were younger, "replacement" partners for all the divorced people who attended the party. Many people at the party disliked each other so intensely that they stayed on opposite sides of the room all night. Martha's interpretation of events is based not on prior or external knowledge, but on her perceptions from observing and interacting with people at the party. And about George's perception that everyone at the party liked him? Martha says, "Think again." She tells George that as soon as he left one group of men in a conversation and walked away, they signaled to one another with their body language that they thought George was a doofus. What's going on here? Who's right, George or Martha?

In actuality, neither is right or both are right. This example illustrates two differing perceptions of the same reality. There's no "truth" to be found, only different "takes" on the same people and set of events. Both sets of perceptions are valid, even though they differ, because varying perceptions are the norm in life. You know this to be true in your own life experience—even people you're very similar to and know quite well can differ from you dramatically in their perceptions of people and events. Your life experiences, how you were raised, and how you developed contribute a great deal to how you perceive things, events, and people in your life. These elements create a filter through which you observe and process the world around you.

Communicate to Enhance Your Powers of Perception

2.6 Summarize three communication strategies that can improve your powers of perception.

Has anyone ever told you that they formed a misperception about you when they first met you, but you proved them wrong over time? On occasion, people who are shy, serious, or simply more quiet in their communication style than others are misperceived as being conceited, aloof, or cocky. Outgoing, extroverted people may be viewed as overbearing when really they just enjoy the company of others.

Sometimes our powers of perception are sharp, but other times we miss the mark.[62] Because our communication is affected by our perceptions of others, it's important to work toward forming the most accurate perceptions you can, because then you have better, more reliable information on which to act. How can you improve your ability to form accurate perceptions? Here are three suggestions: increase your awareness, avoid stereotypes, and check your perceptions against others' perceptions.

Increase Your Awareness

We've made this topic—awareness—our first of five Communication Principles for a Lifetime for a reason. Exercise your senses, especially your sense of hearing. Work at really listening to people—fully listening, without interrupting them to put in your two cents' worth. Try to be more verbally and nonverbally aware; monitor how you communicate with others and how people respond to you. If you don't like the responses you're getting from people, it may be time for a change in *your* behavior, not theirs. You also want to monitor the verbal and nonverbal cues others exhibit. Pay attention to contextual cues, such as where an interaction is taking place, the time of day, the perceived moods of those interacting, and any physical or psychological barriers that impede the communication exchange. Learn from your mistakes, rather than repeating them.

Avoid Stereotypes

"She's a snob." "He's a nerd." "They're a bunch of dumb jocks." These statements reflect **stereotypes**, or generalizations we apply to individuals because we perceive them to have attributes common to a particular group.[63]

What comes to mind when you hear the term *homeless*? Do you associate the word with someone begging on the street, families living in shelters or their cars, or "bums" or "bag ladies" in parks, alleys, or subway stations? If these images came to mind, you've just invoked a stereotype. What may not have come to mind are the many families in the United States who are homeless following an economic recession with high rates of unemployment and home foreclosures. Research shows that many of us hold unfortunate stereotypes about homeless people and homelessness in general.[64]

Some positive or functional aspects of stereotypes emerge from our human nature to simplify and categorize stimuli in our environment, which we described as components of the perception process. Stereotypes serve as a baseline of information. If you know nothing else about a person other than she or he is a "northerner," for instance, then you can think about commonly held characteristics of other persons you've met from the northern part of the United States and go from there. Social psychologist Douglas Kenrick and his colleagues point out that "Stereotyping is a cognitively inexpensive way of understanding others: By presuming that people are like other members of their groups, we avoid the effortful process of learning about them as individuals."[65] But obviously, there's a serious downside.

Have you ever taken a class and, from day one, felt that the teacher pegged you a certain way? The teacher may have perceived you to be a slacker or uninterested in the course topic (on the negative side) or a straight-A student or future Ph.D. (on the positive side). The bottom line is that no one likes to be treated as a stereotype because it's limiting and impersonal. You can also feel pressure to try to live up to a stereotype, such as "all Asian students are exceptionally bright." Stereotypes are often degrading, as in age-old references to dumb blondes, bad women drivers, and dirty old men. Many of the worst stereotypes are related to gender, race/ethnicity, age, and physical appearance.[66]

Research has explored the ways we try to inhibit stereotypical thoughts before they have a chance to affect our behavior.[67] For example, if you grew up hearing family members invoke stereotypes about different ethnic groups, you may decide as an adult that you will not follow suit—that assigning ethnic stereotypes is inappropriate. However, because it's part of your upbringing and ingrained in you, your first thoughts may be stereotypical when you encounter someone from an ethnic group other than your own. You have to assert mental control to suppress the stereotypical thoughts. Remember that there's nothing inherently wrong with a stereotype as a baseline of information. But the rigid way we enforce a stereotype, the expectations we form on the basis of the stereotype, and our ensuing communication with the stereotyped person are problematic.

stereotype
A generalization applied to persons perceived to have attributes common to a particular group.

Check Your Perceptions

You can check the accuracy of your perceptions and attributions indirectly and directly so that you increase your ability to perceive things and people and respond to them effectively. **Indirect perception checking** involves an intensification of your own perceptual powers. You seek additional information to either confirm or refute your interpretations of someone's behavior. If you suspect that your romantic partner wants to end your relationship, for instance, you're likely to look for cues in his or her tone of voice, eye contact, and body movements to confirm your suspicion. You'll probably also listen more intently and pay attention to the language your partner chooses to use. The information you gain is "checked" against your original perceptions.

Direct perception checking involves asking straight out whether your interpretations of a perception are correct. You can accomplish this in two ways: asking people directly for their interpretations of their own actions or asking other observers for their take on a situation (going to a third or outside party). Asking people directly is often more difficult than asking a third party for an interpretation. For one thing, we don't like to admit uncertainty or suspicions to others; we might not trust that they'll respond honestly. And if our interpretations are wrong, we might suffer embarrassment or anger. But asking someone to confirm a perception shows that you're committed to gaining a better understanding.

Perception checking with colleagues, as well as with family members and trusted friends, is an invaluable tool, particularly when emotions are involved. It can be very helpful to discuss situations with other people and get their input as to what happened, why it happened, how they would feel about it if it happened to them, and what you might do about it. This is especially advisable in work settings, when the wisdom of someone else's perceptions can save you professional embarrassment or prevent you from losing your job. The "Can I run something by you?" strategy gives you a broader perspective and a basis of comparison.[68]

indirect perception checking
Using your own perceptual abilities to seek additional information to confirm or refute your interpretations of someone's behavior.

direct perception checking
Asking someone else whether your interpretations of what you perceive are correct.

STUDY GUIDE:
Review, Apply, and Assess Your Knowledge and Skill

Review Your Knowledge

Self-Awareness: How Well Do You Know Yourself?

2.1 Discuss the importance of self-awareness in the process of improving one's communication skills.

Self-awareness is the ability to develop and communicate a representation of yourself to others.

Self-Concept: Who Are You?

2.2 Describe the components of our self-concepts and major influences on the development of self-concept.

Your self-concept is your interior identity or subjective description of who you think you are. Your self-image is your view of yourself in a particular situation. The self-concept contains three components: attitudes, beliefs, and values. Philosopher William James believed that three "selves" exist in each of us:

- Material self: the tangible things you own, such as your body, possessions, home, and so forth;
- Social self: that part of you that interacts with others; and
- Spiritual self: a mixture of your beliefs and your sense of who you are in relationship to other forces in the universe.

Our self-concept develops through our communication with others, our association with various groups, the roles we assume in our lives, and the labels we use to describe ourselves. Our avowed identity is assigned by ourselves, whereas our ascribed identity involves characteristics other people assign or attribute to us.

Self-Esteem: What's Your Value?

2.3 Describe how gender, social comparisons, self-expectations, and self-fulfilling prophecies affect one's self-esteem.

Your assessment of your worth as a person in terms of skills, abilities, talents, and appearance constitutes your level of self-esteem. Self-esteem is affected by many factors, but primary among them are your gender, your comparisons of yourself to others, the expectations you hold for yourself, and your self-fulfilling prophecies.

Communication and the Enhancement of Self-Esteem

2.4 Practice six communication strategies for enhancing one's self-esteem.

Because enhanced self-esteem is a goal for most of us, we recommend the following six means of improving the way you feel about yourself.

- Engage in positive self-talk.
- Visualize the behavior you want to enact or the attributes you wish to acquire.
- Reframe, meaning redefine events and experiences from a different point of view.
- Develop honest relationships, ones in which people tell you the truth about yourself so you can get some growth from the feedback.
- Surround yourself with positive people, not "Debbie Downers."
- Lose your baggage, meaning let go of the past and those experiences that can cause your self-esteem to suffer.

The Perception Process

2.5 Explain the three stages of perception and why people differ in their perceptions of people and events.

Perception, the process of receiving information from your senses, involves three stages:

1. Attention and selection, when you notice and choose stimuli in your environment on which to focus
2. Organization, when you convert stimuli into understandable information
3. Interpretation, when you attach meaning to what you have attended to, selected, and organized

People often differ in their perceptions of things, events, and other people. Your life experiences, how you were raised, and how you developed contribute a great deal to how you perceive the world around you.

Communicate to Enhance Your Powers of Perception

2.6 Summarize three communication strategies that can improve your powers of perception.

If you want to enhance your perceptual accuracy, we recommend the following:

- Increase your awareness by fully listening, observing, and paying attention to your surroundings and other people.
- Avoid stereotypes or generalizations about people.
- Check your perceptions—indirectly and directly—to confirm or refute your interpretations of events or someone's behavior.

Key Terms

Self-Awareness, p. 31
Symbolic Self-Awareness, p. 31
Self, p. 33
Self-Concept, p. 33
Self-Image, p. 33
Attitudes, p. 33
Beliefs, p. 33
Values, p. 33
Material Self, p. 34
Social Self, p. 34
Spiritual Self, p. 34
Avowed Identity, p. 35
Ascribed Identity, p. 35
Self-Reflexiveness, p. 36
Self-Esteem, p. 36
Self-Concept Clarity, p. 36
Gender, p. 37
Social Comparison, p. 38
Self-Expectations, p. 38
Self-Fulfilling Prophecy, p. 39
Narcissism, p. 40
Intrapersonal Communication, p. 40
Self-Talk, p. 40
Visualization, p. 41
Reframing, p. 41
Perception, p. 43
Attention, p. 44
Selection, p. 44
Organization, p. 44
Closure, p. 45
Interpretation, p. 45
Stereotype, p. 47
Indirect Perception Checking, p. 48
Direct Perception Checking, p. 48

The Principle Points

Principle One:

Be aware of your communication with yourself and others.

- Becoming aware of yourself as you develop your self-concept involves communicating with others, associating with groups with whom you identify, assuming social roles, and selecting self-labels that describe who you are.
- Inventory yourself for any negative self-fulfilling prophecies that can be detrimental to your self-esteem.
- Engage in positive intrapersonal communication, or self-talk, because a heightened awareness of how you talk to yourself can help enhance self-esteem.
- Develop your perceptual abilities by becoming more aware of yourself and others.
- Use direct and indirect perception checks to sharpen your perceptual accuracy.

Apply Your Skill

Consider the following questions. Write your answers and/or share them with your classmates:

1. Describe an example of how you or someone you know progressed through Maslow's levels of competence. What skill did you or the other person develop, and how was each level demonstrated in behavior?
2. How has communication with family, friends, teachers, or others influenced your self-concept, either in the past or now?
3. In addition to self-comparisons sparked by media or social media, what situations or stimuli have you noticed tend to make people engage in more self-comparisons?
4. Describe a situation or event in your life for which it would be—or already has been—helpful to use positive self-talk or visualization to enhance your self-esteem.
5. In addition to the example given in this chapter of mistakenly thinking a person was flirting with you, what experiences have you had with inaccurately perceiving other people's communication?
6. What are some stereotypes held by people you know?
7. Read or reread the Communication & Ethics feature in this chapter. Do your own experiences agree with the research conclusions? Have you noticed high or increasing narcissism in yourself or the people you know? What are the consequences of the narcissism you see for the individuals, for people they know, and for society?

Assess Your Skill

Rosenberg Self-Esteem Scale

One of the most widely used scales to measure a person's self-esteem is the Rosenberg Self-Esteem Scale, developed in the 1960s by Dr. Morris Rosenberg, a sociologist. Respond to items on the scale using the following system: SA = Strongly Agree, A = Agree, D = Disagree, and SD = Strongly Disagree. Scoring information follows the scale.

1. I feel that I'm a person of worth, at least on an equal plane with others.	SA	A	D	SD
2. I feel that I have a number of good qualities.	SA	A	D	SD
3. All in all, I am inclined to feel that I am a failure.	SA	A	D	SD
4. I am able to do things as well as most other people.	SA	A	D	SD
5. I feel I do not have much to be proud of.	SA	A	D	SD
6. I take a positive attitude toward myself.	SA	A	D	SD
7. On the whole, I am satisfied with myself.	SA	A	D	SD
8. I wish I could have more respect for myself.	SA	A	D	SD
9. I certainly feel useless at times.	SA	A	D	SD
10. At times, I think I am no good at all.	SA	A	D	SD

Scoring Instructions

To score the scale, assign a value to each of the ten items as follows and total the values:

For items 1, 2, 4, 6, and 7: Strongly Agree = 3, Agree = 2, Disagree = 1, Strongly Disagree = 0.

For items 3, 5, 8, 9, and 10: Strongly Agree = 0, Agree = 1, Disagree = 2, Strongly Disagree = 3.

Scores on the scale range from 0 to 30, with 30 indicating the highest score possible, or the highest level of self-esteem the scale can measure. If you score on the low end of the scale, we suggest that you reread and perhaps try the suggestions in the section in this chapter on self-esteem enhancement.

Source: M. Rosenberg, *Society and the Adolescent Self-Image* rev. ed. (Middletown, CT: Wesleyan University Press, 1989). Reprinted with permission; retrieved from <www.bsos.umd.edu>.

Inventory Your Self-Esteem

One way to begin to improve your self-esteem is to take an honest measure of how you feel about yourself *right at this very point in time.* Take some time to think about yourself—who you used to be, who you were only a short time ago, and who you have developed into at this moment in time. Ponder the relationships that had the greatest effect on your development and maturation, and think about the events that caused you to change in some profound way. Then use the columns below to inventory where you stand and to reveal where you may need to put some energy into making change happen for yourself.

Things I Like About Myself	Things I Don't Like About Myself	How to Make Some Changes

Assessing Some Everyday Stereotypes

Generate statements that reveal common stereotypes about people in the following groups. Try to generate stereotypes that reflect positive as well as negative perceptions. We provide a couple of examples to get you started. Then focus on the damage that stereotypes can do to someone's self-esteem. Also, think about how your communication with someone from each group might be affected by stereotypes.

Group	Positive Stereotype	Negative Stereotype
elderly	Old people are wise.	Old people can't fend for themselves.
women	Women are naturally more loving and nurturing than men.	Women are terrible drivers.
men		
straight-A students		
blondes		
fundamentalist Christians		
bodybuilders		
southerners		
overweight people		
athletes		
rednecks		
video gamers		

Chapter 3
Understanding Verbal Messages

Words—so innocent and powerless as they are, as standing in a dictionary, how potent for good and evil they become in the hands of one who knows how to combine them. —NATHANIEL HAWTHORNE

ampyang/Shutterstock

Chapter Outline

Chapter Objectives

After studying this chapter, you should be able to

3.1 List two reasons why it is important to study verbal communication.

3.2 Summarize how words are used as symbols that have denotative, connotative, concrete, and abstract meanings and are bound by culture and context.

3.3 Identify five primary ways in which words have power.

3.4 Describe the major ways in which language reveals bias about race, ethnicity, nationality, religion, gender, sexual orientation, age, class, and ability.

3.5 Explain how language helps create supportive or defensive communication climates.

"cul8tr"
"j/k"
"v/t/y"
"by4now"

code switching
Changing seamlessly from use of one form of language to use of another form.

Many students are familiar with and comfortable using abbreviated messages, known as *textisms,* in their text messages and e-mails. You probably deciphered the above textisms as shorthand for "see you later," "just kidding," "very truly yours," and "bye for now." But don't assume everyone decodes textisms with equal skill. One comic recently joked about how her mother (a texting novice on her new smart phone) thought "btw" was short for Booker T. Washington. Textisms and acronyms (taking the first letters of words and forming a new word, like the commonly used "lol" for "laugh out loud" and "omg" for "oh my God") make texting, instant messaging, and e-mailing faster. These adaptations of the English language are becoming more popular in everyday communication, especially communication that's mediated by technology.[1] A persistent use of slang may be fine when texting, posting, or talking with friends, but when it becomes such a habit that it slips into other written or oral communication—especially at inappropriate moments (like calling a potential boss at a job interview "dude")—you've got a problem. The key is to be able to develop **code-switching** abilities, skills in shifting from one form of language to another to be better able to adapt to your listeners. It's wise to use more standard or formal language when appropriate (as in college papers, professional resumés, and job interviews) and relegate the shortcuts and "slanguage" to informal texting, posting, online chatting, e-mailing, and conversing with friends who translate.[2]

Figure 3.1 Communication Principles for a Lifetime

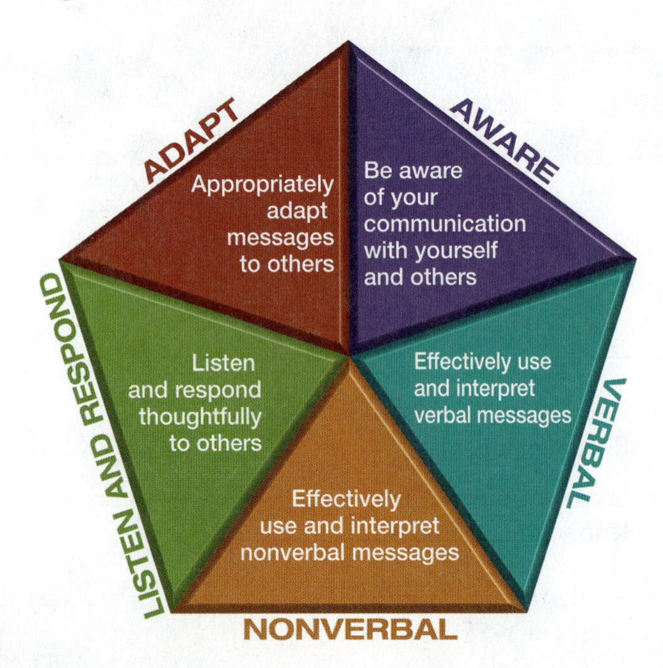

Figure 3.1 depicts our five core principles of communication. In Chapter 2, where we discussed the first of our five Communication Principles for a Lifetime, we explored

ways to become more aware of yourself and your perceptions of things and people with whom you come into contact. An important step in this process of coming to know and understand yourself better is an honest, insightful examination of how you talk.

Consider this: *What you say is who you are.* That may sound like a strong statement, but it's true that the words you use reveal who you are. Granted, you communicate with more than your words. Your background, culture, values, experiences, and the way you express yourself nonverbally reveal who you are as well. But it's a provocative notion that every time we speak, every time we use language, we reveal our thoughts, our very selves to others—no matter how inane, superficial, or emotion-laden the conversation. In addition to their tremendous potential to reveal our selves, our words also carry the power to make and break relationships and careers and to shape cultures. Because of the immense power of words, we've chosen to make verbal communication one of our five key Communication Principles for a Lifetime. And as we explore the power of words, we challenge you to think about the incredible tool you have at your disposal: verbal communication.

Why Focus on Language?

3.1 List two reasons why it is important to study verbal communication.

Take an inventory of your use of language as you read this chapter. Do you use language that accurately and effectively represents to other people who you are? Do some areas need improvement? How do you come across when meeting someone new? When talking with your best friends? What kind of communicator do your closest friends and family members think you are?

On occasion, we do stop to consider the effects of our language on others—usually when we're attempting to persuade or we've said something that has injured or angered someone else. We've all been in situations that made us wish we could get a conversational second chance. One of our main messages in this chapter is this: *Words are powerful.* They affect your emotions, thoughts, actions, and relationships. They affect how you're perceived by others.

In fact, interviews with employers reveal their concern about college graduates' lack of language skills, attributed to growing up in a culture that is more visual than oral, stressing nonverbal cues over language. In recent surveys by both the Association of American Colleges and Universities and the Society for Human Resource Management, employers expressed significant concerns about college graduates' writing and speaking skills.[3] This is clearly a negative trend, in light of other research that has determined that one's ability to use words to effectively participate in conversation with others is a key component in judgments about one's competence as a communicator. In this study, people who talked less in conversation were perceived by others as being less interpersonally skilled than people who comfortably and actively engaged in conversation.[4] If you better understand the nature and power of language and if you attend to your use of language and work to use words with forethought and skill, you can exert great influence and enhance your relationships.

Our second main theme in this chapter is this: *You choose language.* You don't use language as an involuntary reflex to a stimulus, in the way that your knee might jerk when rapped with a doctor's mallet. You choose the language you use—even if you make that choice in the split second it takes your brain to select a symbol (word) to communicate your thought or impulse. At times we go into "default mode," choosing language we've chosen before. We're prone to patterns in our language because, as humans, we prefer regularity. We also choose particular words because we like them, they've worked well for us in the past, or we grew up with those words and have used them for many

Leo Cullum/Cartoon Bank

years. But pattern and history can breed too much comfort, preventing you from asking yourself, "Is this the best way to say this? Should I say this another way?" You have an incredible wealth of words from which to choose and the power to make choices that allow you to communicate who you are to others in the most effective way possible.

The Nature of Language

3.2 Summarize how words are used as symbols that have denotative, connotative, concrete, and abstract meanings and are bound by culture and context.

A **language** is a system of symbols (words or vocabulary) structured by grammar (rules and standards) and syntax (patterns in the arrangement of words) common to a community of people. Two language researchers, Edward Sapir and Benjamin Lee Whorf, developed what has come to be known as the Sapir–Whorf Hypothesis.[5] This hypothesis suggests that human language and thought are so interrelated that thought is actually rooted in and controlled by language. One implication of the supposition is that you cannot conceive of something for which you have no word. As a quick illustration of what we mean by this, think about colors. A woman describes her new dress to her friend using the term *puce,* but if the friend does not have the term *puce* in her frame of reference as a color term, she will be unable to conceive of the color her friend mentions. (For those of you with a possibly underdeveloped color-term repertoire, puce is a brilliant purplish-red color.)

To extend this notion further, one could argue that the quality of one's language reflects the quality of one's thought. Your verbal communication reveals how you think and what you think about. This is only one supposition about how language and thought operate, but it's a provocative notion to consider that language has such a powerful influence on our everyday thinking processes.

language
A system of symbols (words or vocabulary) structured by rules (grammar) and patterns (syntax) common to a community of people.

symbol
A word, sound, gesture, or visual image that represents a thought, concept, object, or experience.

People Use Words as Symbols

As we noted in Chapter 1, words are **symbols** that represent something else. Just as a flag is a symbol of a country, words are symbols that trigger thoughts, concepts, or feelings. For instance, what comes to mind when you see or hear the word *freedom*? Perhaps you think historically, remembering what you studied in grade school about Abraham Lincoln's freeing the slaves, or perhaps you picture U.S. armed forces defending our national freedom. Or maybe you envision something a bit closer to home, like the feeling of freedom you get during a break between semesters at college.

People Attach Meanings to Words

Now imagine that you use the word *freedom* in a conversation, in an effort to convey to the other person the concept or image in your mind. You know what you're thinking when you say the word; the challenge is for the other person to understand your thoughts behind your choice of word. In communication terms, this is the process of creating **meaning**. The meaning of a word is a person's interpretation of that symbol—it's how the person makes sense of the symbol. Meanings don't reside in the words themselves but in the ways in which communicators use the words. You attach a meaning to the word *freedom,* the symbol you choose in conversation; your listener creates meaning for the word when he or she attempts to interpret what you've said. Words aren't the culprits in communication problems; the meanings people create for words lead to successful or problematic communication.

Sometimes a speaker's and a receiver's meanings don't correspond because the same words mean different things to different people; the term for this communication problem is **bypassing**. Using the *freedom* example, think about a couple in a long-term romantic relationship. If one partner said to the other, "I need more freedom in this relationship," what might that mean? It might mean that the relationship is over because one partner wants out completely, to be *free* to explore other relationships. But it might also mean that the partner is suffocating or feeling a lack of *freedom* to do as she or he pleases in the relationship. If the partner is using *freedom* in this latter sense, the relationship might stay intact. The couple might need only to make some changes in the amount of time they spent together. Some conflicts in relationships can be boiled down to a simple difference in the meaning of the words that get exchanged.

meaning
A person's interpretation of a symbol.

bypassing
A communication problem that arises when the same words mean different things to different people.

People Create Denotative and Connotative Meanings for Words

Symbol sharing through language isn't just a simple process of uttering a word and having its meaning clearly understood by another. People create meanings for language on two levels: the denotative and the connotative.[6]

Because different people can attach different meanings to the same word, it's easy to get confused. What can you do to help clarify your own meaning so that others understand you?
Christopher Robbins/Getty Images

The **denotative meaning** of a word conveys content. Denotation is the restrictive, or literal, meaning of a word. For example, one dictionary defines *apartment* as "a room or suite of rooms used as a residence."[7] This definition is a literal, or denotative, definition of the word *apartment;* it describes what the word means in American culture.

By contrast, the **connotative meaning** of a word conveys feelings; people create personal and subjective meanings for words. To you, the word *apartment* might mean a comfortable place to relax at the end of the day or a setting in which to entertain friends. To others, though, the word *apartment* might engender feelings of guilt (if the apartment hasn't been cleaned in a while) or feelings of dread (if apartment rent is draining the wallet or relationships with roommates leave something to be desired). Clearly, the connotative level of language is more individual. While the denotative or objective meaning of the word *apartment* can be found in any dictionary, your subjective response to the word is probably not contained there.

People Convey Concrete and Abstract Meanings through Words

Meanings for words can be placed along a continuum from concrete to abstract.[8] A word's meaning is **concrete** if we can experience what the word refers to (the referent) with one of our senses; if we can see it, touch it, smell it, taste it, or hear it, it's concrete. If we cannot do these things with the referent, the word's meaning is **abstract**. In general, the more concrete the language, the easier it is for others to understand and retain. For example, the word *patriotism* is abstract because we cannot hear or taste patriotism. But a word that suggests a demonstration of patriotism, such as *voting,* is more concrete, because we can physically perform the act of voting. Minimize the use of abstract words when you're trying to clarify a message. Concrete terms help make a message more clear and memorable.[9]

Meanings Are Culture Bound

Culture is a learned system of knowledge, behavior, attitudes, beliefs, values, rules, and norms that is shared by a group of people and shaped from one generation to the next.[10] The meaning of a word, just like the meaning of any symbol, can change from culture to culture and across **co-cultures**, cultural groups that exist within a larger culture. To a European, for example, a *Yankee* is someone from the United States; to a player on the Boston Red Sox baseball team, a *Yankee* is an opponent; and to an American from the South, a *Yankee* is someone from the North. Some years ago, General Motors sold a car called a *Nova.* In English, *nova* means "bright star," and in Latin, *nova* means "new"—both appropriate connotations for a car. In Spanish, however, the spoken word *nova* sounds like the words *no va,* which translate to "It does not go." As you can imagine, this name was not a great sales tool for the Spanish-speaking market.

Sometimes a cultural group will have a need for a completely new word or combination of words because some phenomenon emerges without language to capture or communicate it. New terms introduced into a language are termed **neologisms**. Examples include *sexual harassment,* a term introduced into the English language by feminists in the 1960s who wished to describe sexist treatment experienced primarily by women in the American workforce. Nowadays, it's hard to imagine not having the term *sexual harassment* as a regular form of language, but the term is only about five decades old. Other attempts at new language haven't been as successful, such as efforts in the 1970s to persuade English speakers to use "tay" or "gen" as non-sex-specific pronouns, as in "If a student wants to be successful, *tay* should not get behind in assigned reading."[11]

denotative meaning
The restrictive, or literal, meaning of a word.

connotative meaning
The personal and subjective meaning of a word.

concrete meaning
Meaning that refers to something that can be perceived with one of the senses.

abstract meaning
Meaning that refers to something that cannot be perceived or experienced with one of the senses.

culture
A learned system of knowledge, behavior, attitudes, beliefs, values, rules, and norms that is shared by a group of people and shaped from one generation to the next.

co-culture
A culture that exists within a larger cultural context (e.g., LGBT cultures, Amish culture).

neologism
A new term introduced into a language.

Communication & TECHNOLOGY

Danged Autocorrect!

If you, like many people, use a smart phone to send text messages, you've no doubt encountered the joys and woes of autocorrect, that function that tries to make sense out of our spelling and typing errors and correct them before we hit "send." It's also the function that causes occasional "oops" in this form of mediated communication.[12]

Several websites, such as Damn You Autocorrect, collect and share users' submissions of their funniest autocorrection moments.[13] In entries on this website and others like it, users shared texts in which "the sweetest things" was corrected to "the sweetest nothings," and "group hug" was changed to "grope hug." One texter's complaint about a hard week was autocorrected to "my whole week has been Shatnered" (presumably referring to the actor who played *Star Trek*'s Captain Kirk for many years). Thanks to autocorrect, one romantic man ended up texting his beloved, "I love you. If I could I'd buy you a casket." He immediately sent a correction text, which included an explanation that he meant "castle" instead of "casket," followed by the sentiment, "Damned autocorrect!" One of the funniest autocorrections we've heard was from a student of ours. She sent a text, trying to compliment a friend's daughter named Sarah. The daughter's name was autocorrected to "Satan," so the message read "I really enjoyed having my children play with your Satan."

These "oops" examples are interesting to think about. But maybe we should take a moment to consider the language conveyed in our texts or in our tweets on Twitter. We may have come to view texting or posting as handy shorthand forms of communication with people, but the technology and our use of it may have shaped our perceptions of language and communication ability, perhaps without our realizing it.

Research has found, for example, that receivers of text messages, tweets, and e-mails tend to be somewhat forgiving and blame the technology, not the sender of the message, for spelling, punctuation, and grammar errors as well as the occasional unfortunate autocorrect mishap.[14] But might we rely too much on a receiver's good graces? It's easy to become lulled into thinking that, because a text or tweet is conveyed through our phone or pad, receivers of the message will do the work of translating us as we must have intended. The problem is that communication can become habitual. Just as we tend to use spoken language consistently because our choice of words becomes patterned and comfortable, in our mediated forms of communication, we may come to rely on such features as autocorrect or depend on receivers' translations, rather than working to improve what we send. Research has determined that grammar, spelling, and punctuation help us communicate our feelings and can clarify short messages. For example, a text message or tweet of "great" sends a different message than "GREEEEAAAATTTTT!!!" One study of texting behavior found that women text more than men and are more likely to use first-person language and repeated exclamation points in texts and tweets.[15] Men in the study were more likely than women to share links to other information and include more technologically-related language in their texts and tweets.

Should speed rule accuracy? Should the technology cover a "multitude of sins"? What happens when the receiver of a text message from a too-comfortable sender is someone new, perhaps someone in a position of authority over the sender, such as the person's boss? Should we expect people to overlook or figure out our language, possibly conveying the unintended message that we're too lazy to take care with our texts or e-mails? On the flip side, if your text messages, tweets, and e-mails contain no errors, what message is conveyed to your receivers? Is there a downside to accuracy?

Meanings Are Context Bound

Politicians often claim that the media "takes them out of context," causing the intended meanings of their words to be lost or distorted. Many times, the politicians are right. In an effort to deliver a speedy, pithy sound bite to an audience, reporters often edit politicians' comments, deleting context and sometimes changing a politician's intended message.

The context of verbal messages plays a central role in how accurately our communication is interpreted by receivers. The context includes all of our words, plus the nonverbal elements that are ever present in communication, including the environment or setting in which the communication occurs as well as people's facial expressions, tone of voice, and other

RECAP

The Nature of Language

- People use words as *symbols:* Symbols represent something else.
- People create *meanings* for words: Meaning is a person's interpretation of a symbol.
- Words have both *denotative* and *connotative* meanings: The denotative meaning is a restrictive, or literal, meaning; the connotation is a personal and subjective meaning.
- People convey *concrete* and *abstract* meanings through words: A word's meaning is concrete if we can experience what the word refers to with one of our senses; if not, the meaning is abstract.
- Meanings are *culture bound:* The meaning of a word can change from culture to culture.
- Meanings are *context bound:* The situation or context for communication aids people as they attach meanings to symbols.

nonverbal cues that surround and accompany a verbal message and help us decode it. Removing words from their context distorts their meaning. If you're struggling to figure out what someone must have meant, look to the context of the communication for clues as to the meaning of the message.

The Power of Words

3.3 Identify five primary ways in which words have power.

No doubt you've heard the old schoolyard chant "Sticks and stones may break my bones, but words can never hurt me." We don't know who first came up with that statement, but we imagine it to be someone who never experienced the sting of name calling, the harmful effects of being labeled a "slow reader," or the legacy of an unfortunate family nickname. Words *do* hurt. With all the national headlines about tragic stories of the consequences of bullying, teasing, and harassment, it's important to consider the damage language can do. California educator Jane Close Conoley addressed this subject in her article "Sticks and Stones Can Break My Bones and Words Can Really Hurt Me." She encourages university students who are training to be schoolteachers to pay attention to the language that surrounds bullying, because physical violence usually begins with a verbal assault.[16]

Words have the power to evoke a wide range of emotions in listeners. But words can also heal and inspire and transform the human spirit, which is another reason for making the effective use and interpretation of verbal messages one of our five Communication Principles for a Lifetime. Let's explore five powers of words.

- *The Power to Create and Label Experience*. Alzheimer's, Parkinson's, Tourette syndrome—each of these diseases is named after the person who discovered the condition. The name of a phenomenon has the power to label the experience and make it more real.[17]

- *The Power to Communicate Feelings*. Words help communicate our moods and emotional states, giving labels to feelings that otherwise would be hard to convey.[18] The emotional power of words is not limited to expressing your feelings; your words

This woman's strong reaction to a text shows the power of words to convey our emotions and to affect other people's thoughts and feelings. What steps help you to consider others' feelings when choosing your words?
Zea Lenanet/Fotolia

and corresponding outlook may also have the power to affect your emotional, mental, and physical health. For example, one study found that people who described the world in pessimistic terms when they were younger experienced poorer health in middle age than those who had been optimistic.[19]

- *The Power to Affect Thoughts and Actions.* A few decades ago, a weight-loss product called Ayds came on the market. Ayds were small, brown, chewy squares that manufacturers claimed would help reduce appetite. You can guess why this product disappeared in the 1980s. Given what we now know about the disease AIDS, who today would willingly ingest a product called Ayds? Advertisers have long known that the way a product is labeled greatly affects the likelihood that consumers will buy it, because words affect the way we think about things and react to them.
- *The Power to Shape and Reflect Culture.* International students often puzzle over English slang and ask such questions as "What does it mean to 'cowboy up'?" or "When someone is called 'all that and a bag of chips,' is that a good or a bad thing? Does it mean you're fat?" Cultures and co-cultural groups within them develop unique languages of their own as a way of forging connections and enhancing solidarity, so the language you use both shapes and reflects your culture.
- *The Power to Make and Break Relationships.* Probably we've all had the experience of saying something to another person that we regret. But if you've ever said something so inappropriate that it cost you a romantic relationship or friendship, you know firsthand the power of words to make and break relationships. Granted, some people believe "actions speak louder than words," but both verbal and nonverbal communication are crucial to getting relationships going in the first place and then making them work.

RECAP

The Power of Words to . . .

- *Create and Label Experience.* New experiences may lead to new words. For example, *global weirding* is a newly coined term for strange or not-the-norm weather.
- *Affect Thoughts and Actions.* Words influence how we think. For instance, product names are critical to audience response and sales success. The critically acclaimed film *The Shawshank Redemption* was a box-office failure, which some attributed to the film's obtuse title.
- *Communicate Feelings.* Words help create and communicate our moods and emotional states. Think of how many terms exist for sadness: *blue, down, depressed, in the depths, mopey, bummed, down in the dumps, out of sorts, feeling punk.*
- *Shape and Reflect Culture.* Cultures change; language both creates and reflects the changing nature of culture.
- *Make and Break Relationships.* Verbal communication creates opportunities for us to know and be known by others. It's an important tool for establishing relationships and deepening them; it can also be a catalyst for a relationship to end.

Confronting Bias in Language

3.4 Describe the major ways in which language reveals bias about race, ethnicity, nationality, religion, gender, sexual orientation, age, class, and ability.

We understand that some of you are likely wary about "political correctness" when it comes to people telling others how to talk. For us, as communication professors, improving your linguistic choices isn't about political correctness or conforming to some societal standard of how you should talk; it's about using the best language adapted for your listeners. It's about using language that shows you're a highly educated person with excellent communication skills. Oftentimes, insensitive or stereotypical language usage arises out of ignorance or a lack of education. But even well-meaning, educated people can communicate bias through the language they choose to use. Words that reflect bias toward members of other cultures or groups can create barriers for listeners. In addition, such language ignores the fact that the world is constantly changing. In the following pages, we explore a few categories of language that illustrate the constant evolution of verbal communication and represent areas in which we can all heighten our sensitivity.

Biased Language: Race, Ethnicity, Nationality, and Religion

Think about whether you have ever said or overheard someone say the following:

> "I got a great deal on a car; the sticker price was a lot higher, but I jewed the dealer way down."
> "You can't have that back, you Indian giver!"
> "She's a real Bible banger."
> "He doesn't have a Chinaman's chance to make the team."
> "That divorce settlement gypped me out of what's rightfully mine!"

That last statement tends to puzzle people more than the others. It includes the term *gypped,* which is derived from the word for the nomadic cultural group known throughout the world as gypsies. The stereotype relates to being suckered or cheated out of what one is due.

The language used in each of these examples demonstrates an insensitivity to members of cultural groups and a word barrier known as **allness**, which occurs when words reflect unqualified, often untrue generalizations that deny individual differences or variations. In this chapter, where we examine our day-to-day language, it's important to think about how language reflects your attitudes and reveals how you think.

It seems like every other week you can hear or read a story involving yet another celebrity caught making remarks that others deem racist, whether it's foodie Paula Dean, Justin Bieber, or one of the male contestants on a recent season of *The Bachelorette* being accused of calling the two African American finalists "blackies."[20] Many of us try to stay current with our language, exhibiting sensitivity as we try to use appropriate terminology when referring to members of our own race and ethnicity as well as members of other groups. But occasionally we may hear—both off campus and on—race-related language that's a throwback to an earlier time in our country's evolution. Hearing or even hearing *about* that kind of language is jolting.

Terms pertaining to certain racial and ethnic groups have certainly changed over time. Check out Table 3.1, which provides some racial categories that appeared as options in the U.S. censuses of 1970, 1980, 1990, 2000, and 2010. Not all cultural groups' terms are represented in the table, but you can get a sense for identifiers that have changed for some co-cultures in the United States. You'll see how much more specific our language has become in an attempt to better communicate racial and ethnic identity in this country. Sometimes it's a challenge keep pace as language changes with the changing times, but try not to get lazy with language. It's important to inventory and revolutionize your language with regard to the racial, ethnic, national, and religious affiliations of people, because the language you choose to use is your primary tool for creating the reality of your existence, for revealing how you think, for being known by others, and for knowing them as well.[21]

allness
A word barrier created through the use of language that reflects unqualified, often untrue generalizations that deny individual differences or variations.

Table 3.1 U.S. Census Racial Categories

1970	1980	1990	2000	2010
White	White	White	White	White
Negro or Black	Negro	Black	Black or African American	Black, African American, or Negro
Indian (American)	Indian (American)	Indian (American)	American Indian or Alaska Native (specify tribe)	American Indian or Alaska Native

SOURCES: Table based on information from M. Anderson and S. Feinberg, 2000, "Race and Ethnicity and the Controversy over the U.S. Census," *Current Sociology 48.3*: 87–110; National Research Council, *Measuring Racial Discrimination* (Washington, DC: National Academies Press, 2004); U.S. Census Bureau, 2001, "Population by Race and Hispanic or Latino Origin for All Ages and for 18 Years and Over for the United States: 2000," <www.census.gov/PressRelease/www/2001/tables/st00_1.pdf>; U.S. Census Bureau, 2010, *Questionnaire Reference Book* (Washington, DC: U.S. Department of Commerce, Bureau of the Census, Washington DC), retrieved from <2010census.gov>.

Biased Language: Gender and Sexual Orientation

Language that reveals bias in favor of one sex and against another, termed **sexist** or **exclusive language**, is more prevalent than you'd think. Decades of effort, spurred by the women's liberation movement in the 1960s, have raised the consciousness of American culture regarding exclusive language. But even in this day and age of heightened awareness about sex and gender issues, many people still don't reflect and include both sexes in their verbal communication.

LANGUAGE AND THE SEXES Even though women now constitute 50 percent of the U.S. population, to listen to the language of some people, you'd think it was still a man's world. Sexist language can reflect stereotypical attitudes or describe roles in exclusively male or female terms.[22] Research indicates that exclusive language usage does the following: (1) maintains sex-biased perceptions, (2) shapes people's attitudes about careers that are appropriate for one sex but not the other, (3) causes some women to believe that certain jobs and roles aren't attainable, (4) contributes to the belief that men deserve more status in society than women do, and (5) mutes the voices of many women, because the words and norms formed by the dominant group don't allow for the articulation of women's experiences.[23]

sexist (exclusive) language
Language that reveals bias in favor of one sex and against another.

generic language
General terms that stand for all persons or things within a given category.

Even dictionaries fall into patterns of describing women and men with discriminatory language.[24] Included in the *Oxford English Dictionary* definition for *woman* are (1) an adult female being, (2) female servant, (3) a lady-love or mistress, and (4) a wife. Men are described in more positive and distinguished terms: (1) a human being, (2) the human creation regarded abstractly, (3) an adult male endowed with many qualities, and (4) a person of importance of position.

The most common form of sexism in language is the use of **generic language**, using a masculine term as though it were a term to describe all people. There are two primary ways in which masculine-as-generic language typically appears in written and oral communication: in pronoun usage and in man-linked terminology.[25]

Consistent evidence from research on sexist language shows that people—particularly in American culture—simply do not tend to think in neuter; we think in male or female. We don't tend to think of living entities as *it,* and we rarely use that pronoun to refer to them. When most people read or hear the word *he,* they think of a masculine person, not a sexless person.[26] Using generic masculine language, in essence, turns all persons into male persons. For example, a student giving a speech on how to project a winning, confident style in a job interview said, "When you greet the boss for the first time, be sure to look him straight in the eye, give him a firm handshake, and let him know you're interested in the job." The student's exclusive language choice only allowed for the possibility of a male boss, not a female boss.

We don't know what you were taught in high school or in other college classes about generic language, but publishing standards today require the use of nonsexist language, which allows no masculine terms to stand for all persons.[27] You'll notice that we use inclusive language in this text—because it reflects our value system and because our publisher requires it.

The solution to the problem of sexist language is not to replace each *he* with *she* but to use terms that include both sexes so that your language reflects the contemporary world. If you want to refer to one person—any person of either sex—the most clear, grammatical, nonsexist way to do that is to use *she or he, he/she,* or *s/he.*[28] Other options include (1) omitting a pronoun altogether, either by rewording a message or by substituting an article (*a, an,* or *the*) for the pronoun; (2) using *you* or variations of the indefinite pronoun *one;* or (3) using the plural pronoun *they.*[29]

The gender-neutral term *firefighter* describes both of these people, whereas the sexist term *fireman* excludes the person on the left.
Monkey Business/Fotolia

Communication & DIVERSITY

Sex/Gender Complexity: Facebook's Fifty-Six New Terms for Gender Identity

When exposed to the list of fifty-six new terms Facebook distributed in 2014, some people reacted with new-terminology fatigue: "What? I have to learn all this?" Some users thought Facebook was taking gender sensitivity to a ridiculous degree, creating "much ado about nothing." Others celebrated because the complexity of sex and gender was finally being placed front and center—on the world's most popularly used social media platform, no less.[30]

Whatever your reaction and the level to which you embrace the language, it's hard to argue with the fact that increased attention is being paid to the language we use when we communicate about sex and gender. For many of us, the heightened attention and awareness are welcome developments. Let's explore a few of the terms that Facebook has decided to embrace.

Several of the terms include the prefix *cis,* as in *cisgender* and *cis female/male/man/woman*. *Cis* is Latin for "on this side of" and it refers to someone who identifies with the sex she or he was born with, such as a person who was born female and now identifies as a woman. *Cis* may be a better, less value-laden term than "normal."[31] Multiple entries also appear in the Facebook list for *trans* status, depending on what a person wants to emphasize about his or her transition into a different sex or gender.

Here's one that sometimes stumps people: *agender*. According to various researchers who've attempted to explain some of the terms in the Facebook list, people who describe themselves as agender don't necessarily see themselves as neutered or missing a gender; rather, they don't view their sex or gender as central to their identity.

Although the term *asexual* doesn't appear on the Facebook list, we've heard this term embraced by college students whose gender identity stems, in part, from the fact that they're not sexually attracted to anyone, ever.[32] They may have sexual relations (both heterosexually and homosexually) because their bodies have sexual needs, just like anyone else's, but they don't feel sexual attraction, and therefore they believe they are "a-sexed." (They go by "Ace" or "Ase" for short.) Never heard of such a thing? You're not alone, but AVEN, the Asexual Visibility and Education Network, works to enhance understanding of what some believe to be a fourth sexual orientation, along with bisexuality, homosexuality, and heterosexuality.

We're not the language police here, but we stress throughout this book the importance of taking an other-oriented approach to communication. This means that others' interpretations of your messages, not just your intentions, are central to communication effectiveness. We encourage you to keep an open mind about sex and gender language and to consider the possibility that someone you know and care about might request you to stretch your language usage to include that person's gender identity.

Consciously remembering to use nonsexist, inclusive language brings the following benefits:[33]

- Gender-inclusive language reflects inclusive attitudes. Monitoring your verbal communication for sexist remarks will make you aware of any sexist attitudes or assumptions you may hold.
- Using inclusive language helps you become more other-oriented, which will have a positive effect on your relationships. Consciously ridding your language of sexist remarks reflects your awareness of others and their sensitivities.
- Inclusive language makes your communication more contemporary and unambiguous. If you say *he,* for example, how is a listener to know whether you're referring to a male person or to just any person?
- Nonsexist language strengthens your style and demonstrates sensitivity that can empower others. By eliminating sexist bias from your communication, you affirm the value of all individuals with whom you interact.[34]

LANGUAGE AND SEXUAL ORIENTATION We realize that sexual orientation is one of the more difficult topics to discuss, mainly because people tend to hold strong opinions about it. But no matter your views about sexuality, it's vital to use sensitive, appropriate communication with whomever you encounter.

Insensitivity or intolerance toward persons who are gay, lesbian, bisexual, transgender, or queer (a term of liberation from labels about sexual orientation) is often reflected in **homophobic language**.[35] Homophobic language denigrates people of nonheterosexual orientations and may arise out of a fear of being labeled gay or lesbian.

homophobic language
Language that overtly denigrates persons of nonheterosexual orientations, usually arising out of a fear of being labeled gay or lesbian.

Sometimes homophobic language is obvious, such as calling someone a derogatory term that we've heard all too often. But homophobic language is often more subtle than a terrible epithet, sometimes cloaked in an attempt at humor. Examples include blithe references to a lesbian as "wearing the pants in the family" or a gay man as being "light in the loafers." Such language could be perceived as being more tolerable than something overtly homophobic, particularly if the receiver of such language doesn't know what it means. But both subtle and overt homophobic language reveals insensitive attitudes and a rigid communication style.

Another way to communicate bias is through the use of **heterosexist language**, language that reflects an assumption that the world is (or should be) heterosexual, as if romantic and sexual attraction to those of the same sex or both sexes simply were not possible or acceptable. For example, we often hear students in public speaking classes start a speech something like this: "How many of you ladies have trouble getting your boyfriend to go shopping with you?" In a mixed-sex audience in such a class, what are some possible interpretations of this speech introduction? One take is that the speaker is addressing only those women in the audience that he or she believes to be straight and in possession of a boyfriend, leaving all others in the audience excluded. Another interpretation is that the use of the term "ladies" is derogatory and intended to include some of the men in the audience, particularly the gay men in the audience who might have boyfriends. Either way, such an introduction shows a speaker's assumptions as well as a poor choice of language.

Just as you have learned to avoid racially charged terms that degrade and draw attention to someone's ethnicity, it's important to learn to avoid language that denigrates a person's sexual orientation and draws undue attention to this element of cultural diversity. One of your authors was quite taken aback a few years ago when she received a paper from a first-year student in which the derogatory term *fag* frequently appeared. You've no doubt heard this term, probably bandied about in high school, but its use can be a signal of homophobia—the fear of being labeled or viewed as gay or lesbian. Heterosexist language is more subtle; it often emerges through omission, meaning what *is not* said, rather than commission, or what *is* said. For example, in class, how many of your instructors give dating examples using two people of the

heterosexist language
Language that reveals an assumption that the world is heterosexual, as if homosexuality or bisexuality did not exist.

Communication & ETHICS

"That's So Gay!"

We've said in this chapter that the primary definition of the term *homophobia* is a fear of being labeled or viewed as homosexual. However, research has found two other meanings for the term: A secondary meaning of *homophobia* is a discriminatory attitude toward or hatred of people who are homosexual, and some forms of language certainly reflect this negativity. Yet a third sense of the term occurs when it's used among homosexual persons, as either a form of self-hatred or an aggressive, derogatory term people who share this sexual orientation hurl at each other.[36]

A few years ago, a language usage surfaced that can still be heard, albeit to a much lesser extent than when it first became popular: saying "That's so gay" in response to someone's choice of clothing, accessories, or furnishings (typically things not expected to be owned or used by members of one sex or the other) or in response to someone's communication or actions. The language was made popular by the then-hit TV show *Friends*, whose characters Chandler and Joey could often be heard criticizing something by saying, "That's so gay." College students picked up this language, using the term *gay* to refer to anything disagreeable and often justifying its use by saying that it was just a funny thing to say, not meant to refer to homosexuals or to be discriminatory or inappropriate. Many communication professors, as well as gay rights activists and educators, across the country took a stand to curb the use of this form of language, contending that it was indeed homophobic and discriminatory.[37] You may not hear this language much anymore; if that's the case, we're glad it's on its well-deserved way out of the lexicon, because here's the problem: Substitute any word for the term *gay* and see if it sounds derogatory. Would someone say "That's so Jew" or "That's so black" and dare to think that these phrases weren't racial/ethnic slurs?

RECAP

Confronting Bias in Language

Inventory your language for subtle and not-so-subtle indications of bias in several areas:

- *Race, Ethnicity, and Nationality.* Avoid language that denigrates members of a racial or ethnic group; be careful not to overemphasize race or ethnicity or "mark" a person by using adjectives referring to national origin, as in "that Oriental student in my class."
- *Religion.* Watch stereotypical language pertaining to religious affiliation, such as derogatory references to Jews, Muslims, or fundamentalist Christians, for example.
- *Gender.* Include both sexes in your language, especially in your use of pronouns; avoid masculine generic pronouns and male-linked terms that exclude women.
- *Sexual Orientation.* Be alert to the potential for heterosexism in your language—the assumption that everyone is heterosexual or that heterosexuality is the only possible orientation. Eliminate homophobic language that degrades and stereotypes gays, lesbians, bisexuals, and transgender individuals.
- *Age.* Avoid calling too much attention to a person's age in your verbal communication. Be especially vigilant not to label or stereotype the elderly or to condescend to or glorify youth.
- *Class.* Monitor references to socioeconomic differences, such as distinctions between blue-collar and white-collar workers.
- *Ability.* Avoid verbal communication that draws attention to a person's physical, mental, or learning ability.

same sex? Most examples about relationships that you read or hear about in courses such as Interpersonal Communication or Introduction to Psychology reflect heterosexual romantic relationships. As another example, how often do you hear or use the term *partner* instead of *husband* or *wife*? The first term, *partner,* is inclusive of all forms of couples, while the latter terms, at least in most states, refer only to heterosexual marriage. These forms of language usage can communicate a heterosexist bias and suggest that other sexual orientations are inappropriate or nonexistent.[38]

People sometimes use the word *retarded* in casual conversation to refer to occasions when someone does something foolish or incorrectly. Recent publicity campaigns have helped to curb the use of this biased language, as has the increasing visibility of celebrities with Down syndrome, such as Jamie Brewer, a member of the cast of on *American Horror Story*.
2013 HPA/Hutchins Photo/Newscom

Biased Language: Age, Class, and Ability

"Just turn the car, grandpa!" Ever heard a driver say something like this in irritation or said it yourself? Ever call an elderly person a "geezer" or an "old-timer"? Just as some people contend that Americans are hung up on gender and racial diversity, many believe that Americans are hung up on age. We live in a culture that glorifies youth and tends to put its elders out to pasture.[39] Age discrimination is a very real problem in the workforce—so much so that laws have been enacted to guard against someone's being denied professional opportunities because of age. Likewise, some older people may hold stereotypes of young people and may speak to them as though their youth exempts them from intelligence or responsible action. We recommend that you inventory your language for any terms that either show disrespect for elders or are patronizing or condescending to younger people.

Another factor influencing language that has received research attention is socioeconomic class.[40] Class distinctions typically are revealed in derogatory references to lower-economic-class "blue-collar workers," "manual laborers," "welfare recipients," or upper-class "one percenters." Another class slur is "white trash." In the late 1990s, when Paula Jones filed a sexual harassment lawsuit against then-president Bill Clinton, she was called "white trash" and "trailer trash" as she was ridiculed in the press and in living rooms across the country. Avoid references that reveal a condescending or disrespectful attitude toward someone's education (or lack of it) and socioeconomic status.

Finally, an area of bias in language that most people became conscious of by the turn of the 21st century relates to ability. Some years ago, Helen Keller was described as "deaf, dumb, and blind." Nowadays, the appropriate term for her inability to communicate vocally would be *mute*. Be careful that your language doesn't make fun of or draw attention to someone's physical, mental, or learning disability, such as calling someone a "cripple," "retard," or "slow reader" or describing someone as having an "ADD moment." Research has found that when people with disabilities are called demeaning names, they're perceived as less trustworthy, competent, persuasive, and sociable than when they're described in positive terms.[41]

Using Words to Establish Supportive Relationships

3.5 Explain how language helps create supportive or defensive communication climates.

For more than five decades, communication scholar Jack Gibb's research has been used as a framework for both describing and prescribing verbal behaviors that contribute to feelings of either supportiveness or defensiveness.[42] Gibb spent several years listening to and observing groups of individuals in meetings and conversations, noting that some exchanges seemed to create a supportive climate whereas others created a defensive one. Words and actions, he concluded, are tools we use to let someone know whether we support them or not. Thus, Gibb defined **supportive communication** as communication that uses language to create a climate of trust, caring, and acceptance. The language used in **defensive communication**, in contrast, creates a climate of hostility and mistrust. When someone gets defensive, communication is seriously impeded.

Two specific uses of language tend to engender negative reactions and defensiveness in most of us; thus, we view them as word barriers that can damage even the most secure of relationships.

- **Polarization** occurs when we describe things in extremes or opposites without any middle ground. One romantic partner might say to the other, "You either love me or you don't." Pronouncements of this kind can be interpreted as ultimatums, as though there were only two options and no compromise position. Former President George W. Bush was both praised and criticized for stating in his post–September 11, 2001, speech to Congress, "You're either with us or you're with the terrorists." It's wise to avoid language that creates a false or forced choice for people, making them feel controlled, hemmed in, or manipulated.
- **Trigger words** arouse our emotions. Travis, a former student, described in class a word his wife used during arguments that really sparked his anger more than anything else. When Travis would make a point that would frustrate his wife—one for which she had no comeback—she would look at him, toss her hand in the air, and say, "Whatever." Perhaps this word triggers you too, because it punctuates a conversation; it dismisses the other person and her or his point. Do you know what words trigger your emotions, in both positive and negative directions? Certain uses of language can make us feel accepted and appreciated or disrespected and hostile.[43]

Think about times when your words made someone defensive and how hard you had to work to get the person to let the defenses down. In the following section, we suggest ways to use verbal communication to create a supportive rather than an antagonistic climate.

supportive communication
Language that creates a climate of trust, caring, and acceptance.

defensive communication
Language that creates a climate of hostility and mistrust.

polarization
The tendency to describe things in extremes, as though no middle ground existed.

trigger words
Forms of language that arouse strong emotions in listeners.

Describe Your Own Feelings Rather Than Evaluate Others

Most of us don't like to be judged or evaluated. One way to avoid evaluating others is to attempt to use "I" statements instead of accusatory "you" statements. Statements such as "You always say you'll call, but you never do" or "You need to pick up the dirty clothes in your room" attack a person's sense of self-worth and usually result in a defensive reaction. Instead, use the word *I* to describe your own feelings and thoughts about a situation or event: "I find it hard to believe you when you say you'll call" or "I don't enjoy the extra work of picking up your dirty clothes." When you describe your own feelings instead of berating the receiver of the message, you take ownership of the problem. This approach leads to greater openness and trust because your listener is less likely to feel rejected or as if you are trying to control him or her.

Solve Problems Rather Than Control Others

When you were younger, your parents gave you rules to keep you safe. Even though you may have resented their control, you needed to know that the stovetop was hot, when not to cross the street, and how dangerous it was to stick your finger in a light socket. Now that you're an adult, when people treat you like a child, it often means they're trying to control your behavior, to take away your options.

Most of us don't like to be controlled. Someone who presumes to tell us what's good for us instead of helping us puzzle through issues and problems to arrive at our own solutions or higher understanding is likely to engender defensiveness. In truth, we have little or no control over others. Open-ended questions such as "What seems to be the problem?" or "How can we deal with this issue?" create a more supportive climate than critical comments such as "Here's where you are wrong" or "You know what your problem is?" or commands like "Don't do that!"

Empathize Rather Than Remain Detached from Others

Empathy, one of the hallmarks of supportive relationships, is the ability to understand and actually feel or approximate the feelings of others and then to predict the emotional responses they will have to different situations.[44] You work to put yourself in the other person's shoes, to experience as closely as you can what she or he is experiencing. The opposite of empathy is neutrality. To be neutral is to be indifferent or apathetic toward others. (Even when you express anger or irritation toward another, you're investing some energy in the relationship.) A statement that epitomizes this concept of neutrality is "I don't love you or hate you; I just *don't* you."

Remaining detached from someone when empathy is obviously called for can generate great defensiveness and damage a relationship. Here's an example: You're upset about an argument you just had with someone you're dating, so you seek the support and listening ear of a good friend. But that friend is in "party mode" or in such a good mood that he or she chooses not to concentrate and listen to what's going on with you. Rather than engaging in your situation, your friend remains detached and blows off your concerns. In situations like this, most of us become defensive and frustrated, and the quality of our friendship may suffer. Empathy is a building block of a supportive relationship; it may come naturally to some people, but most of us have to work at it, just like many other skills we can develop with a bit of effort.[45]

Be Flexible Rather Than Rigid Toward Others

Some people are just *always* right, aren't they? (These people spend a lot of time alone, too.) Most people don't like someone who always seems certain that she or he is right. A "You're wrong, I'm right" attitude creates a defensive climate. This doesn't mean

empathy
The ability to understand and feel what another person is feeling.

Being genuine and showing empathy for others' feelings are two ways to help establish supportive relationships. What words can help convey your empathy when a friend is troubled?
Jules Selmes/Pearson Education

that you should have no opinions and go through life passively agreeing to everything. And it doesn't mean that there isn't a clear-cut right and wrong in many situations. But instead of making rigid pronouncements, at times you may want to qualify your language by using phrases such as "I may be wrong, but it seems to me . . ." or "Here's something you might want to consider." Conditional or provisional language gives your opinions a softer edge that allows room for others to express a point of view; it opens the door for alternatives. Declarations tend to shut the door. In those cases when you want to induce supportiveness and reduce the potential for defensiveness, conditional, flexible language works best.

Present Yourself as Equal Rather Than Superior

You can antagonize others by letting them know that you view yourself as better than they are. You may be gifted and extraordinarily intelligent, but it's not necessary to announce or publicize it. Ever hear of the humblebrag? It's language that, at first glance, makes a person sound humble, but upon further inspection, it's a way to tell others about your achievements.[46] Examples include "When I bought my Mercedes, no one told me I'd get pulled over all the time" and this one from comedian Dane Cook: "Being famous and having a fender bender is weird. You want to be upset, but the other driver's just thrilled and giddy that it's you." This subtle style of bragging doesn't typically engender supportiveness in conversations with others; even the humblebrag will eventually be interpreted as pompous and can create defensiveness in listeners.

Here's another use of language to watch out for: Although some people have the responsibility and authority to manage others, "pulling rank" doesn't usually produce a supportive climate. With phrases such as "Let's work on this together" or "We each have a valid perspective," you can avoid erecting walls of resentment and defensiveness. "We" language can be preferable to "you" language; it builds a sense of camaraderie and shared experience, and by using it, you avoid setting yourself apart from listeners.

Avoid using "high-falutin'" (unnecessarily complicated) words just to posture, impress others, or project some image. Sometimes referred to as "bafflegab," this kind of language can come in the form of words, phrases, or verbal shorthand that people use but no one understands. People with particular expertise may use abbreviated terms or acronyms. The military is notorious for its use of language that doesn't easily translate outside of military circles. It's better to use informal language appropriate to the situation and your listeners than to attempt to talk over the heads of everyone in the room.

You can also create defensiveness by using language that is too simplistic for your listeners. Granted, when you communicate with someone from another culture or even from another U.S. co-cultural group, you may need to alter your message to get your meaning across. But this means your verbal communication should be explicit, not condescending. For example, some people use oversimplified words when communicating with elderly people. It's inappropriate to assume that aging diminishes one's capacity to understand. Try to use language to present yourself on equal ground with your listeners and establish a supportive, open climate for communication.

Avoid Gunny-Sacking

Gunny-sacking involves dredging up someone's past mistakes or problems and linking them to a current situation. Suppose your best male friend has just been dumped by his "one true love," but you—being the good friend that you are—remind him that the last three people he dated were also his "one true love," at least at the time. Your friend wants empathy, but you respond by highlighting his tendency to turn "Ms. Right" into "Ms. Right Now." Such an approach will likely make him feel criticized and engender defensive reactions in him. This kind of scenario rarely deepens a relationship.

RECAP

Using Words to Create a Supportive Climate

- Describe your own feelings instead of evaluating the point of view or behavior of others.
- Keep the focus on problem solving rather than controlling others.
- Be genuine rather than manipulative in your communication.
- Instead of ignoring someone's feelings, try to empathize.
- Use conditional language and demonstrate flexibility rather than rigidity in your communication.
- Present yourself as an equal rather than as a superior. Avoid acting like a know-it-all. Don't attempt to talk over the heads of listeners or condescend to them, because either approach can breed defensiveness.
- Avoid gunny-sacking, or reminding someone of past mistakes or issues.

STUDY GUIDE: Review, Apply, and Assess Your Knowledge and Skill

Review Your Knowledge

Why Focus on Language?

3.1 List two reasons why it is important to study verbal communication.

Words are powerful; they affect your emotions, thoughts, actions, and relationships, as well as how you're perceived by others. The better your choices of language, the better your overall communication skill and your relationships.

The Nature of Language

3.2 Summarize how words are used as symbols that have denotative, connotative, concrete, and abstract meanings and are bound by culture and context.

Language is a system of symbols (words or vocabulary) structured by grammar (rules and standards) and syntax (patterns in the arrangement of words) common to a community of people. The Sapir–Whorf Hypothesis suggests that language and thought are so interrelated that thought is rooted in and controlled by language. The limits of your language may be the limits of your thought.

Six important aspects of language are (1) people use words as symbols (something that represents something else); (2) people attach meanings to words, and sometimes meanings differ (bypassing); (3) people use denotative and connotative meanings for words; (4) people convey concrete and abstract meanings through words; (5) meanings are culture bound; and (6) meanings are context bound.

The Power of Words

3.3 Identify five primary ways in which words have power.

Words are extremely powerful. They can create and label our experiences, communicate our feelings, affect our thoughts and actions, shape and reflect our culture, and make and break our relationships.

Confronting Bias in Language

3.4 Describe the major ways in which language reveals bias about race, ethnicity, nationality, religion, gender, sexual orientation, age, class, and ability.

Our language often reveals our biases. Monitor your language to avoid bias in these categories: (1) race, ethnicity, nationality, and religion; (2) gender and sexual orientation; and (3) age, class, and ability.

Using Words to Establish Supportive Relationships

3.5 Explain how language helps create supportive or defensive communication climates.

Supportive communication creates a climate of trust, caring, and acceptance; defensive communication creates a climate of hostility and mistrust. Two uses of language that breed hostility and mistrust are (1) polarization, which occurs when people describe things in extremes or opposites, as though there were no middle ground, and (2) trigger words, which are forms of language that trigger our emotions, in both positive and negative directions.

Here are six tips for developing a supportive communication climate:

- Describe your own feelings rather than evaluate others;
- Solve problems rather than control others;
- Empathize rather than remain detached from others;
- Be flexible rather than rigid toward others;
- Present yourself as equal rather than superior; and
- Stick to the present situation and avoid gunny-sacking (dredging up past mistakes, problems, and issues).

Key Terms

Code Switching, p. 54
Language, p. 56
Symbol, p. 56
Meaning, p. 57
Bypassing, p. 57
Denotative Meaning, p. 58
Connotative Meaning, p. 58
Concrete Meaning, p. 58
Abstract Meaning, p. 58
Culture, p. 58
Co-culture, p. 58
Neologism, p. 58

Allness, p. 62
Sexist (Exclusive) Language, p. 63
Generic Language, p. 63
Homophobic Language, p. 64
Heterosexist Language, p. 65
Supportive Communication, p. 67
Defensive Communication, p. 67
Polarization, p. 67
Trigger Words, p. 67
Empathy, p. 68

The Principle Points

Principle Two:

Effectively use and interpret verbal messages.

- Realize that communication problems may not have to do with the words used, but rather with the meanings people attach to the words.
- Recognize the difference between denotative and connotative language.
- Use concrete terms whenever appropriate, because abstract language is harder to understand and remember than concrete language.
- Understand that words are affected by the culture within which the language is used.
- Pay attention to the words communicators choose to use, and attempt to interpret those words in the spirit and context in which they were intended.
- Avoid biased language when speaking about race, ethnicity, nationality, religion, gender, sexual orientation, age, class, and ability.
- Use words to engender supportiveness rather than defensiveness.

Apply Your Skill

Consider the following questions. Write your answers and/or share them with your classmates:

1. In taking a mental inventory of your use of language, what did you notice that you can change to improve the effectiveness of your communication?
2. Do you find that people's verbal communication to you seems to accurately reflect the quality of their thought? Have you ever run across anybody whose verbal skills did not seem to match his or her thinking skills?
3. Give an example of a time when you became acutely aware of the power of words, because someone said something that either worked miracles or turned out badly for everyone involved.
4. What do you do when someone makes a biased remark around you or to you? How can you effectively respond to show that you don't accept such language?
5. What are your trigger words?
6. Give an example of a time when someone's word choice has had a powerful effect in your own life.

Assess Your Skill

Practicing Denotation and Connotation

Below we review the differences between denotative and connotative meanings of words and provide examples.

Level	Definition	Example
Denotative	Literal, restrictive definition of a word	*Teacher:* the person primarily responsible for providing your education
Connotative	Personal, subjective reaction to a word	*Teacher:* the warm, supportive person who fostered a climate in which you could learn or the cold taskmaster who drilled lessons into you and made you feel inferior

For each of the following terms, provide a denotative, or dictionary-type, definition; then generate connotative meanings of your own.

Term	Denotative Definition	Connotative Meanings
work		
parent		
infidelity		
professionalism		
loyalty		

Your Bias Is Showing

Here's an activity to illustrate how people reveal their biases through their use of language. Generate a list of stereotypical terms, both positive and negative, often associated with each word below. For example, for the word *Democrat,* you might think of positive and negative terms like "liberal," "tax and spend," "big government," "anti-war," "environmentalist," and "populist."

Term	Positive Stereotypical Language	Negative Stereotypical Language
conservatives		
foreign students		
homeless people		
churchgoers		
movie stars		

Chapter 4

Understanding Nonverbal Messages

We respond to gestures with an extreme alertness and, one might say, in accordance with an elaborate and secret code that is written nowhere, known by none, and understood by all. —EDWARD SAPIR

Anna Karwowska/Shutterstock

Chapter Outline

Chapter Objectives

After studying this chapter, you should be able to

4.1 Provide four reasons for studying nonverbal communication.

4.2 Discuss six elements that reveal the nature of nonverbal communication.

4.3 Identify and explain the seven nonverbal communication codes.

4.4 Explain Mehrabian's three-part framework for interpreting nonverbal cues.

SHE: "Uh huh, the minute my back is turned, you're looking at that hoochie mama over there. I SAW you; your eyes were buggin' out of your head."

HE: "Don't give me that tone, woman. I only noticed how cheap she looked, with all that makeup on."

SHE: "Yeah right. You're shifting around in your chair like you know you've been caught."

HE: "Don't get all crazy, accusing me of something I didn't do. Right now I need some space."

The comments in this conflict all reflect a form of human communication that occurs without words—what we term *nonverbal communication.* In this confrontation, comments about eye contact, someone's appearance, shifting around in one's chair, and needing space all relate to nonverbal elements that have a profound effect on how we interact with one another. As we explained in Chapter 1, **nonverbal communication** is communication other than written or spoken language that creates meaning for someone. The one exception to this definition is that to hearing people, sign language appears to be nonverbal communication. However, to people who are deaf, sign language is verbal communication in that certain movements, signs, and facial expressions convey words, phrases, and emphasis.[1]

nonverbal communication Communication other than written or spoken language that creates meaning for someone.

We know you're becoming familiar with our five-sided model of Communication Principles for a Lifetime, shown in Figure 4.1, but let's do a quick recap. In Chapter 2, we explored ways to become more aware of yourself and your perceptions of things and people with whom you come into contact. An important step in this process of coming to know and understand yourself better is an honest, insightful examination of how you talk. In Chapter 3, we challenged you to consider the power of words, to take inventory of your use of language, and to think about ways to improve your verbal communication so that you extend yourself to others and respond to them in an appropriate, effective manner.

Now we get to what most people consider an even greater challenge: understanding and evaluating your nonverbal communication and improving your ability to interpret the nonverbal behavior of others. Nonverbal communication is of great importance; a person who can read others' nonverbal communication with sensitivity and skill

Figure 4.1 Communication Principles for a Lifetime

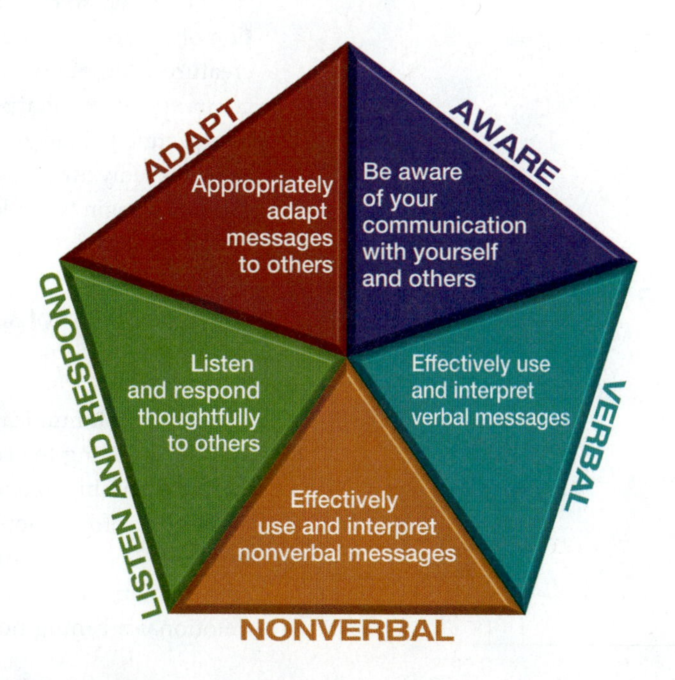

makes a memorable impression on other people. Because of the power of nonverbal communication to complement verbal communication, to further reveal the self—particularly in situations when talking is inappropriate, impossible, or inadequate—and to affect how you connect with others as you initiate and build relationships, we've chosen to make this the third of our five key Communication Principles for a Lifetime.

We have two primary goals in this chapter:

- To help you become more aware of your own nonverbal communication and
- To enhance your nonverbal receiving skills, or your ability to detect and interpret the nonverbal cues of others more accurately.

You first have to become more aware of your own nonverbal behavior; such awareness helps you understand yourself—how and why you behave as you do. Because much nonverbal communication behavior is subconscious, most people have limited awareness or understanding of it. Your heightened awareness will lead to a more skillful use of nonverbal communication as well as greater accuracy in interpreting others' nonverbal cues so that you interact more effectively with other people.

Why Focus on Nonverbal Communication?

4.1 Provide four reasons for studying nonverbal communication.

Have you ever watched a person interact with someone else and thought, "That person just doesn't have a clue"? We've all seen or met people who appear not to pick up on the communication clues of others. For example, have you ever tried to end a conversation because you were late or needed to be somewhere else, and the person you were talking to just wouldn't let you out of the conversation? The person didn't seem to notice you looking at your watch, angling your body away, taking a few steps back, and making minimal vocal responses to what was being said. Now, we all have times when we can't "catch a clue," even if we consider ourselves to be fairly sensitive, perceptive people. Certain people, places, moods, or topics of conversation may impede our ability to give and receive nonverbal communication effectively. But we don't want to be clueless. We want to be able to exhibit effective nonverbal communication and to read and interpret the clues others give us more sensitively and accurately.

However, no one can become a perfect interpreter of the nonverbal communication of others, because human beings are unique, complicated, and ever-changing creatures. Although we encourage you to deepen your understanding of nonverbal communication, sharpen your powers of observation, and develop greater skill in interpreting the meanings behind others' nonverbal actions, we also suggest that you remain keenly aware of the idiosyncratic and complex nature of nonverbal communication. To begin to explore this topic, let's look at four reasons for studying nonverbal communication.

Nonverbal Messages Communicate Feelings and Attitudes

Nonverbal communication is a primary tool for conveying our feelings and attitudes and for detecting the emotional states of others.[2] Nonverbal communication scholar Albert Mehrabian concluded from his research that the most significant source of emotional information is the face, which can channel as much as 55 percent of our meaning. Vocal cues such as volume, pitch, and intensity convey another 38 percent of our emotional meaning. In all, we communicate approximately 93 percent of our emotional meaning nonverbally; as little as 7 percent of the emotional meaning is

How aware are you of the power of your nonverbal communication with others? Think about confrontations you've had in the past. In your opinion, which communicates emotions most effectively: the volume, pitch, and intensity of the voice; nonverbal gestures, facial expressions, and body positions; or the meaning of the actual words spoken?
Monkey Business Images/Shutterstock

communicated through explicit verbal channels.[3] Although these percentages don't apply to every communication situation, Mehrabian's research illustrates the potential power of nonverbal cues to communicate emotion and attitude.

Nonverbal Messages Are More Believable Than Verbal Ones

> "Hey—are you mad or something?" asks Jonas.
>
> (Big sigh.) "Oh, no. I'm not mad," responds Danita (in a subdued tone of voice and without making eye contact).
>
> "You sure? Because you're acting funny, like you're ticked off." (One more try and then Jonas will likely give up.)
>
> "I SAID I'M NOT MAD, OKAY? WILL YOU LEAVE IT ALONE PLEASE?"

Despite Danita's claim to the contrary, the real story is—she's mad. The reason the phrase "actions speak louder than words" is used so often that it's become a cliché is because nonverbal communication is more believable than verbal communication. Verbal communication is a conscious activity; it involves the translation of thoughts and impulses into symbols. Some nonverbal communication is conscious, but a great deal of it is generated subconsciously as we act and react to stimuli in our environment. It's easier to control your words than to control a quiver in your voice when you're angry, the heat and flush in your face when you talk to someone you're attracted to, or shaky knees when you're nervous.

When a person's verbal and nonverbal communication contradict, as in Danita's case, which should an astute observer believe? The nonverbal actions carry the truer message most of the time.

Nonverbal Messages Are Critical to Successful Relationships

One researcher suggests that as much as 65 percent of the way we convey messages is through nonverbal channels.[4] Of course, the message others receive from our behavior may not be the one we intended. But we begin making judgments about people just a fraction of a second after meeting them, based on nonverbal information.[5] We may

Communication & ETHICS

Do We Have a Rhythm or Are You Just Mimicking Me?

People often talk about being "out of synch" with others or having "timing problems" that cause some relationships to end. Sometimes you'll hear people say, "Our relationship went down in flames because we just couldn't get a rhythm." Many of us are very sensitive to the rhythm of relationships and communication with key people in our lives.

In research, this rhythm phenomenon (sometimes termed the "chameleon effect" or "mimicry") is called *interactive synchrony*; it's specifically defined as the coordination of speech and body movement between at least two speakers.[6] Often, people are so in synch that they mirror each other's movements unintentionally. It's a fascinating phenomenon to observe and experience.

However, we can also purposely mirror our conversational partners. Is intentionally mirroring someone ethical, or is it taking synchrony too far?

At times, such purposeful mirroring may be an example of adapting our communication. Adaptation is our fifth principle for a lifetime, and we discuss it fully in Chapter 6. A good deal of our ability to adapt our communication involves nonverbal awareness and sensitivity to how we and others nonverbally communicate.

At other times, our goal may be more self-serving than simply adapting to our conversational partners. People who study persuasion and marketing will tell you that one of the keys to successful selling is to develop camaraderie or rapport so the potential buyer feels a kinship with the seller and a relationship gets established. One technique marketing trainers often teach salespeople is mimicry, mirroring how a potential buyer dresses, stands, walks, gestures, and uses eye contact and facial expressions, and even the rate, volume, and other aspects of the buyer's speech. A customer who perceives the salesperson's matching behavior may feel a rapport and be more likely to buy. For example, waitstaff at some restaurants are trained to squat to be at table level when talking to customers so that they're not hovering and can more easily adapt their behaviors in response to diners. Research has found that this simple adaptation increases waitstaff tips by 3 percent.[7]

Is this form of nonverbal adaptation just smart business, an ethical use of what research reveals about interactive synchrony? Or is it unethical to pretend to be in synch with someone just to win a sale or persuade people to see things your way? Is it really synchrony or is it chicanery?

decide whether a date is going to be pleasant or dull during the first thirty seconds of meeting the person, before he or she has had time to utter more than "Hello."[8]

Consider the handshake, a simple ritualistic greeting between two people used in many cultures. Have you ever considered the power of a handshake to communicate? If you get a half-handed, limp handshake (a.k.a. a "fingerella") from someone, what are you likely to conclude about that person? William Chaplin and his colleagues examined the judgments Americans make about someone's personality based on a handshake and determined that the most positive handshake was strong (but not so strong as to cut off the blood supply), vigorous, not too brief or too long, and complete (meaning that the people gripped each other's hands fully, with palms touching).[9] We form more favorable first impressions of people with good handshakes than of those with lousy ones, so even a simple nonverbal ritual such as a handshake can have a definite and long-lasting impact on how others perceive you.[10]

Nonverbal cues are important not only in the early stages of relationships, but also as we maintain, deepen, and sometimes terminate those relationships. In fact, the more intimate the relationship, the more we use and understand the nonverbal cues of our partners. We also use nonverbal cues to signal changes in the level of satisfaction with a relationship. When we want to cool things off, we may start using a less vibrant tone of voice and cut back on eye contact and physical contact with our partner.

Nonverbal Messages Serve Multiple Functions

Nonverbal messages function in a variety of ways:

- Nonverbal cues can *substitute for* verbal messages. Raising your index and middle fingers in the air can mean "peace" or "V" for victory, or it can simply be someone's way of ordering two of something in a noisy, crowded environment where it's hard to be heard.

- Nonverbal cues delivered simultaneously with verbal messages *complement*, clarify, or extend the meaning of the verbal cues, conveying more information and allowing for a more accurate interpretation. When someone waves, makes eye contact, and says "Hello," the gesture and eye contact are nonverbal complements to the verbal greeting, providing context and revealing emotions and attitudes.
- Sometimes our nonverbal cues *contradict* our verbal cues, as in the case of Danita in our earlier example, whose words said she wasn't mad but whose nonverbal cues showed her true emotional state. In most instances when verbal and nonverbal cues contradict each other, the nonverbal message is the one we should believe.
- We use nonverbal messages to *repeat* our verbal messages. You and a friend head in different directions after class. You yell, "See you at the dorm at 4," but your friend can't hear you over the hall noise, so he makes a face as though he's confused. You point in the direction of the dorm and then raise four fingers in the air, to which your friend nods his head up and down, signaling that he understands your message. In such a situation, the verbal message comes first, but the nonverbal cues repeat the message to create greater understanding.
- Nonverbal cues *regulate* our participation in conversation. When talking with people, we rely on such nonverbal cues as eye contact, facial expressions, audible intakes of breath, vocalizations such as "um," shifts in posture or seating position, and movements closer to or farther away from others.
- We may use nonverbal cues to *accent* or reinforce a verbal message. "We simply must do something about this problem or we will all bear the blame," bellows the mayor. When the mayor says the word *must*, she pounds the podium and increases her volume for emphasis. Such a vocalization and gesture serve to accent or add intensity to the verbal message.

RECAP

Why Focus on Nonverbal Communication?

- Nonverbal communication is our primary means of communicating feelings and attitudes toward others.
- Nonverbal messages are usually more believable than verbal messages.
- Nonverbal communication is critical in the initiation, development, and termination of relationships.
- Nonverbal messages function to substitute for, complement, contradict, repeat, regulate, and accent verbal messages.

The Nature of Nonverbal Communication

4.2 Discuss six elements that reveal the nature of nonverbal communication.

While the benefits of studying and improving one's facility with nonverbal communication are clear, deciphering unspoken messages is a tricky activity. Dictionaries help us interpret words, but no handy reference book exists to help decode nonverbal cues. Below are some of the challenges inherent in the interpretation of nonverbal communication.

The Culture-Bound Nature of Nonverbal Communication

Some evidence suggests that humans from every culture smile when they are happy and frown when they are unhappy.[11] They also all tend to raise or flash their eyebrows when meeting or greeting others, and young children in many cultures wave to signal that they want their parents, raise their arms to be picked up, and suck their thumbs for comfort. These trends indicate some underlying commonality in human emotion. Yet each culture tends to develop unique rules for displaying and interpreting the expression of emotion.[12]

Nonverbal behavior is culture bound. You'll make critical errors in communicating nonverbally, as well as in attempting to interpret the nonverbal behavior of others, if you don't situate nonverbal actions within a cultural context. Intercultural communication scholars teach us that one culture's friendly or polite action may be another culture's obscene gesture.[13]

The Rule-Governed Nature of Nonverbal Communication

You operate according to many rules in your nonverbal communication. You may be unaware that you function according to these rules, but when your rules are violated, you definitely know it. For example, have you ever been in a conversation with someone who got too close, all up in your face? For some reason, the other person's rule about appropriate distance differs from yours.

Communication scholar Judee Burgoon created a theory of how nonverbal communication functions, termed **expectancy violations theory**.[14] The theory suggests that we develop expectations for appropriate nonverbal behavior in ourselves and others, based on our cultural backgrounds, personal experiences, and knowledge of those with whom we interact. When those expectations (or rules) are violated, we experience heightened arousal (we become more interested or engaged in what's happening), and the nature of our interpersonal relationship with the other person becomes a critical factor as we attempt to interpret and respond to the situation.

expectancy violations theory
A theory that suggests that we develop rules or expectations for appropriate nonverbal behavior and react when those expectations are violated.

When someone stands too close to you in conversation, expectancy violations theory claims that you'll react to the nonverbal rule infraction according to the credibility, status, and attractiveness of the person who's violating your space. If the

Communication & DIVERSITY

The Olympics: Winning Medals in Nonverbal Sensitivity?

Every couple of years, the world gets treated to the Olympic Games. Without shared languages, athletes, coaches, staff, volunteers, spectators, and host-country residents must rely primarily on their nonverbal communication skills to make the Olympics function.

Soon after a city is selected—years in advance—as the site for the games, Olympic planners in that city set about the work of helping residents prepare for an influx of people from many different cultures, with their customs, expectations, and unique communication styles in tow. Hosts are concerned with making these guests feel comfortable. For example, in preparation for the summer Olympics in Beijing in 2008, messages went out across China, asking citizens to refrain from wearing clothing that Westerners wouldn't approve of, such as mixes of prints and plaids or color schemes Western visitors would deem clashing.[15] For the summer games in London in 2012, organizers mandated that all 70,000 volunteers and paid staff members working the games attend a four-hour training session in cultural sensitivity.

At an event with the size and complexity of the Olympic Games, however, you can expect the occasional "oops." At the 2012 London games, an international panel of judges ruled that a female Saudi Arabian judo competitor wasn't allowed to wear her traditional headscarf (hijab) during her matches. Rules about clothing and gear worn during competition in the various events are very strict, and the judges ruled that the hijab would compromise the safety of both competitors, given the strangleholds and chokeholds judo competitors perform during matches.[16] The athlete was put in an untenable position: She was being asked to choose between violating her national and religious culture's strict custom about women's headgear and forfeiting her opportunity to compete at the Olympic Games. In the end, she was allowed to compete in a modified hijab.

Another cultural gaffe at the London games caused an even bigger stir: The jumbotron at the soccer stadium flashed a photo in which the wrong flag was shown for the North Korean women's soccer team. The image was the South Korean flag, not the North Korean one. Given that these two countries have been in conflict for more than fifty years, confusing the two flags was a major mistake, one that led to a protest by the North Korean players.[17] Flags are nonverbal symbols of nations—their pride, their history. At international competitions where the whole world is watching, such nonverbal symbols take on even greater meaning than they have at home.

Planners of later Olympic Games, including the 2016 summer games in Rio de Janeiro, Brazil, and the 2018 winter games in PyeongChang, South Korea, have no doubt worked to improve upon the cultural sensitivity of their predecessors. As they have likely learned, attention to nonverbal communication is essential.

person isn't attractive (physically or personally) or of respectable status and credibility, you'll likely compensate for the space invasion nonverbally, usually by stepping back or moving away from the person. Only rarely do most of us resort to a verbal response such as "Please back up; you're violating my personal space." We all violate nonverbal rules from time to time, and at those moments we become acutely aware that rules or expectations of appropriateness have a powerful influence on nonverbal communication.

The Ambiguous Nature of Nonverbal Communication

Most words are given meaning by people within a culture who speak the same language. But the intended meaning of a nonverbal message is known only to the person displaying it. The person may not mean to convey the meaning that an observer sees in it. In fact, the person may not intend for the behavior to have any meaning at all. Some people have difficulty expressing their emotions nonverbally. They may have frozen facial expressions or monotone voices. Often it's a challenge to draw meaningful conclusions about these people's behavior, even if we know them quite well.

perception checking
The skill of asking other observers or the person being observed whether your interpretation of his or her nonverbal behavior is accurate.

One strategy that helps us interpret others' nonverbal cues is called **perception checking**, a strategy we mentioned in Chapter 2 in our discussion of self-awareness. Jonas, whom we read about earlier in this chapter, was trying to check Danita's perceptions when he asked whether she was mad. To check your own perceptions, observe in detail the nonverbal cues, make your own interpretation, and then do one (or both) of two things: (1) Ask the people you're observing how they feel or what's going on, and/or (2) run your interpretation by another observer to get a second opinion or more input before you draw a conclusion.

The Continuous Nature of Nonverbal Communication

Words have a beginning and an end. You can point to the first word in this sentence and underline the last one. Our nonverbal behaviors are not as easily dissected because they're continuous. Imagine you're standing in the hallway after class, talking to a classmate. You both make eye contact as you talk, and your facial expressions coordinate with what you're saying. You stand a certain distance apart, move and change your posture as the conversation flows, add a hand gesture or two to emphasize what you're saying, and change your pitch, volume, and rate of speaking to further make yourself understood. Your classmate's cell phone rings. Your classmate apologizes, looks down into his or her book bag to fish out the phone, and makes eye contact with you once again, along with a facial expression of apology. Your classmate then signals to you with a hand gesture, while talking into the phone, that she or he has to go, and you understand that your conversation is over. You wave goodbye, break eye contact, and go your separate ways, and your nonverbal behaviors go with you. In this simple example, the nonverbal cues are flying faster than the verbal ones, but they're essential in getting the message across. The sheer volume and continuous flow of nonverbal cues—not to mention complications such as culture and emotion—make accurate interpretation a challenge.

We're usually uncomfortable when someone breaks our unwritten rules for nonverbal communication. President Lyndon Johnson, for example, was known for standing too close when he talked to people, giving listeners what came to be called "the Johnson treatment." In this 1966 conversation, civil rights leader Whitney Young seemed to be so uncomfortable with President Johnson's space invasion that he closed his eyes. How do you typically respond when someone violates your nonverbal communication expectations?
White House Photo Office/Lyndon B. Johnson Presidential Library

The Nonlinguistic Nature of Nonverbal Communication

Even though some writers in the 1960s and 1970s tried to make readers think otherwise, there is no "language of the body." Julius Fast, author of the 1970 book *Body Language*, believed that nonverbal communication was a language with pattern and grammar, just like verbal communication.[18] He suggested that if you were savvy and observant enough, you could quickly and easily interpret certain nonverbal behaviors to mean certain things—in any case, at any time. For example, Fast contended that if

Aaron Bacall/Cartoon Stock

"Of course I'm listening to your expression of spiritual suffering. Don't you see me making eye contact, striking an open posture, leaning towards you and nodding empathetically?"

a woman sat cross-legged and pumped her foot up and down while talking to a man, that was a clear-cut sign of her romantic interest in him. If someone didn't make eye contact, she or he was automatically dishonest and untrustworthy. If people crossed their arms in front of them, that indicated hostility.

The problem is that the body language approach didn't take into account the complexities of individual, contextual, and cultural differences. Pumping the foot might be an indication of nervousness or impatience, not attraction. Some people are shy; others come from a culture in which making direct eye contact is considered rude. It's important to remember that nonverbal communication doesn't conform to the patterns of a language.

The Multichanneled Nature of Nonverbal Communication

The "second screen" phenomenon is quite popular these days. Recent research shows that a growing number of TV watchers view (or listen to) programming while also using their mobile phones, tablets, or laptop computers (a.k.a. a "second screen"). According to one survey, 41 percent of people surveyed indicated that they used other devices while watching TV, mainly for the purpose of searching for information related to the TV show they're watching. Others use social media, such as Twitter and Facebook, to comment about the TV programming or just to multitask, perhaps sending e-mail messages while a TV is on in the background.[19] But even with your powers of multitasking and an ability to switch your attention rapidly, you can really focus on only one medium at a time.

Nonverbal communication works the same way; nonverbal cues are communicated in multiples or clusters, but we process the cues individually. Before you try to interpret the meaning of a single nonverbal behavior, look for clusters of corroborating nonverbal cues, in conjunction with verbal behavior, to get the most complete picture possible.

RECAP

The Nature of Nonverbal Communication

- *Nonverbal communication is culture bound.* Nonverbal behaviors vary widely across cultural and co-cultural groups. Interpret nonverbal cues within a cultural context.
- *Nonverbal communication is rule governed.* We develop rules or expectations for appropriate nonverbal behavior in ourselves and others.
- *Nonverbal communication is ambiguous.* Nonverbal behavior is difficult to interpret accurately because the meanings for different actions vary from person to person.
- *Nonverbal communication is continuous.* Unlike the stop-start nature of verbal communication, nonverbal messages flow from one situation to the next.
- *Nonverbal communication is nonlinguistic.* Nonverbal communication does not have the regularities of vocabulary, grammar, and pattern that language has.
- *Nonverbal communication is multichanneled.* Nonverbal cues register on our senses from a variety of sources simultaneously, but we can actually attend to only one nonverbal cue at a time.

Codes of Nonverbal Communication

4.3 Identify and explain the seven nonverbal communication codes.

Many researchers and theorists have long been fascinated with nonverbal communication, but two who have made perhaps the greatest contributions to our understanding are Paul Ekman and Wallace Friesen, sometimes referred to as the "great classifiers" of nonverbal behavior.[20] Below we introduce and explain each code and then provide a few research findings to illustrate how we can apply knowledge of nonverbal communication to further our understanding of human behavior.

Appearance

Many cultures around the world place a high value on appearance—body size and shape, skin color and texture, hairstyle, and clothing—but it seems like Americans *really* emphasize this one nonverbal cue. Cosmetic procedures to modify physical appearance generate billions of dollars annually. In 2012, over ten million surgical and nonsurgical cosmetic procedures were performed in the United States—90 percent of them on women, with breast augmentation being the most prevalent procedure.[21] We put such pressure on ourselves and others to be physically attractive that our self-esteem may decline when we realize we cannot match up with some perceived ideal.[22] Americans elevate onto a pedestal highly physically attractive people (whether or not they actually deserve this kind of accolade), attaching all sorts of desirable qualities to them. Research shows that we tend to think physically attractive people are more credible, happy, popular, socially skilled, prosperous, employable, persuasive, honest, poised, strong, kind, outgoing, and sexually warm than other people.[23] And studies have shown that college students perceive physically attractive teachers to be more approachable than other teachers and give them higher evaluation scores.[24]

Another aspect of physical appearance is clothing, which serves many functions. Chief among them are keeping the body warm and protected; preserving a person's modesty and a society's sense of decency; conveying one's personality, status, and culture; demonstrating one's sexuality; and communicating identification with a group, such as wearing your university's logo on a T-shirt.[25] **Artifacts** such as jewelry, tattoos, piercings, makeup, cologne, and eyeglasses are also displays of culture and personality. These nonverbal elements of appearance affect how we feel about ourselves and how we are perceived by others.[26]

artifact
Clothing or another element of appearance (e.g., jewelry, tattoos, piercings, makeup, cologne).

Body Movement, Gestures, and Posture

Have you ever traveled in a country where you couldn't speak the language? Or have you ever tried to have a conversation locally with a person who didn't speak English or who was deaf and didn't read lips? What do you do in these situations? Chances are that you risk looking foolish by using overexaggerated gestures

Communication & TECHNOLOGY

Talking While Walking: Dangerous Multitasking

You've probably seen the phenomenon: people staring down into their cell phones, perhaps texting, but certainly not watching where they're walking. They meander, veering unpredictably from a straight path; they almost run into you or inanimate objects. Eventually, they may suddenly look up and realize they weren't paying attention to their surroundings. We get it: Cell phones are mesmerizing. We've probably all gotten absorbed in our cell phones, focused on the task of checking messages, texting someone, or looking to see who called us while we were in class.

Most states, if not all by now, have banned texting while driving; many states have banned any kind of cell phone use—even hands free—behind the wheel because of the staggering statistics about cell phone use and car crashes. People who talk or text on cell phones while driving tend to drive under the speed limit (which can be dangerous) and weave across lanes (which is *very* dangerous). But here's something you may not know: Talking or texting on your cell makes you a dangerous, inefficient *walker*.

Just how much does the use of technology compromise this basic nonverbal cue of walking? Eric Lamberg and Lisa Muratori, physical therapists and professors at Stony Brook University in New York, studied the effects of cell phone use on walking behavior.[27] Their results weren't surprising: Like drivers who slow down while texting, students who walked across campus while talking or texting on their cell phones walked more slowly than others who were not engaged in cell phone use. In addition, cell phone walkers evidenced significant "lateral deviation"; they strayed by as much as 61 percent from a straight path as they walked toward their destination. Although both talking and texting caused walking problems, texters were worse at walking than talkers.

We know students are going to use their cell phones on campus—that's not going to change. But we encourage you to try to have more awareness when you're on your phone. Notice your own nonverbal behavior, such as how you walk, how loudly you might be talking, and the amount of time you're engaged in activities related to your phone. You may be motivated to make some changes that can make your life more efficient and productive (or at least keep you from walking into a classmate).

Monkey Business/Fotolia

or slowly and deliberately shouting words the listener can't understand. These responses are nonverbal attempts to compensate for a lack of verbal understanding. Even when we do speak the same language as others, we often use gestures to help us make our point.

Kinesics is a general term for human movements, gestures, and posture. Posture and movement are greatly affected by self-esteem and emotional state. For example, when you're feeling upbeat and good about yourself, you're likely to carry yourself more upright and possibly exhibit a "spring in your step." Conversely, if you're having a bad day, your posture might be more slumped over or stooped, because some days it's just hard to hold your head and shoulders up.

As we said earlier in this chapter, gestures are culture bound, context bound, and rule governed. Nancy Armstrong and Melissa Wagner are the authors of a book entitled *Field Guide to Gestures,* in which they describe and interpret a wide variety of gestures, particularly as used in U.S. culture.[28] They organize gestures into such categories as Arrival and Departure, Approval and Disapproval, Mating, and Offensive and Profane. Among the gestures in the Arrival and Departure category are the Bow, the Blown Kiss, the Fist-Chest Pound, and the Live Long and Prosper gesture (which needs no explanation for *Star Trek* fans).

Some gestures have cross-cultural, widely understood meanings, such as the pointing gesture or "come here" and "stay away" gestures accomplished with the placement of the palms and motion of the hands and arms. But here's our repeated warning with nonverbal cues: *Don't assume.* Don't assume a universal interpretation

kinesics
Human movements, gestures, and posture.

for a gesture you've grown up using in your home culture. These forms of nonverbal communication are complicated.

As one interesting application of the research on kinesics, scholars have explored verbal and nonverbal indications of attraction.[29] One study found fifty-two gestures and nonverbal behaviors that women use to signal their interest in men. Among the top nonverbal flirting cues were smiling, surveying a crowded room with the eyes, and moving closer to the object of one's affection.[30] However, other studies have found that men tend to view flirting as more sexual than women do and misinterpret women's friendly behaviors as signs of sexual attraction and interest.[31] Studies have found that the likelihood for this kind of misinterpretation greatly increases with alcohol consumption.[32]

Eye Contact

Do you agree that the eyes are the "windows to the soul"? What can people tell about you by looking into your eyes? Are you comfortable making eye contact with most people or only with people you know well? Eye contact is extremely important in American culture and in many other cultures around the world. Americans, in particular, make all kinds of judgments about others—particularly about their trustworthiness, truthfulness, and sincerity—on the basis of whether they make or avoid eye contact.[33] Table 4.1 summarizes circumstances under which we're more or less likely to make eye contact with a conversational partner.[34]

Research shows that eye contact plays a significant role in judgments of a public speaker's credibility.[35] In the first televised presidential candidates' debate, John F. Kennedy appeared comfortable and confident as he made eye contact with television cameras. It seemed as though he was making eye contact directly with the American public. In contrast, Richard Nixon darted his eyes nervously from side to side at times and generally made less eye contact with the camera and the viewing audience. This created a perception that Nixon was shifty, untrustworthy, and lacking credibility.

Facial Expressions

Actor/comedian Steve Carell has a very expressive face. Researchers suggest that the human face is capable of producing 250,000 different facial expressions.[36] Steve Carell can probably make them all.

As early as 1872, when Charles Darwin systematically studied the expression of emotion in both humans and animals, scientists realized that nonverbal cues are the primary ways humans communicate emotion.[37] Facial and eye expressions, along

Table 4.1 When Do We Make Eye Contact?

You are more likely to look at your conversational partner when you . . .	You are less likely to look at your conversational partner when you . . .
• are physically distant from the person.	• are physically close to the person.
• are discussing impersonal topics.	• are discussing intimate topics.
• have nothing else to look at.	• have other objects, people, or backgrounds to look at.
• are interested in your partner's reactions.	• aren't romantically interested in or dislike your partner.
• are romantically interested in or like your partner.	• come from a culture that doesn't value visual contact in interaction.
• wish to dominate or influence your partner.	• are an introvert.
• come from a culture that emphasizes visual contact in interaction.	• are embarrassed, ashamed, sorrowful, sad, or submissive.
• are an extrovert.	• are trying to hide something.
• are listening, rather than talking.	• are male.
• are female.	

with posture, gestures, and body movements (such as how we walk) reveal our feelings.[38] Your face tends to express which *kind* of emotion you're feeling, whereas your body reveals the intensity or how *much* emotion you're feeling.

You've downloaded a new app on your phone and show it to your romantic partner or a friend. Or as an interviewer reads your resumé, you sit in silence across the desk. In both of these situations, you scan the other person's face, eagerly awaiting some reaction. To interpret someone's facial expressions accurately, you need to focus on what the other person may be thinking or feeling. It helps if you know the person well, can see her or his whole face, have plenty of time to observe, and understand the situation that prompted the reaction.[39]

How accurately do we interpret emotions expressed on the face? Researchers who have attempted to measure subjects' skill in identifying the emotional expressions of others have found it a tricky business. Classic research by Ekman and Friesen determined that the human face universally exhibits six primary emotions: happiness, sadness, surprise, fear, anger, and disgust or contempt.[40] More recently, however, researchers at Ohio State University have documented people's abilities to consistently express twenty-one recognizable facial expressions that reflect combined, even contradictory or conflicting, emotions, such as "happily disgusted" or "sadly angry."[41]

Even though our faces provide a great deal of information about emotions, we quickly learn to control our facial expressions. One fascinating study examined children's facial expressions when they received either wonderful, new toys or broken, disappointing toys.[42] When they received the disappointing toys, the children showed a flash of disappointment on their faces, but then very quickly they masked their disappointment and changed their facial expressions to reveal a more positive, socially appropriate reaction. Even very young children learn to control the way an emotion registers on their face.

Touch

Touch is the most powerful form of nonverbal communication; it's also the most misunderstood and carries the potential for the most problems if ill used. Consider some moments involving accidental touch. Standing elbow to elbow in an elevator or sitting next to someone in a crowded airplane, you may find yourself in physical contact with total strangers. As you stiffen your body and avert your eyes, a baffling sense of shame and discomfort may flood over you. Why do we sometimes react this way to accidental touching? Normally, we touch to express affection and intimacy. When affection or intimacy isn't our intended message, we instinctively react to modify the impression our touch has created.

haptics
The study of human touch.

touch ethic
A person's own guidelines or standards as to appropriate and inappropriate touch.

Countless studies on touch, termed **haptics** in research, have shown that intimate human contact is vital to our personal development, well-being, and physical health.[43] Think about your role models and the lessons you learned about touch while growing up. If you grew up in a two-parent family, did your parents display affection in front of you? If not, you may have grown up believing that affectionate touching should not be done in front of others. As an adult, you may be uncomfortable with public displays of affection. If you grew up with parents or family members who were affectionate with each other and their children, your **touch ethic**—what you consider appropriate touching—as an adult is influenced by that experience.[44] We don't mean to insinuate that a touch ethic that accepts public affection is somehow more psychologically healthy than one that reserves touching for private moments. But what if you date or partner with someone whose experiences while growing up led to a very

Our views of appropriate touch, termed the *touch ethic*, are typically formed early in life, as we interact with family members.
Andy Dean/Fotolia

different touch ethic than yours? You may be headed for some conflict but, ideally, some compromise as well.

The amount of touch we need, initiate, tolerate, and receive depends also on our cultural background.[45] Certain cultures are high contact—meaning that touching is quite commonplace—such as some European and Middle Eastern cultures in which men kiss each other on the cheek as a greeting and may even hold hands. Other cultures are low contact, such as some Asian cultures in which demonstrations of affection are rare and considered inappropriate.[46]

The Voice

"We have nothing to fear but fear itself."

"Ask not what your country can do for you—ask what you can do for your country."

"I have a dream . . . I have a dream today."

"I am not a crook."

"Mr. Gorbachev, tear down this wall."

If you recognize these statements as having been made by American leaders and you have heard them live or in recordings, you're likely to read them aloud (or hear them in your mind) using the same pauses and changes in pitch, volume, and emphasis as did the famous speakers. John F. Kennedy greatly emphasized the word *not,* as in "Ask NOT what your country. . . ." Martin Luther King Jr. used rising pitch and increased volume as he uttered the word *dream* over and over again in his speech. These leaders learned to use the tremendous capacity and versatility of the voice to create memorable moments.

Like your face, your voice is a major vehicle for communicating your thoughts, your emotions, and the nature of your relationships with others. It also provides information about your self-confidence and influences how you're perceived.[47] The pitch, rate, and volume at which you speak and your use of silence—elements termed **paralanguage** or **vocalics**—all provide important clues. Most of us would conclude, as has research, that a speaker who mumbles, speaks very slowly and softly, continually mispronounces words, and uses "uh" and "um" is less credible and persuasive than one who speaks clearly, rapidly, fluently, and with appropriate volume.[48] Sometimes it's jarring when a person's physical appearance doesn't seem to match her or his voice.[49] A famous example is former boxing champ Mike Tyson, whose high-pitched voice isn't what we tend to expect out of someone with such a muscular physique.

Sometimes it's not what we say or even how we say it that communicates our feelings. Pausing and being silent communicate volumes.[50] You may be at a loss for words or need time to think about what you want to contribute to a conversation, so pausing or being silent may be better than fumbling for the right way to express yourself. Silence can be a sign of respect, but it can also be an indication of anger (as when you give someone "the silent treatment") or discomfort (as in "an awkward silence"). At other times, you may feel so comfortable with someone that words aren't necessary; psychologist Sidney Baker calls these moments "positive silence."[51]

Physical Environment, Space, and Territory

Close your eyes and picture your bedroom as it is right now—whether it's a dorm room you share with one or more roommates, the room you've had since you were a child, your own room, or a bedroom shared with a spouse or partner. Try to get a clear, detailed mental image of how that room looks right now. Then think about this: If one of your professors were to walk into your bedroom right now, what impressions would he or she form about you?

This question has to do with your interaction with the physical environment and the space around you. You may be unused to looking at the environment as a form of nonverbal communication, but the miniworld you create for yourself reveals a good deal about you. Also, your preferred amount of space, the level of

paralanguage (vocalics)
Nonverbal aspects of voice (e.g., pitch, rate, volume, use of silence).

ownership you attach to that space, and your behavior as you delineate and protect that space are fascinating nonverbal elements that researchers continue to study.[52]

THE PHYSICAL ENVIRONMENT What's so great about a corner office with wall-to-wall windows? It's one of many indications in American culture of high status. In a working world increasingly structured into cubicles, an employee's work location serves as a symbol of importance.[53] The environment is important to the study of nonverbal communication in two ways:

- The choices we make about the environments in which we live and operate reveal a good deal about who we are; physical environments are extensions of our personalities.[54] We tend to put our "signature" on our environments by adorning the settings in which we work, study, and reside to make them unique and personal.
- Nonverbal behavior is altered by the various environments in which we communicate.[55] Formal settings may make our movements more restrained, our body posture more rigid, and our speech limited and whispered. Informal settings tend to cause us to expand and relax our nonverbal behaviors.

One of the more cutting-edge and interesting lines of research into the environment as a form of nonverbal communication surrounds designing spaces for people with disabilities.[56] Although college students without physical disabilities might think this area pertains to building ramps and installing elevators in older campus buildings, design for disability means much more. Some examples include placing extensive Braille signage on campuses (not just in elevators), retrofitting computer labs to offer people with disabilities better access to technology, and providing furniture design in classrooms that assimilates into the environment and accommodates learners of all physical types.[57]

proxemics
The study of how close or far away from people and objects we position ourselves.

SPACE Imagine that you're sitting alone at a long, rectangular table in your campus library. As you sit dutifully with your head in a textbook, you're startled when a complete stranger sits directly across from you at the table. Since there are several empty chairs at the other end of the table, you may feel uncomfortable that this unknown individual has invaded *your* area.

Figure 4.2 Edward T. Hall's Four Zones of Space

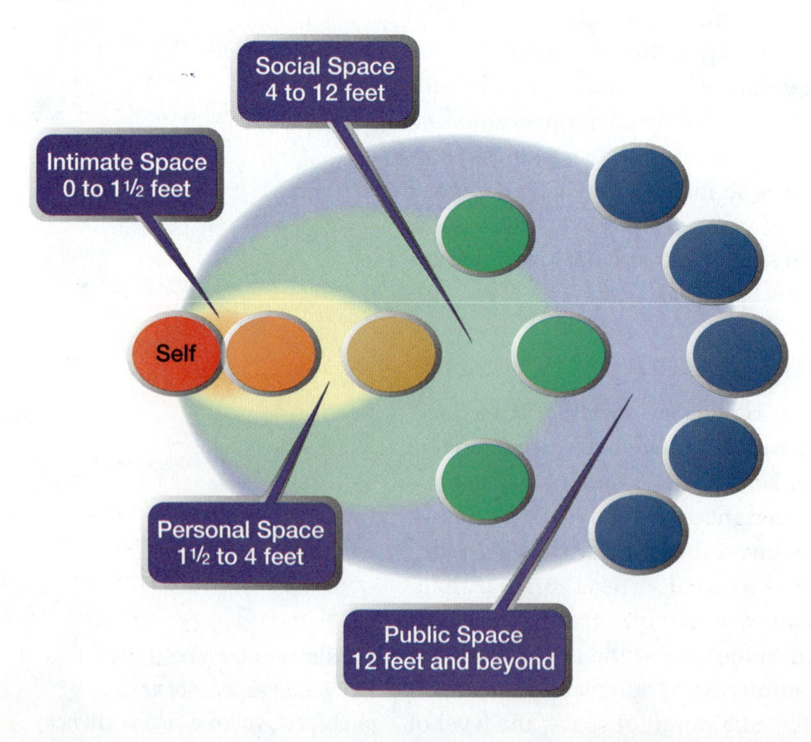

Every culture has well-established ways of regulating spatial relations. How physically close we are willing to get to others relates to how well we know them, to considerations of power and status, and to our cultural background.[58]

A pioneer in helping us understand personal space was Edward T. Hall, who studied **proxemics**, or the distances that people allow between themselves and objects or other people. Hall identified four spatial zones, which are diagrammed in Figure 4.2:[59]

- *Intimate space*. The most personal communication occurs when people are from 0 to 1½ feet apart. Unless we're forced to stand in a crowded space, intimate space is open only to those with whom we are well acquainted.
- *Personal space*. Most of our conversations with family and friends occur when we are

1½ to 4 feet apart. We feel uncomfortable if someone we don't know well enters our personal space zone on purpose.

- *Social space*. The majority of formal group interactions and many of our professional relationships take place in the social space zone, which ranges from 4 to 12 feet.
- *Public space*. Many public speakers position themselves at least 12 feet away from their audiences, but interpersonal communication doesn't usually occur in the public space zone.

The specific space that you and others choose depends on several variables, most specifically your cultural background.[60] Generally, however, the more you like people, the closer you tend to stand to them. Higher-status and larger people are afforded more space than lower-status and smaller people.[61] We also tend to stand closer to others in a large room than we do in a small room. In general, women tend to stand closer to others than men do.[62]

TERRITORY The study of how people use space and objects to communicate occupancy or ownership of space is termed **territoriality**.[63] You assumed ownership of that part of the table in the library and the right to determine who sat with you. You may have reacted negatively not only because your sense of personal space was invaded, but also because the intrusive stranger broke a cultural rule governing territoriality.

You announce your ownership of space with **territorial markers**—things and actions that signify that an area has been claimed. When you arrive at class, for example, you may put your book bag on a chair while you get up and go out into the hall to make a call on your cell phone. That book bag signifies temporary ownership of your seat. If you returned to find that someone had moved your stuff and was sitting in your seat, you would probably become indignant. The most common form of territorial marker is a lock. We lock our doors and windows, cars, offices, briefcases, TVs (using V-chips), and computers (using passwords) to keep out intruders.

While we traditionally think of space as a physical dimension, with increased accessibility and use of technology that links us with cyberspace, we have recently begun to think of space differently.[64] What if someone hacked into your e-mail account or stole your phone and read your messages or texts? You'd probably be very upset and view this as a territorial violation.

RECAP

Codes of Nonverbal Communication

Appearance	Influences perceptions of credibility and attractiveness
Body Movement, Gestures, and Posture	Communicate information, status, warmth, credibility, interest in others, attitudes, and liking
Eye Contact	Conveys trustworthiness, sincerity, honesty, and interest
Facial Expressions	Reveal thoughts and express emotions and attitudes
Touch	Communicates intimacy, affection, and rejection
Voice	Communicates emotion and clarifies the meaning of messages through pitch, rate, and volume
Environment	Communicates information about the person who functions in that environment; provides context that alters behavior
Space	Provides information about status, power, and intimacy
Territory	Provides cues as to use, ownership, and occupancy of space

How to Interpret Nonverbal Cues More Accurately

4.4 Explain Mehrabian's three-part framework for interpreting nonverbal cues.

How do we make sense of all the nonverbal cues we receive from others? If you earnestly want to accurately interpret and sensitively respond to someone's nonverbal communication, you must be willing to spend time and effort to develop this skill. Enhancing your interpretive skills requires, first, an awareness of the importance of nonverbal elements in the communication process. A second requirement is the willingness and emotional maturity to make your own behavior secondary to that of someone else. In other words, if you're so wrapped up in yourself that you can think about and deal only with how *you're* feeling, what *you're* thinking, and what *you* want at a given moment, you can't possibly hope to take in others' nonverbal cues, interpret them accurately, and respond appropriately.

territoriality
The study of how humans use space and objects to communicate occupancy or ownership of space.

territorial marker
A thing or action that signifies that an area has been claimed.

Beyond these suggestions, we recommend that you keep in mind a three-part framework developed by Albert Mehrabian to help you improve your nonverbal interpretive skills. Mehrabian found that we synthesize and interpret nonverbal cues along three primary dimensions: immediacy, arousal, and dominance.[65]

- *Immediacy*. Mehrabian contends that **immediacy**—nonverbal cues that communicate liking and engender feelings of pleasure and closeness—explains why we're drawn to some people but not others.[66] In a social setting, to find out whether someone likes us or views us favorably, we should watch for eye contact, smiling and other pleasant facial expressions, head nods, an open and relaxed posture, a body orientation toward us rather than away from us, close proximity, a rising intonation in the voice, and culture- and context-appropriate touch.[67]
- *Arousal*. Nonverbal cues of **arousal** communicate feelings of interest and excitement. As nonverbal scholar Peter Andersen puts it, arousal is "the degree to which a person is stimulated or activated."[68] Primary arousal cues include increased eye contact; closer conversational distances; increased touch; animated vocal expressions (such as laughing); more direct body orientation, smiling, and active facial expressions; and interactive synchrony (or mimicry, as discussed earlier in this chapter).[69]
- *Dominance*. The third dimension of Mehrabian's framework communicates the balance of power in a relationship. **Dominance** cues indicate status, position, and importance. People who are high in status tend to have a relaxed body posture; less direct body orientation toward lower-status people; a downward head tilt; less direct eye contact; and less smiling, head nodding, and facial animation than lower-status people.[70] As we alluded to earlier, "power people" usually have more space around them; they have bigger offices and more barriers (human and nonhuman) protecting them. They may communicate their sense of power through clothing, possessions, and their use of time.

When you attempt to interpret someone's nonverbal communication, realize that there's a good deal of room for error. Humans are complex, and they don't always send clear signals. But the more you learn about nonverbal communication and the more you become aware of your own nonverbal communication and the nonverbal cues of others, the greater your chances of accurately perceiving and interpreting someone's message.

immediacy
Nonverbal behaviors that communicate feelings of liking, pleasure, and closeness.

arousal
Nonverbal behaviors that communicate feelings of interest and excitement.

dominance
Nonverbal behaviors that communicate power, status, and control.

Who is the most powerful person in this room? What nonverbal cues indicate that person's dominance?
Picture Factory/Fotolia

STUDY GUIDE:
Review, Apply, and Assess Your Knowledge and Skill

Review Your Knowledge

Why Focus on Nonverbal Communication?

4.1 Provide four reasons for studying nonverbal communication.

Nonverbal communication is communication other than written or spoken language that occurs without words. It's important to become more aware of your own nonverbal communication and to enhance your ability to detect and interpret others' nonverbal cues more accurately. Nonverbal messages communicate our feelings and attitudes and are critical to successful relationships. They can substitute for, complement, contradict, repeat, regulate, and accent verbal messages. Nonverbal messages are also more believable than verbal messages.

The Nature of Nonverbal Communication

4.2 Discuss six elements that reveal the nature of nonverbal communication.

Nonverbal communication is:

- Culture bound: Interpret nonverbal cues within a cultural context.
- Rule governed: Expectancy violations theory suggests that you may not know that you have rules or expectations governing appropriate nonverbal communication until those expectations are violated.
- Ambiguous: Exact meanings for nonverbal cues are difficult to determine, but perception checking can help decipher the meaning of a nonverbal message.
- Continuous: Unlike verbal messages that start and stop, nonverbal cues are ongoing.
- Nonlinguistic: Verbal communication consists of language with patterns, grammar, and regularities; nonverbal communication is more complex and does not operate like language.
- Multichanneled: Nonverbal cues register on our senses from a variety of sources simultaneously, but we can attend to only one nonverbal cue at a time.

Codes of Nonverbal Communication

4.3 Identify and explain the seven nonverbal communication codes.

Ekman and Friesen provided the primary codes or categories of nonverbal behavior, which are enacted differently by people depending on their cultural background. Each code has been researched extensively and applied to different contexts and relationships. The seven primary codes include the following:

- Appearance: Body size, shape, skin color and texture, hairstyle, clothing, and other appearance aspects (artifacts) provide protection for our bodies, convey our identity, and communicate our culture.
- Kinesics includes human movements, gestures, and posture.
- Eye contact conveys interest and credibility and is an important nonverbal cue within most cultures.
- Facial expressions reveal our emotions.
- Touch (haptics) is the most powerful nonverbal cue but also the most complex because of the potential for misunderstanding.
- The voice (paralanguage or vocalics) communicates our thoughts, our emotions, and the nature of our relationships.
- The physical environment, space (proxemics), and how we delineate and protect that space (territoriality) are important nonverbal cues.

How to Interpret Nonverbal Cues More Accurately

4.4 Explain Mehrabian's three-part framework for interpreting nonverbal cues.

It takes time and effort to develop our skills in detecting and accurately interpreting others' nonverbal communication. Albert Mehrabian suggested that nonverbal cues can communicate *immediacy,* or liking; *arousal,* or excitement and interest; and *dominance,* or status, position, and importance.

Key Terms

Nonverbal Communication, p. 75
Expectancy Violations Theory, p. 80
Perception Checking, p. 81
Artifact, p. 83
Kinesics, p. 84
Haptics, p. 86
Touch Ethic, p. 86
Paralanguage (Vocalics), p. 87
Proxemics, p. 88
Territoriality, p. 89
Territorial Marker, p. 89
Immediacy, p. 90
Arousal, p. 90
Dominance, p. 90

The Principle Points

Principle Three:

Effectively use and interpret nonverbal messages.

- Realize the importance of physical appearance and attractiveness in American culture.
- Use culturally appropriate body movement, including posture and gestures, to convey messages.
- Work on making appropriate eye contact with others, given that eye contact is the key nonverbal behavior North Americans link with credibility and trustworthiness.
- Become more aware of your and others' facial expressions, because this nonverbal channel is a primary one for conveying emotions.
- Use touch appropriately, given the cultural context within which you communicate.
- Become more aware of the potential you have for vocal expression and how others use their vocal capacities to communicate emotions and ideas.
- Become more aware of your rules regarding space and territoriality so that you may better understand and enact appropriate, effective proxemic nonverbal behaviors when interacting with others.
- Recognize that body movement, eye contact, facial expressions, touch, vocal behaviors, and use of space and territory communicate liking, interest, and dominance.

Apply Your Skill

Consider the following questions. Write your answers and/or share them with your classmates:

1. Give an example of how you or someone you know has used nonverbal communication to substitute for, complement, contradict, repeat, regulate, or accent a verbal message.
2. In addition to the personal space rules described in the chapter, give an example of another nonverbal communication rule you hold and what happens when people violate it.
3. In what situations do you consider it always okay for someone to touch you? When is touching you never okay?
4. What is your opinion about the ethics of purposefully synchronizing your nonverbal communication with someone else's? Do you believe it's manipulative or adaptive? Explain your answer.

Assess Your Skill

Body Movement and Emotion

Describe examples of body movement that reveal each of the six primary emotions listed below. Then generate possible alternative meanings for the same movement. For example, arms crossed across your chest might reveal anger or that you're closed off and not open to conversation; it might also be that you're just chilly. We've provided an example to get you started.

Emotion	Body Movements	Alternative Meaning of Movement
Embarrassment	Covering your face with your hands	Could also indicate deception
Happiness		
Anger		
Surprise		
Fear		
Disgust		
Sadness		

Is This Space Invasion?

We've explored the nonverbal codes of space and territory, and you should now have a better understanding of the range of people's reactions to perceived invasions of their space. Read each situation below, decide whether a proxemic or territorial violation has occurred, and then describe two tactics you might use in response to each situation. (Try to think of things you realistically *would* do in each situation, not just what you *could* do.)

a. You're at a bar or club, sitting alone, waiting for a friend to join you. A stranger sits down beside you and starts a conversation.
b. You're a business executive. You enter your office after lunch and find your administrative assistant sitting in your chair, feet up on the desk, talking on the phone.
c. You're taking racquetball lessons, and it's your turn on the court. A group of people gather to watch your lesson.
d. You're interviewing for a part-time job. As the interview nears a close, the interviewer moves from behind the desk toward you and touches you on the knee.
e. You want to wear your favorite sweater but can't find it. You discover it wadded up in the bottom of the laundry hamper, reeking of cigarette smoke, and you realize your roommate or a family member wore it without your permission.

Chapter 5
Listening and Responding

Listening, not imitation, may be the sincerest form of flattery. —DR. JOYCE BROTHERS

Ilya Andriyanov/Shutterstock

Chapter Outline

- The Importance of Listening and Responding Skills
- How We Listen
- Listening Styles
- Listening Barriers
- Improving Your Listening Skills
- Improving Your Responding Skills
- Study Guide: Review, Apply, and Assess Your Knowledge and Skill

Chapter Objectives

After studying this chapter, you should be able to

5.1 Explain the principle of listening and responding thoughtfully to others.

5.2 Identify the elements of the listening process.

5.3 Describe four listening styles.

5.4 Identify and describe barriers that keep people from listening well.

5.5 Identify and use strategies that can improve your listening skills.

5.6 Identify and use appropriate responding skills.

You spend more time listening to others than doing almost anything else you do. Americans spend up to 90 percent of a typical day communicating with people, and they spend 55 percent of that communication time listening to others.[1] As Figure 5.1 shows, if you're typical, you spend the *least* amount of your communication time writing, yet you receive more training in writing than in any other communication skill.[2] Most people have not had any formal training at all in listening or responding.[3] Reading this chapter will provide you information and skills many people lack.

In this chapter, we focus on the principle of increasing your sensitivity to others—your awareness of and concern for them—by listening. Becoming sensitive to others includes more than just understanding and interpreting their words, thoughts, and ideas—sensitivity also involves understanding the emotions underlying the words and unspoken messages of others. Increasing your skill in listening to others is one of the most productive ways to increase all these aspects of your communication sensitivity.

As shown in our familiar model of the Communication Principles for a Lifetime in Figure 5.2, effective communicators do more than absorb a message; they also provide an appropriate response to the speaker. We'll address both listening and responding to others in this chapter.

Figure 5.1 What You Do with Your Communication Time

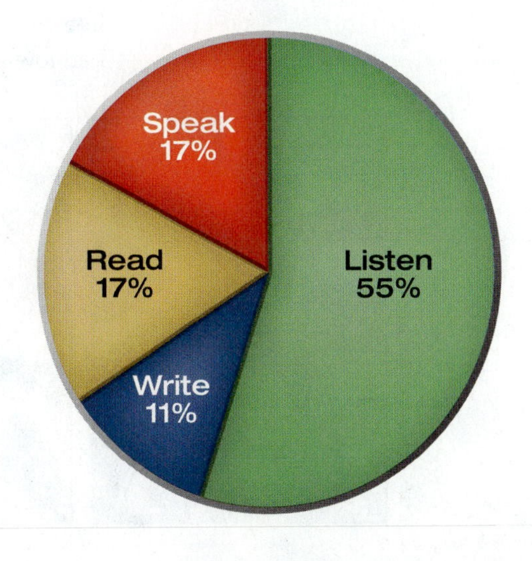

The Importance of Listening and Responding Skills

5.1 Explain the principle of listening and responding thoughtfully to others.

Some researchers suggest that because listening is the first communication skill we learn (we respond to sounds even while in our mother's womb), it's also the most important skill.[4] Listening plays a key role in helping us learn to speak. Listening and responding skills are vital as we develop relationships with others, collaborate, and listen to lectures and speeches.

Figure 5.2 Communication Principles for a Lifetime

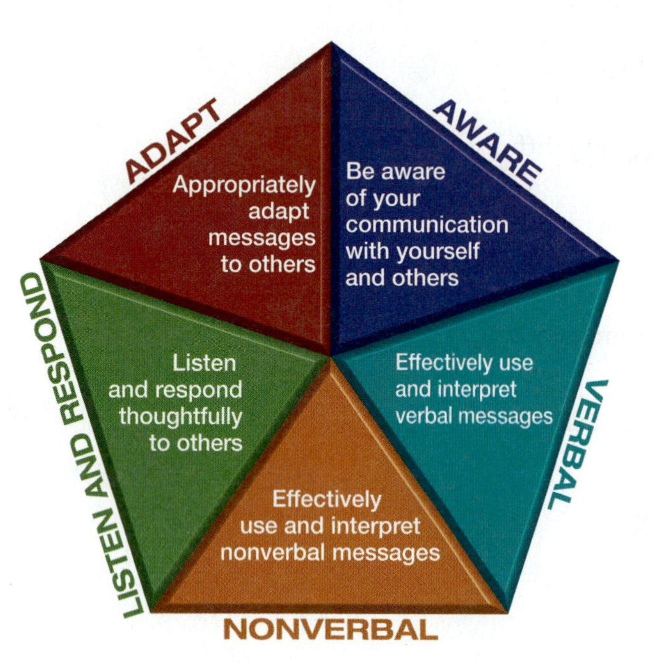

Listening Enhances Our Relationships with Others

Your skill as a listener has important implications for the relationships you establish with others.[5] In interpersonal communication situations, the essence of being a good conversationalist is being a good listener. Rather than focusing only on what to say, a person skilled in the art of conversation listens and picks up on interests and themes of others. Listening well can also earn you some tangible benefits. Some evidence suggests that our ability to listen influences how others respond to us; when people are in the presence of someone whom they perceive to be a good listener, they are likely to respond with greater empathy and interest.[6] One research study found that a key difference between couples who remain married and those who divorce is the ability to listen to each other.[7] Partners in marriages that endure report that being a good listener is key to a satisfying marital relationship.

People who are perceived to be good listeners also enjoy greater success in their jobs than those who are perceived to be poor listeners.[8] For example, physicians, nurses, and others who work in the health professions who are good listeners are perceived to be more competent and skilled than those who listen poorly.[9]

Listening Helps Us Collaborate with Others

One study found that being a good listener was the most important skill to have when working with others in groups and teams.[10] One of the hallmarks of an effective leader is being a good listener.[11]

But your ability to listen and connect to others will affect your value to other group members whether you are the appointed or emerging leader of a group or are a group or team member.[12] Group members who verbally dominate group meetings are not usually held in high esteem. Groups need people who can listen and connect conversational threads that often become tangled or dropped during group dialogue.

Listening Links Speaker and Audience

Without effective listening skills, you'll likely miss some messages in public speaking situations. Listening skills are especially important when you need to understand and retain spoken information. There is evidence, for example, that listening skills correlate with academic ability. One study found that almost half of college students who had low scores on a listening test were on academic probation at the end of their first

Zits/King Features Syndicate

year in college. In comparison, just over 4 percent of the students who had high scores on the same listening test were on academic probation.[13] Improving your listening skills can improve your grade-point average.[14]

Listening is not just for audience members; it is also important for speakers. Good speakers are audience-centered. They consider the needs of their listeners first. They understand what will hold listeners' attention. Many effective speakers acquire this knowledge by listening to audience members one on one before a talk or lecture. Effective speakers also listen to the feedback from their audiences and use the feedback to adjust their speeches while giving them.[15]

How We Listen

5.2 Identify the elements of the listening process.

Do you know someone who is interpersonally inert? Interpersonally inert people are those who just don't "get it." You can drop hints that it's late and you'd rather they head home instead of playing another hand of cards, but they don't pick up on your verbal and nonverbal cues. The physiological processes that let their ears translate sound waves into information in the brain may be working so they can *hear* you, but they certainly aren't listening; they are not making sense out of your symbols.

Hearing is the physiological process of decoding sounds. You hear when the sound waves reach your eardrum. Hearing and listening are two different processes.

Defined succinctly, **listening** is the process we use to make sense out of what we hear; it is a complex process of receiving, constructing meaning from, and responding to verbal and nonverbal messages.[16] Listening involves five activities: (1) selecting, (2) attending, (3) understanding, (4) remembering, and—to confirm that listening has occurred—(5) responding. Understanding these five elements in the listening process can help you diagnose where you sometimes get off track when listening and figure out how to get back on track to increase your listening skill.[17]

Selecting

To listen, you must first **select**, or focus on, one sound among the myriad noises always competing for your attention. Even now, as you are reading this book, there are probably countless sounds within earshot. Stop reading for a moment. What sounds surround you? Do you hear music? Is a TV on? Can you hear traffic noises or birds? Maybe there is the tick of a clock, a whir of a computer, a whoosh of a furnace or an air conditioner. A listener who is sensitive to others selects the sound or nonverbal behavior that symbolizes meaning. The interpersonally inert person does not pick up on the same clues, because he or she is oblivious to the information.

Attending

After selecting a sound, you attend to it. To **attend** is to maintain a *sustained* focus on a particular message. When you change channels on your TV, you first select the channel and then attend to the program you've selected. Just as you tune in to TV programs that reflect your taste in information while you channel surf, you attend to messages of others that satisfy your needs or whims. Attending to a message is vital to being a good listener. There is clear evidence that a person who is skilled in maintaining sustained attention to a message (just listening without interrupting) is perceived as a better listener than is someone with a "restless mind."[18]

What holds our attention? Typically, conflict, new ideas, humor, a good story, or something that we can see or that is concrete holds our attention more easily than abstract ideas that don't relate to us.[19] If you're having difficulty sustaining attention to a message, it may be because what you're listening to does not immediately seem to

hearing
The physiological process of decoding sounds.

listening
A complex process of receiving, constructing meaning from, and responding to verbal and nonverbal messages, which involves selecting, attending, understanding, remembering, and responding.

select
To focus on one sound as you sort through various sounds competing for your attention.

attend
To maintain a sustained focus on a particular message.

relate to you. You may need to work a bit harder, either to concentrate on the message or to consider ways in which the message is relevant or important to you.

Understanding

It's been estimated that we hear more than one billion words each year but understand a mere fraction of that number. To **understand** is to assign meaning to messages—to interpret a message by making sense out of what you hear. You can select and attend to sounds and nonverbal cues but not interpret what you see and hear. Understanding occurs when you relate what you hear and see to your experiences or knowledge.[20] Perhaps you have heard the Montessori school philosophy: I hear, I forget; I see, I remember; I experience, I understand. It is when we can relate our experiences to what we hear and see that we achieve understanding.

Remembering

Remembering information is considered part of the listening process because it's the primary way we determine whether a message was understood. To **remember** is to recall information. But you can't consciously retrieve or remember all the bits of information you experience; your eye is not a camera; your ear is not a microphone; your mind is not a hard drive. Sometimes, even though you were present, you have no recollection of what occurred in a particular situation.

The first communication principle we presented in this book is to become self-aware. When we are not aware of our actions, our thoughts, or what we are perceiving—when we are mindless—our ability to remember what occurs plummets. We increase our ability to remember what we hear by being not only physically present, but also mentally present.

You tend to remember what is important to you (such as the time of a meeting mentioned in a voice message) or something you try to remember or have practiced to remember (like the information in this book for your next communication test). You tend to remember dramatic information (such as where you were when you heard about the September 11, 2001, terrorist attacks) or vital information (such as your phone number or your mom's birthday).

understand
To assign meaning to messages.

remember
To recall information.

asynchronous listening
Listening to recorded messages, such as those on an answering machine or voice mail, which do not allow an opportunity for you to get a response to your feedback.

Communication & TECHNOLOGY

The Vanishing Art of Listening to Voice Messages

As we noted in Chapter 1, if you're under age 25, you are much more likely to text your friends than to phone them.[21] You may not have much training or experience in **asynchronous listening**, which is what you do when you listen to someone's recorded voice message.

Despite the popularity of text messages, however, there are still many occasions, especially in business and professional contexts, when competent communication requires effective use of voice messages.[22] Here are some ways you can improve your skills in listening to and transmitting recorded messages.

When listening to a recorded message,

- *Focus.* Before playing the recorded message, stop what you are doing so that you can focus on the message; while driving, scurrying around the room, or coming in the door after a busy day may not be the best time to listen carefully to recorded messages.
- *Mentally summarize.* If you are listening to several recorded messages, mentally summarize the essence of the message you've just heard before playing the next one. You might also pause to jot down a note.
- *Increase redundancy.* If need be, replay the recorded message to ensure that you've absorbed the details. Save important messages so you can refer back to them later if needed.

When recording a message,

- *Slow down.* When you're leaving a recorded message, speak slowly, clearly, and distinctly.
- *Keep it short.*
- *Leave follow-up information.* Do more than leave a phone number or e-mail address. Indicate when you're most likely to be available, rather than encouraging a game of phone tag.

Responding

As you learned in Chapter 1, communication is a transactive process, not a one-way, linear one. Communication involves responding to others as well as simply articulating messages. You **respond** to people to let them know that you understand their message. Your lack of response may signal that you didn't understand the message. Your predominant response is often unspoken; direct eye contact and head nods let your partner know you're tuned in. An unmoving, glassy-eyed, frozen stupor may tell your communication partner that you are physically present yet mentally a thousand miles away.[23] There is some evidence that there are cultural differences in our perception of how effectively we respond to others. Students from the United States, for example, perceived themselves to be more responsive listeners than students from Iran.[24] As you'll discover in the next section, most people have a certain style of listening and responding to others.

Listening Styles

5.3. Describe four listening styles.

Your **listening style** is your preferred way of making sense out of the messages you hear and see. Listening researchers Debra Worthington, Graham Bodie, and Christopher Gearhart, building on the extensive work of other listening researchers,[25] have found that people tend to listen using one or more of four listening styles: relational, analytic, critical, and task oriented.[26]

Relational Listening Style

Relational listeners tend to prefer listening to people's emotions and feelings. They are quite interested in hearing personal information from others. Perhaps for that reason, evidence suggests that relational-oriented listeners are less apprehensive than people with other listening styles when communicating with others in small groups and interpersonal situations[27] and especially when listening to just one other person.[28]

A person with a relational listening style searches for common interests and seeks to empathize with the feelings of others—she or he connects emotionally with the sentiments and passions others express.[29] These people seem to have greater skill than other listeners in understanding the thoughts and feelings of others.[30] One study found that jurors who are relational listeners (originally described as people oriented) are less likely to find a defendant at fault in a civil court trial, perhaps because of their tendency to empathize with others.[31]

Research also shows that relational listeners have a greater tendency than those with other listening styles to be sympathetic to the person they are listening to.[32] A sympathetic listener is more likely to voice concern about the other person's welfare when that person is sharing personal information or news about a stressful situation. A sympathetic listener says, for instance, "Oh, Pat, I'm so sorry to hear about your loss. You must feel so lonely and sad."

Analytical Listening Style

Analytical listeners listen for facts and tend to withhold judgment before reaching a specific conclusion. Analytical listeners would make good judges; they generally consider all sides of an issue before making a decision or reaching a conclusion. Analytical listeners tend to listen to an entire message before assessing the validity of the information they hear. To help them analyze information, they take the perspective of the person to whom they are listening, which helps them suspend judgment when listening to others. They also like information they hear to be well organized so that

respond
To confirm your understanding of a message.

listening style
A person's preferred way of making sense out of messages.

relational listeners
Those who prefer to focus on the emotions and feelings communicated by others verbally and nonverbally.

analytical listeners
Those who withhold judgment, listen to all sides of an issue, and wait until they hear the facts before reaching a conclusion.

they can clearly and easily analyze it. While listening to a rambling personal story, the analytic listener focuses on the facts and details of the story rather than on the emotions being expressed. Analytical listeners prefer listening to rich message content and then finding ways of organizing or making sense of the information.

Critical Listening Style

Critical listeners are good at evaluating information that they hear. They are able to home in on inconsistencies in what someone says. They are comfortable listening to detailed, complex information and focusing on the facts, yet they are especially adept in noting contradictions in the facts presented. Critical listeners are also likely to catch errors in the overall logic and reasoning being used to reach a conclusion.

Critical listeners tend to be a bit more skeptical and demanding than relational listeners of the information they hear. Researchers call this skepticism **second guessing**—questioning the assumptions underlying a message.[33] It's called second guessing because critical listeners don't always assume that what they hear is accurate or relevant; they make a second guess about the accuracy of the information they are listening to. Accuracy of information is especially important to critical listeners because if they are going to use the information in some way, they want it to be valid.

Task-Oriented Listening Style

Task-oriented listeners are more interested in focusing on a specific outcome or task than on the communication relationship when listening to others. They emphasize completing a specific transaction such as solving a problem, taking action, or making a purchase. Task-oriented listeners focus on verbs—what needs to be done. Consequently, they don't like to listen to rambling, descriptive messages that don't seem to have a point. They appreciate efficient communicators who organize messages so that their listeners can focus on the outcomes—the "bottom line."

critical listeners
Those who prefer to listen for the facts and evidence to support key ideas and an underlying logic; they also listen for errors, inconsistencies, and discrepancies.

second guessing
Questioning the assumptions underlying a message.

task-oriented listeners
Those who look at the overall structure of the message to see what action needs to be taken; they also like efficient, clear, and briefer messages.

The Benefits of Understanding Your Listening Style

There are at least three reasons to think about your listening style and those of others: (1) to enhance your self-awareness, (2) to adapt your own listening style to different situations, and (3) to communicate more effectively.

ENHANCE YOUR SELF-AWARENESS Understanding your preferred listening style can help you become more aware of how you behave in communication situations. Some research suggests that women are more likely to be relational listeners, whereas men have a tendency to assume one of the other listening styles.[34] Your listening style, however, may be less influenced by your gender than by the overall approach you take to interpreting and remembering the information you hear. Your cultural traditions, one research team suggests, may have a major influence on your particular listening style. People from a more individualistic, self-focused cultural perspective (such as people from the United States) tend to be more action-oriented listeners than people from other places. Relational listeners, according to research, are more likely to have collectivistic values, are group oriented, or were raised in a collaborative cultural tradition (such as some Asian cultures).[35]

You may wonder, "Do I have just one listening style, or do I have more than one?" According to listening researchers Larry Barker and Kitty Watson, who have done extensive research into listening styles (using different labels than the styles we've described), about 40 percent of all listeners have one primary listening style that they use, especially if they are under stress. Another 40 percent of listeners use more than one style—for example, they may prefer to listen to evaluate (critical listening

A task-oriented listener is interested in achieving a specific outcome.
CandyBox Images/Shutterstock

style) and also want the information delivered in a short amount of time and focused on the task to be accomplished (task-oriented listening style).

About 20 percent of people do not have a specific listening style preference; these individuals may want to avoid listening altogether because they are shy and don't like to be around others in social situations, they may have receiver apprehension, or they may just have listener burnout—they are weary of listening to other people.[36] Or they may not have a predominant style because they are good at adapting to others.

ADAPT TO DIFFERENT LISTENING SITUATIONS Knowing your own listening style can help you adapt and adjust your listening style to fit the listening situation. Evidence suggests that the occasion, time, and place all have an effect on the listening style or styles people adopt.[37] For example, if you are a relational listener and you're listening to a message that has little information about people but lots of technical details, you will have to work harder than other types of listeners to stay tuned in to the message.

COMMUNICATE EFFECTIVELY Your awareness of others' listening styles can help you communicate messages that they are more likely to listen to. If you know that your spouse is an analytical listener, you should communicate a message that is rich in information because that's what your spouse prefers. Tell the analytical listener, "Here are three things I have to tell you," and then say those three things. The information preview tells your analytical listener that you are about to convey three pieces of information. It may be difficult to determine someone's listening style, especially if you don't know the person very well. But it is worth the time, as well as easier, to consider the listening styles of people you do know well (your family members, your coworkers, your instructors, your boss).

RECAP

Listening Styles

Relational Listening Style	Listeners prefer to attend to feelings and emotions and to search for common areas of interest when listening to others.
Analytical Listening Style	Listeners prefer to withhold judgment, listen to all sides of an issue, and wait until they hear the facts before reaching a conclusion.
Critical Listening Style	Listeners are likely to listen for the facts and evidence to support key ideas and an underlying logic; they also listen for errors, inconsistencies, and discrepancies when listening.
Task-Oriented Listening Style	Listeners are focused on accomplishing something and look at the overall structure of the message to see what action needs to be taken; they also like efficient, clear, and brief messages.

Listening Barriers

5.4 Identify and describe barriers that keep people from listening well.

Although we spend almost half of our communication time listening, some say that we don't use that time well. One day after hearing something, most people remember only about half of what was said. Two days later, our retention drops by another 50 percent. The result: Two days after hearing a lecture or speech, most of us remember only about 25 percent of what we heard.

Our listening deteriorates not only when we listen to speeches or lectures, but also when we interact interpersonally. Even in the most intimate relationships (or perhaps we should say *especially* in the most intimate relationships), we tune out what others are saying. One study reported that we sometimes pay more attention to strangers than to our close friends or spouses. Married couples tend to interrupt each other more often than nonmarried couples and are usually less polite to each other than are strangers involved in a simple decision-making task.[38]

What keeps us from listening well? The most critical elements are (1) self barriers—personal habits that work against listening well, (2) information-processing barriers—the way we mentally manage information, and (3) context barriers—the surroundings in which we listen.

Self Barriers

"We have met the enemy and he is us" is an oft-quoted line from the vintage comic strip *Pogo.* Evidence suggests that we are our own worst enemy when it comes to listening to others. We often attend to our own internal dialogues and diatribes instead of to others' message, and when we do, our listening effectiveness plummets.

SELF-FOCUS Most of us are egocentric—self-focused, though we may develop a consciousness of others' needs as we grow and mature. Scholars of evolution might argue that it is good that we are self-focused; looking out for number one is what perpetuates the human race. Yet an *exclusive* focus on ourselves inhibits effective communication. While trying to listen, we may be carrying on an internal narration, one that is typically about us. "How long will I have to be here for this lecture?" "Wonder what's for dinner tonight?" "I've got to get that report finished." "She's still talking—will we be out of here in ten minutes?" "Do I have a school meeting tonight, or is that tomorrow night?" Focusing on such internal messages often keeps us from selecting and attending to the other person's message.

What can you do to regain your listening focus if you are focused on yourself rather than on the other person's message? Consider these suggestions:

- *Become aware of the problem.* Become consciously competent. Notice when you find yourself drifting off rather than concentrating on the speaker.
- *Concentrate.* Yes, some messages are boring, useless, and stupid. But even if you think you're listening to such a message, avoid mindlessly tuning it out. The habit of quickly dismissing ideas and messages without making an effort to stay focused on them will keep you from being nominated for the Listening Hall of Fame.
- *Be active rather than passive.* The key to concentration is finding ways to be actively involved in the communication process. Taking notes when appropriate and providing nonverbal and even sometimes verbal feedback to the speaker can help keep your focus on the speaker rather than on you. If you don't understand something the speaker says, ask for clarification. Don't just sit there and "take it"; if you find your concentration waning, you'll more than likely "leave it."

EMOTIONAL NOISE Emotions are powerful. What we see and hear affects our emotions. **Emotional noise** occurs when our emotional arousal interferes with communication effectiveness. Certain words or phrases can arouse emotions very quickly, and, of course, the same word may arouse different emotions in different people. You respond emotionally because of your personal experiences, cultural background, religious convictions, or political philosophy. Words that reflect negatively on your nationality, ethnic origin, or religion can trigger strong emotional reactions. Cursing and obscene language may also reduce your listening efficiency. If you grew up in a home in which R-rated language was never used, four-letter words may distract you.

emotional noise
A form of communication noise caused by emotional arousal.

Brian Crane/The Cartoonist Group

Sometimes it's not just a word but a concept or idea that causes an emotional eruption. Third-trimester abortion and public school prayer, for example, are topics guaranteed to get radio talk show hosts' audiences involved in lively discussion.

The emotional state of the speaker may also affect your ability to understand and evaluate what you hear. Research has shown that if you are listening to someone who is emotionally distraught, you will be more likely to focus on his or her emotions than on the content of the message.[39] Another researcher advises that when you are communicating with someone who is emotionally excited, you should remain calm and focused and try simply to communicate your interest in the other person.[40]

What are other strategies to keep your emotions from getting the best of you? Psychologist Daniel Goleman offers several research-based strategies in his best-selling book *Emotional Intelligence*.[41] To be emotionally intelligent is to have the ability to understand, manage, and appropriately express emotions. There is evidence that people who are emotionally intelligent—because of their skill in recognizing, expressing, and managing their emotions—are better listeners than others.[42] Being attuned to the emotions of your listening partner helps you discern the underlying, sometimes not explicitly expressed, meaning of a message.[43] For example, one simple yet powerful strategy to manage emotions when you find you may be about to lose control is to take a deep breath. Yes, just breathe. Taking a deep, slow breath is a way of regaining control by calming down. It helps make you more conscious of your anger or frustration, much like the old technique of counting to ten.

Another strategy for managing emotions is to use the power of self-talk, a concept we discussed in Chapter 2. Tell yourself you won't get angry. Early detection of the emotions bubbling inside you can help you assess and then manage emotions before your nonrational, emotional impulses take control. And sometimes, of course, expressing your frustration is appropriate.

Awareness of the effect that emotions have on your listening ability (such as you now have after reading this section) is a constructive first step to avoid being ruled by unchecked emotions. Becoming consciously aware of our emotions and then talking to ourselves about our feelings is a way to avoid emotional sidetracks and keep your attention focused on the message. When emotionally charged words or actions kick your internal dialogue into high gear, make an effort to quiet it down and steer back to the subject at hand. The principle of self-awareness gives you choice *and* control.

CRITICISM We usually associate the word *criticism* with negative judgments and attitudes. Although critiquing a message can provide positive as well as negative insights, most of us don't like to be criticized. The well-known advocate for the poor, the late Mother Teresa, once said, "If you judge people, you have no time to love them."[44] Being inappropriately critical of the speaker may distract us from focusing on the message.

A person's appearance and speech characteristics can affect your ability to listen to him or her. Many a speaker's droning monotone, lack of eye contact, and distracting mannerisms have contributed to his or her ideas not being well received—even if the ideas are potentially life-changing for the listener. The goal of a sensitive communicator is to be conscious of when the delivery or other distracting features of the message or messenger are interfering with the ability simply to listen. In fact, now that you are studying principles of communication, you may find that this problem looms even larger because you now pay more attention to nonverbal cues.

It would be unrealistic to suggest that you refrain from criticizing speakers and their messages. It is realistic, however, to monitor your internal critiques of speakers to make sure you are aware of your biases. Good listeners say to themselves, "Although this speaker may be distracting, I am simply not going to let appearance or mannerisms keep my attention from the message." For example, Stephen Hawking is a prize-winning physicist at Cambridge University in England; because of a disability, he is able to speak only through computer-synthesized sounds. He is unquestionably brilliant, and if you let his speaking delivery overpower you, you'd miss his marvelous message. Avoid using your mental energy to criticize a speaker unnecessarily; the longer your mental critique, the less you'll remember.

Information-Processing Barriers

In addition to self barriers that contribute to our loss of focus on messages, the way in which we process the information we hear may keep us from being good listeners. Four information-processing listening barriers are (1) processing rate, (2) information overload, (3) receiver apprehension, and (4) shifting attention.

PROCESSING RATE You can think faster than people speak. Most people speak 125 words per minute, give or take a few words. You have the tremendous ability, however, to process four to ten times that amount of information. Some people can listen to 600 to 800 words a minute and still make sense out of what the speaker is saying; another estimate puts the processing rate up to 1,200 words per minute. Yet another estimate claims that we think not just in words but also in images and sounds: We can process 2,000 bits of information a minute for short periods of time. This difference between average speaking rate and your capacity to make sense out of words as they register in your cortical centers can cause trouble. You have extra time on your hands to tune in to your own thoughts rather than focusing on the speaker.[45]

You can use your information-processing rate to your advantage if you use the extra time to summarize mentally what a speaker is saying. By periodically sprinkling in mental summaries during a conversation, you can dramatically improve your listening ability and make the speech-rate/thought-rate difference work to your advantage.

INFORMATION OVERLOAD The one word to describe many beleaguered listeners is "weary." We spend 55 percent of our communication time listening, and the pace at which the information zips toward us exhausts us. The billion words that we hear each year contribute to our fatigue. The pace has only increased now that much of that information is electronic. Incoming e-mail, voice messages, or social media updates on computers and mobile devices can interrupt conversations and distract us from listening to others.

Again we recommend self-awareness. Be on the alert for drifting attention because of information overload. And when the encroaching information dulls your attentiveness, either take a break or consider conducting some *communication triage*—determining what's urgent and what's not urgent—so that you can focus on the information that is most important.

receiver apprehension
The fear of misunderstanding or misinterpreting the messages spoken by others or of not being able to adjust psychologically to messages expressed by others.

RECEIVER APPREHENSION Just as some people are fearful of presenting a speech or speaking up during a meeting, research suggests that some people are fearful of receiving information. **Receiver apprehension** is fear of misunderstanding or misinterpreting the messages spoken by others or of not being able to adjust psychologically to messages expressed by others.[46] Some people may be fearful of receiving new information because they worry about being able to understand it. Or apprehension may be a characteristic of the way some people respond psychologically to information; they may not be able to make sense out of some of what they hear, which causes them to be anxious or fearful of listening to others.[47] If you are fearful of receiving information, you'll remember less information.

If you know that you are fearful of listening to new information, you'll have to work harder than others to understand the information presented. Recording video or audio of a lecture may help you feel more comfortable and less anxious about trying to remember every point. Becoming actively involved in the listening experience by taking notes or mentally repeating information to yourself may also help.[48]

Remaining aware of the dangers of information overload can help you keep electronic messages from distracting you from conversations. It is much harder to give your full attention to another person while continually glancing at your phone for incoming messages.
Rommel Canlas/Shutterstock

SHIFTING ATTENTION Can you multitask? A few people can easily do two things at once, but our performance on at least one of the tasks suffers when most of us try it. Emerging research evidence suggests that men are more likely to have difficulty attending to multiple messages: When they are focused on a message, they may have more difficulty than women in carrying on a conversation with another

Communication & DIVERSITY

Does Gender Influence Listening Skill?

There is evidence that men and women can be equally good listeners, but research suggests that they sometimes (although not always) have different approaches to listening. They also have different approaches to interrupting others when listening. According to one study that reviewed a number of research investigations, men interrupt others more than women do. Specifically, men were sometimes perceived as interrupting to control the conversation. When women interrupted, they were more likely either to express agreement or to add something to the conversation.[49]

Women and men's interruption patterns provide clues to possible differences in listening styles. Listening differences can be characterized as a feminine style (a more relational approach) or a masculine style (more task oriented). The following chart summarizes research conclusions from several studies about feminine and masculine listening styles.[50]

	Feminine Listening Style	Masculine Listening Style
Different Listening Focus	• Tends to search for existing relationships among separate pieces of information • Tends to identify individual facts and other isolated pieces of information • Tends to shift from one idea to another or to shift listening among people who may be speaking at the same time	• Tends to look for a new structure or organizational pattern when listening • Tends to listen for the big picture and seek the major points being communicated • Tends to lock on to a specific message without shifting between two or more conversations
Different Listening Goals	• More likely to listen to new information to gain new understanding and new insights • Tends to use information to develop relationships with listening partners • Tends to have a greater ability and motivation to listen when providing supportive and positive feedback[51]	• More likely to listen to new information to solve a problem • Tends to listen to reach a conclusion; shows less concern about relationship cues and more concern about using the information gained • Tends to have less ability and motivation to listen in situations that call for providing supportive feedback
Different Application of Nonverbal Messages	• Tends to emphasize meaning communicated through nonverbal cues • Typically uses more eye contact with the other person when listening	• Tends to emphasize the meaning of the words and information exchanged • Typically uses less eye contact with the other person when listening

Although not all men and women fit into these categories of listening behavior, it's helpful to be aware of listening differences.[52] When communication differences arise, we may be less critical and more accepting of others if we know that conflicts may result simply because you and your listening partner are focusing on different parts of the message being expressed.

By being aware of whether you fit the general profile of a masculine or a feminine listener, you also can determine whether you need to adapt your listening style. The best listener may be one who is the most flexible and doesn't always default to his or her typical pattern or preferred listening approach but rather combines listening approaches.[53]

Not all researchers agree that there are style differences between men and women. Listening experts Stephanie Sargent and James Weaver suggest that studies of listening style differences between men and women may simply be measuring listening stereotypes[54] or a self-fulfilling prophecy: Men and women assume that they *are* listening the way they think that they *should* listen.[55] Although there are some discernible patterns in masculine and feminine listening styles, the differences may not be as consistently pronounced as was once thought.

By noting some perceived differences in listening style, we don't want to be guilty of promoting gender- or sex-based stereotypes. So we repeat our caution: *Don't assume that all men or all women have typical masculine or feminine listening styles.*

person.[56] Men have a tendency to lock onto a message, whereas women seem more adept at shifting between two or more simultaneous messages. When many men watch a TV program, they seem lost in thought—oblivious to other voices around them. Women, by contrast, are more likely to be carrying on a conversation with one person and also focusing on a message they hear nearby. This difference doesn't mean that women are more likely to eavesdrop intentionally, but it does mean that some women have greater ability to listen to two things at once. What are the implications? It may be especially important for women to stop and focus on the messages of others rather than on either internal or external competing messages. And men may need to be sensitive to others who may want to speak to them rather than becoming fixated on their own internal message or on a single external message such as a program on TV.

CULTURAL DIFFERENCES Different cultures place different emphases on the importance of listening. Some cultures are more source or speaker oriented, whereas others are more receiver or listener oriented. North American communication, for example, often centers on the sender. Much emphasis is placed on how senders can formulate better messages, improve credibility, and polish their delivery skills. Recently, there has been increased interest in listening in the United States. Communication scholars and practitioners recognize that listening is necessary not only to aid comprehension but also, and more important, to provide the speaker the satisfaction of being listened to.[57] However far more U.S. colleges and universities offer courses in speaking than provide courses in listening.

In contrast, the emphasis in East Asia has typically been on listening and interpretation. The Chinese culture, for example, places considerable emphasis on the listener. Communication researcher C. Y. Cheng identified *infinite interpretation* as one of the main principles of Chinese communication.[58] It's understood by both speaker and listener that the listener can make infinite interpretations of what has been said. According to another researcher, a related process called **anticipatory communication** is common in Japan. Instead of the speaker having to explicitly tell or ask for what he or she wants, listeners guess and accommodate the speaker's needs, sparing him or her the embarrassment that could arise if the verbally expressed request could not be met.[59] Thus, foreign students from East Asia may be puzzled about why they are constantly being asked what they want when they are visiting in American homes. In their home countries, a good communicator should anticipate what others want and act accordingly, so the host or hostess should not have to ask what is needed.

With the emphasis on indirect communication in East Asian cultures, the receiver's sensitivity and ability to capture the under-the-surface meaning and to understand implicit meaning become critical. Receivers work to be more sensitive to others by emptying their minds of preconceptions and making them as clear as a mirror.[60] Different levels of emphasis on listening can be a barrier to effective communication unless the communicators understand how much importance the other person places on listening in the communication process.

Context Barriers

In addition to the barriers that relate to how you process information and those that occur when your emotions and thoughts crowd out a message, listening barriers can arise from the communication context or situation. **Noise** is anything that interferes with your ability to listen to a message. Although you may think of it as sounds you hear, noise can be processed by any one of your five senses. Not only sounds, but also sights, the feeling of something touching you, and even tastes and smells can affect your listening ability. Two factors that can increase interfering noise are *when* you listen and *where* you listen.[61]

anticipatory communication
A listening process in which the listener guesses the speaker's needs and accommodates them so that the speaker does not have to say what he or she wants.

noise
Anything that interferes with your ability to listen to a message.

BARRIERS OF TIME Are you a morning person or an evening person? Morning people are cheerfully and chirpily at their mental peak before lunch. Evening people find it easier to tackle major projects after dark; they are at their worst when they arise in the morning.

The time of day can affect your listening acuity. If you know you are sharper in the morning, schedule your key listening times then whenever possible. Evening listeners should try to shift heavy listening to the evening hours. Of course, that's not always practical. If you can't change the time of listening, you can increase your awareness of when you will need to listen with greater concentration.

Vahan Shirvanian/Cartoon Stock

"You can stop saying 'uh-huh'! I stopped talking to you an hour ago!"

Daily activities, such as work, can also cause timing issues. When a person wants to converse with you at a time when you're busy with other things, for example, it may be tempting to try to do two things at once. We have all tried to get away with a few "uh-huhs" and "mm-hmms" to indicate that we're listening to everything that's being said while, in fact, our attention was divided.

Respect the effect of timing on other people, too. Don't assume that because you are ready to talk, the other person is ready to listen. If your message is particularly sensitive or important, you may want to ask your listening partner, "Is this a good time to talk?" Even if he or she says yes, look for eye contact and a responsive facial expression to make sure the positive response is genuine.

BARRIERS OF PLACE Listening takes all the powers of concentration you can muster. A good listener seeks a quiet time and place to maximize listening comprehension. For most people, the best listening environment is one that offers as few distractions as possible.

When *you* want to talk to someone, pick a quiet time and place, especially if you know that you will be discussing a complex or potentially difficult topic. Even in your own home, it may be a challenge to find a quiet time to talk. Closing a door or window, turning off the TV or radio, asking noisy or offensive talkers or texters to converse more quietly or not at all, and simply moving to a less distracting location are steps you may need to take to manage the noise barrier.

RECAP

Managing Listening Barriers

Listening Barriers	What to Do
Self Barriers	
Self-Focus	• Shift attention back to the speaker. • Become actively involved in the message. • Take meaningful notes.
Emotional Noise	• Act calm to remain calm. • Use self-talk to stay focused on the message. • Take a deep breath if you start to lose control.
Criticism	• Focus on the message, not on the messenger.
Information-Processing Barriers	
Processing Rate	• Use the difference between speech rate and thought rate to mentally summarize the message.
Information Overload	• Realize when you or your partner is tired or distracted and not ready to listen. • Assess what is urgent and not urgent when listening.
Receiver Apprehension	• Record the message to be sure you capture it; review the audio later. • Take notes. • Make mental summaries of the information you hear.
Shifting Attention	• Make a conscious effort to remain focused on one message.
Cultural Differences	• Acknowledge that some cultures place greater emphasis on the listener than on the speaker.
Context Barriers	
Barriers of Time	• If possible, schedule difficult listening situations for when you're at your best.
Barriers of Place	• Eliminate distracting noise.

Improving Your Listening Skills

5.5 **Identify and use strategies that can improve your listening skills.**

At the heart of listening is developing sensitivity to focus on the messages of others rather than on your own thoughts. Listening researcher Graham

Bodie and his colleagues discovered that most people define a skilled listener as attentive, friendly, and responsive, someone who maintains the flow of the conversation and provides feedback that the message was understood.[62] In this section, we discuss several specific underlying skills that will increase your sensitivity and result in you being a good listener.

At first glance, the skills we present may look deceptively simple—as simple as the advice given to most elementary students about crossing the street: (1) stop, (2) look, and (3) listen. Despite the appearance of simplicity, these three words summarize decades of research and insight about how to avoid being interpersonally inert. Those steps may seem like common sense, but they are not common practice.[63] Let's consider each separately.

Stop: Turn Off Competing Messages

As we noted earlier, while you are listening, you may also be talking to yourself, providing a commentary about the messages you hear. These internal, self-generated messages may distract you from giving your undivided attention to what others are saying. To stop and focus on a message, you need to (1) be aware of the competing messages, (2) stop the internal competing chatter and attend to the message, and (3) socially decenter to focus on the thoughts of others.

BE AWARE OF COMPETING MESSAGES Becoming aware of our internal dialogue is the first step toward stopping our own running commentary about issues and ideas that are self-focused rather than other-focused.[64] To be aware of what you are doing is to be consciously mindful of what you are attending to. If you aren't aware that you're talking to yourself, you'll likely continue your internal monologue and miss a portion of the message from your listening and speaking partner. How can you increase your awareness of competing messages? At any given moment, you are either on task or off task when listening. Periodically ask yourself, "Am I on task? Am I focused on the speaker or my own internal conversation? Am I aware of what I'm doing?"

Some people find that yoga or quiet meditation helps dissolve the internal barriers that prevent effective listening. What strategies have you used to become more aware of your intrapersonal communication and any internal barriers to listening you may have experienced? What methods have you found helpful for making you conscious of the way your own self-talk affects your ability to listen to and communicate with others?
Chris Collins/Shutterstock

STOP INTERNAL NOISE Two listening researchers conducted a study to identify the specific behaviors that good listeners perform when listening.[65] What they discovered supports our admonition that after being aware of whether you're on task, the next step is to stop focusing on your own mental messages. Specifically, you should be other oriented by taking the following actions during what the researchers called the *preinteraction phase* of listening:

- Put your own thoughts aside.
- Be there mentally, not just physically.
- Make a conscious, mindful effort to listen.
- Take adequate time to listen; don't rush the speaker; be patient.
- Be open-minded.

It may also help if you simply speak less. Members of some religious groups take a vow to be silent and not talk to anyone else. They literally stop talking. Does that make them better listeners than those who do not talk? One research team studied this question by comparing groups of research participants.[66] One group heard a lecture about how to be better listeners—probably like the lectures you hear in this course—and then took a test to assess their overall listening skill. A second group promised not to talk to anyone for twelve hours—they literally gave others the "silent treatment." Then they, too, took a test to assess their listening ability. A third group both heard a listening lecture and were silent for twelve hours; then they also took the listening test. The results: There were no differences in listening test scores among the groups. All groups seemed to listen equally well, according to test results—but those who kept silent for twelve hours reported *thinking* that they were more attentive to others and more conscious of being good listeners. The researchers concluded that literally ceasing to speak can increase our awareness of listening. Their research supports the maxim "You have been given two ears and one mouth so that you will listen more and talk less." No, we're not suggesting that you stop talking entirely; rather, you should increase your awareness of how your own thoughts and talk can interfere with being a good listener. Stop—do your best to eliminate mental messages that keep you from listening well.

SOCIALLY DECENTER After being aware of competing messages and stopping your internal chatter, try a process called social decentering. **Social decentering** involves stepping away from your own thoughts and attempting to experience the thoughts of another. Instead of making yourself the center of your focus, you *decenter*—you place your focus on the other person. In essence, you ask yourself, "If I were the other person, what would I be thinking?" Although the goal is to focus on someone else, decentering first requires you to practice the first principle of communication—self-awareness. You need to become aware that your own thoughts are keeping you from focusing on another's message. Then you can focus on the other person.[67] Of course, we are not suggesting that your own ideas and internal dialogue should be forever repressed; that would be both impossible and inappropriate. We are suggesting that to connect to another, you must focus on the other person rather than on yourself and, while doing so, consider what the other person may be thinking as he or she is communicating with you.

Look: Listen with Your Eyes

Sensitive listeners are aware of nonverbal as well as verbal messages; they listen with their eyes as well as their ears. As we discussed in Chapter 4, nonverbal messages are powerful, especially in communicating feelings, attitudes, and emotions.[68] A person's body movement and posture, for example, communicate the intensity of his or her feelings, whereas facial expression and the vocal cues that accompany spoken words provide clues about the specific emotion being expressed. A competent listener notices these cues; an incompetent listener attempts to decode a message based only on what is said rather than "listening between the lines." When there is a contradiction between the verbal message and the nonverbal message, we will almost always believe the unspoken one; nonverbal cues are more difficult to fake. How do you focus on nonverbal messages? We suggest two strategies: (1) attend to the meta-message, and (2) nonverbally communicate *your* interest in the other person.

ATTEND TO THE META-MESSAGE *Meta-communication* is communication about communication. By attending to your interpersonal partner's unspoken message, you are looking for the **meta-message**—the message about the message. The nonverbal meta-message provides information about the emotional and relational effect of what a speaker is expressing with the verbal message. Accurately decoding unspoken meta-messages helps you understand what people really mean.

Often, a person will express a positive feeling with a nonverbal message, such as smiling, that matches a verbal message, such as "I'm happy to be here." Sometimes, though, the nonverbal communication contradicts the verbal message. Your friend may say, "Oh, that's just great," but may use an exaggerated, sarcastic tone of voice and a facial expression that expresses just the opposite of the content of the verbal message. The sarcasm communicated by the tone of voice and facial expression (relationship cues) modifies the meaning of the verbal message (the actual content of the message).[69] The tone of voice and facial expression are a meta-message about what your friend really means. Your friend may not explicitly say that he or she is angry, upset, or irritated, but the nonverbal cues let you know that your friend is not happy.

social decentering
Stepping away from your own thoughts and attempting to experience the thoughts of another.

meta-message
The message about the message.

How can you clarify the meaning of a nonverbal meta-message? Ask. For example, when you detect a smirk or a grimace from your listening partner, you can seek information about the communication by asking, "Is what I'm saying bothering you?"

NONVERBALLY COMMUNICATE YOUR INTEREST IN THE OTHER PERSON A key aspect of the "look" step of good listening is to actually look at the person you are listening to—establish eye contact, which signals that you are focusing your attention on your partner. Even though mutual eye contact typically lasts only one to seven seconds, when you carry on an interpersonal conversation, your eye contact reveals how attentive and responsive you are to your listening partner.[70] If you look as if you are listening, you will also be more likely to listen. We usually have more eye contact with someone when we are listening than when we are talking.[71]

In addition to eye contact, other nonverbal cues signal whether you are on task and responsive to the messages of others. Remaining focused, keeping your hands and feet still, and even leaning forward slightly communicate to someone that you are listening. Appropriate head nods and verbal responses also signal that you are attending to the other person's message.[72]

Listen: Understand Both Details and Major Ideas

How do you improve your listening skill? Now that you've stopped your own internal dialogue and looked for nonverbal cues, it's time to listen. Here are six additional strategies for improving your listening skill.[73]

IDENTIFY YOUR LISTENING GOAL You listen to other people for a variety of reasons. Knowing your listening goal can increase your self-awareness of the listening process and increase your skill. If you're listening to Aunt Deonna talk about her recent trip to northern Minnesota for the annual bear hunt, you need not worry about taking extensive notes or trying to remember all the details of her expedition. But when your sociology professor tells a story to illustrate a sociological theory, you should be more attuned to the point he or she is making; the theory may be on a test. At other times, you need to be on your guard to evaluate the message of a politician or salesperson. Having a strong motivation to listen for specific kinds of information can enhance your listening effectiveness.[74] There are four primary listening goals: to enjoy, to learn, to evaluate, and to empathize.

- *Listening to enjoy*. Sometimes we listen just because it's fun. You might listen to music, watch TV, go to a movie, or visit with a friend. Because you know you won't be tested on Jimmy Fallon's monologue, you can relax and just enjoy the humor.
- *Listening to learn*. Nothing snaps a class to attention more quickly than a professor's proclamation "This next point will be covered on the test." Another key reason we listen is to learn. But you don't have to be a college student to listen to learn. Phone calls and conversations with family and friends also often contain information that you will want to remember.
- *Listening to evaluate*. When you listen to evaluate, you try to determine whether the information you hear is valid, reliable, believable, or useful. One problem you may have when you listen to evaluate is that you may become so preoccupied with your criticism that you may not completely understand the message.
- *Listening to empathize*. The word *empathy,* which we introduced in Chapter 3 and will discuss in more detail later in this chapter, comes from a Greek word for "passion" and the German word *Einfühlung,* meaning "to feel with." To empathize with someone is to try to feel what he or she is feeling rather than just to think about or acknowledge the feelings.[75] Empathic listening serves an important therapeutic function; just having an empathic listener may help someone out. No, we

are not empowering you to be a therapist, but we are suggesting that sometimes simply listening and feeling with someone can help that person sort things out.

MENTALLY SUMMARIZE THE DETAILS OF THE MESSAGE You can process words more quickly than a person speaks, so you can use the extra time to your advantage by periodically summarizing the names, dates, and facts embedded in the message. If the speaker is disorganized and rambling, use your tremendous mental ability to reorganize the speaker's information into categories or try to place events in chronological order. It is important to have a grasp of the details your communication partner presents. But remember that to listen is to do more than focus on facts. Research suggests that poor listeners are more likely to focus on *only* facts and data, rather than the overall point of the message, than good listeners.[76] If you listen too much for details, you may miss the main point.

LINK MESSAGE DETAILS WITH THE MAJOR IDEA OF THE MESSAGE As we just pointed out, facts and data make the most sense when we can use them to support an idea or point. Mentally weave your summaries of the details into a focused major point or series of major ideas. Use facts to enhance your critical thinking as you analyze, synthesize, evaluate, and finally summarize the key points or ideas your partner makes.

PRACTICE BY LISTENING TO DIFFICULT OR CHALLENGING MATERIAL Learning any skill takes practice. Listening experts suggest that our listening skills deteriorate if we listen only to easy and entertaining material. Make an effort to listen to news or documentary programs. As you listen to a lecture that seems full of content, make a conscious effort to stay focused, concentrate, and summarize facts and major ideas.

WORK TO OVERCOME LISTENING BARRIERS If you can avoid the listening barriers presented earlier, you will be well on your way to improving your listening skill. Avoid being self-focused, letting emotional noise distract you, or criticizing a message before you've understood it. Watch out for information overload. And, when possible, take steps to minimize external noise and provide an environment more conducive to listening.

DON'T INTERRUPT One of the best things you can do to be perceived as a good listener is to not interrupt a speaker when he or she is talking. When we interrupt someone, we are saying, "What I have to say is more important than what you have to say." This translates to the other person as "I'm more important than you are." Interrupting others when listening is more than just rude; it decreases your credibility and lowers your ability to understand the other person. Do you want to make sure you *don't* get hired because of the impression you make during a job interview? Interrupt your interviewer and you're less likely to get the job, according to one research study.[77] To listen without interrupting seems simple, but because thoughts are bouncing around in our heads, we sometimes blurt them out,[78] or we think that we know what the other person is going to say, so we talk over her or him. Resist these temptations.

LISTEN ACTIVELY Our suggestion that you listen actively is a distillation of the other recommendations we've offered. Active listeners are engaged listeners who listen with both their minds and their hearts. They are engaged physically and mentally in the listening process.[79] Active listeners are aware of what they are doing; they stop thinking about things that might take them off track.[80] They also have good eye contact with the speaker and communicate their interest with an intent facial expression and a slight forward lean. By contrast, passive listeners are not involved listeners; they are detached and may fake attention with a frozen, nonexpressive facial expression or a single, unchanging expression that mimics interest. One listening research team noted that a passive listener receives information by being talked *to* rather than as an equal partner in the speaking-listening exchange.[81]

This same team described active listeners as people who do the following:

- Give full attention to others.
- Focus on what is being said.
- Expend considerable energy participating in the listening process.
- Have an alert posture.
- Maintain much direct eye contact.

Another research study found that listeners who offered person-centered comments (comments that acknowledge the feelings of others) and provided immediate nonverbal responses (eye contact, natural forward lean, appropriate head nods) were judged to be better listeners than those who did not use those skills.[82]

It seems that the best listeners are mentally alert, physically focused on the other person, and actively involved in seeking understanding. In short, they stop, they look, and they listen.

RECAP

How to Listen Well

What to Do	How to Do It
Identify your listening goal.	Decide whether you are listening to enjoy, to learn, to evaluate, or to empathize. Your listening goal should determine the strategies you use to achieve it.
Mentally summarize the details of the message.	Every few minutes, take time to create your own mental recap of the key information presented. In just a few seconds, you can summarize much information.
Link message details with the major ideas of the message.	Consciously relate the bits of information you hear to the key points the speaker is developing rather than focusing only on facts and details or only on major points.
Practice by listening to difficult or challenging material.	Periodically make an effort to listen to material that is complex and richer in detail and information than what you typically listen to; while listening to this more complex material, make a conscious effort to stop, look, and listen.
Work to overcome listening barriers.	Identify the key obstacles that keep you from listening at peak effectiveness (self barriers, information-processing barriers, or context barriers); make conscious efforts to overcome their underlying causes.
Don't interrupt.	Increase your awareness of whether you interrupt others. Wait until the other person has finished speaking before you speak.
Listen actively.	Be engaged in the listening process by maintaining good eye contact with the speaker and an alert posture (slight forward lean, sitting up rather than slouching).

Improving Your Responding Skills

5.6 Identify and use appropriate responding skills.

To respond is to provide feedback to another about his or her behavior or communication. Your response can be verbal or nonverbal, intentional or unintentional.

Your thoughtful response serves several purposes. First, it tells a speaker how well you have understood his or her message. Second, your response lets a speaker know how the message affects you. It indicates whether you agree or disagree. Third, it provides feedback about statements or assumptions that you find vague, confusing, or wrong. It helps an individual keep the communication on target and purposeful. Finally, your response signals to the speaker that you are still "with" him or her—that you are still ready to receive messages. We respond to let others know that we understand what we have heard, to empathize with the feelings of others, and to provide support.

Responding to Clarify and Confirm Understanding

The skill of thoughtfully responding to others lets those to whom you are listening know that you have understood their message and that they communicated clearly. There are several ways to ensure that your confirming responses are helpful.

BE DESCRIPTIVE Although one listening goal is to evaluate and make critical judgments about messages, don't evaluate until you're sure you understand the speaker. Effective feedback describes rather than evaluates what you hear. We're not suggesting that it's easy to listen from a nonevaluative perspective or that you should refrain from ever evaluating messages and providing praise or negative comments. But feedback that first acts like a mirror to help the speaker understand what he or she has said is more useful than a barrage of critical comments. Describing your own reactions to what your partner has said rather than pronouncing a quick judgment on his or her message is also more likely to keep communication flowing. "I see that from a different point of view" often evokes more thoughtful responses than "You're wrong, I'm right."

If your partner thinks that your prime purpose in listening is to take potshots at the message or the messenger, the communication climate will cool quickly. Listening researcher Eve-Anne Doohan not surprisingly found that when wives expressed negative emotions and critical evaluative comments to their listening husbands, the husbands were less satisfied with the overall quality of their relationships with their wives.[83]

BE TIMELY Feedback is usually most effective at the earliest opportunity after the behavior or message is presented, especially if the purpose is to teach. Waiting to provide a response after much time has elapsed invites confusion.

Now let us contradict our advice. Sometimes, especially if a person is already sensitive and upset about something, delaying feedback can be wise. Use your critical-thinking skills to analyze when feedback will do the most good. Rather than automatically offering immediate correction, use the just-in-time approach. Provide feedback just before the person might make another mistake, just in time for the feedback to have the most benefit.

BE BRIEF Less information can be more. Cutting down on the amount of your feedback can highlight the importance of what you do share. Don't overwhelm your listener with details that obscure the key point of your feedback. Brief is usually best.

BE USEFUL Perhaps you've heard this advice: "Never try to teach a pig to sing. It wastes your time, it doesn't sound pretty, and it annoys the pig." When you provide feedback to someone, be certain it is useful and relevant. Ask yourself, "If I were this person, how would I respond to this information? Is it information I can act on?" Immersing your partner in information that is irrelevant or that may be damaging to the relationship may make you feel better, but it may not enhance the quality of your relationship or improve understanding.

ASK APPROPRIATE QUESTIONS As you listen for information and attempt to understand how another person is feeling, you may need to ask questions to help clarify your conclusions. Most of your questions will serve one of four purposes: (1) to obtain additional information ("How long have you been living in Buckner?"), (2) to check how the person feels ("Are you frustrated because you didn't get your project finished?"), (3) to ask for clarification ("What do you mean when you say you want to telecommute?"), or (4) to verify that you have reached an accurate conclusion about your partner's intent or feeling ("So are you saying you'd rather work at home than at the office?").

Another way to sort out details and get to the emotional heart of a dialogue is to ask questions to help you (and your communication partner) identify the sequence of events. "What happened first?" and "Then what did he do?" can help both you and your partner clarify a confusing event.

Your ability to ask appropriate questions will demonstrate your supportiveness of your partner and signal that you are interested in what he or she is sharing.

Of course, if you are trying to understand another's feelings, you can just ask how he or she is feeling in a straightforward way—don't ask questions just for the sake of asking questions. Also, monitor how you ask your questions. Your own verbal and nonverbal responses will contribute to the emotional climate of your interaction.

PARAPHRASE MESSAGE CONTENT After you have listened and asked questions, check whether your interpretations are accurate by paraphrasing the content you have heard. **Paraphrasing** is restating in your own words what you think a person is saying. Paraphrasing is different from repeating something exactly as it was spoken; that would be parroting, not paraphrasing. Paraphrase when you need to confirm your understanding of a murky message or to help the speaker sort out a jumbled or confusing situation. Your paraphrase can summarize the essential events, uncover a detail that was quickly glossed over, or highlight a key point. Typical lead-ins to a paraphrase include statements such as the following.

"So here is what seems to have happened. . . ."

"Here's what I understand you to mean. . . ."

"So let me see if I get what you are saying. . . ."

"Are you saying . . . ?"

Does paraphrasing a speaker's message really enhance the overall quality and accuracy of communication? Yes. Several researchers have found considerable support for the value of paraphrasing the messages of others in enhancing communication.[84] Listening researcher Harry Weger and his colleagues found that listeners perceived people who skillfully used paraphrasing as more socially attractive than other people. That is, the listener liked the person who paraphrased more than a person who didn't use the paraphrasing skill. The researchers found that people liked skillful paraphrasers better even when listeners didn't feel well understood or satisfied with the conversation.[85]

Responding to Empathize with Others

Empathy, as was noted earlier in this chapter, is the process of feeling what another person is feeling. To empathize is more than to acknowledge that another person feels a particular emotion. Being empathic involves making an effort to feel the same emotion yourself.[86]

Central to being empathic is being emotionally intelligent, which as we discussed earlier in this chapter includes being able to understand and express emotion, interpret emotions in yourself and others, and regulate or manage emotions.[87] Emotional intelligence theorist Daniel Goleman summarizes the importance of emotions in developing empathy by quoting Antoine de Saint-Exupéry: "It is with the heart that one sees rightly; what is essential is invisible to the eye."[88] Researchers have found evidence supporting Goleman's ideas. Studies suggest that empathic listeners make better salespeople, teachers, counselors, and therapists and develop better relationships with others overall than nonempathic listeners.[89]

At the heart of empathic listening is the ability not only to know when to speak, but also to know when to be silent. Henri Nouwen eloquently expressed both the challenge and the rewards of empathic listening:

> To listen is very hard, because it asks of us so much interior stability that we no longer need to prove ourselves by speeches, arguments, statements, or declarations. True listeners no longer have an inner need to make their presence known. They are free to receive, to welcome, to accept. . . . Listening is a form of spiritual hospitality by which you invite strangers to become friends, to get to know their inner selves more fully, and even to dare to be silent with you.[90]

paraphrasing
Checking the accuracy of your understanding by restating your partner's message in your own words.

Psychologist Carl Rogers suggests that empathic listening is more than a technique; it's a "way of being."[91] Effective empathic listeners make empathy a natural and normal way of interacting with others. Some people are simply better at being empathic than others. Just as you inherit physical qualities from your parents, there is evidence that you inherit communication traits as well.[92] Some people may have a personality and communication traits that result in being a skilled empathic listener.[93] This does not mean that if you are not naturally empathic, you can never develop empathic skills, but it does mean that you may have to work a bit harder than others to enhance these skills. Can people be taught to be more empathic? Research suggests that the answer is a clear "yes." One goal of this book is to enhance your skill in appropriately adapting to others; empathy is at the heart of focusing on the needs and emotions of others.[94]

Being empathic is not a single skill but several related skills that help you predict how others will respond.[95] Two strategies to help you respond empathically are to understand your partner's feelings and to paraphrase his or her emotions.

UNDERSTAND YOUR PARTNER'S FEELINGS If your goal is to empathize, or "feel with," your communication partner, you might begin by imagining how you would feel under the same circumstances. If your roommate comes home from a hassle-filled day at work or school, try to imagine what you might be thinking or feeling if you had had a stressful day. If a friend calls to tell you his mother died, consider how you would feel if the situation were reversed. Even if you have not yet experienced the loss of your mother, you can imagine what it would be like to suffer such a loss. Of course, your reaction to life events is unlikely to be exactly like someone else's response. Empathy is not telepathically trying to become your communication partner.[96] But you do attempt to decenter—to consider what someone may be thinking—by first projecting how you might feel and then asking appropriate questions and offering paraphrases to confirm the accuracy of your assumptions. Considering how others might feel has been called the Platinum Rule—even more valuable than the Golden Rule ("Do unto others as you would have others do unto you"). The Platinum Rule invites you to treat others as *they* would like to be treated—not just as *you* would like to be treated.

PARAPHRASE EMOTIONS The bottom line in empathic responding is to make certain that you understand your communication partner's emotional state. You can paraphrase his or her feelings using common lead-in phrases, such as "So you feel . . .," "So now you feel . . .," and "Emotionally, you are feeling. . . ."

Communication & ETHICS

Paraphrase Properly

If used with wisdom, paraphrasing can help both you and your partner clarify message accuracy. The most essential guideline is to use your paraphrasing skills *only* if you are able to be open and accepting. If you try to color your paraphrased comments to achieve your own agenda, you aren't being ethical.

Also avoid the overuse of paraphrasing. Too much of it can slow down a conversation and make the other person uncomfortable or irritated. A sensitive communicator tries not to let his or her technique show.

Other guidelines to keep in mind when you ask questions and paraphrase content and feelings are the following:

- Use your own words—don't just repeat exactly what the other person says.
- Don't add to the information presented when paraphrasing.
- Be brief.
- Be specific.
- Be accurate.

Using these or other ways of paraphrasing feeling (as well as content) can be especially useful in situations in which messages could escalate emotions or produce conflict, such as the following:

Before you take an important action
Before you argue or criticize
When your partner has strong feelings
When your partner just wants to talk
When your partner is speaking "in code"—using unclear jargon or abbreviations you don't understand
When your partner wants to understand your feelings and thoughts
When you are talking to yourself (you can question and check your own emotional temperature)
When you encounter new ideas[97]

As a final word on responding with empathy, realize that although we have discussed empathic responses and the active listening process using a tidy, step-by-step textbook approach, in practice the process won't be as neat and tidy. You may have to back up and clarify content, ask more questions, and rethink how you would feel before you summarize how your partner feels. Or you may be able to summarize feelings without asking questions or summarizing the content of the message. Be sure to adapt the skills appropriately, and ethically, to each specific communication situation. The Communication & Ethics box offers more advice for when and how to paraphrase.

social support
Sensitive and empathic listening, followed by messages of comfort or confirmation, that lets a person know that he or she is understood and valued.

Responding to Provide Social Support

Responding with empathy is especially important if you are listening to provide social support or encouragement to someone. You provide **social support** to someone when you sensitively and empathically listen to him or her and then offer messages

Table 5.1 Suggestions for Providing Social Support

What to Do	What to Say
Clearly express that you want to provide support.	"I would really like to help you."
Appropriately communicate that you have positive feelings for the other person; explicitly tell the other person that you are her or his friend, that you care about her or him, or that you love her or him.	"You mean a lot to me." "I really care about you."
Express your concern about the situation the other person is in right now.	"I'm worried about you right now, because I know you're feeling ____ [stressed, overwhelmed, sad, etc.]."
Indicate that you are available to help, that you have time to support the person.	"I can be here for you when you need me."
Let the other person know how much you support him or her.	"I'm completely with you on this." "I'm here for you, and I'll always be here for you because I care about you."
Acknowledge that the other person is in a difficult situation.	"This must be very difficult for you."
Paraphrase what the other person has told you about the issue or problem that is causing stress.	"So you became upset when she told you that she didn't want to see you again."
Consider asking open-ended questions to find out whether the other person wants to talk.	"How are you doing now?"
Let the other person know that you are listening and supportive by providing conversational continuers.	"Yes—then what happened?" "Oh, I see." "Uh-huh."
After expressing your compassion, empathy, and concern, just listen.	Say nothing; just establish gentle eye contact and listen.

Table 5.2 What to Avoid When Providing Social Support

What Not to Do	What Not to Say
Don't criticize or negatively evaluate the other person. She or he needs support and validation, not judgmental comments.[98]	"Well, you never were the best judge of people. You should expect this kind of stress if you hang around with him."
Don't tell the other person to stop feeling what he or she is feeling.	"Oh, snap out of it!" "Don't be sad."
Don't immediately offer advice.	"So here's what you should do: Cut off all communication with her."
Don't tell the other person that all will necessarily be well.	"It's going to get better from here." "The worst is over."
Don't tell the other person that she or he really has nothing to worry about.	"Oh, It's no big deal." "Just think happy thoughts."
Don't tell the other person that the problem can be solved easily.	"You can always find another girlfriend."
Don't blame the other person for his or her problems.	"Well, if you didn't always drive so fast, you wouldn't have had the accident."
Don't tell the other person that her or his expression of feelings and emotion is wrong.	"You're just making yourself sick. Stop crying."

of comfort or confirmation that let the person know that he or she is both understood and valued. Providing social support does *not* mean trying to solve the issue or problem your communication partner has. Instead, it means communicating genuine concern rather than just going through the motions of pretending to listen.[99]

How much social support should you offer? One research study suggests that when we are experiencing sadness, disappointment, or trauma, most of us prefer a "midlevel" amount of social support—a moderate level of positive, genuine, supportive communication.[100] Although the women in the study preferred a bit higher level of comforting than did the men, most people studied didn't want over-the-top, dramatic expressions of support. Neither did they like mild or timid expressions of support.

What's the best way to express your support? Tables 5.1 and 5.2 summarize research-based suggestions that can help you say the right thing and avoid saying the wrong thing when you are providing social support to others. Research suggests that following these guidelines as appropriate to the other person's situation can help you develop positive, empathic, comforting messages that are likely to be appreciated by your listener.[101] Remember, however, that there are no magic words or phrases that will always ease someone's stress or anxiety.

Don't be discouraged if your initial attempts to use these skills seem awkward and uncomfortable. Learning to use any new set of skills well takes time. The instructions and samples you have seen here should serve as a guide rather than as hard-and-fast prescriptions to follow every time. Being an empathic listener can be rewarding in both your personal and your professional life.[102] And here's some encouraging news about listening and responding skills: These skills can be improved. People who have received listening training show overall improvement in their ability to listen to others.[103] Reading this chapter, listening to your instructor give you tips on enhancing your skills, and participating in skill-building activities are well worth your time.

The following poem "Listen," by an unknown author, summarizes the essential ideas of how to listen and respond with empathy.

Listen

When I ask you to listen to me and you start giving advice, you have not done what I asked.

When I ask you to listen to me and you begin to tell me why I shouldn't feel that way, you are trampling on my feelings.

When I ask you to listen to me and you feel you have to do something to solve my problems, you have failed me, strange as that may seem.

Listen! All I asked was that you listen. Not talk or do—just hear me.
Advice is cheap: 50 cents will get you both Dear Abby and Billy Graham in the same newspaper.
And I can do for myself; I'm not helpless. Maybe discouraged and faltering, but not helpless.
When you do something for me that I can and need to do for myself, you contribute to my fear and weakness.
But when you accept as a simple fact that I do feel what I feel, no matter how irrational, then I quit trying to convince you and can get about the business of understanding what's behind this irrational feeling.
And when that's clear, the answers are obvious and I don't need advice.
Irrational feelings make sense when we understand what's behind them.
Perhaps that's why prayer works, sometimes, for some people, because God is mute, and doesn't give advice or try to fix things,
God just listens and lets you work it out for yourself.
So, please listen and just hear me, and, if you want to talk, wait a minute for your turn; and I'll listen to you.

—*Anonymous*

STUDY GUIDE:
Review, Apply, and Assess Your Knowledge and Skill

Review Your Knowledge

The Importance of Listening and Responding Skills

5.1 Explain the principle of listening and responding thoughtfully to others.

You spend more time listening than doing any other communication activity. Being a good listener and responding thoughtfully to others will help you

- Enhance the quality of your interpersonal relationships.
- Develop good collaboration skills.
- Forge a stronger link between speaker and audience.

How We Listen

5.2 Identify the elements of the listening process.

Listening is a complex process of receiving, constructing meaning from, and responding to verbal and nonverbal messages. The five activities of listening are (1) selecting, (2) attending, (3) understanding, (4) remembering, and (5) responding.

Listening Styles

5.3 Describe four listening styles.

Each person develops a preferred listening style. The four listening styles are relational, analytical, critical, and task oriented. Knowing your listening style can help you adapt your listening approach for maximum listening effectiveness.

Listening Barriers

5.4 Identify and describe barriers that keep people from listening well.

Many people struggle with the skill of listening. Barriers to effective listening include (1) self barriers: self-focus, emotional noise, and criticism; (2) information-processing barriers: processing rate, information overload, receiver apprehension, shifting attention, and cultural differences; and (3) context barriers: time barriers and place barriers.

Improving Your Listening Skills

5.5 Identify and use strategies that can improve your listening skills.

To become a better listener, consider three simple steps that may sound easy to do but are challenging to put into practice: stop, look, and listen. To stop means to be mindful of the message and avoid focusing on your own distracting inner talk, which may keep you from focusing on the messages of others. To look is to listen with your eyes—to focus on nonverbal information. To listen involves the skill of capturing the details of a message while also connecting those details to a major idea.

Improving Your Responding Skills

5.6 Identify and use appropriate responding skills.

The other half of listening is responding to others accurately and appropriately. To respond thoughtfully means to consider the needs of the other person. Check the accuracy of your listening skills by reflecting your understanding of what your partner has said. To respond effectively, be descriptive, timely, brief, and useful. To listen with empathy is to understand your partner's feelings, ask appropriate questions, paraphrase message content, and paraphrase emotions. When you respond to provide social support, offer messages of comfort and concern that make your partner feel understood and valued.

Key Terms

Hearing, p. 97
Listening, p. 97
Select, p. 97
Attend, p. 97
Understand, p. 98
Remember, p. 98
Asynchronous Listening, p. 98
Respond, p. 99
Listening Style, p. 99
Relational Listeners, p. 99
Analytical Listeners, p. 99
Critical Listeners, p. 100

Second Guessing, p. 100
Task-Oriented Listeners, p. 100
Emotional Noise, p. 102
Receiver Apprehension, p. 104
Anticipatory Communication, p. 106
Noise, p. 106
Social Decentering, p. 109
Meta-Message, p. 109
Paraphrasing, p. 114
Social Support, p. 116

The Principle Points

Principle Four:

Listen and respond thoughtfully to others.

- Stop: Work to turn off competing mental messages that distract your listening focus.
- To overcome self barriers to listening effectively, consciously become aware of your drifting attention. Then, to get back in synch, use self-talk skills and emotion management skills (such as deep breathing) to remain calm and focused on the message, not the messenger.
- To overcome information-processing listening barriers, make mental summaries of the message you hear, recognize when you are tired and not at your listening best, take effective notes, and remain focused.
- To overcome context listening barriers, become aware of your best and worst times of the day for listening; consciously intensify your concentration if you know you're not at your listening best; and assertively take action, such as closing a door or a window, to reduce external noise when listening.
- Look: Listen with your eyes to discern nonverbal information that provides important information about emotions, attitudes, and relationship cues.
- Listen: Work to link facts and details with major ideas you hear.
- Respond: Use effective responding skills by providing feedback that is descriptive, timely, brief, and useful while remaining an active listener.
- Be empathic: Try to imagine how you would feel in a situation like the one your communication partner is in. To confirm your interpretation of his or her message, ask appropriate clarifying questions and then paraphrase both the content and the emotions expressed.
- Paraphrase by briefly summarizing the message in your own words while trying to accurately capture the essence of what your listening partner said; don't add to the information presented when paraphrasing.

Apply Your Skill

Consider the following questions. Write your answers and/or share them with your classmates:

1. Identify specific instances from your own experience in which poor listening skills resulted in a significant communication problem. How would using effective listening skills have diminished or eliminated the problem?
2. What captures and holds your attention when you are listening?
3. What is your usual listening style? How do you adapt your style when situations call for a different one?
4. Which self barrier do you encounter most often when listening? What do you try to do to cope with it?
5. Do you find yourself interrupting or getting interrupted often? What can you do—as a listener or a speaker—to avoid interruptions and deal with them if they happen?
6. Do you usually paraphrase when listening to others in everyday life? If so, how do you summarize messages in a helpful and natural-sounding way? If you don't paraphrase much, what kinds of phrases do you think would help you?
7. If you're doing something at the time someone wants to you to listen, should you be honest and disclose that you're busy and would rather chat (and listen) when you can be more attentive? If so, what sort of verbal strategies might you use?

Assess Your Skill

Listening Journal

Keep a listening journal for a day. During your waking hours, note what you have been listening to each hour of the day. You may have been listening to several different sources or people during the course of an hour. If so, was it primarily a lecture? Were you listening to music or TV? Were you listening to someone during conversation? In addition to noting what you were listening to, evaluate how effectively you listened. Rate your listening on a scale of 1 to 10 (1 = not effective, 10 = very effective) for each one-hour interval. Write a short summary describing what you listened to, how much time you spent listening, and your self-assessment of how effectively you listened during the day.

Assessing Your Listening Style

Complete the following brief assessment of your listening style.

Relational Listeners

1. I am most comfortable listening to people's feelings and emotions. I like to empathize and search for common areas of interest with others when listening; I seek strong interpersonal connections with others.

1	2	3	4	5	6	7	8	9	10
Low									High

Analytical Listeners

2. I wait until all the facts are presented before I reach a conclusion or judgment; I like to see all sides of an issue. I am good at analyzing information that I hear.

1	2	3	4	5	6	7	8	9	10
Low									High

Critical Listeners

3. I am good at critically evaluating the information that I hear; I find inconsistencies and errors in what others say. I listen for the underlying logic and reasoning of what others are saying.

1	2	3	4	5	6	7	8	9	10
Low									High

Task-Oriented Listeners

4. I listen to determine what I need to do to accomplish a task. I like clear, brief messages so that I can efficiently achieve the work that needs to be done.

1	2	3	4	5	6	7	8	9	10
Low									High

After you have completed the scales and analyzed your style, reread the material in the chapter about listening styles, and then write a short summary of the implications of your listening style for you and your listening behavior. As you write you short summary, consider these questions:

- Do you have one predominate listening style, or do you have more than one style? What factors might influence why you may have more than one primary listening style?

- How does your listening style(s) influence your conversations with your friends, family members or others? Does your preferred listening style suggest that you are more comfortable in specific listening situations? Based on your listening style, which listening situations do you sometimes avoid?
- What are ways you might determine what listening style others may have? How might their verbal or nonverbal behavior give you clues as to their listening style?
- What are specific listening situations in which it would be useful to adopt a listening style that is not your predominate listening style?
- Which listening styles might you wish to enhance? What would be advantages to developing greater flexibility in using a variety of listening styles?

For additional insight, ask a close friend, family member, spouse, or significant other to assess his or her listening style, too. You can then discuss the implications of your listening styles upon your relationship and how you could enhance communication between you.

Source: These scales are based on the work of Debra Worthington, Graham D. Bodie, and Christopher Gearhart, "The Listening Styles Profile Revised (LSP-R): A Scale Revision and Validation," paper presented at the Eastern Communication Association, Arlington, VA (April 2011).

Chapter 6

Adapting to Others: Diversity and Communication

There are no ordinary people. —C. S. LEWIS

Gino Santa Maria/Fotolia

Chapter Outline

- Understanding Diversity
- Culture and Communication
- Barriers to Bridging Differences and Adapting to Others
- Adapting to Others Who Are Different from You
- Study Guide: Review, Apply, and Assess Your Knowledge and Skill

Chapter Objectives

After studying this chapter, you should be able to

6.1 Describe how differences of gender, sexual orientation, ethnicity, and age influence communication.

6.2 Define *culture*, and compare and contrast cultural contexts and cultural values.

6.3 Illustrate four barriers that inhibit communication between individuals.

6.4 Describe six strategies that will help bridge differences between people and help them adapt to differences.

Overheard from a student before class:

> I've had it with all this cultural diversity and gender stuff. It seems like every textbook in every class is obsessed with it. My music appreciation class is trying to force the music of other cultures down my throat. What's wrong with Bach, Beethoven, and Brahms? In English lit, all we're reading is stuff by people from different countries. And it seems my history prof talks only about obscure people I've never heard of before. I'm tired of all this politically correct nonsense. I mean, we're all Americans, aren't we? We're not going off to live in Africa, China, or India. Why don't they just teach us what we need to know and cut all this diversity garbage?

Have you heard this kind of sentiment expressed before? Perhaps you've encountered such a "diversity backlash" among some of your classmates, or you may harbor this attitude yourself. Some people may find it unsettling that school curricula and textbooks have increased their focus on issues of culture and gender differences. But these changes are not motivated by an irrational desire to be politically correct. We'll see in this chapter that they are taking place because diversity is increasing in the United States and many other parts of the world. School textbooks and courses are *reflecting* the change, not initiating it. To live comfortably in the 21st century, we must learn ways to appreciate and understand human differences rather than ignore them, suffer because of them, or wish they would disappear.

Figure 6.1 Communication Principles for a Lifetime

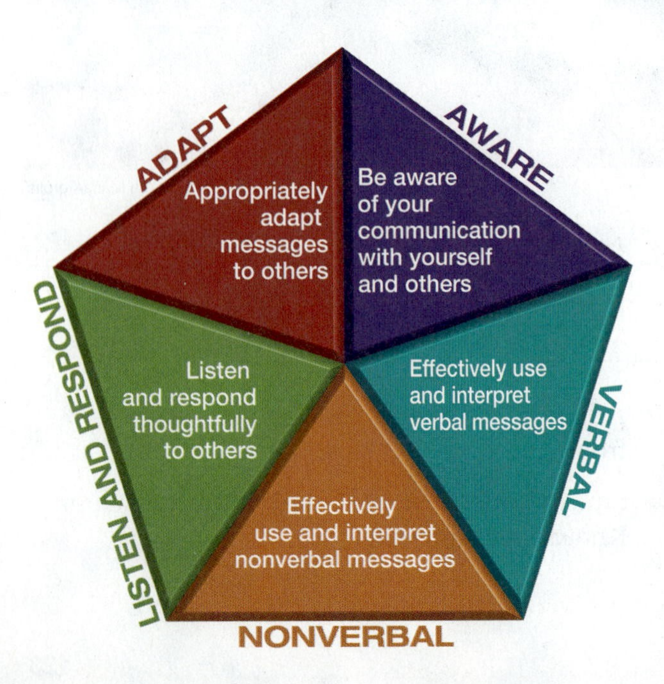

One of life's unprofound principles with profound implications for human communication is this: *We each have different backgrounds and experiences.*[1] Your employers, teachers, religious leaders, best friends, or romantic partners may have grown up with cultural traditions different from your own. And the not-so-startling fact that people *are* different from one another provides the context for discussion of our final Communication Principle for a Lifetime: *Effective communicators appropriately adapt their messages to others.* Figure 6.1 presents our now-familiar model, which includes this final principle of appropriately adapting messages to others.

We introduce this principle last because often people learn how to adapt only after they have learned the other communication principles. Being able to adapt to others requires a relatively sophisticated understanding of the communication process. The ability to adapt suggests that you already have a sense of who you are and a consciousness of the presence of others—self-awareness and other-awareness, the components of the first principle we presented.[2] Studies in developmental communication suggest that the ability to appropriately adapt our behavior to others evolves after we have become aware that there is a "me," after we have learned to use verbal and nonverbal symbols to communicate, and after we have developed an ability to hear and listen to others, all skills that we begin to develop as infants and refine throughout our lives.

The goals of this chapter are to identify human differences that may inhibit communication with others and to suggest adaptive strategies that can improve the quality and effectiveness of our communication with others. To frame our discussion of diversity and communication, we'll note differences in gender, sexual orientation, ethnicity, and age and the implications these differences have for communication. Some of these differences are learned, and some are based on biology—or, in the case of age differences, simply how long someone has lived—but they all have an effect on how we perceive and interact with others. As you read in Chapter 2, each of us perceives the world differently. To some degree, we are each estranged from others. Following our discussion of some of the classic ways we are diverse, we'll turn our attention to cultural differences and then note how human differences create communication barriers.

But simply understanding that there are differences is not enough to improve communication; it is important to learn how to use effective communication skills to adapt to those differences. The phrase "survival of the fittest" is attributed to evolution theorist Charles Darwin, but what Darwin actually said was, "It is not the strongest of the species that survives, nor the most intelligent that survives. It is the one that is the most adaptable to change."[3] We think that Darwin was correct: The ability to adapt is a quintessential communication principle that will serve you well for a lifetime.[4]

The goal of being able to appropriately adapt your communication to other people does not mean you have to abandon your own traditions and preferences. It does suggest that appropriately using communication strategies to understand and bridge differences that exist among people can enhance human understanding. So we'll conclude the chapter by identifying strategies to enhance the quality of communication with others by appropriately adapting to our differences.

Understanding Diversity

6.1 Describe how differences of gender, sexual orientation, ethnicity, and age influence communication.

As we begin this chapter, we'll see that communication researchers have found that differences in our gender, sexual orientation, ethnicity, and age affect the way we interact with one another. Some of these differences among groups of people are learned, and some are based on biology—or, in the case of age differences, simply how long someone has lived—but they all have an effect on how we perceive and interact with others. As we study these group differences, however, keep in mind that groups are made up of individual people, and as we've noted every single person has different experiences. As C. S. Lewis observed in the quotation that opens this chapter, there are no ordinary people—which implies that each of us is unique. Although you may have some things (such as your gender, age, skin color, where you grew up, or your language) in common with a larger group of people, you nonetheless are a unique individual. And so is everybody else.

Sex and Gender

Perhaps the most obvious form of human diversity is gender—the division of human beings into female and male. As we pointed out in Chapter 2, a person's sex is determined by biology. Gender is the culturally constructed and psychologically based perception of one's self as feminine, masculine, **androgynous** (having both feminine and masculine traits) or **transgender** (biologically born one gender while psychologically and culturally living as the other gender). One's gender is learned and is socially reinforced by others as well as by one's life experience and genetics.

At one time or another, you have probably thought, "Why doesn't that person act like people of *my* sex?" You may not think of yourself as stereotyping others on the basis of their sex or gender, but there is evidence that many of us do make snap judgments about someone's behavior on the basis of their sex. You may also have heard (or said), "Vive la différence"—a French expression that celebrates that men and women are different. Why celebrate? Because that difference makes us fascinating and mysterious, and it keeps the world from being awfully dull. Whatever your view of the relationship between the sexes, your day-to-day interaction with members of both sexes is a fact of life (unless you're a hermit). Women and men work, live, and play together, so it's important to explore the effects of gender on communication to improve our ability to relate to one another.

John Gray, author of the book *Men Are from Mars, Women Are from Venus,* would have us believe that the sexes are so different that we approach life from two distinct "planets," or spheres of perspective.[5] Although communication scholars have challenged several of Gray's conclusions because they are not supported by research, there are some research-documented differences in the ways men and women communicate.[6] Deborah Tannen, author of several books on the behavior of the sexes, views men and women as distinctly different cultural groups.[7] She suggests that female–male communication is cross-cultural communication, with all the challenges inherent in exchanging messages with persons of very different backgrounds and value systems.

androgynous
Exhibiting both masculine and feminine characteristics.

transgender
Biologically being born one gender while psychologically and culturally living as the other gender. Being transgender is independent from one's sexual orientation.

Perhaps these viewpoints are a bit extreme and the sexes are actually more alike than different. Research using multiple methods and originating in various disciplines

Have you ever been in a social situation like the one pictured here, in which friends, relatives, or loved ones seem to self-segregate according to gender? What does this common social phenomenon reveal about the nature of gender and communication? How can you appropriately adapt messages to others across gender lines?
BananaStock/SuperStock

consistently shows that differences in men's and women's communication have more to do with *why* we communicate than with *how* we communicate. Research reveals that men tend to approach communication from a content orientation. They view the purpose of communication as primarily goal oriented and tend to talk to accomplish something or complete a task. You talk when you have something to say. This is consistent with the tendency for men to base their relationships, especially their male friendships, on sharing activities rather than talking.

Women, research suggests, tend to use communication for the purpose of relating or connecting to others, of extending themselves to other people to know them and be known by them. What you talk about is less important than that you're talking, because talking implies a relationship. One study found that when interrupted, women are more likely to simply smile, agree, politely nod, and laugh, actions that suggest, according to the researchers, a greater effort, even when interrupted, to maintain a positive relationship and facilitate the flow of conversation.[8]

To summarize this difference: *Men often communicate to report; women often communicate to establish rapport.*[9] So the point of difference isn't in the way the sexes actually communicate but in the motivations or reasons for communicating.[10] Our instrumental and expressive orientations to the world translate into our communication behavior.

To bridge the gap, here's what we suggest you do:

- First, work to understand the differences that may exist.
- Second, make an insightful examination of your own behavior in light of the differences discussed and then determine how you conform to and differ from the description of members of your sex.
- Third, be a gender researcher yourself. Note differences as well as similarities between you and members of the opposite sex. Be careful not to ascribe differences in communication only to gender. Be sure to consider other reasons such as age, personality, or culture, too.
- Finally, make a conscious effort to adapt your behavior appropriately; be mindful of how you interact with others to enhance the quality of your relationships with them.

In a conversation with a member of the opposite sex, try to assess the person's communication motivation: What does the other person view as the purpose for the conversation? Sometimes it's wise simply to ask the person what he or she wants. Then adjust your response accordingly. Just because you're female doesn't mean that you have to take an expressive approach to every interaction; just because you're male doesn't mean that conversations are always about information exchange. By developing the ability to accomplish both content and relational approaches to communication, you broaden what you can do. Your communication skill increases.

RECAP

Gender-Based Approaches to Communication

Masculine Approach	Feminine Approach
• More instrumental; often characterized by assertiveness and getting things done	• More expressive; often characterized by an emphasis on connecting with others and fostering harmonious relationships
• Usually more emphasis on the content of messages and the information being exchanged (the *what*) rather than on relational elements (the *how*) in the message	• Usually more emphasis on the relational elements of messages
• More attention given to verbal than nonverbal messages	• More attention given to nonverbal elements, *how* something is said rather than *what* is said

Sexual Orientation

The lesbian, gay, bisexual, transgender, and queer (LGBTQ) communities are important groups within the larger U.S. culture. Although we are using the terms *lesbian, gay, bisexual, transgender,* and *queer* (a term that communicates a liberation from labels about sexual orientation), Facebook has announced that there are at least fifty-six ways of describing one's gender and sexual orientation on your Facebook page.[11] So rather than thinking about a person's gender and sexual orientation in terms of just a few rigid categories, it's more accurate to consider a wide range of gender and sexual orientation identities.

Regardless of the label, sexual orientation has become a source of pride for some people but remains socially stigmatized for others. Although 92 percent of LGBTQ individuals in a recent survey said that society is becoming more accepting of them, there is evidence that LGBTQ individuals continue to be judged negatively solely on the basis of their sexual orientation.[12] Research has found that a heterosexual person who knows someone who is gay or lesbian is more inclined to be accepting of gays or lesbians and more likely to support same-sex marriage. Still, about 40 percent of LGBTQ individuals report that at some point in their lives they were rejected by a family member or close friend because of their sexual orientation.[13] In addition, people who hold negative attitudes toward gays and lesbians are less likely to communicate with them than are those with more accepting views. Research further suggests that heterosexuals who have negative perceptions of gay and lesbian people are more likely to have rigid views about gender roles and will assume that their peers also hold such rigid views and negative impressions of gays and lesbians.[14] Perhaps related to such perceptions, **homophobia**, fear or aversion toward gay and lesbian people, often accompanied by the fear of being labeled or perceived as LGBTQ, continues to exist among many people.

It is because of the persistence of these negative attitudes toward gays and lesbians, as well as antigay violence and harassment, that some gays and lesbians continue to live "in the closet," concealing their sexual orientations.[15] For example, research has found that LGBTQ individuals are frequent communicators via social media; 80 percent report that they have used Facebook or Twitter, compared to 58 percent of the general public. Yet only 16 percent of LGBTQ people indicate that they regularly discuss LGBTQ issues online.[16]

An effective and appropriate communicator is aware of and sensitive to issues and attitudes about sexual orientation in contemporary society. Just as you have been taught to avoid racially biased expressions that degrade someone's race or ethnicity, it is equally important to avoid using language that demeans a person's sexual orientation. Telling stories and jokes whose point or punch line relies on ridiculing a person because of his or her sexual orientation lowers perceptions of your credibility not only among LGBTQ people, but also among people who dislike bias against gays and lesbians.

What seems helpful is to create a communication climate in which LGBTQ individuals can be themselves and comfortably talk about who they are without fearing rejection or discrimination. Creating a climate of openness and acceptance is important for any human relationship. Family members who have a gay, lesbian, bisexual, transgender, or queer member report more overall relational satisfaction if their family doesn't avoid a discussion of sexual orientation. In addition, there is less anxiety and negativity if issues of sexuality, specifically sexual orientation, are discussed openly and appropriately. Many universities offer training courses, known as ally training, to help faculty and staff members create safe, accepting relationships. Participants are informed about LGBTQ culture and taught how to provide appropriate support. A faculty or staff member who has completed ally training may post a sign on his or her door to indicate that it's safe to be yourself in that person's office or classroom.[17]

Sometimes we unintentionally offend someone through subtle use or misuse of language. For example, gays and lesbians typically prefer to be referred to as *gay* or *lesbian*, rather than as *homosexual*,[18] and the term *sexual orientation* is preferred over *sexual preference* in describing a person's sexual orientation. The key point is this: It is important to be aware of the range of human sexual expression and to be sensitively other oriented as you interact with those whose sexual orientation is different from your own.

homophobia
Fear of, aversion to, or discrimination against gays or lesbians.

Age

Because different generations have experienced different cultural and historical events, they often view life differently. If your grandparents or great-grandparents experienced the Great Depression of the 1930s, they may have different attitudes about bank savings accounts than you or even your parents do. Today's explicit song lyrics may shock older Americans who grew up with such racy lyrics as "makin' whoopee." The generation gap is real and has implications for how we communicate with others.

There is considerable evidence that people hold stereotypical views of others based on others' perceived age.[19] You may see someone with graying or thinning hair and wrinkles and make assumptions about that person's preferences in music, food, or even politics. Similarly, older people who see someone with tattoos, piercings, and wildly colored hair may make stereotypical assumptions about a host of preferences of the younger person. (Even our example of old and young draws on stereotypes and runs the risk of reinforcing those stereotypical images.)

Regardless of the accuracy of the assumptions we make about others on the basis of perceived age, a person's age has an influence on his or her communication with others, including how messages are processed. For example, one study found that older adults have greater difficulty in accurately interpreting the nonverbal messages of others than do younger people.[20] Older adults don't like to be patronized or talked down to (who does?).[21] And younger people seem to value social support, empathic listening, and being mentored more than older people do.[22]

Authors Neil Howe and William Strauss, researchers who have investigated the role of age and generation in society, define a generation as "a society-wide peer group, born over a period roughly the same length as the passage from youth to adulthood, who collectively possess a common persona."[23] Table 6.1. summarizes the labels and common characteristics and values of several generational types. *Baby boomers* is the label for one such generation, of people born between 1943 and 1960. Perhaps your parents or grandparents are "boomers." *Generation X* is the term used for people born between 1961 and 1981. If you were born between 1982 and 2002, you and other

Table 6.1 Summary of Generation Characteristics[24]

Generation Name	Birth Years	Typical Characteristics
Matures	1925–1942	• Work hard • Have a sense of duty • Are willing to sacrifice • Have a sense of what is right • Work quickly
Baby boomers	1943–1960	• Value personal fulfillment and optimism • Crusade for causes • Buy now/pay later • Support equal rights for all • Work efficiently
Generation X	1961–1981	• Live with uncertainty • Consider balance important • Live for today • Save • Consider every job as a contract
Millennials	1982–2002	• Are close to their parents • Feel "special" • Are goal and team oriented • Frequently use social media • Focus on achievement

members of your generation have been labeled *millennials*. Researchers Howe and Strauss suggest that, as a group, "Millennials are unlike any other youth generation in living memory. They are more numerous, more affluent, better educated, and more ethnically diverse. More importantly, they are beginning to manifest a wide array of positive social habits that older Americans no longer associate with youth, including a focus on teamwork, achievement, modesty, and good conduct."[25] Millennials are more comfortable with technology than people in other age groups because the Internet, cell phones, and personal computers have always been part of their lives.[26] According to research by the Pew Research Center, millennials are also less likely to be tied to a specific religious institution and more likely to build their own personal networks using social media. Although recent economic trends have left many millennials financially stressed, as a group, they still feel optimistic about the future.[27] The newest generation—people born since 2002—has been labeled *postmillennials*. Because postmillennials are just emerging, there is less research that identifies the specific attributes of this generation. One clear observation is that postmillennials view technology as an even more seamless method of interacting with others than do millennials. For postmillennials, technological tools to connect socially have always been a way of relating to others.

Your generation of origin has important implications for communication, especially as you relate to others in both family and work situations. Each generation has developed its own set of values, anchored in social, economic, and cultural factors stemming from the times in which the generation has lived. Our values—core conceptualizations of what is fundamentally good or bad and right or wrong—color our way of thinking about and responding to what we experience. Generational and age differences may create barriers and increase the potential for conflict and misunderstanding. For example, one team of researchers, after investigating the role of generations in the workforce, suggests that Generation X workers are paradoxically both more individualistic (self-reliant) and more team oriented than boomers.[28] In contrast, boomers are more likely to have a sense of loyalty to their employers, expect long-term employment, value a pension plan, and experience job burnout from overwork. Generation Xers, by contrast, seek a more balanced approach between work and personal life, expect to have more than one job or career, value working conditions over other job factors, and have a greater need to feel appreciated.[29] This research suggests that if you have a boomer boss and you are a Generation Xer, your boss may not understand why you want to take extra vacation time just to "clear your head" when there is a lot of work that needs to be done. Of course, these broad generalizations do not apply to all people in these categories.

Ethnicity

Ethnicity is a *social classification* based on a variety of factors, such as nationality, religion, and language, as well as biological ancestral heritage (race), that are shared by a group of people with a common geographic origin. Simply stated, an ethnic group is a group of people who have identified themselves as such, based on a variety of factors that may or may not include ancestral heritage or biological characteristics such as skin color.

ethnicity
A social classification based on factors, such as nationality, religion, and language as well as biological ancestral heritage, that are shared by a group of people with a common geographic origin.

Ethnicity fosters common bonds that affect communication patterns. Although ethnic groups bring vitality and variety to American society, members of these groups may experience persecution or rejection by members of other groups in our society.

A concept closely related to ethnicity is **race**, which is based on the genetically transmitted physical characteristics of a group of people who are also classified together because of a common history, nationality, or geographical location.[30] A person's racial classification is typically based on phenotypes, which are such visible

race
Genetically transmitted physical characteristics of a group of people.

physiological attributes as skin color and other physical features, including body type, hair color and texture, and facial attributes. Skin color and other physical characteristics affect our responses and influence the way people of different races interact.

Although it may seem easy to classify individuals genetically as belonging to one race or another, it's not quite that simple. One geneticist has concluded that there is much more genetic variation *within* a given racial category than *between* one race and another.[31] There really aren't vast genetic differences between the people assigned to two racial categories.[32] However, some scholars point out that, in practice, many of us think of race as a category that includes not only biological or genetic characteristics, but also such factors as cultural, economic, social, geographic, and historical elements.[33] The term *race* therefore is a fuzzy, somewhat controversial way of classifying people.

Communication scholar Brenda Allen emphasizes that ethnicity refers in large part to the common culture shared by people who identify with an ethnic group. Ethnicity may include race, but race is a separate category based on more genetic or biological factors that are not clear-cut.[34] A key distinction between race and ethnicity is that ethnicity is a *socially constructed* category that emphasizes culture (learned behaviors, attitudes, beliefs, values, and norms shared by a group of people) and factors other than racial or genetic background.[35] Not all Asians (race), for example, have the same socially constructed cultural background (ethnicity). Nationality and geographical location are especially important in defining an ethnic group. People of Irish ancestry are usually referred to as an ethnic group rather than as a race. The same could be said of Britons, Norwegians, and Spaniards.

One of the most significant problems stemming from attempts to classify people by racial or ethnic type is the tendency to discriminate and unfairly, inaccurately, or inappropriately ascribe stereotypes to racial or ethnic groups. **Discrimination** is the unfair or inappropriate treatment of people based on their group membership. One of the goals of learning about diversity and becoming aware of both differences and similarities among groups is to eliminate discrimination and stereotypes that cause people to rigidly and inappropriately prejudge others.

Culture and Communication

6.2 Define *culture*, and compare and contrast cultural contexts and cultural values.

You need not travel the world to encounter people who are different from you; the world is traveling to you. The Communication & Diversity feature documents how diverse the United States is already, as well as providing evidence that the trend toward greater diversity will continue.[36]

discrimination
The unfair or inappropriate treatment of people based on their group membership.

Communication & DIVERSITY

Diversity Almanac

1. Two-thirds of the immigrants on this planet come to the United States.[37] For example, 60 percent of the residents of Miami, Florida, are foreign-born.[38]
2. "About one in three U.S. residents is a minority," said U.S. Census Bureau Director Louis Kincannon. "To put this into perspective, there are more minorities in this country today than there were people in the United States in 1910. In fact, the minority population in the U.S. is larger than the total population of all but eleven countries."[39]
3. By 2050, more than 50 percent of the U.S. population will be nonwhite; whites will no longer be a majority.[40] Even earlier, by the year 2023, nearly half of all young adults in this country will come from minority groups, according to the U.S. Census Bureau.[41]
4. One in seven U.S. marriages occurs between spouses of different races or ethnicities.[42]
5. It is estimated that more than 40 million U.S. residents learned something other than English as their first language, including 18 million people whose first language is Spanish.[43] One of every eight U.S. residents speaks a language other than English at home, and one-third of children in urban U.S. public schools speak a first language other than English.[44]
6. By 2050, two of every five children under age 5 in the United States will be Hispanic.[45]
7. In 2010, over half of U.S. doctoral degrees granted were earned by women.[46]
8. Estimates of gay and lesbian populations in the United States vary from 1 to 9 percent of the general male population and from 1 to 5 percent of the general female population.[47]
9. There are more millennials (people born between 1982 and 2002) than any other age group in the U.S. The 2003 population included 100 million millennials, 44 million Generation Xers (1961–1981), and 78 million baby boomers (1943–1960).[48]

Globalization, the integration of economics and technology that is contributing to a worldwide, interconnected business environment, is changing the way we work and relate to people around the world.[49] For example, when you call to get technical assistance with your computer or advice on fixing your TV, you are more likely to talk to someone in India than in Indiana. One statistician notes that if the world were a village of 1,000 people, the village would have 590 Asians, 122 Africans, 96 Europeans, 84 Latin Americans, 55 members of the former Soviet Union, and 53 North Americans.[50] Clearly, globalization has increased the probability that you will communicate with someone today who has a cultural background different from your own. Although some people suggest that because of globalization and the merging of cultural traditions, the concept of a "national culture" is obsolete, nonetheless cultural differences do exist. To ignore the range of human cultural differences is to ignore a significant factor, which can mean the difference between effective communication and ineffective communication.

Defining Culture

Culture is a learned system of knowledge, behavior, attitudes, beliefs, values, and norms that is shared by a group of people and shaped from one generation to the next.[51] Communication and culture, says anthropologist Edward T. Hall, are inseparable—you can't talk about one without the other.[52] There is ample evidence that documents the influence of culture on how we work and live.[53] In the broadest sense, culture includes how people think, what they do, and how they use things to sustain their lives. Researcher Geert Hofstede says culture is the "mental software" that helps us understand our world.[54] Like the software and operating system in a computer, our culture provides the framework within which we interpret the data and information that enter our life.

globalization
The integration of economics and technology that is contributing to a worldwide, interconnected business environment.

culture
A learned system of knowledge, behavior, attitudes, beliefs, values, and norms that is shared by a group of people and shaped from one generation to the next.

Cultures are not static; they change as new information and new technologies modify them.[55] We no longer believe that bathing is unhealthy or that we should use leeches as the primary medical procedure to make us healthy. Through research, we have changed our cultural assumptions and values about personal hygiene and medical care.

Some groups of individuals can best be described as a **co-culture**—a cultural group within a larger culture. Examples of co-cultures include people with physical disabilities, different age groups, and various religious groups. Different Christian denominations, such as the Amish or members of the Church of Jesus Christ of Latter-day Saints (Mormons), have distinct traditions and cultural norms. A person's gender places her or him in one of the co-cultures that researchers have used to analyze and investigate the influence of communication on our relationships with others. Gay, lesbian, bisexual, and transgender people constitute another example of an important co-culture in our society.

Intercultural communication occurs when individuals or groups from different cultures communicate. The transactional process of listening and responding to people from different cultural backgrounds can be challenging; the greater the difference in culture between two people, the greater the potential for misunderstanding and mistrust. There is evidence that studying the role of culture in our lives can help us adapt when we encounter cultural differences—whether those differences occur in our hometown or when we are living in a culture different from our own.[56] Understanding the nature of culture and cultural differences helps us develop strategies to make connections and adapt to others with different "mental software."[57]

When you encounter a culture that has little in common with your own, you may experience **culture shock**, a sense of confusion, anxiety, stress, and loss.[58] If you are visiting or actually living in the new culture, your uncertainty and stress may take time to subside as you learn the values and message systems that characterize the culture. Research has found that one of the ways we seek to adapt to a new culture is by using various social media. International exchange students, for example, often use Skype or Facebook to make them feel closer to their friends and family back home and feel less stress when in a new culture. Research has found that students were more likely to Skype with family and close friends.[59]

co-culture
A culture that exists within a larger cultural context (e.g., GLBT cultures, Amish culture).

intercultural communication
Communication between people who have different cultural traditions.

culture shock
Feelings of confusion, loss, stress, and anxiety that a person may experience when encountering a culture different from his or her own.

Communication & TECHNOLOGY

Adapting to Differences When Making E-Connections

As we have noted, it is increasingly likely that you communicate with people who are far from where you work and live. It's not unusual to e-mail or text people from another culture. With the advent of Facebook and other social media, as well as Skype and other easy-to-use videoconference methods, it's also not surprising to see and hear the person you're talking with. According to a *Business Week* survey, most people believe that they will be working with someone in an international location by 2017.[60]

A team of communication researchers points out that when we communicate via e-mail or phone, it takes a bit longer to interpret information about relationships, because often there are fewer nonverbal cues available.[61] Evidence also shows that, because of the limited cues, we are more likely to inaccurately stereotype others, especially on the basis of gender, when interacting via electronic channels than we are when communicating face to face.[62]

Given the importance and prevalence of e-communication and the increased potential for misunderstanding, how can you enhance the quality of your relationships online? Consider these suggestions:

- If you are using a "lean" communication channel, such as e-mail or texting, to interact with a person who is from a high-context culture, you may need to provide more explicit references to your feelings and emotions by telling your partner how you feel or using emoticons.
- When appropriate, consider asking more questions to clarify meanings.
- Consciously make more small talk about the weather or other topics that may not directly be related to the task at hand. Such interaction helps connect you to others, makes the interaction less task oriented, and provides a balance of relational information that humanizes the communication.
- Use paraphrasing to confirm that you understand what others are saying.
- Finally, you simply may need to be more patient with others; relationships may take longer to develop because of the diminished nonverbal cues. Be mindful of the differences and consciously develop other-oriented skills.

Our culture and life experiences determine our **worldview**—the general cultural perspective that shapes how we perceive and respond to what happens to us. A culture's worldview, according to intercultural communication scholar Carley Dodd, encompasses "how the culture perceives the role of various forces in explaining why events occur as they do in a social setting."[63] These beliefs shape our thoughts, language, and actions. Your worldview permeates all aspects of how you interact with society; it's like a lens through which you observe the world. Since, as we noted in Chapter 1, communication is how we make sense of the world and share that sense with others, our worldview is one of the primary filters that influence how we make sense out of the world. Two frameworks for describing how culture influences our worldview are cultural contexts and cultural values.

Cultural Contexts

The **cultural context** of any communication consists of the nonverbal cues that surround and give added meaning to the message. In this sense, *all* nonverbal cues are part of a cultural context. Some cultures give more weight to the surrounding nonverbal context than to the explicit verbal message in interpreting the overall meaning of a message. Other cultures place less emphasis on the nonverbal context and greater emphasis on what someone says.

For example, when you interview for a job, you may be scanning the face of your interviewer and looking for nonverbal messages to provide cues about the impression you are making on the interviewer. These contextual cues (in this case, the nonverbal messages) give meaning to help you interpret the message of your interviewer. Edward T. Hall helped us understand the importance of cultural context when he categorized cultures as either high- or low-context.[64]

HIGH-CONTEXT CULTURES In **high-context cultures**, nonverbal cues are extremely important in interpreting messages. Communicators rely heavily on the context of subtle information such as facial expression, vocal cues, and even silence in interpreting messages—hence the term *high-context cultures,* to indicate the emphasis placed on the context. Asian, Arab, and southern European peoples are more likely to draw on context for message interpretation.

LOW-CONTEXT CULTURES People in **low-context cultures** rely more explicitly on language and the meaning of words and use fewer contextual cues to send and interpret information. Individuals from low-context cultures, such as North Americans, Germans, and Scandinavians, may perceive people from high-context cultures as less attractive, knowledgeable, and trustworthy because they violate unspoken low-context cultural rules of conduct and communication. Individuals from low-context cultures often are less skilled in interpreting unspoken contextual messages.[65] Figure 6.2 describes differences in communication style between high-context and low-context cultures.

worldview
A perspective shared by a culture or group of people about key beliefs and issues, such as death, God, and the meaning of life, that influences interaction with others; the lens through which people in a given culture perceive the world around them.

cultural context
Additional information about a message that is communicated through nonverbal and environmental cues rather than through language.

high-context culture
A culture in which people derive much information from nonverbal and environmental cues and less information from the words of a message.

low-context culture
A culture in which people derive much information from the words of a message and less information from nonverbal and environmental cues.

Cultural Values

Ancient Egyptians worshiped cats. The Druids of England believed they could tap into spiritual powers in the shadow of the mysterious rock circle of Stonehenge at the summer solstice. Some would say contemporary Americans place a high value on accumulating material possessions and making pilgrimages to sports arenas on weekends. By paying attention to what a culture values, we can get important clues about how to respond to communication messages, establish relationships, and avoid making embarrassing errors when interacting with people from a given

Figure 6.2 A Scale of High-Context and Low-Context Cultures

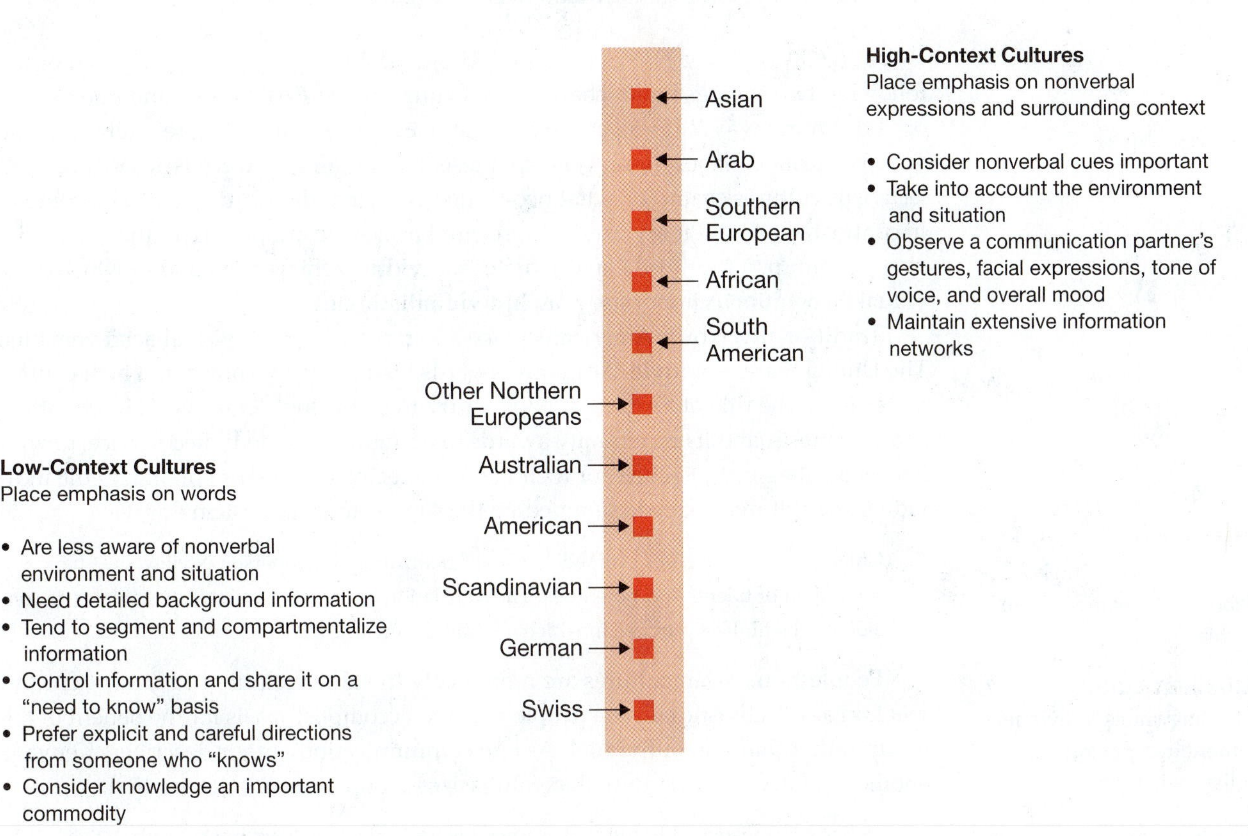

culture. Identifying what a particular group of people values or appreciates can give us insight into the behavior of an individual raised within that culture. Although there are considerable differences among the world's **cultural values**—clearly, not all cultures value the same things—Geert Hofstede has identified five categories for measuring values that are important in almost every culture.[66] These generalizations are based on several surveys that he developed and administered to more than 100,000 people. Even though his data were collected more than thirty-five years ago and sampled only employees (predominantly males) who worked at IBM—a large international company with branch offices in many countries—Hofstede's research remains one of the most comprehensive studies to help us describe what people from a culture may value.

According to Hofstede's research, every culture establishes values relating to (1) individualism versus collectivism, (2) distribution of power (either centralized or shared), (3) avoidance of uncertainty versus tolerance for uncertainty, (4) masculine or feminine cultural perspectives, and (5) long-term and short-term orientation to time. An overview of Hofstede's research conclusions for several countries is included in Table 6.2 at the end of this section, but first we'll consider each of these five categories of values in more detail.

As we discuss the five cultural values, keep in mind that we are applying generalizations to a cultural group. There are vast differences *within* a culture as well as between cultural groups; certainly not all the people within the cultural group will hold the cultural values we will discuss. Think of these values as explaining cultural *group* differences viewed from an anthropological perspective rather than *individual* differences viewed from a psychological perspective.[67] Using Hofstede's five cultural values to describe a given culture or geographic region is a bit like flying over

cultural values
Whatever a given group of people values or appreciates.

a country at 35,000 feet; at that height, you can't see the details and notice nuances of difference, but you can gain a broad overview of the landscape.

INDIVIDUALISTIC AND COLLECTIVISTIC CULTURAL VALUES Which of the following two sayings better characterizes your culture: "All for one and one for all" or "I did it my way"? If you chose the first one, your culture is more likely to value group or team collaboration—it is what researchers call a **collectivistic culture**. Collectivistic cultures champion what people do together and reward group achievement. In contrast, the "I did it my way" phrase emphasizes the importance of the individual over the group.[68] A culture that celebrates individual achievement and in which individual recognition is important is an **individualistic culture**.

Traditionally, North Americans place a high value on individual achievements. The United States—with its Academy Awards; its reality TV shows in which contestants vie for the title of "American Idol" or try to be the lone "Survivor"; its countless sports contests; and its community awards to firefighters for dedicated service, to winners of spelling bees, to chefs for their barbecue recipes—perhaps epitomizes the individualistic culture. Hofstede summed up the American value system this way:

> Chief among the virtues claimed . . . is self-realization. Each person is viewed as having a unique set of talents and potentials. The translation of these potentials into actuality is considered the highest purpose to which one can devote one's life.[69]

collectivistic culture
A culture that places a high value on collaboration, teamwork, and group achievement.

individualistic culture
A culture that values individual achievement and personal accomplishments.

People from Asian cultures are more likely to value collective or group achievement. In a collectivistic culture, people strive to accomplish goals for the benefit of the group rather than the individual. As one communication author describes, Kenya is another country with a culture that emphasizes group or team collaboration:

> Nobody is an isolated individual. Rather, his [or her] uniqueness is a secondary fact. . . . In this new system, group activities are dominant, responsibility is shared and accountability is collective. . . . Because of the emphasis on collectivity, harmony and cooperation among the group tend to be emphasized more than individual function and responsibility.[70]

Awards for individual achievements are one indicator of how much North American cultures tend to value individualism.
FOX/Getty Images

Some researchers believe that the values of individualism and collectivism are the most important values of any culture—they determine the essential nature of every other facet of how people behave.[71] Other researchers, however, caution that cultures are complex and that it is dangerous to label an entire culture as individualistic or collectivistic.[72] We agree—as we've pointed out, not everyone in a given culture fits a single label. But in trying to understand the role of culture and its effect on human communication, we believe that Hofstede's concept of cultural values, with special emphasis on individualism and collectivism, can help to explain and predict how people may send and interpret communication.[73]

DECENTRALIZED AND CENTRALIZED APPROACHES TO POWER AND CULTURAL VALUES Some cultures are more comfortable with a broad distribution of power than other cultures. People from such cultures prefer a decentralized approach to power. Leadership is not vested in just one person. Decisions in a culture that values decentralized power distribution, as found in countries such as Australia and Ireland, are more likely to be made by consensus in a parliament or congress rather than by decree from a monarch or dictator.

Cultures that place a high value on centralized power, such as those found in Indonesia, India, and the Philippines, are more comfortable with a more structured form of government and with managerial styles that feature clear lines of authority. Hierarchical bureaucracies are common, and the general assumption is that some people will have more power, control, and influence than others.

UNCERTAINTY AND CERTAINTY AND CULTURAL VALUES "Why don't they tell me what's going on?" exclaims an exasperated student. "I don't know what my grades are. I don't know what my SAT score is. I'm in a complete fog." Many people like to know "what's going on." They like to avoid uncertainty and to have a general sense of what's going to happen. Too much uncertainty makes them uncomfortable. Others tolerate more ambiguity and uncertainty.

Cultures in which people need certainty to feel secure are likely to develop and enforce more rigid rules for behavior and establish more elaborate codes of conduct. People from cultures with a greater tolerance for uncertainty have more relaxed, informal expectations for others. "It will sort itself out" and "Go with the flow" are phrases that characterize their attitudes.[74]

Again, we remind you that although there is evidence for the existence of the general cultural value of uncertainty avoidance, not all people in a given culture or country find this cultural value equally important. There is considerable variation within a culture as to how people respond to uncertainty.

MASCULINE AND FEMININE CULTURAL VALUES Some cultures emphasize traditional "male" values such as getting things done and being assertive; other cultures place greater emphasis on traditional "female" values such as building relationships and seeking peace and harmony with others. These values are not really about biological sex differences but about general assumptions that underlie the values of interacting with others. People from **masculine cultures** also tend to value more traditional roles for men and women. People (both men and women) from masculine cultures value achievement, heroism, material wealth, and making things happen. Men and women from **feminine cultures** tend to value such things as caring for the less fortunate, being sensitive toward others, and enhancing the overall quality of life.[75] Later in this chapter, we will discuss how gender contributes to the development of a culture, but for now it is enough to realize that whole cultures can be typified by whether they identify with or emphasize masculine or feminine values.

We caution you once more to avoid making sweeping generalizations about every person in any cultural group. Just as there are differences between and among cultures, there are differences within a cultural group. For centuries, most countries have had masculine cultures. Men and their conquests are featured in history books and all aspects of society more than women are. But today's cultural anthropologists see some shift in these values. There is some movement toward the middle, with greater equality between masculine and feminine roles.

LONG-TERM AND SHORT-TERM TIME ORIENTATION AND CULTURAL VALUES A culture's orientation to time falls on a continuum between long-term and short-term.[76] People from a culture with a long-term orientation to time place an emphasis on the future and tend to value perseverance and thrift because these are virtues that pay off over a long period of time. A long-term time orientation also implies a greater willingness to subordinate oneself for a larger purpose, such as the good of society or the group.

In contrast, a culture that tends to have a short-term time orientation values spending rather than saving (because of a focus on the immediate time rather than the future), tradition (because of the value placed on the past), and preserving face of both self and others (making sure that an individual is respected and that his or her dignity is upheld) and has an expectation that results will soon follow the actions and effort expended on a task. Short-term cultures also place a high value on social and status obligations.

masculine culture
A culture that values achievement, assertiveness, heroism, material wealth, and traditional male and female roles.

feminine culture
A culture that values being sensitive toward others and fostering harmonious personal relationships with others.

Table 6.2 Five Categories of Cultural Values

Cultural Value	Countries Where People Scored Higher on This Cultural Value	Countries Where People Scored Lower on This Cultural Value
Individualism: Societies with higher individualism scores generally value individual accomplishment rather than the collective or collaborative achievement valued by societies with lower scores.	United States, Australia, Great Britain, Canada, Netherlands, New Zealand, Italy, Belgium, Denmark, Sweden, France	Guatemala, Ecuador, Panama, Venezuela, Colombia, Indonesia, Pakistan, Costa Rica, Peru, Taiwan, South Korea
Power Distribution: Societies with higher power distribution scores generally value greater power differences between people; they are generally more accepting of fewer people having authority and power than are those with lower scores on this cultural dimension.	Malaysia, Guatemala, Panama, Philippines, Mexico, Venezuela, Arab countries, Ecuador, Indonesia, India	Australia, Israel, Denmark, New Zealand, Ireland, Sweden, Norway, Finland, Switzerland, Great Britain
Uncertainty Avoidance: Societies with higher uncertainty avoidance scores generally prefer to avoid uncertainty; they like to know what will happen next. Societies with lower scores are more comfortable with uncertainty.	Greece, Portugal, Guatemala, Uruguay, Belgium, Japan, Peru, France	Singapore, Jamaica, Denmark, Sweden, Hong Kong, Ireland, Great Britain, Malaysia, India, Philippines, United States
Masculinity: Societies with higher masculinity scores value high achievement, men in more assertive roles, and more clearly differentiated sex roles than people with lower scores on this cultural dimension.	Japan, Australia, Venezuela, Italy, Switzerland, Mexico, Ireland, Jamaica, Great Britain	Sweden, Norway, Netherlands, Denmark, Costa Rica, Finland, Chile, Portugal, Thailand
Orientation to Time: Societies with higher scores have a longer-term orientation to time; they tend to value perseverance and thrift. Societies with lower scores have a shorter-term orientation to time; they value the past and present, respect for tradition, saving face, and spending rather than saving.	China, Hong Kong, Taiwan, Japan, Vietnam, South Korea, Brazil, India, Thailand, Hungary, Singapore, Denmark, Netherlands	Pakistan, Czech Republic, Nigeria, Spain, Philippines, Canada, Zimbabwe, Great Britain, United States, Portugal, New Zealand

SOURCE: Adapted with permission from Geert Hofstede, Gert Jan Hofstede, and Michael Minkov, *Cultures and Organizations, Software of the Mind,* Third Revised Edition (New York: McGraw Hill, 2010). ISBN 0-07-166418-1 © Geert Hofstede BV.

As shown in Table 6.2, cultures or societies with a long-term time orientation include many Asian cultures, such as China, Hong Kong, Taiwan, and Japan. Cultures with a short-term time orientation include Pakistan, the Czech Republic, Nigeria, Spain, and the Philippines. Both Canada and the United States are closer to the short-term time orientation than the long-term time orientation, which suggests an emphasis on valuing quick results from projects and greater pressure toward spending rather than saving, as well as a respect for tradition.[77]

RECAP

Cultural Values

Individualistic vs. Collectivistic	• Individualistic cultures value individual accomplishments and achievement. • Collectivistic cultures value group and team collaboration.
Decentralized vs. Centralized Power	• Centralized power cultures value having power in the hands of a smaller number of people. • Decentralized power cultures favor more equality and a more even distribution of power in government and organizations.
Uncertainty vs. Certainty	• Cultures that value certainty do not like ambiguity and value feeling secure. • Cultures with a greater tolerance for uncertainty are comfortable with ambiguity and less information.
Masculine vs. Feminine	• Masculine cultures value achievement, assertiveness, heroism, material wealth, and more traditional sex roles. • Feminine cultures value relationships, caring for the less fortunate, overall quality of life, and less traditional distinctions between sex roles.
Long-Term vs. Short-Term Orientation to Time	• Cultures with a long-term orientation to time tend to be future oriented and value perseverance and thrift. • Cultures with a short-term orientation to time tend to value the past and present, respecting tradition, preserving face, and fulfilling social obligations.

Barriers to Bridging Differences and Adapting to Others

6.3 Illustrate four barriers that inhibit communication between individuals.

Now that we've paid attention to some of the ways people are different from one another, let's identify barriers that *increase* the differences that exist between people. Differences, whether based in culture or gender, often breed misunderstanding, which can lead to feelings of distrust, suspicion, and even hostility. The headlines continue to chronicle the prevalence of terrorism, war, and conflict around the globe, which are due, in part, to different cultural perspectives.

Is it possible to develop effective relationships with people who are different from ourselves? The answer is "Of course." Although almost every relationship experiences some degree of conflict, most of the world's people do not witness annihilating destruction each day. Bridging culture and gender differences is possible. To develop effective strategies to adapt to others who are different from ourselves, we'll examine some of the barriers that often separate us from one another.

Assuming Superiority

One of the most powerful barriers to adapting to others is the belief that one's own culture or gender is better than that of others. **Ethnocentrism** is the attitude that our own cultural approaches are superior to those of other cultures.[78] Extreme ethnocentrism is the opposite of being other oriented. When fans from two rival high schools at a Friday night football game scream, "We're number one!" they are hardly establishing high-quality communication. Competition is, of course, expected in sports; but when the mind-set of unquestioned superiority is created through cultural or religious identification, the resulting mistrust and suspicion are breeding grounds for conflict. Ethnocentrism and cultural snobbery create a barrier that inhibits rather than enhances communication.

It would probably be impossible to avoid feeling most comfortable with our own culture and people who are like us. In fact, some degree of ethnocentrism can play a useful role in perpetuating our own cultural traditions; we form communities and groups based on common traditions, beliefs, and values. A problem occurs, however, if we become so extremely biased in favor of our own cultural traditions that we fail to recognize that people from other cultural traditions are just as comfortable with their approach to life as we are with ours. And when we mindlessly attack someone else's cultural traditions (which may be a prelude to physical aggression), we erect communication barriers.

A person who assumes superiority may also assume greater power and control over others. Conflicts are often about power—who has it and who wants more of it. Differences in power are therefore breeding grounds for mistrust and conflict. Nineteenth-century British scholar Lord Acton said that absolute power corrupts absolutely; although this may not always be the case, an ethnocentric mind-set that assumes superiority may add to the perception of assumed power over others. It's true that there are cultural differences in attitudes toward power (whether power is centralized or decentralized), but world history documents that people who are consistently pushed and pulled and pummeled eventually revolt and seek greater equity of power.

Assuming Similarity

We've all done it. On meeting a new acquaintance, early in the conversation we usually explore what we may have in common. "Do you watch 'The Simpsons'?" "Oh,

ethnocentrism
The belief that one's own cultural traditions and assumptions are superior to those of others.

Hagar © King Features Syndicate

you're from Buckner. Do you know Mamie Smith?" The search for similarities helps us develop a common framework for communication. But even when we find a few similarities, it's a mistake to make too many assumptions about our new friend's attitudes and perceptions. Because of our human tendency to develop categories and use words to label our experiences, we may lump people into a common category and assume similarity where no similarity exists. Even if they appear to be like you, people do not all behave the same way.[79] As an ancient Greek proverb tells us, "Every tale can be told in a different way."

Anthropologists Clyde Kluckhohn and Henry Murray suggested that every person is, in some respects, (1) like all other people, (2) like some other people, and (3) like no other people.[80] Our challenge when meeting another person is to sort out how we are alike and how we are unique. Focusing on superficial factors such as appearance, clothing, and even a person's occupation can lead to false impressions. Instead, we must take time to explore the person's background and cultural values before we can determine what we really have in common.

Our cultural worldview has a profound effect on how we describe ourselves and people in other cultures. Each of us perceives the world through our own frame of reference. We not only see the world differently, but also express those differences in the way we talk, think, and interact with others. For example, research has found that English-speaking people describe themselves and others by identifying individual personality traits ("Matt is friendly") rather than merely describing behavior ("Matt brings snacks to the meeting").[81] If we fail to be mindful of others' cultural values and individual worldviews, we may take communication shortcuts, use unfamiliar words, and assume that our communication will be more effective than it is.

Assuming Differences

Although it may seem contradictory to say so, given what we just noted about assuming similarities, another barrier that may keep you from bridging differences between yourself and someone else is to automatically assume that the other person will be different from you. It can be just as detrimental to communication to assume that someone is essentially different from you as it is to assume that someone is just like you. The fact is, human beings *do* share common experiences and characteristics despite their differences. So we suggest that although you don't want to assume that everyone is just like you, it also hinders communication to assume that you have nothing in common with others.

We are all members of the human family. If we don't seek to connect with those factors that make us all human, we may miss opportunities for bridging the real differences that exist. The words *communication* and *common* resemble each other. We communicate effectively and appropriately when we can connect to others based on discovering what we hold in common. Identifying common cultural issues and similarities can also help you establish common ground with your listeners when speaking before an audience.

How are we all alike? Cultural anthropologist Donald Brown has compiled a list of hundreds of "surface" universals of behavior.[82] According to Brown, people in all cultures:

- Have beliefs about death.
- Have a childhood fear of strangers.
- Have a division of labor by sex.
- Experience certain emotions and feelings, such as envy, pain, jealousy, shame, and pride.
- Use facial expressions to express emotions.
- Experience empathy.

- Value some degree of collaboration or cooperation.
- Experience conflict and seek to manage or mediate conflict.

Of course, not all cultures have the same beliefs about death or the same way of dividing labor according to sex, but all cultures address these issues.

Communication researcher David Kale believes that the dignity and worth of other people are universal values. Therefore, he suggests that all people can identify with the struggle to enhance their own dignity and worth, although different cultures express it in different ways.[83] Another common value that Kale notes is world peace.

Intercultural communication scholars Larry Samovar and Richard Porter assert that there are other elements that cultures share.[84] They note that people from all cultures seek physical, emotional, and psychological pleasure and seek to avoid personal harm. It's true that each culture and each person decides what is pleasurable or painful; nonetheless, Samovar and Porter argue, all people operate somewhere on this pleasure-pain continuum.

People from many different cultures similarly value close, happy families, but they may have different ideas about what makes a family close and happy. How can you discover the similarities and differences in your values when you communicate with someone from another culture?
Jane September/Shutterstock

Another advocate for common human values was Oxford and Cambridge professor and widely read author C. S. Lewis. In his book *The Abolition of Man,* Lewis argued for the existence of universal, natural laws, which he called the Tao, that serve as benchmarks for all human values.[85] Lewis identified such common values as do not murder; be honest; hold parents, elders, and ancestors with special honor; be compassionate to those who are less fortunate; keep your promises; and honor the basic human rights of others.

What are the practical implications of trying to identify common human values or characteristics? If you find yourself disagreeing with another person about a particular issue, identifying a larger common value such as the value of peace and prosperity or the importance of family can help you find common ground so that the other person will at least listen to your ideas. Discovering how we are alike can provide a starting point for human understanding.

Communication effectiveness is diminished when we assume that we're all different from one another in every aspect, just as communication is hindered if we assume that we're all alike. We're more complicated than that.

Stereotyping and Prejudice

Closely related to ethnocentrism and feelings of cultural and gender superiority is the barrier of making a rigid judgment against a class or type of people.

> All Russians like vodka.
> All men like to watch wrestling.
> All Asians are good at math.
> All women like to go shopping.

These statements are stereotypes. They are all inaccurate. To **stereotype** someone is to place him or her in an inflexible, all-encompassing category. The term *stereotype* started out as a printing term to describe a process in which the typesetter uses the same type to print text again and again. When we stereotype, we "print" the same judgment over and over again, failing to consider the uniqueness of individuals, groups, or events. Such a "hardening of the categories" becomes a barrier to effective communication and inhibits our ability to adapt to others.

stereotype
To place a person or group of persons into an inflexible, all-encompassing category.

Communication & ETHICS

Can Stereotyping Others Ever Be a Good Idea?

Reaching conclusions about someone before you get to know him or her can hinder communication and result in a dishonest relationship. Most people are taught not to be prejudiced toward others. Yet might stereotypes sometimes serve a useful purpose, especially when a quick decision is needed and you have only partial information?

Imagine, for example, that you are driving your car late at night and have a flat tire in a neighborhood that's known to have a high crime rate. While wondering what to do, you see two people who have observed your plight and are moving toward you. Do you hop out of your car and seek their help? Or do you lock your doors and be thankful that you have your cell phone to call for assistance? Could a case be made that the ability to respond stereotypically may be useful in times of stress when quick thinking is needed?

We never know all the facts about a situation, and we sometimes (maybe even often) have to respond with only the partial information we have at hand. Malcolm Gladwell, author of *Blink: The Power of Thinking without Thinking,* describes how people often make snap decisions and argues that sometimes these "thin-sliced," momentary decisions can be quite accurate.[86] Of course, snap judgments can also sometimes be way off base.

What do you think? Is it ever appropriate to hold stereotypical views of others and to make judgments about them without knowing all the facts? Why or why not? When do stereotypical evaluations hinder communication? When is it preferable to avoid stereotypical decisions?

RECAP

Barriers to Bridging Differences and Adapting to Others

Assuming Superiority	Becoming ethnocentric—assuming that one's own culture and cultural traditions are superior to those of others
Assuming Similarity	Assuming that other people respond to situations as we respond; failing to acknowledge and consider differences in culture and background
Assuming Differences	Assuming that other people are always different from ourselves; failing to explore common values and experiences that can serve as bridges to better understanding
Stereotyping and Prejudice	Rigidly categorizing others and prejudging others on the basis of limited information

A related barrier, **prejudice**, is a judgment based on the assumption that we already have all the information we need to know about a person. To prejudge someone as inept, inferior, or incompetent on the basis of that person's ethnicity, race, sexual orientation, gender, or some other factor is a corrosive practice that can raise significant barriers to effective communication. Some prejudices are widespread. Although there are more women than men in the world, one study found that even when a man and a woman held the same type of job, the man's job was considered more prestigious than the woman's.[87] Even though it is illegal in the United States to discriminate because of a person's gender, race, or age in offering employment or promotions, women and members of minority groups may still be discriminated against. Stereotyping and prejudice are still formidable barriers to communicating effectively with others.

Mark Twain once said, "It is discouraging to try and penetrate a mind such as yours. You ought to get out and dance on it. That would take some of the rigidity out of it." Learning how to break rigid stereotypes and overcome prejudice is an important part of the process of learning how to adapt to others.

Adapting to Others Who Are Different from You

6.4 Describe six strategies that will help bridge differences between people and help them adapt to differences.

prejudice
A judgment of someone based on an assumption that you already know relevant facts or background information about the person.

Eleanor Roosevelt once said, "We have to face the fact that either we, all of us, are going to die together or we are going to live together, and if we are to live together we have to talk."[88] In essence, she was saying that we need effective communication skills to overcome our differences. It is not enough just to point to the barriers we have identified and say, "Don't do that." Identifying the causes of misunderstanding is a good first step, but most people need more concrete advice with specific strategies to help them overcome these barriers.[89]

Aim for Intercultural Communication Competence

To have **intercultural communication competence** is to be able to adapt your behavior toward another person in ways that are appropriate to the other person's culture. As we've stressed, intercultural competence involves more than merely being aware of what is appropriate or being sensitive to cultural differences.[90] The interculturally competent person *behaves* appropriately toward others. Research has found that people who are interculturally competent do these three things: (1) They prepare by doing things such as learning the language and studying cultural traditions of others, (2) they thoughtfully engage in conversations with others, and (3) they evaluate and periodically reflect on their interactions with others.[91]

One team of intercultural communication researchers has developed a framework for describing the stages of interpersonal communication competence. Before we are able to behave appropriately toward others, we need to have knowledge about other cultures and the motivation to adapt or modify our behavior.[92] This framework has six stages, progressing from least to most competent behavior.[93]

Stage One: Denial In this stage, a person believes that there is only one real, authentic culture: his or her own culture. The interculturally incompetent person, characterized by extreme ethnocentrism, denies that there are other ways of doing things or other ways of behaving.

Stage Two: Defense In this stage, a person acknowledges the presence of other cultures but still believes that his or her culture has the best way of doing things and that other culturally based views are wrong. So the person defends his or her own culture as the best culture.

Stage Three: Minimization In this stage, a person recognizes that there are other cultural perspectives but minimizes them, suggesting that there are no real differences in the way people behave and interact. He or she simply doesn't see the nuances or the major differences reflected in culture.

Stage Four: Acceptance In this stage, the person's ethnocentrism (perception of cultural superiority) is diminished, and he or she recognizes and accepts cultural differences.

Stage Five: Adaptation In this stage, intercultural competence emerges in full blossom. A person consciously seeks to adapt his or her behavior appropriately in response to cultural differences.

Stage Six: Integration At this highest stage of intercultural competence, a person moves freely in and out of his or her own cultural mind-set while adapting to others. The person skillfully modifies his or her behavior to appropriately adapt to other cultures because the person's focus on his or her own cultural identity is minimized; instead, the focus is on others.

The first three stages of this six-stage framework reflect an **ethnocentric cultural perspective**, in which a person assumes that her or his own culture is superior to all other cultures. Ethnocentric people believe that their appearance (for example whether or not they have tattoos and piercings), the style of music they listen to, or the specific holidays they celebrate are superior to (rather than just different from) those of other cultures.

intercultural communication competence
The ability to adapt one's behavior toward another person in ways that are appropriate to the other person's culture.

ethnocentric cultural perspective
The view that one's own culture is superior to all other cultures.

The last three stages of cultural competence reflect a more **ethnorelative cultural perspective**. This perspective requires an appreciation for and sensitivity to cultural differences; one's own cultural perspective is not viewed as always superior to other cultural perspectives.[94] An ethnorelative person understands that there are wide ranges of perceptions about what is stylish or beautiful, that other people listen to a variety of musical genres, and that holidays other people celebrate may be different from theirs. You need not abandon your own preferences, tastes, and cultural traditions; but it is important to acknowledge that other people act, speak, and think in ways that are different from—and just as good as—your own ways.

To become competent at any task, you need three things: knowledge, motivation, and skill. The remaining portion of this chapter presents the following specific strategies to help you develop your intercultural communication competence:[95]

To increase your knowledge about others,

- Seek information about a culture.
- Ask questions and listen to the responses.

ethnorelative cultural perspective
An appreciation for and sensitivity to cultural differences.

To motivate yourself to adapt when communicating with others who are different from you,

- Be patient.
- Strive to tolerate ambiguity and uncertainty.
- Become mindful of differences.

To develop your communication skill set,

- Become other oriented.
- Learn appropriate ways to adapt your communication.

A good way to understand people from other cultures is to learn all you can about their culture. If you were planning a visit to another country, how would you find out about its culture and people?
Image Source/Getty Images

Seek Information

Philosopher André Gide said, "Understanding is the beginning of approving." Prejudice often is the result of ignorance. Learning about another person's values, beliefs, and culture can help you understand that person's messages and their meaning. Researchers have found, not surprisingly, that if you have increased contact and experience interacting with someone from another culture, you will be more sensitive, mindful, and other oriented when communicating with that person.[96] The more you know about someone and can comfortably anticipate how he or she will respond, the more interculturally competent you are likely to be. As you speak to a person from another culture, think of yourself as a detective, watching for implied, often unspoken messages that provide information about the values, norms, roles, and rules of that person's culture.

You can also prepare yourself by studying other cultures. If you are going to another country, start by reading a travel guide or another general overview of the culture. You may then want to learn more detailed information by studying the history, art, or geography of the culture. The Internet offers a wealth of information about the cultures and traditions of others. In addition, talk to people from other cultures. If you are trying to communicate with someone closer to home who is from a different background, you can learn about the music, food, and other aspects of the culture. Given the inextricable link between language and culture, the more skilled you become at speaking another language, the better you will understand the traditions and customs of the culture where it is spoken.[97]

Ask Questions and Listen

Communication, through the give-and-take process of listening, talking, and asking questions, helps reduce the uncertainty present in any relationship. When you meet people for the first time, you are typically not certain about their likes and dislikes, including whether they like or dislike you. When you communicate with a person from another culture or co-culture, the uncertainty level escalates. When you talk with people who are different from you, you may feel some discomfort and uncertainty. This is normal. We are more comfortable talking with people we know and who are like us. However, as you begin to talk with this person, you exchange information that helps you develop greater understanding. If you continue to ask questions, eventually you will feel less anxiety and uncertainty. You will be more able to predict how the person will behave.

When you meet a person who is different from you, ask thoughtful questions and then pause to listen.[98] This is a simple technique for gathering information and confirming the accuracy of your expectations and assumptions. Just asking questions and sharing information about yourself is not sufficient to remove communication barriers and bridge differences in culture and background, but it is a good beginning. The skills of stopping (focusing on the message of the other person), looking (observing nonverbal cues), and listening (noting both details and major ideas) that we presented in Chapter 5 will serve you well in enhancing communication with people from cultural traditions different from your own.

Tolerate Ambiguity

Many people become uncomfortable when faced with uncertainty and ambiguity—especially if they are from a low-context culture such as those in North America. As we discussed earlier in the chapter, people from low-context cultures prefer a more direct approach to getting information. North Americans, for example, often say things like "Tell it to me straight," "Don't beat around the bush," or "Just tell me what you want."

Communicating with someone from a culture that does not value such directness produces uncertainty. It may take time and several exchanges to clarify a message. If you are from a cultural tradition that values certainty and you are uncomfortable with uncertainty, you may have to acknowledge the cultural difference. Be patient and work at tolerating more ambiguity. Don't be in a hurry to have all the details nailed down. Remind yourself that the other person does not have the same attitudes about knowing the future or appreciating details.

Develop Mindfulness

To be **mindful** is to be aware of how you communicate with others. A mindful communicator puts into practice the first communication principle presented in this book: *Be aware of your communication with yourself and others.* To be a mindful communicator, you should constantly remind yourself that other people are not like you. Also, you should be aware that other people do not use different communication strategies to offend or to be rude; they just have different culturally based strategies of interacting with others. Intercultural communication scholars William Gudykunst and Young Kim suggest that being mindful is one of the best ways to approach any new cultural encounter.[99] Mindfulness is a conscious state of mind, a realization of what is happening to you at a given moment. If you are not mindful, you are oblivious to the world around you. You are on mental cruise control.[100]

How can you cultivate the skill of being mindful? You can become more mindful through **self-talk**, something discussed earlier in the book. Self-talk consists of messages you tell yourself to help you manage your discomfort, emotions, or negative thoughts about situations. For example, acknowledging cultural differences through self-talk, rather than emotionally and mindlessly becoming offended, can help you

mindful
Aware of what you are doing and how you are communicating with others.

self-talk
Inner speech; communication with the self; the process of mentally verbalizing messages that help a person become more aware or mindful of how he or she is processing information and reacting to life situations.

maintain your composure and communicate in a manner appropriate to the circumstances. There is also evidence that mindfully reflecting on different cultural experiences that you have can also improve your intercultural competence.[101] Consider keeping a journal of your thoughts and reactions to cultural differences you experience as a tool to help you reflect.

Become Other Oriented

Other-oriented communication is communication in which we take into account the needs, motives, desires, and goals of our communication partners while still maintaining our own integrity. Most of us are **egocentric**—focused on ourselves.[102] Our first inclination is to focus on meeting our own needs before addressing the needs of others.[103] Scholars of evolution might argue that our tendency to look out for number one is what ensures the continuation of the human race. But as we noted earlier, assuming superiority is a major barrier to communicating with others. If we focus exclusively on ourselves, it is very unlikely that we will be effective communicators.

We should consider the thoughts and feelings of others when forming messages and selecting the time and place to deliver them. If we fail to adapt our message to listeners, especially listeners who are different from us (and isn't everyone different from you?), it is less likely that we will achieve our communication goal. As we noted earlier, adapting messages to others doesn't mean that we tell others only what they want to hear. That would be unethical, manipulative, and ineffective. Nor does being considerate of others mean we abandon all concern for our own interests.

How do you become other oriented? We suggest a two-stage process, using skills discussed previously. The first stage, which we previewed in Chapter 5, is called social decentering—consciously *thinking* about another's thoughts and feelings. The second stage is developing empathy, a set of skills we also discussed in Chapter 5. To empathize is to respond *emotionally* to another's feelings and actions. We'll discuss each of these two stages in more detail.

SOCIAL DECENTERING **Social decentering** is a *cognitive process* through which we take into consideration another person's thoughts, values, background, and perspectives. It is seeing the world from the other person's point of view. To socially decenter is not to be a mind reader but to use past experiences and the ability to interpret the clues of others to understand what they may be thinking or how they may be perceiving issues or situations. According to Mark Redmond, a scholar who has extensively studied the process of social decentering, there are three ways to socially decenter.[104]

1. *Consider how you have responded in the past.* Develop an understanding of the other person based on how you have responded when something similar has happened to you.[105] For example, when someone you know says that he or she feels frazzled because he or she was late for a major meeting, you can think about what would be going through your mind if the same thing happened to you.
2. *Consider how the other person has responded in the past.* Base your understanding of what another person might be thinking on your knowledge of how that person has responded in similar situations. In communicating with someone who is different from you, the more direct experience you have interacting with that person, the better able you usually are to make predictions about how that person will react and respond. For example, suppose that you have never known a particular friend to be late for a meeting; you know that this friend is generally punctual. You can therefore guess that your friend would be quite frustrated by being late for a meeting.
3. *Consider how most people respond to similar situations.* The more you can learn about others' cultural or gender perspectives, the more accurate you can become in socially decentering. If your friend is from Germany and you have some general idea of the high value many Germans place on punctuality, your ideas about how

other-oriented communication
Communication in which we focus on the needs and concerns of others while maintaining our personal integrity; achieved through the processes of socially decentering and being empathic.

egocentric
Focused on oneself and one's importance.

social decentering
A cognitive process through which we take into account another person's thoughts, values, background, and perspectives.

most German people would react to being late for a meeting might help you understand how your friend feels. It is important, however, not to develop inaccurate, inflexible stereotypes and labels for others or to base your perceptions of others only on generalizations.

DEVELOPING EMPATHY Socially decentering involves attempting to understand what another person may be thinking. Developing **empathy**, a second strategy for becoming other oriented, is feeling the *emotional* reaction that the other person may be experiencing. When we feel empathy, we feel what another person feels.

Empathy is also different from **sympathy**. When you sympathize, you acknowledge someone's feelings or let the person know that you recognize the way he or she feels. When you empathize, however, you experience an emotional reaction that is similar to the other person's; as much as possible, you strive to feel what he or she feels. Emotional intelligence, which includes accurately assessing the emotions of others, is essential to both sympathy and empathy, which in turn help us establish high-quality relationships with others, especially when there are cultural differences.[106]

As we discussed in Chapter 5, you develop the ability to empathize by being sensitive to your own feelings, assessing how you feel during certain situations, and then projecting those feelings onto others.[107]

The late author and theologian Henri J. M. Nouwen suggested that empathy lies at the heart of enhancing the quality of our relationships with others. As Nouwen phrased it, to bridge our differences, we need to "cross the road for one another":

> We become neighbors when we are willing to cross the road for one another. There is so much separation and segregation: between black people and white people, between gay people and straight people, between young people and old people, between sick people and healthy people, between prisoners and free people, between Jews and Gentiles, Muslims and Christians, Protestants and Catholics, Greek Catholics and Latin Catholics.
>
> There is a lot of road crossing to do. We are all very busy in our own circles. We have our own people to go to and our own affairs to take care of. But if we could cross the road once in a while and pay attention to what is happening on the other side, we might indeed become neighbors.[108]

RECAP

How to Become Other Oriented

Socially Decenter	View the world from another person's point of view. • Develop an understanding of someone based on your own past experiences. • Consider what someone may be thinking, based on your previous association with the person. • Consider how most people respond to the situation at hand.
Develop Empathy	Consider what another person may be feeling. • Stop: Avoid focusing only on your own ideas or emotions. • Look: Determine the emotional meaning of messages by observing nonverbal messages. • Listen: Focus on what the other person says. • Imagine: Consider how you would feel in a similar situation. • Paraphrase: Summarize your understanding of the other person's thoughts and feelings.

Ethically Adapt to Others

After you have thought about how you may be different from others and have identified your own potential barriers to communication, you reach this question: So now what do you *do?* What you do is appropriately and ethically adapt.

To **adapt** is to adjust your behavior in response to the other person or people you are communicating with. Adapting to others gets to the bottom line of this chapter. You don't just keep communicating in the same way you always did. Instead, make an effort to change how you communicate, to enhance the quality of communication. Whether you are in an interpersonal interaction, a group, or a presentational speaking situation, adapting your message to others makes common sense. Even so, being sensitive to others and wisely adapting behaviors to others are often not common.

Adapting to others does not mean that you do or say only what others expect or that your primary goal in life is always to please others. You don't have to abandon

empathy
An emotional reaction that is similar to the reaction being experienced by another person.

sympathy
An acknowledgment that someone is feeling a certain emotion, often grief; compassion.

adapt
To adjust behavior in response to someone else.

Today's technology can help you adapt your communication. Your phone can translate your words or show a map when you don't speak the local language, for example. But you must still be aware of what adaptations are appropriate and ethical.
Image Source/Getty Images

your own ethical principles and positions. In fact, it would be unethical to change your opinions and point of view just to avoid conflict and keep the peace—like a politician who tells audiences only what they want to hear.[109] As President Harry Truman said, "I wonder how far Moses would have gone if he'd taken a poll in Egypt?"[110] When we encourage you to adapt your messages to others, we are not recommending that you become a spineless jellyfish. We are suggesting that you be sensitive and mindful of how your comments may be received by others.

We do not advocate adapting communication in any way that is false or manipulative. You have a responsibility to *ethically* adapt your messages to others. To be ethical is to be truthful and honest while also observing the rights of others. Ethical communication is responsible, honest, and fair; enhances human dignity; and maintains listener options rather than coerces or forces someone to behave against his or her will. Ideally, both (or all) parties' goals are met.

We adapt messages to others for several reasons: to enhance their understanding of the message, to help us achieve the goal or intended effect of our communication, to ensure that we are ethical in our communication with others, and to establish and develop satisfying relationships. Your goal can help you choose from among the following adaptation strategies.

To . . .	You may need to . . .
Enhance understanding	• Slow down or speed up your normal rate of speech. • Use more examples. • Speak in a very structured, organized way.
Meet your own communication goals	• Use evidence that is most valuable to your listener; statistics may prove your point to some listeners, but others may be more moved by a story that poignantly illustrates your point.
Ensure ethical communication	• Give your partner choices and identify options rather than coercing the person or making demands. • Tell the truth, without withholding information.
Establish and develop relationships	• Use communication that generates positive feelings. • Clearly demonstrate your regard for others.

It is not possible to prescribe how to adapt to others in all situations, but you can draw on the other four Communication Principles for a Lifetime presented in this book:

1. *Be aware of your communication with yourself and others.* You will be more effective in adapting to others if you are aware of your own cultural traditions and gender-related behavior and how they are different from those of other people.
2. *Effectively use and interpret verbal messages.* To be able to interpret spoken information accurately is a linchpin of competence in adapting to others.
3. *Effectively use and interpret nonverbal messages.* Being able to "listen with your eyes" to unspoken messages will increase your ability to adapt and respond to others.
4. *Listen and respond to others thoughtfully.* The essential skills of listening and responding to others are key competencies in being able to adapt to others—to be oriented toward others.

Can the skills and principles we have suggested here make a difference in your ability to communicate with others? The answer is a resounding "yes."[111] Several research studies document the importance and value of skillfully being able to adapt your communication behavior.[112] Communication researcher Lori Carrell found, for example, that students who had been exposed to lessons in empathy as part of their study of interpersonal and intercultural communication improved their ability to empathize with others.[113] There is also evidence that if you master these principles and skills, you will be rewarded with greater ability to communicate with others who are different from you—which means everyone.[114]

RECAP

Adapting to Others

Develop Knowledge	
Seek Information	Learn about a culture's worldview.
Ask Questions and Listen	Reduce uncertainty by asking for clarification and listening to the answer.
Develop Motivation	
Tolerate Ambiguity	Take your time and expect some uncertainty.
Develop Mindfulness	Be consciously aware of cultural differences rather than ignoring the differences.
Develop Skill	
Become Other Oriented	Put yourself in the other person's mental and emotional frame of mind; socially decenter and develop empathy.
Adapt to Others	Listen and respond appropriately.

STUDY GUIDE:
Review, Apply, and Assess Your Knowledge and Skill

Review Your Knowledge

Understanding Diversity

6.1 Describe how differences of gender, sexual orientation, ethnicity, and age influence communication.

Human differences result in the potential for misunderstanding and miscommunication. Differences in gender, sexual orientation, age, and ethnicity contribute to the challenges of communicating with others. To overcome these challenges, you must employ Communication Principle Five: Effective communicators appropriately adapt their messages to others.

Culture and Communication

6.2 Define *culture*, and compare and contrast cultural contexts and cultural values.

Culture is a system of knowledge that is shared by a group of people. Because of the powerful role culture plays in influencing our values, culture and communication are clearly linked. Cultural values reflect how individuals regard stereotypically masculine perspectives (such as achieving results and being productive) and stereotypically feminine perspectives (such as consideration for relationships), their tolerance of uncertainty or preference for certainty, their preference for centralized or decentralized power structures, the value they place on individual or collective accomplishment, and their long-term or short-term orientation to time.

Barriers to Bridging Differences and Adapting to Others

6.3 Illustrate four barriers that inhibit communication between individuals.

By doing the following, we create barriers that inhibit our communication with others:

- *Assuming superiority.* When one culture or gender assumes superiority or is ethnocentric, communication problems often occur.
- *Assuming similarity.* It is not productive when individuals or groups from different backgrounds or cultures assume that others behave with responses similar to their own.
- *Assuming differences.* Don't automatically assume that other people are different from you.
- *Stereotyping and being prejudice.* We stereotype by placing a group or person into an inflexible, all-encompassing category. Stereotyping and prejudice can keep us from acknowledging others as unique individuals and therefore can hamper effective, open, and honest communication.

Adapting to Others Who Are Different from You

6.4 Describe six strategies that will help bridge differences between people and help them adapt to differences.

You develop intercultural communication competence when you are able to adapt your behavior toward another person in ways that are appropriate to the other person's culture. Specific strategies for becoming interculturally competent include the following:

- Seek information.
- Ask questions and listen.
- Tolerate ambiguity.
- Be mindful.
- Become other oriented by socially decentering and empathizing with others.
- Appropriately and ethically adapt your communication to others.

Key Terms

Androgynous, p. 126
Transgender, p. 126
Homophobia, p. 128
Ethnicity, p. 130
Race, p. 130
Discrimination, p. 131
Globalization, p. 132
Culture, p. 132
Co-Culture, p. 133
Intercultural Communication, p. 133
Culture Shock, p. 133
Worldview, p. 134
Cultural Context, p. 134
High-Context Culture, p. 134
Low-Context Culture, p. 134
Cultural Values, p. 135
Collectivistic Culture, p. 136
Individualistic Culture, p. 136
Masculine Culture, p. 137
Feminine Culture, p. 137
Ethnocentrism, p. 139
Stereotype, p. 141
Prejudice, p. 142
Intercultural Communication Competence, p. 143
Ethnocentric Cultural Perspective, p. 143
Ethnorelative Cultural Perspective, p. 144
Mindful, p. 145
Self-Talk, p. 145
Other-Oriented Communication, p. 146
Egocentric, p. 146
Social Decentering, p. 146
Empathy, p. 147
Sympathy, p. 147
Adapt, p. 147

The Principle Points

Principle 5:

Appropriately adapt messages to others.

- Appropriately adapt messages based on gender differences in communication by doing the following: (1) Seek to understand differences between genders as well as acknowledge similarities; (2) consider your own preferences, needs, and communication goals; (3) avoid assuming that differences you observe are solely the result of gender; and (4) consider both your needs and goals and those of the other person.
- Appropriately adapt your messages, paying particular attention to your verbal messages, to reflect differences in sexual orientation.
- Appropriately adapt your messages to respond to differences in age and ethnicity.
- Appropriately adapt messages to others on the basis of whether an individual is from a high-context culture, in which emphasis is placed on nonverbal messages and the surroundings, or a low-context culture, in which emphasis is placed on words and explicitly communicated messages.
- Appropriately adapt messages to others on the basis of the cultural value of individualism versus collectivism, preference for certainty versus tolerance of uncertainty, tendency to emphasize stereotypically masculine versus stereotypically feminine values, preference for centralized or decentralized power, and a long-term or short-term orientation to time.
- Acknowledge differences. Don't assume that everyone does things the same way you do or holds the same attitudes, beliefs, or values that you hold.
- Seek to explore and establish common ground with others. Don't assume that because someone is from another culture or geographic area, you don't have anything in common with the person.
- Seek to bridge differences between yourself and others who speak a different language or have different interpretations for nonverbal expressions; learn the language of others.
- Bridge cultural differences by learning as much as you can about another culture.
- Listen and ask questions to enhance your understanding of others.
- Be patient and tolerate some ambiguity and uncertainty when you communicate with people who are different from you.
- Become mindful, or aware that differences will exist, to help yourself better tolerate differences.
- Develop your skills at being other oriented. Focus on the needs and concerns of others while maintaining your personal integrity.

- Socially decenter. Think about how your communication partner would respond to information and situations; take into account people's thoughts, values, background, and perspectives.
- Empathize. Try to imagine how you would feel if you were in the other person's position.

Apply Your Skill

Consider the following questions. Write your answers and/or share them with your classmates:

1. In addition to the differences described in this chapter—gender, sexual orientation, age, ethnicity, and culture—can you think of other differences among people that affect the way we communicate with each other?
2. Describe the context and values of a co-culture to which you belong. For example, do you and people in your group tend to be high-context or low-context? Are you and your group more individualist or collectivist? More masculine or feminine? What is the overall attitude toward power distribution, uncertainty, and time?
3. Describe an example of a time when you experienced one of the barriers mentioned in this chapter. For example, have you tried to communicate with someone who assumed that you were more like them than you actually are? Or did you ever find yourself assuming that people were much more different from you than they turned out to actually be?
4. You've been assigned to work on a semester-long research project with a partner who has told you that his or her sexual orientation is different from your own. How could you use the skills in this section of the chapter to appropriately adapt your communication with your research partner?
5. What's your opinion about discussing diversity? Is it done too much? Not enough? Explain your answer.

Assess Your Skill

Assessing Your Culture Values and Adapting to Others

Based on the descriptions of cultural values described in this chapter, use the scales below to evaluate your own cultural values. Place an X or other mark to indicate where your culture falls on each scale.

Individualistic ____ ____ ____ ____ ____ ____ ____ Collectivistic

Decentralized ____ ____ ____ ____ ____ ____ ____ Centralized

Uncertainty ____ ____ ____ ____ ____ ____ ____ Certainty

Masculine ____ ____ ____ ____ ____ ____ ____ Feminine

Long Term ____ ____ ____ ____ ____ ____ ____ Short Term

After assessing your cultural values, think of a friend, teacher, classmate, family member, or colleague who may have a different cultural value profile than yourself. Based on the discussion of ways to enhance intercultural competence that you studied in this chapter, what specific strategies could you use to adapt to someone whose cultural values are different from your own?

Assessing Your Intercultural Skill

This chapter presented six specific strategies to help bridge differences in between people. Rank order these strategies in terms of what you need to improve in your interactions with people from different backgrounds. Give a rank of 1 to the skill that you most need to develop, a rank of 2 to the next area you feel you need to work on, and so on. Rank yourself on all eight strategies.

Seek information	____
Ask questions and listen	____
Tolerate ambiguity	____
Be mindful	____
Become other oriented (socially decenter and empathize)	____
Appropriately and ethically adapt to others	____

Chapter 7
Understanding Interpersonal Communication

The best of life is conversation, and the greatest success is confidence, or perfect understanding between sincere people. —RALPH WALDO EMERSON

Digital Vision/Getty Images

Chapter Outline

- What Is Interpersonal Communication?
- Initiating Relationships
- Maintaining Relationships
- Study Guide: Review, Apply, and Assess Your Knowledge and Skill

Chapter Objectives

After studying this chapter, you should be able to

7.1 Define interpersonal communication and discuss its three unique attributes.

7.2 Describe the roles of communication in revealing interpersonal attraction and initiating relationships.

7.3 Explain the roles of self-disclosure and emotional expression in maintaining face-to-face and online relationships.

"Hi. I'm ____. Nice to meet you." This simple statement can strike fear in the heart of even the most outgoing individual. Yet we know that meeting and getting to know people, as well as becoming known, are some of the most rewarding experiences in this life. If we cannot break out of our comfort zones to communicate with others, we won't survive.

Interpersonal communication is the form of communication we experience most often in our lives, and it involves all five of our Communication Principles for a Lifetime, shown in Figure 7.1. *In the remaining chapters of the book, you'll see a small version of the communication principles model in the margin to highlight our reference to one or more of the communication principles that we discuss.*

Effective interpersonal communication begins with an *awareness* of oneself. As you interact with people, you make mental notes of what works well and what doesn't. You learn from these experiences and develop a personal style of communication. We continue this process by reshaping our communication styles throughout our lives with the goal of becoming better communicators. The second and third principles involve the *effective use of verbal and nonverbal messages.* We experiment with verbal and nonverbal communication as we interact with people, form and develop relationships, and, in some cases, let go of those relationships. A major element that enhances relationships is the ability to *listen and respond thoughtfully* to others, our Principle Four. Finally, few interpersonal relationships last without *adaptation.* We live in an extremely diverse world. It's imperative to learn to adapt our communication to others' cultural backgrounds and values, personalities, communication styles, needs, and goals.

interpersonal communication
Communication that occurs between two people who simultaneously attempt to mutually influence each other, usually for the purpose of managing relationships.

Figure 7.1 Communication Principles for a Lifetime

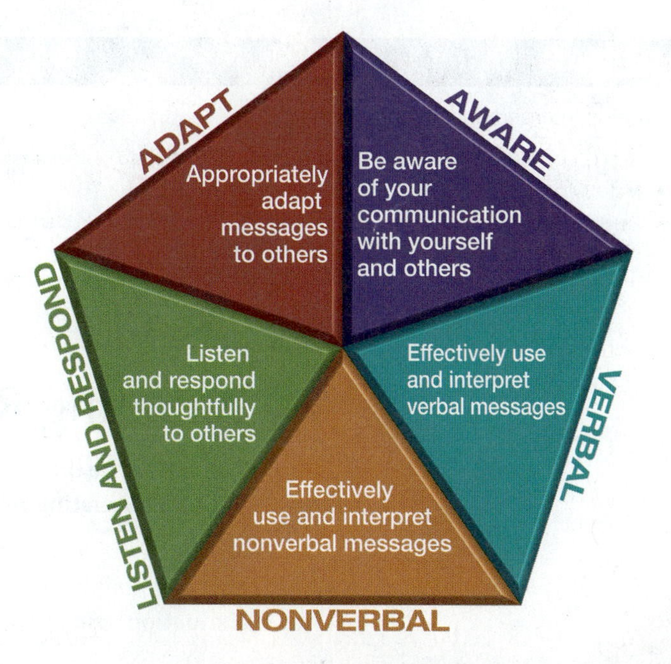

What Is Interpersonal Communication?

7.1 Define interpersonal communication and discuss its three unique attributes.

Interpersonal communication is a special form of human communication that occurs when two people interact simultaneously and attempt to mutually influence each other, usually for the purpose of managing relationships. Traditionally, interpersonal communication research has focused primarily on the face-to-face (FtF) encounter. However, given greater accessibility, affordability, and the ease of using technology, it's important to also study how interpersonal communication occurs through mediated channels such as cell phones and computers.[1]

In Chapter 1, we defined **mediated communication** as communication carried out using some channel other than those used in face-to-face encounters. It then follows that **mediated interpersonal communication** is communication that occurs when two people attempt to mutually influence each other through the use of a mediated channel, usually for the purpose of managing relationships. In this chapter, we'll explore some similarities and differences between mediated interpersonal communication and FtF interpersonal communication.

mediated communication
Communication that is carried out using some channel other than those used in face-to-face encounters.

mediated interpersonal communication
Communication that occurs when two people attempt to mutually influence each other through the use of a mediated channel, usually for the purpose of managing relationships.

impersonal communication
Communication that treats people as objects or that responds only to their roles rather than to who they are as unique people.

relationship
An ongoing connection made with another person.

relationship of circumstance
A relationship that forms situationally, simply because one life overlaps with another in some way.

Let's begin by considering three attributes that help us better understand the nature of interpersonal communication:

- *Interpersonal communication involves quality.* If you're having dinner with a friend, let's hope that your communication with your friend is different from communication with your waiter. The quality of the communication makes the difference. Interpersonal communication occurs not just when we interact with someone, but when we treat the other as a unique human being. Conversely, **impersonal communication** occurs when we treat people as objects or respond to their roles rather than to who they are as unique people.[2] In terms of mediated interpersonal communication, e-mailing or texting a friend is interpersonal communication; by contrast, responding to a mass text or e-mail message is impersonal communication because you likely don't know all the receivers of your message.
- *Interpersonal communication involves mutual influence.* We don't mean to imply that interpersonal communication exclusively involves persuasion—changing someone's mind or swaying someone's opinion. We simply mean that people who interact affect each other in some way. During that dinner with a friend, you might ask where your friend grew up. You've both been affected by this question—there's something you want to know and information your friend can provide. But what if your friend doesn't hear you because of a distracting noise in the restaurant? In this case, interpersonal communication hasn't really occurred because there's no mutual interaction; you have been affected by your attempt at communication, but your friend has not.
- *Interpersonal communication helps manage relationships.* **Relationships** are ongoing connections we make with others through interpersonal communication. For some people, the term *relationship* signals something serious and usually romantic, but we use the word in a much broader sense in this text. You probably have a wide variety of relationships, such as those with family members, coworkers, classmates, friends, and romantic interests. Some relationships are formed and maintained solely through mediated channels; others involve a combination of FtF and mediated interaction.

RECAP

What Is Interpersonal Communication?

- High quality: Interpersonal communication is superior to impersonal communication.
- Mutually influential: Both people in the relationship are affected.
- Relationship managing: We use interpersonal communication to help start, maintain, and sometimes end our interpersonal relationships.

Initiating Relationships

7.2 Describe the roles of communication in revealing interpersonal attraction and initiating relationships.

Relationships form for different reasons. **Relationships of circumstance** form situationally, simply because our lives overlap with others' lives in some way or because a situation brings us into contact. Relationships with family members, teachers, classmates, and coworkers typically fall into this category. An online relationship of circumstance might be formed between members of a group, such as students enrolled in an online or blended class. In contrast, relationships that we seek out and intentionally develop are termed **relationships of choice**. These relationships typically include those with friends, lovers, and spouses or relational partners. These categories of relationships are not mutually exclusive. Relationships of circumstance can change into relationships of choice; your sister or brother can turn out to be your best friend. Most of your online relationships are probably relationships of choice.

Some people make relationships look easy; they just seem to meet people and make positive impressions effortlessly. For others, meeting and getting to know people is a huge challenge. We'll let you in on a little secret: Initiating relationships really isn't all that easy for anyone. Let's explore the nature of attraction—what draws us into a conversation in the first place.

relationship of choice
A relationship that is sought out and intentionally developed.

attraction
A motivational state that causes someone to think, feel, and behave in a positive manner toward another person.

interpersonal attraction
The degree to which one desires to form or maintain an interpersonal relationship with another person.

physical attraction
The degree to which one finds another person's physical self appealing.

Interpersonal Attraction: Why We Like Whom We Like

What does it mean to say that you're attracted to another person? Most of the time, we tend to think of physical or sexual attraction. But there are many forms of attraction besides physical and sexual, including intellectual, spiritual, and personality attraction. **Attraction**, in general, is a motivational state that causes someone to think, feel, and behave in a positive manner toward another person.[3] More specifically, **interpersonal attraction** is the degree to which you desire to form and possibly maintain an interpersonal relationship with another person. Several factors come into play when you decide to act on your attraction and establish a relationship.

PHYSICAL AND SEXUAL ATTRACTION Volumes have been written about the role that physical and sexual attraction play in the formation of relationships.[4] While these forms of attraction are often lumped together or viewed as the same thing, actually they're different. In FtF situations, the degree to which we find another person's physical self appealing represents our **physical attraction** to that person, which is a powerful nonverbal cue. That appeal might be based on height, size, skin tone and texture, clothing, hairstyle, makeup, or vocal qualities. By this definition, even if you're heterosexual, you can still be attracted to a person of your own sex because you admire her or his physical attributes.

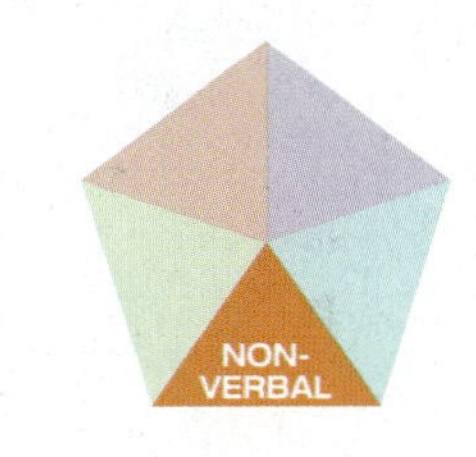

Attraction is fascinating to observe, as well as to feel for another person. How do you typically communicate the attraction you feel for someone? Do your nonverbal cues reveal your attraction, or do you use language to convey your feelings?
Monkey Business/Fotolia

Communication & DIVERSITY

Straight Women and Gay Men: What's Up with the Friendship?

Many straight women seem to have a special and interesting affinity for gay men and vice versa. What's the draw? Is it just that they're both attracted to men, so that commonality links them as friends? Is it that, because gay men and straight men have maleness in common, straight women seek advice on things "man"-kind from their gay male friends, viewing them as relationship advisors who have some sort of special insight? Another confusing observation is that you rarely see straight men having lots of lesbian friends. Why doesn't the trend seem to work in reverse?

Researchers in communication, psychology, and other disciplines have studied the increasingly common connection between straight women and gay men.[5] One study found that straight women were drawn to friendships with gay men because with their gay male friends, women didn't experience the same loss of self-esteem and sense of being judged for their attractiveness and sex appeal that they often felt with straight men (and other straight women). The straight female/gay male friendship was just easier, some women in the study reported.[6] Another element seems to be the fact that, since gay male friends are "off limits" sexually for straight women, the lack of sexual tension takes the heat off the relationship, leaving the friends to just *be*.

Gay men sometimes describe a feeling of tension in their friendships with many straight men, depending on the self-awareness and self-confidence of the straight men. Friendships seem to work if the straight men are completely comfortable with their own sexuality and their gay friends' sexuality and aren't concerned about being labeled gay or being the subjects of speculation and gossip. Those restrictions on the kind of straight man who can feel comfortable in a friendship with a gay man tend to make this profile of friendship the exception rather than the rule. So it's common for gay men to feel more comfortable being friends with straight women.

How do these research findings compare with your own observations and experiences?

Is physical attraction a factor in establishing online relationships? Research reveals that many online communicators find the *lack* of emphasis on physical appearance and attractiveness in online relationships to be one of the most positive features of this approach to relationship development.[7] One set of researchers described the Internet as "a world where what you write, not how you look or sound, is who you are."[8]

Sexual attraction has been defined as "the desire to engage in sexual activity with someone," a desire that "typically is accompanied by feelings of sexual arousal in the presence of the person."[9] You may be physically attracted to someone but not sexually attracted, as we stated before. But can you be sexually attracted but not physically attracted? We're not sure about the answer to that one because it may be a uniquely individual judgment. You may find another person's online communication sexually arousing even if you've never seen the person in the flesh. Suffice it to say that these two forms of attraction usually operate in tandem, even though they represent different kinds of appeal.

Our perceptions about others' physical attractiveness affect relationship possibilities. In general, although we may be attracted to a range of people, we tend to seek out individuals who represent the same level of physical attractiveness we do.[10] In research, this tendency is termed the **matching hypothesis**.[11] Perhaps you perceive yourself to be average looking, not model-beautiful but not unattractive. You may be physically or sexually attracted to extremely good-looking people; but if you're average looking, you're more likely to seek someone who is also average looking to date and even partner with or marry.

sexual attraction
The desire to have sexual contact with a certain person.

matching hypothesis
The theory that one tends to seek out individuals who represent the same level of physical attractiveness as oneself.

SIMILARITY Opposites certainly do attract, and differences between people can be interesting. But we like to add another phrase to the "opposites attract" cliché: "Opposites attract, but dramatic opposites seldom last." People who are significantly different from one another in dispositions and preferences may intrigue each other and teach each other something in the short run, but similarity appears to be a more important factor in highly committed, long-term relationships than in short-term, noncommitted relationships.[12]

Video chats, Facebook usage, texts, and other technological innovations have redefined the meaning of proximity in attraction. How do your face-to-face relationships compare to your mediated ones in terms of proximity?
Art Family/Fotolia

In general, you're attracted to people with whom you have **similarity**—those whose personality, values, upbringing, experiences, attitudes, or interests are similar to yours.[13] You may also be attracted more to people who are similar to you in age, intelligence, and life goals. The Internet allows people with similar interests to find one another easily and form online relationships.[14] In the initial stages of an online or FtF relationship, we try to emphasize positive information about ourselves to create a positive and attractive image. We reveal those aspects of ourselves that we believe we have in common with the other person, and the other person does the same.[15]

PROXIMITY In a traditional sense, the principle of **proximity** in interpersonal relationships refers to the fact that we're more likely to be attracted to people who are nearer to us physically and geographically than to those who are farther away.[16] You're more likely to form relationships with the classmates sitting on either side of you than those at the opposite end of the room. Physical proximity increases our communication opportunities, and opportunities to interact are likely to increase attraction.

similarity
The degree to which one's characteristics, values, attitudes, interests, or personality traits are like those of another person.

proximity
The likelihood of being attracted to people who are physically close rather than to those who are farther away.

Technology has turned the notion of proximity on its head, however, with virtual access to people around the globe in an instant. Those of you who are "digital natives" grew up in a world of computers where online information was always easily found at your fingertips. You have a different sense of boundaries, geographic limitations, and globalism than previous generations—those known as "digital immigrants," who discovered and adopted technology along the way.[17] People who have never met (and may never meet) in the physical world can come to feel a sense of proximity and develop relationships with people in the virtual world. In fact, some scholars contend that the instantaneous and pervasive nature of online communication bridges physical distance, creating a virtual closeness that FtF relationships might not achieve.[18]

COMPLEMENTARITY Although we tend to like people with whom we have much in common, most of us wouldn't find it very exciting to spend the rest of our lives with someone who had identical attitudes, needs, and interests. We tend to be

RECAP

Elements of Interpersonal Attraction

Physical Attraction	This form of attraction is based on another person's physical self.
Sexual Attraction	This form of attraction is based on the desire to have sexual contact with another person.
Similarity	Attraction increases if our characteristics, values, attitudes, interests, and personality traits are similar to those of another person.
Proximity	We are more likely to be interpersonally attracted to people who are physically close to us.
Complementarity	We may be attracted to someone whose abilities, interests, and needs differ from but balance or round out our own.

attracted to someone who is similar to us in important things such as our values, but when we consider less essential characteristics, we may be more interested in someone with whom we share **complementarity** of abilities and needs.[19] For example, if you're highly disorganized by nature (and that's fine by you), you might be attracted to someone who's very organized because you appreciate that person's sense of structure.

Communicating Our Attraction

According to research, we can size up a potential romantic partner or good future friend within the first three minutes of meeting the person.[20] That's impressive as well as daunting. What kind of impression do you make in the first three minutes of meeting someone? What kind of vibe do you get from someone in the first three minutes that lets you know whether you'd like to talk with the person further or whether there's a chance of something more meaningful developing?

When we're attracted to people, we use both verbal and nonverbal strategies to communicate our liking. Verbally, we ask questions to show interest, listen responsively, probe for details when others share information, and refer to information shared in past interactions in an attempt to build a history with people. But we most often communicate our attraction nonverbally, through indirect cues referred to as **immediacy**. As described in Chapter 4, immediacy behaviors reduce the physical and psychological distance between people.[21] Research on speed dating shows that nonverbal immediacy is a primary factor in determining whether a future date is desired.[22] Some examples of nonverbal immediacy cues include the following:

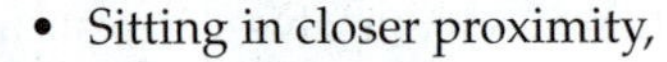

- Sitting in closer proximity,
- Increasing our eye contact,
- Increasing our use of touch,
- Leaning forward,
- Keeping an open body orientation rather than a closed-off position,
- Using more vocal variety or animation,
- Smiling more often than we do normally, and
- Preening (adjusting clothing, playing with our hair) as a means of attracting attention.[23]

How do we convey attraction in an online or mediated context? One study asked approximately 6,000 people how they flirt in person as well as online.[24] The majority of people in the study reported that flirting was accomplished online similarly to how it's done in person, meaning that people translate physical actions into text for mediated communication such as typing LOL or inserting an emoticon into a text, e-mail message, or post. With the rise in webcam use and video chatting, the more traditional nonverbal cues associated with flirtation can be effective, except, of course, cues that involve actual physical contact (though people often touch the screen of their computers or tablets during video chats to try to create the sensation of a touch).

Getting That First Conversation Going

In some ways, online interpersonal relationships have an advantage over FtF relationships in that they develop out of conversation, meaning that an online conversation is probably what launched the relationship in the first place.[25] In an FtF situation, the various steps of noticing someone interesting, realizing that you're interested (physically, sexually, or interpersonally), finding a way to meet the person, and starting up the first conversation can all be nerve-racking.[26] But these steps don't happen the same

complementarity
The degree to which another person's different abilities, interests, and needs balance or round out one's own.

immediacy
Nonverbal cues, such as eye contact, a forward lean, touch, and open body orientation, that communicate feelings of liking, pleasure, and closeness.

What nonverbal immediacy cues are these two people using to communicate their liking to each other? What immediacy cues do you exhibit when you find yourself attracted to someone?
Siri Stafford/Getty Images

way in online interactions. Initial online interactions are critical in that they can make or break future exchanges. With repeated virtual contact, online topics of discussion often become very personal, and intimacy often develops at a more rapid pace than it typically does in FtF relationships. If rapport develops, it may lead to telephone conversations or FtF meetings.[27]

In FtF settings, once you realize you're attracted to someone, what do you do next? Research indicates that people who meet and have that all-important first conversation feel enduring effects of the encounter even months later, no matter what direction the relationship took (if it took any direction at all).[28] We have some practical suggestions for how to approach those first conversations so that you feel confident and keep your self-esteem intact while communicating effectively.

REDUCING UNCERTAINTY Even though most of us like surprises from time to time, human beings are much more comfortable with certainty than with uncertainty. We prefer the known to the unknown, the predictable to the chaotic. Communicating in a new FtF or online relationship can involve *uncertainty*, or a fear of not knowing what to expect in a potential relationship. One communication research team developed **uncertainty-reduction theory**, an explanation of how we use information as we endeavor to reduce our uncertainty, especially as it relates to communicating with people we don't know (or know well). Communication researchers Charles Berger, Richard Calabrese, and James Bradac contend that this driving motivation among humans to reduce our uncertainty prompts us to communicate.[29]

We typically respond to uncertainty in three ways:

- **Passive strategy**: We seek information by observing people and scoping out situations before more actively working to reduce uncertainty. Suppose you just started a new job, a transition that creates a level of uncertainty in most of us. One way to begin to reduce your uncertainty is to simply observe how your coworkers and supervisors interact. In an online context, you may read a person's tweets or Facebook postings to get a sense of the person before communicating with her or him directly.
- **Active strategy**: After making passive observations, we might decide to check our perceptions of things with a third party. You might ask a coworker about

uncertainty-reduction theory
A driving human motivation to increase predictability by reducing the unknown in one's circumstances.

passive strategy
A noncommunicative strategy for reducing uncertainty by observing others and situations.

active strategy
A communicative strategy for reducing uncertainty by getting information from a third party.

something associated with your new job or colleagues, for example. Finding out others' perceptions increases your knowledge, reduces your uncertainty, and helps you decide how to behave. People often network online in an attempt to learn more information from a third-party source before making a decision about contacting a person online directly. Online daters often conduct background checks on their online partners before ever even thinking about arranging for more contact, such as one-on-one video chats or FtF meetings.

- **Interactive strategy**: The final strategy is going "straight to the horse's mouth," communicating directly with the person who has the most potential to reduce our uncertainty. At your new job, this person might be your boss, a coworker who's been on the job a while, or perhaps someone in personnel or human relations. Online, many people reduce their uncertainty directly by asking a person for more information about himself or herself, an interaction that may have less risk than an FtF meeting.

These strategies don't necessarily have to be used in order. You might bypass the active strategy and head to interactive, deeming it better to get the "straight scoop" from a direct source. We also don't always need to use all three strategies. In some cases, uncertainty can be reduced enough through passive and active strategies; there may be no cause for an interactive approach.[30]

Interactive strategies are frequently used in online relationships because starting up an online conversation or exchanging e-mails with someone tends to evoke less uncertainty than FtF first conversations. Online exchanges usually happen in private, with less potential for embarrassment than in FtF situations, when such factors as physical appearance and nervousness are in play. But one element can inject uncertainty into the online situation: the potential for deception. Because you stare at a computer monitor rather than into someone's eyes when you "meet" online, you really don't know whom you're talking to. Research has shown people's tendencies to give false information or to omit pertinent facts in their online communication.[31] Subjects in studies reported lying about age, weight, details of physical appearance, marital status, and even their sex, meaning that some gender-bending experimentation certainly occurs.

WHAT DO YOU SAY FIRST? In some contexts, the first words you exchange with someone may be fairly scripted or expected. For example, in a job interview, introductions and ritualistic greetings typically take up the first few minutes. (See Appendix A for helpful information on communicating in interviews.) But what about situations in which there are no prescribed, explicit rules or expectations for behavior? Our students tell us that the official "date" is a dying institution—they just don't date much anymore. More common than dating is "hanging out," in which two people meet somewhere or a group of people gather together, many of whom are "talking," "seeing each other," or have a special connection that goes beyond what they have with other people.

This first-conversation business used to be easier in the past, though perhaps not particularly satisfying. Men were taught by their fathers or older brothers how to use opening or pickup lines to attract women; women were schooled by their mothers or older sisters about how to respond (or ignore).[32] You might think such opening lines as "Come here often?" "Haven't I met you before?" and (the post-1960s all-time favorite) "What's your sign?" are relics of the past, but research has examined how well opening lines work to get a conversation going.[33] Researchers tested the effectiveness of three categories of opening lines said by men to women: (1) flippant and flirtatious, such as "You must be tired, because you've been running through my mind all day"; (2) direct and complimentary, such as "It took a lot of courage to approach you, so can I at least ask your name?"; and (3) innocuous, meaning that the line masked the man's interest, as in "What do you think of the band?" The women in the study liked the

interactive strategy
A strategy of communicating directly with the source who has the greatest potential to reduce one's uncertainty.

Mark Stivers

direct complimentary line the most, believing that it conveyed more trustworthiness and intelligence than other forms.

We don't recommend a one-size-fits-all approach to first conversations as in the use of a stereotypical pickup line. Instead, rely on our fifth Communication Principle for a Lifetime, which encourages communicators to appropriately adapt their messages to others. Each situation and the unique qualities of each person you meet should dictate how you communicate.

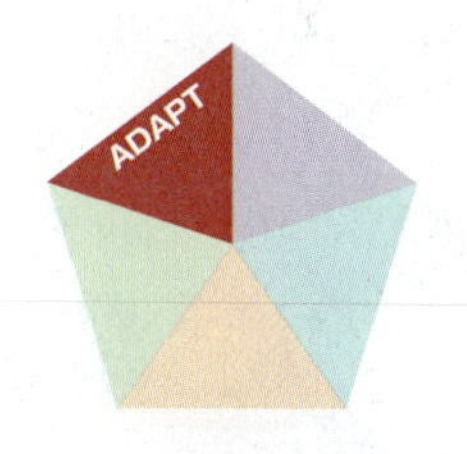

THE ART AND SKILL OF ASKING GREAT QUESTIONS When students ask us, as they frequently do, "What makes someone a good conversationalist?" a variety of things come to mind. All five of our Communication Principles for a Lifetime could be reflected in our answer, but one important element is the ability to ask a great question of another person. This skill doesn't just magically appear. It takes time, maturity, and experience with a variety of people and relationships to develop fully.[34]

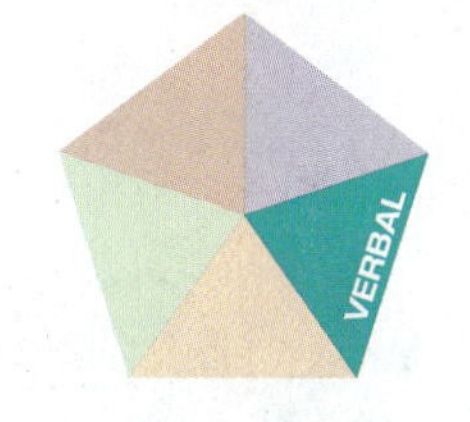

What do we mean by "asking great questions"? We don't mean tossing rapid-fire, superficial questions at someone as though you were in the first five minutes of a job interview or gathering data for the census. Asking a great question means, first, tailoring the question to the person as much as possible. Use what you've observed and what you've learned from other sources to formulate your questions. Online, it's typical to ask basic information just to break the ice, but the use of too many "yes/no" questions or questions requiring one-word responses is not likely to advance a conversation. Avoid questions that might be too personal or probing in the early stages of developing FtF and online relationships.

A second, very critical skill to develop is really listening to the person's answers to your questions. Then pose a follow-up question based on the person's response to your question. You can offer your opinion on something, but opinions work best when followed up with "Do you agree?" or "That's what I think, but what do you think?" Great conversationalists are great because they listen and then form responses that show they're listening—responses that are designed to draw other people out and let them shine.

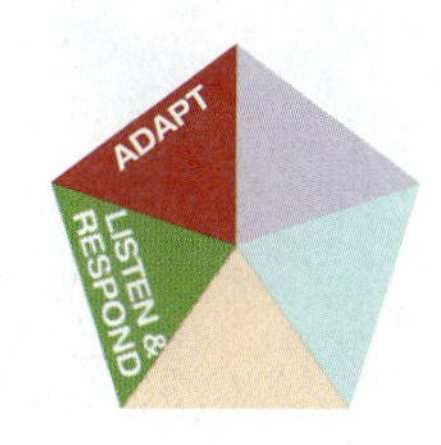

AVOIDING SELF-ABSORPTION Too many people think the best way to be conversationally impressive is by talking glibly, smoothly, confidently, and virtually nonstop *about themselves*. In an online context, when one person's messages are consistently five times as long as the another's and the content rambles on and on about the person, it's a definite turnoff. Researchers use the terms **conversational narcissism** or a **self-absorbed communicator style** for people who communicate like they are the center of the universe. Some people always (or predominantly) communicate this way, which is termed **trait conversational narcissism**; the style may be an outgrowth of a personality trait in which oneself is the constant focus.[35] Other times, the behavior reflects **state conversational narcissism**, not trait, meaning a temporary style of interacting rather than a more pervasive characteristic of a person. We're all likely to be self-absorbed from time to time, but if the self-absorbed communication continues, if it moves from a temporary state into a more permanent trait or style of a person, the likelihood that the person will be positively perceived seriously declines.

conversational narcissism (self-absorbed communicator style) A dominating communication style in which one focuses attention on oneself.

trait conversational narcissism Habitual use of a narcissistic or self-absorbed communicator style in which one focuses attention on oneself.

state conversational narcissism Occasional use of a narcissistic or self-absorbed communicator style in which one focuses attention on oneself.

Some verbal indications of self-absorption include the number of times a person uses the pronoun *I* instead of *you* or *we*. Narcissistic communicators converse mostly about themselves and typically provide more detail in their narratives than necessary (perhaps because they enjoy the sound of their own voice).[36] They talk more in statements than questions and constantly try to top someone's story or to draw the topic of conversation toward themselves, as in "Oh, you think *you're* tired—let me tell you about the kind of day *I* had." No one's day is as bad, no one's opinion as valuable or information as correct as the self-absorbed communicator's. The person may feign empathy in a conversation: "Oh, I know exactly how you feel." This usually leads to "The same thing happened to me," followed by a long story that takes attention away from the original communicator. Another indication of self-absorption is talking ad nauseam on topics about which one has some particular knowledge or expertise but that may bore the socks off listeners. Many times, these types of communicators are driven by insecurity and uncertainty rather than a belief that they truly are the center of the universe.

In FtF encounters, self-absorbed communicators use nonverbal cues such as increasing volume and dominant body postures to hold their turns at talk and stave off interruptions from others. They may even physically block another person from attempting to leave the conversation and are generally insensitive to others' nonverbal cues. Online, self-absorbed communicators attempt to dominate the contributions of others, control the topic of conversation, seem to post "selfies" every five seconds, and make their postings more frequent and lengthier than others'. People with self-absorbed personalities soon find themselves with few FtF or online friends because few of us can tolerate such an out-of-balance relationship.

In sum, the best conversationalists aren't great talkers—they're great listeners and responders (as articulated in Principle Four). In other words, it's not what *you* say, but how you respond to what *others* say that makes you a good conversationalist.

THE ART AND SKILL OF GIVING AND RECEIVING COMPLIMENTS Sometimes it seems as though people don't comment about one another unless it's to criticize. That's unfortunate because positive reinforcement and support from others are central to our self-esteem. British linguistic scholar Janet Holmes calls compliments "social lubricants."[37] She explains that the most common purpose of a compliment is to make someone feel good by offering praise and encouragement, but an important by-product is a sense of increased goodwill and solidarity between the complimenter and the receiver. Research shows that compliments between romantic partners can enhance self-esteem and are viewed as a form of intimate talk and that the sharing of positive feelings is linked to how satisfied partners are with the relationship.[38]

However, giving compliments is a tricky business because some attempts at flattery can be taken in ways other than you intend. For example, many female professionals tire of receiving workplace compliments on their looks while their male coworkers are more often complimented on their work. Some compliments are too personal and can make people feel uncomfortable. A pattern of personal compliments may be grounds for a claim of sexual harassment. But these are extreme examples. We encourage you to think about complimenting as a communication skill and a strategy particularly useful in first conversations, whether online or face to face. You don't want to come across as a phony or a predator, but a well-thought-out compliment can open the door to further conversation.

It's also important to know how to receive a compliment graciously—not by agreeing with the complimenter (and sounding cocky) or by disagreeing or attempting to talk the person out of his or her compliment, as in "This old outfit? I've had it for years—I just threw it on today." The best response is a simple "thank you" that acknowledges that something nice was said about you.[39]

Maintaining Relationships

7.3 Explain the roles of self-disclosure and emotional expression in maintaining face-to-face and online relationships.

Not only do relationships bring us life's greatest joy, but they also dramatically improve our physical health. Research examining data from more than 300,000 people found that a lack of strong relationships increased one's risk of premature death by 50 percent. This statistic represents a health risk comparable to smoking up to fifteen cigarettes a day and a greater risk than obesity or physical inactivity.[40]

Many forms of interpersonal communication are necessary to maintain successful, satisfying relationships. People in geographically separated relationships, such as couples whose careers require them to live in different locations, college students in long-distance relationships, or partners separated because of wartime deployments, have extraordinary challenges when it comes to relationship maintenance.[41]

Relationship experts John Harvey and Ann Weber describe relationship maintenance as "minding the close relationship," which they define as "thought and behavior patterns that interact to create stability and feelings of closeness in a relationship."[42] In this section, we explore the forms of communication most central to relationship maintenance, which also represent some of the most heavily researched topics in the communication discipline.

Self-Disclosure: Revealing Yourself to Others

Imagine you're hanging out with someone or are on a first date and things are going fairly well. But as you're talking, your date starts describing sexual details about his or her last date or romantic partner—information that is just too intimate and private for a first date or, by some people's standards, for *any* date. How would you react?

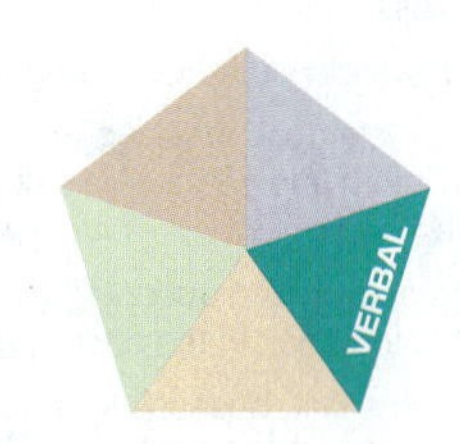

Self-disclosure, originally studied by psychologist Sidney Jourard, occurs when we voluntarily provide information to others that they would not learn unless we told them.[43] Communication scholar David Johnson provides eight reasons why people self-disclose:

- We begin and deepen a relationship by sharing reactions, feelings, personal information, and confidences.
- Self-disclosure improves the quality of relationships.
- Self-disclosure allows us to validate our perceptions of reality.
- Self-disclosure clarifies our understanding of ourselves.
- The expression of feelings and reactions is a freeing experience.
- We may disclose or withhold information about ourselves as a means of social control.
- Self-disclosing is an important part of managing stress and adversity.
- Self-disclosure fulfills a human need to be known intimately and accepted.[44]

self-disclosure
Voluntarily providing information to others that they would not learn if one did not tell them.

Properties of Self-Disclosure

Self-disclosure is a building block of intimacy, and greater intimacy generally leads to enhanced relationships, whether those relationships are developed face to face or online.[45] Because of the importance of self-disclosure, we first need to understand three properties of this unique form of interpersonal communication.

- *Reciprocity.* When we share information about ourselves with others, we expect them to share information similar in risk or depth about themselves, that is, to provide **reciprocity**. Sharing information about yourself gives others a certain amount of power over you. If the other person reciprocates by disclosing similar information, it helps maintain a balance of power. Over time, unreciprocated self-disclosure may cause someone to end a relationship. The reciprocity aspect applies to the online context as well. If someone doesn't respond to our social media posts or e-mail messages with as much depth of disclosure as we'd like, we may reduce or end our online communication with that nonreciprocating person.[46]
- *Appropriateness.* It's sometimes hard to gauge what's appropriate to talk about and what's not while you're in the process of getting to know someone.[47] Some information isn't right for the early stages of a relationship but is appropriate to disclose at a later stage. People vary a good deal on this judgment. Unwanted disclosures may emerge because one person misjudges the nature of the relationship, assuming or wanting a greater level of intimacy than his or her partner assumes or wants. Be sensitive when you choose what and when to disclose; consider how the recipient of your disclosure will react. Conversely, when someone reveals information to you, try to determine whether it's highly personal to her or him and respond appropriately. Sometimes an appropriate response is to (gently but assertively) explain to the person that her or his level or topic of disclosure will be better suited to your relationship later in its development, rather than at the current moment.
- *Risk.* Self-disclosure can be extremely rewarding because of its potential to deepen a relationship and enhance trust. But self-disclosure is not without its risks because, in our increasingly open culture, protecting our privacy is a challenge.[48] For example, even in a society that is becoming more accepting of homosexuality, bisexuality, and transgenderism, "coming out of the closet" as a form of self-disclosure is still a risky prospect. Relationships with family members and friends can be hurt by the revelation, and the potential for rejection of and hostility toward the discloser is very real.[49] When we disclose, we make ourselves vulnerable and forfeit control of information. We might offend, hurt, or insult another person by our disclosure, thus damaging the relationship. In relationships, we typically seek a balance between the potential risks and rewards of disclosing personal information.

RECAP

Self-Disclosure

. . . is providing someone with information about yourself that she or he couldn't learn about you unless you revealed it.

. . . is highly rewarding in that it is a building block of relational intimacy.

. . . should be reciprocal, meaning that the person you reveal something to should respond with information about himself or herself that is similar in depth. The frequency with which partners self-disclose should be reciprocal as well.

. . . should be appropriate, meaning that it can be a mistake to reveal information that is too personal too soon in the development of a relationship.

. . . involves some risk, because knowledge is power. By revealing information to another person, you give that person a degree of power over you.

reciprocity
Sharing information about oneself with another person, with the expectation that the other person will share information that is similar in risk or depth.

social penetration model
A model of self-disclosure that asserts that both the breadth and the depth of information shared with another person increase as the relationship develops.

Two Models of Self-Disclosure

Research has explored the way in which self-disclosure works to move a relationship toward intimacy. Here we examine two of the more prominent models that illustrate the process by which this happens.

THE SOCIAL PENETRATION MODEL Irwin Altman and Dalmas Taylor developed the **social penetration model**, which illustrates how much and what kind of information we reveal in various stages of a relationship.[50] According to their theory, interpersonal communication in relationships moves gradually from the superficial to the more intimate. Two aspects of this communication increase: the breadth of the

Communication & TECHNOLOGY

Do You Need a Boyfriend/Girlfriend *That* Badly?

We were appalled to learn of Invisible Girlfriend and its proposed counterpart, Invisible Boyfriend—services that, for a fee, let single people deceive everyone around them into thinking they have a significant other.

Fees range from about 10 to 50 dollars per month, depending on how deep a user wants the deception to go. At the lower end of the range, users receive e-mails, texts, postings to social media sites, and/or voice mail messages from an entirely fictional girlfriend or boyfriend, which they can read or play within earshot of their parents, boss, or friends who might feel comforted by knowing that the user is in a romantic relationship. At upper tiers of services, the company will provide live phone calls from the fake "beloved," as well as gifts, even "premium" gifts. The company claims that the service helps users who want to avoid pressure or awkward questions from their friends and family.[51] It has even advertised on Craigslist, seeking selfie photos from young women to use as "evidence" to support male users' claims of having a girlfriend.[52]

Invisible Girlfriend and Invisible Boyfriend may sound humorous and ridiculous, but stop and think about the deception that forms the core of such a service. With this company's help, users are duping people into presumably thinking better of them because they're in a romantic relationship. What does the perceived need for a business that caters to people's insecurities and feelings of competitiveness about singlehood and relationships say about our culture? Why are their customers willing to pay money and lie just so that others don't think they are single? Do we actually question or worry about people who aren't in a relationship? Do we think more positively about those who are? If so, why? Is that how it should be?

What about gay, lesbian, bisexual, and transgender people who might turn to such a service because they feel they can't be open about their sexuality? At first blush, it sounds like a way to reduce pressure people might feel from others who become curious about their sexuality. As we've discussed in this chapter, disclosing your sexuality can be risky. But most people who have survived a coming out process will tell you that deception is deadly—the real self-esteem killer. Most believe that, no matter the pain they or their loved ones may have felt when they were honest about their sexuality, doing so was the right call for them, rather than continuing a life of deception.

We continue to emphasize that self-disclosure is truly an individual decision. But we're not staying neutral about "invisible" boyfriends and girlfriends. Companies that make money by peddling deception are reprehensible.

information (the variety of topics discussed) and the depth (the personal significance of what is discussed).

As shown in Figure 7.2, the Altman and Taylor model is a configuration of rings, or concentric circles. The outermost circle represents breadth, or all the potential information about yourself that you could disclose to someone—information about athletic activities, spirituality, family, school, recreational preferences, political attitudes and values, and fears. Then there are a series of inner circles, which represent the depth of information you could reveal about yourself. The innermost circle represents your most personal information.

Figure 7.2 Altman and Taylor's Model of Social Penetration

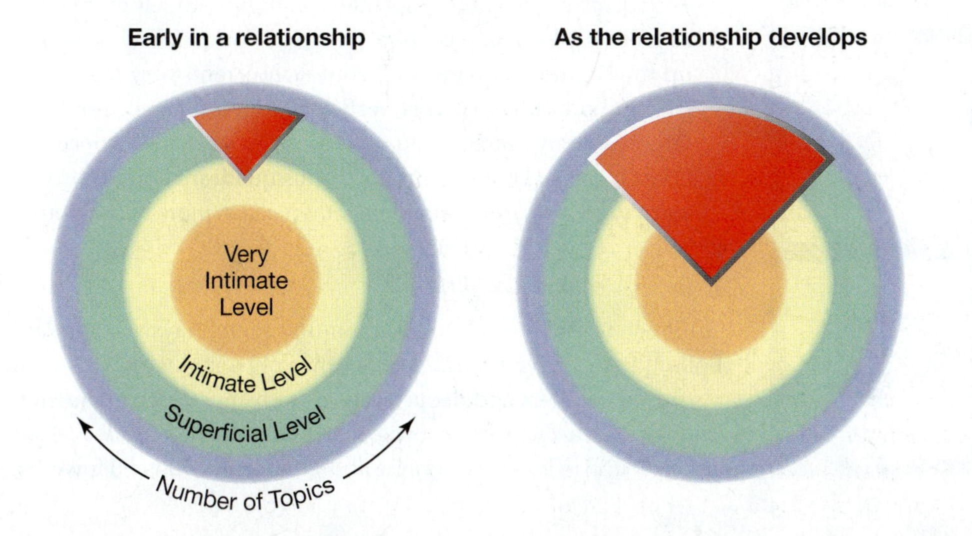

As an online or FtF relational partner interacts with you, that interaction can be seen as a wedge that's at first narrow (few topics are discussed) and shallow (topics are fairly superficial). People who have just started dating might talk about commonalities (such as being students at the same college), hobbies, interests, and favorite activities. As the relationship progresses, the wedge becomes broader (as more topics are discussed) and deeper (as more personal topics are discussed). After several dates or conversations about hobbies and interests, topics might turn more to values, such as the importance of family and friendships or attitudes about politics or social issues. Self-disclosure causes your layers to be penetrated as you penetrate the layers of the other person.

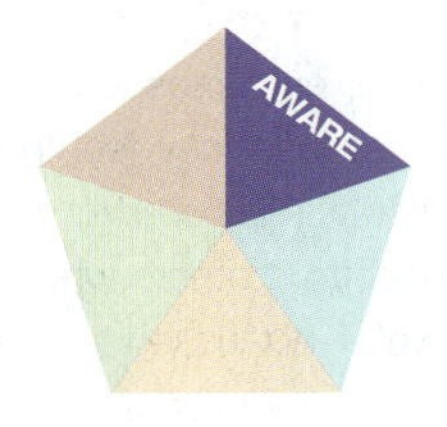

Each of your relationships exhibits a certain degree of social penetration, determined by the extent to which the other person has entered your concentric circles. Some relationships reflect a narrow, shallow wedge because they don't involve a great deal of personal disclosure. A few relationships represent almost complete social penetration, the kind you achieve in an intimate, well-developed relationship in which a large amount of in-depth self-disclosure has occurred. This model is a helpful way to assess your relationships in terms of whom you allow or encourage to get close to you and why.

THE JOHARI WINDOW The **Johari Window** in Figure 7.3 is another model of how self-disclosure varies from relationship to relationship. It reflects various stages of relational development, degrees of self-awareness, and others' perceptions of us. Its name comes from the first names of the two men who developed it (Joe Luft and Harry Ingham) and from its window-like appearance.[53] The large square window represents the self, which encompasses everything about you, including things you don't see or realize. A vertical line divides the square into what you have come to know about yourself and what you don't yet know about yourself. A horizontal line divides the square into what another person knows about you and doesn't know about you. The intersection of these lines divides the Johari Window into the following four quadrants:

Johari Window
A model that explains how self-disclosure varies from relationship to relationship; the model reflects various stages of relational development, degrees of self-awareness, and others' perceptions.

- *The Open quadrant.* The part of yourself that you know and have revealed to another person is the Open quadrant. As a relationship becomes more intimate, the Open quadrant grows larger.
- *The Blind quadrant.* Information that another person knows about you but that you fail to recognize is in your Blind quadrant. For example, your closest friends may be able to tell when you're attracted to someone even before you are aware of the attraction yourself. Before someone knows you well, the Blind quadrant is usually small; it grows larger as that person observes more information that's in your Unknown quadrant.
- *The Hidden quadrant.* Information that you know about yourself but haven't shared with another person makes up the Hidden quadrant. Initially fairly large, the Hidden quadrant shrinks and the Open quadrant grows as you disclose more and more.
- *The Unknown quadrant.* Information about yourself that you—as well as other people—have yet to discover or realize makes up the Unknown quadrant. People who aren't very introspective and don't have a very well-developed sense of self have larger Unknown areas than do those who've made a concerted effort to get to know themselves. This quadrant shrinks as you learn more about yourself or as others learn more about you.

Figure 7.3 Johari Window

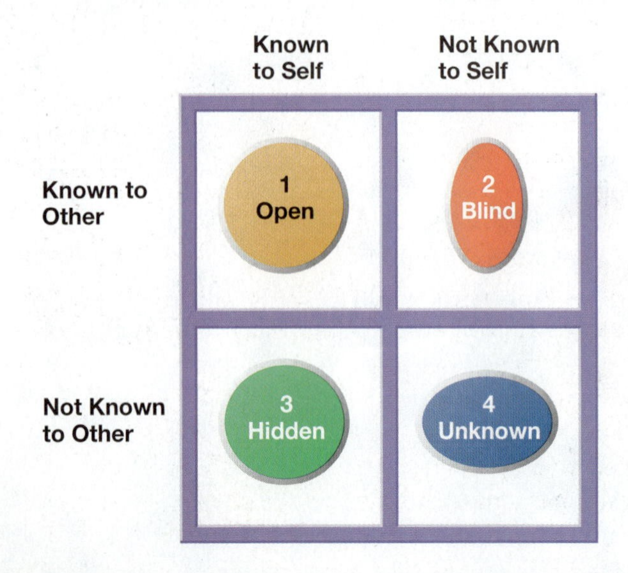

Expressing Emotions

"Emotion is the fuel of human communication," says scholar Paul Bolls.[54] Expressing emotions is another powerful way we reveal ourselves to others and deepen our relationships. Such expression comes more easily to some people than others, but it's a skill that can be improved in both your online and FtF relationships.[55] However,

Communication & ETHICS

Are You a Blurter?

Is honesty always the best policy in communication? People often say "I'm just being honest" as a way to soften or excuse something they just said that shocked or offended others. As a judge on *American Idol* and other television talent competitions, Simon Cowell was notorious for this behavior, frequently delivering brutal put-downs of well-intentioned young contestants. When people booed him or looked at him as though he was the cruelest person on Earth, he shrugged off the criticism with a glib "I'm just being honest." Cowell may have played up his tactlessness to improve ratings, but we all know someone in real life who also seems to lack a social filter on their honesty.

We've probably all also, at some time, blurted out something we thought. Many times, we regret our unfiltered remarks, and think or say, "It just came out. I don't know what came over me." One team of communication researchers has studied blurting, which they define for research purposes as the "production of speech that is spontaneous, unedited, and negative in its repercussions."[56] As Hample, Richards, and Skubisz explain, "Blurters say the first (only) thing that occurs to them."[57] As instructors, we've seen our share of students forget something or have an "oops" moment while making speeches in class. Occasionally, a from-the-gut "sh_t" flies out of the student's mouth before the student realizes that she or he just cursed in front of an audience (for a grade). Such blurting, it turns out, is *very* human. It's often connected to our emotional and attitudinal states. People giving speeches often have heightened emotions, for example.

Sometimes, however, blurting is habitual and can be an indication of a lack of self-awareness or self-control in one's communication. Not surprisingly, in Hample et al.'s study, subjects who were self-described blurters were high in verbal aggression and low in their ability to take the perspective of others.

Honesty is a prized value for most people, often more valued than tact, which some perceive as potentially deceptive. What's your opinion? Where's the line between politeness and honesty? If you blurt out your uncensored thoughts, are you "just being honest"? If you apply a filter to what you say, so as to not hurt someone's feelings, are you being dishonest?

there are cultural barriers to achieving this skill in that many cultures designate particular emotions as appropriate for only some people to display in certain situations.[58] If you placed emotional expression on a continuum according to cultural groups, with an open approach to emotional display at one end and the suppression of emotional display at the other end, American culture would fall somewhere in the middle.[59]

Families teach children very specific rules about the appropriateness of emotional display, rules that often perpetuate gender distinctions related to emotions.[60] Many American men are taught to contain their emotions for fear that emotional expression may make them appear weak. In fact, the male tendency to suppress emotion is so pronounced that it led Sidney Jourard (who first studied self-disclosure) to entitle one of his book chapters "The Lethal Aspects of the Male Role."[61] Jourard found that men who had difficulty expressing their feelings had high levels of stress-related disease.

Women in American culture, in most settings, are allowed the emotional display of crying that can be prompted by sadness, fear, or joy. But many women receive negative reactions when they display anger. While these trends and expectations have changed somewhat with recent generations, there is still a significant tendency for men (as well as many women) to believe that emotional expression of any kind is more appropriate in women than in men.[62]

As relationships become more intimate, we have a greater expectation that our partner will disclose emotions openly. The amount of risk associated with such emotional disclosure varies from person to person.[63] Most of us are comfortable sharing the emotions of happiness and joy but are more reserved or hesitant about sharing fear or disappointment. While emotional expression can sometimes be difficult to handle, we generally want to know how our partners in intimate relationships are feeling, even if those feelings are negative.

In this chapter, we've explored several aspects of interpersonal communication, yet we've only scratched the surface of the complexities of relationships—those connections that give us life's greatest joys, as well as challenges. In the next chapter, we examine key aspects of communication that are critical to ongoing relationships with regard to our five Communication Principles for a Lifetime.

Many American men learn at an early age to mute their expressions of most emotions, whereas American women often learn to express a wide range of feelings. What were you taught about emotional expression that affects the way you communicate in relationships today?
IKO/Shutterstock

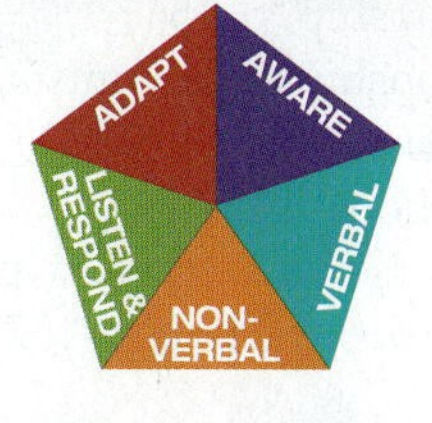

STUDY GUIDE:
Review, Apply, and Assess Your Knowledge and Skill

Review Your Knowledge

What Is Interpersonal Communication?

7.1 Define interpersonal communication and discuss its three unique attributes.

Interpersonal communication occurs when two people interact simultaneously and attempt to mutually influence each other, usually for the purpose of managing relationships. Interpersonal communication research has traditionally focused on the face-to-face relationship, but more recently, studies have investigated how online relationships are initiated and maintained through mediated interpersonal communication.

Interpersonal communication has three attributes:

- Interpersonal communication involves quality, which can be contrasted with impersonal communication, in which people are treated as objects or are communicated with based on the roles they hold.
- Interpersonal communication involves mutual influence.
- Interpersonal communication helps manage relationships of choice and circumstance.

Initiating Relationships

7.2 Describe the roles of communication in revealing interpersonal attraction and initiating relationships.

We are drawn to other people because of physical, sexual, and interpersonal attraction; similarity; proximity; and complementarity. We use nonverbal immediacy cues to convey our attraction and communicate to reduce uncertainty as we initiate and develop relationships. Besides listening, adapting, and being sensitive to nonverbal cues, good interpersonal communicators ask great questions, avoid self-absorbed communication, and give and receive compliments graciously.

Maintaining Relationships

7.3 Explain the roles of self-disclosure and emotional expression in maintaining face-to-face and online relationships.

Many forms of interpersonal communication are necessary to maintain successful, satisfying relationships. An important communication skill is self-disclosure, or voluntarily providing information to others that they wouldn't learn if you didn't tell them. Self-disclosure is characterized by three aspects: (1) reciprocity, (2) appropriateness, and (3) risk.

Two models of self-disclosure help us understand how relationships progress toward intimacy. Social penetration suggests that interpersonal communication in relationships moves gradually from the superficial to the more intimate. The breadth and depth of communication increase as intimacy increases in relationships. The Johari Window depicts various stages of relational development, degrees of self-awareness, and others' perceptions.

Emotional expression is another powerful mechanism for revealing ourselves to others and deepening our relationships.

Key Terms

Interpersonal Communication, p. 155
Mediated Communication, p. 156
Mediated Interpersonal Communication, p. 156
Impersonal Communication, p. 156
Relationship, p. 156
Relationship of Circumstance, p. 156
Relationship of Choice, p. 157
Attraction, p. 157
Interpersonal Attraction, p. 157
Physical Attraction, p. 157
Sexual Attraction, p. 158
Matching Hypothesis, p. 158
Similarity, p. 159
Proximity, p. 159
Complementarity, p. 160
Immediacy, p. 160
Uncertainty-Reduction Theory, p. 161
Passive Strategy, p. 161
Active Strategy, p. 161
Interactive Strategy, p. 162
Conversational Narcissism (Self-Absorbed Communicator Style), p. 164
Trait Conversational Narcissism, p. 164
State Conversational Narcissism, p. 164
Self-Disclosure, p. 165
Reciprocity, p. 166
Social Penetration Model, p. 166
Johari Window, p. 168

The Principle Points

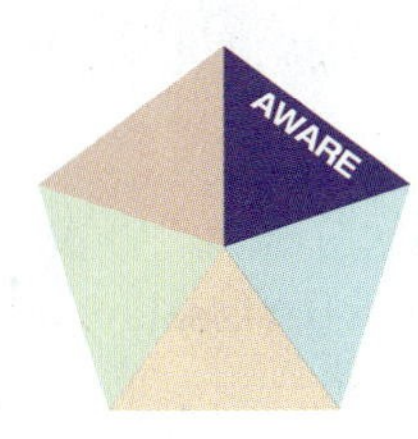

Principle One:

Be aware of your communication with yourself and others.

- Attraction emerges in several different forms; it's important to discover what traits in other people are attractive to you.
- Early in an online or FtF relationship, be aware of aspects of your personality that you want to emphasize to another person to create a positive and attractive image.
- One strategy to reduce uncertainty in interpersonal contexts is to be aware of your surroundings and situation as you passively observe others' interactions.
- The social penetration model and the Johari Window can help you become more aware of your relationships and your interpersonal communication.

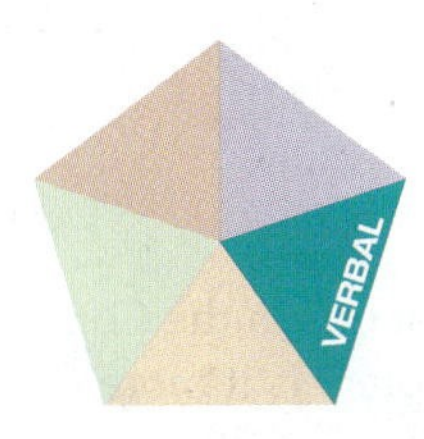

Principle Two:

Effectively use and interpret verbal messages.

- In initial interactions, honest, direct approaches are preferable to canned opening lines.
- When initiating online or FtF relationships, use questions that will engage and draw out the other person.
- You may verbally reveal your liking for another person by using informal, personal, and inclusive language.
- You may verbally reveal your liking for another person by asking questions, probing for further information, and directly expressing your feelings.
- An active strategy to reduce uncertainty in interpersonal contexts is to ask third parties for their perceptions and knowledge.
- An interactive information-seeking strategy involves direct communication with the source who has the greatest potential for reducing your uncertainty.
- Asking great questions in a conversation draws a person out and helps a communicator avoid creating a perception of being self-absorbed.
- Practice giving sincere compliments generously and receiving others' compliments graciously.
- One of the key variables in relationship development is self-disclosure.
- As relationships grow more intimate, the expectation of deeper, more personal self-disclosure increases.
- As online and FtF relationships grow more intimate, the expectation of emotional expression increases.

Principle Three:

Effectively use and interpret nonverbal messages.

- Physical attraction is the degree to which you find another person's physical self appealing, whereas sexual attraction is the desire to have sexual contact with a certain person.
- In an FtF relationship, you may nonverbally reveal your liking for another person through the display of immediacy cues.
- Certain nonverbal behaviors such as increasing speech volume to ward off interruptions or sending lengthy texts can signal a self-absorbed communication style.

Principle Four:

Listen and respond thoughtfully to others.

- Early in online and FtF relationships, it's important to concentrate on and listen to your partner's responses to your questions so that you can offer an appropriate follow-up response.
- You may verbally reveal your attraction and liking for other people by listening, asking questions to elicit more detail, and then responding appropriately and sensitively to the added information.
- The best conversationalists aren't great talkers; they're great listeners and responders.
- The formulation of great questions in conversation requires listening carefully and responding appropriately to someone's communication.

- It's important to attend carefully to someone's self-disclosure because it comes with an expectation of reciprocity, meaning that the receiver is expected to self-disclose in response to the sender's self-disclosure.

Principle Five:

Appropriately adapt messages to others.

- Adapt to others' communication, especially in first conversations, by attending to what is said and following up with great questions.
- Self-absorbed communication involves little adaptation.
- Adapt your self-disclosure to the other person and the context so that your revelations are appropriate.

Apply Your Skill

Consider the following questions. Write your answers and/or share them with your classmates:

1. Give an example of the mutual influence of interpersonal communication from your own life in the past twenty-four hours.
2. Give examples of when you have used passive, active, and interactive strategies to reduce your uncertainty in a new situation or before meeting a new person.
3. What are your responses to the questions in the Communication & Ethics box in this chapter? Is it more honest to say whatever you're thinking? Is filtering your comments dishonest?
4. What pickup lines have you heard or heard about? What approach would be better than using a canned line?

Assess Your Skill

Learning to Ask Great Questions

Because we think that learning to ask great questions is so important, we want to provide an opportunity for you to practice this art and skill. For each of the situations and snippets of conversation that follow, generate effective follow-up questions that would deepen and extend the conversation. We've provided an example to get you started.

Sample Situation and Conversation: The situation is a first conversation between two classmates who have never met. They are seated in the classroom before class begins.

Bob: Hi. My name's Bob. What's yours?
Sue: Hi. I'm Sue.
Bob: I've never taken a philosophy course before, have you? What do you think this course will be like?
Sue: Well, I've never taken one either, but I expect lots of reading. And I've heard the professor's tests are tough.
Bob: Oh, great! Is it too late to drop? When you say the tests are tough, tough in what way? Do you mean they cover lots of material, the prof's a hard grader, or what?

1. *Practice Situation:* At a fraternity/sorority mixer, a woman and a man are introduced to each other for the first time by other members of their organizations.
2. *Practice Situation:* After a staff meeting, two new coworkers who will be working on the same important project introduce themselves to each other.

Too Private to Talk About—Unless It's on Facebook?

For the following topics, check the column to indicate in which situation you would freely disclose the information to another person you were trying to get to know: face to face (FtF), online, neither, or both. Then analyze your answers. What information would you share anytime? What information are you unlikely to reveal to anyone in either context?

Topic	Would Disclose FtF	Would Disclose Online
Weight		
Racial/ethnic background		
Sexual history		
Family details		
Relationship status		
Weaknesses/strengths		
Religious/spiritual beliefs		
Political views		

Chapter 8

Enhancing Relationships

If civilization is to survive, we must cultivate the science of human relationships . . . —FRANKLIN D. ROOSEVELT

berc/Fotolia

Chapter Outline

- The Importance of Relationships: Friends, Family, and Colleagues
- Stages of Relationship Development
- Relationship Dissolution (a.k.a. the Breakup)
- Tensions in Relationships: The Dialectical Perspective
- Managing Interpersonal Conflict
- Study Guide: Review, Apply, and Assess Your Knowledge and Skill

Chapter Objectives

After studying this chapter, you should be able to

8.1 Explain how the five Communication Principles for a Lifetime apply to interpersonal communication among friends, family members, and colleagues.

8.2 Identify and describe the stages of relational escalation and de-escalation.

8.3 Summarize research findings on relationship dissolution, including communication in the on-again/off-again relationship and the postdissolutional relationship.

8.4 Discuss relational dialectics and three primary tensions in relationships.

8.5 Summarize the definition and seven types of interpersonal conflict; key characteristics of nonconfrontational, confrontational, and cooperative styles of conflict management; and ways in which people can cooperate in conflict situations by managing their emotions, managing information, managing goals, and managing the problem.

What makes you happy? Staring at a computer screen? Working on a project for your job? Reading a great book? Playing a video game? Being by yourself, writing in your journal? Taking a long walk? Let us venture a guess: While any one of these things might bring some level of pleasure into your life, none of them could be considered *the* thing in life that gives you the most enjoyment. Probably most of us would answer that question with some response that involves other people or perhaps only one other person.

In Chapter 7, we examined some fundamental aspects of interpersonal communication that help us initiate online and face-to-face relationships. In this chapter, we move forward to discuss interpersonal communication as it occurs in ongoing relationships. Where appropriate, we discuss online relationships, but our primary focus in this chapter is how our five Communication Principles for a Lifetime apply to the good old-fashioned face-to-face relationship.

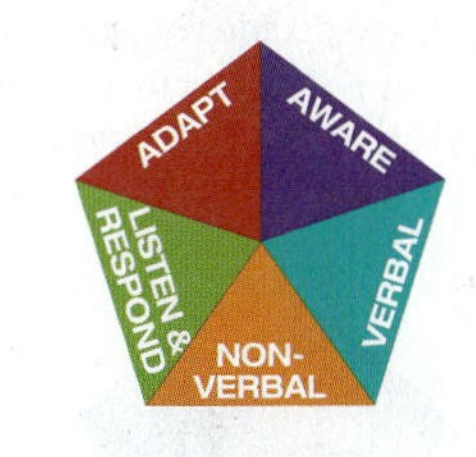

The Importance of Relationships: Friends, Family, and Colleagues

8.1 Explain how the five Communication Principles for a Lifetime apply to interpersonal communication among friends, family members, and colleagues.

Our family members, friends, and coworkers are very important to us. We don't have to lecture students on the value of friendship. As for family, to some degree we all come from dysfunctional families—there's no such thing as a perfect or "functional" family. No matter how imperfect our families are, how crazy our siblings

These two friends may have met just moments ago. Our earliest friendships are usually based on momentary sharing of activities. How long does it take now for you to decide someone is your friend? What influences that decision?
Thinkstock Images/Stockbyte/Getty Images

still make us, or how far apart we've grown, almost all of us would agree that family relationships are extremely important. On the job front, when people talk about what they like best about their jobs, most often they talk about the people they work with. So, disregarding the few true hermits out there, most of us are "people who need people."

Friendship Matters

One of the best definitions of a friend, attributed to Aristotle, is "a soul that resides in two bodies." A friend is someone we like and who likes us. We trust our friends and share good and bad times with them. We expect a certain level of sacrifice from our friends. For example, you know you've got a good friend when he or she gives up something (like a hot date) to help you through a tough time.

Researchers have examined some differences among friendships at four stages in life: childhood, adolescence, adulthood, and old age.[1] When we start to talk (around age two) and interact with others, our first friendships are typically superficial, self-centered, and fleeting because they're based on momentarily shared activities.[2] As we grow and mature, we develop more of a give-and-take in friendships. During adolescence we move away emotionally from relationships with parents, and peer relationships have more influence on our behavior.[3]

Adult friendships are among our most valued relationships, even though they may be few in number. Research has found that, on average, adults have ten to twenty casual friends, four to six close friends, and only one to two best friends.[4] Rather than progressing through a series of stages in which intimacy deepens, which is typical of romantic relationships, friendships often alternate between periods of development and deterioration.[5] As Americans continue to spend more hours at work each year, we often find that our closest friends are also our coworkers.[6]

Friendships are extremely important in old age.[7] During retirement, when many individuals have more time for socializing, friendships become increasingly critical. Older adults tend to rely on enduring friendships and maintain a small, highly valued network of friends.

Our familiar five Communication Principles for a Lifetime can help you enhance your friendships.

- **Principle One: Be Aware of Your Communication with Yourself and Others** Knowing your own interests, likes, and dislikes is a first step if you're trying to expand your circle of friends.
- **Principle Two: Effectively Use and Interpret Verbal Messages** Our verbal communication tends to become more frequent and deepens as friendships develop.
- **Principle Three: Effectively Use and Interpret Nonverbal Messages** We also use nonverbal immediacy cues to establish friendships—behaviors that reveal our liking of other people, such as leaning forward, moving closer, making eye contact, smiling, and nodding.
- **Principle Four: Listen and Respond Thoughtfully to Others** Probably no other communication skill develops a friendship more than the ability to listen and respond appropriately. Most of us don't stay friends with people who don't seem to listen to us or who listen but respond inappropriately.

- **Principle Five: Appropriately Adapt Messages to Others** We extend different parts of ourselves and communicate differently with various friends. Having a wide range of friends taps into different parts of your personality, which, in turn, helps you develop your skills of adaptation.

Family Matters

To say that family life has changed is an understatement. Family units are dramatically different from what they were in the 20th century, when the predominant profile was a two-parent, father-as-breadwinner, mother-as-homemaker arrangement.[8] In the 1980s, the New York Supreme Court provided a very broad definition of a family, stating, "The best description of a family is a continuing relationship of love and care, and an assumption of responsibility for some other person."[9] The most common profile of the American family in the 21st century is the step-family, or blended family, with rising rates of extended family or multigenerational arrangements.[10] As more states legalize same-sex marriage, we're witnessing another paradigm shift in our basic views of what constitutes a family.[11]

Of all the relationships we experience in our lifetimes, none are more complicated than family relationships. All five Communication Principles for a Lifetime come into play when we interact with our families.

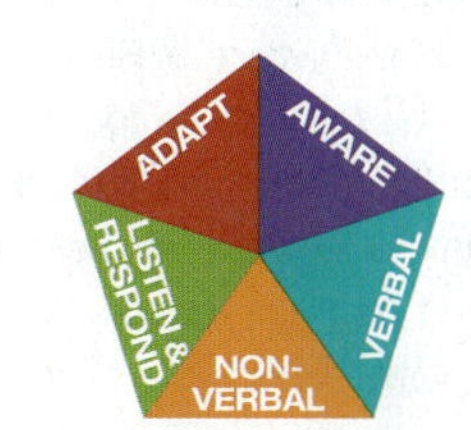

- **Principle One: Be Aware of Your Communication with Yourself and Others** Growing up in families, we begin to discover who we are and how we should communicate with others. Family members have more power to shape our self-concepts and affect self-esteem than other people do. Granted, at some point we can choose to lessen the effect family members can have on our lives. But for most of us, those early messages we received as children remain in our psyches and affect who we are today.
- **Principles Two and Three: Effectively Use and Interpret Verbal and Nonverbal Messages** Renowned family therapist Virginia Satir has conducted extensive research on family communication.[12] She suggests that the following elements are present in healthy families:
  - Self-worth of members is high.
  - Communication is direct and honest.
  - Rules are flexible.
  - People listen actively.
  - Family members look *at* one another, not *through* one another.
  - Family members treat children as people.
  - They touch one another affectionately regardless of age.
  - They openly discuss disappointments, fears, hurts, angers, and criticism, as well as joys and achievements.
- **Principle Four: Listen and Respond Thoughtfully to Others** One of the characteristics Satir recommends is active listening. Healthy family relationships are built on foundations of trust, which involves listening to one another and responding helpfully. Many conflicts arise because family members don't listen well to one another and respond on the basis of that faulty listening.[13]
- **Principle Five: Appropriately Adapt Messages to Others** Finally, family relationships involve a good deal of adaptation, particularly when, as adults, we visit our parents. Sometimes our parents and extended family members talk a certain way mainly because they've always talked that way.[14] But if you're the family member who has moved away, attended college, and adapted your communication to meet the changing times, relate to friends, and demonstrate professionalism at work, it can be quite awkward to be immersed once again in the family setting and realize how much you've changed. Reintegration into family patterns of communication can also be a challenge for military personnel who've served overseas and are returning to family life in the United States.[15]

Communication & TECHNOLOGY

The Joys (and Woes) of the Video Chat

How cool was it when comic strip detective Dick Tracy used his "2-way wrist radio" and, later, his "2-way wrist TV" to talk to his police chief? How about the Jetsons, who had a videophone in their home? (Yes, we're old.) Several decades ago, having a video watch or phone was the stuff of futuristic cartoons. Now we just have to fire up our laptops or cell phones and we're video chatting. Stop and think for a moment how truly remarkable this technology is.

Applications such as Skype and FaceTime that let us see as well as hear our communication with people at a distance are especially helpful for family members who are geographically separated because of work demands or relationship change, such as divorce.[16] Researchers have found that video chatting can be therapeutic for children who are living apart from one or both parents.[17] Adult family members benefit, too. A bride-to-be can model wedding dresses for an ailing or far-away parent who can't be there to enjoy the shopping moment. Family members separated by work or military deployment might meet a new baby for the first time via Skype. And we can all enjoy being more "up close and personal" with people we care about who don't live where we live.

A good deal of research has focused on military families in which one member has been deployed to a war zone.[18] Findings from such research contribute to skills-training modules for service members and their families. Service members are trained in such topics as how to avoid the effects on spouses and children of having a video chat interrupted by gunfire or other noises that signal danger to their loved one.[19] Families of deployed personnel learn how and when to disclose a problem to a deployed family member.[20] One of the leading causes of suicides among members of the armed forces is a major crisis that occurs at home. It might be necessary, for example, to tell a soldier halfway around the world that his or her parent has been diagnosed with cancer. Training helps help family members find the least distressing way possible to share such news.

Blend Images/Ariel Skelley/Getty Images

Colleagues Matter

For many of us, our work is our livelihood, our most time-consuming activity. In fact, many Americans are working longer hours—10 percent more time on the job in the 21st century than thirty years ago.[21] Many things make a job worthwhile and rewarding, but most people say that relationships with people at work make the difference between job satisfaction and dissatisfaction.

What are the most important skills people need to be successful on the job? Year after year, the number-one skill employers look for in new hires is the ability to communicate effectively with others.[22] You land your job through an interview; you keep your job on the basis of your ability to do the work and get along with coworkers, bosses, and clients, which usually involves a large amount of interpersonal interaction. The higher you go in an organization, the more your job involves communicating with others, both online and in person. You'll likely apply all five Communication Principles for a Lifetime to help you succeed at your job.

Our familiar five Communication Principles for a Lifetime can help you enhance your work relationships.

- **Principle One: Be Aware of Your Communication with Yourself and Others** When we start a new job, we experience uncertainty. We need to learn the basics like where to park and how the organization functions. We also need to figure out more important things, such as how to do your job well, who's who in the chain of command, and which colleagues have the potential to develop into friends.[23]

We're most likely to observe our surroundings and how people interact on the job as a way of becoming more aware so that we'll know how to behave appropriately. Perception checking with our colleagues, supervisors, and trainers also increases awareness.

- **Principles Two and Three: Effectively Use and Interpret Verbal and Nonverbal Messages** As we begin to interact with people of varying status in the organization, we draw on our most effective verbal and nonverbal communication skills so that we make positive impressions on others.
- **Principle Four: Listen and Respond Thoughtfully to Others** It's important to listen patiently, fully, and nonjudgmentally at work and essential to exercise caution before responding so that you respond appropriately.
- **Principle Five: Appropriately Adapt Messages to Others** Finally, our Principle Five about adaptation is critical to successful coworker relationships. You won't be successful on the job if you communicate the same way to your boss as you do to your peers, subordinates, clients, and others in your life—including long-term friends, intimates, and family members.[24] This may seem obvious, but we find that people sometimes experience isolation on the job because they can't get along with coworkers. They don't adapt to the situation, and it often costs them their jobs.

Stages of Relationship Development

8.2 Identify and describe the stages of relational escalation and de-escalation.

In this chapter, we explore aspects of communication that are critical to the successful functioning of ongoing relationships, but it's helpful to first understand that relationships tend to develop in discernible stages.[25] Although the research on relational stages is most often applied to dating or romantic relationships, the information can also apply to other types of relationships.

Understanding relationship stages is important for two main reasons:

- Interpersonal communication is affected by the stage of a relationship. For instance, people in advanced stages discuss topics and display nonverbal behaviors that rarely appear in the early stages of a relationship.
- Interpersonal communication facilitates movement between the various stages. Ongoing relationships change and are constantly renegotiated by those involved. Interpersonal communication moves a relationship forward—possibly from friends to romantic partners to marital or committed partners. Ideally, communication can also move a relationship back to a previous stage, although regressing a relationship or changing a relationship's definition is difficult to accomplish.[26]

Think of relational stages as floors in a high-rise (see Figure 8.1). The bottom floor represents a first meeting; the penthouse is intimacy. Relational development is an elevator that stops at every floor. As you ascend, you might get off the elevator and wander around for a while before going to the next floor. Each time you get on the elevator, you don't know how many floors up it will take you or how long you'll stay at any given floor. If you fall head over heels in love, you might want to escalate quickly from floor to floor toward intimacy, possibly even skipping some

Figure 8.1 Relationship Stages

SOURCE: From Steven A. Beebe, Susan J. Beebe, and Mark V. Redmond, *Interpersonal Communication: Relating to Others*, 7th edition. Reprinted and electronically reproduced by permission of Pearson Education, Inc., Upper Saddle River, New Jersey. Copyright © 2013.

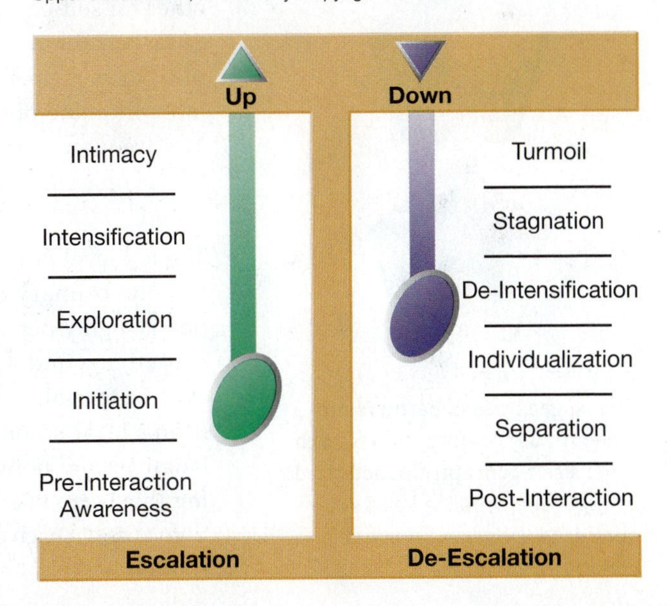

floors. Other times, you stop at a particular floor and never get back on the elevator, electing instead to stay at a particular stage of relational development. This may represent stability or stagnation. Stability is not the same as stagnation; stability may simply mean that a relationship has reached a comfortable point for both partners.

If one partner believes that the relationship has stabilized and the other partner believes that it has stagnated, dissatisfaction and conflict are often the result, and they may trigger de-escalation. The process of de-escalating a relationship doesn't always occur, but if it does, it may be a slow or a quick descent through various floors.

The best approach to relationship development is to share this elevator with your partner or friend so that the two of you make decisions about how high you will ride, how long to stay at each floor, and whether to take the elevator back down. But often partners don't share decisions about movement within the relationship. Sometimes one of the partners rides the elevator alone.

Relational Escalation

According to Mark Knapp and Anita Vangelisti, the communication scholars who developed the model of developmental stages within relationships, relational escalation occurs in the following five stages:[27]

- **Pre-interaction awareness** is the first stage, one in which potential partners or friends observe each other and talk with other people about each other without having any direct interaction. If your impressions of a potential friend or relational partner aren't favorable or circumstances aren't right, you might not move beyond this first stage.
- In the **initiation stage,** first conversations occur between potential friends or romantic partners, with each person responding to the other's questions as both try to determine what they have in common. Nonverbal cues are important at this stage because they signal interest.
- **The exploration stage** occurs next as partners or friends begin to share more in-depth information. Minimal physical contact is typical, and the amount of time people spend together tends to be fairly limited as the relationship begins to build.
- If people proceed to the **intensification stage,** they start to depend on each other for self-confirmation, meaning that each partner's or friend's opinion of or feeling about the other weighs more heavily than the opinions of other people. Partners spend more time together in a wider variety of activities, adopt more intimate physical distance and contact, and personalize their language. The frequency and level of shared personal information increase, and the two people may decide to label their connection. (Friends may move to "best friend" status.)
- The top level of relationship escalation is the **intimacy stage,** in which partners provide primary confirmation of each other's self-concept and communication is highly personalized and synchronized. Partners talk about anything and everything, and a commitment to maintaining a romantic relationship might even be formalized and socially recognized, such as with a decision to marry or form a legal union. Romantic partners share an understanding of each other's language and nonverbal cues and have a great deal of physical contact. Reaching this stage takes time—time to build trust, share highly personal information, observe each other in various situations, and create an emotional bond and commitment.

pre-interaction awareness stage
The stage of becoming aware of one's attraction to another person and observing that person but not actually interacting.

initiation stage
The first contact with a person with whom one desires a relationship; usually characterized by asking and answering questions.

exploration stage
The stage that involves more in-depth interactions.

intensification stage
The stage in which partners begin to depend on each other for self-confirmation; characterized by more shared activities, more time spent together, more intimate physical distance and contact, and personalized language.

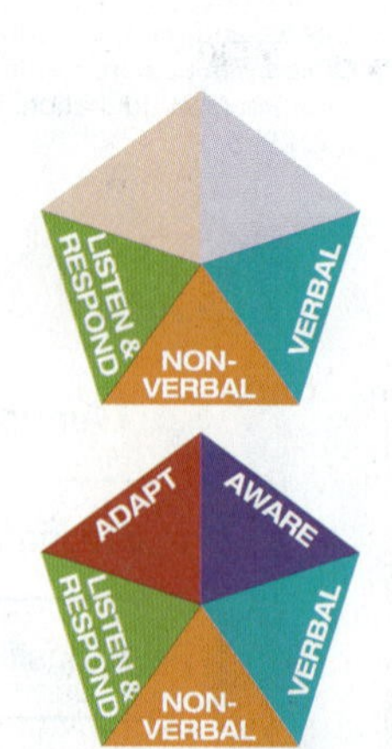

intimacy stage
The stage in which partners provide primary confirmation of each other's self-concept; characterized by highly personalized and synchronized verbal and nonverbal communication.

This is a nice and tidy model of what *may* happen as a relationship progresses, but we all know that relationships can be messier than this. Some people move through relational stages very quickly. We probably all know people whose relationships were extremely physical and perhaps sexual from the very start. Are those relationships doomed because they didn't follow set or prescribed paths for development? No, some relationships may just proceed through stages faster than others. Extremely physical or sexual relationships may burn out quickly, however, because they lack the emotional foundation necessary to survive. Partners may have difficulty developing an emotional connection or finding things in common once the physical spark wanes.

At the intensification stage, a couple's relationship becomes the central focus of their lives.
Jupiterimages/Stockbyte/Getty Images

Relational De-Escalation

Sometimes relationships begin to unravel, some to the point of termination. But as you may already know, a relationship in decline doesn't simply go down the same way it went up; it's not a mere reversal of the escalation process.[28] Relational de-escalation contains the following six stages:

- The **turmoil stage** comes first in a relationship's demise and is characterized by increased conflict as partners find faults in each other. The definition of the relationship loses clarity, and mutual acceptance declines. Conversations are tense, difficult, and forced.
- The **stagnation stage** occurs when the relationship loses its vitality and partners take each other for granted. Communication and physical contact decrease. Partners or friends spend less time together but don't necessarily engage in conflict. People in a stagnating relationship go through the motions of an intimate relationship without the commitment or joy. But a stagnating relationship can be salvaged. People can repair, redefine, and revitalize their relationship and return to intimacy.
- If turmoil or stagnation continues, friends or partners will likely experience the **de-intensification stage,** which involves increased physical, emotional, and psychological distance; significantly decreased interaction; and decreased dependence on each other for self-confirmation. Partners might discuss the definition of their relationship, question its future, and assess each other's level of dissatisfaction.
- After de-intensification, the **individualization stage occurs**, in which partners tend to define their lives more as individuals and less as a couple or unit. Interactions are limited; both partners tend to turn to others for self-concept confirmation.

turmoil stage
The stage characterized by increased conflict, less mutual acceptance, a tense communication climate, and an unclear relationship definition.

stagnation stage
The stage in which a relationship loses its vitality, partners begin to take each other for granted, and communication and physical contact decline.

de-intensification stage
The stage involving significantly decreased interaction, increased distance, and decreased dependence on one's partner for self-confirmation.

individualization stage
The stage in which partners define their lives more as individuals and less as a couple.

RECAP

Relational Escalation

Stage	Explanation
Pre-Interaction Awareness	You become aware of your attraction to someone and begin to observe that person.
Initiation	You initiate contact with the person with whom you want a relationship.
Exploration	Interactions deepen as questions and answers elicit more information from partners.
Intensification	Partners begin to depend on each other for confirmation of their self-concepts. They spend more time together, engage in more intimate touch, and personalize their language.
Intimacy	Partners provide primary confirmation of each other's self-concept. Verbally, language is highly personalized; nonverbal behaviors are synchronized.

Communication & ETHICS

Infidelity in Cyberspace: Is It Cheating If You Don't Actually Touch?

This topic may be more about morality than ethics, but it always sparks lively debate. What's your view of cyberinfidelity? Should technologically mediated liaisons outside of one's primary romantic relationship be viewed as breaches of ethics or morals or simply as signs of the times?

We all know that technology helps us keep in touch with important people in our lives, including our romantic partners. But another use is to establish and maintain romantic connections with people other than our primary romantic partners.[29] As one source suggests, "Fueling our sexual freedom is our ability to pursue a fling without even opening the front door; we can simply open a laptop."[30] Such external liaisons may form through common interests and not begin as sexual relationships, but cyberrelationships can quickly escalate. How many relationships have gone down in flames because one partner checked text messages or voice mail on the other's phone and found evidence of infidelity?

Most people view in-person relational infidelity as a deal breaker. Even people who haven't experienced it say that they would respond negatively to a partner's infidelity.[31] But some people view **cyberinfidelity** (online sexual activity outside of one's in-person, monogamous relationship) differently because no physical consummation actually occurs. In this view, if the connection is virtual, it's not real; therefore, it's not cheating.[32] Do you find this logic persuasive?

What if the cybersex involves sexting not just words but also explicit photos? What about making sexual use of the computer or phone device's video chat capabilities? Does that activity now qualify as infidelity because people can see each other being sexual, whereas text is just words that spark the imagination?

Researchers have asked people these questions.[33] One study found that 41 percent of respondents didn't believe online sexual activity was cheating on a partner under any circumstances. Some deemed it cheating only if a person engaged in cybersex repeatedly with the same person, if webcams were used, or if the online sex led to phone sex. Thirty-three percent believed that any form of online sex was cheating and that it was just as much an act of infidelity as in-person sex with someone other than one's partner. Where do you stand on the issue?

cyberinfidelity
Online sexual activity outside of one's in-person, monogamous relationship.

separation stage
The stage in which individuals make an intentional decision to minimize or eliminate further interpersonal interaction.

post-interaction stage
The bottom, or final, stage in relational de-escalation, which represents the lasting effects of a relationship on the self.

For romantic partners, physical intimacy is at an all-time low, if not nonexistent, and nonverbal distance is easily detected.

- In the **separation stage,** individuals make an intentional decision to minimize or eliminate further interaction. If they share custody of children, attend mutual family gatherings, or work at the same place, the nature of their interaction noticeably changes. They divide property, resources, and friends. Interactions in this stage are increasingly tense and difficult, especially if the relationship has been intimate.
- The final level in de-escalation is the **post-interaction stage**. It represents the lasting effects the relationship has on the self and others. Relationships—even failed ones—are powerful experiences in our lives, so the effects continue even after the relationship has ended. In this stage, partners engage in "grave dressing," meaning that they create a public statement for people who ask why they broke up or are no longer friends.[34] Sometimes self-esteem gets battered during the final stages of a relationship, so partners work to regain a healthy sense of self.

RECAP

Relational De-Escalation

Stage	Explanation
Turmoil	Partners take each other for granted and have more conflict. They exhibit less mutual acceptance, their communication climate is tense, and their relationship definition is unclear.
Stagnation	The relationship loses its vitality, partners begin to take each other for granted, and communication and physical contact decline.
De-Intensification	Partners significantly decrease their interaction and their dependence on each other for self-confirmation; they increase their physical distance.
Individualization	Partners define their lives more as individuals and less as a couple.
Separation	Partners make an intentional decision to minimize or eliminate further interpersonal interaction.
Post-Interaction	This is the bottom or final level in relational de-escalation; it represents the lasting effects of a relationship on the individuals.

Relationship Dissolution (a.k.a. the Breakup)

8.3 Summarize research findings on relationship dissolution, including communication in the on-again/off-again relationship and the postdissolutional relationship.

Friendships can fade away, marriages can end in divorce, and romantic partners can break up—we

United Media/Universal Uclick

all know this. **Relationship dissolution** is the research term for relational endings, possibly preferred because "relationship termination" has connotations of death.[35] Since ending relationships is an inescapable part of everybody's life, let's take a moment to think about communication and breakups, as well as what happens to a relationship after a breakup.

Best Practices in Breaking Up

Friendships tend to end (or transition into a different level) more gradually than romantic relationships, sometimes just fading away because of distance or changed circumstances or priorities. But it's bewildering when romantic relationships just fade away (a phenomenon known as "ghosting"). People are usually left wondering what happened.[36] Without knowing what happened, it's hard to gain some growth from the experience. So let's focus here on what research can teach us about appropriate romantic relationship endings.

With the popularity of texting, you may know someone who was broken up with via text message; perhaps you have been on the short end of that stick. Let's be clear (and blunt) about this: It's a coward's way to end a relationship. We understand that it saves the "dumper" time and emotional angst, not having to witness in person the "dumpee's" reaction, but even in a superficial, short-term relationship, breaking up at a distance shows no respect for the other person. It also doesn't do your reputation any favors, since perpetrating a text breakup reveals to others the kind of relational partner you are, even in short-term liaisons.

One study examined college students' methods of delivering a breakup message.[37] The researchers found that 43 percent of subjects' breakups were accomplished face to face; 32 percent were handled through a phone call; 10 percent were conveyed through instant messaging via computer; 8 percent were done in an e-mail message; 2 percent used a written letter; and another 2 percent used a third party, such as a friend, to be the bearer of the bad news. (Who would volunteer for *that* gig?) Some students used combinations of these methods. None said that they'd broken up with someone via text, explaining that they would be even angrier and more upset if someone broke up with them by text. The takeaway from this study is that the predominant breakup method reported by these students was the good old-fashioned face-to-face conversation, which is also how they would prefer someone break up with them.

So on the basis of what research tells us, here's some advice on communication and breaking up, should you find yourself needing to end a romantic relationship someday (or processing how someone broke up with you):

- *Don't be a ghost.* Avoid simply expanding distance by not calling someone back (ever), ignoring messages, avoiding places and situations where you might run into the person, and hoping the person will get the hint. These methods generate

relationship dissolution
Ending a relationship.

confusion and ambiguity, causing undue hurt to the target of the breakup.[38] Relational fuzziness can also keep both parties from moving on.

- *Give the other person a chance to respond.* Using a mediated channel to end a relationship may make it easier on the dumper but is terrible for the dumpee (and, some would argue, unethical). Without even a short conversation, the person is cut off from a full explanation, a chance at negotiation, and the opportunity to express her or his feelings.[39]
- *Do it face to face.* A face-to-face interaction offers a chance to exercise your communication skills. Although the "dreaded conversation" is rarely pleasant, resist the instinct to duck out or postpone. Force yourself to have a conversation with the person.[40] Thinking to yourself, "If I see the person, I might not be able to go through with it" is no excuse to avoid or put off the inevitable. Both parties will retain more dignity and self-respect through a breakup conversation than by being denied the opportunity to talk.
- *Avoid the trite "let's still be friends" line.* For most people in the position of being dumped, the last thing they want to do or can even conceive of is being friends with a former romantic partner.[41] It's understandable for a dumper to try to soften the blow or retain some kind of connection to the dumpee, but it's selfish to expect the other person to change relationship definition easily or quickly. Maybe, with time, something can be salvaged that works for both parties.
- *Also avoid the dreaded and trite "It's not you—it's me" explanation.* People getting dumped don't tend to believe that anyway. When someone says to us, "It's not you, it's me," most of us will think, "That means it's me." Granted, there are times when we may agree with the person—it really *is* them. But this line is overused, hurtful, and simply not believable in most circumstances. It does more damage than it saves hurt.
- *Don't use the infamous "timing" explanation either.* You may be tempted to trot out the classic line "It's just not a good time for me right now to be in a relationship." Most of us don't believe that. Instead, most dumpees would prefer that the dumper be honest enough to tell them that the relationship just isn't what the dumper wants.

After the Breakup: Communicating with an Ex

People may change the profile of their relationship, but that doesn't mean it can't change *again.* How many people do you know who "break up to make up"?

Research has begun to investigate the **on-again/off-again relationship** (also called "cyclical" or "habitual"), which is quite common.[42] Communication scholar René Dailey has conducted extensive research on this form of dating relationship, which occurs when people get back together with the same partner, sometimes over and over again. Some people return to a partner out of habit or because the relationship is comfortable or known, even if it's not great. Others experience turning points, key events such as infidelity and the forgiveness that can come with a relational transgression, that cause breakups and reconciliations.[43]

Studies also focus on the ways people create or reinvent a connection once they've broken up. Yes, some people actually want to have a relationship of some form with an ex, as challenging as that may be. The **postdissolutional relationship** has been defined as "the relationship formed between dating partners after their romance terminates."[44] (The term doesn't apply to divorced couples who negotiate a connection once their marriage has ended.) The factors that may determine whether this form of relationship can be successful include how much the partners like each other, how long the partners were together romantically (the longer the romantic relationship, the less successful the postrelationship), and how much the partners hope they will get back together romantically.[45]

on-again/off-again relationship
A relationship characterized by repeated breakups and reconciliations.

postdissolutional relationship
The relationship formed between dating partners after their romance terminates.

Tensions in Relationships: The Dialectical Perspective

8.4 Discuss relational dialectics and three primary tensions in relationships.

Relationships are living, breathing, evolving, dynamic entities; no two are the same. One way to view relationships, known as **relational dialectics** or the dialectical perspective, was developed by communication scholars Leslie Baxter and Barbara Montgomery.[46] Dialectics help us understand the messy, often illogical nature of interpersonal relationships. The theory describes tensions people in relationships commonly face, but by *tensions,* we don't mean to imply something negative. A dialectical perspective suggests that relationship issues are better understood in terms of push–pull dynamics.[47] Although tensions can occur in all sorts of relationships—among family members, between coworkers, within friendships—they're arguably most revealing of the romantic relationship.

Researchers have identified multiple tensions. We focus on the following three primary issues that most relational partners face:

- *Integration–separation: autonomy versus connection.* Although people want to be connected to others and feel they're part of a couple or group, they also want to be self-sufficient and independent. The amount of autonomy partners desire varies widely, making this tension one of the most difficult to confront. Early on, relational partners tend to spend as much time together as possible, but when a time-consuming activity or work intrudes, friends or family members demand some time, or one partner wants a night out without the other, autonomy-versus-connection conflict can arise.[48] Partners can benefit from honest, open, nondefensive communication about this tension, proactively negotiating how much time they expect to spend together and apart. Even the amount of cell phone or text contact may need to be negotiated between partners, as research shows that calling, texting, and overuse of mobile phones between partners can heighten this tension.[49]
- *Stability–change: predictability versus novelty.* Although people are drawn to stability and consistency in a relationship, we're also drawn to excitement and unpredictability. Becoming comfortable with a relationship's ebb and flow can be a challenge.[50] Typically, at the start of a relationship, people are happy with the status quo, emphasizing a partner's positive points and glossing over less-desirable personality traits or behaviors. Over time, however, people may have more difficulty accepting each other as they are; one partner may try to change the other. Being aware that this tension is likely to emerge at some point—or several points—within a relationship is key, because the amount of persuasion or influence that goes on in a relationship is associated with satisfaction.
- *Expression–privacy: openness versus closedness.* We all differ in how open we wish to be (or are comfortable being) and our need for privacy. If relational partners are dramatically different in this area, they'll need to be proactive and work hard to manage this tension, or it might be a deal breaker. Couples, friends, even family members may feel a push–pull, with one person in the relationship wanting complete openness and equating openness with trust while the other wants to retain a degree of privacy and connects privacy with individual identity.[51] One topic in particular illustrates this tension: the discussion between romantic relational partners of past relationships, especially sexual ones. One partner may want to reveal all and know all, whereas the other may not wish to bring the past into the present. Both positions—and all points in between—are legitimate, but differences in partners' positions create a tension that typically has to be addressed for a relationship of any kind to flourish.

relational dialectics
A perspective that views interpersonal relationships as constantly changing rather than stable and that revolves around how relational partners manage tensions.

As the novelty wears off in relationships, we may find that we are bored with the predictability of our partner. How can you balance stability and change in your own relationships?
Rido/Shutterstock

Managing Interpersonal Conflict

8.5 Summarize the definition and seven types of interpersonal conflict; key characteristics of nonconfrontational, confrontational, and cooperative styles of conflict management; and ways in which people can cooperate in conflict situations by managing their emotions, managing information, managing goals, and managing the problem.

We live in a world full of conflict. Whether it's a political coup in a foreign country or a disturbance generated by extremist groups right here at home, conflict on a global scale seems inevitable. Although conflicts have always existed throughout the world, developing an understanding of conflict and effective communication skills to manage it begins one on one, in our day-to-day relationships. Conflict is rooted in interpersonal communication.

Interpersonal conflict is a struggle that occurs when people cannot agree on a way to meet their needs. If needs or goals are incompatible, if there are too few resources to satisfy them, or if individuals opt to compete rather than to cooperate to satisfy them, conflict occurs. The intensity of a conflict usually relates to the intensity of the unmet needs. The bedrock of all conflict is differences—different goals, experiences, expectations, and so forth.[52] Before we explore how to better manage and resolve conflict, let's first examine the nature of conflict and how it functions in interpersonal relationships.

Types of Conflict

interpersonal conflict
A struggle that occurs when people cannot agree on a way to meet their needs.

constructive conflict
Conflict characterized by cooperation in dealing with differences; helps build new insights and patterns in a relationship.

destructive conflict
Conflict characterized by a lack of cooperation in dealing with differences; dismantles relationships without restoring them.

Conflict can be constructive or destructive.[53] To construct something is to build or make something new. Characterized by cooperation in dealing with differences, **constructive conflict** can help identify which elements of a relationship need to change or be improved so that new patterns are established. Here's an example:

Jake: You know, I'm getting tired of always going to your parents' on Sundays. It's like we're in a rut or something. Just one weekend, I'd like to have a Sunday with no schedule or agenda.

Julie: Jake, I thought you liked going over there, because my mom's such a good cook and you and dad are working on that project together. Plus, it's one of the few times I get to spend time with my folks.

Jake: Well, I do like going over there, but not every weekend.

Julie: I didn't realize you were starting to resent it or feel like we were in a rut. Let's figure something out.

Notice that Julie transforms the issue of disagreement into a topic for discussion and relational adjustment. If Jake hadn't expressed his dissatisfaction, the issue might have taken on larger proportions. He might have expressed his feelings of being in a rut in a more hurtful way later on. A well-managed disagreement that includes expressing one's own needs or revising goals can lead people to examine and then revitalize their relationship. Constructive conflict enables both people to view a disagreement from different perspectives, even if the information shared seems negative at first.

A rapidly spiraling **destructive conflict** can do a great deal of damage. A conflict that starts over a seemingly small issue can increase in intensity as other issues and differences are brought into the discussion. Such destructive escalation blocks off options for managing differences and makes a win–win solution more elusive. The primary characteristic of destructive conflict is a lack of flexibility in responding to others.[54] Combatants view their differences from a win–lose perspective rather than looking for solutions that allow each individual to gain. This form of conflict dismantles relationships without restoring them. If both individuals are dissatisfied with the outcome of the conflict, it has been more destructive than constructive.

In their book on interpersonal conflict, William Wilmot and Joyce Hocker discuss six hallmarks of constructive conflict:[55]

1. *People change.* In relationships, people are involved with each other. In conflict, people must work hard to stay involved with each other, because an interaction that escalates into conflict can pull people apart. Flexibility and a willingness to change are key.
2. *People interact with an intent to learn instead of an intent to protect themselves.* You can learn a great deal about yourself, your partner, and your relationship if you approach conflict as a learning experience—one that will take your relationship forward instead of allowing it to stagnate or regress. Protecting yourself against conflict doesn't help a relationship grow.
3. *People don't stay stuck in conflict when the conflict is constructive.* Destructive conflict can make you feel stuck in one place in a relationship. Constructive conflict is a dynamic process that emerges, plays out, and recedes.
4. *Constructive conflict enhances self-esteem in the participants.* You probably don't associate conflict with enhanced self-esteem, because most of us think of conflict as negative and destructive. However, constructive conflict brings energy and productivity to a relationship and provides partners with a more honest, complete picture of themselves.
5. *Constructive conflicts are characterized by a relationship focus instead of a purely individualistic focus.* If parties in a conflict focus on the relationship instead of themselves, the conflict will more likely be constructive than destructive. Participants should emphasize the "we" over the "I" so that conflict is seen as an experience that builds the relationship.
6. *Constructive conflict is primarily cooperative.* Conflict built on competition, power struggles, and self-interest will destroy a relationship. Conversely, a cooperative, win–win approach to conflict will open the door for greater growth.

Communication scholars Gerald Miller and Mark Steinberg provide three categories of conflict:[56]

- **Pseudoconflict** reflects a basic lack of understanding; one person misunderstands the meaning in a message.
- **Simple conflict** stems from differences in ideas, definitions, perceptions, or goals.
- **Ego conflict** occurs when conflict gets personal, such that people attack each other's self-esteem.

pseudoconflict
Conflict stemming from a lack of understanding.

simple conflict
Conflict over differences in ideas, definitions, perceptions, or goals.

ego conflict
Conflict based on personal issues in which people attack each other's self-esteem.

serial arguments
Argumentative episodes focused on the same issue that occur at least twice.

Let's use an example to help distinguish these types. Two people start out with a simple misunderstanding about the time they were supposed to meet (pseudoconflict). If the misunderstanding escalates, they might argue over their varying perceptions of what being "on time" means (simple conflict), especially if they come from different cultural backgrounds. If the disagreement degenerates and becomes personal, such as one person accusing the other of something deeper than mere misunderstanding (as in "You did this on purpose" or "You're *always* late"), an ego conflict has erupted out of a simple conflict.

Two other types of conflict are worthy of note. First, people in ongoing relationships often have **serial arguments**, defined as "argumentative episodes focused on a given issue that occur at least twice."[57] How many times have you heard someone complain, "We have this same argument over and over"? Serial arguments typically involve repetitious, highly negative verbal communication (such as name calling) and negative nonverbal cues (yelling or aggressive movements). They usually spiral and are rarely productive. They engender mutual hostility in the partners and create a pattern that's very hard to break. Over time, unchecked serial arguments have an adverse effect on relationships and can erode self-esteem.

Dave Coverly/The Cartoonist Group

Communication & DIVERSITY

Coping with Conflict across Cultures

Interpersonal conflict is difficult to manage, but cross-cultural conflict can be overwhelming. Some people are trained in negotiation and mediation techniques so that they can facilitate peaceful relations between nations and peoples. But what if you're not planning to become an international negotiator? What if you simply want to know a few things to keep from being tossed in jail in a foreign country?

Intercultural communication scholars have written extensively on this subject and have produced some insightful information that can help you anticipate and avoid intercultural conflict.[58] People from individualistic cultures, such as the United States, emphasize the importance of the individual over the group. Those in collectivistic cultures, such as Japanese people, emphasize group rather than individual achievement. These differing values contribute to intercultural conflict.

Below are seven assumptions about conflict that individualistic cultures hold and seven assumptions about conflict that collectivistic cultures hold. Compare the lists, assessing the differences. Members of different cultural groups not only have different views of conflict, but also have different ways of dealing with or managing conflict. Research any countries you'll be visiting or moving to so that you understand how the basic cultural values differ from those of your home country.

Individualistic Cultures

1. The purpose of conflict is to air major differences and problems.
2. Conflict can be either functional or dysfunctional.
3. Repressed, unconfronted problems can lead to dysfunctional conflict.
4. Functional conflict provides an opportunity for solving problems.
5. Substantive or informational issues should be handled separately from relational issues.
6. Conflict should be handled directly and openly.
7. Effective conflict management should be a problem-solving activity with a win–win outcome.

Collectivistic Cultures

1. Conflict is damaging to self-respect and relational harmony; it should be avoided as much as possible.
2. For the most part, conflict is dysfunctional.
3. Conflict signals emotional immaturity and a lack of self-discipline.
4. Conflict provides a testing ground for skillful negotiation and face-saving.
5. Substantive and relational issues are always intertwined.
6. Conflict should be handled discreetly and subtly.
7. Effective conflict management should be a face-saving negotiation game with a win–win outcome.

Another form of conflict that occurs within interpersonal relationships is the **irresolvable or intractable conflict**, which occurs when one or both of the parties deem the conflict impossible to resolve.[59] A person who holds the view that an argument is irresolvable may not necessarily state that view out in the open, choosing simply to believe that compromise is impossible. She or he may adopt a "go along to get along" approach to appease the other person, or tolerate the situation rather than confronting the person and attempting to resolve it.

Properties of Conflict

It's surprising (and disconcerting) when people in relationships say, "We just get along so well. We belong together because we've never even had a fight." Conflict is a normal, inevitable element of relationships. While we don't advocate staging or picking a fight with a partner as an experiment, we do believe that it's worrisome to commit to a person when you don't know how she or he handles conflict. If your partner or close friend is a screamer and you prefer to walk away from a conflict in silent protest, your relationship is headed for very rough waters. One of the best ways to improve a relationship is to understand conflict—how it functions; how each person in a relationship approaches, processes, and responds to conflict; and how we can better manage conflict when it inevitably arises.[60]

irresolvable (intractable) conflict
A conflict that one or both parties deem impossible to resolve.

CONFLICT INVOLVES POWER One of the most significant elements in interpersonal relationships is power.[61] We might not realize it, but distributing power between partners requires a lot of subtle negotiation. Without this negotiation, conflict can become rampant. Power has been defined in a variety of ways, but for our purposes, **interpersonal power** means the ability to influence another in the direction we desire—to get another person to do what we want.[62] It also involves the ability to resist others' influences on us.[63] Perhaps it's easier to think of it in terms of who has more *control* in a relationship rather than to use the term *power.*

Most interactions, including conflicts, involve some level of power or control. If you ask a friend to go to a movie with you, you are attempting to influence him or her. If the answer is no, your friend is mustering resistance and demonstrating power over you. If you don't like the negative response, you might attempt to assert control once more, perhaps by offering to buy your friend's ticket or to drive.

CONFLICT MAY INVOLVE ASSERTIVE OR AGGRESSIVE COMMUNICATION

Sometimes our emotions cause us to communicate aggressively when assertive communication would be preferable. You may think of assertive and aggressive communication as being the same thing, but they're actually different. **Assertive communication** takes the other person's feelings and rights into account; **aggressive communication** doesn't. Let's say you experience a mix-up with a close friend over plans for the weekend. You get your signals crossed and don't end up getting together. When you next see your friend, you have the choice of responding to your frustration over the situation in a passive, assertive, or aggressive manner. You could be passive and say nothing, which some people choose to do even when they've been wronged, a phenomenon known as self-silencing.[64] The passive approach tends merely to internalize frustration, which may build into rage that erupts later.

Another option is to blow up at your friend in an aggressive, self-oriented approach that doesn't take into account your friend's rights. Unfortunately, this is the tactic of choice for some people, especially if they have a great deal of anxiety and feel justified taking out their frustrations on others. An aggressive approach rarely achieves one's objectives.

Clearly, an assertive approach to conflict is best—for ourselves and for the people we interact with. It's important to assert yourself and express your perception of a problem to the person who can best correct or clear it up rather than blowing off steam to an innocent bystander or third party. Communicating assertively means that you explain your concerns or cause for disagreement in a direct and firm manner, staying in control of your emotions but not allowing yourself to be bullied or discounted, while also taking your receiver's rights into account.[65]

An assertive response to the mix-up with your friend might be something like this: "Hey, we were supposed to get together last weekend, but you never called. What happened?" In this statement, you express your perception of the situation, but you ask the other person for her or his perception, rather than aggressively saying something in an angry tone that would make the other person defensive, such as "Why did you leave me hanging when we made plans?" If the person offers a lame excuse, an assertive follow-up might be "Well, I just want you to know that I don't like what happened. It's too late now but I just hope it doesn't happen again." If you communicate in this manner, you're far more likely to reach a positive resolution to any conflicts than if you behave passively or aggressively.[66]

Styles of Managing Conflict

Scholars in the communication discipline like to talk about conflict in terms of *management,* meaning that interpersonal communication can help people work through and handle conflict so that something positive results. What's your approach to managing interpersonal conflict: fight or flight? Do you tackle conflict head-on or seek ways to remove yourself from it? Most of us don't have a single way of dealing with disagreements, but we do have a tendency to manage conflict by following patterns we learned early in life and have used before.[67]

interpersonal power
The ability to influence another in the direction one desires; getting another person to do what one wants.

assertive communication
Communication that takes a listener's feelings and rights into account.

aggressive communication
Self-serving communication that does not take a listener's feelings and rights into account.

nonconfrontational style
A conflict management style that involves backing off, avoiding conflict, or giving in to the other person.

confrontational style
A win–lose approach to conflict management in which one person wants control and to win at the expense of the other.

cooperative style
A conflict management style in which conflict is viewed as a set of problems to be solved rather than as a competition in which one person wins and another loses.

Researchers have attempted to identify styles of conflict management. One widely accepted approach organizes conflict styles into three types: (1) nonconfrontational, (2) confrontational or controlling, and (3) cooperative (also known as a *solution orientation*).[68]

NONCONFRONTATIONAL STYLE One conflict management style is to avoid conflict altogether, becoming aloof or giving in to the other person before or when a conflict emerges, which can have a chilling or silencing effect on a relationship.[69] Research shows that when conflict arises during problem-solving discussions, people who exhibit a **nonconfrontational style** are perceived as incompetent.[70] This dynamic often creates a lose–lose situation, where neither party feels the issue has been effectively addressed; instead, it has perhaps merely been postponed.

CONFRONTATIONAL STYLE Each of us has some need to control others, but some people always want to dominate and make sure their objectives are achieved. In managing conflict, people with a **confrontational style** have a win–lose philosophy. They want to win at the expense of others, claim victory over their opponents, and control people and situations. They focus on themselves and usually ignore the needs of others. Confronters often resort to blaming or seeking a scapegoat rather than assuming responsibility for a conflict. For example, a confronter may claim, "I didn't do it," "Don't look at me," or "It's not my fault." If this strategy doesn't work, confronters may try hostile name calling, personal attacks, or threats.

COOPERATIVE STYLE Those who have a **cooperative style** of conflict management view conflict as a set of problems to be solved rather than as a competition in which one person wins and another loses. They work to foster a win–win climate by using the following techniques:[71]

- *Separate the people from the problem.* Leave personal grievances out of the discussion. Describe problems without making judgmental statements about personalities.
- *Focus on shared interests.* Emphasize common interests, values, and goals by asking such questions as "What do we both want?" "What do we both value?" and "Where do we already agree?"
- *Generate many options to solve the problem.* Use brainstorming and other techniques to generate alternative solutions.
- *Base decisions on objective criteria.* Try to establish standards for an acceptable solution to a problem. These standards may involve costs, timing, and other factors.

People with a confrontational or win–lose approach to conflict may spend more effort trying to assign or avoid the blame for a problem than solving it.
Mario Beauregard/Fotolia

Conflict Management Skills

As we saw in the previous section, nonconfrontational and confrontational styles of conflict management don't solve problems effectively, nor do they foster healthy relationships. Managing conflict, especially emotionally charged conflict, isn't easy. Even with a fully developed set of skills, you shouldn't expect to melt tensions and resolve disagreements instantaneously. However, the following skills that we touched on in our discussion of the cooperative style can help you generate options that promote understanding and provide a framework for cooperation.[72]

MANAGE EMOTIONS Suppose you've been working for weeks on a group project for an important class. The project has a firm deadline that your professor will no doubt enforce. You submitted your portion of the project to your group members two weeks ago. Today you check in with the group and discover that very little has been done since you completed your portion. Your grade is on the line; you feel angry and frustrated. How should you respond? Maybe you're tempted to scream at your classmates. Maybe you decide to go to the professor and complain. Here's our best advice at a moment like this: Try to avoid taking action when you're in an emotional state. You may regret what you say, and you'll probably escalate the situation into a heated conflict, making things worse.

The first sign that we're in a conflict situation may be a combination of anger, frustration, and fear that sweeps over us. In actuality, anger often isn't the predominant emotion generated by conflict. Many of us are unprepared for the aching, lonely, sad, and forlorn feelings that can emerge in conflict.[73] As tall an order as it is, it's important to try to understand the other person's feelings and take the emotion of the situation seriously.[74] Here are some specific strategies you can draw on when an intense emotional response to conflict clouds your judgment and decision-making skills:[75]

RECAP

Conflict Management Styles

Nonconfrontational	A person avoids conflict and may become aloof or give in to another person just to stave off a conflict. This approach can be viewed as a lose–lose framework because issues aren't dealt with and conflict is likely to recur.
Confrontational	A person wants to manipulate others by blaming and making threats. This approach sets up a win–lose framework.
Cooperative	A person seeks mutually agreeable resolutions to manage differences and works within a win–win framework. This is a cooperative approach. It: • Separates people from problems. • Focuses on shared interests. • Generates many options to solve problems. • Bases decisions on objective criteria.

- *Select a mutually acceptable time and place to discuss a conflict.* If you're upset or tired (or really hungry), you're at risk for an emotion-charged confrontation. If you ambush someone with an angry attack, you can't expect that person to be in a productive frame of mind. Give yourself time to cool off, rest, or have a meal before you try to resolve a conflict. In the case of the group project, you could call a meeting for later in the week. Take the intervening time to gain control of your feelings and think things through.
- *Plan your message.* If you approach someone to discuss a disagreement, take care to organize your message, perhaps even on paper. Identify your goal and determine what outcome you would like; don't barge in unprepared and dump your emotions on others.

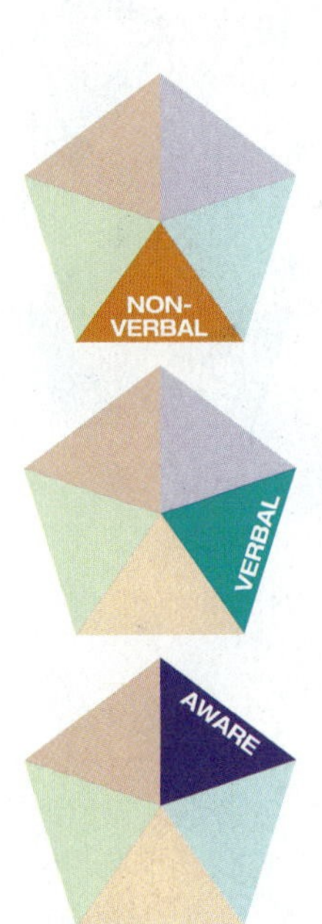

- *Monitor nonverbal messages.* Nonverbal communication plays a key role in managing an emotional climate. Monitor your own and others' nonverbal cues to defuse an emotionally charged situation. Speak evenly, use direct eye contact, and maintain a calm facial expression and body position to signal that you wish to collaborate rather than control.
- *Avoid personal attacks, name calling, profanity, and emotional overstatement.* Threats and bad language can turn a minor conflict into an all-out war. When people feel attacked, they usually respond defensively. Avoid exaggerating your emotions. If you say you're *irritated* or *annoyed* rather than *furious,* you can still communicate your feelings, but you'll take the sting out of your description.
- *Use self-talk.* Instead of lashing out at someone, the better tactic is to pause, take a slow deep breath, and talk yourself down off your emotional ledge. You may think that talking to yourself is an eccentricity, but thoughts are directly linked to feelings. The messages we tell ourselves play a major role in how we feel and respond to others.[76]

MANAGE INFORMATION Because uncertainty, misinformation, and misunderstanding are often by-products of conflict and disagreement, skills that promote mutual understanding are important components of cooperative conflict management. The following skills can help you enhance the quality of communication during conflict:

- *Clearly describe the conflict-producing events.* Instead of blurting out complaints in a random order, try to deliver a brief, well-organized, chronological presentation. In our example of the group project situation, you could offer your perspective

When communicating to resolve a conflict, try to "own" your communication by using "I" language rather than accusatory "you" language.
Jack Hollingsworth/Photodisc/Getty Images

on what created the conflict, sequencing the events and describing them dispassionately so that your fellow group members end up sharing your understanding of the problem.

- *"Own" your statements by using descriptive "I" language.* Use "I" language instead of "you" language to create a supportive climate. "I feel upset when it seems as if little is getting done and we're running the risk of not making our deadline" is an example of an "I" statement you could make to your group members. The statement describes your feelings as your own and keeps the issue manageable.
- *Use effective listening skills.* Managing information is a two-way process. Whether you're describing a conflict situation to someone or that individual is bringing a conflict to your attention, good listening skills are invaluable. Give your full attention to other speakers so that you can fully understand their perspectives, and then respond appropriately.
- *Check your understanding of what others say and do.* Checking perceptions is vital when emotions run high. If you're genuinely unsure about facts, issues, or major ideas addressed during a conflict, ask questions instead of barreling ahead with solutions. Then summarize your understanding of the information, checking key points to make sure that you comprehend the message.

MANAGE GOALS Conflict is goal-driven; people involved in an interpersonal conflict want something, and for some reason—competitiveness, scarce resources, or lack of understanding—goals appear to be in conflict. To manage conflict, here are some techniques that will help you seek an accurate understanding of everyone's goals and identify where they overlap:

- *Identify everyone's goals.* Most goals can be phrased in terms of wants or desired outcomes. In the group project example, suppose you express to your fellow group members your goal of turning the project in on time. Next, it's useful to identify the goals of other people involved in the conflict. Use effective describing, listening, and responding skills to determine what each conflict partner wants. Obviously, if goals are kept hidden, it will be difficult to resolve the conflict.
- *Identify where your goals and everyone else's goals overlap.* Authorities on conflict negotiation stress the importance of focusing on shared goals in seeking to

manage differences.[77] Suppose that after you explain your goal about the project deadline, another group member states that her or his goal is to make the project the best it can possibly be. These goals may be compatible, so you've identified a commonality that can help unify the group rather than keeping it splintered. But what if the goal of making the project the best means that your group will have to ask the professor for an extension on the deadline? Now you may have competing goals, but at least you've identified a central part of the problem. Framing the problem as "How can we achieve our mutual goal?" rather than arguing over differences of opinion moves the discussion to a more productive level.

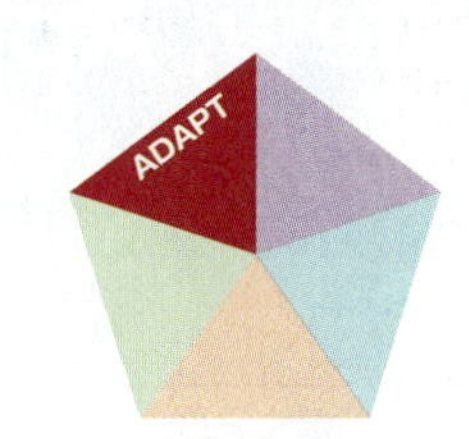

MANAGE THE PROBLEM If you can view conflicts as problems to be solved rather than battles to be won or lost, you'll better manage the issues that confront you in your relationships. Of course, not all conflicts can be easily managed and resolved. But a rational, logical approach to conflict management is more effective than emotionally flinging accusations and opinions at someone. Structuring a disagreement as a problem to solve helps manage emotions that often erupt, while also keeping the conversation focused on issues rather than personalities. As you apply a problem-solving approach to managing conflict, consider the following suggestions:

- *Define the problem before trying to solve it.* When a problem needs to be solved, we typically want to head directly for solutions. Resist that temptation, and make sure everyone fully understands the problem at hand before trying to fix it.
- *Think of lots of possible solutions.* The more possible solutions you identify and consider, the greater the likelihood that conflict will be managed successfully. If you're just batting around one or two solutions, you're limiting your options in managing the conflict.
- *Systematically discuss together the pros and the cons of each possible solution, arriving at the best decision.* After you have a list of possible solutions, honestly identify advantages and disadvantages of each solution. Determine which solution or combination of solutions best achieves the goals you and your feuding partners are trying to accomplish.

STUDY GUIDE: Review, Apply, and Assess Your Knowledge and Skill

Review Your Knowledge

The Importance of Relationships: Friends, Family, and Colleagues

8.1 Explain how the five Communication Principles for a Lifetime apply to interpersonal communication among friends, family members, and colleagues.

Relationships of all types are important in our lives, but those with friends, family, and colleagues are most critical to our overall enjoyment. The five Communication Principles for a Lifetime can be applied to each form of relationship and can improve how we communicate interpersonally with others.

Stages of Relationship Development

8.2 Identify and describe the stages of relational escalation and de-escalation.

Research has determined that relationships, particularly intimate or romantic ones, tend to develop in stages of escalation and de-escalation. Interpersonal communication is affected by the stage of a relationship; in turn, movement through the stages is facilitated by interpersonal communication.

The five stages of relational escalation are (1) preinteraction awareness, (2) initiation, (3) exploration, (4) intensification, and (5) intimacy.

The six stages of relational de-escalation are (1) turmoil, (2) stagnation, (3) de-intensification, (4) individualization, (5) separation, and (6) post-interaction.

Relationship Dissolution (a.k.a. the Breakup)

8.3 Summarize research findings on relationship dissolution, including communication in the on-again/off-again relationship and the postdissolutional relationship.

Not all relationships last, so communication skills are important when a romantic relationship, friendship, or other form of connection ends. Research shows that most people use and prefer a face-to-face channel of communication when being on both the sending and receiving end of relationship dissolution.

Tensions in Relationships: The Dialectical Perspective

8.4 Discuss relational dialectics and three primary tensions in relationships.

One approach to studying interpersonal communication in relationships is the relational dialectics perspective, which examines sets of tensions that emerge in ongoing relationships, especially romantic or intimate ones. Three tensions are particularly critical:

- Integration–separation: autonomy versus connection
- Stability–change: predictability versus novelty
- Expression–privacy: openness versus closedness

Managing Interpersonal Conflict

8.5 Summarize the definition and seven types of interpersonal conflict; key characteristics of nonconfrontational, confrontational, and cooperative styles of conflict management; and ways in which people can cooperate in conflict situations by managing their emotions, managing information, managing goals, and managing the problem.

Conflict is inevitable in relationships and is rooted in interpersonal communication. Interpersonal conflict occurs when people cannot agree on a way to meet their needs. Conflict can be constructive or destructive in a relationship, and it occurs in multiple forms: pseudoconflict, simple conflict, ego conflict, serial arguments, and irresolvable (intractable) conflict.

Conflict involves power, which may manifest itself in assertive communication or aggressive communication. Research has revealed three general styles of managing conflict: nonconfrontational, confrontational, and cooperative. In managing conflict, it's important to manage your emotions, manage the information surrounding the dispute at hand, manage competing goals that may be the root of the problem, and manage the problem rather than the emotion of the situation or the people involved in the conflict.

Key Terms

Pre-Interaction Awareness Stage, p. 180
Initiation Stage, p. 180
Exploration Stage, p. 180
Intensification Stage, p. 180
Intimacy Stage, p. 180
Turmoil Stage, p. 181
Stagnation Stage, p. 181
De-Intensification Stage, p. 181
Individualization Stage, p. 181
Cyberinfidelity, p. 182
Separation Stage, p. 182
Post-Interaction Stage, p. 182
Relationship Dissolution, p. 183
On-Again/Off-Again Relationship, p. 184
Postdissolutional Relationship, p. 184
Relational Dialectics, p. 185
Interpersonal Conflict, p. 186
Constructive Conflict, p. 186
Destructive Conflict, p. 186
Pseudoconflict, p. 187
Simple Conflict, p. 187
Ego Conflict, p. 187
Serial Arguments, p. 187
Irresolvable (Intractable) Conflict, p. 188
Interpersonal Power, p. 189
Assertive Communication, p. 189
Aggressive Communication, p. 189
Nonconfrontational Style, p. 190
Confrontational Style, p. 190
Cooperative Style, p. 190

The Principle Points

Principle One:

Be aware of your communication with yourself and others.

- Know your own interests, likes, and dislikes as you expand your circle of friends.
- Awareness and an understanding of self begin in your family.
- Perception checking with colleagues increases your awareness of yourself and your workplace.
- The first stage of relational escalation, the pre-interaction awareness stage, begins with an awareness of the self and the other person you're interested in.
- Be aware that relationships continue to affect our self-concepts even after they end.
- It's important to know your conflict management style, especially if your style differs from that of other conflict partners.
- Self-talk is appropriate in conflict because it can help you manage your emotions and think clearly.
- Check your perceptions of a conflict with trusted others.
- Be aware of your own and others' goals in conflict situations.

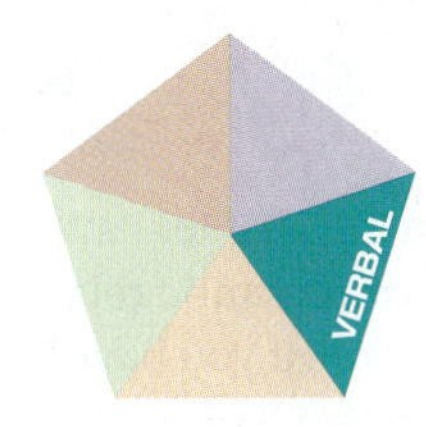

Principle Two:

Effectively use and interpret verbal messages.

- Language patterns learned as children stay with us into adulthood.
- People in advanced stages of relationships tend to use verbal communication to discuss topics that typically aren't discussed in early stages.
- When a relationship terminates or dissolves, most people prefer a face-to-face conversation rather than mediated breakup messages or having the relationship simply fade away.
- Relational partners should use effective verbal communication to work through relational dialectics or tensions in a relationship.
- Assertive communication takes a receiver's rights into account; aggressive communication doesn't.
- Managing the verbal expression of your emotions in conflict situations is an important skill.
- Plan your message carefully in a conflict situation.
- Avoid personal attacks, name calling, profanity, and emotional overstatements in conflict situations.
- Use "I" language instead of "you" language in a conflict so as to lessen defensiveness.

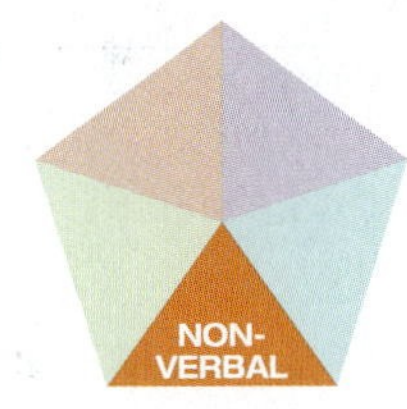

Principle Three:

Effectively use and interpret nonverbal messages.

- Nonverbal immediacy behaviors, such as eye contact and a forward body lean, are important in the maintenance of friendships, family relationships, and workplace relationships.
- People in advanced stages of relationships tend to display nonverbal behaviors that typically aren't in evidence in early stages.
- Nonverbal skills are important in your first conversations with people as you attempt to establish and escalate relationships.

- Nonverbal immediacy cues diminish when a relationship de-escalates and then terminates.
- Monitor and adapt your nonverbal behaviors in conflict situations.
- Monitor the nonverbal cues of conflict partners.

Principle Four:

Listen and respond thoughtfully to others.

- Listening is important in friendships, family relationships, and workplace relationships.
- Listening and responding appropriately are key skills that potential employers value.
- Destructive conflict is characterized by a lack of listening.
- Conflict often escalates because the parties don't listen to one another; continue to listen, even if you feel yourself becoming emotional in the conflict.

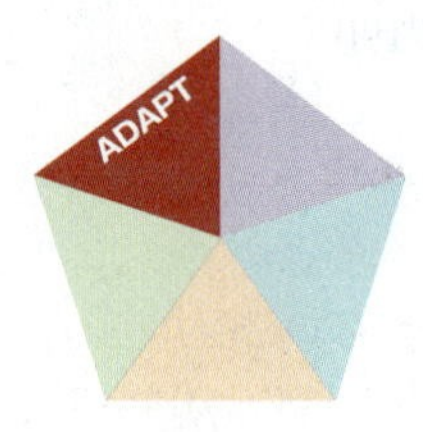

Principle Five:

Appropriately adapt messages to others.

- It's important to learn to adapt our communication in friendships, family relationships, and workplace relationships.
- Adaptation is critical for couples who face relational tensions.
- Both the on-again/off-again relationship and the postdissolutional relationship involve a good deal of adaptation in order to be successful.
- In conflict situations, partners often have to adapt to each other and admit they were wrong. Destructive conflict often involves a reluctance to adapt to other people and see the problem from their point of view.
- Be flexible and adapt to other cultures' approaches to conflict. Don't assume that your home culture's approach to conflict management is applicable in conflicts with members of other cultural groups.
- After checking your perceptions of a conflict with trusted others, adapt your communication accordingly.
- One way to adapt in a conflict is to look for overlaps between your goals and the goals of your conflict partners.

Apply Your Skill

Consider the following questions. Write your answers and/or share them with your classmates:

1. How have your friendships changed since you were younger? How do you expect your long-term friendships to develop as you get older?
2. How well does the description of relational escalation in this chapter match how your relationships have developed? How did your process differ, if it did?
3. Imagine one your friends wants to break up with a romantic partner. Using the advice in this chapter, what suggestions would you give your friend for accomplishing the breakup ethically and with as little pain as possible for both parties?
4. Which of the three tensions described in this chapter have you experienced in your friendships or romantic relationships? How did you resolve the tension, if you have?
5. Have you experienced or witnessed a serial argument or intractable conflict in a relationship? What was the problem? How did the parties respond?
6. What's your opinion about post-breakup relationships? Can former romantic partners still have some kind of relationship? Should they? Explain your answer.

Assess Your Skill

Am I an Aggressive or an Assertive Communicator?

Sometimes it's hard to discern the difference between assertive and aggressive communication. To gain some practice, consider the following situations. For each one, first generate aggressive and inappropriate communication. Then rethink the situa-ion and generate an assertive form of communication that would be more effective. /e've provided an example to get you started.

Sample Situation: You're expecting a raise at work but find out that a coworker, who has less time on the job than you, received a raise and you didn't.

Aggressive Communication: You interrupt a staff meeting that your boss is holding, storm about the room, and demand an explanation of why you didn't receive the expected raise.

Assertive Communication: You make an appointment with your boss for a meeting. At the meeting, you calmly ask the boss to assess your value to the company, leading up to the question of why you didn't receive the expected raise.

Situation: Two people have been in a monogamous dating relationship for several months when one partner finds out that the other person has cheated.

Situation: A student receives a disappointing grade on a paper. After reading the papers of a few other classmates and finding that poorer-quality papers received higher grades, the student decides to confront the teacher about the grade.

What's My Style?

In intimate relationships, in which a great deal is on the line, knowing how you usually tend to handle conflict, as well as how your partner handles it, can save you some major heartbreak. Below, we give you a sample situation along with samples of nonconfrontational, confrontational, and cooperative responses. Supply responses reflecting these three conflict management styles for the other two hypothetical conflict situations. (If you're really brave, pose these same situations to your relational partner and compare your responses to hers or his. That exercise can lead to a constructive, proactive discussion about how to handle conflict in your relationship.)

Conflict Situation 1: Your roommate is *wild,* partying every night, coming home late, and disrupting your study time and your sleep. This behavior is starting to affect your ability to get your schoolwork done and concentrate on your studies. You're not a fuddy-duddy, but you're not a nightly partier either. How do you communicate in response to this conflict situation?

Nonconfrontational Response: Ignore it. It's not my problem; it's my roommate's life to live as he (she) pleases. I would rather have more quiet time, but if I bring up my objections to my roommate's behavior, the situation will escalate and get worse, and I'll regret mentioning anything in the first place.

Confrontational Response: I have rights; I live in this place and pay my fair share of the rent, so I should be able to have some peace and quiet so at least one of us doesn't flunk out of college. When my roommate comes home, I'm going to lay down the law on the late-night partying. If the problem persists, I'll threaten to move out.

Cooperative Response: My roommate and I both have rights because we both live in this apartment. When my roommate is sober and alone here at the apartment, not with a group of partying friends, I'll bring up the problem and ask for solutions we can both live with. I want to respect my friend's right to enjoy life, but I want to set limits so my goals can also be reached.

Conflict Situation 2: You work part time at a restaurant near campus. Thus far, the managers have been flexible and understanding about your class schedule and commitments at the university, but now—just when you've got three exams and two papers coming up—they decide to load you up with extra hours. You need this job and want to keep it, so how do you communicate to address the conflict between what you can do and what management wants you to do?

Nonconfrontational Response:

Confrontational Response:

Cooperative Response:

Conflict Situation 3: You've been dating someone fairly steadily for a few months but have recently developed a romantic interest in a classmate. You'd like to keep dating your current relational partner but renegotiate your relationship so that you can start hanging out with other people, such as the attractive classmate. How do you communicate to manage this situation?

Nonconfrontational Response:

Confrontational Response:

Cooperative Response:

Chapter 9

Understanding Group and Team Performance

Teamwork is . . . the fuel that allows common people to attain uncommon results. —ANDREW CARNEGIE

Igor Mojzes/Fotolia

Chapter Outline

- Groups and Teams Defined
- Group and Team Dynamics
- Group and Team Development
- Study Guide: Review, Apply, and Assess Your Knowledge and Skill

Chapter Objectives

After studying this chapter, you should be able to

9.1 Describe types of groups and teams, differences between groups and teams, concerns that confront real-life groups and teams, and when groups and teams should be avoided.

9.2 Identify and describe group and team dynamics, including roles, rules, norms, status, power, and cohesiveness.

9.3 Summarize the four stages of group and team development.

Do you like working with others in groups? Although you may be one of those people who relish working on team projects and going to meetings, many people don't like collaborating with others. Here are some typical sentiments people sometimes have about working in groups:

> To be effective, a committee should be made up of three people. But to get anything done, one member should be sick and another absent.
>
> A committee is a group of people who individually can do nothing and who collectively decide nothing can be done.
>
> A group task force is a collection of the unfit chosen from the unwilling by the incompetent to do the unnecessary.

Whether you are one of those people who likes group work or one who finds it frustrating and a waste of time, evidence suggests that groups are here to stay. Human beings collaborate.[1] We are raised in groups, educated in groups, and entertained in groups; we worship in groups and work in groups. Today's technology makes it easier for us to collaborate in teams, even when we're not meeting face to face. There is evidence that you're likely to spend about one-third of your time on the job working in groups or teams and attending meetings or preparing for meetings.[2] And if you

We are raised and educated in groups and continue to communicate in groups and teams throughout our lives, so strengthening your group communication skills now will provide lasting benefits.
Erik Isakson/Tetra Images/Alamy

aspire to upper-management leadership positions, you'll spend up to two-thirds of your time in meetings.[3] One study found that more than 80 percent of organizations use teams to accomplish a major portion of the work.[4] Your work will be based on that kindergarten skill called "getting along with others."

To help you with the group and team projects that will inevitably come your way, this chapter offers descriptions of how groups and teams work. In Chapter 10, we'll offer specific strategies for improving group and team performance. As we examine concepts and strategies of group skills and theories, we'll remind you how the core of group communication research can be discussed in terms of the five principles we've used to frame our presentation of human communication:

1. *Be aware of your communication with yourself and others.* Your awareness of your own behavior and the behavior of other group members is often the first step in understanding why you and other group members behave as you do and adjusting your behavior for improved group performance.
2. *Effectively use and interpret verbal messages.* The verbal messages you and other group members use are pivotal in shaping the roles you assume and how the group accomplishes its work.
3. *Effectively use and interpret nonverbal messages.* The social climate of a group is influenced by the way group members behave nonverbally; eye contact, tone of voice, facial expression, and the use of space and time influence what it feels like to be in a group.
4. *Listen and respond thoughtfully to others.* How group members interact (or don't interact) is directly shaped by group members' skill in listening and responding to what others say and do. One survey found that effective listening was the skill most valued by those who work in groups and teams.[5]
5. *Appropriately adapt messages to others.* The ability to modify messages and adjust to the behavior of others is especially important when communicating with three or more people in a small group.

Groups and Teams Defined

9.1 Describe types of groups and teams, differences between groups and teams, concerns that confront real-life groups and teams, and when groups and teams should be avoided.

What makes a group a group? Is a collection of people waiting for an elevator a group? How about students assigned to a class project—do they meet the technical definition of a group? Is there a difference between a group and a team? By exploring these questions, you can better understand what groups and teams do and develop strategies for improving group and team performance.

Communicating in Small Groups

A **small group** consists of three to fifteen people who share a common purpose, feel a sense of belonging to the group, and exert influence on one another.[6] Let's look at this definition more closely.

A GROUP CONSISTS OF A SMALL NUMBER OF PEOPLE A small group generally needs at least three people. Two people do not usually exhibit the characteristics of group behavior. A group is not *small* anymore when more than fifteen people meet together, however. In a larger group, it can become difficult for all members to participate, and a few members often will monopolize the discussion.[7] A large group frequently operates as a collection of subgroups rather than as a single body. Large groups need formal rules, such as parliamentary procedure, to provide structure that will help the group stay focused on the task at hand.

A GROUP HAS A COMMON PURPOSE To be a group, people need to be united by a common goal or purpose. They must all seek the same thing. A collection of people waiting for an elevator may all want to go somewhere, but they probably haven't organized their efforts so that they all are going to the same place. If you are assigned to a class project by an instructor, your classmates do have a common goal: to complete the project and earn a good grade. This class project group would meet our definition of a group.

Groups can be classified according to their purposes into two general categories: primary and secondary. A **primary group** exists to fulfill basic human needs. It's called a primary group because the group meets a primary human need to socialize or just be together. Your family and many **social groups**—groups that provide opportunities for members to enjoy an activity with others—are primary groups.

Secondary groups are more focused on accomplishing a specific task or goal than are primary groups. Secondary groups include:

- **Study groups**, groups that exists to enhance learning;
- **Therapy groups**, groups that provide treatment, or mutual support, including groups like Alcoholics Anonymous;
- **Problem-solving groups**, groups that seek to solve a problem by overcoming one or more obstacles to achieve a goal; and
- **Focus groups**, groups of people who are brought together so others can listen and learn from them—they're like group interviews to gather information and opinions from group members.

GROUP MEMBERS FEEL A SENSE OF BELONGING To be a group, the members must realize that they are part of the group. The people waiting for the elevator probably do not feel an obligation to others around them. Group members develop a sense of identity with their group. They know who is in their group and who is not in the group.

GROUP MEMBERS EXERT INFLUENCE ON OTHERS IN THE GROUP When you are in a group, your presence and participation influence other people in the group. Group members are interdependent; what one group member says or does affects other group members. Your comments and even your silence help shape what the group does next. If you meet in person, your nonverbal messages have a powerful effect on personal relationships. Even silence, facial expressions, and eye contact (or lack of it) affect what the group does. As described in Communication & Technology, each member of the group still has the potential to influence the others even if you "meet" electronically, as a virtual group.

small group
Three to fifteen people who share a common purpose, feel a sense of belonging to the group, and exert influence on one another.

primary group
A group, such as a family, that exists to fulfill basic human needs.

social group
A group that exists to provide opportunities for group members to enjoy an activity in the company of others.

secondary group
A group formed to accomplish a specific task or goal.

study group
A group that exists to help group members learn new information and ideas.

therapy group
A group that provides treatment for problems that group members may have.

problem-solving group
A group that meets to seek a solution to a problem and achieve a goal.

focus group
A group that is asked to discuss a particular topic or issue so that others can better understand how the group members respond to the topic or issue presented to them.

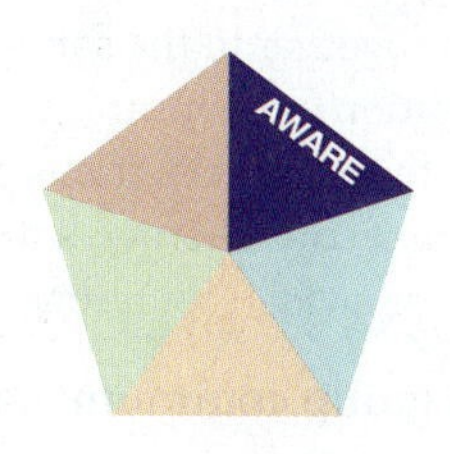

Communication & TECHNOLOGY

Virtues (and Vices) of Virtual Groups

Chances are that you will work in a **virtual group or team**—a group or team that doesn't meet face to face but is instead connected via some electronic channel. What pluses and minuses might you experience as a member of a virtual team?[8]

Advantages of Working in Virtual Teams

- Working in a virtual team can save members travel time and expense.
- Virtual teams can develop the same degree of trust among members as face-to-face groups, especially if team members meet face to face before working virtually.[9]
- In computer-mediated meetings, ideas can be captured and recorded quickly and accurately.
- Technology can help structure a group's process and keep the group focused.
- Some team members may feel more comfortable sharing ideas electronically—or even anonymously—than they do in person.

Disadvantages of Working in Virtual Teams

- Developing trust among group members can take longer than is the case with in-person groups.[10]
- When only some members participate virtually in a team, a special effort must be made to integrate these long-distance members into the fabric of the team.
- Cultural differences in a virtual group may result in less participation among group members.[11]
- The increased speed of information transfer can allow little time for reflection. Thus, technology may sometimes help us make mistakes faster.
- Some group members do not thoroughly evaluate the pros and cons of alternatives when using computer-mediated technology.
- The application of technology does not inherently result in better solutions and decisions. Problems are solved and decisions are made by people.[12]

Small group communication is the transactive process of creating meaning among three to fifteen people who share a common purpose, feel a sense of belonging to the group, and exert influence on one another. Regardless of the type of group, communicating in small groups is sometimes a challenge because of the potential for misunderstanding. But don't assume that working in a group will inevitably be a frustrating experience. People accomplish much when working together. As anthropologist Margaret Mead said, "Never doubt that a small group of concerned citizens can change the world. Indeed, it's the only thing that ever has." In this chapter and the next, we'll provide concepts and strategies to enhance the quality of your collaborations with others.

Communicating in Teams

Most of us have participated on a sports team at some time. The goal of a sports team is to win the game or competition. A work team has some of the same characteristics as a sports team.[13] Instead of winning the game, the goal may be to get the contract, build the best mousetrap, or achieve some other objective. A **team** is a coordinated group of people organized to work together to achieve a specific, common goal.[14]

Often the terms *team* and *group* are used interchangeably. Is there a difference? Yes. Given the increased importance teams have in the workforce today, it's important to know precisely how groups and teams are different from each other.[15] Although groups and teams both are made up of a small number of people who work to achieve a goal, teams are often structured deliberately to achieve the goal. Also, teams spend a great deal of time coordinating their efforts to accomplish the goal.[16] Every team is a group, but not every group is highly organized or coordinated enough to meet the definition of a team. Let's consider several specific characteristics of teams.

TEAMS DEVELOP CLEARLY DEFINED RESPONSIBILITIES FOR TEAM MEMBERS On a sports team, most team members have specifically assigned duties, such as shortstop, pitcher, quarterback, or fullback. On a work team, team members' duties and roles are usually explicitly spelled out. Team members may perform more than one function or role, but they nonetheless have well-defined duties.[17]

virtual group or team
A group or team whose members are not together in the same physical location but who are typically connected via an electronic channel such as the Internet, a telephone, or a video conference.

small group communication
The transactive process of creating meaning among three to fifteen people who share a common purpose, feel a sense of belonging to the group, and exert influence on each other.

team
A coordinated group of people organized to work together to achieve a specific common goal.

Communication & ETHICS

How Far Would You Go to Achieve a Team Goal?

Without a clear goal, teams falter. But sometimes you may be part of a team whose goal or means of achieving the goal you don't support.

Assume that you're a salesperson and part of a sales team. To get a raise in salary, everyone on the team has to meet the sales goal assigned to the team. To get the sales, one team member doesn't always tell the truth to customers about the company's product. That team member's sales success helps make the whole team look good in terms of sales, but bad in terms of ethics.

What would you do? Would you keep quiet and enjoy the benefits of being part of a "successful" sales team? Or would you bring the unethical behavior of the team member to the attention of your supervisor, even though it would place other team members in jeopardy for knowingly "going along to get along"? The ethical question is: Are team goals more important than individual ethical standards?

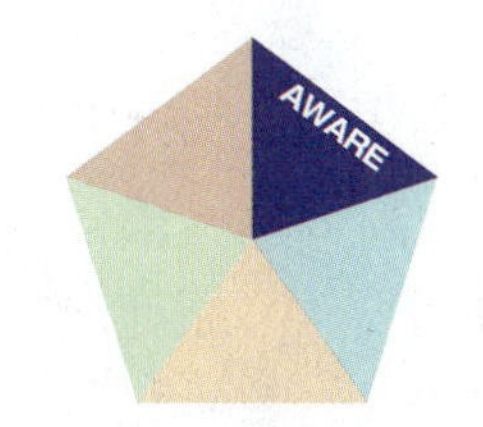

TEAMS HAVE CLEARLY DEFINED RULES FOR TEAM OPERATION Team members develop explicit rules for how the work should be done. A rule is a followable prescription for acceptable behavior.[18] Just as there are written rules in the game of *Monopoly*, there are usually explicit rules for how a team will function. For example, a team may establish a rule that a member who will be absent from a meeting must tell another team member beforehand. Team members know what the rules are and know how those rules affect the team.

TEAMS DEVELOP CLEAR GOALS A third way to characterize a team is to look at the importance and specificity of the team goal.[19] A team goal is usually stated in such a way that the goal can be measured: to win the game, to sell more cornflakes than the competition, or to get to the North Pole before anyone else, for example.

TEAMS DEVELOP A WAY OF COORDINATING THEIR EFFORTS Team members spend time discussing how to accomplish the goals of the team. Their work is coordinated to avoid duplication of effort.[20] A sports team spends considerable time practicing how to work together. Watching a sports team at work is like watching a choreographed dance. Team members have developed a system of working together rather than at cross-purposes. Just as a football team develops a list of the plays to get the ball down the field, a work team develops collaborative strategies to achieve its goal.

Although we have differentiated between groups and teams, don't get the idea that they are completely exclusive entities. Think of groups and teams as existing on a continuum. Some deliberations will make the people seem more like a group, whereas other behavior—a more coordinated and structured process with clear rules and explicit goals—will make the people appear to be a team. Since every team is a small group, whenever we refer to a team, we are suggesting that it's a group as well.

When Not to Collaborate in Groups and Teams

Although we've joined the chorus singing the praises of working in groups and teams, at times one head may be better than two or more. In what

RECAP

Comparing Groups and Teams

	Groups	Teams
Roles and Responsibilities	Individual responsibilities of group members may not always be explicitly defined.	Expectations, roles, and responsibilities of team members are clearly developed and discussed.
Rules	Rules are often not written down or formally developed; rules evolve, depending on the group's needs.	Rules and operating procedures are clearly identified to help the team work efficiently and effectively.
Goals	Group goals may be discussed in general terms.	Clearly spelled-out goals are the focus of what the team does.
Methods	Group members may or may not decide to divide the work among group members.	Team members develop clear methods of collaborating and coordinating their efforts to achieve the team's goals.

situations may it be best *not* to collaborate? The following are four situations in which it is better to work individually rather than collectively:[21]

- *When the group or team has limited time.* Sometimes you may not have time to gather a group together to discuss options; action may be needed immediately. If a very quick decision must be made, delegating an individual to make the decision may be better than convening a group. In times of extreme crisis or emergency, it may be best to have a leader ready to provide some initial direction.
- *When an expert already has the answer.* If you want to know what tomorrow's weather will be, ask a meteorologist. Don't collaboratively puzzle through questions that can be readily answered by someone else. You don't need a group to hash through the process of finding an answer if an individual already has the answer.
- *When the information is available from other research sources.* Using the power of the Internet, you can find vast amounts of information. If you want a bit of data, a specific date, or more information about something, doing individual research may be better than commissioning a group, team, or task force to get the answers. Some groups find it useful for individual members to gather information and then meet with the rest of the group to analyze and discuss the information. But if you just need information and need it fast, click your mouse or head to the library.
- *When the group or team is entrenched in unmanageable conflict.* We don't suggest that you avoid group and team conversations just because they may arouse conflict and disagreement. In fact, it's normal for groups to experience conflict; an absence of conflict can be a sign of an ineffective group. But if the conflict is so entrenched that group members can't listen and thoughtfully respond, it may be advisable to take a break from group deliberations. Convening a dysfunctional group or team that can't or won't work together may not be the best way to reach a decision. If the conflict is so pervasive that no progress is likely, a more structured conversation, such as mediation or negotiation with a trained facilitator, may be needed to help sort things out.

bona fide perspective
A perspective that focuses on how groups actually operate within organizations.

Working in Real Groups and Teams

Textbooks have a tendency to describe things in tidy ways, which may make it appear as if the world were neatly organized into orderly categories and clear-cut definitions. Although we've defined groups and teams and have described distinctly different types of groups—as they operate in real-world businesses and other organizations—real groups and teams don't always neatly fit textbook categories.

If conflicts among group members prevent thoughtful discussion, it's probably not a great idea to collaborate.
Syda Productions/Fotolia

It is likely that in today's multitasking workforce you will be participating in many different types of teams and groups at the same time. Most people do not belong to just one team at a time or focus all their energy and talent on one primary task. The **bona fide perspective** of groups suggests that the context and boundaries for the groups in which we participate move and change. The term *bona fide* simply means authentic, true, or genuine. Thus, a bona fide perspective is concerned with how groups actually operate in work, school, and other real-world situations.

According to communication scholar Linda Putnam, who has done extensive research and writing about bona fide groups, we need to be more sensitive to how groups really operate in natural settings.[22] Most groups and teams do not work in isolation from other groups; they are connected to and influenced by what else is happening in the larger organization. If, for example, an organization is losing money and is on a tight budget, the lack of money will affect how a group operates within the organization. Or if you're working on a group project in your college or university, group members are doing more than just working on one group project. They have lives and are communicating in a number of groups (family, social, study, work) simultaneously. Therefore, Putnam suggests that two elements need to be addressed when considering bona fide groups: (1) how the group is connected to other groups and the organization and (2) how the group operates in relationship to its external context.

How can you apply a bona fide perspective to help you with groups and teams to which you belong? Consider these observations:

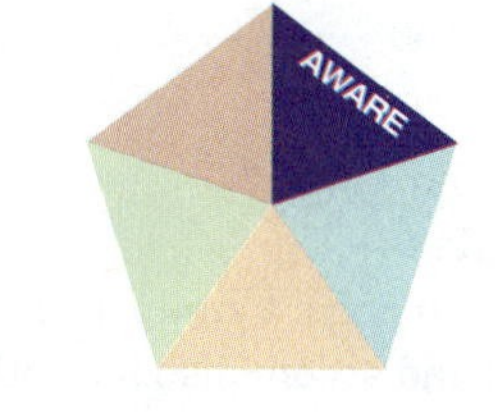

- If you're a group or team leader, a bona fide perspective suggests that you need to be aware that the people who work with you have multiple roles and multiple jobs. Just as your instructor needs to remember that you're likely taking more than one class, so should a group or team leader realize that her or his fellow members are working on multiple projects (both individual and collaborative projects) at the same time.
- Remember that the teams you're working with today may not be the same teams you'll be working with tomorrow. Team membership changes. The changing composition of the group may require that the group go through numerous periods of reorientation as new group members come and others go.
- When some members participate in a virtual team via e-mail, video conference (such as Skype), or phone rather than face to face, special effort must be made to integrate these long-distance group members into the fabric of the team.
- Remember that when you work on a group or team task, you're bound by the constraints of the larger organization in which you work. You're not just working in isolation; you're connected to the whole, although all you may experience is the interaction in the group or team in which you're working.

Naturally occurring groups are complex, with changeable boundaries and changes in group membership. The bona fide, or authentic, approach reminds us to be realistic when we apply definitions, principles, and practices of group theory to groups and teams.

Group and Team Dynamics

9.2 Identify and describe group and team dynamics, including roles, rules, norms, status, power, and cohesiveness.

Groups and teams are dynamic; their structure changes. The study of group dynamics includes a discussion of the roles, norms, status, power, and cohesiveness of groups. We'll examine each concept and note how it is related to the five Communication Principles for a Lifetime.

Roles

Your **role** is the consistent way you communicate with others in a group. It is based on your expectations of yourself and the expectations others place on you. Do you often become a leader of a group, or are you more comfortable just blending in and taking directions from others? Or are you the one who makes sure the group gets the work done instead of just having a good time? There may also be group members who seem especially gifted at smoothing conflict and disagreement. Or perhaps there is no typical pattern to what you do in a group; maybe your role depends on the group and who else is in it.

role
The consistent way a person communicates with others in a group.

TYPES OF ROLES The following are three classic categories of group roles:

- **Task roles** are behaviors that help the group achieve its goal and accomplish its work, such as gathering and sharing research conclusions with the group, taking minutes of meetings, and writing ideas on a chalkboard.
- **Social roles** focus on behavior that manages relationships and affects the group climate; these roles help resolve conflict and enhance the flow of communication. Smoothing hurt feelings and helping the group celebrate its accomplishments are examples of social-role behavior.
- **Individual roles** focus attention on the individual rather than the group. They do not help the group; they emphasize individual accomplishments and issues, not those of the entire group.[23] Dominating group discussions to talk about personal issues or concerns, telling frequent jokes that get the group off track, and constantly complaining or whining about how one's individual needs aren't being met are examples of individual roles.

task role
A role that helps a group achieve its goal and accomplish its work.

social role
A role that helps a group manage relationships and affects the group climate.

individual role
A role that focuses attention on the individual rather than on the group.

LEADERSHIP ROLES The role of leader, a person who influences others in the group, is a special kind of role, and more than one person can assume it. Some leaders focus on assisting with the team's task and therefore assume more task roles to get the job accomplished. Other leaders assume more social roles to help manage the quality of relationships in the group. Usually, a person who assumes an individual, self-focused role doesn't emerge as a natural leader. Being overly dominant or aggressive or blocking the team's progress may focus attention on an individual, but such self-focused behavior doesn't wear well over time, and people who focus on themselves rather than on the team aren't perceived as effective leaders.

SPECIFIC ROLES Helping to develop clear role expectations for you and other team members enhances overall performance.[24] Seventy years ago, group researchers Kenneth Benne and Paul Sheats came up with a list of group roles that remains a classic way of dividing up the roles that group and team members typically assume.[25] As you review the roles and their descriptions, summarized in Table 9.1, note whether you usually assume roles in the task, social, or individual category. Or perhaps you'll see yourself in a variety of roles in all three categories.

Table 9.1 A Classification of Group Roles

Task Roles	Description	Example
Initiator/contributor	Offers new ideas or approaches to the group; suggests ways of getting the job done.	"How about developing an agenda to help us organize our work?"
Information seeker	Asks for additional clarification, facts, or other information that helps the group with the issues at hand.	"Can anyone tell me how many times the university has threatened to close the fraternities and sororities on campus because of the problem of underage drinking?"
Opinion seeker	Asks group members to share opinions or express a personal point of view.	"So what do you all think of the new dress code the school board is proposing?"
Information giver	Provides facts, examples, statistics, or other evidence that relates to the task confronting the group.	"Within the past year, the vice president for student affairs has given a special award to three fraternities and one sorority for developing a program to combat underage drinking."
Opinion giver	Offers opinions or beliefs about what the group is discussing.	"I think the new school dress code proposed for first graders is unworkable."
Elaborator	Provides comments or examples to extend or add to the comments of others.	"Tom, that's a good point. I had the same thing happen to me when my children were attending a private school in New York last year."
Coordinator	Clarifies and notes relationships among the ideas and suggestions that have been offered by others.	"Tyrone, your ideas sound a lot like Juanita's suggestion. Juanita, could you elaborate on your idea so that Tyrone can decide whether he agrees or disagrees with you?"

Orienter	Summarizes what has occurred and seeks to keep the group focused on the task at hand.	"I think we're getting a bit off track here. Let's go back to the issue on the agenda."
Evaluator/critic	Assesses the evidence and conclusions that the group is considering.	"How recent are those statistics? I think there are newer figures for us to consider."
Procedural technician	Helps the group accomplish its goal by handling tasks such as distributing reports, writing ideas on a chalkboard, or performing other tasks.	"I'll write your ideas on the board as you suggest them. After the meeting, I'll copy them and summarize them in an e-mail message to each of you."
Recorder	Makes a written record of the group's progress by writing down specific comments, facts, or the minutes of the meeting.	"I'll take the minutes of today's meeting."
Social Roles	**Description**	**Example**
Encourager	Offers praise and support and confirms the value of other people and the ideas they contribute.	"You're doing a wonderful job."
Harmonizer	Manages conflict and mediates disputes among group members.	"Tynesha, you and Mandy seem to be agreeing more than you are disagreeing. Both of you have the same goal. Let's brainstorm some strategies that can help you both get what you want."
Compromiser	Resolves conflicts by trying to find an acceptable solution; seeks new alternatives.	"Jane, you want us to meet at 7:00 p.m., and Sue, you'd like us to start at 8:00. What if we started at 7:30? Would that work?"
Gatekeeper	Encourages people who talk too much to contribute less and invites those who are less talkative to participate.	"Tim, we've not heard what you think. What do you suggest we do?"
Follower	Goes along with the suggestions and ideas of other group members.	"I can support that option. You have summarized the issues about the same way I see them."
Emotion expresser	Verbalizes how the group may be feeling about a specific issue or suggestion.	"We seem to be frustrated that we are not making more progress."
Group observer	Summarizes the group's progress or lack of progress.	"We are making great progress on all the issues except how much salary we should offer."
Tension reliever	Monitors stress within the group and offers suggestions for breaks, using humor or other appropriate strategies.	"Hey, what we need is a good laugh. Here's a joke I saw on the Internet today."
Individual Roles	**Description**	**Example**
Aggressor	Deflates or disconfirms the status of other group members or tries to take credit for the work of others.	"Lee, your idea is the pits. We all know that what I suggested two meetings ago is the only way to go."
Blocker	Is negative, stubborn, and disagreeable without an apparent reason.	"I just don't like it. I don't have to tell you why. I just don't like it."
Recognition seeker	Seeks the spotlight by dwelling on his or her personal accomplishments; seeks the praise of others.	"Don't you remember this was my idea? And say, did you see my picture in the paper? I won the grand prize at the science fair."
Self-confessor	Uses the group as a forum to disclose unnecessary personal feelings and personal problems unrelated to the group's task.	"I can't deal with this stuff right now. My parents are being so unfair. They won't let me live off campus next year. They just don't understand me."
Joker	Wants to crack jokes, tell stories, and just have fun instead of focusing on the task or what the group needs.	"Hey, let's forget this project and go to the mall. I'll tell you the gossip about Professor Smith. What a kook!"
Dominator	Tries to take control of the group, talks too much, and uses flattery or aggression to push his or her ideas off on the group.	"Now, here's what we're going to do: Marcie, you will take notes today; Phil, you go get us some pizza; and Russ, I want you to just sit there in case I need you to run an errand."
Special-interest pleader	Seeks to get the group to support a pet project or personal agenda.	"My service club would like it if we would support the new downtown renovation project. I'll stand a good chance at club president if I can get you on board."
Help seeker	Seeks to evoke a sympathetic response from others; often expresses insecurity stemming from feelings of low self-worth.	"I don't know if I can participate in this project. I'm not very good with people. I just feel like I don't relate well to others or have many friends."

As you look at the list of roles in Table 9.1, you may think, "Yes, that's what I usually do. That's the role I usually take." You can probably see roles that fit other group members. Most group members don't assume only one or two roles during group meetings. Most of us assume several roles when we interact in a group. A role is worked out jointly between us and the group, and the roles we assume change depending on which group we're in. Your personality and the personality characteristics of other team members also have major influences on team role development.[26]

Effective group members adapt their behavior to what is happening or needed in the group. In some groups, your expertise may give you the confidence to give information and share your opinions freely. In other groups, you may assume a role to maintain social harmony and peace.

BALANCING ROLES What are the best or worst roles to assume? We don't recommend that you assume any individual role; by definition, these roles focus attention on an individual rather than the group. The group needs a balance of task and social roles, instead of attention drawn to an individual. At the same time, however, don't ignore the contributions of your fellow group members. One study found that one of the most negative things a group member can do is ignore comments another group member makes, isolating a group member.[27]

What is the proper balance between task and social concerns? Some experts recommend a 60–40 balance between task and social roles.[28] In general, more comments need to be about getting the work done than about having fun or managing the social climate, but it is also important to make sure that there are good working relationships among group members. If your group seems unduly focused on the task and members are insensitive to the harmony of the group relationships, the group will not be as effective as it might be. Conversely, an out-of-balance group that focuses just on having a good time is not going to achieve its task goals.

Use two of the Communication Principles for a Lifetime to help you balance roles.

Principle 1: Be aware of your communication:	Monitor what roles are being assumed and not assumed in your group.
Principle 5: Adapt appropriately:	Adapt your behavior to the group's needs by helping meet a need or fill an unfilled role.

Rules

As we noted both in Chapter 1 and earlier in this chapter, *rules* are followable prescriptions that indicate what behavior is expected or preferred.[29] Rules also clearly specify what behavior is inappropriate. By college, most students are quite familiar with rules. Leaders or members of groups and teams often develop rules that specify how people should behave.

In particular, teams often develop ground rules that help them function more smoothly. **Team ground rules** are a way to talk about the behaviors that are expected of group members. They are important to help manage uncertainty when working with others. Rules are needed to ensure that a team is both efficient and effective. Although most informal groups do not develop explicit, written rules, more formal, highly structured teams may take time to develop such rules as that everyone should attend all meetings, meetings will start on time, and each member should follow through on individual assignments. Making the rules explicit makes it easier to foster appropriate behavior and prevent inappropriate behavior. Research has found that when people are working in virtual teams, in which uncertainty is often high, clear rules help a team operate more efficiently.[30]

team ground rules
The behaviors that are expected of team members, often spelled out in explicit rules of acceptable behavior developed by team members working together.

norms
Standards that determine what is appropriate and inappropriate behavior in a group.

Norms

Although not all groups develop explicit rules, most groups and teams develop norms. **Norms** are general standards that determine what is appropriate and inappropriate behavior in a group. As their name implies, norms reflect what's normal behavior in the group; they influence a variety of group member behaviors, such as the type of language that is acceptable, the casualness of members' clothing, or the acceptability of using first names. Is it normal for group members to raise their hands before speaking in your group? Is it acceptable to move around while the group is in session or to get a cup of coffee while someone is talking?

NORMS AND RULES How do norms differ from rules? Rules are more explicit. Group and team rules are written down or at least verbalized. Here's an example of a rule: Any member of this team who does not pay his or her dues on time will pay an extra $5 in dues. Norms are more general standards or expectations that are not as clearly spelled out. It may be a norm in your group that no one uses four-letter words; there's probably no written policy that prohibits expletives, and group members may never have said, "No one should ever use a curse word during our discussions," but even without such specific admonitions, group members don't use offensive or obscene words.

SOURCES OF NORMS Norms develop on the basis of norms that you and other team members have experienced in other groups as well as behavior that occurs naturally as group members interact. If after a couple of meetings no one is uttering a swear word, a norm has begun to gel.

The norms that emerge in a group are also strongly influenced by the larger cultural context in which group members live. Norms relating to how attentive the group is to deadlines and punctuality, for example, are anchored in the overall cultural expectations. Some people approach time from a **monochronic time perspective**; they are more likely to develop norms to do only one thing at a time, to pay attention to deadlines and schedules, and to make plans to use time efficiently. Others prefer a **polychronic time perspective**; they do many things at a time, don't worry about deadlines and schedules, believe relationships are more important than work, change plans frequently, and are less concerned about deadlines than are monochronic individuals.[31] Many people from North America and northern Europe tend to be monochronic; deadlines and timelines are valued.[32] People from Latin America, southern Europe, and the Middle East often tend to be polychronic; deadlines and strict adherence to schedules are less important.[33]

monochronic time perspective
Preferring to do one thing at a time, to pay attention to deadlines and schedules, and to use time efficiently.

polychronic time perspective
Preferring to do many things at once, to place less emphasis on deadlines and schedules, and to consider relationships to be more important than work and meeting deadlines.

If you find yourself in a group whose members have cultural approaches to time or other norms that are different from yours, what should you do? Consider these suggestions:

- Take time to talk about those differences. Share your concerns and assumptions.

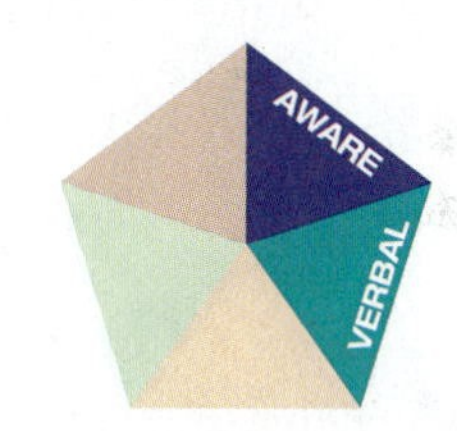

Cultural norms about the use of time are just one source of diversity you may encounter when communicating in groups or teams. How can you start a discussion about group norms?
Pio3/Fotolia

- Don't pounce on other team members and accuse them of being laggards or taskmasters.
- Make the issue a group concern rather than an issue between just one or two people.

Conversation and compromise can accomplish a lot when you find yourself facing cultural differences.

ENFORCING NORMS Noticing when someone breaks a norm can help you spot a norm. If a member waltzes into a meeting twenty minutes late and several folks grimace and point toward the clock on the wall, that's a sure sign that a norm has been violated. The severity of the punishment for violating a norm corresponds to the significance of the norm.[34] Mild punishment is usually unspoken—such as silent glances or frowning stares. More serious punishment might include a negative comment about the behavior in front of other group members or even expulsion from the group.

You don't have to worry about whether your group will have norms or not; norms happen. You should, however, monitor the group norms to ensure that your behavior doesn't distract from the work of the group and to notice the possible development of any unproductive group norms (such as spending too much time socializing) that the group should talk about.

Status

As she walks into the room, all eyes are fixed on her. Group members watch every move. As the chairperson, she has much influence. Without her support, no new issues will come before the board. She has high status. **Status** refers to an individual's importance and prestige. Your status in a group influences to whom you talk, who talks to you, and even what you talk about. Your perceived importance affects both your verbal and your nonverbal messages. A person with high status typically

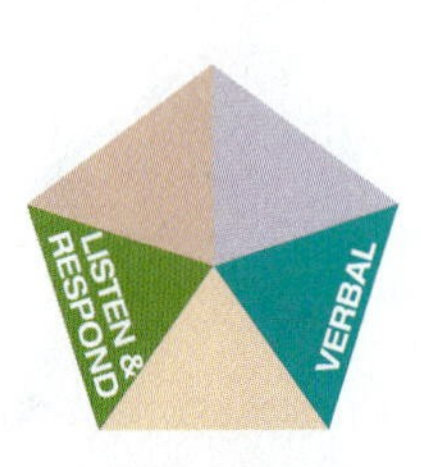

- Talks more than low-status members,
- Directs comments to other high-status group members,
- Has more influence on the decisions the group makes,
- Is listened to by group members, and
- Addresses more comments to the entire group than to individuals.[35]

Because high-status people enjoy more privileges, most people want to be in the "in-group"—the group with high status and influence. Being aware of status differences can help you predict who talks to whom. If you can discern status differences, you'll also be better able to predict the type of messages communicated. Although some people underestimate their perceived level of status and influence in a group, research suggests that you are probably quite perceptive at knowing your own status level when communicating with others.[36]

But just because a person has status doesn't mean that his or her ideas are good. Some groups get into trouble because they automatically defer to the person with more status without reviewing the validity of the ideas presented. Don't let status differences influence your perceptions of and critical thinking about the merit of the ideas presented. Conversely, don't dismiss ideas simply because the person who suggested them doesn't have high status or prestige. Focus on the quality of the message, not on the messenger.

status
An individual's importance and prestige.

power
The ability to influence other people's behavior.

Power

Status refers to perceived importance, whereas **power** is the ability to influence others' behavior. Although status and power often go hand in hand, a group member can have high status and still not be able to influence how others behave. People have power if they can affect what others do. Their power stems from the resources available to them to influence others. Who does and doesn't have power in a group influences how people relate to one another.

A group in which the power is not balanced may have problems; the "power people" may dominate the discussion. In any group or team, when one or more members dominate the discussion, the group loses the contributions and insights of others. People with less power tend to participate less in group discussion unless they're trying to gain power. A power struggle often creates ripples of conflict and contention through a group. Power struggles also often focus attention on individual group members rather than on the group as a whole. Research supports the conclusion that groups with equal power distribution usually have better-quality outcomes than other groups.[37]

According to a classic discussion of how individuals become powerful, there are five power bases: legitimate, referent, expert, reward, and coercive power. These power bases explain why certain people have power and why others don't.[38]

"I've called this meeting because it's a big ego trip having the authority to call you all together whenever I want to."

Patrick Harden/Cartoon Stock

LEGITIMATE POWER You have **legitimate power** if someone elected or appointed you to a position of power. Your power source comes from holding a position of responsibility. The president of your university or college has the legitimate power to establish and implement school policy. U.S. senators and your mayor are other examples of people who have legitimate power. A group or team member who has been elected chair or president of the group is given legitimate power to influence how the group operates.

REFERENT POWER You have **referent power** if people like you. Put simply, people we like have more power over us than people we do not like. If you are working on a committee with your best friend, your friend exerts power over you in the sense that you will tend to give more credence to what your friend recommends than to other recommendations. Just the opposite occurs if you are working with someone you don't like. You will be more likely to ignore the advice that comes from someone you don't admire than from someone you do.

EXPERT POWER Knowledge is power. People who have **expert power** are perceived as informed or knowledgeable. They have more influence in a group or team than do people who are perceived as uninformed. Suppose you are working with a group to develop strategies to clean up the river that runs through your town. Your colleague who is majoring in aquatic biology will probably have more power than other, less knowledgeable group members.

REWARD POWER People who can grant favors, money, or other rewards have more power than people who can't provide such rewards; those who can bestow rewards have **reward power**. People who have greater power to reward are typically sent more positive, supportive messages than people who don't have the ability to reward others. Someone also has reward power if he or she can take away a punishment or other unpleasant experience. But reward power is effective only if the person being rewarded finds the reward satisfying or useful. What is rewarding to one person may not be rewarding to another person.

COERCIVE POWER You have coercive power if you can punish others. **Coercive power** is the flip side of reward power. The ability to influence comes from the ability

legitimate power
Power that stems from being elected or appointed to a position of authority.

referent power
Power that stems from being liked.

expert power
Power derived from having expertise and information.

reward power
Power that comes from the ability to provide rewards or favors.

coercive power
Power that stems from being able to punish others.

RECAP

Types of Power

Legitimate Power	Power that results from being elected, appointed, or ordained to lead or make decisions for a group or a team.
Referent Power	Power that results from being popular and well liked.
Expert Power	Power that results from having information or being knowledgeable about issues or ideas.
Reward Power	Power that results from having the resources to bestow gifts, money, recognition, or other rewards that group members value.
Coercive Power	Power that results from having the ability to punish others.

to make others uncomfortable. If someone can cut your salary, lower your grade, demote you, put you in jail, or force you to do unpleasant jobs, that person has coercive power. The power results from the perception that the person with the power will actually use the power. If a person has the authority to punish but group members don't perceive that the person will use this power, there really is no coercive power.

Even though we have categorized power into five different types, don't get the idea that group members may exert just one type of power. In reality, group or team members often have more than one type of power. For example, because a group member is the elected leader (legitimate power), he or she may also be able to offer rewards (reward power) or punishments (coercive power).

Cohesiveness

If you have ever read about the Three Musketeers or seen a movie about them, you know that their motto was "All for one, one for all." They were a cohesive group—they liked to be around one another. **Cohesiveness** is the degree of attraction that members of a group feel toward one another and the group.

CHARACTERISTICS OF COHESIVE GROUPS In a highly cohesive group, the members feel a high degree of loyalty to one another; the goal of the group is also the goal of the individual.[39] Cohesive group members listen to one another. Members of a cohesive group are more likely to use words and phrases that have a unique meaning to group members than all members of less cohesive groups; they are also more likely to tell inside jokes—jokes that mean something only to them.[40] Groups that are cohesive generally are more effective than groups that are not cohesive.[41]

Groups become cohesive because of a variety of forces that attract people to the group and to one another. Similarity of goals, feelings of genuine liking, and similarity of backgrounds and culture are variables that influence group cohesiveness.

HOW TO ENHANCE GROUP COHESIVENESS Table 9.2 summarizes some strategies that enhance group cohesiveness and other strategies that make a group less cohesive. The common element in cohesive groups is the manner in which group members communicate with one another. Cohesiveness is more likely to occur if group members have the opportunity to talk with one another freely about a goal all members have in common and if this interaction increases group members' affection and liking for one another. Teams that have greater control over how they conduct their work are also likely to be more cohesive than other teams.[42]

cohesiveness
The degree of attraction group members feel toward one another and toward their group.

Table 9.2 Suggestions for Enhancing Group Cohesiveness[43]

Cohesive Groups	Uncohesive Groups
Talk about the group in terms of "we" rather than "I"; stress teamwork and collaboration.	Emphasize the individual contributions of group members; stress individual accomplishment.
Reinforce good attendance at group meetings.	Make little effort to encourage group members to attend every meeting.
Establish and maintain group traditions.	Make little effort to develop group traditions.
Set clear short-term and long-term goals.	Avoid setting goals or establishing deadlines.
Encourage everyone in the group to participate in the group task.	Allow only the most talkative or high-status members to participate in the group task.
Celebrate when the group accomplishes either a short-term or a long-term goal.	Discourage group celebration; make sure group meetings are all work and little or no fun.

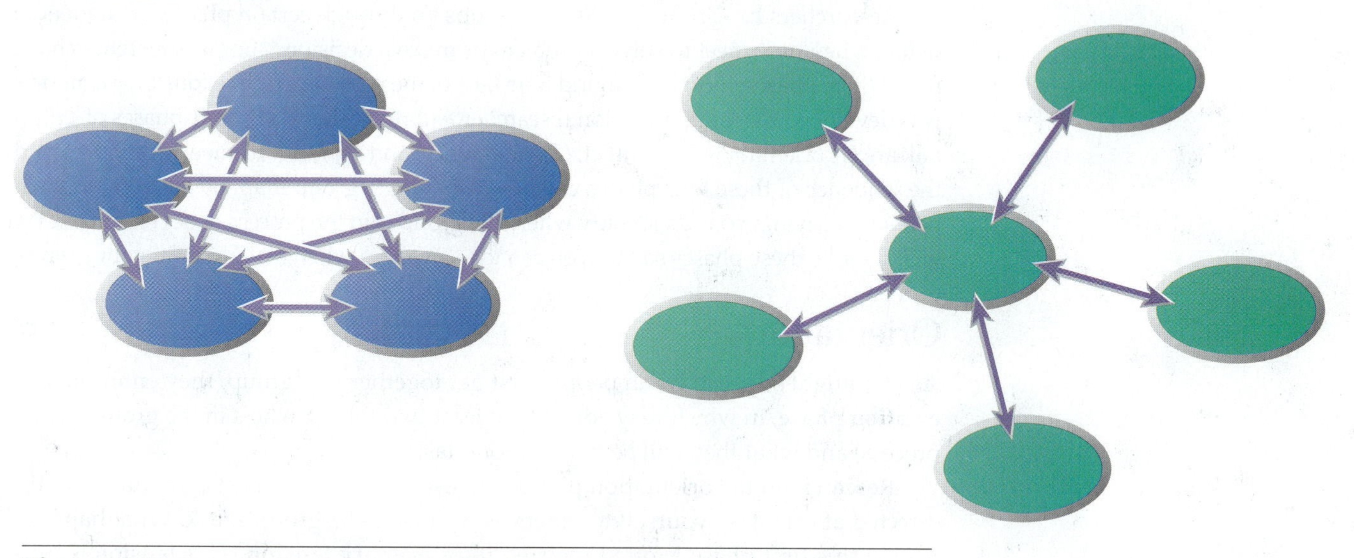

Figure 9.1 All-Channel Small Group Communication Network

Figure 9.3 Wheel Small Group Communication Network

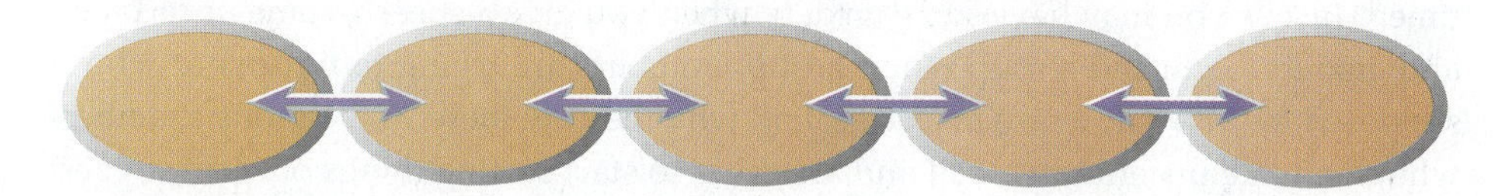

Figure 9.2 Chain Small Group Communication Network

A **communication interaction pattern** is a consistent pattern of who talks to whom. The all-channel network pattern shown in Figure 9.1, in which everyone talks to everyone else, is most likely to enhance group cohesiveness. The chain interaction pattern in Figure 9.2 illustrates a form of group communication in which people convey a message to one person at a time rather than communicating with all group members at once. Groups in which a great deal of communication occurs within a **clique**, a smaller group of people within a group who form a common bond among themselves, are also usually less cohesive than groups with communication among all members.

Sometimes, a great deal of communication is directed to one person in the group who holds an opinion different from that of the rest of the group. This person is called a **group deviate**. Other group members may spend considerable time trying to change that person's opinion. The wheel interaction pattern, shown in Figure 9.3, occurs when one person is the focal point of communication with all other group members. The focal person in a wheel pattern is not always a group deviate; a quarterback speaking to other football team members is another example of the wheel pattern. However, the wheel pattern, like the chain pattern, is less likely than the all-channel pattern to foster group cohesiveness.

Can a group be too cohesive? Yes. Although usually cohesiveness is a good thing, a group can have too much of a good thing. If group members are focused only on having fun and developing a positive, cohesive relationship to the exclusion of getting their work done, group productivity can suffer. Strive for group cohesiveness, but balance it with concern for accomplishing the group's task.

communication interaction pattern
A consistent pattern of who talks to whom.

clique
A smaller, cohesive group within a group.

group deviate
A group member who holds an opinion, attitude, or belief that is different from that of other group members.

Group and Team Development

9.3 Summarize the four stages of group and team development.

Small group communication can be a disorganized, messy process, especially if the all-channel network is the predominant communication pattern. Although the free flow of ideas is a good thing, it may seem as though there is no order or structure to the way group members interact. But what may look like chaotic talk may, in fact, be just a normal aspect of how groups behave.

Researchers have found that some groups go through certain phases or sequences of talk when they meet to solve a problem or make a decision.[44] Some researchers have found three phases; most have found four. One of the most descriptive four-phase models was developed by communication researcher Aubrey Fisher.[45] His four phases of group talk are (1) orientation, (2) conflict, (3) emergence, and (4) reinforcement. To understand the sequence of these four phases can be like having a group map. By listening to what people are saying, you can identify where the group is in the process of development. We will describe these phases so that you can identify them when they occur in your group.

Orientation

As you might suspect, when people first get together in a group, they enter the **orientation phase**, in which they adjust to at least two things: who's in the group (group process) and what they will be doing (group task).

Research on the orientation phase suggests that your earliest communication is directed at orienting yourself to others as well as to the group's task. What happens during this first phase is often referred to as **primary tension**. This tension results from the uncertainty and discomfort people experience when they meet for the first time.[46] Just as you may have some anxiety when you give a speech, some uncertainty and anxiety occur in a group when group members are trying to figure out who is supposed to do what, who's in charge, and why they are there. Some group members who don't like uncertainty at all and are eager to start sorting things out will suggest an agenda: "Hello, my name is Steve. Let's each introduce ourselves." Other group members are quite content to sit quietly in the background and let others take the lead. As people begin to become acquainted and start talking about the group's purpose, typical groups experience the second phase: conflict.

orientation phase
The first phase of group interaction, in which members become adjusted to one another and to the group's task.

primary tension
Tension arising from the uncertainty and discomfort that occur when a group first meets.

Conflict

As we pointed out, people are different—and nowhere is that more evident than in a group discussion after the group gets down to business. As group members become more comfortable and oriented toward the task and one another, they start asserting opinions about what the group should be doing, how it should be done, and who should be doing it. They have tested the water in the first phase and are now ready to jump in. This second phase, which is characterized by increased disagreement, is known as the **conflict phase**. Groups may experience **task conflict** in which they disagree about how to accomplish the task at hand; **process conflict** about the procedures and methods of working on the task; or **relational conflict**, in which disagreement about who does what results in personal disagreement.[47] The relational conflict that arises in this phase is sometimes called **secondary tension**. This secondary tension or conflict occurs when there is a struggle for leadership or when the conflict becomes personal and group members disagree with one another.

Conflict isn't always bad—it occurs when people are honest about sharing their opinions. If there is no conflict, it usually means that people aren't honest about how they really feel.[48] As journalist Walter Lippman once said, "When we all think alike, then no one is thinking." The conflict phase is necessary for solving problems and maintaining group relationships. When ideas aren't challenged and tested, groups are more likely to make unwise decisions. We are not suggesting that you celebrate when you have conflict, only that you take some comfort in knowing that conflict is an expected part of group deliberations. The amount and intensity of the conflict vary, depending on how important the issues are to the group. The more important the issues are to group members, the greater the intensity of the conflict is likely to be.

conflict phase
The second phase of group interaction, in which group members experience some degree of disagreement about social and task issues.

task conflict
Conflict that occurs because of differences about how to accomplish what the group is trying to achieve.

process conflict
Disagreement about the procedures or methods for accomplishing the task.

relational conflict
Conflict that becomes personal because group members do not like, value, or respect one another.

secondary tension
The conflict that occurs, after the members of a group have become acquainted with one another, over group norms, roles, leadership, and differences among member opinions.

Taking a time-out might help to resolve this team's conflict. What other strategies have you found useful for dealing with conflict in groups?
Stockbyte/Getty Images

Research suggests that when intense conflict arises in your group, especially conflict that results in heightened emotions and tension because of cultural differences, it may be best to "cool it."[49] Taking time to back off rather than continuing to hash out issues verbally may be helpful in managing the tension. Regardless of the issue or trigger for the conflict, when emotions are aroused, rational discussion is hard to achieve. Especially if the group you're in includes people from a variety of cultural backgrounds, it may be best to let the group "breathe" rather than continuing to hammer out meaning with more talk. We're not suggesting that all conflict should be managed by avoiding it. We are suggesting that when emotions become aroused, it's difficult to make headway on the issues with words that may expand the conflict.

When conflict in virtual groups and teams stems from differences in cultural values or perceptions, it's important that team members feel connected to the team and empowered to participate rather than feel marginalized or discounted. Research suggests that having virtual team members vote on decisions or the value and importance of contributions is a useful way to keep them engaged with the team.[50]

Emergence

You know you are in the **emergence phase** when the group begins to solidify a common point of view. Decisions emerge, and conflict is reduced. Although conflict is still evident in this third phase, what sets the emergence phase apart from the conflict phase is the way in which group members manage conflict. Norms, roles, and leadership patterns that have been established in the group now help the group get work accomplished. In the emergence phase, the group settles on norms and moves closer to agreement. The group begins to get a clearer glimpse of how issues will be resolved and what the group outcome will be.

Not all of what emerges may be productive. The group could decide that the conflict is so intense that the best decision is to disband the group, or an individual could decide to leave the group.

emergence phase
The third phase of group interaction, in which conflict or disagreement is managed, decisions are made, and group problems begin to be solved or managed.

Reinforcement

Group members become more unified in the **reinforcement phase**. During the orientation, conflict, and emergence phases, group members struggle through getting acquainted, developing cohesiveness, competing for status and prominence, puzzling

reinforcement phase
The fourth phase of group interaction, in which group members express positive feelings toward one another and toward the group.

Communication & DIVERSITY

The Impact of Individualism and Collectivism on Groups and Teams

As we mentioned in Chapter 6, individualistic cultures tend to focus on individual achievement. Most North Americans value individual accomplishment over group or team achievement. In general, people from the dominant cultural groups in the United States, Great Britain, and Australia savor and celebrate individual accomplishment. Collectivistic cultures, which include cultures in Asia, Latin America, and some parts of Eastern Europe, emphasize group or team accomplishment rather than individual achievement.[51]

People who hold individualistic cultural values may find it more difficult to work collaboratively than people from collectivistic cultures. The following summary compares individualistic assumptions with collectivistic assumptions about working in groups and teams.[52] These differences can sometimes explain why groups and teams have difficulty collaboratively accomplishing their tasks. If you're from a culture that places a high value on individual achievement, you may find it challenging to work well with others.

Individualistic Assumptions	**Collectivistic Assumptions**
The best decisions are made by individuals.	The most effective decisions are made by teams.
Planning should be done by leaders.	Planning is best done by the entire group.
Individuals should be rewarded.	Groups or teams should be rewarded.
Individuals should work primarily for themselves.	Individuals should work primarily for the team.
Healthy competition among group and team members is more important than teamwork.	Teamwork is more important than competition.
Meetings are for sharing information with others.	Meetings are for making group or team decisions.
To get something accomplished, you should work with individual people.	To get something accomplished, you should work with the entire group or team.
The prime objective of meetings is to advance your own ideas.	The prime objective of meetings is to reach consensus or agreement.
Group or team meetings are often a waste of time.	Group or team meetings are the best way to achieve a quality goal.

over action the group could take, and making decisions. The group eventually emerges from those struggles and develops a new sense of direction. This accomplishment results in a more positive feeling about the group. The group more clearly develops a sense of "we." In fact, one way you can identify the reinforcement phase is when group members use more collective pronouns (*we, us, our*) than personal pronouns (*I, me, my*) to talk about the group.

The Process Nature of Group Phases

Even though we have identified four distinct phases that groups can experience, don't get the idea that all groups progress neatly through these phases in exactly the same way. They don't.[53] Some researchers have found that only about one-third of all groups experience these distinct stages.[54] Other studies have had difficulty identifying four phases and found just one or two. Even if you have trouble identifying these phases in your group, you will probably see some elements of the four phases during your group meetings.

Some groups get stuck in one of the phases. For example, have you ever participated in a group that could never quite figure out what it was supposed to do? It was stuck in the orientation phase. Some groups remain in the conflict phase for long periods of time, perhaps bouncing between orientation and conflict. The group either seems torn by personal conflict between group members or just can't reach agreement or make a decision.

As we've noted, the group will eventually reach phase three, when something will emerge, even if it is not a wise decision or high-quality solution. The group may decide, for example, to disband and never meet again because it is so dysfunctional. Although this was not the original objective of the group, something emerged: The group members quit.

Reinforcement is likely to occur because we like to make sense out of what happens to us. Even if the group disbands, we are likely to celebrate its demise or reinforce the decision to disband. Because of our culture's emphasis on efficiency and productivity, many groups quickly gloss over the reinforcement aspects of group celebration. Wise group leaders and participants make sure that accomplishments are celebrated and both group and individual efforts are recognized. The cohesiveness and positive feelings that result from such celebrations will be helpful as the group prepares for its next task.

RECAP

A Map of Group Phases

Phase One: Orientation
- What are we doing here?
- What is our goal?
- Who are these people?
- What is my role?

Phase Two: Conflict
- Who put that person in charge?
- I see the goal differently.
- I have different ideas.
- I have different strategies.

Phase Three: Emergence
- Something happens.
- Decisions are made.
- Issues are managed.
- The group moves forward.

Phase Four: Reinforcement
- The group is aware it is making progress.
- Members seek to justify their actions.
- Members reward others.
- The team celebrates its success or rationalizes its failure.

STUDY GUIDE:
Review, Apply, and Assess Your Knowledge and Skill

Review Your Knowledge

Groups and Teams Defined

9.1 Describe types of groups and teams, differences between groups and teams, concerns that confront real-life groups and teams, and when groups and teams should be avoided.

Small group communication is the transactive process of creating meaning among a small number (three to fifteen) of people who share a common purpose, feel a sense of belonging to the group, and exert influence on one another. Primary groups, such as family groups and social groups, exist to fulfill primary human needs to socialize and live together. Secondary groups form to achieve a specific goal. Secondary groups include study groups, therapy groups, focus groups, and problem-solving groups. Groups and teams are similar in that they are collections of a small number of people who meet to achieve a goal. A team can be differentiated from a group in that it is more highly organized and the members' collaborative efforts are more coordinated to achieve the team goal.

Group and Team Dynamics

9.2 Identify and describe group and team dynamics, including roles, rules, norms, status, power, and cohesiveness.

A variety of factors influence the ever-changing nature of members' interactions in groups and teams. One factor is the role you assume in a group—the consistent way you communicate with others. There are three primary types of roles in small groups and teams: (1) task roles help the group do its work, (2) social roles help the group members relate to one another, and (3) individual roles inappropriately divert the group's focus to individual concerns rather than group concerns. Other factors that affect the dynamic nature of groups and teams include norms (standards of what is normal or expected), rules (explicit statements about appropriate and inappropriate behavior), status (a person's importance or prestige), power (the ability to influence others), and cohesiveness (the degree of loyalty and attraction the group members feel toward one another).

Group and Team Development

9.3 Summarize the four stages of group and team development.

The four stages of group and team development are (1) orientation, (2) conflict, (3) emergence, and (4) reinforcement. During the orientation phase, group members get acquainted with both the task and one another. The second phase, conflict, occurs when group members recognize that they have differing ideas and opinions about both the group's task and its procedures for accomplishing the task. The third phase, emergence, is evident when the group begins to make decisions and starts to complete the task. The reinforcement phase occurs when the group has accomplished its task and takes some time to recognize and confirm the group's actions.

Key Terms

Small Group, p. 201
Primary Group, p. 201
Social Group, p. 201
Secondary Group, p. 201
Study Group, p. 201
Therapy Group, p. 201
Problem-Solving Group, p. 201
Focus Group, p. 201
Virtual Group or Team, p. 202
Small Group Communication, p. 202
Team, p. 202
Bona Fide Perspective, p. 204
Role, p. 205
Task Role, p. 206
Social Role, p. 206
Individual Role, p. 206
Team Ground Rules, p. 208
Norms, p. 208
Monochronic Time Perspective, p. 209
Polychronic Time Perspective, p. 209
Status, p. 210
Power, p. 210
Legitimate Power, p. 211
Referent Power, p. 211
Expert Power, p. 211
Reward Power, p. 211
Coercive Power, p. 211
Cohesiveness, p. 212
Communication Interaction Pattern, p. 213

Clique, p. 213
Group Deviate, p. 213
Orientation Phase, p. 214
Primary Tension, p. 214
Conflict Phase, p. 214
Task Conflict, p. 214
Process Conflict, p. 214
Relational Conflict, p. 214
Secondary Tension, p. 214
Emergence Phrase, p. 215
Reinforcement Phase, p. 215

The Principle Points

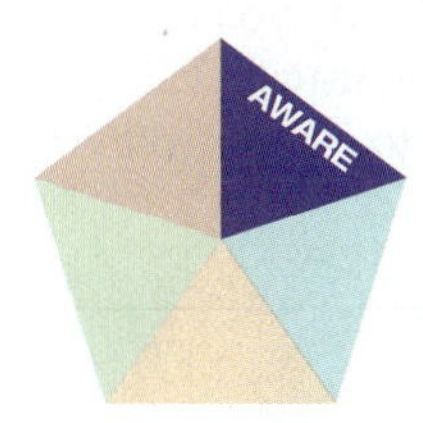

Principle One:

Be aware of your communication with yourself and others.

- Be aware of your role and the roles of others in groups and teams.
- Be aware of how you and your group develop and maintain group norms.
- Be mindful of how your power and the power of others influence group interaction.
- Be aware of the forces that affect group and team cohesiveness.
- Be aware of and sensitive to the stages of orientation, conflict, emergence, and reinforcement that influence group interaction.

Principle Two:

Effectively use and interpret verbal messages.

- Be verbally supportive of other team members to foster a collective sense of team spirit.
- Verbally help clarify team goals. Clear, elevating goals are the hallmark of an effective team.
- Express realistic optimism when working with others in groups and teams. Groups and teams with a positive outlook are more effective than those with a pessimistic perspective.
- Help the group or team set clear ground rules and clarify norms that may be ambiguous.
- Talk about your group or team in terms of "we" rather than "I."

Principle Three:

Effectively use and interpret nonverbal messages.

- Nonverbal cues help you understand group and team norms.
- Observe group and team members' use of space, touch, and eye contact to pick up clues about status and power.
- Be supportive of other group members nonverbally as well as verbally. Reinforce statements with positive facial expressions, eye contact, and head nods to indicate agreement when appropriate.

Principle Four:

Listen and respond thoughtfully to others.

- Listening well is a very important way to help a group. Listening skills help you identify your roles and the roles of others.
- Listen to others to help identify group and team norms and rules.
- Listen attentively to other group members to help foster a climate of cohesiveness.

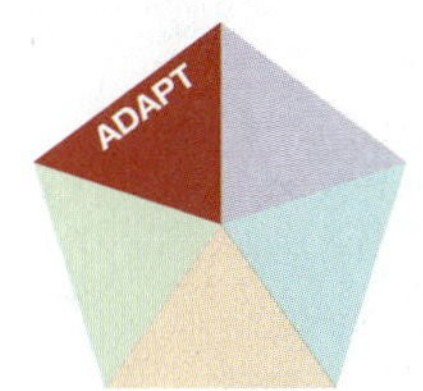

Principle Five:

Appropriately adapt messages to others.

- Adapt to group roles, norms, rules, and status differences.
- Adapt to help the group become oriented to the task, manage conflict, facilitate emergent decisions, and reinforce group behavior.
- Adapt appropriately to cultural differences within the group.

Apply Your Skill

Consider the following questions. Write your answers and/or share them with your classmates:

1. What do you find most rewarding about working in groups and teams? What do you find most challenging?
2. What other advantages and disadvantages of virtual groups and teams can you add to the list in this chapter's Communication & Technology box, either from experience or based on your observations and analysis?
3. Do you sometimes feel uncertain and uncomfortable when joining a new group? How do you typically try to resolve discomfort when you meet new group members? How successful is your method?
4. Which of the roles described in Table 9.2 do you fill most often in groups? Why do you think you usually take that role? Which roles would you like to fill more often?

Assess Your Skill

Communication researchers Katherine Hawkins and Bryant Fillion surveyed personnel managers to find out what the managers considered the most important skills for successful groups and teams. The items in the following list of skills are among those the personnel managers deemed important. Rate each member of a group you are in on the following skills, using a scale from 1 to 5 (1 = not at all effective, 2 = generally not effective, 3 = uncertain, 4 = effective, and 5 = very effective).

Scoring Instructions

Total the score for each group member. A perfect score is 65; the lowest possible score is 13. Your instructor may invite you to share your ratings of other group members anonymously. If you don't share your ratings, simply note how you evaluate your skill in comparison to your ratings of other group members.

	Group Member				
Skill	**A**	**B**	**C**	**D**	**E**
1. Listens effectively	___	___	___	___	___
2. Understands roles and responsibilities	___	___	___	___	___
3. Actively contributes to the group	___	___	___	___	___
4. Asks clear questions	___	___	___	___	___
5. Establishes and maintains rapport with others	___	___	___	___	___
6. Is sensitive to people with different cultural backgrounds	___	___	___	___	___
7. Uses clear, concise, accurate, and professional language	___	___	___	___	___
8. Communicates well with people who have different professional backgrounds	___	___	___	___	___
9. Gives clear and accurate instructions	___	___	___	___	___
10. Presents a positive professional image nonverbally (through appropriate grooming and attire)	___	___	___	___	___
11. Helps resolve conflicts	___	___	___	___	___
12. Accurately summarizes information for the group	___	___	___	___	___
13. Gives brief, clear, well-organized, and informative presentations to the group when appropriate	___	___	___	___	___
Total	___	___	___	___	___

Chapter 10

Enhancing Group and Team Performance

Never doubt that a small group of concerned citizens can change the world; it's the only thing that ever has. —MARGARET MEAD

Monkey Business Images/Shutterstock

Chapter Outline

- What Effective Group and Team Members Do
- Structuring Group and Team Problem Solving
- Enhancing Group and Team Leadership
- Enhancing Group and Team Meetings
- Study Guide: Review, Apply, and Assess Your Knowledge and Skill

Chapter Objectives

After studying this chapter, you should be able to

10.1 Identify six functions that effective group members perform.

10.2 List and describe the five steps of group problem solving (reflective thinking).

10.3 Compare and contrast the trait, functional, styles, situational, and transformational approaches to understanding leadership.

10.4 Develop and use strategies to structure meetings appropriately, keep meetings on track, and promote appropriate dialogue and interaction.

What's so great about groups? Why does every organization, from the U.S. Congress to the local Parent Teacher Association, use groups, teams, and committees to get things done? The simple fact is: Groups work. Collaborating with other people produces clear benefits that just don't happen when a task is given to an individual. Research clearly supports the following conclusions:

- Groups and teams come up with more creative solutions to problems than a person does working alone.
- Working with others in groups improves group members' comprehension of the ideas presented.
- Group and team members are more satisfied with the group's conclusions and recommendations if they participated in the discussion than if they did not.
- Groups have access to more information when they tap into the experience of group members.[1]

All these advantages sound wonderful. But these benefits of collaboration don't occur automatically when people work in groups and teams. Sometimes there are significant disadvantages to working collaboratively:

- Overly talkative or insensitive, overbearing people may speak too much. The advantage of working collaboratively is lost when one or more people dominate the conversation.
- Group members sometimes feel pressure to conform to what other members are doing and saying. It can be difficult to stick up for your own ideas when everyone else sees issues differently.
- It may be easy for some people to loaf and not do their share of the work. If not enough people carry part of the load, the advantages of working together as a group don't materialize.
- Working in groups and teams takes more time than working individually.[2]

This chapter is designed to help you achieve the advantages of working in groups and minimize the disadvantages of working collaboratively. We can't claim that if you follow all the strategies we suggest, your life will be free of unpleasant and unproductive group experiences. We do believe, however, that group members who both understand how groups work (see Chapter 9) and know principles and strategies for enhancing the quality of group work are much more likely to avoid the pitfalls and reap the benefits of working in groups.

Underpinning all the suggestions we offer in this chapter are the same five Communication Principles for a Lifetime that we introduced in Chapter 1 and have been discussing throughout the book. Effective group members are aware of what they are doing. They effectively use verbal and nonverbal messages, listen and respond, and then appropriately adapt their messages to others.

What Effective Group and Team Members Do

10.1 Identify six functions that effective group members perform.

"I hate groups," mutters an exasperated group member who has just finished a two-hour meeting in which nothing was accomplished. "Not me," chirps another group member. "Meetings and team projects are fun. I like the energy and productivity that occur when we work together." What does the second person know that the first one doesn't? As we noted at the start of this chapter, working in groups can have drawbacks, but you can reduce those disadvantages if you and other group members learn some fundamental ways to perform effectively as group members.

Identify a Clear, Elevating Goal

Among the first questions that a vigilant-thinking group asks relates to the group's goal: What are we trying to do?[3] According to one research team, the goal should be not only clear, but also *elevating*, or exciting to the group.[4] The group needs to know that it is pursuing a goal that is significant; the group goal needs to be something more exciting and important than anything a group member could achieve individually. A professional baseball team during spring training camp may hang up signs in the locker room that say "World Series Champs!" A professional football team may see itself as a Super Bowl contender at the beginning of preseason. Groups also need to identify a clear, exciting, yet realistic goal that drives all aspects of what the group does.[5] Without a goal and a results-driven structure to achieve it, group performance sputters. Research has found that it's important not only to set goals, but also to develop contingency plans in case a

Groups offer a lot of advantages in trying to solve problems, so it pays to learn how to overcome some of the challenges to effective group communication.
Wavebreakmedia/Shutterstock

goal is not reached. Being able to react and adjust the group's plans to achieve a goal is especially important.[6]

Develop a Results-Driven Structure

A group or team may have a clear goal, such as winning the Super Bowl, getting an "A" on a group assignment, or selling more widgets than other groups in the company, but just having a clear, elevating goal doesn't mean that the group will achieve what it wants to achieve. The group also has to carry out actions that contribute to reaching the goal. If you want to win the Super Bowl, you have to invest time in becoming physically fit and working on executing successful football plays. If you want to get an "A" on the assignment, you need to be doing what the instructor wants you to do rather than socializing and just having fun.

A group with a **results-driven structure** is organized around the action steps it needs to take to achieve its goal.[7] To be driven by results means "keeping your eyes on the prize" and then developing a group or team structure to secure the prize. Perhaps you've been part of a group or team that was quite busy but didn't seem to accomplish much; that kind of activity reflects a non-results-driven structure. Results-driven groups focus on verbs—action words—that provide the road map to success.

Gather and Share Appropriate Information

Another question that vigilantly thinking groups ask is "Does something need to be changed?" To answer that question, high-performing groups and teams don't just rely on the unsupported opinions of group members. Instead, they gather information and analyze the situation.[8] Sharing information is just as important in virtual groups as it is in face-to-face groups.[9]

To analyze an issue, an effective group should do at least three things:

1. *Gather the information the group members need.* Computer programmers are familiar with the acronym GIGO: "Garbage in, garbage out." If you develop a computer program using bad information or a bad program command (garbage), you're likely to get low-quality output (more garbage). Information is the fuel that makes a group function well.[10]
2. *Share the information among group and team members.* Group members have a tendency to share with other group members information that everyone already knows. Research has found that better decisions are made when group members make an effort to share information that others may *not* know.[11] So if you are uncertain whether other group members know what you know, don't hesitate to share that information with the entire group.
3. *Draw accurate conclusions from the information.* Having too little evidence—or no evidence at all—is one reason groups sometimes fail to analyze their current situation correctly.[12] Even if group members do have plenty of evidence, however, it may be bad evidence, or perhaps they have not tested the evidence to see whether it is true, accurate, or relevant.

One team of researchers found that when there is missing or unknown information, effective group members will do their best to make inferences or to find the missing or unknown information.[13] Group members who use evidence to support their well-reasoned arguments are more likely to have their conclusions accepted by the entire group than group members who do not.[14] Group members who don't gather and use information effectively are more likely to make bad and less creative decisions than others.[15] Here are some tips for gathering and using information effectively:

- In group deliberations, ask for expert advice sooner rather than later. Seeking expert advice results in better group outcomes.

results-driven structure
A structure that causes a group to focus its efforts on the actions it needs to take to achieve its goals.

- If you find that just a few people are doing the talking and sharing information, invite quieter group members to participate. Groups that have more equal participation by all group members generally are more effective than other groups.
- Don't rush to make a quick decision. To reach a better outcome, take your time and sift through the information you have.

Develop Options

Another hallmark of a vigilantly thinking group is that the members generate many ideas and potential solutions after gathering information and analyzing a situation. Effective groups don't just settle on one or two ideas and then move on. They list multiple creative approaches.

Sometimes groups get stuck, and ideas just don't flow. If that happens to your group, you may want to take a break from the difficult issues or problems rather than continue to hammer away at them. Taking a break gives you space to thrash through the issues. You may generate a breakthrough solution when you are not actively trying to; perhaps you've had a great idea come to you when you were taking a walk or driving. The principle of self-awareness operates here: As a group member, you have a responsibility to become aware of the group's ability to generate high-quality ideas. Be sensitive to the group's need to take a fresh look at the problem or issue.

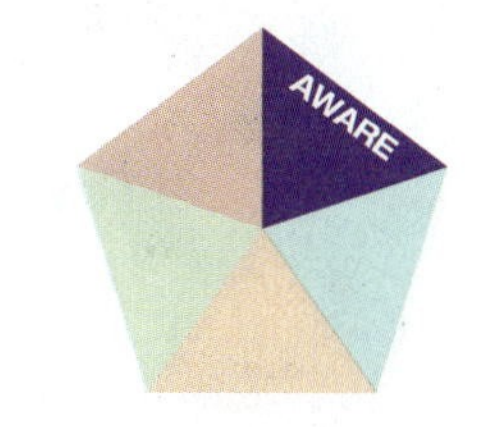

Evaluate Ideas

High-performing groups know a good idea when they see it. They are able to evaluate evidence, opinions, assumptions, and solutions to separate good ideas from bad ones. Low-performing groups are less discriminating. A group that does not critically evaluate ideas because members are too eager to make a decision just so they can get a job done usually comes up with low-quality decisions.

As we've seen, a group of vigilant thinkers examines the advantages and disadvantages of an idea, issue, or opinion.[16] When the group is zeroing in on a particular course of action, the effective group has at least one member who suggests, "Let's consider the positive and negative consequences of this decision." Research reveals that it's especially important to talk about the negative consequences of a specific proposal.[17] Some groups use a chalkboard or flipchart and make a written list comparing

Members of high-performing groups and teams are likely to enjoy spending time together. A good balance of social and task focus makes it more fun for group members to be together. How else can you make group membership more enjoyable for yourself and other members?
Pressmaster/Fotolia

the pros and the cons. Groups that do so are likely to come up with a better decision than groups that don't systematically evaluate the good and bad aspects of a potential solution or decision.

Not only is it a good idea to evaluate the conclusions of the group, but research suggests that it is useful to evaluate the team's process periodically and talk about how well team members are coordinating the work. Don't wait until the project is finished to evaluate the team's process; discuss how well the team is achieving its goals as the team is working on a project.[18]

Develop Sensitivity Toward Others

Most of the functions we've described so far focus on getting work done effectively and efficiently, but group success is about more than just focusing on the task. Being solely task oriented is not beneficial to the way a group functions. Effective group members balance concern for the task with concern for the feelings of others.

Fostering a climate of fairness and supportiveness is essential to developing a well-functioning team.[19] In groups that function effectively, members are aware of how their comments might be perceived by others. Effectively functioning group members make comments that confirm the value of others' contributions and nonverbally show that they are genuinely interested in what others are saying. Group members also listen to what each group member has to say—even members who hold a minority opinion. One benefit of working in a group is that you can hear a variety of ideas. If opinions of some members are quickly squelched because they are not what most other group members think or believe, the group loses the power of many different points of view.

A recent study found that one sign of a competent group is that group members simply like spending time with one another.[20] They also explicitly talk about the importance of trusting one another, clarify misunderstandings by collaboratively defining key terms, listen effectively, consciously talk about what makes the group effective, share personal information, and use humor and laugh together.[21] In summary, competent group members are sensitive to how individual members relate to one another.

Develop a Positive Personal Style

You may have heard the story about a boy who awoke on the morning of his birthday to find only a large pile of manure where he'd hoped to find birthday presents. Undaunted, he smiled and said, "With this much horse manure, there's got to be a pony here somewhere!" Effective team members are optimistic like that boy: Even in bad times, they find something to be positive about.

One thing effective team members are optimistic about is themselves. Researchers have found that effective teams and effective team members *believed* that they were effective, that they had the skills and resources to accomplish their task. Teams that were less effective *thought* that they were less effective.[22] Was the team effective because of a self-fulfilling prophecy (just expecting to be effective caused the team to act effectively)? Or did team members think that they were effective because they really were a top-notch team? We're not quite sure what the precise cause-and-effect relationship is between self-perceptions of being effective and actually being effective. We do know, however, that teams that have a positive, can-do attitude perform better than teams whose members have doubts, worries, and uncertainties about whether they will get the job done. The bottom line is that optimism enhances effectiveness.

As we've seen, being driven by results also makes a group member more productive. Furthermore, perhaps not surprisingly, team members also like colleagues who are encouraging, patient, enthusiastic, and friendly. To be perceived as an *ineffective* team

Table 10.1 How to Collaborate with Difficult Group Members

Problem	Suggestions
Dominator: A group member talks too much.	**1.** Consider giving the group member responsibility for a specific task. **2.** Use gatekeeping skills to invite others to talk. **3.** Privately ask the "oververbalizer" to give others an opportunity to talk. **4.** If necessary, the group may collectively decide to confront the domineering member.
Blocker: A group member has a negative attitude and consistently suggests what can't be done.	**1.** Consider defusing the tension with appropriate humor. **2.** Ask the blocker to be the devil's advocate, a role that gives the blocker permission to be negative at certain times rather than all the time. **3.** Ask for evidence to support the blocker's claims. **4.** Gently confront the blocker, noting how the negative attitude is affecting the entire group.
No Follow-Through: A group member is irresponsible and doesn't perform assigned tasks.	**1.** Assign a mentor to help the group member. **2.** Clarify that only those who do the work will be recognized for accomplishing the task. **3.** Privately ask the irresponsible group member to do his or her share of the work. **4.** If need be, confront the irresponsible group member as a group, explaining how the lack of follow-through is hurting the group.
Bully: A group member is unethically aggressive and verbally abusive and tries to take the credit for work others do.	**1.** Support those who are bullied. **2.** Don't tolerate unethical behavior; describe the offensive behavior to the bully and explain its effect on the group. **3.** As a group, confront the bully, explaining how the bullying behavior is hurting the group's climate. **4.** If need be, seek help from someone of authority outside the group (supervisor or instructor); sometimes a bully responds only to a person with greater power.

member, argue with others frequently, be intolerant and impatient, and cultivate skills that will help you win the "pain-in-the-neck" award. To be an effective team member, you need to find a way to deal with group members who may dominate, block, bully, or have no follow-through. Table 10.1 offers suggestions.

You may wonder whether these attributes of team effectiveness can be enhanced through study and training. There's good news: Evidence suggests that by learning more about teams and participating in training development courses, you can indeed improve your team skills.[23]

RECAP

What Effective Group and Team Members Do

Group Function	Description of Function
Identify a Clear, Elevating Goal	A clear, elevating, or important goal provides an anchor for group discussion.
Develop a Results-Driven Structure	Structure helps the group stay on task and do the things that will help it achieve its goal.
Gather and Share Appropriate Information	Effective teams conduct research, share information with all group members, and take steps to confirm that they have accurate information.
Develop Options	Effective groups expand the number of options before choosing a course of action.
Evaluate Ideas	Effective groups or teams examine the pros and cons of an option before implementing the strategy.
Develop Sensitivity toward Others	Members of effective groups express sensitivity to the needs and concerns of group members by using appropriate verbal and nonverbal messages, listening, responding, and adapting messages to others.
Develop a Positive Personal Style	Effective group members have optimistic attitudes about the prospects for overall group success and use effective strategies to change ineffective member behavior.

Structuring Group and Team Problem Solving

10.2 List and describe the five steps of group problem solving (reflective thinking).

How many of us have uttered the plea "Just tell me what to do"? When we do, we are usually looking for simple techniques or steps to help us achieve our goal. Several researchers have sought to identify the sequence that works best to help groups solve problems and achieve their goals. In fact, more than seventy methods or sequences of steps and techniques have been prescribed for structuring problem solving in groups and teams.[24] Despite all of these recommendations, however, researchers have concluded that there are no magic techniques that always enable a group of team members to come up with the right solution to a problem. No single prescriptive method or series of steps works best in every situation. There is some good news, though: Research shows that *having some structured sequence of steps or questions works better than having no structure.*[25]

Another important conclusion of group researchers is that whatever structure the group uses must be balanced with interaction.

- **Structure** is the way a group or team discussion is organized to follow a prescribed agenda. Groups and teams need structure to keep them on task and on track. According to research, groups that engage in free-ranging discussion without an agenda change topics about once a minute.[26] Besides having difficulty staying focused, a group without adequate structure or focus is more likely than a well-structured group to take excessive time to do its work, jump at the first solution recommended, find that one or more people dominate discussions, and have problems managing conflict.[27]
- **Interaction** includes give-and-take discussion and the responsiveness of group members to the comments of others. In an interactive group, there are fewer long utterances, more people contribute, and more people take turns talking. People listen and thoughtfully respond to one another. In a highly structured meeting, there is more control over who talks, about what and for how long; overly structured meetings include less interaction.

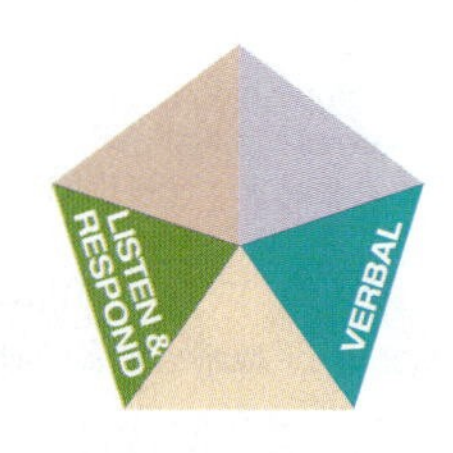

As Figure 10.1 suggests, the key is to find the right balance between structure and interaction. When there is too much interaction, the group experiences the chaos of unbridled talk, which might not be focused; group and team members may need help focusing on one idea at a time rather than bouncing from topic to topic. When there is too much structure, however, the group loses the freedom to listen and respond with sensitivity to what others are saying.

In the pages that follow, we present a set of steps that can help you develop a sequence of things group members should be talking about. These five steps are inspired by educator and philosopher John Dewey, who in 1910 wrote a book called *How We Think*.[28] His book described how individuals go about the problem-solving process. In essence, he described the scientific method that scientists still use to solve problems: defining and analyzing a problem, identifying solutions, picking a solution, and putting the solution into practice. He called this process **reflective thinking**. We present these steps here not as a one-size-fits-all prescription that you should always follow, but as a way of structuring the problem-solving process to manage uncertainty and ensure that the key functions we talked about earlier are accomplished during your discussion. These steps incorporate the ideas we presented earlier in the chapter when describing what effective group members do. In addition to describing each step of the reflective thinking process, we present several techniques to help you structure discussion.

structure
The way a group or team discussion is organized, focusing on the group's agenda and the task that needs to be achieved.

interaction
The give-and-take discussion and responsiveness to other group members.

reflective thinking
A problem-solving process based on the scientific method.

Figure 10.1 Groups Need a Balance of Structure and Interaction

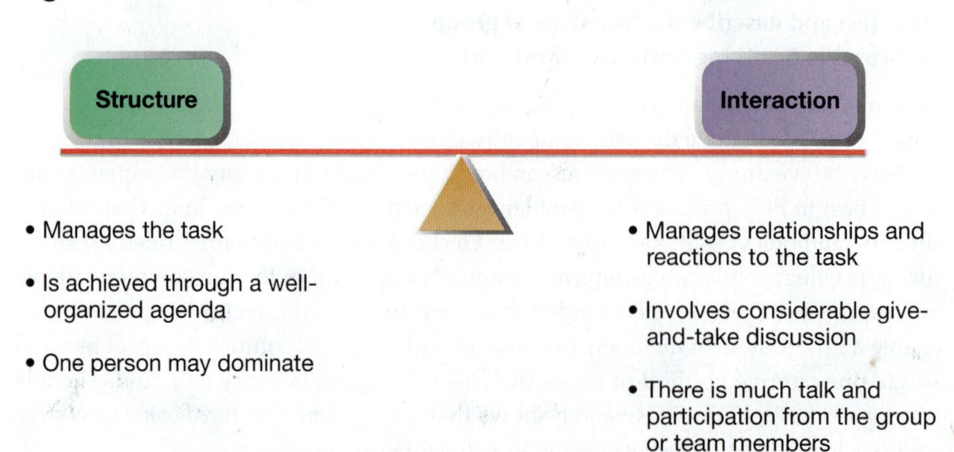

Step 1: Identify and Define the Problem

"What's your problem?" As we noted earlier, groups work best when they have identified a clear, elevating goal that unites their effort. Whatever method or technique a group uses, it is essential that the group members know precisely what problem they are trying to solve. To reach a clear statement of the problem, consider asking the following questions:

- What is the specific problem that concerns us?
- What do we want more of or less of?
- What terms, concepts, or ideas do we need to define so as to understand the problem?

It is also helpful to phrase the problem as a question and to clarify the problem.

DEVELOP A QUESTION Most group experts recommend that an effective way to give your problem-solving task appropriate structure is to phrase your problem in the form of a policy question. A policy question is phrased so that the group will recommend some action (policy) to eliminate, reduce, or manage the problem. Policy questions begin with the words "What should be done about . . ." or "What could be done to improve . . . ."

Here are some examples:

- What should be done to lower the cost of tuition at our university?
- What could be done to decrease property taxes in our state?
- What should be done to make health care more affordable for all U.S. citizens?

CLARIFY THE PROBLEM One specific technique for clarifying the problem is to use the journalists' six questions method.[29] Most news reporters are taught to include the answers to six questions—who, what, when, where, why, and how—when writing a news report. Answering each of these six questions about the problem the group has identified can help further define and limit the problem. For example, a group might ask *who* and *when* questions such as "Who is harmed by the problem?" and "When do the harmful effects of the problem occur?" The group's answers can also help it move to the next step in the process: analyzing the problem.

One way to help your group fully identify and define a problem is to use these six questions about the problem.
iQoncept, 2010/Shutterstock.com

Step 2: Analyze the Problem

Many groups want to "cut to the chase" quickly and start spinning out solutions without taking the time to analyze the problem thoroughly. Resist this temptation. Analyzing a problem well is an important prerequisite to finding an effective solution. To analyze something is to break it down into smaller pieces. To analyze a problem is to consider the causes, effects, symptoms, history, and other information that will inform the group about how to best solve the problem. Essential questions that can help you analyze problems include the following:

- How long has the problem been in existence?
- How widespread is the problem?
- What are the causes of the problem?
- What are the effects of the problem?
- What are the symptoms of the problem?
- Who is harmed by the problem?
- What methods already exist for managing the problem?
- What are the limitations of existing methods?
- What obstacles keep the group from achieving the goal?

ESTABLISH CRITERIA In addition to considering these questions, group members should develop criteria for an acceptable solution. **Criteria** are standards for an acceptable solution to a problem. Identifying clear criteria can help you spot a good solution when you see one. Sample criteria for solutions include the following:

- The solution should be inexpensive; the cost should not exceed a specified percentage of the budget.
- The solution should be implemented by a certain date.
- The solution should be agreed on by all group members.
- The solution should be agreed on by all individuals affected by the recommendations.

Don't rely on your memory when you verbalize criteria. Write down on a highly visible chalkboard, flipchart, or projected image the list of criteria your group has identified, and include the list in the minutes or notes that summarize the meeting.

criteria
Standards for an acceptable solution.

force field analysis technique
A method of analyzing a problem or issue by identifying forces that increase the likelihood that the desired goal will occur (driving forces) and forces that decrease the probability that the goal will occur (restraining forces).

ANALYZE PROBLEM ELEMENTS After you have gathered information and developed criteria, your group may need to develop a systematic way of analyzing the information you've gathered. One technique that can help structure the analysis of your problem and also help your team identify criteria is the **force field analysis technique** shown in Figure 10.2.[30] This technique works best when your group has identified a clear goal and needs to assess what is happening now that would increase the probability that the goal will be achieved.

After identifying a goal, the group lists all the driving forces currently at work that would help achieve the goal. Then the group does just the opposite: It identifies the restraining forces that are keeping the group from achieving the goal. When complete, the task of the group in developing solutions is now clear: Increase the driving forces and decrease the restraining forces.

Figure 10.2 Force Field Analysis

This analysis was conducted by a group that wanted to increase the number of students who volunteer for community projects. The goal is written on the top. Driving forces, shown on the left, are factors that increase the group's chance of achieving its goal. Restraining forces, listed on the right, are factors that reduce the group's ability to get more students to volunteer.

SOURCE: Adapted from Julius E. Etington, *The Winning Trainer* (Houston: Gulf Publishing, 1989).

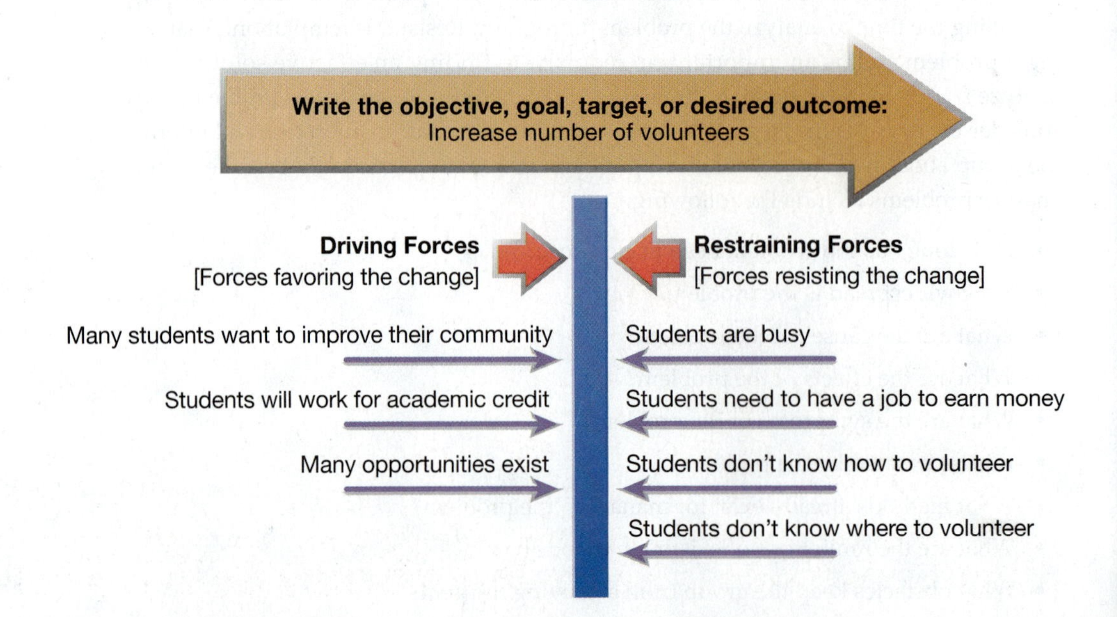

Step 3: Generate Creative Solutions

Now that you've identified a specific problem, analyzed its causes and history, and established clear criteria for solutions, you're ready to generate creative options to solve the problem. **Creativity** is the generation, application, combination, and extension of new ideas. Researchers have found that your entire group is more likely to be creative if individual group members are creative, are open to new ideas, have diverse backgrounds, and believe that they can be creative; it's important not to rely on others to be creative but to develop your own creative skill.[31] It's simply not true that only a few gifted and talented people are creative. Creative ideas can come from anyone. Author Malcolm Gladwell believes that our powers of intuition and creativity harbor the greatest potential for generating the breakthrough ideas that can change the world.[32] Your group is more likely to be creative if you do the following things:[33]

- Make sure everyone in the group knows the precise nature of the problem.
- Review and summarize the analysis of the problem.
- Promote a climate of freedom; let people experiment and play with ideas.
- Don't judge and evaluate the ideas of others prematurely.
- Listen to minority points of view; you never know who may have the next great insight.
- Provide enough time for creativity to occur; don't rush the creative process.

Brainstorming is the classic technique for identifying possible solutions to a problem. This technique, in which group members try to generate, without evaluating them, as many ideas as possible within a set period of time, was developed by an advertising executive about fifty years ago to encourage a group to be creative.[34] You've probably used brainstorming before. Many groups, however, don't use the technique effectively.

creativity
The generation, application, combination, and extension of new ideas.

brainstorming
A technique for generating many possible solutions to a problem by withholding evaluation while group members suggest ideas. Ideas are evaluated after suggestions have been offered.

PROBLEMS WITH BRAINSTORMING The key to making brainstorming work—to generating many creative ideas—is to *separate the generation of ideas from the evaluation of ideas.* This means that group members should feel free to offer ideas without fear of criticism, snickering, or being made to feel foolish. Reality, however, may be quite different. When group members start suggesting ideas, there may be verbal or, more likely, nonverbal evaluation of ideas. People may laugh at the more offbeat suggestions; or when someone announces a suggestion, others may frown, sneer, voice an editorial comment, or talk over the person and ignore the suggestion. Another subtle form of evaluation occurs when some group ideas are praised and some are not. Group members whose ideas are not praised may feel that their ideas are considered stupid. Clearly, when ideas are evaluated as soon as they're offered, brainstorming doesn't work well; members may be reluctant to share ideas. This is

Stephan Pastis/Universal UClick

especially true of group members who are shy or uncomfortable talking in a group; however, these people may have great ideas that are worth sharing.

BETTER BRAINSTORMING One solution to this problem is to have a period of **silent brainstorming** before members share their ideas verbally. Another name for silent brainstorming is the **nominal group technique**.[35] For a few moments, people work individually, and for that period of time, they are a group in name only (hence the term *nominal*). After group members have brainstormed individually, they share their ideas with the group.

Several variations of silent brainstorming can also be effective. You may ask group members to do some individual brainstorming before they come to the group meeting. For example, you could say, "Each group member should bring five or ten suggestions for solving our problem." Group members can also be asked to do some private brainstorming and e-mail their responses to the group leader or other group members. Electronic brainstorming websites and apps can help virtual groups share ideas without meeting in person.

For groups that do meet in person, group members can brainstorm ideas silently for a few minutes and then move into small groups to share and piggyback ideas before the entire group comes back together. When groups use silent brainstorming, it's usually best to go around the group one at a time to have group members share what they have written down.

Another creative way to generate ideas is to have group members first write each of their ideas or suggestions on a sticky note.[36] Once the ideas are on the sticky notes, group members can stick them to the wall and then arrange them in groups. Seeing other group members' ideas may trigger additional creative ideas from the group.

In all variations, the goal is to separate generating or listing ideas from critiquing the ideas. Evaluate the ideas *after* all the group members have finished sharing. When the two parts of brainstorming get mixed together, fewer ideas flow because of group members' fear of being criticized.

As we've noted, the purpose of brainstorming is to think of as many ideas as possible. To generate a lot of options, encourage members to piggyback each other's ideas. List all ideas where everybody can see them; referring to the list can fuel more ideas. Try to identify one or more zany or wild ideas—this triggers creativity and may lead to a less zany but workable idea.

RECAP

Brainstorming Steps

1. Select a problem that needs to be solved.
2. Discuss the history, causes, and background of the problem. Make sure the group knows precisely what options are needed.
3. Tell the group to develop a creative mind-set:
   - Put aside judgments and evaluations.
   - Stress quantity of ideas.
   - Avoid criticizing ideas, including your own.
   - Try to come up with one or more wild ideas—stretch your imagination; it's easier to modify wild ideas.
   - Piggyback someone else's ideas.
4. Start brainstorming. Give the group a time limit.
5. To reduce the possibility that people will evaluate ideas, consider using a period of silent brainstorming before having people verbalize their ideas.
6. Write all the ideas on a chalkboard, flipchart, or computerized projection.
7. Keep reminding the group not to evaluate the ideas of others when they are first expressed.
8. Evaluate the ideas after all ideas have been presented.

Step 4: Select the Best Solution

After the group has generated a long list of ideas, the next step is to evaluate the ideas that were generated to determine which ones best meet the criteria the group identified when they analyzed the problem. It's really important that group members have both a clear goal and specific criteria. Without them, the group members will have difficulty recognizing a good solution when they see it.

It is usually easier for groups to expand alternatives (brainstorm) than to narrow alternatives. The methods that groups use to whittle a long list down to a manageable number for more serious debate include these five approaches:

1. *Decision by expert.* Let someone who has high credibility narrow the list.
2. *Rank.* Tell group members to rank their top five choices from 1 to 5.

silent brainstorming (nominal group technique)
A method of generating creative ideas; group members brainstorm individually and write down their ideas before meeting together to share them.

Communication & ETHICS

What If Someone Can't Stop Judging?

Sarah likes to be in charge of group meetings. She has lots of good ideas, and other group members benefit from her leadership and wealth of suggestions. But during traditional brainstorming sessions, she can't stop criticizing other people's ideas. One or two group members have asked Sarah not to evaluate others' ideas because they have noticed how some members don't share as frequently because of her criticism, but she just can't seem to stop critiquing ideas during the brainstorming sessions.

Sarah makes important contributions to the group and is a good leader except for this one flaw of continually evaluating what others say. What would you do if you were in this group with Sarah? Would you speak to Sarah, as other group members have done, to ask her to stop critiquing? Or would you say nothing? What are your ethical obligations to help the group perform as effectively as possible?

Some members have suggested asking Sarah to leave the group during brainstorming sessions, since her behavior hurts group creativity. On the basis of what you've read so far in this chapter, what other ideas might help Sarah avoid critiquing ideas as they are generated?

3. *Rate.* Ask group members to evaluate each solution on a scale from 1 to 5; the solutions that are rated best get the most serious discussion.
4. *Majority vote.* Group members vote for the ideas they like.
5. *Consensus.* Group members seek a solution that all group or team members can accept.

DEVELOP CONSENSUS **Consensus** occurs when there is enough agreement that group members will all support a decision. Consensus doesn't mean that everyone agrees enthusiastically and completely with what the group has decided, but at least group members won't stand in the way of what the group has decided. Reaching a consensus decision has the advantage that all group members can verbalize support for the decision. But reaching consensus takes time.

The three primary strategies summarized in Table 10.2 can help groups reach consensus:[37]

1. Be goal oriented.[38]
2. Listen.
3. Promote honest dialogue and discussion.

consensus
Agreement among all members of a group or team to support an idea, proposal, or solution.

Table 10.2 Suggestions for Reaching Group and Team Consensus

Effective Group Members	Ineffective Group Members
Keep the Group Oriented Toward Its Goal	
Remind the group what the goal is.	Go off on tangents and do not stay focused on the agenda.
Write facts and key ideas on a flipchart or chalkboard.	Fail to summarize or rely on oral summaries to keep group members focused on the goal.
Talk about the discussion process, and ask questions that keep the group focused on the agenda.	Do little to help clarify group discussion.
Listen to the Ideas of Others	
Clarify misunderstandings.	Do not clarify misunderstandings or check to see whether others understand their message.
Emphasize areas of agreement.	Ignore areas of agreement.
Maintain eye contact when listening to someone and remain focused on the speaker without interrupting.	Do not have eye contact with the speaker, do not focus attention on the speaker, or interrupt the speaker.
Promote Honest Dialogue and Discussion	
Seek out differences of opinion.	Do not seek other opinions from group members.
Do not change their minds quickly to avoid conflict.	Quickly agree with other group members to avoid conflict.
Try to involve everyone in the discussion.	Permit one person or just a few people to talk too much and dominate the conversation.

AVOID GROUPTHINK Be cautious if all group members agree too quickly or too consistently. You may be experiencing groupthink instead of consensus. **Groupthink** occurs when group members seem to agree but primarily just want to avoid conflict. On the surface, it seems as though group members have reached consensus, but it may be an illusion of agreement. Another way of describing groupthink is to call it faulty consensus; too little disagreement often reduces the quality of group decisions. If a group does not seriously examine the pros and cons of an idea, the quality of the decision it makes is likely to suffer because the group has not used its full power to analyze and evaluate ideas.[39]

Failure to test ideas and the resulting groupthink can have serious consequences in the form of wrong, dangerous, or stupid decisions. The following list identifies a few well-known disasters or problems in which groupthink was a key factor:

- In 1986, American TV viewers watched in horror as the *Challenger* space shuttle, carrying the first teacher in space, exploded on their screens. The tragedy resulted from both faulty engineering and groupthink: Some people knew that the shuttle might not fly in cold temperatures but, because of pressure to stay on schedule, decided not to stop the launch.[40]
- In 1999, several students were killed in a traditional pre–football game bonfire at Texas A&M University. Some people thought the bonfire construction unsafe before the accident occurred, but because of tradition the bonfire continued to be built, and tragedy was the result.[41]
- The commission that investigated the September 11, 2001, terrorist attacks concluded that the nation's lack of preparedness for the attacks was attributable in part to groupthink.[42] The commission found that evidence of a terrorist threat existed before the attacks, yet not enough action was taken to address the problem fully.

groupthink
A faulty sense of agreement that occurs when members of a group fail to challenge an idea; a false consensus reached when conflict is minimized and group members do not express concerns or reservations about an idea or proposal.

The headlines are not the only places to look for examples of groupthink. If you think about it, you'll find plenty of examples in groups and teams you've worked with.

"All those in favor say 'Aye.'" "Aye." "Aye." "Aye." "Aye." "Aye."

Henry Martin/Cartoon Bank

Causes of Groupthink Groupthink is more likely to occur in your group under the following conditions:

- The group feels apathetic about its task.
- Group members don't expect to be successful.
- One group member has very high credibility—group members tend to believe what he or she says.
- One group member is very persuasive.
- Group members don't usually challenge ideas—it's expected that group members will agree with one another.[43]

Be on the lookout for these symptoms in your groups and teams.

Of course, as the saying goes, "Hindsight is 20/20." After the fact, it can be easy to spot an example of groupthink. The hard part is to be aware of groupthink when it is occurring in your group. Knowing the causes and symptoms of groupthink can help you spot it and then put an end to it.

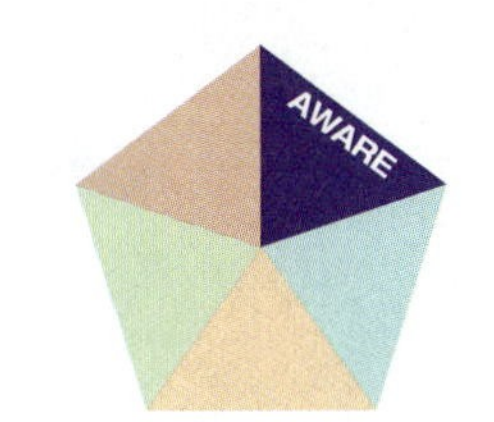

How to Avoid Groupthink The first thing to do is to be aware that groupthink is occurring. In addition to awareness, here are several additional strategies to avoid groupthink:[44]

- Don't agree with someone just because that person has high status; examine the ideas of others carefully, regardless of their position.
- Consider asking someone from outside the group to evaluate the group's decisions and decision-making process.
- Assign someone to be a devil's advocate—to look for disadvantages to a proposed idea. One of the hallmarks of effective decision making is verbalizing the negative, as well as positive, consequences of an idea or suggestion.[45]
- Ask group members to break into smaller teams or pairs to consider both the pros and the cons of a proposed solution. An easy way to structure a discussion of pros and cons is to list the pros in one column of a two-column T-chart and the cons in the second column.

Step 5: Take Action

Once you have identified your solution or solutions, your group needs to consider the question "Will it work?" You may want to do a pilot test (practice test) or ask a small group of people what they think of your idea before you "go public" with it. Bouncing your proposed solution off an expert and checking to see whether your solution has been successful when others have adopted it can help you test the solution's effectiveness.

If your group has to not only identify a solution but also put it into action, your group will need structure to make sure that details don't get overlooked in getting the job done. Perhaps you know the people in the following story:

> This is a story about four people: Everybody, Somebody, Anybody, and Nobody. There was an important job to be done, and Everybody was asked to do it. Everybody was sure Somebody would do it. Anybody could have done it, but Nobody did it. Somebody got angry about that because it was Everybody's job. Everybody thought Anybody could do it, but Nobody realized that Everybody wouldn't do it. It ended up that Everybody blamed Somebody when actually Nobody asked Anybody.

RECAP

Reflective-Thinking Steps and Techniques

Steps	Techniques
1. Identify and define the problem.	• Phrase the problem as a policy question. • Use the journalists' six questions (Who? What? When? Where? Why? How?) to help define the issues.
2. Analyze the problem.	• Use force field analysis to identify driving and restraining forces. • Develop clear criteria that clarify the issues and can help in evaluating solutions.
3. Generate creative solutions.	• Use brainstorming. • Use silent brainstorming (nominal group technique) or electronic brainstorming.
4. Select the best solution.	• Narrow alternatives using expert decision, ranking, rating, majority vote, or consensus. • Reach consensus by being goal oriented, by listening, and by promoting honest dialogue.
5. Take action.	• Develop a clear action plan. • Make a written list of who should do what.

Make a written list of who should do what. Follow up at the next group meeting to see whether the assignments have been completed. Effective groups and teams develop an action plan and periodically review it to make sure Anybody asked Somebody.

Enhancing Group and Team Leadership

10.3 Compare and contrast the trait, functional, styles, situational, and transformational approaches to understanding leadership.

Leadership is the ability to influence others through communication. Some people view a leader as someone who delegates and directs the group. Others see a leader as someone who is primarily responsible for ensuring that whatever task is assigned

leadership
The ability to influence the behavior of others through communication.

or designed by the group is completed. Actually, most groups have many leaders, not just one person who influences others. In fact, each group or team member undoubtedly influences what the group does or does not achieve. Regardless of who serves as leader, research suggests that the quality of group and team leadership has a significant effect on how satisfied team members are.[46] Members of an effectively led team feel greater satisfaction, are more productive, and are less likely to be absent than members of less effective groups.[47] The quality of team leadership influences virtually every aspect of what it feels like to be a team member. The prevailing approaches to analyzing the behavior of effective leaders are the trait, functional, styles, situational, and transformational approaches to leadership.

Trait Approach

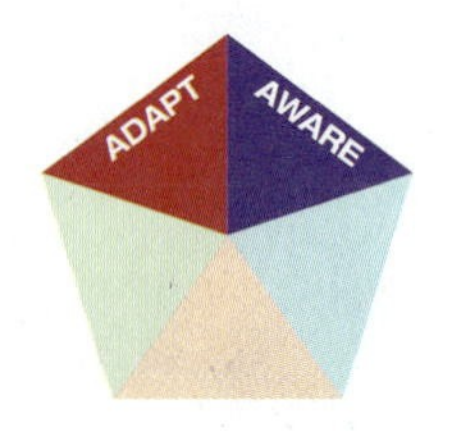

Are leaders born or made? The **trait approach to leadership** suggests that there are certain attributes or traits that make leaders. According to this approach, if you are born with these traits or if you cultivate leadership skills, you will be a leader. Research has identified intelligence, confidence, social skills, general administrative skill, physical energy, and enthusiasm as some of the traits effective leaders possess.[48] Researchers have also found that effective leaders develop persuasive arguments and are comfortable expressing their ideas to others.[49] Another research study found support for two of the Communication Principles for a Lifetime presented in this book: Effective leaders are self-aware and adapt to the people they lead and the context in which they lead.[50] Although many leaders do seem to have traits or special skills that can enhance their ability to influence others, just having these traits does not mean that you will be an effective leader. Traits alone will not ensure effective leadership behavior. Leadership is more complicated than that.

trait approach to leadership
A view of leadership that identifies specific qualities or characteristics of effective leaders.

functional approach to leadership
A view of leadership that identifies the key task and process roles that need to be performed in a group.

Functional Approach

Rather than identifying personality characteristics or other traits, the **functional approach to leadership** categorizes the essential leadership behaviors or functions that need to be performed to enhance the workings of a group. According to the

According to the trait approach to leadership, personal characteristics such as intelligence, confidence, social skills, physical energy, and enthusiasm make good leaders. However, positive traits alone do not guarantee that someone will be a good leader.
Viorel Sima/Fotolia

functional approach, there are two broad leadership functions: (1) task functions and (2) process functions. These two functions should look familiar. They are similar to the types of group roles discussed in Chapter 9.

Task functions include behaviors that help the group or team get the work done. Whether the leader is appointed or elected, one of the responsibilities of leaders is to ensure that the group completes the task it is tackling. The functional approach to leadership suggests that several people can share the leadership functions. These are some of the jobs that often need to be done:

- Helping set the group's agenda
- Recording what the group does
- Determining when meetings begin and end
- Preparing and distributing handouts
- Initiating or proposing new ideas
- Seeking and giving information
- Suggesting options
- Elaborating on the ideas of others
- Evaluating ideas

In most groups, these key functions are assumed by many if not most group members. A group member who rarely helps with any of these tasks often earns the uncoveted title of "slacker."

Process functions are the second major type of function leaders assume in groups. Process leaders seek to maintain a friendly environment that promotes honest, frank discussion. Process leaders have "people skills." They listen sensitively to others and are observant of nonverbal cues. They focus on managing relationships by adapting to the needs of individual members. Another key process leadership task is to seek support from people and resources outside the team. An effective team leader keeps the team informed about how external influences affect the team's work goals.[51] Although a single person can perform all these functions, just as with task leadership, it is more than likely that several people will help maintain the group's process. Specific process roles include the following:

- Energizing the team by encouraging team members to keep at it
- Mediating conflict
- Compromising or helping others to compromise
- Gatekeeping: monitoring discussion to ensure that some members don't talk too much and others too little

In most groups or teams, these process roles are not formally assigned. Although some of the task functions may be explicitly assigned ("Daria, would you make copies of this report?"), process roles are assumed when needed; they emerge according to the needs of the group and the personality, skills, sensitivity, and past experiences of the group members who are present. It is unlikely that you will start a meeting by saying, "Okay, Janice, you're in charge of settling the arguments between Ken and Daryl. And Carl, you try to encourage Muriel and Russell to talk more." Effective leaders look for opportunities to enhance the overall climate of the group. They try to catch people doing something right and then offer sincere praise and recognition.

task function
A leadership behavior that helps a group accomplish its job.

process function
A leadership behavior that helps maintain a positive group climate.

Styles Approach

The **styles approach to leadership** suggests that leaders operate in one of three primary styles: (1) authoritarian, (2) democratic, or (3) laissez-faire. The methods used to influence group members usually fall into one of these broad categories, outlined in Table 10.3.[52]

styles approach to leadership
A view of leadership that identifies three methods of interacting when leading others: authoritarian, democratic, and laissez-faire.

Table 10.3 Leadership Styles

Authoritarian	Democratic	Laissez-Faire
The leader makes all policy decisions.	The leader discusses all policy decisions with group members. The group makes decisions by consensus.	The leader gives minimal direction to discussions of policy decisions. Group members must initiate discussions about policy and procedures.
The leader determines what will happen one step at a time; future steps are unclear or uncertain.	The group discusses what steps need to be taken. Group members work together to develop both short-term and long-term action steps.	The leader may supply information about what steps need to be taken, if asked. The leader does not volunteer information.
The leader tells people what to do.	The leader serves as a facilitator to develop a collaborative approach to accomplishing the group's work.	The leader does not participate in making work assignments.

Authoritarian leaders influence by giving orders and controlling others. Dictators and military officers assume this leadership style. But you don't have to be in the military or living in a dictatorship to experience an authoritarian leadership style. Perhaps you've felt like mumbling, "Who put *her* in charge?" during a group meeting. Or maybe you have observed that some action needed to be taken and asked someone in the group to do what you thought was needed. As we discussed, groups need a certain amount of structure. The authoritarian leader assumes that he or she knows the type and amount of structure the group needs and proceeds to tell others what to do. Authoritarian leaders may be self-aware and may use appropriate verbal and nonverbal messages, but they are not always known for listening and responding to others; they also may not be worried about adapting their messages to those whom they lead. They often speak and expect others to follow. Of the three primary leadership styles, the authoritarian leader is least effective over a long period of time.[53] Yet when a group or team experiences increased stress, a decisive leader is perceived as more charismatic than other types of leaders.[54] Group members don't like an authoritarian leader all the time, but they may tolerate or even appreciate a bold, charismatic leader when there's a need for someone to make an important decision quickly.

The **democratic leader**, as you might guess from the name, consults with the other group members before issuing edicts. The democratic leader listens and adapts messages to others. This type of leader seeks to join in the process of influencing without bulldozing or shoving the group into action its members may resent. Sometimes formal votes are taken in larger groups or assemblies; in smaller groups, the leader or leaders gauge the reaction of the group through dialogue and nonverbal cues. The democratic leader leads by developing a consensus rather than telling people what to do or think.

The **laissez-faire leader** takes a hands-off, laid-back approach to influencing. This type of leader shies away from actively influencing the group. He or she influences only when pushed to lead. Like the authoritarian leader, this type of leader often does not adapt to the needs of the group. A laissez-faire approach is easiest to spot when an elected or appointed leader simply won't lead. Sometimes, a laissez-faire approach may fit the group's needs. In other instances, laissez-faire leaders fear making a mistake, or they just want to be liked and don't want to ruffle anyone's feathers. But as the slogan goes, "Not to decide is to decide." The laissez-faire leader is influencing the group by his or her silence or inactivity. The team may have a problem to unravel, but the laissez-faire leader leaves the task entirely to the rest of the group members.

Which leadership style works best? As we discuss next, it depends on the situation. It also depends on the leader and the members. One study found that a democratic, collaborative leadership style works best when the leader is perceived as credible and charismatic.[55] And as we'll see, a more directive, authoritarian style of leadership is generally more effective when group members doubt that they can effectively accomplish the work and value direct assistance and guidance. Remember that leadership in groups and teams is usually shared by several people. Even when someone has been appointed or elected to be "the leader," leadership roles are often assumed by several group members.

authoritarian leader
One who leads by directing, controlling, telling, and ordering others.

democratic leader
One who leads by developing a consensus among group members; a leader who asks for input and then uses the input when leading and making decisions.

laissez-faire leader
One who fails to lead or who leads or exerts influence only when asked or directed by the group.

Situational Approach

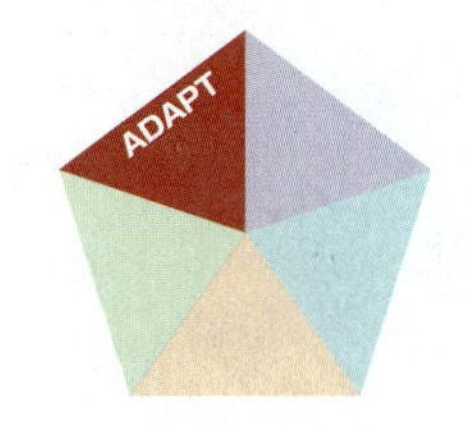

The **situational approach to leadership** views leadership as an interactive process in which such factors as culture, time limitations, group member personalities, and the work the group needs to do determine a particular style of leadership. The situational leadership approach is based on Principle Five: Appropriately adapt messages to others. The effective leader adapts his or her style to fit the needs of the group and the task at hand. Sometimes a group needs a strong, authoritarian leader to make decisions quickly so that the group can achieve its goal. Although most groups prefer a democratic leadership style, during times of crisis a group needs a decisive leader who can help manage uncertainty and provide appropriate structure. An authoritarian style may be acceptable then.[56]

Groups with highly structured goals and a high level of stress also may operate best with a more authoritarian leadership style. For example, firefighters who are battling a house fire with a family of five people inside have a clearly structured goal: to save lives. In this situation, the group needs decisive authoritarian leadership. If the group's task is to solve a problem or make a decision collaboratively, the group will likely benefit from a democratic leadership style. If a group's goal is primarily social or creative, a laissez-faire leader may be best. Compared to the firefighters, for example, a book club that is trying to select its next reading selection has less structured goals (there are many possible options) and a less stressful situation (there is no fire!). This less structured and less stressful task calls for a more participative democratic style of leadership or a hands-off, laissez-faire style of leadership. So according to the situational approach, the answer to the question "What's the best leadership style?" is "It depends."[57]

The readiness of the group also plays a major role in which leadership style would work best.[58] *Readiness* refers to a group member's ability to assume responsibility to accomplish a task; his or her overall knowledge, background, and experience; and his or her general level of motivation. Leadership experts Paul Hersey and Ken Blanchard suggest that a directive or more authoritative, "telling" style of leadership seems to

situational approach to leadership
A view of leadership as an interactive process in which a leader gauges how to lead based on such factors as the quality of the relationships among group members, the power of the leader, the nature of the task, and the maturity of the group.

surface-level diversity
Human differences that are easily visible to us, such as differences in ethnicity, race, age, sex, gender, and other social and observable features.

deep-level diversity
Human differences that aren't always visible on the surface, such as differences in attitudes, opinions, values, information, culture, and other factors that take time to become evident in groups.

Communication & DIVERSITY

Deep and Surface Diversity: Which Differences Make a Difference?

People work in groups because "two heads are better than one." More people bring more—and more varied—approaches to solving a problem or illuminating an issue. But are all differences created equal?

Researchers have found that some differences among group members are more significant than others.[59] **Surface-level diversity** encompasses the human differences that are easily visible to us, such as differences in ethnicity, race, age, sex, gender, and other social and observable features. **Deep-level diversity** involves differences that aren't always visible on the surface, such as differences in attitudes, opinions, values, information, culture, and other factors that take time to become evident in groups. Group communication researcher Ralph Rodriguez has found that these differences in underlying values or approaches to problems affect a group's performance more than do differences in such surface characteristics as race, gender, and ethnicity. Rodriguez also suggests that groups can enhance the quality of their outcomes if they discuss their differences.[60]

- *Be cautious of making sweeping generalizations about people who are from a culture that appears to be similar to yours.* Researchers have found that we often expect people who look like us at the surface level to agree with us. Yet the deep-level differences may be the best predictors of whether someone agrees or disagrees with our perspective.[61]
- *Take time to explore group members' deep-level differences in perspectives and approaches.* These deep-level differences are noticed only after people spend time with one another and are engaged in conversation.
- *Encourage people to share ideas and information via e-mail or text messages.* Because some members of a group may be quieter than others, the opportunity to respond individually rather than orally in the presence of others may bring out more differences in perspective that can help a group reach a better outcome.
- *Group members need the benefit of different perspectives.* If you're in the surface-level minority or the deep-level minority in a group, make sure that you tactfully yet assertively express your ideas, opinions, facts, and information to the group.

work best when groups have a low level of readiness. A high degree of readiness suggests that a more delegating style of leadership would help the group function well. An exceptionally ready or mature group may need minimal direction—more of a laissez-faire leadership style. Wise leaders also consider the cultural backgrounds of those whom they lead. Research supports the important role of culture in influencing the style of leadership that seems to be best suited to a team.[62] Group members from collective cultures seem to appreciate more participative styles of leadership.

One simple rule for determining your leadership style is that when the leader emerges naturally from the group or leads a one-time-only group, the group will permit him or her to be more directive. If the group will be together for some time and the quality of group relations is important to the functioning of the group, a more participative, democratic leadership style is in order.[63]

Transformational Leadership

One of the newer leadership approaches to emerge is called the **transformational approach to leadership**.[64] The transformational leader influences the group or organization by *transforming* the group—giving it a new vision, energizing or realigning the group culture, or giving the group a new structure. The leader leads by helping the group see all the possibilities within the group. The transformational leader also develops a relationship with those whom he or she leads.[65] Author Peter Senge suggests three fundamental skills of transformational leadership: (1) Build a shared vision, (2) challenge existing ways of thinking, and (3) be a systems thinker—help a group or team see that everything is connected to everything else.[66] Articulating a shared, or collective, vision is an important part of what a transformational leader does. An authoritarian leader would just tell the group, "Here's your vision; now get to work." The democratic leader would ask, "What vision do you want?" The laissez-faire leader would do nothing about a vision unless asked to do something. The situational leader would say, "Let me see what type of group I'm leading and listen to group members, and then I'll share a vision."

transformational approach to leadership
A view of leadership that defines a leader as one who leads by shaping the vision of the group and by developing trust through high-quality interpersonal relationships with group members.

Research suggests that transformational leaders can enhance team cohesiveness and improve perceptions of team performance.[67] They achieve these benefits by linking with other groups and teams either inside or outside the organization, helping the group span boundaries and stay connected with issues and forces that influence the group.[68]

Another skill of transformational leaders is the ability to encourage new ideas. Teams that emphasize learning do a better job of both accomplishing the task and fostering positive, supportive interpersonal relationships.[69] Transformational leaders like to think of themselves as coaches or mentors rather than leaders who dictate or even just facilitate interaction. They are sometimes viewed as the "guide on the side" rather than the "sage on the stage."

Can transformational leadership skills—or any leadership skills—be taught, the way you can teach someone to drive a car? Some researchers suggest that experience is the best teacher.[70] You can learn how to communicate, listen, relate, and solve problems, but having an opportunity to practice these skills in real-life settings may be the best way to develop your leadership skills. Whether you learn leadership skills and principles from a

RECAP

Leadership Approaches

Approach to Leadership	Guiding Principle
Trait	Leaders possess certain traits or characteristics that contribute to leadership effectiveness.
Functional	Leaders influence others through two primary functions: • Task functions, which help accomplish the work • Process functions, which help establish a positive climate
Styles	Leadership is enacted in three primary styles: • Authoritarian leaders direct and control others. • Democratic leaders solicit input from others and seek to lead by involving others in the decisions. • Laissez-faire leaders intentionally influence others only when asked or directed by others to lead.
Situational	Leadership is an interactive process in which a leader adapts his or her approach based on such factors as • The quality of group member relationships. • The nature of the task. • Time limitations.
Transformational	A leader influences others by • Developing a shared vision. • Using listening and relationship-building skills to create a climate of trust.

book or from the "school of life," the role of a good leader is that of a servant, helping others accomplish a goal. This ancient description of a wise leader offers considerable insight into what makes a leader great:

> The wicked leader the people despise.
> The good leader the people revere.
> Of the great leader the people say,
> "We did it ourselves."
> —Lao Tsu

Enhancing Group and Team Meetings

10.4 Develop and use strategies to structure meetings appropriately, keep meetings on track, and promote appropriate dialogue and interaction.

Humor columnist Dave Barry said, "If you had to identify, in one word, the reason why the human race has not achieved, and never will achieve, its full potential, that word would be *meetings*."[71] Meetings are an inescapable fact of life for most people and will undoubtedly be inescapable for you as well.

Why does meeting participation inspire such a negative reaction—not just from Dave Barry, but from many people? Often, it's because meeting leaders and participants have not mastered the principles we've stressed as fundamental to communication success in any context. Meetings are more productive if participants are aware of their behaviors and the behaviors of others and if they believe they have the necessary skill to make meetings effective.[72] Using and interpreting verbal and nonverbal messages effectively are also vital for meeting effectiveness, as are listening and responding to messages with sensitivity. Because of the complexity and uncertainty that arise when people collaborate, being able to adapt message content and message structure is essential.[73] We conclude this chapter by providing some tips for managing one of the most likely collaborative contexts you'll encounter: meetings.

What specific problems occur most frequently in meetings? According to a survey of meeting participants, the most common meeting "sin" is getting off the subject.[74] The second-biggest problem is not having clear goals or a meeting agenda. Meeting goers also reported that often meetings were too long, people weren't prepared, nothing really happened, meetings started late, and there were no follow-up action plans.

agenda
A written plan for achieving the goals during a group meeting, which typically includes items for discussion, action, and information.

Meetings need two essential things to be effective: *structure* and *interaction*. Sound familiar? As we noted earlier in this chapter, groups also need a balance of these two things.

Manage Meeting Structure

The essential weapon to combat disorganized, rambling meetings is a clear, well-developed **agenda**, a list of the key issues, ideas, and information that will be discussed, in the order of discussion. How do you develop a well-crafted agenda? Consider these three steps.

STEP ONE: DETERMINE YOUR MEETING GOALS

Every meeting seeks to accomplish something. (If you don't have something to accomplish, don't hold a meeting!) Most meetings have one or more of the following three goals: (1) giving information, (2) discussing information, and (3) taking action.

- *Giving information.* An information-giving meeting is like a briefing or a series of short speeches. If the only

Aaron Huw/CARTOONSTOCK

"I fear we may have strayed from the agenda somewhat."

task is to share information, you may not really need a meeting at all; a written memo or an e-mail message will suffice. If you want to emphasize the importance of the information by sharing with others face to face, however, then giving information is an appropriate primary meeting goal.

- *Discussing information.* An information-discussion meeting is one in which there is considerable give and take. The key to this type of meeting is not to let it become a series of long-winded speeches. Also, if you're not careful, discussions digress from the topic. The meeting leader or meeting participants should be aware of the goals of the discussion so that the comments remain relevant.
- *Taking action.* A meeting may involve making a decision, solving a problem, or implementing a decision or solution. If the purpose of the meeting is to take action, it's helpful if group members know before they arrive for the meeting that they will be asked to take some action.

STEP TWO: IDENTIFY WHAT NEEDS TO BE DISCUSSED TO ACHIEVE THE GOAL After you have determined your goal(s), you need to determine how to structure the meeting to achieve the goal. What topics need to be covered to achieve the goal? What information do you need? What issues do you need to focus on? Brainstorm answers to these questions, but don't worry about the precise order of the items yet; focus on organizing the agenda after you know what you need to discuss.

STEP THREE: ORGANIZE THE AGENDA Once you have identified your meeting goals (giving information, discussing information, taking action) and assessed what you need to talk about, take time to arrange the items in the most effective way to achieve your goals. Table 10.4 identifies several meeting problems and possible solutions. In addition, here are several specific strategies for organizing effective meetings:[75]

- Organize the agenda around your meeting goals. If you're meeting to solve a problem, you could use the five problem-solving steps as an agenda-setting guide: (1) Identify and define the problem, (2) analyze the problem, (3) generate creative options, (4) select the best option, and (5) take action. A single meeting may focus on only one or two of those steps; don't feel that you have to cram all five problem-solving steps into every meeting.
- Use the subheads "Information Items," "Discussion Items," and "Action Items" as you construct your agenda to signal to group members the goal of the discussion, as shown in the sample meeting agenda.
- Consider putting your most important agenda item first, because what is introduced first usually takes the most time.

Table 10.4 Solving Meeting Agenda Problems

Potential Meeting Agenda Problem	Suggested Meeting Agenda Strategy
Meeting participants tend to spend more time on the first or second agenda item than on later items.	Make sure that the early agenda items are something the group needs to spend time on.
Meeting participants want to talk, even if the meeting leader wants them to just listen.	Take advantage of the desire to participate by inviting input and discussion early in the meeting rather than trying to squelch discussion or having to deal with interruption of group members.
Meeting participants aren't prepared. They haven't done their "homework."	Allow a few minutes for silent reading. Let members get up to speed by reviewing information or quickly looking at key pieces of data.
Meeting participants won't stick to the agenda.	Continue to remind the group of the agenda and the overall goal of the meeting. Make sure to distribute a written agenda ahead of the meeting.
There is an agenda item that may produce conflict and disagreement.	Help the group develop a sense of success by putting one or more noncontroversial items on the agenda ahead of the item that may produce conflict. Build on the group's ability to reach agreement.

- There may be times when you will want to put your most challenging issue for discussion in the middle of the meeting. This gives the group a chance to get oriented at the beginning and ease out of the discussion at the end.[76]
- Consider making your first agenda item something that will immediately involve all meeting participants in active discussion. If you start with routine reports (a common practice), you establish a norm of passivity, and boredom is the usual result.
- If you are going to discuss a conflict-producing topic, you may want to put that agenda item after an issue on which you think the group will reach agreement. Groups may be more likely to reach agreement on a contentious issue if they have already reached agreement on another point.
- Start the meeting by asking meeting participants whether they have any other agenda items to consider. That way, you aren't as likely to be surprised by people who want to add something after you've planned the meeting agenda.
- After you've prepared your agenda, estimate how long you think the group will take to discuss each agenda item. Most groups take more time than you would expect to talk about issues and ideas.

Sample Meeting Agenda

Meeting Goals:

1. Discuss new product proposal: evaluate the pros and cons.
2. Decide whether to implement the personnel policy and mentor program.
3. Receive updates from committees.

I. Discussion Items
- A. How should we revise today's agenda?
- B. Identify new problems: What new issues or problems have you identified?
- C. React to new product team proposal (distributed by e-mail): What are the pros and cons of the proposal?

II. Action Items
- A. Should we approve the new personnel policy (distributed by e-mail)?
- B. Issue: Should we implement the new mentor program? If so, what should the program policies be?

III. Information Items
- A. New employee orientation report
- B. Planning committee report
- C. Finance committee report
- D. Announcements

A sample agenda is shown above. Notice that the meeting has clear goals. Also notice how many of the agenda items are phrased as questions. Questions give an agenda focus and help to manage discussion.

When your job is to lead the meeting, you have several specific tasks to perform, including the following:

1. Call the group together; find out when is the best time to meet (finding time is often a major problem for busy people).
2. Develop an agenda, using the steps already described.
3. Determine whether there is a **quorum**—the minimum number of people who must be present at a meeting to conduct business.
4. Call the meeting to order.
5. Keep notes (or delegate note-taking). Use a flipchart, chalkboard, or dry-erase board or a computer projection method to make notes visible to members during the meeting. Such written notes of the meeting become the "group mind" and help keep the group structured.
6. Decide when to take a vote.
7. Prepare a final report or delegate to a group member the preparation of a report or minutes.

Manage Meeting Interaction

Interaction, as you recall, is the back-and-forth dialogue and discussion in which participants engage during meetings. Without interaction, meetings would be like a monologue, a speech, or a seminar rather than a lively discussion. It's important for people in a meeting to be involved in the discussion and share the information that they have with one another.[77] Research has found that meetings that have more equal

quorum
The minimum number of people who must be present at a meeting to conduct business.

Communication & TECHNOLOGY

Virtual Meeting Tips

A virtual meeting occurs when you use the Internet or some other electronic means of connecting with others rather than meeting face to face. Increased globalization of the economy, rising travel costs, and technological advances in electronic collaboration make it likely that you will hold meetings in cyberspace. What are ways to maximize your electronic collaboration? Here are several research-supported tips to help you make the most of mediated meetings:[78]

- *Start live.* If at all possible, make your first meeting a face-to-face meeting. Getting to know your team members in person helps to develop positive relationships at the outset of a longer project in which you will be interacting over a period of time.[79]
- *Develop communication ground rules.* Aside from communicating during a planned virtual meeting, determine how and when you will communicate with other team members.[80] Will you call someone on the phone? Skype? Use only e-mail? Clarify communication expectations about the method of communication and when it's best to reach your fellow team members.
- *Communicate frequently.* One ground rule we suggest is to contact team members when questions or issues arise even if you're not in a scheduled meeting. Don't hesitate to send virtual meeting members short notes and messages. Resist the temptation to hold onto information until you have a longer message. Frequent communication helps virtual meeting participants get to know one another.
- *Use technology to monitor team progress.* Invite team members to provide periodic reports via e-mail or on the team home page. Also distribute meeting minutes via e-mail very soon after the group has held a virtual meeting.
- *Encourage the development of relationships.* Virtual meetings have a tendency to be task oriented. To foster good team relationships, allow time at the beginning of a virtual meeting for relationship building; during this time, encourage meeting participants to engage in off-task talk, communicating personal information. During the meeting, ensure that every person is heard from and that all are engaged and participating in the meeting.
- *Be positive.* Research suggests that, like members of face-to-face groups, virtual group members who have a positive perception of their own abilities to achieve results are more effective. So fostering a can-do spirit in a group or team is a good thing to do.[81]

participation by all participants generally are more effective than meetings dominated by a few people.[82] But too much unfocused interaction can result in a disorganized, chaotic discussion. To keep a meeting on track, meeting leaders and participants need facilitation skills. The most important facilitation skills include being a gatekeeper, using metadiscussion, monitoring discussion time, and structuring discussion techniques to keep discussion focused.

USE GATEKEEPING SKILLS A gatekeeper encourages less-talkative members to participate and tries to limit long-winded contributions by other group members. Gatekeepers need to be good listeners so that they can help manage the flow of conversation. Gatekeepers make such comments as "Ashley, we haven't heard your ideas yet. Won't you share your thoughts with us?" or "Mike, thanks for sharing, but I'd like to hear what others have to say." Polite, tactful invitations to talk or limit talk usually work. As we noted earlier in this chapter, you may need to speak privately with chronic oververbalizers to let them know that you would appreciate a more balanced discussion.

USE METADISCUSSION **Metadiscussion** literally means "discussion about discussion."[83] It's a comment about the discussion process rather than about the topic under consideration. Metadiscussional statements include "I'm not following this conversation. What is our goal?" "Can someone summarize what we've accomplished so far?" and "Peggy, I'm not sure I understand how your observation relates to our meeting goal." These comments contain information and advice about the communication process rather than about the issues being discussed.

metadiscussion
Discussion about the discussion process; comments that help the group remain focused on the goals of the group or that point out how the group is doing its work.

Metadiscussional phrases are helpful ways to keep the team or group focused on the task. Obviously, metadiscussional statements should not be phrased to personally attack others. Don't just blurt out "You're off task" or "Oh, let's not talk about that anymore." Instead, use tactful ways of letting other group members know that you'd like to return to the issues at hand. Use "I" messages rather than "you" messages to bring the group back on track. An **"I" message** begins with the word *I*, such as "I am not sure where we are in our discussion" or "I am lost here." A **"you" message** is a way of phrasing a message that makes others feel defensive—for example, "You're not following the agenda" or "Your point doesn't make any sense." Another way to express these same ideas, but with less of a negative edge, is to use "I" messages such as "I'm not sure where we are on the agenda" or "I'm not sure I understand how your point relates to the issue we are discussing." The ability to carry on metadiscussion is an exceptionally powerful skill because you can offer metadiscussional statements even if you are not the appointed leader.

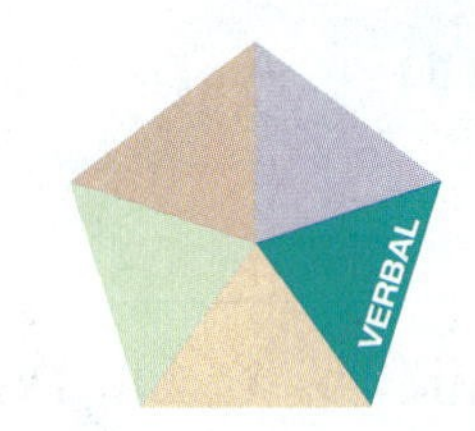

MONITOR TIME Being sensitive to the time the group is spending on an issue is yet another skill that is necessary to manage meeting interaction. Think of your agenda as a map, helping you plan where you want to go. Think of the clock as your gas gauge, telling you the amount of fuel you have to get where you want to go. In a meeting, keeping one eye on the clock and one eye on the agenda is analogous to focusing on the map and the gas gauge on a car trip. If you are running low on fuel (time), you will need to either get more gas (budget more time) or recognize that you will not get where you want to go. Begin each meeting by asking how long members can meet. If you have two or three crucial agenda items and one-third of your group has to leave in an hour, you may need to reshuffle your agenda to make sure that you can achieve your goals.

"I" message
A message in which you state your perspective or point of view.

"you" message
A message that is likely to create defensiveness in others because it emphasizes how another person has created a problem rather than describing the problem from one's own perspective ("I" message).

USE STRUCTURE TO MANAGE INTERACTION Another way to manage interaction is to use some of the prescriptive structures talked about earlier. For example, you can use silent brainstorming is a way to gain maximum participation from everyone. Yet another strategy is to ask people to come to the meeting with written responses to questions you posed in the agenda, which group members received in advance of the meeting. This signals that you want people to prepare for the meeting beforehand rather than doing their "homework" at the meeting.

An essential task of the meeting facilitator is to orchestrate meaningful interaction during the meeting so that all group or team members have the opportunity to share. Another structured method of inviting involvement is to have group members first write individually and then share their ideas with the group. Having members write before speaking is like providing them with a script, which can be effective in garnering contributions from all group members, not just the people who talk the most or who aren't shy about speaking up.

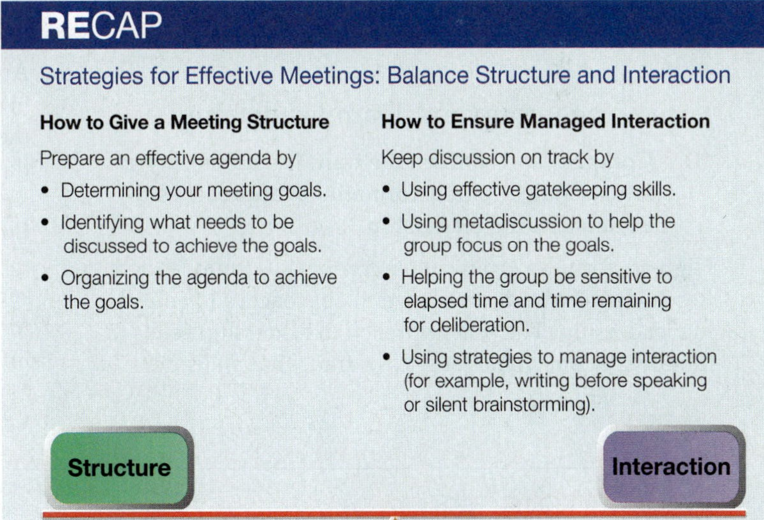

What are the best strategies to make yourself a valuable meeting leader or participant? The five Communication Principles for a Lifetime that we emphasize throughout the book will serve you well. In general, be aware of your own behavior and the behavior of others. Monitor your verbal and nonverbal messages to make sure that you are making comments relevant to the task at hand, but also be sensitive to the needs of the people in your group. You develop that sensitivity by listening to others and responding thoughtfully. Ineffective meeting participants make little effort to link their comments to what others are saying. They also don't adapt to the messages of others. Effective communicators adapt what they say and do to help achieve the goals of the group. There is evidence that putting these principles into practice will enhance group and team performance.[84]

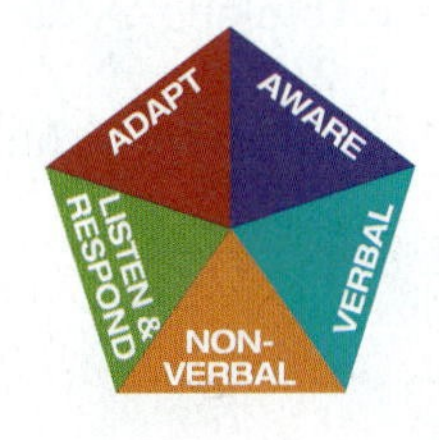

STUDY GUIDE:
Review, Apply, and Assess Your Knowledge and Skill

Review Your Knowledge

What Effective Group and Team Members Do

10.1 Identify six functions that effective group members perform.

Effective group members identify a clear, elevating goal; develop a results-driven structure; gather, share, and use information effectively; develop options; evaluate ideas; and are sensitive to group social and relationship concerns.

Structuring Group and Team Problem Solving

10.2 List and describe the five steps of group problem solving (reflective thinking).

Although there is no single series of steps that will ensure high performance, five classic steps can help groups organize the problem-solving process: (1) identify and define the problem, (2) analyze the problem, (3) generate creative solutions, (4) select the best solution, and (5) take action.

Enhancing Group and Team Leadership

10.3 Compare and contrast the trait, functional, styles, situational, and transformational approaches to understanding leadership.

High-performing groups have competent group leaders. Researchers have devised several approaches to analyzing leadership. The trait approach to leadership seeks to identify certain characteristics or traits that all leaders possess. The functional approach to leadership suggests that leaders need to be concerned with both task functions and group process functions. A third approach to understanding leadership, the styles approach, identifies leaders as authoritarian, democratic, or laissez-faire. No one style seems to work best all the time. The situational leadership approach suggests that the best leadership style depends on a variety of factors, including the readiness of the group, cultures of group members, the urgency of the problem, and the type of issue the group is discussing. Finally, transformational leadership is an approach that encourages leaders to help shape the vision and goals of the group by being in touch with followers.

Enhancing Group and Team Meetings

10.4 Develop and use strategies to structure meetings appropriately, keep meetings on track, and promote appropriate dialogue and interaction.

An effective meeting needs a balance of structure and interaction. Groups maintain appropriate structure if meeting planners develop and use an agenda to keep the discussion focused and on track. Meetings also need appropriate amounts of dialogue and discussion. Effective meeting participants monitor the amount of participation from other group or team members and serve as gatekeepers to ensure that oververbalizers don't monopolize the discussion and quiet members don't feel intimidated.

Key Terms

Laissez-Faire Leader, p. 238
Situational Approach to Leadership, p. 239
Surface-Level Diversity, p. 239
Deep-Level Diversity, p. 239
Transformational Approach to Leadership, p. 240
Agenda, p. 241
Quorum, p. 243
Metadiscussion, p. 244
"I" message, p. 245
"You" message, p. 245

The Principle Points

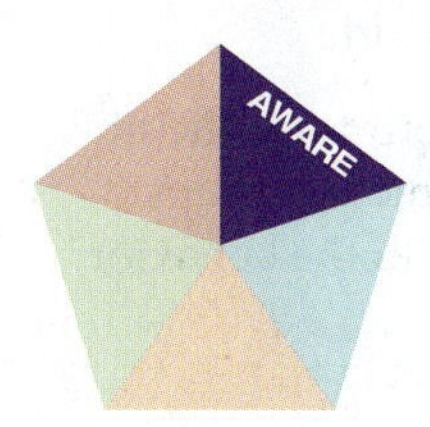

Principle One:

Be aware of your communication with yourself and others.

- Be sensitive to your group's need for appropriate structure to organize and focus the discussion or interaction and to encourage dialogue.
- Be aware of the appropriate leadership style to meet your group's needs.

Principle Two:

Effectively use and interpret verbal messages.

- Clearly describe the goal of the group.
- Evaluate the merits of ideas by verbalizing both the pros and the cons.
- Use verbal "I" messages to express your need for information and your sensitivity to other group members' feelings.
- Develop and use written agendas to give meetings structure.
- Manage the amount of interaction in a group by encouraging quiet members to participate and overly dominant members to let others express ideas.
- Use metadiscussion to keep a meeting on track.

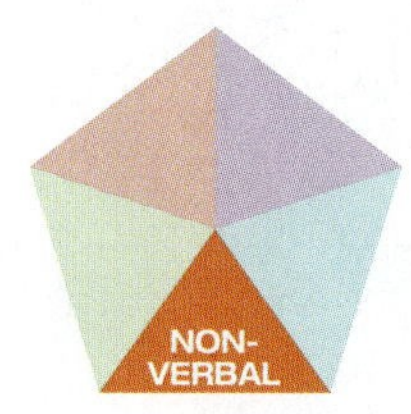

Principle Three:

Effectively use and interpret nonverbal messages.

- Use appropriate nonverbal messages to establish and maintain a positive group climate.
- When brainstorming, do your best to avoid nonverbally expressing your evaluation of other people's ideas.

Principle Four:

Listen and respond thoughtfully to others.

- Listen to other group members to determine whether your group is accomplishing the appropriate group functions.
- Listen and respond to others to express your sensitivity to others' ideas and opinions.
- To be an effective leader, listen and thoughtfully respond to all members.
- Listen and respond to provide appropriate contributions to group meetings and problem-solving discussions.

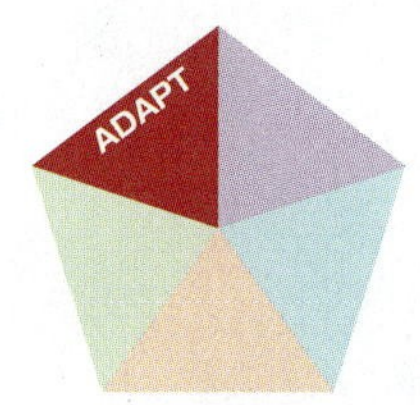

Principle Five:

Appropriately adapt messages to others.

- Adapt your leadership and group membership styles to achieve the goals of the group.
- Adapt your messages to help the group identify, define, and analyze the problem; create solutions; select the best solution; and take action.
- Adapt your messages to give group meetings appropriate structure and to foster interaction.

Apply Your Skill

Consider the following questions. Write your answers and/or share them with your classmates:

1. Describe the best group member or teammate you have encountered. How did that person's behavior compare to this chapter's description of effective team members?
2. Think of a successful brainstorming session or a session with problems in which you've participated as a group leader or member. What factors caused the success or led to the problems? If there were problems, what could be done to address them?
3. How can group members adapt to work effectively if the leader is using an authoritarian style and the group would prefer a more democratic style?
4. Using the suggestions and following the examples presented in this chapter, draft a brief agenda for an upcoming meeting of a group you're in.
5. Review Table 10.1. What other patterns of difficult group behavior have you encountered in groups? How would you suggest dealing with the behavior?

Assess Your Skill

Assessing Group and Team Problem-Solving Competencies[85]

Use the evaluation form on pages 250 to 251 to assess the presence or absence of small group communication competencies in a group or team discussion. *Competencies* are specific behaviors that group and team members perform. The assessment form includes nine competencies organized into four general categories. Here's how to use the form:

1. Observe a group or team that is attempting to solve a problem. Write the names of the group members at the top of the form. (If the group includes more than five members, photocopy the form so that each group member can be evaluated.)
2. When using the form, first decide whether each group member has performed each competency. Circle NO if the group member was not observed performing the competency. Circle YES if you did observe the group member performing the competency (for example, defining the problem, analyzing the problem, identifying criteria).
3. For each competency for which you circled YES, determine how effectively the competency was performed. Use a scale from 0 to 3:

   0 = The group member performed this competency but did so inappropriately or inadequately. For example, the person observed tried to define the problem but did so poorly.
   1 = Overall, the person's performance of this competency was adequate.
   2 = The person performed this competency twice.
   3 = The person performed this competency three or more times.
4. Total the score for each group member in each of the following four categories.

   Problem-oriented competencies consist of items 1 and 2. These are behaviors that help the group or team define and analyze the problem. If a group member performed the competencies, his or her point total for this category ranges from 0 to 6. The more points the person scores, the better he or she performed this competency.
   - Communicate your sensitivity to other group members through your nonverbal behavior.
   - Use appropriate eye contact and other nonverbal cues to regulate the flow of interaction in group and team meetings.

   Solution-oriented competencies include items 3, 4, and 5; the point total for this category ranges from 0 to 9. These competencies focus on how well the group or team member helped to develop and evaluate a solution to the problem.

Discussion management competencies, competencies that helped the group or team remain focused or helped the group manage interaction, are items 6 and 7. The point total for this category ranges from 0 to 6.

Relational competencies are behaviors that focus on dealing with conflict and developing a positive, supportive group climate. Items 8 and 9 reflect this competency; point total for this category ranges from 0 to 6.

5. You can also assess the group's or team's overall ability to perform these competencies. The column marked "Group Assessment" can be used to record your overall impressions of how effectively the group or team behaved. Circle NO if no one in the group performed a particular competency. Circle YES if at least one person in the group or team performed this competency. Then evaluate how well the entire group performed this competency, using the scale already described.

Sometimes it is difficult to make so many judgments about group competencies by just viewing a group discussion once. Many people find that it's easier to make a video recording of the group discussion so that they can observe it more than once.

Competent Group Communicator

Problem-Solving Group Communication Competencies	Group Member A		Group Member B	
COMPETENCIES				
Problem-Oriented Competencies				
1. **Defined the problem** the group attempted to solve.	NO	YES 0 1 2 3	NO	YES 0 1 2 3
2. **Analyzed the problem** the group attempted to solve. Used relevant information, data, or evidence; discussed the causes, obstacles, history, symptoms, or significance of the problem.	NO	YES 0 1 2 3	NO	YES 0 1 2 3
Solution-Oriented Competencies				
3. **Identified criteria** for an appropriate solution to the problem.	NO	YES 0 1 2 3	NO	YES 0 1 2 3
4. **Generated solutions** or alternatives to the problem.	NO	YES 0 1 2 3	NO	YES 0 1 2 3
5. **Evaluated solution(s):** Identified positive or negative consequences of the proposed solutions.	NO	YES 0 1 2 3	NO	YES 0 1 2 3
Discussion Management Competencies				
6. **Maintained task focus:** Helped the group stay on or return to the task, issue, or topic the group was discussing.	NO	YES 0 1 2 3	NO	YES 0 1 2 3
7. **Managed group interaction:** Appropriately initiated and terminated discussion, contributed to the discussion, or invited others to contribute to the discussion. Didn't dominate or withdraw.	NO	YES 0 1 2 3	NO	YES 0 1 2 3
Relational Competencies				
8. **Managed conflict:** Appropriately and constructively helped the group stay focused on issues rather than personalities when conflict occurred.	NO	YES 0 1 2 3	NO	YES 0 1 2 3
9. **Maintained climate:** Offered positive verbal comments or nonverbal expressions that helped maintain a positive group climate.	NO	YES 0 1 2 3	NO	YES 0 1 2 3

Scoring

NO = Not observed

YES
0 = Overall inappropriate or inadequate performance of competency
1 = Overall adequate performance of competency
2 = Person performed this competency twice
3 = Person performed this competency three or more times

Group Member C	Group Member D	Group Member E	Group Assessment
NO YES 0 1 2 3	NO YES 0 1 2 3	NO YES 0 1 2 3	NO YES 0 1 2 3
NO YES 0 1 2 3	NO YES 0 1 2 3	NO YES 0 1 2 3	NO YES 0 1 2 3
NO YES 0 1 2 3	NO YES 0 1 2 3	NO YES 0 1 2 3	NO YES 0 1 2 3
NO YES 0 1 2 3	NO YES 0 1 2 3	NO YES 0 1 2 3	NO YES 0 1 2 3
NO YES 0 1 2 3	NO YES 0 1 2 3	NO YES 0 1 2 3	NO YES 0 1 2 3
NO YES 0 1 2 3	NO YES 0 1 2 3	NO YES 0 1 2 3	NO YES 0 1 2 3
NO YES 0 1 2 3	NO YES 0 1 2 3	NO YES 0 1 2 3	NO YES 0 1 2 3
NO YES 0 1 2 3	NO YES 0 1 2 3	NO YES 0 1 2 3	NO YES 0 1 2 3
NO YES 0 1 2 3	NO YES 0 1 2 3	NO YES 0 1 2 3	NO YES 0 1 2 3

Problem-Oriented Competencies (0–6)
Solution-Oriented Competencies (0–9)
Discussion Management Competencies (0–6)
Relational Competencies (0–6)

Chapter 11
Developing Your Speech

Freedom of speech is of no use to a man who has nothing to say. —FRANKLIN D. ROOSEVELT

Bronwyn Photo/Shutterstock

Chapter Outline

Chapter Objectives

After studying this chapter, you should be able to

11.1 List and explain the components of the audience-centered public speaking model.

11.2 Apply specific strategies for becoming a more confident speaker.

11.3 Select and narrow a topic for a speech.

11.4 Write an audience-centered specific-purpose statement for a speech.

11.5 Develop a central idea for a speech.

11.6 Generate main ideas from a central idea.

11.7 Describe four potential sources and seven types of supporting material for a speech, and use each type effectively.

A good friend of ours who has lived in Hong Kong for several years recently remarked that she found traveling back to the United States exhausting. Her reason? It was not so much the long plane trip or the thirteen-hour time difference, but, as she explained, "When I begin to hear airport public announcements in English instead of Cantonese, I suddenly feel compelled to pay attention to every word. All that listening wears me out!"

Few of us can take for granted that others will listen to us merely because we are speaking their native language. However, when we study the public speaking process and learn its component skills and principles, we increase the likelihood that others will listen to us out of genuine, compelling interest.

Far from being a rare talent possessed only by an inspired few, the skill of **public speaking,** or **presentational speaking**, is a teachable, learnable process of developing, supporting, organizing, and orally presenting ideas. The skills you will develop as you learn and practice this process will be of practical use in the future. They will give you an edge in other college courses that require oral presentations. They may help you convince a current or future boss that you deserve a raise. They may even land you a job.

Let's begin our discussion with an overview of the public speaking process. Then we will offer suggestions for building your confidence as a public speaker before focusing specifically on the first five stages of the public speaking process—discovering and narrowing your topic, identifying your purpose, developing a central idea, generating main ideas, and gathering supporting material for your speech—all firmly grounded in the five Communication Principles for a Lifetime.

Overviewing the Public Speaking Process

11.1 List and explain the components of the audience-centered public speaking model.

public speaking (presentational speaking)
A teachable, learnable process of developing, supporting, organizing, and orally presenting ideas.

You don't have to read an entire book on public speaking before you give your first speech. An overview of the public speaking process can help you with your early assignments even if you have to speak before you have a chance to read Chapters 11 through through 15. Figure 11.1 illustrates the public speaking process. At the center of the model is "Consider the audience." Double arrows connect this center with every other stage, illustrating that at any point, you may revise your ideas or strategies as you learn more about your audience. Your audience influences every decision you make.

Audience-centered public speakers are inherently sensitive to the diversity of their audiences. While guarding against generalizations that might be offensive, they acknowledge that cultural, ethnic, and other traditions affect the way people process messages. They apply the fundamental principle of appropriately adapting their messages to others. How? They might choose to use pictures to help them communicate. They might select topics and use illustrations with universal themes such as family and friendship. They might adjust the formality of their delivery and even their clothing to whatever is expected by the majority of the audience members. The fundamental communication principle of adapting to the audience is central to the success of any speech.

audience-centered public speaker
Someone who considers and adapts to the audience at every stage of the public speaking process.

public speaking anxiety
Also known as stage fright or speaker anxiety; anxiety about speaking in public that is manifested in physiological symptoms such as rapid heartbeat, butterflies in the stomach, shaking knees and hands, quivering voice, and increased perspiration.

Now view the model as a clock, with "Select and narrow topic" at 12 o'clock. From this stage, the process proceeds clockwise in the direction of the arrows, to "Deliver speech." Each stage is one of the tasks of the public speaker:

1. Select and narrow topic.
2. Determine purpose.
3. Develop central idea.
4. Generate main ideas.
5. Gather supporting material.
6. Organize speech.
7. Rehearse speech.
8. Deliver speech.

Figure 11.1 An Audience-Centered Model of the Public Speaking Process

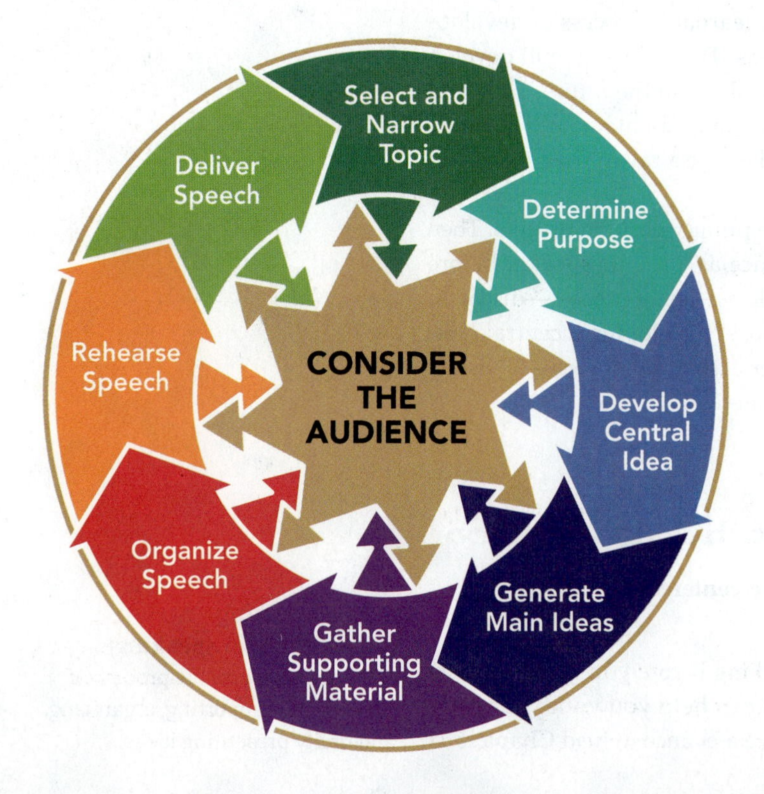

Building Your Confidence

11.2 Apply specific strategies for becoming a more confident speaker.

The above overview of the stages of the public speaking process should help you understand how to prepare for your first speaking assignment, but if you still feel nervous at the prospect, you are definitely not alone.[1] Communication apprehension may have a genetic basis: Some people may inherit a tendency to feel anxious about speaking in public.[2] One study found that more than 80 percent of us feel anxious when we speak to an audience.[3] Other surveys have discovered that the fear of public speaking is more common than the fear of death![4]

If you are taking a communication class online, you might think you will experience less **public speaking anxiety** than you would if you were speaking to a live audience. But recent research suggests that in fact slightly *more* students report feeling anxious about web-based speech delivery than the number who report anxiety about face-to-face delivery.[5]

Developing Your Speech Step by Step

Considering Your Audience

A well-known Chinese proverb says that a journey of a thousand miles begins with a single step. Developing and delivering a speech may seem like a daunting journey. But if you take it one step at a time and keep your focus on your audience, you'll be rewarded with a well-crafted and well-delivered message.

To help you see how the audience-centered speaking process unfolds, this Developing Your Speech Step by Step feature will provide a window through which you can see how one student prepared and delivered a speech. Lario Albarran, a student at the University of Texas, developed the informative speech entitled "Poverty and the Brain" that is outlined in Chapter 12.[6] In the pages ahead, we'll walk through the process Lario used to develop his speech.

Lario thought about his audience even before selecting his topic. Realizing that his listeners would include both university students and faculty, he knew that he could discuss complex issues, using a fairly advanced vocabulary. His concern was to find a topic that would interest both groups.

Fortunately, even if you are predisposed by genetics or course delivery mode to experience public speaking anxiety, you can learn strategies to help you manage your apprehension. If, on the other hand, the prospect of giving a speech makes you feel a sense of heightened excitement rather than fear, you can use these same strategies to make your excitement help rather than distract you.

Understand Public Speaking Anxiety

It is important to understand first that public speaking anxiety results from your brain signaling your body to help with a challenging task. Your body responds by increasing your breathing rate and blood flow and by pumping more adrenaline, which in turn result in the all-too-familiar symptoms of a rapid heartbeat, butterflies in the stomach, shaking knees and hands, quivering voice, and increased perspiration.

Although these physical symptoms may annoy and worry you, the increased oxygen, blood flow, and adrenaline that cause the uncomfortable symptoms can actually be helpful. For example, you may find that you speak with heightened enthusiasm. Your brain thinks faster and more clearly than you would have believed possible. Your state of increased physical readiness can help you speak better.

Keep in mind, too, that most speakers feel more nervous than they look. Although the antiperspirant advertising slogan "Never let 'em see you sweat" suggests that our increased perspiration, along with our shaking hands and knocking knees, is likely to be visible to our audience, rarely is that true. Communication researchers call this mistaken belief the **illusion of transparency** and have found that simply informing speakers that their nervousness is not as apparent as they think can improve the quality of their speeches.[7]

Harry Potter creator J. K. Rowling has admitted experiencing public speaking anxiety. We all need to take positive steps to control anxiety before a performance.
Seth Wenig/AP Images

Know How to Develop a Speech

Communication researchers have found that instruction in public speaking decreases students' perception of their own public speaking anxiety.[8] If you have read the first part of this chapter, you have already taken this first step toward managing the anxiety: learning about the public speaking process. Just knowing what you need to do to develop an effective speech can boost your confidence in being able to do it.

Be Prepared

Being well prepared will decrease your public speaking anxiety. Communication researchers have found that one way for speakers to manage anxiety is to follow the recommended steps for preparing a speech, which include developing a logical and

illusion of transparency
The mistaken belief that the physical manifestations of a speaker's nervousness are apparent to an audience.

clear outline.[9] Being prepared also involves discovering an appropriate topic and researching that topic thoroughly. Perhaps most important, it includes rehearsing your speech. Research suggests that people who spend more time rehearsing experience less public speaking anxiety than do people who rehearse less.[10]

When you rehearse your speech, imagine that you are giving it to the audience you will actually address. Stand up. Speak aloud rather than rehearsing silently. If you cannot rehearse in the room where you will deliver the speech, at least imagine that room. If you will be video recording your speech, practice it—and later deliver it—in a professional setting rather than a kitchen or bedroom.[11] Thorough preparation that includes realistic rehearsal will increase your confidence when it is time to deliver your speech.

Focus on Your Audience

The fundamental communication guideline of audience centeredness is key to reducing public speaking anxiety. As you prepare your speech, consider the needs, goals, and interests of your audience. The more you know about your listeners and how they are likely to respond to your message, the more comfortable you will feel about delivering that message. As you rehearse your speech, visualize your audience members and imagine how they may respond; practice adapting your speech to the responses you imagine. And as you finally deliver your speech, look for positive, reinforcing feedback from audience members.[12] The more you concentrate on your audience, the less you attend to your own nervousness.

Focus on Your Message

Focusing on your message can be another anxiety-reducing strategy. Like focusing on your audience, it keeps you from thinking too much about how nervous you are. In the few minutes before you begin your speech, think about what you are going to say. Mentally review your main ideas. Silently practice your opening lines and your conclusion. Once you are speaking, maintain your focus on your message and your audience rather than on your fears.

Give Yourself a Mental Pep Talk

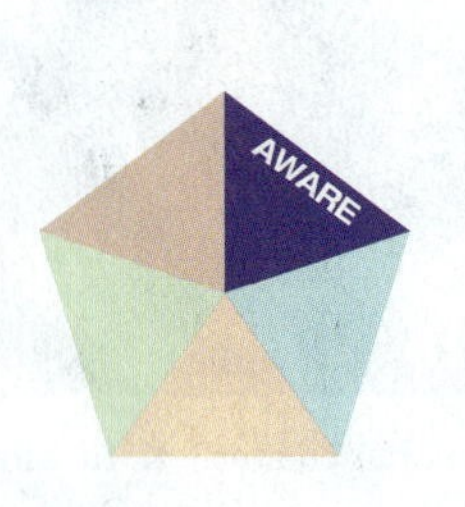

A recent study found that speakers who recast their anxiety as excitement by stating, "I am excited" actually *felt* more excited and were perceived by their listeners as more confident than speakers who tried to tell themselves, "I am calm."[13]

Rather than allowing yourself to dwell on how nervous you are, make a conscious effort to think positively. Remind yourself that you have chosen a topic you know something about. Give yourself a mental pep talk before getting up to speak: "I know I can give this speech. I have prepared and practiced, and I'm going to do a great job." Researchers have suggested that such "prespeaking exercises" may be the most effective antidotes for anxiety both before and during the speech.[14]

Use Deep-Breathing Techniques

Two physical symptoms of nervousness are shallow breathing and rapid heart rate. To counter these symptoms, draw on the breathing techniques employed by practitioners of yoga.[15] Take a few slow, deep breaths before you get up to speak. As you slowly inhale and exhale, try to relax your entire body. These simple strategies will increase your oxygen intake and slow your heart rate, making you feel calmer and more in control.

Take Advantage of Opportunities to Speak

As you gain public speaking experience, you will feel more in control of your nervousness. Communication researchers have found that most public speakers become progressively more comfortable as they speak, a phenomenon they call **habituation**.[16] Past successes build confidence. Your communication course will provide opportunities for frequent practice, which will increase your skill and confidence.

RECAP

Building Your Confidence

- Understand public speaking anxiety.
- Know how to develop a speech.
- Be prepared.
- Focus on your audience.
- Focus on your message.
- Give yourself a mental pep talk.
- Use deep-breathing techniques.
- Take advantage of opportunities to speak.
- Explore additional resources.

Explore Additional Resources

For a few people, the above strategies may not be enough help. These people may still experience a level of public speaking anxiety that they consider debilitating. If you believe that you may be such a person, ask your communication instructor for additional resource recommendations. For example, some college or university departments of communication have communication labs that teach students additional strategies to help manage counterproductive anxiety.

Selecting and Narrowing Your Topic

11.3 Select and narrow a topic for a speech.

Sometimes a speaker is invited or assigned to speak on a certain topic and doesn't have to think about selecting one. Other times, however, a speaker is given some guidelines—such as time limits and perhaps the general purpose for the speech—but otherwise is free to choose a topic. When that happens to you, as it almost certainly will in your communication class, your task may be made easier by exploring three questions: Who is the audience? What is the occasion? What are my interests and experiences?

Who Is the Audience?

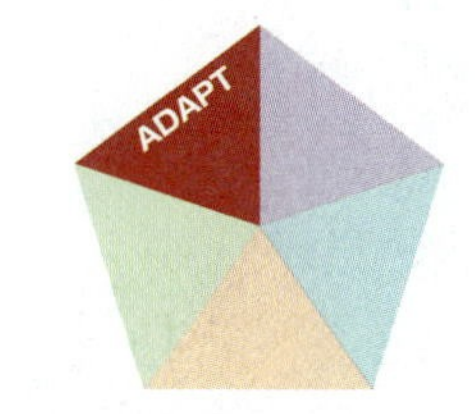

As we have noted several times throughout this book, the principle of appropriately adapting messages to others is central to the communication process. In public speaking, that adaptation begins with topic selection. Who are the members of your audience? What interests and needs do they have in common? Why did they ask you to speak?

One professional speaker calls the answers to such questions "actionable intelligence"—information that you can use as you select your topic.[17] Your college classmates are likely to be interested in such topics as college loans and the job market. Older adults might be more interested in hearing a speaker address such topics as the cost of prescription drugs and investment tax credits. Thinking about your audience can often yield an appropriate topic.

What Is the Occasion?

You might also consider the occasion for which you are being asked to speak. A Veterans' Day address calls for such topics as patriotism and service to one's country. A university centennial address will focus on the successes in the institution's past and a vision for its future.

What Are My Interests and Experiences?

Self-awareness, another communication principle you already know, can also help you discover a topic. Exploring your own interests, attitudes, and experiences may suggest topics about which you know a great deal and feel passionately, resulting in a

habituation
The process of becoming more comfortable as you speak.

speech you can deliver with energy and genuine enthusiasm. One speaker's thinking about her own interests and experiences quickly produced the following list of possible topics.

San Diego, California: city of cultural diversity

Hybrid cars

The reconstructed Globe Theatre

Working at Schlitterbahn water parks

What a sociologist does

Even after considering audience, occasion, and personal interests and experiences, you may still find yourself facing a speaking assignment for which you just cannot come up with a satisfactory topic. When that happens, you might try silent brainstorming, scanning web directories and web pages, or listening and reading for topic ideas.

Conducting Silent Brainstorming

Silent brainstorming, discussed in Chapter 10 as a technique used by small groups to generate creative ideas, is a useful strategy for generating possible topics for speeches. A silent brainstorming session of about three minutes yielded the eleven potential topics shown in Figure 11.2.

Having generated a list of topics, you can now go back and eliminate topics that don't have much promise or that you know you would never use. For example, you may not have any real interest in or reason for discussing European settlement in the Australian Outback. However, perhaps your film course has given you good background for discussing films with both live action and animation. Keep the topics you like in your class notebook. You can reconsider them for future assignments.

Figure 11.2 Brainstorming a Topic

Creating a concept map such as this one might help you visualize connections between ideas and generate more topic ideas as you brainstorm.

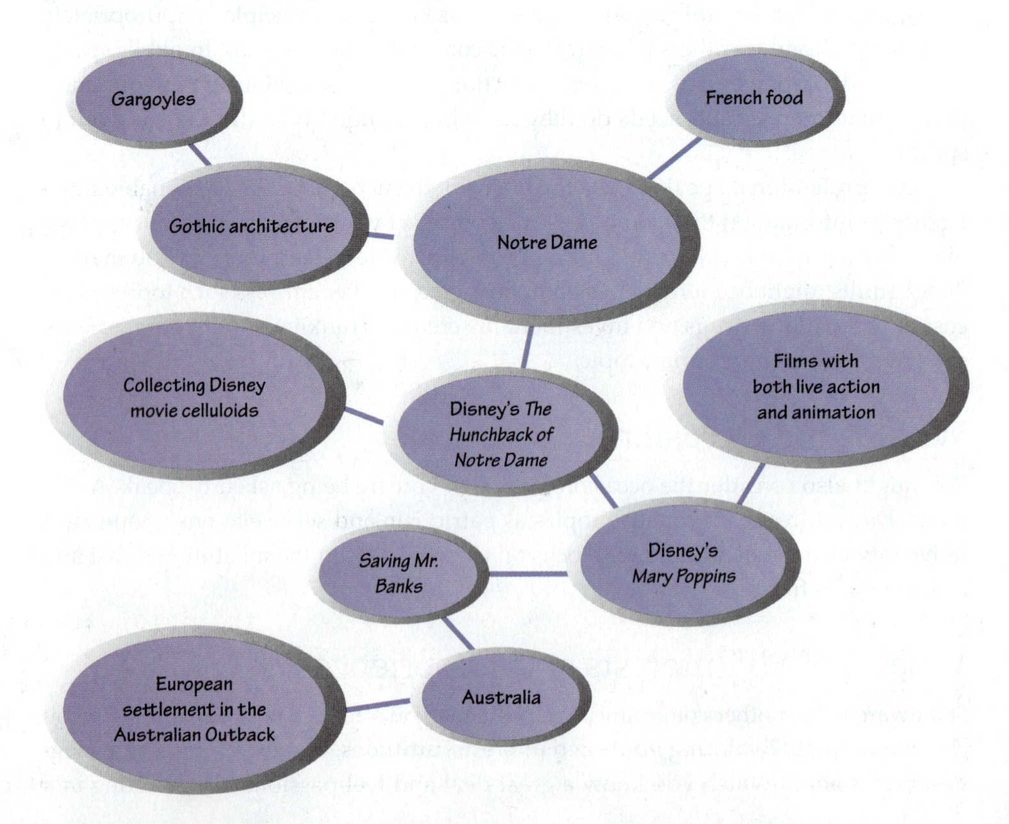

Scanning Web Directories and Web Pages

You know how addicting it can be to surf the web, following various categories and links out of interest and curiosity. What may seem an idle pastime can actually be a good way to discover potential speech topics. For example, a recent random search on Yahoo Directory, starting with the general menu heading *Science*, yielded the following categories and possible topics, arranged from broad to narrow:

Ecology
Sustainable development
Corporate accountability

An additional advantage of this strategy is that you now have both a broad topic and one or more potential sources for your speech.

Listening and Reading for Topic Ideas

It is not unusual to see on television or read in a news source something that triggers an idea for a speech. For example, the following list of quite varied topics was suggested by recent headlines:

Tighter government controls on carbon pollution
Mapping with drones
Veterans' health care
North Korean detention of American citizens

You might also discover a topic in material you have studied for a class. Perhaps you recently had an interesting discussion in your criminology class about minimum mandatory sentencing. It might make a good topic for a speech, and your criminology instructor would probably be happy to suggest additional resources.

Even a subject that comes up in casual conversation with friends may make a good speech topic. Perhaps everyone in your dorm seems to be sniffling and coughing all at once. "It's sick-building syndrome," gasps one. Sick-building syndrome might be an interesting topic for a speech.

The point is to keep your eyes and ears open. You never know when you might see or hear a potential topic. When you do, write it down. Nothing is as frustrating as knowing that you had a good idea for a topic but now can't remember what it was.

Even if you discover potential topics through brainstorming, surfing the web, or listening or reading, you should still consider the communication principles of adapting to your audience and being aware of your own interests and experiences before you make your final topic selection. You will also need to consider the time limits of the speaking assignment. Many good topics need to be narrowed before they are appropriate for a given assignment.

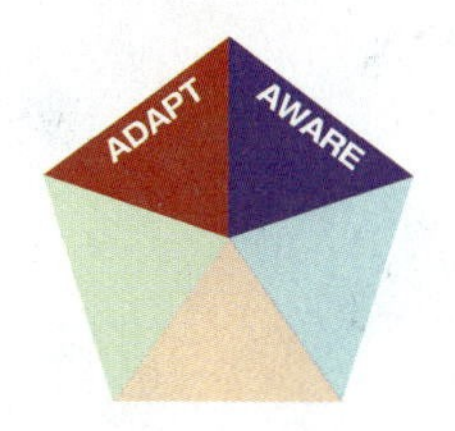

One strategy for narrowing topics is to construct the kinds of categories and subcategories created by web directories. Write your general topic at the top of

Developing Your Speech Step by Step

Selecting and Narrowing Your Topic

While online one afternoon in January, Lario comes across a *New York Times* opinion column inspired by the fiftieth anniversary of President Lyndon B. Johnson's announcement of a "War on Poverty."

As Lario scans the column, he is surprised by the claim that poverty permanently changes the human brain. As he ponders this idea, another thought goes through his mind: Maybe poverty and the brain would make a good topic for his upcoming informative speech. He is personally interested and thinks his audience will be, as well.

Figure 11.3 Narrowing a Broad Topic

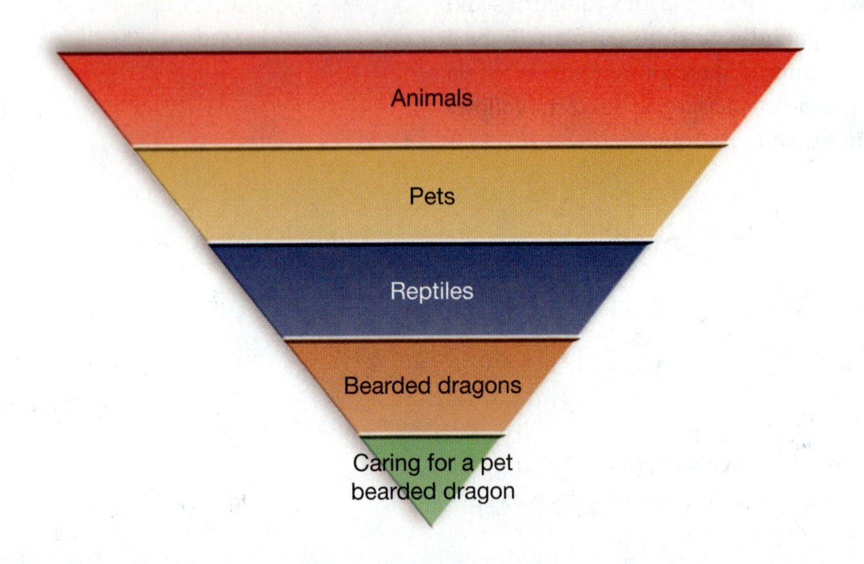

a list, making each succeeding word or phrase more specific and narrow. Figure 11.3 illustrates how the broad topic *animals* might be narrowed to a workable topic for a speech.

If you have ten minutes for your speech, you might decide that the last topic is too narrow. If so, just go back one step. In ten minutes, you may be able to discuss the characteristics and habits of bearded dragons, as well as how to care for them as pets.

RECAP

Selecting and Narrowing Your Topic

- Consider the audience, the occasion, and your interests and experiences.
- Practice silent brainstorming.
- Scan web directories and web pages.
- Listen and read for topic ideas.
- Narrow your topic by generating increasingly specific categories and subcategories.

Identifying Your Purpose

11.4 Write an audience-centered specific-purpose statement for a speech.

Now that you have a topic in mind, you need to determine your purpose for your speech. A clear purpose can help you select main ideas, an organizational strategy, and supporting material. It can even influence how you deliver your speech. You should determine both your general purpose and your specific purpose for every speech you give.

General Purpose

Your **general purpose** is the broad reason for giving your speech: to inform, to persuade, or to entertain.

- *To inform.* When you inform, you teach. You define, describe, or explain a thing, person, place, concept, or process. Although you may use some humor in your speech or encourage your audience to seek out further information about your topic, your primary purpose for speaking is to give information.
- *To persuade.* If you are using information to try to change or reinforce your audience's ideas or convictions or to urge your audience to do something, your general purpose is persuasive. The insurance representative who tries to get you to buy life insurance, the candidate for state representative who asks for your vote, and the coordinator of Habitat for Humanity who urges your school organization to get involved in building homes all have persuasive general purposes. They may offer information, but they use it to convince you or to get you to do something. Their primary purpose is persuasive.
- *To entertain.* The speaker whose purpose is to entertain tries to get the members of his or her audience to smile, laugh, and generally enjoy themselves. For the audience members, learning something or being persuaded about something is secondary to having a good time. Most after-dinner speakers speak to entertain, as do most stand-up comedians and storytellers.

general purpose
The broad reason for giving a speech: to inform, to persuade, or to entertain an audience.

The three main general purposes for public speaking are to inform, to persuade, and to entertain. Which appears to be this speaker's purpose?
Comstock/Stockbyte/Getty Images

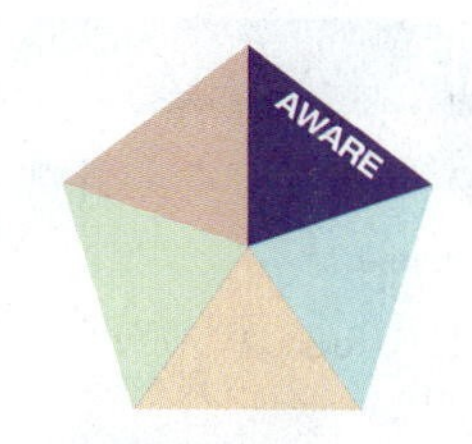

In your speech class, the general purpose for each assignment will probably be set by your instructor. Because the general purpose influences the way you develop and organize your speech, as well as the way you deliver it, it is important to be aware of your general purpose throughout the process of developing and delivering your speech.

Specific Purpose

Knowing whether you want to inform, persuade, or entertain clarifies your general purpose for speaking. You also need to determine your specific purpose. A **specific purpose** is a concise statement of what your listeners should be able to do by the time you finish your speech. In other words, a specific purpose is an audience-centered behavioral goal for your speech. Table 11.1 shows examples of general and specific purposes.

specific purpose
A concise statement of what listeners should be able to do by the time the speaker finishes the speech.

Table 11.1 Examples of General and Specific Purposes

General Purposes	Specific Purposes
To inform	At the end of my speech, the audience will be able to list two benefits for adults learning to play a musical instrument.
To persuade	At the end of my speech, the audience will enroll in a music appreciation course.
To entertain	At the end of my speech, the audience will be laughing at my misadventures as an adult cello student.

Communication & ETHICS

Is It Ethical to Buy a Speech?

An online "speech mill" advertises that for $13 per page, "highly qualified writers" will prepare a custom speech for you. The ad goes on to claim that the speeches are "original" and "from scratch," designed to "let you escape the whole preparation process."

Would it be ethical to use this or a similar website to prepare a speech for a class assignment? Why or why not? Are you comfortable with the site's "plagiarism-free guarantee"? Would it be ethical to buy a speech from such a site for a personal occasion, such as a great-aunt's funeral or your cousin's wedding? How do online speechwriters for hire compare, ethically, with professional speechwriters, who are regularly hired by executives and politicians?

A specific-purpose statement is intended not to become part of your speech, but to guide your own preparation of the speech. You can begin a specific-purpose statement for any speech with the words

At the end of my speech, the audience will . . .

Then you can specify a behavior. For example, if you are giving an informative speech on eating disorders, you might state:

At the end of my speech, the audience will be able to explain the causes and most successful treatments for anorexia and bulimia.

If your topic is Zen meditation and your general purpose is to persuade, you might say:

At the end of my speech, the audience will try Zen meditation.

Wording your specific purpose as in the examples above will help you keep your audience foremost in your mind during the entire speech preparation process.

Every subsequent decision you make while preparing and delivering your speech should be guided by your specific purpose. As soon as you have formulated it, write it on a note card and keep it with you while you are working on your speech. Think of it as a compass pointing true north—toward your audience. Refer to it often.

central idea
A definitive point *about* a topic.

RECAP

Identifying Your Purpose

General Purpose

• To inform	To define, describe, or explain a thing, person, place, concept, or process
• To persuade	To change or reinforce audience members' ideas or convictions, or to urge them to do something
• To entertain	To amuse an audience

Specific Purpose

- Specifies what you want audience members to be able to do by the end of your speech
- Guides you in developing your speech
- Uses the words "At the end of my speech, the audience will . . . ."

Developing Your Central Idea

11.5 Develop a central idea for a speech.

Your specific purpose indicates what you want your audience to know or do by the end of your speech, but your **central idea**

Developing Your Speech Step by Step

Identifying Your Purpose

Lario's assignment is to prepare and deliver an informative speech, so he knows that his general purpose is to inform. He will explain both the short-term and long-term effects of poverty on the brain, and explore how these changes limit people's lives.

Lario also knows that his specific purpose should begin with the phrase "At the end of my speech, the audience will. . . .," so he jots down,

At the end of my speech, the audience will know about poverty and the brain.

As Lario thinks further about his draft specific purpose, he sees some problems with it. How can he determine what his audience "knows" at the end of his speech? And what, specifically, might his listeners learn about poverty and the brain? He edits his purpose statement to read,

At the end of my speech, the audience will voice their support for a war on poverty.

Although more specific, this version is perhaps more appropriate for a persuasive speech than for an informative one. Lario wants his audience to demonstrate their understanding of new information, but not necessarily to take action. Maybe a better statement would be

At the end of my speech, the audience will be able to explain poverty's short-term and long-term effects on the brain and the implications of those effects for people's lives.

Lario is pleased with this third version. It specifies *what* he wants his audience members to know at the end of his speech and *how* they can demonstrate their knowledge.

makes a definitive point *about* your topic. It focuses on the content of the speech.

Sometimes, as in the following example, wording the central idea can be as simple as copying the part of the specific-purpose statement that specifies what the audience should be able to do.

TOPIC:	Foreign-language education
SPECIFIC PURPOSE:	At the end of my speech, the audience will be able to explain two reasons foreign-language education should begin in the elementary grades.
CENTRAL IDEA:	Foreign-language education should begin in the elementary grades.

Although they may seem similar, the specific purpose and central idea are used in quite different ways.

Specific Purpose	Central Idea
• Guides the speaker in preparing a speech	• Guides the audience in listening to a speech
• Is not stated in the speech	• Is stated at or near the end of the speech introduction

Professional speech coach Judith Humphrey explains the importance of a central idea:

> Ask yourself before writing a speech . . . "What's my point?" Be able to state that message in a single clear sentence. Everything else you say will support that single argument.[18]

To be most useful to both speaker and listeners, the "single clear sentence" to which Humphrey refers should be an audience-centered sentence; reflect a single topic; be a complete declarative sentence; and use direct, specific language.

An Audience-Centered Idea

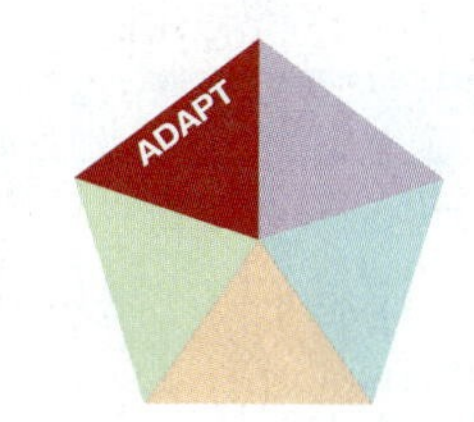

If your specific purpose is focused on your audience, your central idea probably will be, too. It should reflect a topic in which the audience has a reason to be interested and should provide some knowledge that they do not already have or make some claim about the topic that they may not have previously considered. Consider the appropriateness of these central ideas for an audience of college students.

INAPPROPRIATE:	Taking Advanced Placement classes in high school can help fulfill your general education requirements. *(Inappropriate because taking Advanced Placement classes is something college students either did or did not do in the past. They cannot make any decisions about them at this point.)*
APPROPRIATE:	Taking online college classes can help fulfill your general studies requirements. *(Appropriate because students are probably looking for various options for completing required courses. They can choose to take classes online.)*

declarative sentence
A complete sentence that makes a statement as opposed to asking a question.

main ideas
Subdivisions of the central idea of a speech that provide detailed points of focus for developing the speech.

A Single Topic

A central idea should reflect a single topic. Trying to cover more than one topic, even if the multiple topics are related, only muddles your speech and confuses the audience.

MULTIPLE TOPICS:	Clubbing and running in marathons are two activities that appeal to many college students.
SINGLE TOPIC:	Clubbing appeals to many college students.

A Complete Declarative Sentence

Your central idea should be more than just the word or phrase that is your topic; it should also make a claim about your topic. Questions may help you come up with a central idea, but because they don't make any kind of claim, questions themselves are not good central ideas. A central idea should be a complete **declarative sentence**, not a topic and not a question.

TOPIC:	Study abroad
QUESTION:	Should students consider opportunities to study abroad?
CENTRAL IDEA:	Studying abroad provides significant advantages for students in most fields of study.

Direct, Specific Language

A good central idea uses direct, specific language rather than qualifiers and vague generalities.

VAGUE:	Crop circles are not what they seem to be.
SPECIFIC:	Although they have been attributed to alien forces and unknown fungi, crop circles are really just a clever hoax.

Generating Main Ideas

11.6 Generate main ideas from a central idea.

If the central idea of a speech is like the thesis statement of a paper, the **main ideas** of a speech correspond to the paragraph topics of a paper. They support or subdivide the central idea and provide more detailed points of focus for developing the speech.

Getting from the central idea to related but more specific main ideas can seem challenging, but actually you can use the central idea to generate main ideas. Here's how.

Write the central idea at the top of a sheet of paper or a word-processing document. Then ask yourself three questions:

RECAP

The Central Idea Should . . .

- Be audience-centered.
- Reflect a single topic.
- Be a complete declarative sentence.
- Use direct, specific language.

Developing Your Speech Step by Step

Developing Your Central Idea

Lario knows from reading Chapter 11 of this book that his central idea should be a complete declarative sentence that states a single audience-centered idea. He knows, too, that sometimes you can develop your central idea by copying the part of your specific-purpose statement that specifies what the audience should do. So he writes,

> Poverty's short-term and long-term effects on the brain have major implications for people's lives.

1. Does the central idea have *logical divisions*?
2. Can I think of several *reasons* the central idea is true?
3. Can I support the central idea with a series of *steps* or a *chronological sequence*?

You should be able to answer yes to one of these questions and to write down the corresponding divisions, reasons, or steps. Let's apply this strategy to several examples.

Does the Central Idea Have *Logical Divisions*?

Suppose that your central idea is "Most accomplished guitarists play three types of guitars." The phrase *three types* is a flag that indicates that this central idea does indeed have logical divisions—in this case, the three types of guitars. You list the three that come to mind:

1. Acoustic
2. Classical
3. Electric

You don't need to use Roman numerals or to worry particularly about the order in which you have listed the types of guitars. Right now, you are simply trying to generate main ideas. They aren't set in concrete, either. You may revise them—and your central idea—several times before you actually deliver the speech. For example, you may decide that you need to include steel guitars in your list, so you revise your central idea to read "four types of guitars" and add "steel" to your list. If your central idea has logical divisions, you may organize those logical divisions topically, spatially, or according to cause–effect or problem–solution, organizational strategies that will be discussed in Chapter 12.

Can You Think of Several *Reasons* the Central Idea Is True?

If your central idea is "Everyone should study a martial art," you may not be able to find readily apparent logical divisions. Simply discussing judo, karate, and tae-kwondo would not necessarily support the argument that everyone should study one of them. However, the second question is more productive: You can think of a number of *reasons* everyone should study a martial art. You quickly generate this list:

1. Martial arts teach responsibility.
2. Martial arts teach self-control.
3. Martial arts teach a means of self-defense.

Unlike the list of types of guitars, this list is written in brief complete sentences. You may or may not use full sentences in your own list. The purpose of your first list of main ideas is just to get the ideas in written form, whether words, phrases, or sentences. You can and will revise them later. If your main ideas are reasons your central idea is true, you will probably organize them according to effect–cause.

Can You Support the Central Idea with a Series of *Steps* or a *Chronological Sequence*?

"The events of September 11, 2001, were the climax of a decade of deadly terrorist attacks against the United States." That sentence seemed like a pretty good central idea when you came up with it, but now what do you do? It doesn't have any logical divisions. You couldn't really develop reasons that it is true. You could, however, probably support this central idea with a chronological sequence or a history of the problem. You jot down the following list:

1. 1993—Bomb explodes in the underground parking garage of the World Trade Center, killing six people.
2. 1995—Car bomb in Riyadh, Saudi Arabia, kills seven people, five of them U.S. military and civilian National Guard advisors.
3. 1996—Bomb aboard a fuel truck explodes outside a U.S. Air Force installation in Dhahran, Saudi Arabia, killing nineteen U.S. military personnel.
4. 1998—Bombs destroy the U.S. embassies in Nairobi, Kenya, and Dar es Salaam, Tanzania. Three hundred and one people are killed, including thirteen Americans.
5. 2000—Bomb damages the *USS Cole* in the port of Aden, Yemen, killing seventeen American sailors.
6. 2001—Hijacked airliners crash into the World Trade Center in New York, the Pentagon outside Washington, D.C., and a field in Pennsylvania, killing more than 3,000.[19]

These six fatal terrorist attacks, arranged in chronological order, could become the main ideas of your speech.

How many main ideas should you have? Your topic and time limit will help you decide. A short speech (three to five minutes) might have only two main ideas. A longer one (eight to ten minutes) might have four or five. If you have more potential main ideas than you can use, decide which main ideas are likely to be most interesting, relevant, and perhaps persuasive to your audience or combine two or more closely related ideas.

Gathering Supporting Material

11.7 Describe four potential sources and seven types of supporting material for a speech, and use each type effectively.

supporting material
Verbal or visual material that clarifies, amplifies, and provides evidence to support the main ideas of a presentation.

By the time you have decided on your main ideas, you have a skeleton speech. Your next task is to flesh out that skeleton with **supporting material**, both verbal and visual. Verbal supporting material includes illustrations, explanations, descriptions, definitions, analogies, statistics, and opinions—material that will clarify, amplify, and provide evidence to support your main ideas and your thesis. Visual supporting material includes objects, charts, graphs, posters, maps, models, and computer-generated

Developing Your Speech Step by Step

Generating Your Main Ideas

With his central idea in hand, Lario knows that he next needs to generate main ideas for his speech. He asks three questions:

- Does the central idea have logical divisions?
- Can I think of several reasons the central idea is true?
- Can I support my central idea with a series of steps or a chronological sequence?

Lario recognizes that his central idea contains three ideas that are likely logical divisions. Again, he jots down his central idea:

Poverty's short-term and long-term effects on the brain have major implications for people's lives.

Then he lists the logical divisions:

1. Poverty's short-term effects on the brain
2. Poverty's long-term effects on the brain
3. Implications for people's lives of poverty's effects on the brain

Lario feels confident that he has three main ideas that both support his central idea and fulfill his specific purpose.

graphics. You can also support your speech with audio aids such as music or sounds from your smart phone, tablet, or laptop. The speaker who seeks out strong verbal and visual supporting material is adhering to the fundamental communication principles of using verbal and nonverbal messages effectively.

A smart phone lets you do Internet research for your speech anywhere, but there are also times you may need to visit a library or interview someone to get information for your speech.
scyther5/Shutterstock

Sources of Supporting Material

Like a chef who needs to know where to buy high-quality fresh fruits and vegetables for gourmet recipes, you need to know where to turn for supporting material that will effectively develop your speech and achieve your specific purpose. We will discuss four potential sources of supporting material: yourself, the Internet, online databases, and the library.

YOURSELF If you were self-aware as you selected your topic, you may be your own source. You may have chosen a topic based on your passionate interest in cataloging cat videos, raising cockatiels, or cooking. You may have chosen a topic with which you have had some personal experience, such as undergoing plastic surgery or negotiating a favorable apartment lease. You may have chosen a topic for which you have conducted an online survey among your classmates, using simple, free software such as SurveyMonkey. Or you may have conducted a live interview with an expert. (Appendix A provides information and guidelines for participating in an information-gathering interview.)

The point is that you don't necessarily need to consult the Internet or run to the library for every piece of supporting material on every topic on which you speak. It is true that most well-researched speeches will include some objective material gathered from the Internet or from library resources, but your listeners will respect your authority if they realize that you have firsthand knowledge of, or have consulted primary sources about, your topic.

THE INTERNET Although easy to use and generally helpful, general search engines like Google and Yahoo! can yield an overwhelming number of resources. The following relatively simple strategies can help you narrow thousands or even millions of hits to a more workable number:

- *Vertical search engines.* One way you can narrow your search is to use a **vertical search engine**, a specialized tool that may index, for example, only academic sources (Google Scholar) or job websites (Indeed).
- *Boolean searches.* Another way to narrow a search is to conduct a **Boolean search**, which allows you to enclose phrases in quotation marks or parentheses so that a search yields only those sites on which all words or the phrase appear in that exact order and eliminates sites that contain the words at random. Boolean searches

vertical search engine
A website that indexes information on the World Wide Web in a specialized area.

Boolean search
A web search that ties words together so that a search engine can hunt for the resulting phrase.

Communication & TECHNOLOGY

Check Facts from the Internet . . . or Else

When television news journalist Ann Curry was invited to deliver the commencement address at Wheaton College in Norton, Massachusetts, a few years ago, her research strategy led to her self-confessed most embarrassing moment:

> I decided to include a mention of all the great people who graduated from the school.
>
> I went to the computer and added the names: Dennis Hastert, Billy Graham, Wes Craven. It was only later that I discovered that none of those people had gone to Wheaton College in Norton, Mass. They had graduated from Wheaton College in Wheaton, Ill.[20]

Curry acknowledged her mistake and wrote a letter of apology to the school. The lesson? Don't assume that the hits produced by Internet search engines necessarily yield the information you are seeking. Check your facts.

Table 11.2 Six Criteria for Evaluating Internet Resources

Criterion	Applying the Criterion	Drawing Conclusions
ACCOUNTABILITY: Who is responsible for the website?	• Look to see whether the website is signed. • Follow hyperlinks or search the author's name to determine the author's expertise and authority.	• If you cannot identify or verify an author or sponsor, be wary of the website.
ACCURACY: Is the information correct?	• Consider whether the author or sponsor is a credible authority. • Assess the care with which the website has been written. • Conduct additional research into the information on the site.	• If the author or sponsor is a credible authority, the information is more likely to be accurate than inaccurate. • A website should be relatively free of writing errors. • You may be able to verify or refute the information by consulting another resource.
OBJECTIVITY: Is the website free of bias?	• Consider the interests, philosophical or political biases, and source of financial support of the author or sponsor of the website. • Does the website include advertisements that might influence its content?	• The more objective the author and sponsor of the website, the more credible the information.
DATE: Is the site current?	• Look at the bottom of the page on the website for a statement of when the page was posted and when it was last updated. • If you cannot find a date on the page of a website, click on the Tools menu at the top of your browser screen and go down to Page Info. When you click on Page Info, you will find a Last Modified date. • Enter the title of the website in a search engine. The resulting information should include a date.	• In general, when you are concerned with factual data, the more recent, the better.
USABILITY: Do the layout and design of the website facilitate its use?	• Does the website load fairly quickly? • Is a fee required to gain access to any of the information on the website?	• Balance graphics and any fees against practical efficiency.
DIVERSITY: Is the site inclusive?	• Do language and graphics reflect and respect differences in gender, ethnicity, race, and sexual orientation? • Do interactive forums invite divergent perspectives? • Is the website friendly to people with disabilities (e.g., offering a large-print or video option)?	• A website should be free of bias, representative of diverse perspectives, and accessible by people with disabilities.

also let you exclude words or phrases from your search or restrict the dates of documents to a specified time frame.

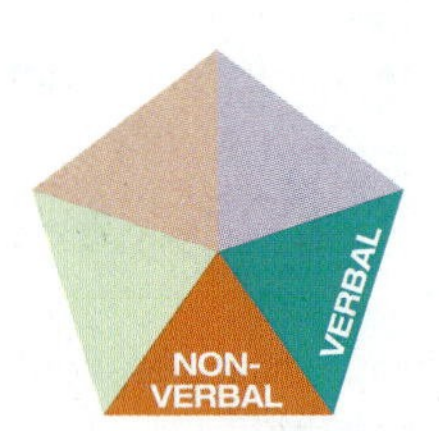

- *Criteria for evaluating web resources.* A third strategy for sorting through information you discover on the Internet has to do with the principles of appropriately interpreting verbal and nonverbal messages. Specifically, you need to evaluate the sites you discover according to a consistent standard. The six criteria in Table 11.2 can serve as such a standard.[21]

ONLINE DATABASES **Online databases** provide access to bibliographic information, abstracts, and full texts for a variety of resources, including periodicals, newspapers, government documents, and even books. Like websites, online databases are accessed via a networked computer. Unlike websites, most databases are restricted to the patrons of libraries that subscribe to them. Your library may subscribe to several or all of the following popular full-text databases:

- *ABI/Inform Global.* This resource offers many full-text articles in business and trade publications from 1971 to the present.
- *Academic Search Complete.* This popular database offers many full-text articles from 1865 to the present, covering a wide variety of subjects.
- *JSTOR.* This multisubject full-text database offers journal articles from the first volume to fairly recent ones, although not usually the most current issues.
- *LexisNexis Academic.* Focusing on business, industry, and law, this database provides many full-text articles from newspapers, magazines, journals, newsletters, and wire services. Dates of coverage vary.

online database
A subscription-based electronic resource that may offer access to abstracts or the full texts of entries, in addition to bibliographic data.

TRADITIONAL LIBRARY HOLDINGS Despite the explosion of Internet and database resources in recent years, the more traditional holdings of libraries, both paper and electronic, remain rich sources of supporting material. Spend some time becoming familiar with your library's services and layout so that you know how and where to access books and reference materials.

- *Books.* Libraries' collections of books are called the **stacks**. The stacks are organized by call numbers, which are included in electronic catalog entries. A location guide can tell you the floor or section of the stacks that houses books with the call numbers in which you are interested.
- *Reference resources.* Print **reference resources**—which include encyclopedias, dictionaries, atlases, almanacs, and books of quotations—are indexed in a library's card catalog with a *ref* prefix on their call numbers to show that they are housed in the reference section of the library. Like periodicals, newspapers, and microfilm, print reference resources are usually available only for in-house research and cannot be checked out. Reference librarians are specialists in the field of information science. They are often able to suggest additional print or electronic resources that you might otherwise overlook. If you plan to use the reference section, visit the library during daytime working hours. A full-time reference librarian is more likely to be on hand and available to help you at that time than in the evenings or on weekends.

stacks
The collection of books in a library.

reference resources
Material housed in the reference section of a library, such as encyclopedias, dictionaries, atlases, almanacs, and books of quotations.

Types of Supporting Material

If you have explored your own knowledge and insights and those of people you know, discovered material on the Internet, consulted databases, and examined a variety of library resources, you probably have a wealth of potential supporting material. Now you will need to decide what to use in your speech.

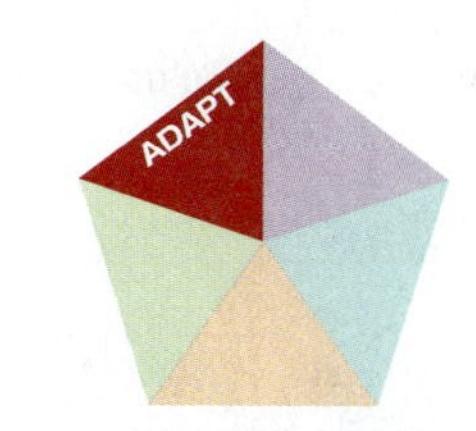

Keeping in mind your listeners' knowledge, interests, and expectations will help you determine where an illustration might stir their emotions, where an explanation might help them to understand a point, and where statistics might convince them of the significance of a problem. Let's discuss these and other types of supporting material and consider suggestions for using them effectively.

RECAP

Sources of Supporting Material

1. *Yourself.* Take advantage of your own expertise.
2. *The Internet.* Use vertical search engines, conduct Boolean searches, and apply evaluation criteria to choose the best information.
3. *Online databases.* For access to abstracts and full texts for a variety of resources, explore the databases to which your library subscribes.
4. *Traditional library holdings.* Get to know your reference librarian for help mining traditional library resources.

ILLUSTRATIONS **Illustrations** offer an example of or tell a story about an idea, issue, or problem a speaker is discussing. Illustrations can be as short as a word or phrase or as long as a well-developed paragraph. Sometimes speakers will offer a series of brief illustrations, as President George W. Bush did in his final state of the union address in January 2008:

> In the past seven years, we've also seen images that have sobered us. We've watched throngs of mourners in Lebanon and Pakistan carrying the caskets of beloved leaders taken by the assassin's hand. We've seen wedding guests in blood-soaked finery staggering from a hotel in Jordan, Afghans and Iraqis blown up in mosques and markets, and trains in London and Madrid ripped apart by bombs. On a clear September day, we saw thousands of our fellow citizens taken from us in an instant.[22]

illustration
A story or anecdote that provides an example of an idea, issue, or problem the speaker is discussing.

Other speakers offer longer and more detailed illustrations. Still others will use instead a **hypothetical illustration**—one that has not actually occurred. If you decide to use a hypothetical illustration, it is important to make clear to your

hypothetical illustration
An example or story that has not actually occurred.

Everybody loves a good story. Garrison Keillor is famous for illustrations that keep the attention of his audiences. What principles can you use from this chapter to hold your listeners' attention?
Dan Harr/Splash/Corbis

audience that the scene you describe never really happened. Notice how Matthew uses the word *imagine* to make clear to his audience that his illustration is hypothetical:

> Imagine an evening outing: You and your two children decide to have a fun night out. You look up to your rearview mirror to see a car slam into the back of your car—WHAM—killing your children. You survive the crash and so does the individual who rear-ended you.[23]

Whether you choose to use brief or extended illustrations, true or hypothetical ones, remember this principle: Everybody likes to hear a story. An illustration almost always ensures audience interest. In addition, communication researchers have found that listeners are less likely to generate counterarguments to a persuasive message supported by examples and personal narratives than one not so supported.[24]

The following suggestions should help you use illustrations effectively in your speeches:

- Be sure that your illustrations are directly relevant to the idea or point they are supposed to support.
- Choose illustrations that are typical, not exceptions.
- Make your illustrations vivid and specific.
- Use illustrations with which your listeners can identify.
- Remember that the most effective illustrations are often personal ones.

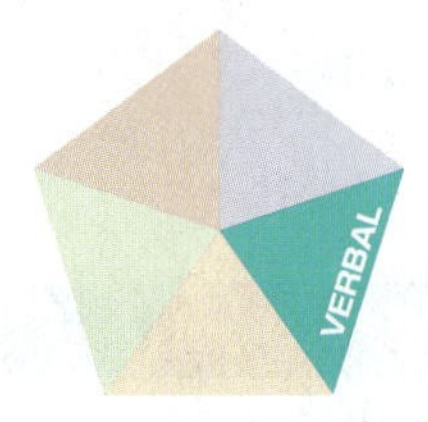

DESCRIPTIONS A **description** provides detailed images that allow an audience to see, hear, smell, touch, or taste whatever you are describing. Descriptions can make people and scenes come alive for an audience. In her Nobel Prize acceptance speech, writer Doris Lessing described Africa as she remembered it:

> the banks of the Zambesi, where it rolls between pale grassy banks, it being the dry season, dark-green and glossy, with all the birds of Africa around its banks . . . . elephants, giraffes, lions and the rest . . . the sky at night, still unpolluted, black and wonderful, full of restless stars.[25]

EXPLANATIONS An **explanation** of how something works or why a situation exists can help an audience understand conditions, events, or processes. Speaking to an audience of supervisors about managing stress and increasing personal productivity, author Jeff Davidson explained why people tend to be most productive in the morning:

> Doctor Norbert Myslinski, a neuroscience professor at the University of Maryland, found that cortisol peaks around the time you wake up. Cortisol, a naturally occurring stress hormone that affects your ability to respond to challenges, increases your blood-sugar level, better enabling you to handle tasks energetically and with enough momentum to carry you through their completion.[26]

Although descriptions and explanations are part of most speeches, they lack the inherent interest factor that illustrations have. The following suggestions may help you keep audiences from yawning through your descriptions and explanations:

- Avoid too many descriptions and explanations.
- Keep your descriptions and explanations brief.
- Describe and explain in specific and concrete language.

description
A word picture.

explanation
A statement that makes clear how something is done or why it exists in its present or past form.

DEFINITIONS Speakers should offer **definitions** of all technical or little-known terms in their speeches, but they do not need to define terms that most or all audience members are likely to find familiar. If you determine that you should define a word or phrase for your audience, consider whether you can best define it by **classification**, the format of a standard dictionary definition, or by an **operational definition**, explaining how the word or phrase works or what it does. Discussing his role in an investigation of unlawful interrogation practices, New York attorney Scott Horton used this operational definition of *torture*:

> The following techniques were the focus of our concern: waterboarding, long-time standing, hypothermia, sleep deprivation in excess of two days, the use of psychotropic drugs and the sensory deprivation/sensory overload techniques first developed for the CIA at McGill University.[27]

To use definitions effectively, consider the following suggestions:

- Use definitions only when necessary.
- Be certain that your definitions are understandable.
- Be sure that any definition you provide accurately reflects your use of the word or phrase throughout the speech.

ANALOGIES An **analogy** demonstrates how unfamiliar ideas, things, and situations are similar to something the audience already understands. Speakers can use two types of analogies in their speeches. The first is a **literal analogy**, or comparison of two similar things. Kristen uses a literal analogy to offer a solution to America's complex income tax system:

> According to many experts, following in Europe's fiscal footsteps could bring the American tax system up to speed. With a flat income tax, the U.S. could keep fairness while gaining simplicity and efficiency in its taxing burden.[28]

The second type of analogy is a **figurative analogy**, a comparison of two seemingly dissimilar things that in fact share a significant common feature. In his much-acclaimed "Last Lecture," Carnegie Mellon professor Randy Pausch created a memorable figurative analogy between one's outlook on life and the outlooks of two beloved characters from *Winnie the Pooh*:

> You just have to decide if you're a Tigger or an Eeyore. I think I'm clear where I stand on the great Tigger/Eeyore debate. Never lose the childlike wonder. It's just too important.[29]

Two suggestions can help you use analogies more effectively in your speeches:

- Be certain that the two things you compare in a literal analogy are very similar.
- Make the similarity between the two things compared in a figurative analogy apparent to the audience.

STATISTICS **Statistics**, or numerical data, can represent hundreds or thousands of illustrations, helping a speaker express the significance or magnitude of a situation. Statistics can also help a speaker express the relationship of a part to the whole. In this brief excerpt from a speech on bogus airline parts, Jon uses both types of statistics:

> 26 million parts are installed on airplanes every year in the U.S., and the FAA estimates that at least 2% of these parts are counterfeits.[30]

Skilled speakers learn how to use statistics to their greatest advantage. For example, they try to make huge numbers more dramatic for their audiences. AFL-CIO

definition
A statement of what something means.

classification
A type of definition that first places a term in the general class to which it belongs and then differentiates it from all other members of that class.

operational definition
A definition that shows how a term works or what it does.

analogy
A comparison between two ideas, things, or situations that demonstrates how something unfamiliar is similar to something the audience already understands.

literal analogy
A comparison between two similar things.

figurative analogy
A comparison between two seemingly dissimilar things that share some common feature on which the comparison depends.

statistics
Numerical data that summarize examples.

president John J. Sweeney dramatized the danger of unsafe bridges in the United States by making a statistic personal:

> Since I was coming to work from Washington to New Rochelle this morning, I asked my staff to check out my route.
>
> We found that traveling the I-95 corridor between Washington, D.C. and New York City, I would cross or come within two-tenths of a mile of 30 bridges that are rated either functionally obsolete or structurally deficient.[31]

A student speaker heightened the effect of the incredible 300-mile distances run by the Tarahumaran tribes of northern Mexico by comparing that statistic with another figure familiar to her listeners:

> To put that into perspective, that's like running 12 marathons back to back to back to back . . . to back to back to back to back . . . to back to back to back to back.[32]

And a recent commencement speaker dramatized a statistic by **exploding** it to enhance its significance:

> . . . if every one of you changed the lives of just ten people—and each one of those folks changed the lives of another ten people—just ten—then in five generations—125 years—the class of 2014 will have changed the lives of 800 million people.[33]

In addition to dramatizing statistics, you can use statistics more effectively if you apply the following suggestions:

- Round off large numbers.
- Use visual aids to present your statistics.
- Cite the sources of your statistics.

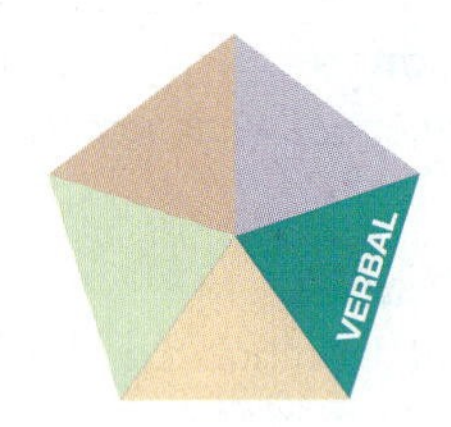

OPINIONS The opinions of others can add authority, drama, and style to a speech. A speaker can use three types of opinions: expert testimony, lay testimony, and literary quotations.

Expert testimony is the type of opinion most frequently employed by speakers. If you lack authority on your topic, cite someone who can offer such expertise. In preparing her speech on the college credit card crisis, Jeni realized that her audience might not believe that the misuse of credit cards by college students is a widespread problem. So Jeni quoted an expert:

> Ruth Suswein, executive director of the Bankcard Holders of America, told the . . . *Pittsburgh Post Gazette*, "I defy you to go on any college campus and find any student who doesn't know some other student who has messed up using credit cards."[34]

After an F5 tornado ravaged Joplin, Missouri, television audiences were moved by the compassionate reporting of Weather Channel journalist Mike Bettes, who was one

exploding
Adding or multiplying related numbers to enhance their significance.

expert testimony
The opinion of someone who is an acknowledged expert in the field under discussion.

Developing Your Speech Step by Step

Gathering Supporting Material

With a draft of his specific purpose, central idea, and main ideas in hand, Lario begins to research the effects of poverty on the brain. The *New York Times* column that launched his topic includes several links to articles, books, and websites.

As he scans and electronically bookmarks these resources, he decides to do a Google search, as well. He discovers related recent articles from *CNN* and *USA Today*. Lario adds electronic bookmarks for these additional sources to the bookmark file he had already begun.

Then he begins to read each resource more carefully and to take notes. As he does so, he puts quotation marks around any material he copies verbatim and makes sure that he has copied it accurately.

of the first reporters on the scene. For a speaker, as well as a news organization, such **lay testimony** can provide the most memorable moments of a speech, stirring an audience's emotions.

Finally, speakers may wish to include **literary quotations** in their speeches. Salem State College Professor Robert Brown quoted architect Buckminster Fuller to make a point about how the English language has become increasingly visual and kinesthetic:

> As the architectural visionary Buckminster Fuller was fond of saying, "I am a verb." In English, with every innovation that comes to market, we transform things into actions, and nouns into verbs, as when I say: "Let me friend you. Let me cell phone you."[35]

Whether you use expert testimony, lay testimony, or literary quotations, consider the following suggestions for using opinions effectively in your speeches:

- Be certain that any authority you cite is actually an expert on the subject you are discussing.
- Identify your sources.
- Cite unbiased authorities.
- Cite opinions that are representative of prevailing opinion. If you cite a dissenting viewpoint, identify it as such.
- Quote or paraphrase your sources accurately and note the context in which the remarks were originally made.
- Use literary quotations sparingly.

RECAP

Supporting Your Speech

Type of Supporting Material	Guidelines for Use
Illustrations	• Make illustrations directly relevant to the idea or point they support. • Choose illustrations that are typical. • Make illustrations vivid and specific. • Use illustrations with which your listeners can identify. • Remember that the most effective illustrations are often personal ones.
Descriptions and Explanations	• Avoid too many descriptions and explanations. • Keep descriptions and explanations brief. • Describe and explain in specific and concrete language.
Definitions	• Use definitions only when necessary. • Be certain that definitions are understandable. • Be sure that a definition accurately reflects your use of the word or phrase.
Analogies	• Be certain that the two things you compare in a literal analogy are very similar. • Make apparent to the audience the similarity between the two things compared in a figurative analogy.
Statistics	• Round off large numbers. • Use visual aids. • Cite your sources.
Opinions	• Be certain that any authority you cite is actually an expert on the subject you are discussing. • Identify your sources. • Cite unbiased authorities. • Cite representative opinions, or identify dissenting viewpoints as such. • Quote or paraphrase accurately and in context. • Use literary quotations sparingly.

As you select your illustrations, descriptions, explanations, definitions, analogies, statistics, and opinions, be guided not only by the suggestions provided in this chapter for each type of supporting material but also by the five Communication Principles for a Lifetime:

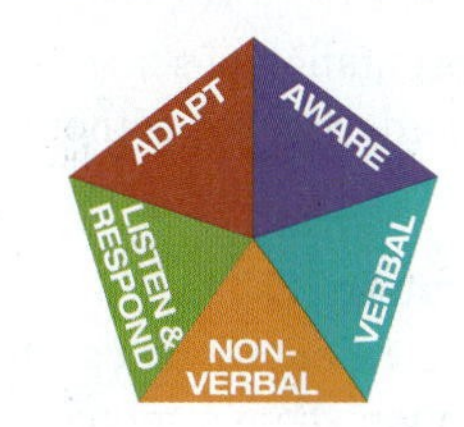

- **Be aware of your communication with yourself and others.** The best supporting material reflects self-awareness, taking advantage of your own knowledge and experience.
- **Effectively use and interpret verbal messages.** Effective verbal supporting material is appropriately worded, concrete, and vivid enough that your audience can visualize what you are talking about.
- **Effectively use and interpret nonverbal messages.** Use visual aids to present statistics.
- **Listen and respond thoughtfully to others.** If listeners find a speech boring, the speaker has probably not used the fundamental principles of communication as criteria for selecting supporting material.
- **Appropriately adapt messages to others.** Sensitivity to your audience will help you choose the verbal and visual supporting material that is most appropriately adapted to them.

lay testimony
The opinion of someone who experienced an event or situation firsthand.

literary quotation
A citation from a work of fiction or nonfiction, a poem, or another speech.

Communication & DIVERSITY

How to Adapt to Your Diverse Audience

Here are some ideas to help you adapt when you speak to an audience of people who have cultural backgrounds different from your own.[36]

- *Adapt your supporting materials.* Telling a good story to illustrate your ideas is an especially effective strategy to appeal to a wide range of audience preferences.
- *Adapt your visual support.* You might want to use more visual aids to illustrate your talk. Pictures and images can communicate universal messages, especially emotional ones.
- *Adapt your speech organization.* People from the predominant culture in North America usually prefer a structured speech that follows an outlined pattern. They also prefer an introduction that previews the ideas you'll present and a conclusion that crisply summarizes the essential points you've made. A Russian or Eastern European audience would expect a less tightly structured speech, however. When you're in doubt about listener preferences, we recommend being structured and organized.
- *Adapt your delivery style.* One study found that members of some cultures prefer a more formal oratorical style of delivery than the conversational, extemporaneous style that is usually taught in American public speaking classes.[37]

Our overarching suggestion is to be aware of who will be in your audience. Before you develop or deliver your speech, if you're unsure of your listeners' speaking-style preferences, ask for tips and strategies from audience members or people you trust.

Acknowledgment of Supporting Material

In the United States and most other Western cultures, using the words, sentence structures, or ideas of another person without crediting the source is a serious breach of ethics. Once you have supporting material in hand, you must decide whether and how to acknowledge the source.

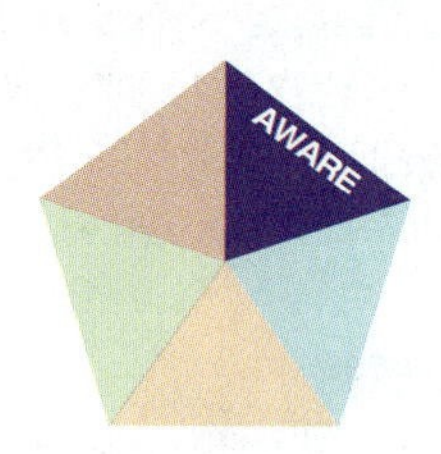

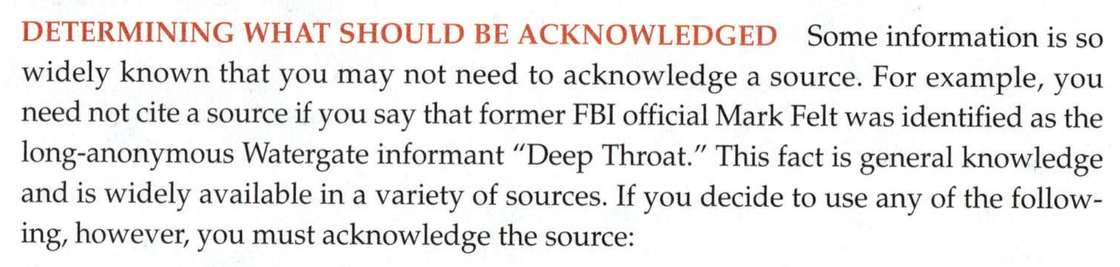

DETERMINING WHAT SHOULD BE ACKNOWLEDGED Some information is so widely known that you may not need to acknowledge a source. For example, you need not cite a source if you say that former FBI official Mark Felt was identified as the long-anonymous Watergate informant "Deep Throat." This fact is general knowledge and is widely available in a variety of sources. If you decide to use any of the following, however, you must acknowledge the source:

- Direct quotations, even if they are only brief phrases
- Opinions, assertions, or ideas of others, even if you paraphrase them rather than quote them verbatim
- Statistics
- Any nonoriginal visual materials, including graphs, tables, and pictures

plagiarism
The presentation of someone else's words or ideas without acknowledging the source.

oral citation
The oral presentation of such information about a source as the author, title, and publication date.

UNDERSTANDING PLAGIARISM AND ITS CONSEQUENCES Presenting someone else's words or ideas without acknowledging the source constitutes **plagiarism**, a breach of academic honesty that can have dire consequences.

A few years ago, one of your authors heard a student's excellent speech on the importance of detecting cancer early. The only problem was that she heard the same speech again in the following class period! On finding the "speech"—actually a *Reader's Digest* article that was several years old—both students were certain that they had discovered a shortcut to an A. Instead, they failed the assignment, ruined their course grades, and lost their instructor's trust. The consequences of plagiarism in other arenas can be even more severe, including the loss of a job or the end of a promising career.

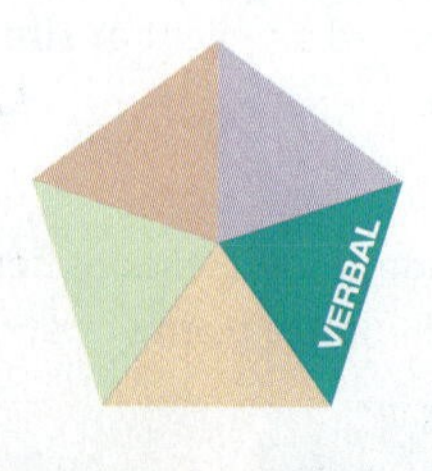

ACKNOWLEDGING SOURCES IN ORAL CITATIONS To acknowledge your source, you can integrate an **oral citation** into your speech. In her speech on domestic abuse, Farrah provided this oral citation:

> The February 3, 2014, *Washington City Paper* recounts the story of a nameless mother who explained, "I would have rather endured getting hit every day than to be homeless with four children."[38]

STUDY GUIDE:
Review, Apply, and Assess Your Knowledge and Skill

Review Your Knowledge

Overviewing the Public Speaking Process

11.1 List and explain the components of the audience-centered public speaking model.

The stages of the public speaking process center on consideration of audience members, who influence every decision a speaker makes. A speaker's tasks include selecting and narrowing a topic, identifying a general and specific purpose for speaking, developing the central idea of the speech, generating main ideas, gathering supporting material, organizing the speech, and rehearsing and delivering the speech.

Building Your Confidence

11.2 Apply specific strategies for becoming a more confident speaker.

Focusing on your audience and message and giving yourself mental pep talks can help you become a more confident speaker, as can knowing how to develop a speech, being well prepared, and seeking out opportunities to speak.

Selecting and Narrowing Your Topic

11.3 Select and narrow a topic for a speech.

As you begin to prepare your speech, you will first have to select and narrow your topic, keeping in mind the audience, the occasion, and your own interests and experiences. You may find helpful such strategies as silent brainstorming, scanning web directories and websites, and listening and reading for topic ideas.

Identifying Your Purpose

11.4 Write an audience-centered specific-purpose statement for a speech.

Once you have a topic, you need to identify both your general purpose and your specific purpose. General purposes include to inform, to persuade, and to entertain. Specific purposes are determined by the general purpose, the topic, and the audience.

Developing Your Central Idea

11.5 Develop a central idea for a speech.

Your central idea will focus on the content of your speech. It should be centered on your audience; reflect a single topic; be a complete declarative sentence; and use direct, specific language.

Generating Main Ideas

11.6 Generate main ideas from a central idea.

The main ideas of a speech support or subdivide the central idea. They are usually logical divisions of the central idea, reasons the central idea is true, or a series of steps or a chronological sequence that develops the central idea.

Gathering Supporting Material

11.7 Describe four potential sources and seven types of supporting material for a speech, and use each type effectively.

You have at least four potential sources of supporting material: yourself, the Internet, online databases, and traditional library resources. Personal knowledge and experience increase the likelihood that the audience will find you a credible speaker. To supplement your own knowledge and experience, you can turn to the vast resources of the Internet. Online databases provide both bibliographic information and full texts to subscribers. You will also most likely use traditional library resources—books, periodicals, newspapers, and reference resources—as sources of supporting material. The types of supporting material you can use in a speech include illustrations, descriptions, explanations, definitions, analogies, statistics, and opinions. Simple guidelines can help you use each type of supporting material effectively and cite your sources correctly.

Key Terms

Public Speaking (Presentational Speaking), p. 253
Audience-Centered Public Speaker, p. 254
Public Speaking Anxiety, p. 254
Illusion of Transparency, p. 255
Habituation, p. 257
General Purpose, p. 260
Specific Purpose, p. 261
Central Idea, p. 262
Declarative Sentence, p. 264
Main Ideas, p. 264
Supporting Material, p. 266
Vertical Search Engine, p. 267
Boolean Search, p. 267
Online Database, p. 268
Stacks, p. 269
Reference Resources, p. 269
Illustration, p. 269
Hypothetical Illustration, p. 269
Description, p. 270
Explanation, p. 270
Definition, p. 271
Classification, p. 271
Operational Definition, p. 271
Analogy, p. 271
Literal Analogy, p. 271
Figurative Analogy, p. 271
Statistics, p. 271
Exploding, p. 272
Expert Testimony, p. 272
Lay Testimony, p. 273
Literary Quotation, p. 273
Plagiarism, p. 274
Oral Citation, p. 274

The Principle Points

Principle One:

Be aware of your communication with yourself and others.

- Understand that public speaking anxiety results from your body working to help you perform better.
- Give yourself a pep talk before getting up to speak.
- Consider your own interests and experiences when selecting a topic.
- Remember that the best supporting material often draws on your own knowledge and experience.

Principle Two:

Effectively use and interpret verbal messages.

- Focus on your message to help you become a more confident speaker.
- Search for topics on the Internet, in the media, and in books.
- Word your specific purpose in terms of your audience to help you keep your focus on them.
- Make sure that your central idea reflects a single topic, is a complete declarative sentence, and uses specific language.
- Consider the accountability, accuracy, objectivity, date, usability, and sensitivity to diversity of verbal material you find on websites.
- Make your illustrations vivid and specific.
- Keep descriptions and explanations brief.
- Describe and explain in specific and concrete language.
- Make your definitions readily understandable, and be certain that they accurately reflect how you use the word or phrase in the speech.
- Round off large numbers to make them more understandable.
- Cite unbiased authorities who represent prevailing opinion.
- Quote or paraphrase accurately and in context.
- Integrate oral citations of your sources into your speech.

Principle Three:

Effectively use and interpret nonverbal messages.

- Remember that nonverbal indicators of public speaking anxiety are rarely visible to an audience.
- Consider the accountability, accuracy, objectivity, date, usability, and sensitivity to diversity of pictures and graphics you find on websites.
- Use visual aids to make statistics more readily understandable to your listeners.

Principle Four:

Listen and respond thoughtfully to others.

- To increase your confidence when speaking in public, seek out information about your listeners and how they are likely to respond to your message.
- Listen for topic ideas in the course of casual conversation with friends.

Principle Five:

Appropriately adapt messages to others.

- As you learn more about your audience, you can revise ideas or strategies for your speech at any point in your preparation process.
- Be centered on your audience to increase your confidence.
- Be sensitive to and adapt to the diversity of your audience.
- Consider your audience's interests and expectations as you select the topic for your speech.
- Keep in mind your audience's knowledge, interests, and expectations as you select supporting material for your presentation.

Apply Your Skill

Consider the following questions. Write your answers and/or share them with your classmates:

1. How is the behavior of a speaker who adapts to his or her audience different from that of a speaker who doesn't adapt to the audience?
2. What are your biggest concerns about giving a speech in public?
3. List some of your own interests and experiences. Use them to brainstorm some possible speech topic ideas.
4. Write your own examples of specific-purpose statements that tell what an audience will do after listening to a speech to inform, a speech to persuade, and a speech to entertain.
5. Following the guidelines in this chapter, write a central idea statement for a speech on the topic of buying car insurance.
6. Divide the central idea statement you wrote about buying car insurance into two or more main ideas, using the three questions recommended in this chapter.
7. What is one illustration, statistic, or other piece of supporting material from a speech you heard that you found highly memorable? Why was it so effective?
8. Is it ever ethical to invent supporting material if you have been unable to find what you need for your speech?

Assess Your Skill

Personal Report of Public Speaking Anxiety (PRPSA)

The first scale developed by James C. McCroskey during his extensive work on communication apprehension, the Personal Report of Public Speaking Anxiety, remains the most reliable measure of public speaking anxiety.

Directions: Below are thirty-four statements that people sometimes make about themselves. Please indicate whether or not you believe each statement applies to you by marking whether you:

Strongly Disagree = 1; Disagree = 2; Neutral = 3; Agree = 4; Strongly Agree = 5.

_____ 1. While preparing for giving a speech, I feel tense and nervous.

_____ 2. I feel tense when I see the words "speech" and "public speech" on a course outline when studying.

_____ 3. My thoughts become confused and jumbled when I am giving a speech.

_____ 4. Right after giving a speech, I feel that I have had a pleasant experience.

_____ 5. I get anxious when I think about a speech coming up.

_____ 6. I have no fear of giving a speech.

_____ 7. Although I am nervous just before starting a speech, I soon settle down after starting and feel calm and comfortable.

_____ 8. I look forward to giving a speech.

_____ 9. When the instructor announces a speaking assignment in class, I can feel myself getting tense.

_____ 10. My hands tremble when I am giving a speech.

_____ 11. I feel relaxed while giving a speech.

_____ 12. I enjoy preparing for a speech.

_____ 13. I am in constant fear of forgetting what I prepared to say.

_____ 14. I get anxious if someone asks me something about my topic that I don't know.

_____ 15. I face the prospect of giving a speech with confidence.

_____ 16. I feel that I am in complete possession of myself while giving a speech.

_____ 17. My mind is clear when giving a speech.

_____ 18. I do not dread giving a speech.

_____ 19. I perspire just before starting a speech.

_____ 20. My heart beats very fast just as I start a speech.

_____ 21. I experience considerable anxiety while sitting in the room just before my speech starts.

_____ 22. Certain parts of my body feel very tense and rigid while giving a speech.

_____ 23. Realizing that only a little time remains in a speech makes me very tense and anxious.

_____ 24. While giving a speech, I know I can control my feelings of tension and stress.

_____ 25. I breathe faster just before starting a speech.

_____ 26. I feel comfortable and relaxed in the hour or so just before giving a speech.

_____ 27. I do poorer on speeches because I am anxious.

_____ 28. I feel anxious when the teacher announces the date of a speaking assignment.

_____ 29. When I make a mistake while giving a speech, I find it hard to concentrate on the parts that follow.

_____ 30. During an important speech I experience a feeling of helplessness building up inside me.

_____ 31. I have trouble falling asleep the night before a speech.

_____ 32. My heart beats very fast while I present a speech.

_____ 33. I feel anxious while waiting to give my speech.

_____ 34. While giving a speech, I get so nervous I forget facts I really know.

Scoring:

To determine your score on the PRPSA, complete the following steps:

Step 1. Add scores for items 1, 2, 3, 5, 9, 10, 13, 14, 19, 20, 21, 22, 23, 25, 27, 28, 29, 30, 31, 32, 33, and 34.

Step 2. Add the scores for items 4, 6, 7, 8, 11, 12, 15, 16, 17, 18, 24, and 26.

Step 3. Complete the following formula:

PRPSA* = *72* − *Total from Step 2* + *Total from Step 1

High = > 131
Low = < 98
Moderate = 98–131
Mean = 114.6; SD = 17.2

Source: J. McCroskey, "Measures of Communication-Bound Anxiety," *Speech Monographs* 37 (1970): 269–277.

Chapter 12

Organizing and Outlining Your Speech

Don't agonize. Organize. —FLORYNCE R. KENNEDY

Kantver/Fotolia

Chapter Outline

Chapter Objectives

After studying this chapter, you should be able to

12.1 List and explain five strategies for organizing the main ideas of a speech.

12.2 Explain six ways to organize the supporting material for a main idea.

12.3 Use signposts to organize your speech for the ears of others.

12.4 Explain the functions of, and several strategies for, speech introductions and conclusions.

12.5 Develop a preparation outline and speaking notes for a speech.

One study found that college students report spending, on average, nearly half of their total speech preparation time outlining and revising their speeches.[1] This chapter will be key in helping you use that preparation time effectively.

You have already completed the first five stages of audience-centered speech preparation:

- Select and narrow a topic.
- Determine your purpose.
- Develop your central idea.
- Generate main ideas.
- Gather supporting material.

Now it is time to put your speech together. You will need to consider first how best to organize your main ideas. Then you will organize your supporting material for maximum effect, and devise signposts to lead your audience through your speech. You will develop an effective introduction and conclusion. Finally, once you have made the necessary decisions about these component parts, you will be ready to outline the entire speech and prepare your speaking notes.

Organizing Your Main Ideas

12.1 List and explain five strategies for organizing the main ideas of a speech.

A logically organized speech includes an introduction, a body, and a conclusion. The body presents the most important content of the speech—the main ideas that you generated with the help of your central idea. At least five strategies can help you determine an effective order in which to present those main ideas.

Organizing Ideas Topically

topical organization
Organization determined by the speaker's discretion or by recency, primacy, or complexity.

If your main ideas are logical divisions of your central idea, you will probably arrange them according to **topical organization**, the strategy that is used most frequently. Topical organization may be simply an arbitrary arrangement of main ideas that are fairly equal in importance. For example, if you are giving an informative speech on the various instrument families in the modern symphony orchestra, your main ideas will probably be strings, woodwinds, brass, and percussion. The order in which you discuss these instrument groups may not really matter.

At other times, topical organization is less arbitrary. Three principles may help you arrange your main ideas effectively.

RECENCY The principle of **recency** suggests that audiences remember best what they hear *last*. If you want to emphasize the string section of an orchestra, you will purposefully place that instrument family last in your informative speech.

PRIMACY Another principle that can help guide your topical organization is **primacy**, which suggests that you discuss your most convincing or least controversial idea *first*. To adapt to an audience that may be skeptical of some of your ideas, discuss first the points on which you all agree. If you are speaking to an anti-gun-control audience about ways to protect children from violence in schools, don't begin by advocating gun control. Instead, begin by affirming family values and education in the home, perhaps move on to the importance of an antiviolence curriculum and adequate counseling in schools, and only then discuss gun control as a possible preventive measure.

COMPLEXITY Organization according to **complexity** moves from simple ideas and processes to more complex ones. You have learned many life skills in order of complexity. In first grade, you learned to read easy words first and then moved on to more difficult ones. In third grade, you learned single-digit multiplication tables before moving on to more complex double- and triple-digit multiplication problems. Similarly, if you are giving a speech on how to trace your family's genealogy, you might discuss readily available, user-friendly Internet sources before explaining how to access old courthouse records or parish registries of births, deaths, and baptisms.

recency
Arrangement of ideas from least important to most important or from weakest to strongest.

primacy
Arrangement of ideas from most important to least important or from strongest to weakest.

complexity
Arranging ideas from simple to more complex.

Organizing Ideas Chronologically

If you determine that you can best develop your central idea through a series of steps, you will probably organize those steps—your main ideas—chronologically. **Chronological organization** is based on time or sequential order according to

chronological organization
Organization by time or sequence.

Which organization is the best choice for this speaker's presentation about the worldwide operations of his organization?
Rawpixel/Fotolia

when each step or event occurred or should occur. If you are explaining a process, you will want to organize the steps of that process from first to last. If you are providing a historical overview of an event, movement, or policy, you might begin with the end result and trace its history backward in time. Topics that lend themselves to chronological organization include the process for stripping and refinishing a piece of furniture, the five deadliest U.S. tornadoes on record, and the three golden ages of journalism.[2]

Organizing Ideas Spatially

"Go down the hill two blocks and turn left by the florist. Then go three blocks to the next stoplight and turn right. The place you're looking for is about a block farther, on your right." When you offer someone directions, you organize your ideas spatially. **Spatial organization** means arranging items according to their location, position, or direction. It is another strategy by which you might organize main ideas that are logical divisions of your central idea.

Speeches that rely on description are especially good candidates for spatial organization. For example, a discussion of the route taken by Sir Edmund Hillary and Tenzing Norgay when climbing Mount Everest in 1953 or of the molecular structure of DNA would lend itself to spatial organization. You might choose to organize your speech on the three deadliest U.S. tornadoes spatially (according to where each tornado occurred) rather than chronologically (by year).

Organizing Ideas to Show Cause and Effect

Cause-and-effect organization actually refers to two related patterns: identifying a situation and then discussing the resulting effects (cause–effect), and presenting a situation and then exploring its causes (effect–cause).

If your main ideas are logical divisions of your central idea, you might organize them according to cause–effect. A speaker discussing the consequences of teenage pregnancy might use a cause–effect pattern, first establishing that teenage pregnancy is a significant social issue and then discussing various consequences or effects.

If your main ideas are reasons your central idea is true, you will probably organize them according to effect–cause. A speaker who wants to explore the reasons for the high rate of teen pregnancy would probably use an effect–cause pattern, first discussing teenage pregnancy as an effect and then exploring its various causes.

As the recency principle would suggest, a cause–effect pattern emphasizes effects; an effect–cause pattern emphasizes causes.

Organizing Ideas by Problem and Solution

If, instead of exploring causes or consequences of a problem or issue, you want either to explore how best to solve the problem or to advocate a particular solution, you will probably choose **problem–solution organization**. This strategy is appropriate for organizing logical divisions of a central idea. For example, if you are speaking on how listeners can protect themselves from mountain lion attacks in the western United States, you might first establish that a significant problem exists, and then talk about solutions to that problem. Or if you are talking about ending discrimination against overweight people, you could first establish that such discrimination exists and then talk about solutions that would end the discrimination.

You can use problem–solution organization for either informative or persuasive speeches. When your general purpose is to persuade, you will go on to urge your audience to support or adopt one or more of the solutions you discuss.

How do you decide which organizational pattern to use? For example, both the mountain lion and the weight discrimination topics lend themselves to

spatial organization
Organization according to location, position, or direction.

cause-and-effect organization
Organization by discussing a situation and its causes, or a situation and its effects.

problem–solution organization
Organization by discussing first a problem and then various solutions.

Communication & DIVERSITY

Acknowledging Cultural Differences in Organizing Messages

What's the shortest distance between two points? Going in a straight line, of course. In organizing a message, it may seem that the most logical strategy is to develop a structure that moves from one idea to the next in a logical, "straight" way. But not every culture organizes ideas using that logic. In fact, each culture teaches its members particular patterns of thought and organization that are considered appropriate for various occasions and audiences.

In general, speakers in the United States tend to be more linear and direct than do Semitic, Asian, Romance language, or Russian speakers.[3] Semitic language speakers support their main points by pursuing tangents that might seem "off topic" to many U.S. listeners. Asians may allude to a main point only through a circuitous route of illustrations and parables. And speakers from Romance language and Russian cultures tend to begin with a basic principle and then move to facts and illustrations that only gradually are related to the main point. The models in Figure 12.1 illustrate these culturally diverse patterns of organization.[4]

Of course, these generalizations are very broad. As an effective speaker who seeks to adapt to your audience, you should investigate and perhaps acknowledge, or even consider adopting, the customary organizational strategy of your particular audience. In addition, when you are listening to a speech, recognizing the existence of cultural differences can help you appreciate and understand the organization of a speaker from a culture other than your own.

Figure 12.1 Organizational Patterns by Culture

SOURCE: Lieberman, Devorah, *Public Speaking in the Multicultural Environment*, 2nd Ed., © 1997. Reprinted and Electronically reproduced by permission of Pearson Education, Inc., Upper Saddle River, New Jersey.

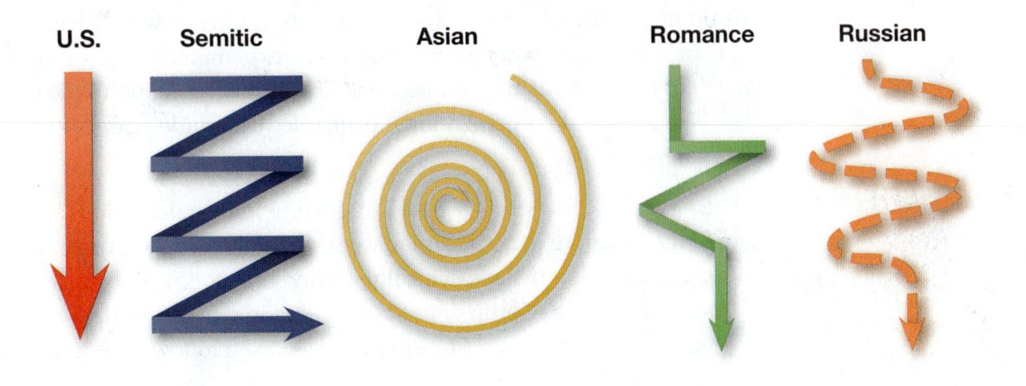

organization by cause and effect, as well as problem–solution. For example, you could discuss mountain lion attacks as an effect and explore why the frequency of such attacks has increased in recent years (causes), or you could talk about discrimination against overweight people as a cause and discuss the harmful effects of such discrimination. Your specific purpose can help you make the decision. If you want your audience to be able to explain how to end discrimination against overweight people, select the problem–solution organizational strategy. If you want your audience to be able to explain the harmful effects of discrimination against those who are overweight, use the cause-and-effect strategy. Let both your general and your specific purpose continue to guide your speech as you organize your main ideas.

RECAP

Organizing Your Main Ideas

Strategy	Description	Applicable to Main Ideas That Are . . .
Topical	Arbitrary arrangement of topics or organization according to recency, primacy, or complexity	Logical divisions
Chronological	Organization by time or sequence	Steps or a chronological sequence
Spatial	Organization according to location or position	Logical divisions
Cause-and-effect	Organization by discussing a situation and its causes (effect–cause) or a situation and its effects (cause–effect)	Reasons (effect–cause) Logical divisions (cause–effect)
Problem–solution	Organization by discussing a problem and then various solutions	Logical divisions

Communication & ETHICS

The Ethics of Primacy and Recency

Nico knows that according to the principle of recency, he should discuss last what he wants his audience to remember best. In his speech on the risk of counterfeit prescription drugs, however, Nico thinks that it may be more ethical to reveal immediately to his audience how costly the problem is in terms of both dollars and human lives. Is it ethical for Nico to save that important statistic for last?

Organizing Your Supporting Material

12.2 Explain six ways to organize the supporting material for a main idea.

Once you have organized your main ideas, you are ready to organize the supporting material for each idea. Suppose you have two brief illustrations, a statistic, and an opinion in support of your first main idea. How should you organize these materials to communicate your verbal message most effectively?

The now-familiar strategies of chronology, primacy, recency, and complexity can also help you organize your supporting material. For example, you might arrange a group of brief illustrations *chronologically*. At other times, you might apply the principle of *recency* and save your most convincing statistic for last. If you decide to present first the opinion with which you are certain your audience will agree, you apply the principle of *primacy*. Or you might arrange two explanations according to the principle of *complexity*, presenting the simplest one first and working up to the more complex one.

Two additional organizational principles can guide your organization of supporting material.

- **Specificity.** Sometimes your supporting material includes both specific illustrations and more general explanations or statistics. The principle of **specificity** suggests that you offer a specific illustration first, followed by a general explanation or statistics, or—as Kerlin does in his speech to raise awareness of poverty—give your general explanation or statistics first and then follow with a specific illustration:

  In New Orleans, 38 percent of children live in poverty, which is more than double the national child poverty rate of 17 percent. In the state of Louisiana, 13 percent of children live not in poverty—but extreme poverty. Let me tell you about the 6-year-old hero in the aftermath of Katrina. Deamonte Love . . . walked down the road, holding a 5-month-old infant. He had no clues whatsoever where his parents were, while surrounded by five toddlers, and one was wearing only diapers.[5]

- **Soft to Hard Evidence.** Another principle that can help you organize your supporting material is moving from "soft" to "hard" evidence. Illustrations, descriptions, explanations, definitions, analogies, and opinions are usually considered **soft evidence**, whereas statistics are **hard evidence**. In his speech on providing asylum to victims of systematic rape, Samin moves from soft evidence to a hard statistic:

  On New Year's Eve, the Congolese army went to the village of Fizi and raped 62 women from 7 p.m. to 6 a.m. . . . The 2010 International Statistics on Crime and Justice Report laments that nearly 200,000 women worldwide face the threat of repeated rape by their government or military in countries such as Zimbabwe, Sudan, and Guatemala.[6]

specificity
Organization from specific information to a more general statement or from a general statement to specific information.

soft evidence
Illustrations, descriptions, explanations, definitions, analogies, and opinions.

hard evidence
Statistics.

RECAP

Organizing Your Supporting Material

Strategy	Description
Chronology	Organization by time or sequence
Recency	Most important material last
Primacy	Most convincing or least controversial material first
Complexity	From simple to more complex material
Specificity	From specific information to general overview or from general overview to specific information
Soft to Hard Evidence	From hypothetical illustrations and opinions to facts and statistics

Signposting: Organizing Your Speech for the Ears of Others

Kamagurka/Cartoon Stock

12.3 Use signposts to organize your speech for the ears of others.

You now have a fairly complete, logically organized plan for your speech, but if you tried to deliver it at this point, your audience would probably become confused. What are your main ideas? How is one main idea related to the next? What supporting material develops which main idea? To adapt your logically organized message to your audience, you need to provide **signposts**, organizational cues for the audience's ears. You do this by adding previews, transitions, and summaries that provide coherence as you move from one idea to the next throughout the speech.

Previews

A **preview** "tells them what you're going to tell them"; it is a statement of what is to come. Previews help your audience members anticipate and remember the main ideas of your speech. They also help you move smoothly from the introduction to the body of your speech and from one main idea to the next.

INITIAL PREVIEW The **initial preview** is usually presented in conjunction with, and sometimes as part of, the central idea. Consider Kevin's speech calling for an end to the FBI's practice of making information requests without first getting search warrants. Notice how he states his central idea and then previews his three main ideas near the end of the introduction:

> It is imperative that we stop the use of warrantless requests of records by the federal government for mere convenience of information. We will first examine the reasons for the FBI's abuse of power; next, explore the damage the bureau's dangerous activities have done; before finally, we discover solutions to abolish a system that . . . allows the FBI to make sending you a subpoena for information as easy as writing a request on a Post-it note.[7]

INTERNAL PREVIEW In addition to offering an initial preview, a speaker may also offer, at various points throughout a speech, an **internal preview**. Internal previews introduce and outline ideas that will be developed as the speech progresses. Meleena provides an internal preview just before the final main idea of her speech on sexual harassment in schools:

> Now . . . we can look at some things that we can all do, as parents, teachers, and students, to stop sexual harassment in our schools. There are two ways to prevent these causes from recurring. The first is education and the second is immediate action.[8]

When Meleena delivers this preview, her listeners know that she is going to talk about two possible solutions to the problem she has been discussing. Their anticipation increases the likelihood that they will hear and later remember these solutions.

signpost
A verbal or nonverbal organizational signal.

preview
A statement of what is to come.

initial preview
First statement of the main ideas of a speech, usually presented with or near the central idea.

internal preview
A preview within the speech that introduces ideas still to come.

transition
A word, phrase, or nonverbal cue that indicates movement from one idea to the next or the relationship between ideas.

verbal transition
A word or phrase that indicates the relationship between two ideas.

Verbal and Nonverbal Transitions

A **transition** signals to the audience that a speaker is moving from one idea to the next.

VERBAL TRANSITION To use verbal messages effectively, include **verbal transitions**, words or phrases that show relationships between ideas in your speech. They

Simply telling listeners you are making your first (or second or third) point can help them understand the organization of your speech.
R. Gino Santa Maria/Shutterstock

include simple enumeration (*first, second, third*); synonyms or pronouns that refer to earlier key words or ideas (the word *they* at the beginning of this sentence refers to the phrase "verbal transitions" in the previous sentence); and words and phrases that show relationships between ideas (*in addition, not only . . . but also, in other words, in summary, therefore, however*). As you begin to rehearse your speech, you might need to experiment with various verbal transitions to achieve a flow that seems natural and logical to you. If none of the verbal alternatives seems quite right, consider a nonverbal transition.

NONVERBAL TRANSITION Sometimes used alone and sometimes used in combination with verbal transitions, an effective **nonverbal transition** might take the form of a facial expression, a pause, a change in vocal pitch or speaking rate, or movement. Most good speakers will use a combination of verbal and nonverbal transitions to help them move from one idea to the next throughout their speeches.

nonverbal transition
A facial expression, vocal cue, or physical movement that indicates that a speaker is moving from one idea to the next.

summary
A recap of what has been said.

internal summary
A recap within the speech of what has been said so far.

final summary
A recap of all the main points of a speech, usually occurring just before or during the conclusion.

Summaries

Like previews, a **summary**—a recap of what has been said—provides an opportunity for the audience to grasp a speaker's most important ideas. Most speakers use two types of summaries: internal summaries and a final summary.

INTERNAL SUMMARY Like internal previews, **internal summaries** occur within and throughout a speech. After you have discussed two or three main ideas, you might want to use an internal summary to ensure that the audience keeps them firmly in mind before you move on to another main idea. You can combine an internal summary with an internal preview. In her speech comparing the Brothers Grimm and Disney versions of *Cinderella*, Grace combined an internal summary and preview in this way:

> So now that we've talked a little bit about the differences in the characters between the two versions and the differences in the royal ball scene, I'd like to discuss the way that Disney omitted some violence from their version of *Cinderella* compared to the Brothers Grimm version.[9]

FINAL SUMMARY In your conclusion, you may want to provide your audience with a final opportunity to hear and remember your main ideas. Whereas your initial preview gave your audience members their first exposure to your main ideas, your **final summary** will give them their last exposure to those ideas. Near the end of Stephanie's speech on cruise ship violence, she provides this final summary of her three main ideas:

> Today we outlined violence on cruise ships and the need for recourse; we then discussed the nature of these criminal environments and lack of laws; and finally, we explored solutions for handling or avoiding these crimes even if the authorities are not supportive.[10]

Adding previews, transitions, and summaries to your well-organized speech applies the fundamental principles of using both verbal and nonverbal messages effectively and of adapting your message to others. It increases the likelihood that your audience will grasp your main ideas and the logic of your organizational strategy.

Introducing and Concluding Your Speech

12.4 Explain the functions of, and several strategies for, speech introductions and conclusions.

At this point, you have developed and organized the ideas and content of the body of your speech, but you might not have thought about how you are going to begin and end the speech. That's okay. Even though you will deliver your introduction first, you usually plan it last. You need to know what you're introducing—especially your central idea and main ideas. Once you do, it is time to plan how you will introduce and conclude your speech. Although your introduction and conclusion make up a relatively small percentage of the total speech, they provide your audience with first and final impressions of you and your speech. They are important considerations in adapting your message to others.

Introductions

Your **introduction** should convince your audience to listen to you. More specifically, it must perform six functions: getting the audience's attention, introducing the topic, giving the audience a reason to listen, establishing your credibility, stating your central idea, and previewing your main ideas. Let's briefly consider each of these functions.

GET THE AUDIENCE'S ATTENTION If an introduction does not capture the attention of audience members, the rest of the speech may be wasted on them. You have to use verbal messages effectively to wake up your listeners and make them want to hear more.

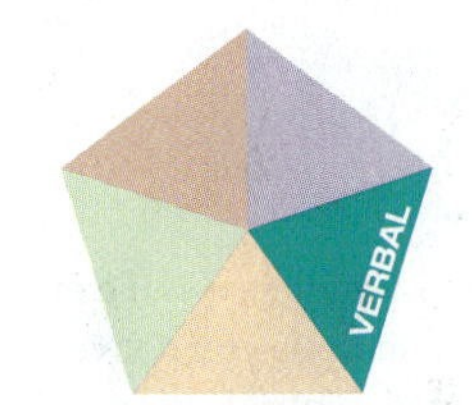

There are several good ways to gain an audience's attention. One commonly used and quite effective way is to open with an illustration. Buey Ruet opens his speech on the bloodshed in Sudan with this moving personal illustration:

> On October 15, 1994, a woman by the name of Workinsh Admasu opened a letter, which required her 8- and 13-year-old boys to immediately report to military training camp. Three weeks after basic training, the boys, along with another 300,000 8- to 14-year-olds, strapped on AK47s that were half of their body weight and headed off to fight in Sudan's civil war. . . . That 8-year-old boy was me. . . . My 13-year-old brother and I were forced to experience things that no other child should ever have to experience.[11]

Other strategies are to ask a rhetorical question, relate a startling fact or statistic, quote an expert or a literary text, tell a humorous story, or refer to historical or recent events. Comedian Conan O'Brien used humor in the introduction to (and throughout) his 2011 commencement address at Dartmouth College:

> New Hampshire is such a special place. When I arrived, I took a deep breath of this crisp New England air and thought, "Wow, I'm in the state that's next to the state where Ben and Jerry's ice cream is made."[12]

Still other speakers might get their audience's attention by referring to a personal experience, the occasion, or something said by a preceding speaker. Speaking to a diverse audience about Alzheimer's disease, brain surgeon Keith Black began by sharing his personal experience:

> For me, this really became personal because my mother was diagnosed with Alzheimer's disease about 12 years ago. And so I realized firsthand how devastating this disease can be and that we really need to accelerate trying to come up with a solution for it.[13]

Although not all these strategies will work for all speeches, at least one of them should be an option for any speech you make. With a little practice, you may be able to choose from several good possibilities for a single speech.

introduction
Opening lines of a speech, which must catch the audience's attention, introduce the topic, give the audience a reason to listen, establish the speaker's credibility, state the central idea, and preview the main ideas.

INTRODUCE THE TOPIC Within the first few seconds of listening to you, your audience should have a pretty good idea of what your topic is.

GIVE THE AUDIENCE A REASON TO LISTEN Not only do you have to get your audience's attention and introduce your topic, but you also have to motivate your listeners to continue to listen. Show the listeners how your topic affects them and those

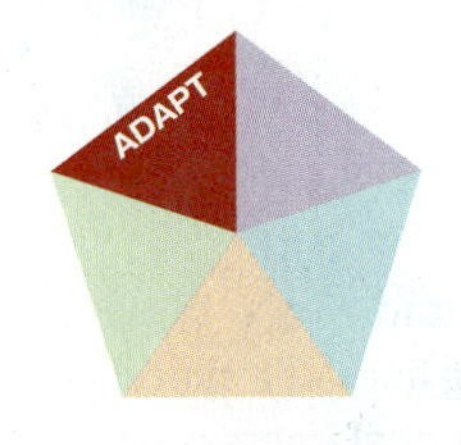

Looking the audience in the eye with a friendly smile as you deliver your well-prepared introduction can help establish your credibility.
Laflor/E+/Getty Images

they care about. Catherine uses rhetorical questions to drive home to her audience the relevance and importance of her speech on a healthy diet:

> What if I told you that, by decreasing one food item in your and your loved ones' diet, you could significantly lessen the chance for metabolic syndrome (or obesity); heart disease; coronary artery disease; osteoporosis due to calcium depletion; high blood pressure; colon, kidney, breast, prostate, and liver cancer? Would you change the menu at your and your loved ones' next meal?[14]

By the end of your introduction, your audience should be thinking, "This concerns *me*!"

ESTABLISH YOUR CREDIBILITY A credible speaker is one whom the audience judges to be believable, competent, and trustworthy. Be aware of the skills, talents, and experiences you have had that are related to your topic. You can increase your credibility by telling your audience about your expertise. For example, in your introduction to a persuasive speech on studying abroad, you might say:

> I know firsthand how studying abroad can broaden your worldview, increase your understanding of another culture, and enrich your academic studies. Last fall, I studied at the Sorbonne in Paris.

STATE YOUR CENTRAL IDEA Your central idea usually appears at or near the end of your introduction, as in the following example from Aaron's speech on post-traumatic stress disorder:

> Hundreds of combat veterans . . . are being dismissed from the Armed Services without the medical benefits needed to treat combat stress.[15]

PREVIEW YOUR MAIN IDEAS Previewing your main ideas allows your listeners to anticipate and begin to listen for those main ideas. You can provide your initial preview immediately after your central idea. Here is the initial preview of main ideas that follows Aaron's central idea, quoted above:

> So in today's speech we will uncover the problems associated with the denial of benefits to discharged veterans suffering from Post-traumatic Stress Disorder. Next we will investigate the causes of these problems before finally understanding what can be done to solve this flaw in the policies of the VA.[16]

Conclusions

Your introduction creates a critically important first impression, and your **conclusion** leaves an equally important final impression. Long after you finish speaking, your audience will hear the echo of effective final words. An effective conclusion serves four functions: to summarize the speech, to reemphasize the main idea in a memorable way, to motivate the audience to respond, and to provide closure. Let's consider each of these functions.

SUMMARIZE THE SPEECH The conclusion offers a speaker a last chance to repeat his or her main ideas. Most speakers summarize their main ideas between the body of the speech and its conclusion or in the first part of the conclusion.

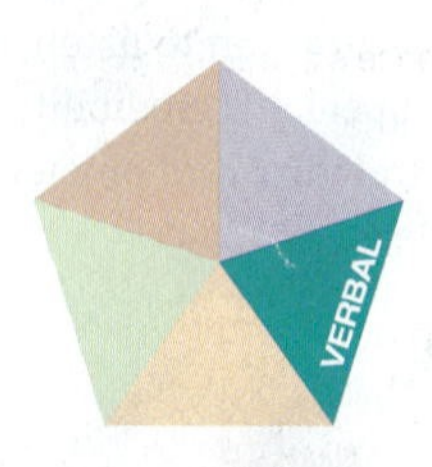

REEMPHASIZE THE CENTRAL IDEA IN A MEMORABLE WAY The conclusions of many famous speeches contain many of the lines we remember best:

> that government of the people, by the people, for the people, shall not perish from the earth. *(Abraham Lincoln)*[17]

Old soldiers never die; they just fade away. *(General Douglas MacArthur)*[18]

Use your final verbal message effectively. Word your thoughts so that your audience cannot help but remember them.

conclusion
Closing lines of a speech, which leave a final impression.

MOTIVATE THE AUDIENCE TO RESPOND Think back to your specific purpose. What do you want your audience to be able to do by the end of your speech? If your

Effective speakers often save their most important idea—the one they want the audience to walk away with—for last.
Ron Chapple/Photolibrary

purpose is to inform, you may want your audience to think about your topic or seek more information about it. If your purpose is to persuade, you may want your audience to take some sort of action, such as write a letter, make a phone call, or volunteer for a cause. Your conclusion is where you can motivate your audience to respond. Travis closes his speech on sleep deprivation with this admonition:

> Before we are all, literally, dead on our feet, let's take the easiest solution step of all. Tonight, turn off your alarm, turn down your covers, and turn in for a good night's sleep.[19]

PROVIDE CLOSURE You may have experienced listening to a speech and not being certain when it was over. If so, you were listening to a speaker who did not achieve the last purpose of an effective conclusion: providing **closure**, or a sense that the speech is finished.

closure
The sense that a speech is finished.

You can provide closure by referring back to your introduction and finishing a story, answering a rhetorical question, or reminding your audience of where you started. Steven had opened his speech on reducing DUI occurrences with an extended illustration about a Wyoming highway patrol officer who was forced to kill a woman in self-defense when the inebriated woman brutally attacked him. He provides memorable closure to his speech by finishing the story:

> Whenever I heard about someone being killed during an alcohol-related traffic incident, I used to shrug it off, thinking, "How does this affect me?" . . . When the Wyoming highway patrolman took the life of Alyssa Harriet, I learned how drinking and driving affects me, because that highway patrolman is my brother.[20]

RECAP

The Purposes of Introductions and Conclusions

Your introduction should . . .	Get your audience's attention.
	Introduce your topic.
	Give your audience a reason to listen.
	Establish your credibility.
	State your central idea.
	Preview your main ideas.
Your conclusion should . . .	Summarize your speech.
	Reemphasize your central idea in a memorable way.
	Motivate your audience to respond.
	Provide closure.

You can also achieve closure by using verbal and nonverbal signposts. For example, you might use such transitions as *finally* and *in conclusion* as you move into your conclusion. You might pause before you begin the conclusion, slow your speaking rate as you deliver your final sentence, or signal by falling vocal inflection that you are making your final statement. Experiment with these strategies until you are certain that your speech "sounds finished."

Outlining Your Speech

12.5 Develop a preparation outline and speaking notes for a speech.

With your introduction and conclusion planned, you are almost ready to begin rehearsing your speech. By this point, you should have your preparation outline nearly complete. A **preparation outline** is a fairly detailed outline of your central idea, main ideas, and supporting material. It may also include your specific purpose, introduction, and conclusion. A second outline, which you will prepare shortly, makes up the speaking notes from which you will eventually deliver your speech.

Preparation Outline

Although few speeches are written in manuscript form, most speakers develop a fairly detailed preparation outline to help them ensure that their main ideas are clearly related to their central idea and are logically and adequately supported. A speaker who creates a preparation outline is applying the first fundamental principle of communication: becoming increasingly aware of his or her communication. In addition to helping the speaker judge the unity and coherence of the speech, the preparation outline also serves as an early rehearsal outline and is usually handed in as part of a class requirement.

Instructors who require students to turn in a preparation outline will probably have their own specific requirements. For example, some instructors ask for the introduction and conclusion as part of the outline, whereas others ask for an outline only of the body of the speech. Some instructors ask that you incorporate signposts into the outline or write your specific purpose at the top of the outline. Be certain that you carefully listen to and follow your instructor's specific requirements regarding which elements to include.

preparation outline
A detailed outline of a speech that includes the central idea, main ideas, and supporting material, and may also include the specific purpose, introduction, and conclusion.

standard outline format
Conventional use of numbered and lettered headings and subheadings to indicate the relationships among parts of a speech.

Almost certainly, your instructor will require that you use **standard outline format**. Standard outline format lets you become more aware of the exact relationships among various main ideas, subpoints, and supporting material in your speech. Even if you haven't had much experience with formal outlines, the following guidelines can help you produce a correct outline.

USE STANDARD NUMBERING Outlines are numbered with Roman and Arabic numerals and uppercase and lowercase letters followed by periods, as follows:

Communication & TECHNOLOGY

Using Outlining Software

Word-processing programs such as Microsoft Word have features that allow you to set the style of an outline and various levels within it. The feature will then apply the appropriate number, letter, and indentation to each heading you provide.

Try using one of these outlining resources to prepare either your preparation outline or your speaking notes for your next speech. Then evaluate whether using the tool made outlining easier or harder for you than outlining by hand.

I. First main idea
  A. First subdivision of I
  B. Second subdivision of I
    1. First subdivision of B
    2. Second subdivision of B
      (a) First subdivision of 2
      (b) Second subdivision of 2
II. Second main idea

You will probably not need to subdivide beyond the level of lowercase letters in most speech outlines.

USE AT LEAST TWO SUBDIVISIONS, IF ANY, FOR EACH POINT You cannot divide anything into fewer than two parts. On an outline, every I should be followed by a II, every A should be followed by a B, and so on. If you have only one subdivision, fold it into the level above it.

LINE UP YOUR OUTLINE CORRECTLY Main ideas, indicated by Roman numerals, are written closest to the left margin. The *periods* following these Roman numerals line up so that the first letters of the first words also line up:

I. First main idea
II. Second main idea
III. Third main idea

Letters or numbers of subdivisions begin directly underneath the first letter of the first *word* of the point above:

I. First main idea
  A. First subdivision of I
  B. Second subdivision of I

If a main idea or subdivision takes up more than one line, the second line begins under the first letter of the first word of the preceding line:

I. First main idea
  A. A rather lengthy subdivision that runs more than one line
  B. Second subdivision

WITHIN EACH LEVEL, MAKE THE HEADINGS GRAMMATICALLY PARALLEL Regardless of whether you write your preparation outline in complete sentences or in phrases, be consistent within each level. In other words, if I is a complete sentence, II should also be a complete sentence. If A is an infinitive phrase (one that begins with *to* plus a verb, such as "to guarantee greater security"), B should also be an infinitive phrase.

We have included in this chapter a sample preparation outline for the speech we've been watching Lario Albarran prepare in the Developing Your Speech Step by Step feature.[21] Your instructor may have additional or alternative requirements for what your preparation outline should include or how it should be formatted.

Speaking Notes

As you rehearse your speech, you will need to look at your preparation outline less and less. You have both the structure and the content of your speech quite well in mind. At this point, you are ready to develop a shorter outline to serve as your speaking notes.

Your speaking notes should provide all the information you will need to make your speech as you have planned, but should not be so detailed that you will be

Sample Preparation Outline

Purpose

At the end of my speech, the audience will be able to explain the short-term and long-term effects of poverty on the brain, and the implications of these effects for people's lives.

Writing the purpose statement at the top of the outline helps the speaker keep it in mind, but always follow your instructor's specific requirements for how to format your preparation outline.

Introduction

With the nickname "Bull Johnson" and a propensity for making other politicians cry, President Lyndon B. Johnson is one of the last people you would want to tick off—which is probably why the January 27, 2014, *Washington Post* waited until he was six feet under to proclaim that he delivered the second best State of the Union address ever. Despite its runner-up status, the February 15, 2014, *New York Times* explains that Johnson's speech in 1964 revolutionized domestic politics by declaring a "War on Poverty." Now, on the fifty-year anniversary of Johnson's proclamation, scientists have discovered that poverty profoundly impacts another area of our lives, one that we would never expect: our brains.

Lario catches his listeners' attention by referring to a historical event. Other strategies for effectively getting audience attention were discussed earlier in the chapter.

Central Idea

Poverty's short-term and long-term effects on the brain have major implications for people's lives.

Lario writes out and labels his central idea and preview. Again, follow your instructor's requirements.

Preview

Let's first explore poverty's short-term effects on our brain; and next, examine the long-term changes it causes; before finally, discussing some implications of brain changes.

Body

I. Poverty has short-term effects on our brains.
   A. Cognitive capacity is rapidly depleted by poverty.
      1. Cognitive capacity, as defined by *The Guardian* on August 8, 2013, is the total amount of information our brains are capable of processing at any particular moment. It's like brain bandwidth.
      2. Consequences of poverty impose such a cognitive load that the poor have little bandwidth left to do things that might lift them out of poverty.

The first main idea of the speech is indicated by the Roman numeral I. This main idea has two subpoints, indicated by A and B.

Subpoints 1 and 2 provide supporting material for A.

Signpost: Second, from a physical standpoint,

   B. Living in poverty shrinks your brain. The November 2013 *JAMA Pediatrics* reports findings that suggest stress from childhood poverty increases cortisol and adrenaline, which reduce the size of those areas of the brain used for short-term memory, long-term memory, cognitive ability, and decision-making.

Lario has written citations of his sources available for his instructor or any other audience member who might want them.

Signpost: As the March 4, 2014, *National Geographic* explains, even if poverty is temporary, its handprint on our brains isn't.

II. Poverty has long-term effects on our brains.
   A. Poverty's effects are permanent. In a study reported in the May 2, 2013, *Proceedings of the National Academy of Sciences*, adults who were poor as

Lario uses signposts to organize his speech for the ears of his listeners—in this case, transitioning from his first main idea (I) to his second (II).

Sample Preparation Outline *(continued)*

children had more problems regulating emotions, remembering things, and grappling with spatial reasoning tasks as adults, even after they had escaped poverty.

B. The impacts of poverty on the brain last for generations.
   1. As the 2013 *Quarterly Review of Biology* reports, the symptoms of poverty alter hereditary segments in our DNA that are then passed on.
   2. Think of it this way: If you inherit a house from your parents, you aren't given a brand new copy of the house. You get the house as-is. Our genetic code works the same way.

Lario uses a figurative analogy to clarify for his listeners how the human genetic code works.

Signpost: After identifying how the stress of poverty damages the brain, we should consider two implications.

III. Poverty's effects on the brain have implications for our approach to fixing education and our understanding of poverty as a disease.
   A. Poverty's effects on the brain challenge the argument that bad schools and ineffective teachers are the cause of declining test scores. The December 10, 2013, *USA Today* argues that unsatisfactory international test results are not a condemnation of our school systems, but of our poverty problem.
   B. Research on how poverty changes the brain may spark a movement to classify these changes as a disease.

Conclusion

As a child, LBJ watched his father struggle to keep their family farm afloat and later spent two years as a debate coach for low-income students. These experiences became his inspiration for later declaring that the War on Poverty could not be won in Washington, but must be won in every private home, and in every public office, from the courthouse to the White House. Today, we've gained a better understanding of poverty's short-term effects on the brain, long-lasting changes, and greater implications. It's clear that we should add another place that the War on Poverty must be won: the laboratory.

In his conclusion, Lario brings closure to his speech by referring back to his introduction. His final sentence drives home the importance of his topic to his student audience and "sounds finished."

tempted to read rather than speak to your audience. Here are a few suggestions for developing speaking notes.

USE NOTE CARDS, A SMARTPHONE, OR A TABLET You want notes that are small enough to hold in one hand, that won't rustle as you handle them, and on which the letters and words are large enough to be read easily.

If you decide to use paper note cards, prepare them according to logical blocks of material, using one note card for your introduction, one or two for the body of your speech, and one for your conclusion. Number your note cards in case they get out of order while you are speaking. If you choose instead to put your speaking notes on an electronic device, you will be able to scroll through your outline as you progress through the speech.

USE STANDARD OUTLINE FORMAT Standard outline format will help you find your exact place when you glance down at your speaking notes. You will know, for example, that your second main idea is indicated by "II."

INCLUDE YOUR INTRODUCTION AND CONCLUSION IN ABBREVIATED FORM Even if your instructor does not require you to include your introduction

Figure 12.2 Sample Speaking Notes

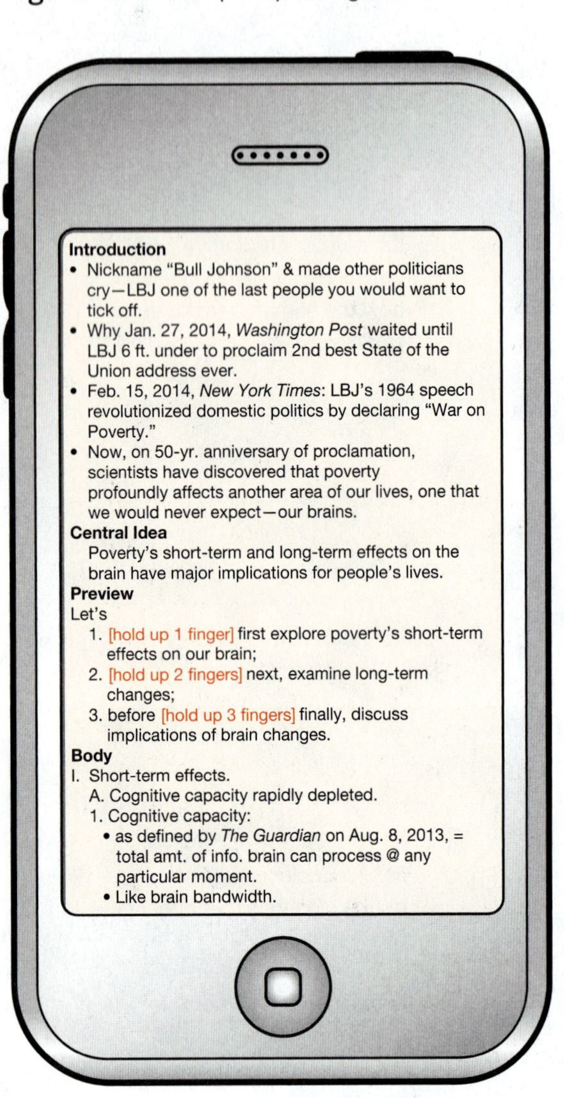

and conclusion on your preparation outline, include shortened versions of them in your speaking notes. You might even feel more comfortable delivering the speech if you have your first and last sentences written out in front of you.

INCLUDE YOUR CENTRAL IDEA, BUT NOT YOUR PURPOSE STATEMENT Be sure to include your central idea in your speaking notes. Do not include your purpose statement because you will not actually say it during your speech.

INCLUDE SUPPORTING MATERIAL AND SIGNPOSTS Write out in full any statistics and direct quotations and their sources. Write your key signposts—your initial preview, for example—to ensure that you will not grope awkwardly as you move from one idea to another.

INCLUDE DELIVERY CUES Writing such cues as "Louder," "Pause," or "Walk two steps left" will remind you to communicate the nonverbal messages you have planned. Use a different color font or ink so that you don't confuse your delivery cues with your verbal content.

Figure 12.2 illustrates speaking notes for Lario's speech on the effects of poverty on the brain.

RECAP

Two Types of Speech Outlines

Type	Purpose
Preparation Outline	Allows speaker to examine speech for completeness, unity, coherence, and overall effectiveness. May serve as first rehearsal outline.
Speaking Notes	Include supporting material, signposts, and delivery cues.

STUDY GUIDE:
Review, Apply, and Assess Your Knowledge and Skill

Review Your Knowledge

Organizing Your Main Ideas

12.1 List and explain five strategies for organizing the main ideas of a speech.

Once you have found supporting material, you are ready to organize your ideas and information. Depending on your topic, purpose, and audience, you can organize the main ideas of your speech chronologically, topically, spatially, by cause and effect, or by problem and solution.

Organizing Your Supporting Material

12.2 Explain six ways to organize the supporting material for a main idea.

You can often organize supporting material according to one of the same patterns used to organize main ideas: chronology, recency, primacy, or complexity. You can also organize supporting material by specificity or from soft to hard evidence.

Organizing Your Speech for the Ears of Others

12.3 Use signposts to organize your speech for the ears of others.

With your speech organized, you will want to add signposts—previews, transitions, and summaries—to make your organization clearly apparent to your audience.

Introducing and Concluding Your Speech

12.4 Explain the functions of, and several strategies for, speech introductions and conclusions.

A carefully planned introduction will get your audience's attention, introduce your topic, give the audience a reason to listen, establish your credibility, state your central idea, and preview your main ideas. An equally carefully planned conclusion will summarize your speech, reemphasize the central idea in a memorable way, motivate your audience to respond, and provide closure.

Outlining Your Speech

12.5 Develop a preparation outline and speaking notes for a speech.

A final step before beginning to rehearse your speech is to prepare a detailed preparation outline and speaking notes. Your preparation outline should follow the instructions provided by your instructor.

Key Terms

Topical Organization, p. 280
Recency, p. 281
Primacy, p. 281
Complexity, p. 281
Chronological Organization, p. 281
Spatial Organization, p. 282
Cause-and-Effect Organization, p. 282
Problem–Solution Organization, p. 282
Specificity, p. 284
Soft Evidence, p. 284
Hard Evidence, p. 284
Signpost, p. 285
Preview, p. 285
Initial Preview, p. 285
Internal Preview, p. 285
Transition, p. 285
Verbal Transition, p. 285
Nonverbal Transition, p. 286
Summary, p. 286
Internal Summary, p. 286
Final Summary, p. 286
Introduction, p. 287
Conclusion, p. 288
Closure, p. 289
Preparation Outline, p. 290
Standard Outline Format, p. 290

The Principle Points

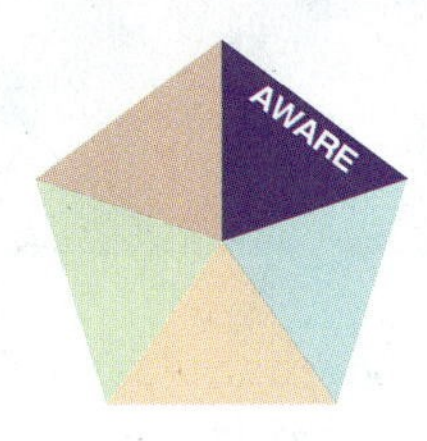

Principle One:

Be aware of your communication with yourself and others.

- Be aware of the skills, talents, and experiences you have that can enhance your credibility with your listeners.
- Use a preparation outline to demonstrate to yourself that your main ideas are clearly related to your central idea and are logically and adequately supported.

Principle Two:

Effectively use and interpret verbal messages.

- To communicate your verbal message effectively, organize your speech logically.
- Use verbal transitions to show relationships between ideas in your speech.
- Introduce your topic and preview your main ideas in your introduction.
- Use stories, examples, illustrations, statistics, a quotation, or other techniques to capture your listeners' attention when you begin your talk.
- In your conclusion, summarize your speech and reemphasize your main idea in a memorable way.

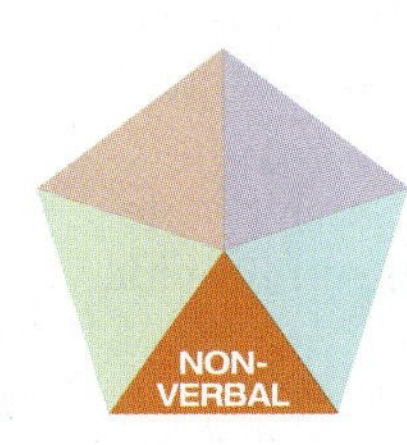

Principle Three:

Effectively use and interpret nonverbal messages.

- Use nonverbal transitions—pauses, facial expression, altered vocal pitch or speaking rate, and movement—to indicate when you are moving from one idea to the next.
- Use nonverbal cues—such as pausing, slowing your rate of speech, and letting your vocal inflection fall—to signal closure in the final sentence or two of your conclusion.
- Add delivery cues and reminders to your final speaking notes.

Principle Four:

Listen and respond thoughtfully to others.

- As you listen to speeches, be aware that their organization may reflect patterns considered appropriate in cultures other than your own.

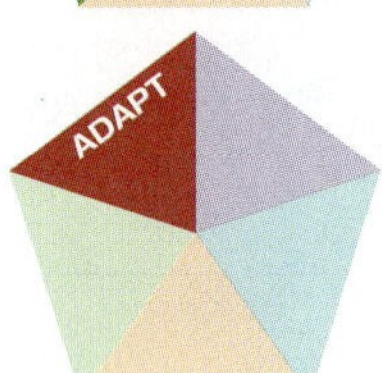

Principle Five:

Appropriately adapt messages to others.

- Investigate and consider using the customary organizational strategy of your audience's culture.
- In most cases, discuss last the idea that you most want your audience to remember.
- If you know that your audience members will be skeptical of some of your ideas, present first the ideas on which you and the audience can agree.
- Provide signposts as organizational cues for your audience.
- Use your introduction and conclusion to help adapt your speech to your audience.

Apply Your Skill

Consider the following questions. Write your answers and/or share them with your classmates:

1. For each of the five patterns of organization discussed, suggest a topic of interest to you that might be organized according to that pattern.
2. Describe the supporting materials in a recent persuasive or informative speech. What principle did the speaker use to organize the order of the supporting material?
3. Recall a recent speech or take notes on an upcoming lecture or a TED talk. Give an example of the speaker's use of signposts.
4. Give an example of an introduction you've heard that effectively caught your attention and gave you a reason to listen.
5. What alternative method of formatting speaking notes might work for speakers who do not wish to use a standard outline?
6. Look again at the Communication & Ethics feature in this chapter and answer the question at the end. Is it ethical to save important supporting material for last? Why or why not?

Assess Your Skill

Listening to and Outlining a Speech

Take notes as you listen to a speech, either live or recorded. Then organize your notes into an outline that you think reflects both the speaker's organization and the intended relationship among ideas and supporting material.

Analyzing the Organization of a Speech

Read one of the speeches in Appendix B. Answer the following questions:

1. How are the main ideas organized?
2. Look closely at the supporting materials. If two or more are used to support any one main idea, what strategy do you think the speaker used to organize them?
3. Is there an initial preview statement? If so, what is it?
4. Is there a final summary? If so, what is it?
5. Find at least one example of each of the following:
   - A transition word or phrase
   - An internal preview
   - An internal summary

Developing a Practice Introduction

Draft an introduction for a speech on one of the following topics:

- Strategies for surviving a tornado
- Private-school vouchers
- Mars up close
- Celebrities and the press

In addition to introducing the topic and previewing your main ideas, be sure to plan strategies for getting the attention of audience members and giving them a reason to listen. Also devise a way to establish your own credibility as a speaker on that topic.

Chapter 13

Delivering Your Speech

O the orator's joys! To inflate the chest, to roll the thunder of the voice out from the ribs and throat, to make the people rage, weep, hate, desire. —WALT WHITMAN

Laflor/E+/Getty Images

Chapter Outline

- Methods of Delivery
- Effective Verbal Delivery
- Effective Nonverbal Delivery
- Effective Presentation Aids
- Some Final Tips for Rehearsing and Delivering Your Speech
- Criteria for Evaluating Speeches
- Study Guide: Review, Apply, and Assess Your Knowledge and Skill

Chapter Objectives

After studying this chapter, you should be able to

13.1 List and describe the four methods of delivery, and provide suggestions for effectively using each one.

13.2 List and explain five criteria for effective verbal delivery.

13.3 Identify and illustrate characteristics of effective nonverbal delivery.

13.4 Discuss how to prepare and use presentation aids effectively.

13.5 Make the most of your rehearsal time, and deliver your speech effectively.

13.6 Understand and apply criteria for evaluating speeches.

Which is more important, the content of a speech or the way it is delivered? Speakers and speech teachers have argued about the answer to this question for thousands of years, and the debate continues.

One researcher has concluded that delivery is almost twice as important as content when students give self-introduction speeches and three times as important when students give persuasive speeches.[1] Other scholars have found that delivery provides important information about a speaker's feelings and emotions and will in turn affect listeners' emotional responses to the speaker.[2] Most speech teachers today agree that both content and delivery contribute to the effectiveness of a speech. As a modern speechwriter and communication coach suggests,

> In the real world—the world where you and I do business—content and delivery are always related. And woe be to the communicator who forgets this.[3]

In this chapter, we will discuss how you can apply the five Communication Principles for a Lifetime to your verbal and nonverbal delivery of speeches. We will also discuss how to determine what presentation aids might be effective for your audience, and we'll offer guidelines for both preparing and using various presentation aids. We'll offer tips for making the most of your rehearsal time and delivering your final speech as effectively as possible. Finally, we'll talk briefly about evaluating both your own speeches and those you hear.

Methods of Delivery

13.1 List and describe the four methods of delivery, and provide suggestions for effectively using each one.

Different audiences expect and prefer different delivery styles. For example, if you are using a microphone to speak to an audience of 1,000 people, your listeners may expect a relatively formal delivery style. On the other hand, your communication class would probably find it odd if you delivered a formal oration to your twenty-five classmates.

People from different cultures also have different expectations of speakers' delivery. Listeners from Japan and China, for example, prefer subdued gestures to a more flamboyant delivery. British listeners expect a speaker to stay behind a lectern and use relatively few gestures.

Speakers should consider and adapt to their audience's expectations, their topic, and the speaking situation as they select from four basic methods of delivery: manuscript speaking, memorized speaking, impromptu speaking, and extemporaneous speaking.

Manuscript Speaking

Perhaps you remember the first speech you ever had to give, maybe as long ago as elementary school. Chances are that you wrote out your message and read it to your audience. Unfortunately, **manuscript speaking** is rarely done well enough to be interesting. Most speakers who rely on a manuscript read it either in a monotone or with a pattern of vocal inflection that makes the speech "sound read." They are so afraid of losing their place that they keep their eyes glued to the manuscript and seldom look at the audience. These challenges are significant enough that most speakers should avoid reading from a manuscript most of the time.

Occasions when effective verbal messages depend on careful and exact phrasing are the few exceptions to the general rule of avoiding manuscript speaking. For example, because an awkward statement made by the U.S. Secretary of State could cause an international crisis, his or her remarks on critical issues are usually carefully scripted. If you ever have to speak on a sensitive, critical, or controversial issue, you too might need to deliver a manuscript speech. If so, consider the suggestions in Table 13.1.[4]

Memorized Speaking

After that first speech you read in elementary school, you probably became a more savvy speaker. The next time you had to give a speech, you wrote it out and memorized it. You thought that no one would be able to tell. What you didn't know then, but probably do now, is that most **memorized speaking** sounds stiff and recited. In addition, you run the risk of forgetting parts of your speech and having to search awkwardly for words in front of your audience. By doing so, you forfeit the ability to adapt to your audience while you are speaking.

On occasion, speaking from memory is justifiable. If you must deliver a short speech within narrow time limits, memorizing and rehearsing it will allow you to time it more accurately. The three guidelines in Table 13.2 can help you use nonverbal messages effectively when you deliver a speech from memory.

manuscript speaking
Reading a presentation from a written text.

memorized speaking
Delivering a speech word for word from memory without using notes.

Table 13.1 Tips for Effective Manuscript Speaking

Tip	Rationale
• Type your manuscript in short, easy-to-scan phrases on the upper two-thirds of the paper.	You won't have to look too far down the page.
• Practice with your manuscript before you deliver your speech.	You'll know where paragraph breaks and page turns occur.
• Unobtrusively use your index finger to keep your place in the text.	You'll be less likely to lose your place in the manuscript.
• Try to take in an entire sentence at a time.	You can maintain eye contact with your audience throughout each sentence—an appropriate nonverbal message.
• Use a slash mark (/) or some other symbol to remind you to pause in strategic places.	Planned pauses will help prevent you from reading too quickly.
• Vary the rhythm, inflection, and pace of your delivery.	Your speech will sound less as if it is being read.
• Use gestures and movement.	Your message will have nonverbal interest and emphasis.

Table 13.2 Tips for Effective Memorized Speaking

Tip	Rationale
• Avoid speaking too rapidly.	Rapid delivery can sound "recited."
• Record and listen to a rehearsal of your speech to ensure that your vocal inflection sounds like a conversation rather than a recitation.	The rise and fall of your voice should emphasize important words and phrases and reflect the structures of your sentences.
• Use gestures and movement.	Gestures and movement add interest and emphasis to your message.

Impromptu Speaking

During President Bill Clinton's first State of the Union address, the teleprompter scrolled the wrong text of his speech for nine minutes. Drawing on his years of experience, the president kept speaking. As political advisor and commentator Paul Begala marveled, "Nine minutes the guy went without a note, and no one could tell."[5]

Although you may plan your speeches, there are times—as illustrated by Clinton's experience—when the best plans go awry. A more likely possibility is that you will be asked to answer a question or respond to an argument without advance warning or time to prepare. At such times, you will have to call on your skills in **impromptu speaking**, or speaking "off the cuff."

impromptu speaking
Delivering a presentation without advance preparation.

extemporaneous speaking
Delivering a well-developed, well-organized, carefully rehearsed speech without having memorized exact wording.

Having a solid grasp of the topic on which you are asked to speak can help you in such instances. The six additional guidelines in Table 13.3 can also help you avoid fumbling for words or rambling.

Extemporaneous Speaking

We have saved for last the method of speaking most appropriate for most circumstances, preferred by most audiences, and most often taught in public speaking classes: **extemporaneous speaking**. The extemporaneous speech is a well-developed and well-organized message delivered in an interesting and vivid manner. It reflects your understanding of how to use both verbal and nonverbal messages effectively and your ability to adapt these messages to your audience.

Table 13.3 Tips for Effective Impromptu Speaking

Tip	Rationale
• Think about your audience.	A quick mental check of who your audience members are and their interests, expectations, and knowledge can help ensure that your impromptu remarks are centered on them.
• Be brief. One to three minutes is probably a realistic time frame for most impromptu speeches.	As one leadership consultant points out, "You're merely expected to hit a theme, say a few nice words, and then depart."[6]
• Organize. Think quickly about an introduction, body, and conclusion. If you want to make more than one point, use a simple organizational strategy such as chronological order—past, present, and future. Or construct an alphabetical list in which your main ideas begin with the letters A, B, and C.[7]	You will stay on track, and your audience will comprehend and remember your main ideas.
• Draw on appropriate and relevant personal experience and knowledge.	Audiences almost always respond favorably to personal illustrations.
• Use gestures and movement that arise naturally from what you are saying.	Your impromptu speech will seem more natural and authentic.
• If your subject is at all sensitive or your information is classified, be noncommittal in what you say.	Be aware of the potential impact of your communication.

Table 13.4 Tips for Effective Extemporaneous Speaking

Tip	Rationale
• Use a full-content preparation outline when you begin to rehearse your extemporaneous speech.	Using your preparation outline at first will help ensure that you practice your full content, including supporting materials and oral citations of sources.
• Prepare speaking notes. Using this new outline, continue to rehearse.	As you grow less dependent on your notes, be aware of your growing confidence in delivering your speech.
• Even as you become increasingly familiar with your message, do not try to memorize it word for word.	Varying the ways in which you express your ideas and information will help you keep your delivery natural.
• As you deliver your speech, use gestures and movement that arise naturally from what you are saying.	Adapt your speech delivery to your audience.

RECAP

Methods of Delivery

Manuscript	Reading a speech from a written text
Memorized	Giving a speech word for word from memory without using notes
Impromptu	Delivering a speech without advance preparation
Extemporaneous	Speaking from a written or memorized outline without having memorized the exact wording of the speech

Although the public speaking chapters in this book offer numerous guidelines for extemporaneous speaking, consider the four tips in Table 13.4 when you reach the rehearsal and delivery stages.

Effective Verbal Delivery

13.2 List and explain five criteria for effective verbal delivery.

In an examination of some 125 years' worth of student speeches prepared for intercollegiate competition, researchers Leah White and Lucas Messer found remarkable consistency in students' use of stylized language. White and Messer explain, "Style and delivery are often tightly connected. Speeches rich in language strategies lend themselves to engaging deliveries."[8] Although you will not write out most speeches word for word, you will want to plan and rehearse words, phrases, and sentences that accurately and effectively communicate your ideas. At the same time, you will want to give your message a distinctive and memorable style. Let's examine some guidelines for effectively using and understanding words and word structures in a speech.

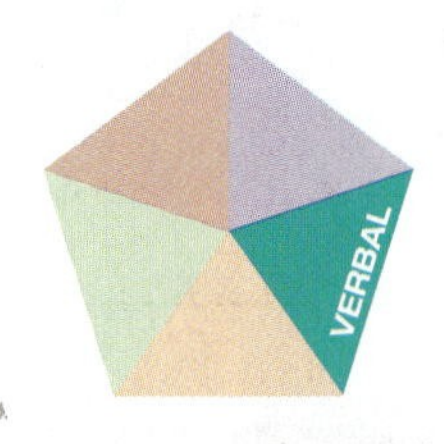

Using Words Well

The most effective words are specific and concrete, unbiased, vivid, simple, and correct. Building on our discussion in Chapter 3 of the power of verbal messages, we'll examine each of these characteristics in turn.

specific word
A word that refers to an individual member of a general class.

concrete word
A word that refers to an object or describes an action or characteristic in the most specific way possible.

unbiased word
A word that does not stereotype, discriminate against, or insult either gender or any racial, cultural, or religious group.

SPECIFIC, CONCRETE WORDS A **specific word** refers to an individual member of a general class—for example, *ammonite* as opposed to the more general term *fossil*, or *sodium* as opposed to *chemical*. Specific words are often **concrete words**, appealing to one of the five senses and communicating an image clearly, as Figure 13.1 demonstrates.

In each case, the second word is more specific and concrete than the first and better communicates the image the speaker intends. For maximum clarity in your speeches, use more specific, concrete words than general, abstract ones.

UNBIASED WORDS **Unbiased words** do not disparage, either intentionally or unintentionally, any gender or racial, cultural, or religious group, nor do they offend any audience member who may belong to one of these groups.

Although speakers can fairly easily avoid overtly offensive language, they must be more mindful to avoid language that subtly stereotypes or discriminates. As

National Transportation Safety Board Chair Deborah Hersman told attendees at the International Women in Aviation Conference,

> I don't want to hear anybody say "I saw a woman mechanic!"
> Or "I saw an all-woman flight crew!"
> Or "I saw a woman engineer!"
> Or "I saw a woman CEO!"
> Or "I saw a woman in space exploration!"
> Not because there are none of us there, but because there are so many of us there![9]

When possible, adapt to your audience by choosing unbiased gender-neutral language.

Figure 13.1 Which word in each of the following pairs creates a more specific mental picture?

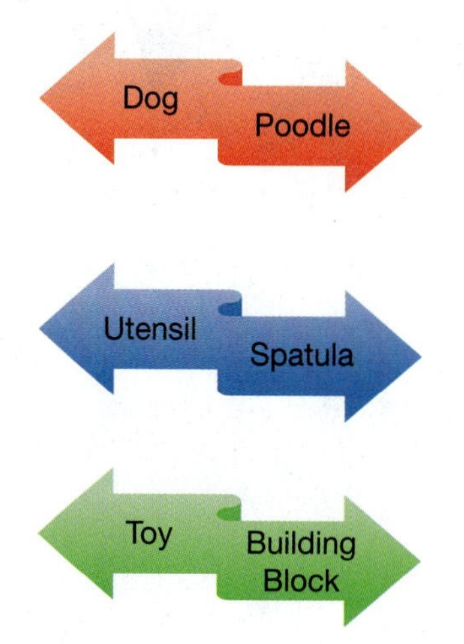

VIVID WORDS **Vivid words** add color and interest to your language. Like concrete words, they help you communicate mental images more accurately and interestingly. Most speakers who try to make their language more vivid think first of adding adjectives to nouns—for example, *distressed oak table* instead of *table, scruffy tabby cat* instead of *cat*—and certainly the first phrase of each example is more vivid than the other. Less frequently considered is the potential power of substituting vivid verbs for "blah" verbs—for example, *sprout* instead of *grow, devour* instead of *eat*.

When searching for a vivid word, you might want to consult a **thesaurus**, or collection of synonyms, but do not assume that the most obscure or unusual synonym you find will necessarily be the most vivid. Sometimes a simple word can evoke a vivid image for your audience.

vivid word
A colorful word.

thesaurus
A list of synonyms.

SIMPLE WORDS **Simple words** are generally an asset to a speaker. They will be immediately understood by an audience. In his classic essay "Politics and the English Language," George Orwell includes this prescription for simplicity:

> Never use a long word where a short one will do. . . . Never use a foreign phrase, a scientific word, or a jargon word if you can think of an everyday English equivalent.[10]

Selected thoughtfully, simple words can communicate with both accuracy and power.

simple word
A word known to most people who speak the language.

correct word
A word that means what the speaker intends and is grammatically correct in the phrase or sentence in which it appears.

CORRECT WORDS Finally, and perhaps most obviously, you should use **correct words** when you speak. Grammatical and usage errors communicate a lack of preparation and can lower your credibility with your audience. Be aware of errors that you make habitually. If you are uncertain about how to use a word, look it up in a dictionary or ask someone who knows. If you are stumped by whether to say, "Neither the people nor the president *knows* how to solve the problem" or "Neither the people nor the president *know* how to solve the problem," seek assistance from a good English handbook. (By the way, the first sentence is the correct one.)

RECAP

Using Words Well

- Use specific, concrete words to communicate clearly and specifically.
- Use unbiased words to avoid offending people of either gender or from any racial, cultural, or religious group.
- Use vivid words to add color and interest to your language.
- Use simple words to be understood readily.
- Use correct words to enhance your credibility.

This word cloud visualizes the frequency with which Pope Francis used various words in his May 2014 speech on his arrival in Israel. Note that many of the larger words, which are those the Pope used most, are simple words that tend to evoke vivid emotions. How can you use simple, specific words to drive home your messages?
Source: Based on speech delivered May 25, 2014, at Ben Gurion Airport in Tel Aviv, Israel by Pope Francis

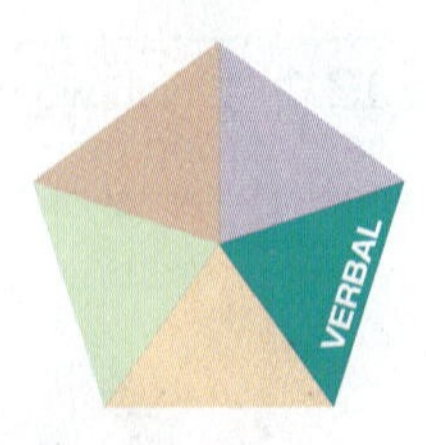

Crafting Memorable Word Structures

We have discussed the importance of using words that are concrete, unbiased, vivid, simple, and correct. Now we will turn our attention to word structures—phrases and sentences that create the figurative language, drama, and cadences needed to provide what one marketing communication specialist calls "ear appeal."[11]

FIGURATIVE LANGUAGE One way to make your message memorable is to use **figurative language**, including **metaphors** (implied comparisons), **similes** (overt comparisons using *like* or *as*), and **personification** (the attribution of human qualities to nonhuman things or ideas). Such language is memorable because it is used in a way that is a little different from its ordinary, expected usage.

Nineteenth-century Missouri senator George Graham Vest used all three types of figurative language to good advantage in his short but memorable "Tribute to the Dog," delivered in Warrensburg, Missouri, in 1870, and nominated by columnist William Safire as one of the greatest speeches of the second millennium.[12] Memorable at least in part because of the figurative language Vest employs, this speech is available online in the Great Speeches collection at the History Place.

- *Metaphors.* Vest makes the abstract concept of malice more concrete with the metaphor "the stone of malice."
- *Similes.* Vest uses a simile to compare the dog's master to a prince: "He guards the sleep of his pauper master as if he were a prince."
- *Personification.* Finally, Vest personifies death, which "takes [the dog's] master in its embrace."

DRAMA Another way to make your word structures in your speech more memorable is to use language to create **drama** by phrasing something in an unexpected way. Three specific devices that can help you achieve verbal drama are omission, inversion, and suspension:

- *Omission.* When you strip a phrase or sentence of nonessential words that the audience expects or with which they are so familiar that they will mentally fill them in, you are using **omission**. Journalist Bill Moyers described modifications in the format of a major American newspaper with the succinct phrase "More money, less news."[13]
- *Inversion.* **Inversion**—reversing the normal order of words in a phrase or sentence—can also create drama in a speech. John F. Kennedy inverted the usual subject–verb–object sentence pattern to object–subject–verb to make this brief declaration memorable: "This much we pledge."[14]
- *Suspension.* A third way to create drama through sentence structures is to employ verbal **suspension**, saving an important word or phrase for the end of a sentence rather than placing it at the beginning. In his second presidential inaugural address, Barack Obama used suspension to dramatize the obligation of the present generation of Americans: "With common effort and common purpose, with passion and dedication, let us answer the call of history. . . ."[15]

CADENCE A final way to create memorable word structures is to create **cadence**, or language rhythm. A speaker does so not by speaking in a sing-song pattern, but by using such stylistic devices as parallelism, antithesis, repetition, and alliteration:

- *Parallelism.* **Parallelism** occurs when two or more clauses or sentences have the same grammatical pattern. In his 2014 "state of the state" address, New Jersey Governor Chris Christie used parallel structures to help his audience recall the damage caused by Superstorm Sandy: "flooding our homes, turning off our power and destroying our roads."[16]

figurative language
Language that deviates from the ordinary, expected meaning of words to make a description or comparison unique, vivid, and memorable.

metaphor
An implied comparison between two things.

simile
An overt comparison between two things that uses the word *like* or *as*.

personification
The attribution of human qualities to inanimate things or ideas.

drama
A characteristic of a speech created when something is phrased in a way that differs from the way the audience expects.

omission
Leaving out a word or phrase the audience expects to hear.

inversion
Reversing the normal word order of a phrase or sentence.

suspension
Withholding a key word or phrase until the end of a sentence.

cadence
The rhythm of language.

parallelism
Using the same grammatical structure for two or more clauses or sentences.

- *Antithesis.* Similar to parallelism, except that the two structures contrast in meaning, **antithesis** is often marked by the conjunctions "not only . . . but (also)." In a speech marking the fiftieth anniversary of John F. Kennedy's "Moon Shot" speech, Vice President Joe Biden noted that Kennedy's character "was a reflection not only of his generation, but of America's character."[17]
- *Repetition.* **Repetition** of an important word or phrase can add emphasis to a key idea and memorability to your message. In her moving convocation address to a grieving Virginia Tech community after the April 2007 campus shootings, poet and Virginia Tech professor Nikki Giovanni repeated five times the stirring affirmation "We are Virginia Tech."[18]
- *Alliteration.* A final strategy for creating cadence is to use **alliteration**, the repetition of an initial consonant sound several times in a phrase, clause, or sentence. In his June 2014 speech commemorating the seventieth anniversary of D-Day, President Barack Obama used the alliterative phrase "blood soaked the water, and bombs broke the sky."[19] Repeating the *b* sound added cadence—and memorability—to the passage.

RECAP

Crafting Memorable Word Structures

To make your message memorable, use . . .

Figurative Language	
Metaphor	Making an implied comparison
Simile	Making a comparison using *like* or *as*
Personification	Attributing human qualities to nonhuman things or ideas
Drama	
Omission	Leaving nonessential words out of a phrase or sentence
Inversion	Reversing the normal order of words in a phrase or sentence
Suspension	Withholding the key words in a phrase or sentence until the end
Cadence	
Parallelism	Using two or more clauses or sentences with the same grammatical structure
Antithesis	Using a two-part parallel structure in which the second part contrasts in meaning with the first
Repetition	Using a key word or phrase more than once
Alliteration	Repeating a consonant sound

Effective Nonverbal Delivery

13.3 Identify and illustrate characteristics of effective nonverbal delivery.

At this point, you understand how important it is to deliver your speech effectively and what delivery style most audiences today prefer. You are familiar with the four methods of delivery and know how to maximize the use of each one. You also have some ideas about how to use effective and memorable language. Still, you may wonder, "What do I do with my hands?" "Is it all right to move around while I speak?" "How can I make my voice sound interesting?" To help answer these and similar questions, and to help you use nonverbal messages more effectively, we'll examine five major categories of nonverbal delivery: eye contact, physical delivery, facial expression, vocal delivery, and personal appearance. This discussion further develops the fundamental principle of using and interpreting nonverbal messages that we introduced in Chapter 4.

Eye Contact

Of all the nonverbal delivery variables discussed in this chapter, the most important one in a public speaking situation for North Americans is **eye contact**. Eye contact with your audience members lets them know that you are interested in and ready to talk to them. It also permits you to determine whether they are responding to you. In addition, most listeners will think that you are more capable and trustworthy if you look them in the eye than if you avoid eye contact. Some studies document a relationship between eye contact and speaker credibility, as well as between eye contact and listener learning.[20]

How much eye contact do you need? One study found that speakers with less than 50 percent eye contact are considered unfriendly, uninformed, inexperienced, and even dishonest by their listeners.[21] On the other hand, is there such a thing as

antithesis
Contrasting the meanings of the two parts of a parallel structure.

repetition
Emphasizing a key word or phrase by using it more than once.

alliteration
The repetition of a consonant sound (usually the first consonant) several times in a phrase, clause, or sentence.

eye contact
Looking at an audience during a presentation.

Communication & DIVERSITY

The Academic Quarter

When speaking at a Polish university a few years ago, one of your authors expected to begin promptly at 11:00 a.m., as announced in the program and on posters. By 11:10, it was clear that the speech would not begin on time, and your author began to despair of having any audience at all.

In Poland, it turns out, both students and professors expect to adhere to the "academic quarter." In other words, most lectures begin at least fifteen minutes (a quarter of an hour) after the announced starting time.

If your author had asked a Polish professor about the audience's expectations, he would have known about this custom in advance. One way to avoid such misunderstandings is to talk with people you know who are familiar with the cultural expectations. Try to observe other speakers presenting to similar audiences. Ask specific questions, including the following:

1. Where does the audience expect me to stand while speaking?
2. Do listeners expect direct eye contact?
3. When will the audience expect me to start and stop my talk?
4. Will listeners find movement and gestures distracting or welcome?
5. Do listeners expect presentation aids?

Keep cultural differences in mind as you rehearse and deliver speeches to diverse audiences.

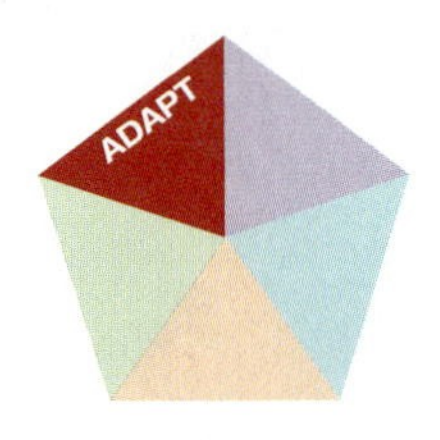

too much eye contact? For North American audiences, the answer is probably not. Be aware, though, that not all people from all cultures prefer as much eye contact as North Americans do. Asians, for example, generally prefer less.

If you are recording your speeches for an online class, you will need to establish eye contact with the device you're using to record your speech, which can be challenging. Although doing so may seem easier than looking at a live audience, more than two-thirds of respondents in a recent study felt that it was actually more difficult.[22] The following suggestions can help you use eye contact effectively when you speak in public:

- Establish eye contact with your audience before you say anything. Eye contact sends listeners a message to tune in as you start your talk.
- Maintain eye contact with your audience as you deliver your opening sentence without looking at your notes.
- Try to establish eye contact with people throughout your audience, not just with the front row or only one or two people. Briefly look into the eyes of an individual, and then transfer your eye contact to someone else.
- Do not look over your listeners' heads. They will notice if you do so and may even turn around to try to find out what you are looking at.

Physical Delivery

Gestures, movement, and posture are the three key elements of **physical delivery**. A good speaker knows how to use effective gestures, make meaningful movements, and maintain appropriate posture while speaking to an audience.

GESTURES The hand and arm movements you use while speaking are called **gestures**. Nearly all people from all cultures use some gestures when they speak. In fact, research suggests that gesturing is instinctive and that it is intrinsic to speaking and thinking.[23] Yet even if you gesture easily and appropriately in the course of everyday conversation, you may feel awkward about what to do with your hands when you are in front of an audience. To minimize this challenge, consider the following guidelines:

- Focus on the message you want to communicate. As in ordinary conversation, when you speak in public, your hands should help emphasize or reinforce your verbal message. Your gestures should coincide with what you are saying.

physical delivery
A person's gestures, movement, and posture, which influence how a message is interpreted.

gestures
Movements of the hands and arms to communicate ideas.

This speaker's gesture acknowledging his fellow graduates is simple, natural, and definite. Focusing on your audience and your message during rehearsals can help you to gesture effectively when you deliver your speech to an audience.
Comstock/ Getty Image

- Again, as in conversation, let your gestures flow with your message. They should appear natural, not tense or rigid.
- Be definite. If you want to gesture, go ahead and gesture. Avoid minor hand movements that will be masked by the lectern or that may appear to your audience as accidental brief jerks.
- Vary your gestures. Try not to use the same hand or one all-purpose gesture all the time. Think of the different gestures you can use, depending on whether you want to enumerate, point, describe, or emphasize ideas.
- Don't overdo your gestures. You want your audience to focus not on your gestures, but on your message.
- Make your gestures appropriate to your audience and situation. When speaking to a large audience in a relatively formal setting, use bolder, more sweeping, and more dramatic gestures than you would use when speaking to a small audience in an informal setting. Also consider the culture-based expectations of your audience. Americans in general tend to use more gestures than do speakers from other cultures. If you are speaking to a culturally diverse audience, you may want to tone down your gestures.

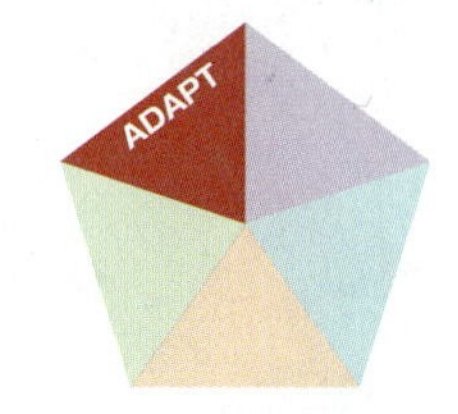

MOVEMENT Another element of physical delivery is **movement**. You may wonder, "Should I walk around during my speech, or should I stay in one place?" "Should I stay behind the lectern, or could I stand beside or in front of it?" "Can I move around among the audience?" The following criteria may help you determine the answers to the preceding questions:

- Like gestures, any movement should be purposeful. It should be consistent with the verbal content of your message; otherwise, it will appear to be aimless wandering. You might signal the beginning of a new idea or major point in your speech with movement, or you might move to signal a transition from a serious idea to a more humorous one. The bottom line is that your use of movement should make sense to your listeners. No movement at all is better than random, distracting movement.
- If a physical barrier such as a lectern, a row of chairs, or an overhead projector makes you feel cut off from your listeners, move closer to the audience. Studies suggest that physical proximity enhances learning.[24]

movement
A change of location during a presentation.

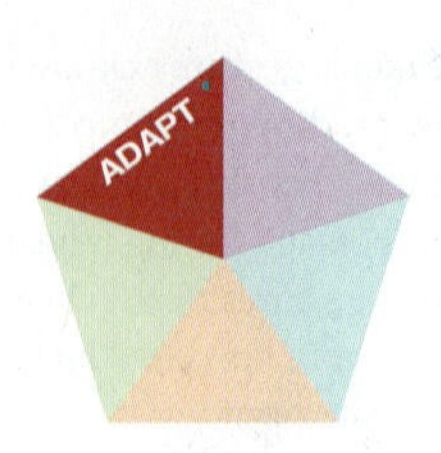

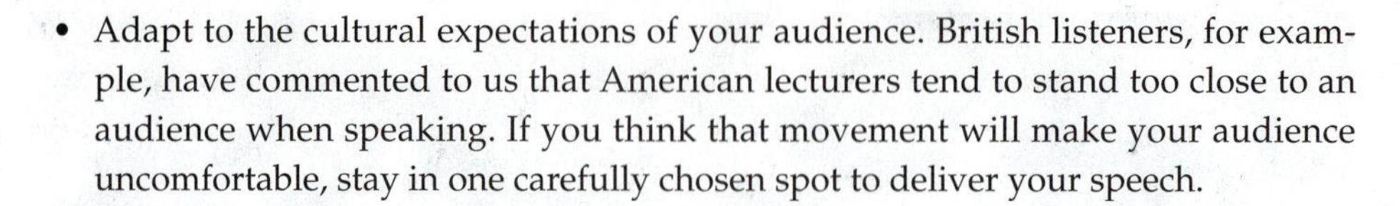

- Adapt to the cultural expectations of your audience. British listeners, for example, have commented to us that American lecturers tend to stand too close to an audience when speaking. If you think that movement will make your audience uncomfortable, stay in one carefully chosen spot to deliver your speech.

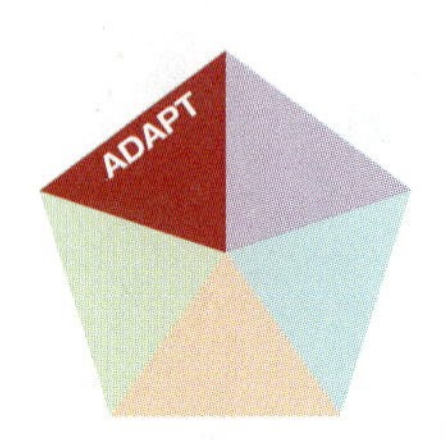

POSTURE **Posture** is the third element of physical delivery to consider when delivering a speech. One study suggests that your posture may reflect on your credibility as a speaker.[25] Another study suggests that "fear contagion," the spread of fear throughout a crowd, is largely a response to posture cues.[26] Certainly, slouching lazily across a lectern does not communicate enthusiasm for or interest in your audience or your topic. On the other hand, you should adapt your posture to your topic, your audience, and the level of formality of the speaking occasion. For example, during a very informal speech, it may be perfectly appropriate, as well as comfortable and natural, to lean against the edge of a desk.

Few speech teachers or texts advocate specific speaking postures. Instead, you should observe some commonsense guidelines about posture:

- Avoid slouching, shifting from one foot to the other, or drooping your head.
- Unless you have a disability, do not sit while delivering a speech. An exception might be perching on or leaning against the edge of a desk or stool (which would still elevate you slightly above your audience) during a very informal speech.

Like your gestures and movement, your posture should not call attention to itself. Rather, it should reflect your interest in and attention to your audience and your message.

Facial Expression

Your **facial expression** plays a key role in expressing your thoughts, emotions, and attitudes.[27] Your audience sees your face before they hear what you are going to say, giving you the opportunity to set the tone for your message even before you begin to speak. Social psychologist Paul Ekman has found that facial expressions of primary emotions are virtually universal, so even a culturally diverse audience will be able to read your facial expressions clearly.[28]

Throughout your speech, your facial expression, like your body language and eye contact, should be appropriate to your message. Present somber news wearing a serious expression. Relate a humorous story with a smile. To communicate interest in your listeners, keep your expression alert and friendly. To ensure that you are maximizing the use of this important nonverbal delivery cue, rehearse your speech in front of a mirror; better yet, record and analyze video of yourself rehearsing your speech. Consider as objectively as possible whether your face is reflecting the emotional tone of your ideas.

Vocal Delivery

We have already discussed the importance of selecting words and phrases that will most effectively communicate your ideas, information, and images. We referred to this element of delivery as verbal delivery. **Vocal delivery**, on the other hand, involves nonverbal vocal cues—not the words you say, but the way you say them. Effective vocal delivery requires you to speak so that your audience can understand you and will remain interested in what you are saying. Nonverbal vocal elements include volume, pitch, rate, and articulation.

VOLUME **Volume** is the softness or loudness of your voice. It is the most fundamental determinant of audience understanding. If you do not speak loudly enough, even the most brilliant presentation will be ineffective, because the audience simply

posture
A speaker's stance.

facial expression
An arrangement of the facial muscles to communicate thoughts, emotions, and attitudes.

vocal delivery
Nonverbal voice cues, including volume, pitch, rate, and articulation.

volume
The softness or loudness of a speaker's voice.

will not hear you. In addition, volume can signal important ideas in your speech; for example, you can deliver a key idea either more loudly or more softly than you have been speaking. Consider these guidelines to help you appropriately adapt the volume of your voice to your audience's needs:

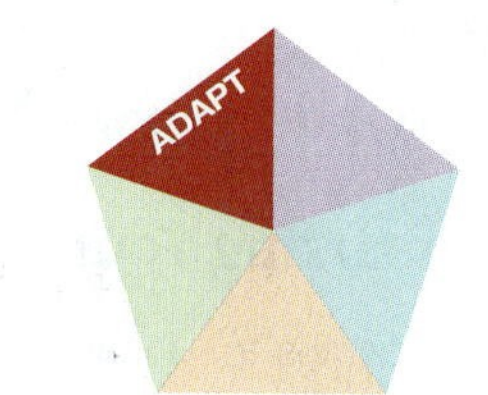

- Speak loudly enough that the members of your audience farthest from you can hear you without straining. Doing so will ensure that everyone else in the room can hear you, too.
- Vary the volume of your voice in a purposeful way. Indicate important ideas by turning your volume up or down.
- Be aware of whether you need a microphone to amplify your volume. If you do and one is available, use it.

There are three kinds of microphones, only one of which demands much technique:

- *Lavaliere or Wireless Hand-Held.* Both lavaliere and wireless hand-held microphones allow a speaker to move freely while speaking. Often worn on the front of a shirt or a jacket lapel by news reporters and interviewees, a lavaliere microphone requires no particular care other than not thumping it or accidentally knocking it off.
- *Boom.* A boom microphone is used by makers of movies and TV shows. It hangs over the heads of the speakers and is controlled remotely, so the speakers need not be particularly concerned with it.
- *Stationary.* A stationary microphone may be attached to a lectern, sit on a desk, or stand on the floor. Generally, today's stationary microphones are multidirectional. Even so, you will have to keep your mouth at about the same distance from the microphone at all times to avoid distracting fluctuations in the volume of sound. You can turn your head from side to side and use gestures, but you will have to limit other movements.

Under ideal circumstances, you will be able to practice with your microphone. If you have the chance, figure out where to stand for the best sound quality and to determine how sensitive the mike is to extraneous noise. Practice will accustom you to any voice distortion or echo that might occur so that these sound qualities do not surprise you during your presentation.

PITCH Whereas volume is the loudness or softness of your voice, **pitch** refers to how high or low your voice is. To some extent, pitch is determined by physiology. The faster the folds in your vocal cords vibrate, the higher the habitual pitch of your voice. In general, female vocal folds vibrate much faster than do those of males. You can, however, raise or lower your habitual pitch within a certain range.

Variation in pitch, called **inflection**, is a key factor in communicating the meaning of your words. You know that a startled "Oh!" in response to something someone has told you communicates something quite different from a lower-pitched, questioning "Oh?" Your vocal inflection indicates your emotional response to what you have heard.

Vocal inflection also helps to keep an audience interested in your message. If your pitch is a monotone, the audience will probably become bored quickly. To help you monitor and practice your pitch and inflection as you prepare to speak, record and play back your speech at least once as you rehearse. Listen carefully to your pitch and inflection. If you think that you are speaking in too much of a monotone, practice again with exaggerated variations in pitch. Eventually, you will find a happy medium.

pitch
How high or low a speaker's voice is.

inflection
Variation in vocal pitch.

RATE Another vocal variable is **rate**, or speed. How fast do you talk? Most speakers average between 120 and 180 words per minute. Good speakers vary their rate to add interest to their delivery and to emphasize key ideas. To determine whether your speaking rate is appropriate and purposeful, become conscious of it. Record your

rate
How fast or slowly a speaker speaks.

Developing Your Speech Step by Step

Rehearsing Your Speech

Lario begins to rehearse his speech. From the beginning, he stands and speaks aloud, practicing gestures and movement that seem appropriate to his message.

At first, Lario rehearses from his preparation outline (see Chapter 12). These early rehearsals go quite well, but the speech runs a little short. Lario knows that he tends to speak fairly rapidly, so he decides to plan more pauses throughout the speech—some to allow his listeners to think about an important point he has just made, and others to provide nonverbal transitions. When he prepares his speaking notes, Lario writes the delivery cue "Pause" in several strategic places.

pause
A few seconds of silence during a speech, used both to slow a fast pace and to signal a key idea.

articulation
The production of clear and distinct speech sounds.

dialect
A consistent style of pronunciation and articulation that is common to an ethnic group or geographic region.

appearance
A speaker's dress and grooming.

presentation during rehearsal and listen critically to your speech speed. If it seems too fast, make a conscious effort to slow down. Use more **pauses** after questions and before important ideas. If you are speaking too slowly, make a conscious effort to speed up.

ARTICULATION **Articulation** is the enunciation of sounds. As a speaker, you want to articulate distinctly to ensure that your audience can determine what words you are using. Sometimes we fall into the habit of mumbling or slurring—saying *wanna* instead of *want to*, or *chesterdrawers* instead of *chest of drawers*. Some nonstandard articulation may be part of a speaker's **dialect**, a speech style common to an ethnic group or a geographic region. One dialect with which most of us are familiar is the dialect of the southern United States, characterized by a distinctive drawl.

Although most native speakers of English can understand different English dialects, studies have shown that North American listeners assign more favorable ratings to, and can recall more information presented by, speakers with dialects similar to their own.[29] If your dialect is significantly different from that of your listeners, or you suspect that it could be potentially distracting, you may want to work to improve your articulation or standardize your dialect. To do so, be aware of words or phrases that you have a tendency to drawl, slur, or chop. Once you have identified them, practice saying them distinctly and correctly.

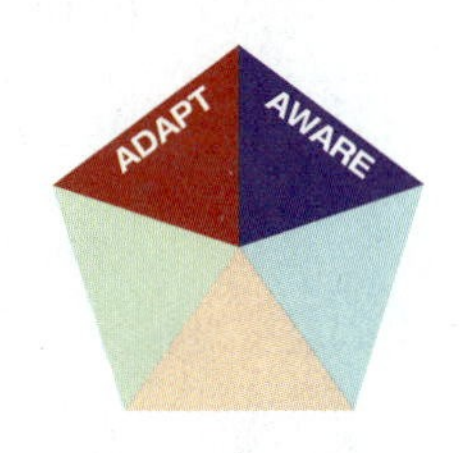

Appearance

What would you wear to deliver a speech to your class? To address your city council? The fact that you would probably wear something different for each of these occasions suggests that you are already aware of the importance of a speaker's **appearance**. There is considerable evidence that your personal appearance affects how your audience will respond to you and your message. If you violate your audience's expectations, you will be less successful in achieving your purpose. The following guidelines may make selecting a wardrobe a bit easier when you are next called on to speak:

- Never wear anything that is potentially distracting, such as a T-shirt with writing on it. You want your audience to listen to you, not read you.
- Consider appropriate clothing to be a presentation aid. For example, if you are a nurse or emergency technician, wear your uniform when you speak about your profession. (We'll discuss presentation aids in more detail shortly.)

RECAP

Characteristics of Effective Nonverbal Delivery

- Eye contact should be established before you say anything and should be sustained as much as possible throughout your speech.
- Gestures should be relaxed, definite, varied, and appropriate to your audience and the speaking situation.
- Movement should be purposeful and adapted to the audience's cultural expectations.
- Posture should feel natural and should be appropriate to your topic, your audience, and the occasion.
- Facial expression should be alert, friendly, and appropriate to your message.
- Volume should be loud enough that you can be easily heard and should be purposefully varied.
- Pitch should be varied so that the inflection in your voice helps sustain your audience's interest.
- Rate should be neither too fast nor too slow and can be varied to add interest and emphasize key ideas.
- Articulation should be clear and distinct.
- Your appearance should conform to what the audience expects.

- Take cues from your audience. If you know that they will be dressed in business attire, dress similarly. If anything, you want to be a bit more dressed up than members of your audience.
- When in doubt about what to wear, select something conservative.

Effective Presentation Aids

13.4 Discuss how to prepare and use presentation aids effectively.

We have already discussed two elements of delivery: verbal delivery and nonverbal delivery. A third element used with increasing frequency in this era of sophisticated computer presentation software is the **presentation aid**. The term *presentation aid* refers to anything your audience can listen to or look at to help them understand your ideas. Charts, photographs, posters, drawings, graphs, audio and video recordings, and PowerPoint™ slides are some of the types of presentation aids frequently used by speakers.

As long as they *aid* the speaker, rather than *replace* the speaker, presentation aids can be invaluable. They help you gain and maintain your audience's attention.[30] They communicate your organization of ideas. They illustrate sequences of events or procedures. They help your audience understand and remember your message. In addition, chances are that for at least one of the assignments in your communication class, you will be required to use a presentation aid. Because presentation aids are valuable supplements to your speeches and because students of communication are so often required to use them, let's discuss first the types of available presentation aids, including computer-generated ones. Then we will discuss guidelines for preparing presentation aids and provide some general suggestions for using them effectively.

Types of Presentation Aids

If you are required to use a presentation aid for an assignment or you think that a presentation aid might enhance your message, you have a number of options from which to select. You might decide to use an object or a model; a person; two-dimensional presentation aids such as drawings, photographs, maps, charts, or graphs; or audiovisual aids.

OBJECTS The first type of presentation aid you ever used—perhaps as long ago as preschool "show and tell"—was probably an object. You took to school your favorite teddy bear or the new remote-control car you got for your birthday. Remember how the kids crowded around to see what you had brought? Objects add interest to a talk because they are real. Whether the members of your audience are in preschool or

presentation aid
Any tangible item used to help communicate ideas to an audience.

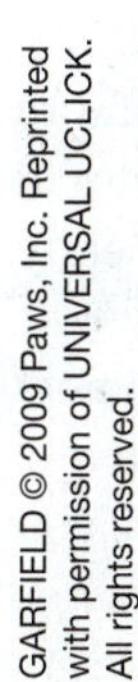

college, they like tangible, real things. If you use an object as a presentation aid, consider these guidelines:

- Make certain that the object can be handled easily. If it is too large, it may be unwieldy; if it is too small, your audience won't be able to see it.
- Don't use dangerous or illegal objects as presentation aids. They may make your audience members uneasy or actually put them at risk.

MODELS If it is not possible to bring an object to class, you may be able to substitute a model. You cannot bring a 1956 Ford Thunderbird into a classroom, but you may be able to construct and bring a model. You could probably not acquire a dog's heart to bring to class, but you might be able to find a model to use for your explanation of how heartworms damage that vital organ. If you use a model as a presentation aid, be sure that the model is large enough to be seen by all members of your audience.

PEOPLE You might not think of people as potential presentation aids, but they can be. George W. Bush used ordinary people as visual aids for some of his most important presidential speeches, "asking them to stand and then telling stories of their sacrifices or heroism . . . a way of coming down from the stage, as it were, and mingling with the crowd."[31] In other instances, people can model costumes, play a sport with you, or demonstrate a dance. If you are going to ask someone to assist you by acting as a presentation aid for a speech, consider the following guidelines:

- Rehearse with the person who will be helping you.
- Don't have the person stand beside you doing nothing. Wait until you need your presentation aid to have your assistant come to the front.
- Don't let your presentation aid steal the show. Make his or her role specific and fairly brief. As the speaker, you should remain the "person of the hour."

DRAWINGS You can use simple drawings to help illustrate or explain ideas that you are talking about. For example, you could sketch the tunnels of a fire ant mound to show your audience why it is so difficult to eradicate an entire ant colony. You could sketch the plants and animals that are crucial to the life cycle of the Florida Everglades. If you use a drawing as a visual aid, consider these suggestions:

- Keep your drawings large and simple. Line drawings are often more effective than more detailed ones.
- One way to show the audience your drawing is to scan it and then put it into a PowerPoint or other computer-generated slide.
- Your drawing does not have to be original artwork. You could ask a friend to help you prepare a drawing, or you could use computer software to generate a simple image. Just be sure to credit your source if you use someone else's sketch.

PHOTOGRAPHS If you are giving a speech on urban forestry, you might want to show your audience good color pictures of trees that are appropriate for urban sites in your area. In this case, photographs would show color and detail that would be nearly impossible to achieve with drawings.

The biggest challenge to using photographs as presentation aids is size; most printed photos are simply too small to be seen clearly from a distance. If you want to use photographs, store them on a flash drive. Then, when you want the photos, you can bring them up on a computer screen and use a video projection system to enlarge them for your audience.

MAPS Like photographs, most maps are too small to be useful as presentation aids; to be effective, they must be enlarged in some way. Consider these suggestions for using maps effectively during a speech:

- Enlarge your map by transferring it to a PowerPoint slide.
- Highlight on your map the areas or routes you are going to talk about in your speech.

CHARTS Charts can summarize and organize a great deal of information in a small space. Consider using a chart anytime you need to present information that could be organized under several headings or in several columns. The chart in Figure 13.2 displays the percentage of American colleges and universities with dedicated offices for active military duty and veteran students.[32] You can prepare charts quite easily by using the Table feature in your word-processing program. Keep in mind these guidelines:

- Be certain that your chart is big enough to be seen easily.
- Keep your chart simple. Do not try to put too much information on one chart. Eliminate any unnecessary words.

GRAPHS Graphs are effective ways to present statistical relationships to your audience and help make data more concrete. You are probably already familiar with the three main types of graphs illustrated in Figure 13.3.

Figure 13.2 Chart

Percentage of American Colleges and Universities with Dedicated Offices for Active Military Duty and Veteran Students	
2009	49%
2012	71%

Figure 13.3 Three Types of Graphs: (A) Bar Graph, (B) Pie Graph, and (C) Line Graph

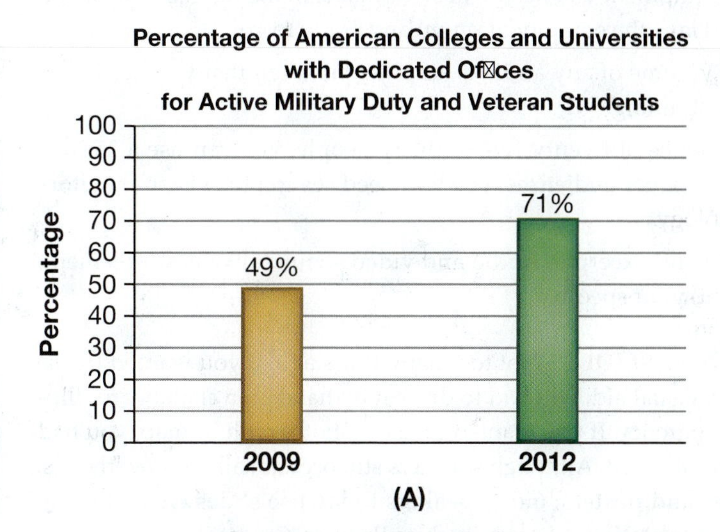

(A)

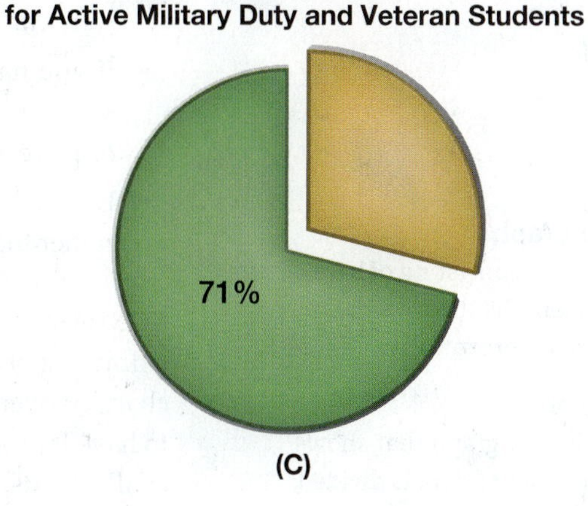

(C)

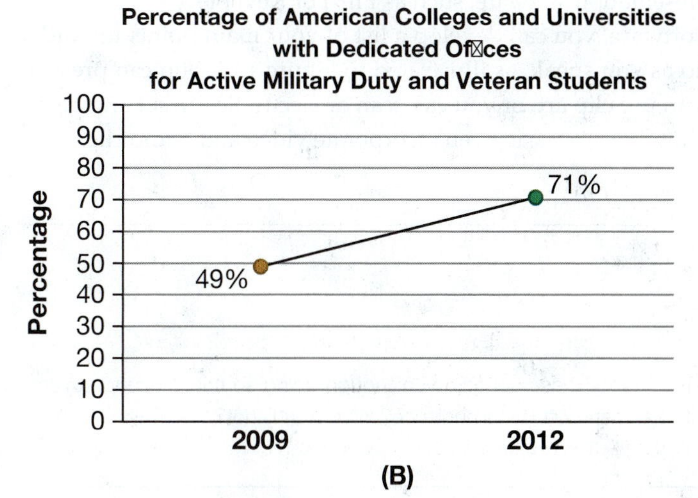

(B)

- *Bar graph.* A **bar graph** consists of bars of various lengths that represent percentages or numbers. It is useful for making comparisons.
- *Pie graph.* A round **pie graph** shows how data are divided proportionately.
- *Line graph.* A **line graph** can show both trends over a period of time and relationships among variables.

Figure 13.3 illustrates all three types of graphs, displaying data from the chart in Figure 13.2. All three graphs were created using Microsoft Excel.

The following guidelines will help you use graphs more effectively in your speeches:

- Keep your graphs simple and uncluttered.
- Remember that many computer programs will generate graphs from statistics. You often don't need to find already-prepared graphs or draw your own.

AUDIO AND VIDEO If you want to use audio presentation aids—say, music or excerpts from speeches or interviews—you might want to play a CD or an MP3 file. Both are readily available, and their sound can be amplified. Similarly, modern video technologies allow you to show scenes from a movie, an excerpt from a training film, or a brief original video. Recordings stored on DVDs, phones, or computer devices, or streamed from the Internet generally offer good picture and sound quality and permit freeze-frame viewing. Most audio and video devices also allow you to replay a scene several times if you want your audience to listen or watch for different specific elements.

If you plan to use an audio or video presentation aid, consider these suggestions:

- Be certain that the equipment you need will be available in the room in which you are going to speak. Have the equipment set up and ready to go.
- Be certain that the volume of any audio is amplified enough that your audience can hear it without straining.
- If you have an audience of twenty-five to thirty people, you can use a 25-inch screen for video. For larger audiences, you will need several television monitors or projection technology.
- Use only brief clips and excerpts. Audio and video should always supplement, rather than supplant, your speech.

bar graph
A graph consisting of bars of various lengths that represent numbers or percentages.

pie graph
A circular graph that shows how a set of data is divided proportionately.

line graph
A graph that shows trends over a period of time and relationships among variables.

COMPUTER-GENERATED SLIDES Not too many years ago, if you wanted to use a drawing or graph as a visual aid, you had to draw it by hand on a chalkboard, flipchart, or overhead transparency. If you wanted to use a photograph or map, you had to have it professionally enlarged. Although speakers still occasionally use overheads, chalkboards, flipcharts, and posters, most speakers today use slides created using PowerPoint or similar presentation software, such as Prezi or Keynote.

With presentation software, you can develop a list of your main points for audience members to refer to as you speak, as illustrated in Figure 13.4. You can present graphs and charts. You can use clip art, or you can scan or electronically cut and paste photographs, maps, or drawings. You can even incorporate video and audio clips.

Communication & ETHICS

Profanity in an Audio Presentation Aid

Matt wants to talk to his college classmates about the use of profanity in rap music. He plans to play sound clips of several profane lyrics from current hits to illustrate his point. Should Matt play these songs, even though doing so might offend several members of his audience? Why or why not?

Although these software tools help you adapt your message to audiences who increasingly expect sophisticated technical support, don't use them simply to project your notes for others. One technology expert explains,

> For example, say you're talking about something that often confuses students. Don't just repeat the words coming out of your mouth on the screen. Instead, project an image of a confused student in order to focus your audience's attention on your message with an emotional driver.[33]

Also guard against letting your slides *become* your presentation. Use them to *supplement* it. Finally, keep the following tips in mind:[34]

- Don't use too many slides.
- Make certain that the slides you do use contain significant information in a simple, uncluttered style.
- Don't overuse bulleted text. Some experts suggest no more than seven lines of text on any single slide.
- Make informed decisions about fonts, color, and layout. A light background with darker-colored words in a simple 28-point or larger font usually works well.
- Finally, practice with your slides so that you can time them to coincide with your oral presentation.

Figure 13.4 Computer-Generated Slide

"Pilot was the grandest position of all"
(Mark Twain, *Life on the Mississippi*).

RECAP

Types of Presentation Aids

- Use *objects* that you can handle easily and that are safe and legal.
- Be sure that any *models* you use are large enough to be seen easily.
- Rehearse with *people* who will serve as presentation aids, and don't let them steal the show.
- Keep *drawings* simple and large.
- Be sure that *photographs* are large enough to be seen easily.
- Highlight on a *map* the geographic areas you will discuss.
- Limit the amount of information you put on any single *chart*.
- Keep *graphs* simple and uncluttered.
- Use only brief *audio and video clips*, make sure they can be easily seen or heard, and have equipment ready to go before you speak.

Guidelines for Preparing Presentation Aids

In addition to the specific guidelines for preparing and using various types of presentation aids, four general guidelines can help you prepare all types of presentation aids more effectively.

SELECT THE RIGHT PRESENTATION AIDS As is evident from the above discussion, you have a number of options for presentation aids. If you are trying to decide which to use, consider these suggestions:

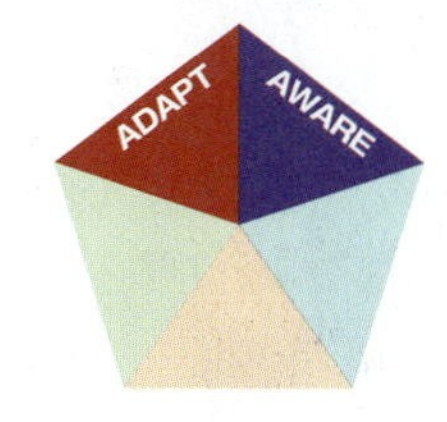

1. Be constantly aware of your specific purpose. Be certain that your presentation aid contributes to it.
2. Adapt to your listeners. Let their interests, experiences, and knowledge guide your selection of presentation aids. For example, an audience of accountants would readily understand arbitrage charts that might be incomprehensible to a more general audience. If you will be speaking to a large audience, be certain that everyone will be able to see or hear your presentation aid.
3. Consider your own skill and experience. Use equipment with which you have had experience, or allow yourself ample time to practice.
4. Take into account the room in which you will speak. If it has large windows and no shades, for example, do not plan to use a visual presentation aid that will require a darkened room. If you plan to use PowerPoint slides, be sure that both hardware and software are available and in good working order.

MAKE YOUR PRESENTATION AIDS EASY TO SEE You have probably experienced the frustration of squinting and straining to read a speaker's too-small presentation aid. If you are going to remember only one thing about using a presentation aid, remember to make it big.

KEEP YOUR PRESENTATION AIDS SIMPLE Don't cram too much information on any single presentation aid. Limit text to key words or phrases. Leave plenty of white space.

USE PRESENTATION AIDS THOUGHTFULLY One speechwriter and presentation coach warns against this bleak but all-too-common scenario:

> The presenter says, "And now, I'd like to talk about quality." And lo and behold . . . the word *quality* flashes on a screen. Now, folks, does this slide offer any new information? Does it clarify a complex point? Does it strengthen the bond between presenter and audience? You know the answer: a resounding "no."[35]

Be sure that the aids you use help you communicate your message.

Guidelines for Using Presentation Aids

Once you have prepared potentially effective presentation aids, you will want to use them effectively as well. In addition to the guidelines offered earlier in this chapter, the following suggestions will help you adapt various types of presentation aids to your audience more effectively.

REHEARSE WITH YOUR PRESENTATION AIDS The day of your speech should not be the first time that you deliver your presentation while holding up your model, advancing your PowerPoint slides, or cueing your MP3 player. Practice setting up and using your presentation aids until you feel at ease with them. Consider during rehearsal what you would do at various stages of the speech if you had to carry on without a particular presentation aid. Electricity fails, equipment fails to show up, and bulbs burn out. Have contingency plans.

MAINTAIN EYE CONTACT WITH YOUR AUDIENCE, NOT WITH YOUR PRESENTATION AIDS You can glance at your presentation aids during your talk, but do not talk to them. Keep looking at your audience.

EXPLAIN YOUR PRESENTATION AIDS Always talk about and explain your presentation aids. Do not assume that the audience will understand their relevance and how to interpret them.

Although this speaker has developed a compelling PowerPoint presentation aid, she is losing eye contact with her audience as she presents it. How can you learn to handle your presentation aids with confidence, while maintaining effective eye contact with your audience?
Creativa Images/Shutterstock

TIME THE DISPLAY OF YOUR PRESENTATION AIDS TO COINCIDE WITH YOUR DISCUSSION OF THEM Don't put a presentation aid in front of your audience until you are ready to use it. Likewise, remove or cover your presentation aid after you are finished with it. Keeping presentation aids in front of an audience before or after you use them will only serve to distract from your message.

DO NOT PASS OBJECTS, PICTURES, OR OTHER SMALL ITEMS AMONG AUDIENCE MEMBERS Passing things around distracts audience members. Either people are focused on whatever they are looking at, or they are counting the number of people who will handle the object before it reaches them. If the item is too small for everyone to see it when you hold it up, it is not a good presentation aid.

USE HANDOUTS EFFECTIVELY Handing out papers during your speech can distract your audience. If possible, wait to distribute handouts until after you have spoken. If your audience needs to refer to the material while you are speaking about it, go ahead and pass out the handouts; then, at various points in your speech, tell audience members where in the handout they should focus.

USE SMALL CHILDREN AND ANIMALS WITH CAUTION Small children and even the best-trained animals are unpredictable. In a strange environment, in front of an audience, they may not behave in their usual way. The risk of having a child or animal detract from your message may be too great to justify using either as a presentation aid.

Some Final Tips for Rehearsing and Delivering Your Speech

13.5 Make the most of your rehearsal time, and deliver your speech effectively.

Throughout this chapter, we have described and offered suggestions for effective verbal and nonverbal delivery and use of presentation aids. In addition to those tips, the following suggestions will help you make the most of your rehearsal time and ultimately deliver your speech successfully:

- *Finish your preparation outline several days before you must deliver the speech.* Begin to rehearse from the preparation outline. Revise the speech as necessary, and then outline your speaking notes. Continue to rehearse and modify your speaking notes as necessary.
- *Practice, practice, practice.* Rehearse aloud as often as possible. Only by rehearsing will you gain confidence in both the content of the speech and your delivery of it. As the author of the bestselling book *Quiet: The Power of Introverts in a World That Can't Stop Talking* points out,

> If you went to a job interview without fixing your tie or applying your lipstick in front of the mirror, you would hope that there's no scarlet lip gloss smeared across your teeth, but how could you know for sure? Better to take the guesswork out of it.[36]

- *Use good delivery skills while rehearsing.* Rehearse your speech standing up. Pay attention to your gestures, posture, eye contact, facial expression, and vocal delivery, as well as the verbal message. Rehearse with your presentation aids.
- *If possible, practice your speech for someone.* Researchers in one study found that students who practice their speeches before an audience

He took every chance to practice his talk.

Andrewgenn/Fotolia

Communication & TECHNOLOGY

The Um Counter

A $0.99 app that is compatible with the iPhone, iPod Touch, and iPad is designed to help a speaker rehearse his or her presentation or, as the app maker points out, "to, like, help eliminate, y'know, those irritating non-words from your vocabulary." A similar app called Word Counter is available for other smart phones.

Marco Benassi, http://umlikeyknow.com

score higher on evaluation instruments than do students who practice without an audience.[37]

- *Use audio or video technology to record your speech, but try not to be overly critical when you listen to or watch yourself, as many of us tend to be.* Notice whether you use too many filler sounds or words, such as "uh," "er," "okay," "you know," and "like." Realize, however, that you're developing a delivery style unique to you, so don't try to change too much.
- *Prepare the room and equipment.* You may want to rearrange the furniture. If you are using technology, check to see that it is working properly, and set up your presentation aids carefully.
- *Re-create the speaking situation in your final rehearsals.* Try to rehearse in a room similar to the one in which you will deliver the speech. Use the speaking notes you will use the day you deliver the speech. Give the presentation without stopping. The more realistic the rehearsal, the more confidence you will gain.
- *Get plenty of rest the night before you speak.* Being well rested is more valuable than squeezing in a frantic, last-minute rehearsal.
- *Arrive early.* If you don't know for certain the location of the room in which you'll make your presentation, give yourself plenty of time to find it. Rearrange any furniture or equipment, and set up and check your presentation aids.
- *Review and apply the suggestions offered in Chapter 11 for becoming a more confident speaker.* As the moment for delivering your speech nears, remind yourself of the effort you have spent preparing it. Visualize yourself delivering the speech

Developing Your Speech Step by Step

Delivering Your Speech

The long-awaited day of Lario's speech has arrived at last. He got a full night's sleep last night and ate a light breakfast before setting out for class.

As he waits to speak, Lario visualizes himself delivering his speech calmly and confidently. When his name is called, he rises, walks to the front of the room, and establishes eye contact with his audience before he begins to speak. Lario focuses on adapting his message to his listeners. He looks at individual members of his audience, uses purposeful and well-timed gestures, and speaks loudly and clearly.

Even before he hears his classmates' applause, Lario knows that his speech has gone well.

When a small boy insisted on participating in one of Pope Francis's early speeches, the Pope seemed delighted rather than distracted. How can you prepare to deliver your speech with similar composure?
AP Photo/L'Osservatore Romano

effectively. Silently practice your opening lines. Think about your audience. Breathe deeply. Relax.

- *If something unforeseen (a ringing cell phone, for example) briefly interrupts your speech, remain composed as you pause briefly and then pick up where you left off.* If the incident is amusing, you can laugh along with your audience. When the presidential seal fell off Barack Obama's lectern and crashed to the stage during a speech, he quipped, "That's all right, all of you know who I am."[38]
- *After you have delivered your speech, seek feedback from members of your audience.* Use the information you gain to improve your next presentation.

Criteria for Evaluating Speeches

13.6 Understand and apply criteria for evaluating speeches.

What makes a speech successful? Our purpose here is not to take you through the centuries of dialogue and debate about this issue, but rather to offer practical ways to evaluate your own speeches as well as those of others.

Your instructor will probably use a rubric or evaluation form that lists precise criteria. Underlying any list of what a successful speaker should do, however, are two fundamental goals: A successful speech should be *effective,* and it should be *ethical.*

- *Effective.* To be effective, a speech should be understandable to listeners and should achieve the speaker's intended purpose.[39]
- *Ethical.* A good speaker is an ethical speaker—one who tells the truth, cites sources for nonoriginal words and ideas, and is sensitive and responsive to listeners. Even if a message can be understood clearly and achieves the speaker's purpose, if the speaker has used unethical means to achieve that purpose, the speech is not successful.

More specific criteria for determining whether a speech is effective and ethical, presented within the context of the model of audience-centered public speaking, are presented in the resources at the end of this chapter.

STUDY GUIDE:
Review, Apply, and Assess Your Knowledge and Skill

Review Your Knowledge

Methods of Delivery

13.1 List and describe the four methods of delivery, and provide suggestions for effectively using each one.

As you consider how you will deliver your presentation speech, you will select from four methods of delivery: manuscript speaking, memorized speaking, impromptu speaking, and extemporaneous speaking. Extemporaneous speaking is the style taught today in most presentational public speaking classes and preferred by most audiences.

Effective Verbal Delivery

13.2 List and explain five criteria for effective verbal delivery.

Once you know what method of delivery you will use, you should think about and rehearse words, phrases, and sentences that will best communicate your intended message and give it a distinct and memorable style. The most effective language is concrete, unbiased, vivid, simple, and correct. You can also make your message memorable by using figurative language and language that creates drama and cadence.

Effective Nonverbal Delivery

13.3 Identify and illustrate characteristics of effective nonverbal delivery.

Nonverbal variables are critical to effective delivery. Physical delivery includes a speaker's gestures, movement, and posture. Eye contact is perhaps the most important delivery variable, determining to a large extent your credibility with your audience. Facial expression plays a key role in expressing thoughts, emotions, and attitudes. Vocal delivery includes such elements as volume, pitch, rate, and articulation. Finally, your personal appearance can affect how your audience responds to you and your message.

Effective Presentation Aids

13.4 Discuss how to prepare and use presentation aids effectively.

Presentation aids include objects or models, people, drawings, photographs, maps, charts, graphs, and audio or video presentations. Today, most presentation aids can be created and displayed by using PowerPoint slides. Guidelines for using any type of presentation aid include selecting the right one for the audience, occasion, and room, and making the presentation aid easy to see and simple. Be sure to rehearse with your presentation aid, maintain eye contact with your audience, explain your presentation aid, time your use of your presentation aid, refrain from passing things around or using handouts indiscriminately, remember that small children and animals are unpredictable presentation aids, and use technology thoughtfully.

Some Final Tips for Rehearsing and Delivering Your Speech

13.5 Make the most of your rehearsal time, and deliver your speech effectively.

Final suggestions for rehearsing your speech include allowing ample time, rehearsing aloud and standing as often as possible, practicing your speech for someone, recording and listening to or watching your speech, and re-creating in your final rehearsals the actual speaking situation. Final tips for delivering your speech include getting plenty of rest the night before you speak, arriving early, and applying the suggestions offered in Chapter 11 for becoming a more confident speaker.

Criteria for Evaluating Speeches

13.6 Understand and apply criteria for evaluating speeches.

Underlying any list of what a successful speaker should do are two fundamental goals: A successful presentation should be effective, and it should be ethical.

Key Terms

Manuscript Speaking, p. 300
Memorized Speaking, p. 300
Impromptu Speaking, p. 301
Extemporaneous Speaking, p. 301
Specific Word, p. 302
Concrete Word, p. 302
Unbiased Word, p. 302
Vivid Word, p. 303
Thesaurus, p. 303
Simple Word, p. 303
Correct Word, p. 303
Figurative Language, p. 304
Metaphor, p. 304
Simile, p. 304
Personification, p. 304
Drama, p. 304
Omission, p. 304
Inversion, p. 304
Suspension, p. 304
Cadence, p. 304
Parallelism, p. 304
Antithesis, p. 305
Repetition, p. 305
Alliteration, p. 305
Eye Contact, p. 305
Physical Delivery, p. 306
Gestures, p. 306
Movement, p. 307
Posture, p. 308
Facial Expression, p. 308
Vocal Delivery, p. 308
Volume, p. 308
Pitch, p. 309
Inflection, p. 309
Rate, p. 309
Pause, p. 310
Articulation, p. 310
Dialect, p. 310
Appearance, p. 310
Presentation Aid, p. 311
Bar Graph, p. 314
Pie Graph, p. 314
Line Graph, p. 314

The Principle Points

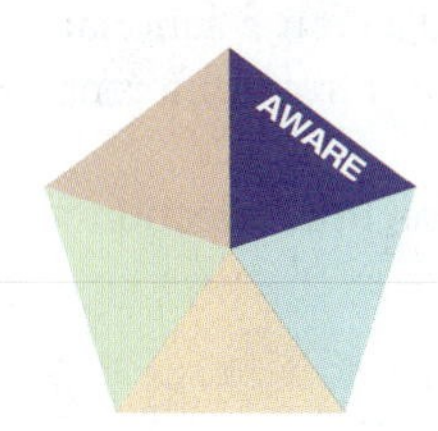

Principle One:

Be aware of your communication with yourself and others.

- If your subject is sensitive or your information is classified, be cautious and noncommittal in any impromptu remarks you make.
- As you become increasingly comfortable rehearsing an extemporaneous speech, you can decrease your reliance on your notes.
- Usage and articulation errors communicate a lack of preparation. If you are uncertain how to use or pronounce a word or phrase, look it up or ask someone.
- Use a microphone if you need one and one is available. Be sure to rehearse with it.
- Be aware of your speaking rate, and adjust it if necessary.
- Be certain that your presentation aids, especially those that use technology, contribute to your specific purpose.
- Pay attention to your nonverbal delivery when you rehearse your speech.
- During rehearsal, record your speech. In reviewing your recording, objectively and critically observe your gestures, posture, eye contact, facial expression, and vocal delivery, as well as your verbal message; and make necessary adjustments.
- When you deliver your speech, apply the suggestions offered in Chapter 11 for becoming a more confident speaker.

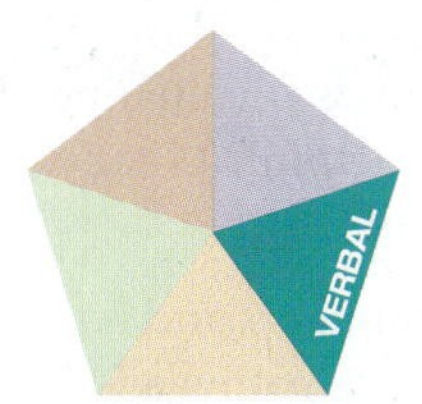

Principle Two:

Effectively use and interpret verbal messages.

- When exact wording is critical, you may want to deliver a manuscript or memorized speech.
- Do not try to memorize an extemporaneous speech word for word; vary the ways in which you express ideas and information.
- Phrase your ideas so that they will be clear, accurate, and memorable.
- Use words that are concrete, unbiased, vivid, simple, and correct.
- Make your message memorable with figurative images, drama, and cadence.

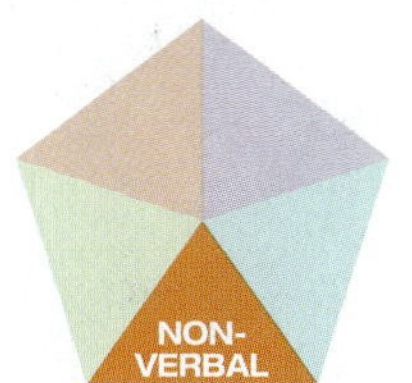

Principle Three:

Effectively use and interpret nonverbal messages.

- When you deliver a manuscript speech, try to look at an entire sentence at a time so that you can maintain eye contact with your audience as you deliver the sentence.
- Do not read a manuscript speech too rapidly; vary the rhythm, inflection, and pace of delivery so that the speech does not sound as though it is being read.

- Deliver a memorized speech at a moderate pace, and avoid patterns of vocal inflection that make the speech sound recited.
- Use gestures and movement to add interest and emphasis to both manuscript and memorized speeches.
- To heighten your credibility and increase listener learning, use eye contact to let your audience know that you are interested in and ready to talk to them.
- Use gestures to reinforce your verbal message.
- Move during your speech to signal the beginning of a new idea or major point or to signal a transition between a serious idea and a humorous one.
- Speak loudly enough to be heard easily by all members of your audience.
- Vary the volume of your voice to emphasize ideas and sustain the audience's interest.
- Vary your speaking rate to add interest to your delivery and emphasize key ideas.
- Articulate your words clearly.

Principle Four:

Listen and respond thoughtfully to others.

- Use eye contact to help you determine how your audience members are responding to you.
- If possible, rehearse your speech for someone and seek feedback about both your content and your delivery.

Principle Five:

Appropriately adapt messages to others.

- Although audiences today generally expect speakers to use everyday language and a conversational delivery style, you will need to adapt your delivery to audiences of different sizes and from different cultures.
- Let your audience's interests, experiences, and knowledge guide your preparation and selection of presentation aids.

Apply Your Skill

Consider the following questions. Write your answers and/or share them with your classmates:

1. Answering an instructor's question or presenting a summary of a small group discussion to the larger class may call for impromptu speaking skills. Based on your observations and experiences in such situations, what tips can you add to the list in Table 13.3?
2. A friend asks for advice on making the word choice in her speech as effective as possible. Offer her at least three suggestions, based on the material in this chapter, for using words effectively.
3. Which of the characteristics of nonverbal delivery described so far—eye contact, gesturing, movement, posture, or facial expression—are you confident you can use effectively? Which are most challenging for you? Which of the tips in this chapter do you plan to use to help you overcome your challenges?
4. What is the least effective use of presentation aids you've witnessed? Based on this chapter, what advice would you give to that speaker to help improve his or her use of presentation aids?
5. How can you determine when you have rehearsed long enough that you can extemporaneously deliver your key ideas to your listeners, but not so long that you are giving a memorized speech?
6. What kinds of comments from classmates evaluating your speeches would you find most helpful? What types of remarks would be *least* useful?
7. Is it ethical to make only positive comments and no suggestions for improvement when evaluating a classmate's speech?

Assess Your Skill

Evaluating a Speech

The following questions, linked to the audience-centered model first presented in Chapter 11 and included in Figure 13.5, can help you evaluate any speech, whether your own or another speaker's.

Figure 13.5 Asking yourself these questions will help you evaluate any speech.

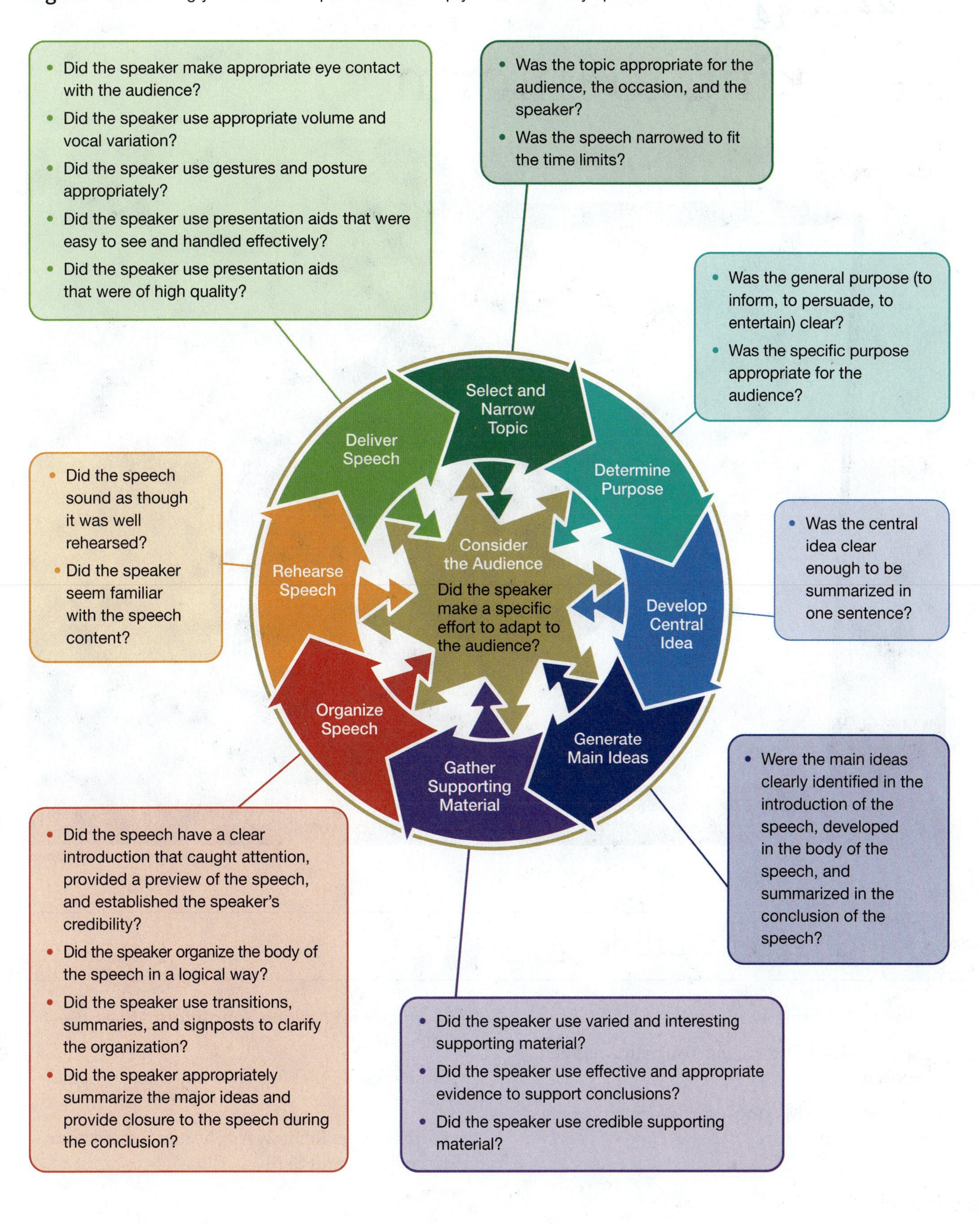

Chapter 14

Speaking to Inform

If education is expensive, ignorance is still more costly. —P. B. DE LA BRUÈRE

Comstock Images/Getty Images

Chapter Outline

- Types of Informative Speeches
- Strategies for Organizing Your Informative Speech
- Strategies for Making Your Informative Speech Clear
- Strategies for Making Your Informative Speech Interesting
- Strategies for Making Your Informative Speech Memorable
- Study Guide: Review, Apply, and Assess Your Knowledge and Skill

Chapter Objectives

After studying this chapter, you should be able to

14.1 Describe five types of informative speeches.

14.2 Identify and use appropriate strategies for organizing informative speeches.

14.3 Identify and use strategies for making informative speeches clear.

14.4 Identify and use strategies for making informative speeches interesting.

14.5 Identify and use strategies for making informative speeches memorable.

One survey of both speech teachers and students who had taken a communication course found that the single most important skill taught in a public speaking class is how to give an informative speech.[1] Given the importance in our lives of sending and receiving information, this finding is not surprising.

The purpose of a message to **inform** is to share information with others to enhance their knowledge or understanding of the information, concepts, or ideas you present.

Informing or teaching others can be a challenge because of a simple fact: *Presenting information does not mean that communication has occurred.* One of the co-founders of Common Craft, a company known for explaining complex ideas and processes in short, easy-to-understand videos, says that

> Creating a great explanation involves stepping out of your own shoes and into the audience's. It is a process built on empathy, on being able to understand and share the feelings of another.[2]

inform
To share information with others to enhance their knowledge or understanding of the information, concepts, and ideas you present.

In other words, a speaker must be audience-centered to communicate information successfully.

In this chapter, we will examine different types of informative tasks and identify specific strategies to help you organize your messages and make them clear, interesting, and memorable. Throughout our discussion, we will continue to apply the five Communication Principles for a Lifetime.

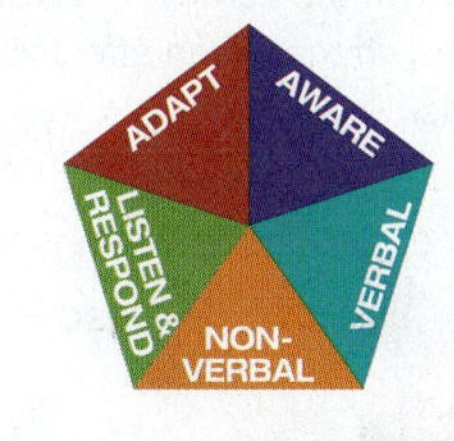

Michael Baldwin/CartoonStock

"I don't have any yet. We just opened."

Types of Informative Speeches

14.1 Describe five types of informative speeches.

Identifying the type of informative speech you will deliver can help you select and narrow your topic, organize your message, and select appropriate supporting material.

Speeches about Objects

A speech about an object might be about anything tangible—anything you can see or touch. You may or may not show the actual

Communication & ETHICS

Confidential or Potentially Dangerous Information

Mike, a computer engineering major, understands how a computer hacker recently accessed confidential personal information files on faculty members at his university. The procedure is actually simple enough that even people without sophisticated technical ability could understand and replicate it. Mike thinks that the procedure might be a good topic for an interesting informative speech. Meanwhile, Mike's classmate Paul, a chemistry major, considers whether to give an informative speech on how to create homemade explosives. If you are privy to confidential or potentially dangerous information, is it ethical to share it with others in an informative speech?

object to your audience while you are talking about it. Objects that could form the basis of an interesting speech include the following:

Items from your own collection (antiques, vintage vinyl, baseball cards)
The Eiffel Tower
Cellos
Digital cameras
The Franklin Delano Roosevelt Memorial in Washington, D.C.
Toys

Speeches about Procedures

A speech about a procedure discusses how something works (for example, how blood travels through the human circulatory system) or describes a process that produces a particular outcome (such as how grapes become wine). At the close of such a presentation, your audience should be able to describe, understand, or perform the procedure you have described. Here are some examples of procedures that could be topics of effective informative speeches:

How to access television network programming on your iPad
How state laws are made
How to refinish furniture
How to select a cell phone
How to plant an organic garden
How to select and purchase stocks

Notice that all these examples start with the word *how.* A speech about a procedure usually focuses on how a process is completed or how something can be accomplished. Speeches about procedures are often presented in workshops or other training situations in which people learn skills.

One good way to teach people a skill is to follow the acronym T-E-A-C-H, as shown in Figure 14.1.[3]

Many speeches about procedures include visual aids. Whether you are teaching people how to install a WiFi router or how to give a speech, showing them how to do something—the *Example* step of the T-E-A-C-H acronym—is almost always more effective than just telling them how to do it.

Figure 14.1 Remember TEACH to teach.

The letters in the acronym TEACH stand for Tell-Example-Apply-Coach-Help and summarize an effective process you can use to teach people new skills.

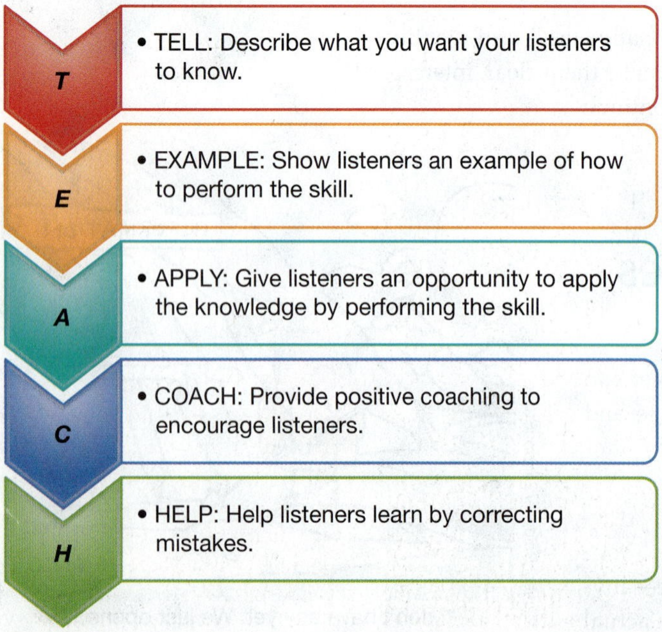

Speeches about People

Most of us enjoy hearing about the lives of real people, whether famous or unknown, living or dead, who have some special quality. The key to making an effective biographical speech is to be selective. Don't try to cover every detail of your subject's life. Relate the key elements in the person's career, personality, or other significant life features so that you build to a particular point, rather than just recite facts about the individual. One speaker gave a memorable speech about his friend:

> To enter Charlie's home was to enter a world of order and efficiency. His den reflected his many years as an Air Force officer; it was orderly and neat. He always knew exactly where everything was. When he finished reading the morning paper, he folded it so neatly by his favorite chair that you would hardly know that it had been read. Yet for all of his efficiency, you knew the minute you walked into his home that he cared for others, that he cared for you. His jokes, his stories, his skill in listening to others drew people to him. He never met a stranger. He looked for opportunities to help others.

Notice how the details capture Charlie's personality and charm. Speeches about people should give your listeners the feeling that the person is a unique, authentic individual.

One specific type of speech about a person is an introduction of another speaker and his or her topic. There are two cardinal rules for introducing another speaker: Be brief and be accurate. Remember that the audience has come to hear the main speaker, not you. In addition, be certain that you know how to pronounce the speaker's name and that you have accurate information about him or her.

Speeches about Events

Have you experienced a natural disaster such as an earthquake, hurricane, or tornado? Have you witnessed the inauguration of a president, governor, or senator? A major event, whether it is one you have experienced firsthand or one you have researched, can form the basis of a fascinating informative speech. Your goal as a speaker is to describe the event in concrete, tangible terms, bringing the experience to life for your audience.

You may have seen a recording of the CBS news bulletin on the assassination of John F. Kennedy. Legendary newscaster Walter Cronkite's ability to describe the event while reflecting the incredible emotion of the moment has made that broadcast a classic. Just as Cronkite was able to do, your purpose as an informative speaker describing an event is to make that event come alive for your listeners.
CBS Photo Archive/Getty Images

Speeches about Ideas

By nature, speeches about ideas are more abstract than other types of speeches. The following principles, concepts, and theories might be topics of idea speeches:

Principles of time management
Freedom of speech
Evolution
Theories of communication
Buddhism
Animal rights

As you look at this list, you may think that these topics seem boring, but as British writer G. K. Chesterton once said, "There is no such thing on earth as an uninteresting subject; the only thing that can exist is an uninterested person."[4] The selection and use of illustrations, examples, and anecdotes to make an otherwise abstract idea seem both interesting and relevant to your listeners are keys to gaining and maintaining interest in your speech about an idea.

Strategies for Organizing Your Informative Speech

14.2 Identify and use appropriate strategies for organizing informative speeches.

As with any presentation, your audience will better understand your informative speech if you organize your ideas logically. Regardless of the length or complexity of your message, you must follow a logical pattern to be understood. The topic of your informative speech may lend itself to a particular organizational pattern.

Organizing Speeches about Objects

Speeches about objects may be organized topically; a topical pattern is structured around the logical divisions of the object you're describing. Here is a sample topical outline for a speech about an object—a nuclear power plant:

I. The reactor core
  A. The nuclear fuel in the core
  B. The placement of the fuel in the core
II. The reactor vessel
  A. The walls of a reactor vessel
  B. The function of the coolant in the reactor vessel
III. The reactor control rods
  A. The description of the control rods
  B. The function of the control rods

Speeches about objects may also be organized chronologically. A speaker might, for example, focus on the history and development of nuclear power plants, and such a speech would probably be organized chronologically. Or, depending on the speaker's specific purpose, the speech could be organized spatially, describing the physical layout of a nuclear power plant.

Organizing Speeches about Procedures

Speeches about procedures are usually organized chronologically, according to the steps involved in the process. Anita chose a chronological organization for her explanation of how to develop a new training curriculum in teamwork skills:

I. Conduct a needs assessment of your department.
  A. Identify the method of assessing department needs.
  B. Implement the needs assessment.

II. Identify the topics that should be presented in the training.
   A. Specify topics that all members of the department need.
   B. Specify topics that only some members of the department need.
III. Write training objectives.
   A. Write objectives that are measurable.
   B. Write objectives that are specific.
   C. Write objectives that are attainable.
IV. Develop lesson plans for the training.
   A. Identify the training methods you will use.
   B. Identify the materials you will need.

Notice that Anita grouped the tasks into steps. Her audience members will remember the four general steps much more easily than they could have hoped to recall the curriculum development process if each individual task had been listed as a separate step.

Organizing Speeches about People

One way to talk about a person's life is in chronological order: birth, school, career, family, professional achievements, death. However, if you are interested in presenting a specific theme, such as "Winston Churchill, master of English prose," you may decide instead to organize Churchill's life experiences topically:

I. Journalist
II. Author
III. Orator

Organizing Speeches about Events

Most speeches about an event follow a chronological arrangement, but a speech about an event might also describe the complex issues or causes behind it and be organized topically. For example, if you were to talk about the Civil War, you might choose to focus on three causes of the war:

I. Political
II. Economic
III. Social

Chefs who teach classes in person or on television, such as Bobby Flay, often arrange their speeches chronologically, to show the procedure of following a recipe from start to finish. What procedures could you describe to an audience?
Vespasian/Alamy

Although these main points are topical, specific subpoints may be organized chronologically. However you choose to organize your speech about an event, remember that your goal should be to ensure that your audience is enthralled by your vivid description.

Organizing Speeches about Ideas

Most speeches about ideas are organized topically (by logical subdivisions of the central idea) or according to complexity (from simple ideas to more complex ones). The following example illustrates how Thompson used a topical organization for his informative speech about philosophy:

I. Definition of philosophy
  A. Philosophy as viewed in ancient times
  B. Philosophy as viewed today
II. Three branches of the study of philosophy
  A. Metaphysics
    1. The study of ontology
    2. The study of cosmology
  B. Epistemology
    1. Knowledge derived from thinking
    2. Knowledge derived from experiencing
  C. Logic
    1. Types of reasoning
    2. Types of proof

Thompson decided that the most logical way to give an introductory talk about philosophy was first to define it and then to describe three branches of philosophy. Because of time limits, he chose to describe only three.

Table 14.1 summarizes typical organizational patterns used for major categories of informational speech topics.

Table 14.1 Organizing Informative Speeches

Speech Type	Description	Typical Organizational Patterns	Sample Topics
Objects	Present information about tangible things	Topical Spatial Chronological	The Rosetta Stone MP3 players International space station The U.S. Capitol
Procedures	Review how something works or describe a process	Chronological Topical Complexity	How to . . . clone an animal operate a nuclear power plant use a computer trap lobsters
People	Describe either a famous person or a personal acquaintance	Chronological Topical	Rosa Parks Nelson Mandela Indira Gandhi Your grandmother Your favorite teacher
Events	Describe an actual event	Chronological Topical Complexity Spatial	Chinese New Year Inauguration Day Cinco de Mayo
Ideas	Present abstract information or information about principles, concepts, theories, or issues	Topical Complexity	Communism Economic theory Tao Te Ching

Strategies for Making Your Informative Speech Clear

14.3 Identify and use strategies for making informative speeches clear.

Think of the best teacher you ever had. He or she probably possessed a special talent for making information clear, interesting, and memorable. Some speakers, like some teachers, are better than others at presenting information clearly.

A message is clear when the listener understands it in the way the speaker intended. As described in Communication & Diversity, translating your speech into the audience's language is a basic step toward helping listeners understand.

How else do you make your messages clear to others?[5] You can help your audience make sense of your message by expressing your ideas simply, presenting information at a reasonable pace, and relating new information to what the audience already knows.

Simplify Ideas

Your job as a public speaker is to communicate with your audience, not to see how many complex words and ideas you can cram into your speech. The simpler your ideas and phrases, the greater the chance that your audience will understand and remember them.

Let's say that you decide to talk about state-of-the-art tablet computers. That's a fine topic, but don't try to make your audience as sophisticated as you are about tablets in a five-minute speech. Discuss only major features and name one or two leaders in the field. Don't load your speech with complex details. Edit ruthlessly.

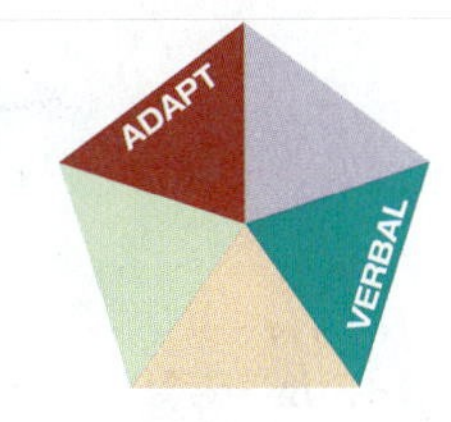

Pace Your Information Flow

If you present too much new information too quickly, you may overwhelm your listeners, and their ability to understand may falter. Arrange your supporting material

Communication & DIVERSITY

Using an Interpreter

It is quite possible that you may at some time be asked to speak to an audience of people who do not understand English or who cannot hear. In such a situation, you will need an interpreter to translate your message so that your audience can understand you. When using an interpreter, consider the following tips:

1. *Edit your message to fit within the time limit.* A speech that may take you thirty minutes to deliver without an interpreter will take at least an hour to present with an interpreter.
2. *Slow your speaking rate a bit.* Pause after every two or three sentences to give the interpreter time to translate your message.
3. *Don't say anything that you don't want your audience to hear.* Don't assume that your audience doesn't understand you just because you're using an interpreter.
4. *Give your interpreter a written copy of any facts, figures, or other detailed data.*
5. *Use humor with caution.* Humor often doesn't translate well. Even a very skilled interpreter may have difficulty communicating the intended meaning of your humor.
6. *Avoid slang, jargon, or terms that will be unfamiliar to your listeners or the interpreter.*
7. *When possible, talk with your interpreter before you deliver your speech.* Tell him or her the general points you will present. Give the interpreter an outline or, if you are using a manuscript, a transcript of your speech.

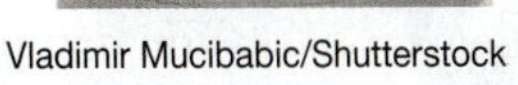
Vladimir Mucibabic/Shutterstock

so that you present an even flow of information rather than bunching up many significant details around one point. Remember that signposts offer your listeners both a break from listening to new information and help in processing that information. Preview your main ideas in your introduction, and use frequent internal summaries.[6]

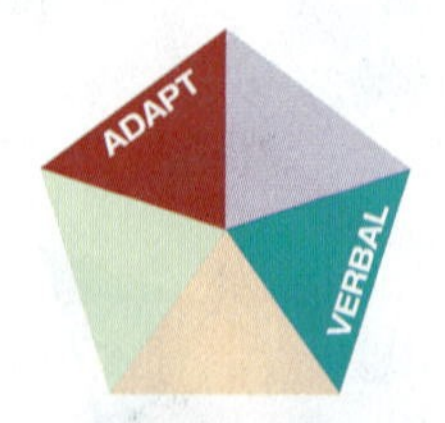

Relate New Information to Old

Most of us learn by building on what we already know. When you are presenting new information to a group, help your listeners associate your new idea with something that is familiar to them. Use an analogy. For example, tell bewildered new college students how their new academic life will be similar to high school and how it will be different. Or describe to young 4-H members how raising cattle is similar to taking care of any animal; they all need food, water, and shelter. By building on the familiar, you help your listeners understand how your new concept or information relates to their experience.

RECAP

Strategies for Making an Informative Speech Clear

- Simplify ideas.
- Pace the information flow.
- Relate new information to old.

Strategies for Making Your Informative Speech Interesting

14.4 Identify and use strategies for making informative speeches interesting.

He had them. No one moved. They hung on every word.

How can you create such interest when *you* speak? Here are several strategies to keep your audiences listening for more.

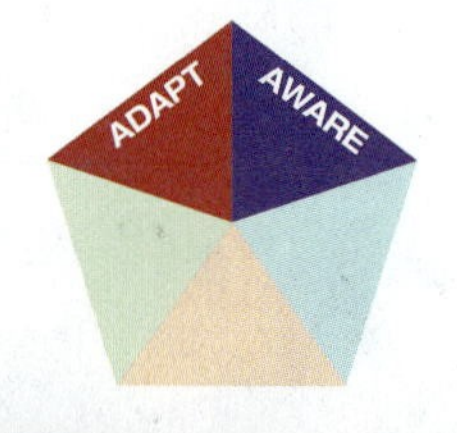

Relate to Your Listeners' Interests

Your listeners may be interested in your topic for a variety of reasons. It may affect them directly, it may add to their knowledge, it may satisfy their curiosity, or it may entertain them. These reasons are not mutually exclusive. For example, if you were giving a lecture on fifteenth-century Benin sculptures to a middle-class audience at a public library, your listeners would be interested because your talk would add to their knowledge, satisfy their curiosity, and entertain them.

Another way to make your message interesting is to think about why you yourself are interested in the topic. Once you are aware of your own interests and background, you can often find ways to establish common bonds with your audience.

Theresa McCracken/CartoonStock

Use Attention-Getting Supporting Material

Consider the following tips for selecting supporting material to best capture and keep your listeners' attention:

- Research suggests that you can increase audience interest if you first provide a simple overview with an analogy, model, picture, or vivid description.[7]

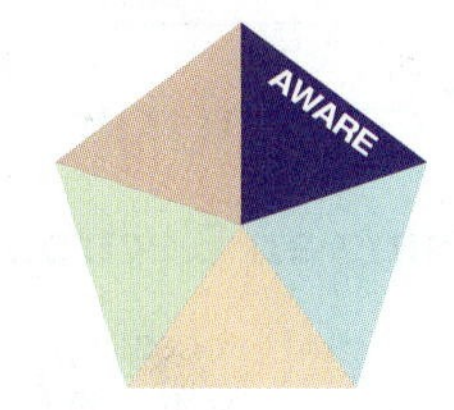

- As you discuss the object, process, person, event, or idea, keep in mind the *who, what, when, where, and why* questions:

  Who is involved?

  What is the object, process, event, or idea that you want to describe?

  When and *where* does or did the object exist, the process take place, the person live, the event occur, or the idea evolve?

  Why does or did the object, process, event, or idea occur, or *why* is it important to the audience?

Establish a Motive for Your Audience to Listen to You

> There will be a test covering my lecture tomorrow. It will count as 50 percent of your semester grade.

Such statements may not make a teacher popular, but they will certainly motivate the class to listen. Lacking the power of a teacher to assign grades, you will need to find more creative ways to get your audience to listen to you. These include the strategies of questioning, engaging, and relating:

- *Question:* One way to arouse the interest of your listeners is to ask them a question, such as one of the following:

  "How many of you are interested in saving tuition dollars this year?"

  "Who would like to save money on their income taxes?"

  "How many of you would like to learn an effective way of preparing your next speech?"

  These questions could stimulate your listeners' interest and motivate them to give you their attention.
- *Engage:* A second way to get your listeners' interest is to begin your speech with an anecdote, a startling statistic, or some other attention-getting strategy.
- *Relate:* Finally, you can tell your listeners explicitly how the information you present will be of value to them.

Use Word Pictures

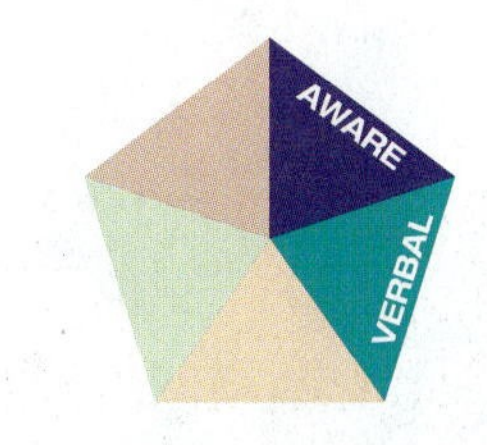

A **word picture** is a vivid description that helps your listeners form a mental image by appealing to one or more of their senses of sight, sound, smell, touch, and taste. Such powerful images can gain and hold an audience's attention. Use as many of your senses as possible to construct effective word pictures:

- *Sight.* Use lively language to describe the flaws, foibles, bumps, and beauties of the people, places, and things you want your audience to see.
- *Sound.* Use colorful, onomatopoetic words, such as *buzz, snort, hum, crackle,* or *hiss,* to imitate the sound you want your listeners to hear with their "mental ear."
- *Smell.* What fragrance or aroma do you want your audience to recall? For example, the first day of school may evoke the scents of new shoe leather, unused crayons, and freshly painted classrooms. The associated smells greatly enhance the overall word picture.
- *Touch.* Describe how an object feels when touched. Rather than saying that something is rough or smooth, use a simile, such as "the rock was rough as sandpaper" or "the pebble was as smooth as a baby's skin."
- *Taste.* Thinking about your grandmother may evoke memories of her buttery homemade noodles or her sweet, fudgy nut brownies. Such description can help you paint for your listeners an accurate, vivid image of your grandmother.

word picture
A vivid description that invites listeners to draw on their senses.

Communication & TECHNOLOGY

Using an Electronic Thesaurus

Most word-processing programs include an electronic thesaurus. To use this tool in Microsoft Word, highlight a word in your text for which you would like to find a synonym and then click on "Thesaurus" in the "Tools" menu. You will get a pop-up box with several alternatives for your highlighted word. If one of these synonyms creates a better word picture, you might want to replace your original word with the new one.

A word of caution, however, about using any thesaurus, whether electronic or traditional: Be sure that you know the alternative word well enough to understand its connotations and grammatical usage. A thesaurus should remind you of a word with which you are already familiar, not launch you into an uncharted adventure in diction!

In addition to providing sensory images, you can enhance a word picture by describing the emotion a listener might feel if he or she were to experience the situation you relate. Use specific adjectives rather than general terms such as *happy* or *sad*. One speaker, talking about receiving her first speech assignment, described her reaction with these words:

> My heart stopped. Panic began to rise up inside. Me? . . . For the next five days I lived in dreaded anticipation of the forthcoming event.[8]

Notice how effectively such words and phrases as "my heart stopped," "panic," and "dreaded anticipation" invoke the speaker's terror at the prospect of giving a speech, much more so than had she simply said, "I was scared."

Create Interesting Presentation Aids

Each day, audiences are exposed to a barrage of messages conveyed through such highly visual electronic media as streaming video. They have grown to depend on more than words alone to help them remember ideas and information. Research suggests that presentation aids can help you get and maintain audience members' attention, as well as increase their retention of the information you present.[9] When you present summaries of data, a well-crafted line graph can quickly and memorably reinforce the words and numbers you cite.

Use Humor

"Humor is the spice of speeches," says comedian Michael Klepper. "Too little and your message may be bland or lifeless, too much and it can burn the mouth."[10] The challenge is to use just the right kind of humor in the right amounts. The following suggestions can help you use humor wisely:[11]

- *Be certain your humor is appropriate to your listeners.* Because your audience "gives attempts at humor their success or failure,"[12] you should avoid topics or language that might offend your listeners and create so much emotional noise for them that they cannot focus on your message.
- *Use humor to make a point.* Don't tell a joke just for the sake of getting a laugh. Make sure that your story or punch line relates to your message. Here's an example of how one presenter used a brief joke to make a point about the value of teamwork:

> I read recently about a veterinarian and a taxidermist who decided to share a shop in a small town in Ohio. The sign in the front window read: "Either way, you get your dog back."
>
> There is an important lesson there. We need to work together to solve our problems. People from marketing need to work with operations people. Designers need to work with engineers. Then, when we find a problem that one part of the organization

Judicious use of humor will help keep your audience's attention and can help them remember and understand your points. Before using humor, be sure to evaluate carefully whether the joke or story you want to use is appropriate for the occasion and the audience, and whether you have the ability to tell it well.
Digital Vision/Getty Images

can't solve, someone else may suggest a solution. It doesn't matter who comes up with the solution. The important thing is to "get your dog back.[13]

- *Poke fun at yourself.* Audiences love it when you tell a funny or embarrassing story about yourself. In addition, if the joke's on you, you don't have to worry about whether you will offend someone else.[14]
- *Use humorous quotations.* You don't have to be a comedy writer to be funny. Quote humorous lines of proverbs, poetry, or sayings from others. Remember, however, that what may be funny to you may not be funny to your audience. Try out your quotes and jokes on others before you present them from behind the lectern. And don't try to pass off a quotation from someone else as one of your own; always give credit for quotations you use.
- *Use cartoons.* A cartoon may be an effective way to make a point. Make sure that your cartoon is large enough to be seen by everyone in the audience. As with any humor, though, don't overdo your use of cartoons.

RECAP

Strategies for Making an Informative Speech Interesting

Relate to your listeners' interests.
Use attention-catching supporting material.
Establish a motive for your audience to listen to you.
Use word pictures.
Create interesting presentation aids.
Use humor.

Strategies for Making Your Informative Speech Memorable

14.5 Identify and use strategies for making informative speeches memorable.

If you have made your message clear and interesting, you're well on your way to ensuring that your audience members will remember what you say. Presenting a

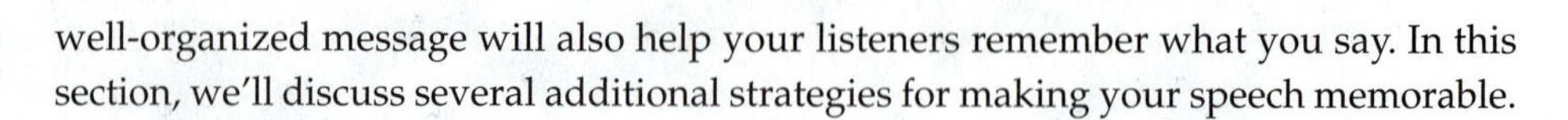

well-organized message will also help your listeners remember what you say. In this section, we'll discuss several additional strategies for making your speech memorable.

Build in Redundancy

Seldom do writers need to repeat themselves. If readers don't quite understand a passage, they can go back and read it again. However, most speech teachers advise their students to structure their speeches as follows:

1. *Tell them what you're going to tell them.* In the introduction of your speech, provide a broad overview of the purpose of your message. Identify the major points you will present.
2. *Tell them.* In the body of your speech, develop each of the main points mentioned during your introduction.
3. *Tell them what you've told them.* Finally, in your conclusion, summarize the key ideas discussed in the body of your speech.

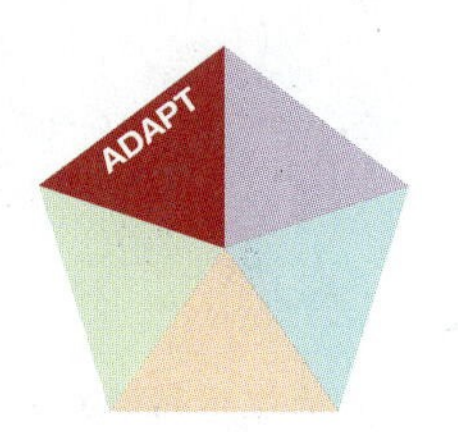

Use Adult Learning Principles

People remember what is important to them, so it is not surprising that one key to making your message memorable is to adapt it to your listeners. If your audience comprises adult listeners, you should make sure that you deliver your message in the way that adults learn best. **Adult learning principles** suggest that adults prefer the following:[15]

- Relevant information that they can use immediately
- Active involvement in the learning process
- Connections between the new information and their life experiences

Most people with office jobs have in-boxes (or "in-piles") on their desks, where they place work that needs to be done. Similarly, adult learners tend to have "mental in-boxes"; as audience members, they have mental agendas of what they want or need to gain from listening to a speech. Remember the characteristics of adult learners, as well as the important principle of adapting your message to others. If you tailor your information to address *their* agenda, you will make your message memorable and also have more success in informing your audience.

Reinforce Key Ideas Verbally

Suppose you have four suggestions for helping your listeners chair a meeting, and your last suggestion is the most important one. How can you make sure that your audience knows that? Just tell them. You can reinforce an idea by using a phrase such as "This is the most important point" or "Be sure to remember this next point; it's the most crucial one." Be careful, however, not to overuse this technique. If you claim that every other point is a key point, soon your audience will not believe you.

Reinforce Key Ideas Nonverbally

You can also signal the importance of a point with nonverbal emphasis. Gestures can accent or emphasize key phrases, just as italics do in written communication. A well-placed pause can emphasize and reinforce a point. Pausing just before or just after you make an important point will focus attention on your thought. Raising or lowering your voice can also reinforce a key idea.

adult learning principles
Preferences of adult learners for what and how they learn.

Movement can help to emphasize major ideas. Moving from behind the lectern to tell a personal anecdote can signal that something special and more intimate is about to be said. Remember that your movement and gestures should be meaningful and natural, rather than seeming arbitrary or forced. Your need to emphasize an idea can provide the motivation to make a meaningful movement.

The sample informative speech about a person (Elvis Presley) that appears later in this chapter is organized chronologically. In this speech, student speaker Angelitta Armijo applies a number of strategies for making an informative speech clear, interesting, and memorable:

- *Clear.* Angelitta makes her speech clear by providing signposts at strategic points to give her audience opportunities to process new information.
- *Interesting.* Angelitta took an important step in making her speech interesting when she initially selected her topic. By speaking on a subject in which she is personally interested and to which her listeners can relate, Angelitta captures and sustains their attention.
- *Memorable.* Finally, Angelitta makes her speech memorable by relating key information to her listeners and using main ideas to focus that information, by dramatizing statistics, and by closing with a line that her listeners will relate to Elvis.

RECAP

Strategies for Making an Informative Memorable

Build in redundancy.

Use adult learning principles.

Reinforce key ideas verbally.

Reinforce key ideas nonverbally.

Sample Informative Speech

Elvis

Angelitta Armijo[16] *Texas State University*

Can you imagine being a singer with 150 different albums and singles that have been certified gold, platinum, or multiplatinum? Neither can I. But according to Elvis.com, that's the reality for Elvis Presley.

Angelitta introduces her speech with a rhetorical question.

Although Elvis is no longer with us, his influence on the rock industry remains prevalent today. After all, he paved the way for groups such as the Beatles and Led Zeppelin. I personally have been an Elvis fan for as long as I can remember. I grew up on him, and I own many of his albums on CD, cassette, and vinyl. I also own every movie that he's ever starred in, including some of his TV specials, which I'll talk about later.

Angelitta establishes a motive for her audience to listen to her by sharing her personal interest in Elvis.

Elvis Presley was an American kid who grew up on the wrong side of the tracks and later became the King of Rock-N-Roll. To better understand Elvis, you need to know about his early days of life before he was famous, his early career, and his shift in career focus, which was prevalent until the end of his life.

Angelitta previews the three main ideas of her presentation, organized chronologically.

Let's begin with Elvis's humble beginnings. Elvis was born into a poor family, but he kept his eyes on his dreams and his love of music. Elvis Aaron Presley was born January 8, 1935, in Tupelo, Mississippi, to Gladys and Vernon Presley. Actually, Elvis was born as a twin but his brother, Jesse Garon, died at birth, leaving Elvis to be raised as an only child, according to the A&E Network. Also according to A&E Network, Elvis was very dedicated to his family and especially to his mother, whom he loved very much. His family encouraged him to be active in church, and it was in church that he discovered his love of singing and music. When he was ten years old, he received his first guitar, and throughout his childhood and young adult life, he was involved in many talent shows.

Angelitta provides her audience with details about Elvis's early life, having selected those that influenced his music career.

According to Elvis.com, the family moved to Memphis in 1948 to seek financial security and job security. Soon after graduating high school in 1953 in Memphis, Elvis became a truck driver. It was during his truck driving years that Elvis recorded a few songs at Sun Records for his mother for her birthday. It was at Sun Records where his career began, because Sam Phillips asked him to record more songs, in hopes of finding a star.

So now that you know about Elvis's beginnings, we can discuss his rise to fame and early successes. Elvis's career began at Sun Records and grew as his fans wanted to see him on stage, on TV, and on the silver screen. According to *Rolling Stone*, one of the recordings requested by Sam Phillips, "That's Alright Momma," became Elvis's first single in 1954. This single, and many of Elvis's other singles, showed the influence of blues music, which he discovered in Memphis. By 1955, Elvis was signed to RCA, a premier record label. In 1956, his first album was released, titled *Elvis Presley*. According to Elvis.com, this record was #1 on the Billboard Pop Charts for 10 weeks and was also Elvis's first gold album, selling over a million copies.

Angelitta provides a signpost to summarize her first main idea and preview her second one.

Throughout the rest of the '50s, Elvis appeared on many variety shows such as the *Ed Sullivan Show* and starred in his first movie, *Love Me Tender*. In 1960, after two years in the army, Elvis taped a special *Welcome Home Elvis* edition of Frank Sinatra's TV show. He received $125,000 for appearing on the show—which, according to Elvis.com, was a record sum of money for an appearance at that time. According to IMDb, Elvis released 27 films throughout the '60s. This was obviously his career focus at that time. He also put out many soundtracks for these movies; some of them include *GI Blues*, *Blue Hawaii*, and *Viva Las Vegas*.

Angelitta knows that the key to making an effective biographical speech is to be selective. To support her second main idea, she has selected the key events of Elvis's meteoric rise to fame.

(continued)

Sample Informative Speech *(continued)*

After covering Elvis's early life and career, we can now discuss his career change. The obvious shift from movies to music came with Elvis's 1968 *Comeback Tour Special*, initially entitled *Elvis*. Elvis used the 1968 *Comeback Special* to be taken more seriously, and he ended the special on a personal note, by closing with the song *If I Can Dream*. This song was in response to the tragedies that had occurred in the 1960s, such as the assassination of JFK, Martin Luther King Jr., and Bobby Kennedy, all men whom Elvis respected. This was a sign he was ready to be taken more seriously. His movies changed as well; he finished up his acting career with a few movies that were less cheesy and had more serious plots.

Angelitta provides another signpost to summarize her second main idea and preview her third one.

Again, Angelitta is selective in relating details about Elvis's later career, focusing on those that emphasize the increasingly serious nature of his work.

In 1973, Elvis made history. His *Aloha from Hawaii Special* was broadcast via satellite to 40 countries and viewed by 1 to 1.5 billion people, according to Elvis.com. Also according to Elvis.com, 51% of Americans viewed the *Aloha from Hawaii Special*. That means it was seen in more American households than the walk on the moon was! Elvis continued to sell out shows and venues such as Madison Square Garden and Las Vegas until his career ended in 1977 with his death.

Having provided data about the viewership of Elvis's 1973 Aloha from Hawaii Special, Angelitta makes these numbers more dramatic for her listeners by comparing them with the numbers of American households who watched the first moon walk.

You can see that Elvis's life is something for the history books. He came from humble beginnings and catapulted himself into a thriving career to become the King of Rock-N-Roll. Now you know about his life before fame, his early fame and rise to stardom, and a career shift that he focused on. Now—as Elvis would say—"Thank you, thank you very much."

After summarizing her main ideas, Angelitta provides closure to her speech with Elvis's signature sign-off.

STUDY GUIDE: Review, Apply, and Assess Your Knowledge and Skill

Review Your Knowledge

Types of Informative Speeches

14.1 Describe five types of informative speeches.

There are five basic types of informative speeches. Messages about objects discuss tangible things. Messages about procedures explain a process or describe how something works. Messages about people can be about either the famous or the little known. Messages about events describe major occurrences or personal experiences. Messages about ideas are often abstract and generally discuss principles, concepts, or theories.

Strategies for Organizing Your Informative Speech

14.2 Identify and use appropriate strategies for organizing informative speeches.

Strategies for organizing your informative speech will vary according to the type of informative speech and your specific purpose. A speech about an object may be organized topically, chronologically, or spatially. A speech about a procedure will usually be organized chronologically. Speeches about either people or events are also usually organized chronologically but can be organized topically. A speech about an idea will probably be organized topically.

Strategies for Making Your Informative Speech Clear

14.3 Identify and use strategies for making informative speeches clear.

To make your message clear, use simple rather than complex ideas, pace the flow of your information, and relate new information to old ideas.

Strategies for Making Your Informative Speech Interesting

14.4 Identify and use strategies for making informative speeches interesting.

To increase interest in your speech, relate information to your listeners' interests, find and use attention-getting supporting material, establish a motive for your audience to listen to you, use vivid word pictures, create intriguing and clear presentation aids, and use humor appropriately.

Strategies for Making Your Informative Speech Memorable

14.5 Identify and use strategies for making informative speeches memorable.

To make messages memorable, build in some redundancy (tell your audience what you're going to tell them, tell them, and then tell them what you've told them), apply principles of adult learning, and reinforce key ideas both verbally and nonverbally.

Key Terms

Inform, p. 325

Word Picture, p. 333

Adult Learning Principles, p. 336

The Principle Points

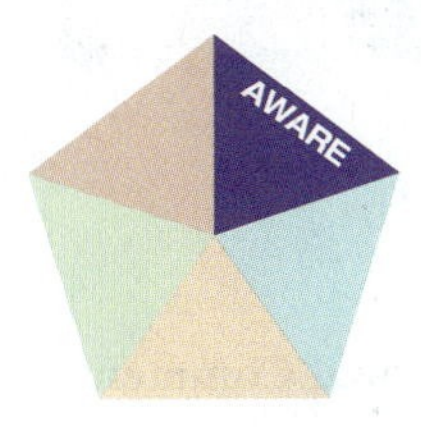

Principle One:

Be aware of your communication with yourself and others.

- To determine how best to organize your message, be conscious of the type of informative speech you are developing (speech about an object, a procedure, a person, an event, or an idea).
- Be mindful of strategies that will make your informative messages clear, interesting, and memorable.

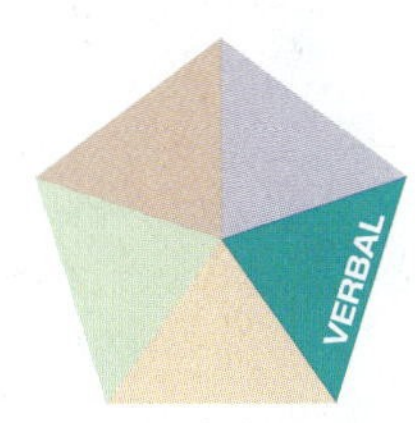

Principle Two:

Effectively use and interpret verbal messages.

- Use supporting material such as stories, examples, and illustrations to gain and maintain attention.
- Create word pictures to make images and stories interesting and memorable.
- Pace the flow of the information you present to enhance message clarity.
- Relate new information to old information to increase clarity and retention.
- To help make your message memorable, reinforce ideas verbally.
- Use simple rather than complex ideas to make your message clear.
- Build in message redundancy to enhance message retention.

Principle Three:

Effectively use and interpret nonverbal messages.

- Use presentation aids to make messages clear, interesting, and memorable.
- Observe the nonverbal behavior of your audience to help you determine whether your message has been communicated clearly.
- Nonverbally reinforce ideas to make your message memorable.

Principle Four:

Listen and respond thoughtfully to others.

- Before you deliver your speech to an audience, talk and listen to audience members to help you customize your message for them.

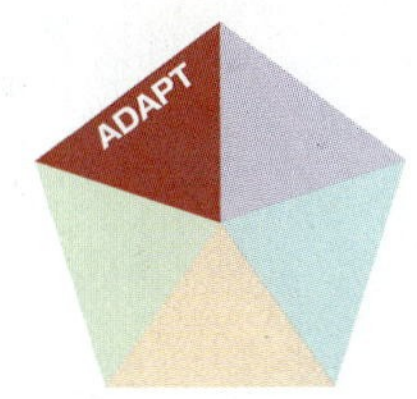

Principle Five:

Appropriately adapt messages to others.

- To enhance message clarity, adapt the structure and flow of your speech to your listeners.
- To help gain and maintain interest and attention, adapt your examples and illustrations to your listeners.

Apply Your Skill

Consider the following questions. Write your answers and/or share them with your classmates:

1. Which type of informative speech have you heard most often? Which type do you think you're most likely to give?
2. How could you organize a speech informing listeners about a brain-imaging project in which you've been involved?
3. How could you simplify the ideas in a speech informing listeners how about the role of the Electoral College in U.S. elections?
4. Think about something you've seen or experienced recently. Draft a word picture that describes the sight or experience.
5. What strategies does your public speaking teacher use in class to make information memorable?
6. Before giving a speech to your class in which you share a humorous or interesting story that includes information about a friend, should you ask that friend's permission?

Assess Your Skill

Checklist for an Informative Speech

Figure 13.5 at the end of Chapter 13 includes speech evaluation questions linked to the audience-centered model. You may also find it useful to refer to the following checklist, which is specific to informative speaking.

Element	Criteria	Additional Comments
Audience	______ Adapted to needs, interests, and background of audience	
Topic	______ Appropriate to audience, occasion, and speaker	
	______ Focused on objects, procedures, people, events, or ideas	
	______ Narrowed to fit the time limits	
Purpose	______ Informative general purpose—to share information by teaching, defining, illustrating, describing, or explaining	
	______ Audience-centered specific purpose	
	______ General and specific purposes achieved	
Central Idea	______ Clear one-sentence declarative summary of the speech	
Main Ideas	______ Related to central idea as natural divisions, reasons, or chronological steps	
	______ Previewed in introduction of speech	
	______ Developed in body of speech	
	______ Summarized in conclusion of speech	
	______ Ideas simplified	
Supporting Material	______ Information flow appropriately paced	
	______ New information related to old	
	______ Use of attention-catching supporting material	
	______ Use of word pictures	
	______ Appropriate use of humor	
Organization	______ Introduction that caught attention, established motive for audience to listen, stated central idea, previewed main ideas	
	______ Body organized in a logical way	
	______ Redundancy and reinforcement of key ideas evident	
	______ Conclusion that restated central idea, summarized main ideas, and provided closure	
Delivery	______ Nonverbal reinforcement of key ideas	
	______ Eye contact with listeners	
	______ Appropriate volume and vocal inflection	
	______ Appropriate gestures, movement, and posture	
	______ Interesting and effectively prepared presentation aids, if any	

Chapter 15

Speaking to Persuade

Give me the right word and the right accent and I will move the world. —JOSEPH CONRAD

Junial Enterprises/Shutterstock

Chapter Outline

Chapter Objectives

After studying this chapter, you should be able to

15.1 Define persuasion and describe five ways listeners may be motivated.

15.2 Explain how to select and narrow a persuasive topic, identify a persuasive purpose, and develop and support a persuasive proposition.

15.3 Use credibility, logical reasoning, and emotional appeals to make your persuasive speech more effective.

15.4 Organize your persuasive message.

15.5 Provide specific suggestions for adapting to receptive audiences, neutral audiences, and unreceptive audiences.

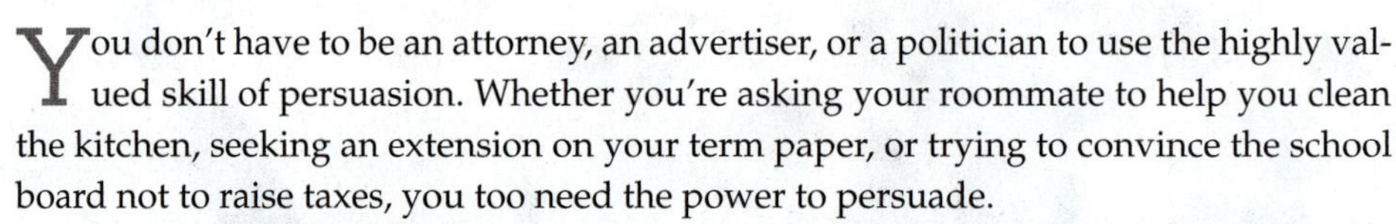

You don't have to be an attorney, an advertiser, or a politician to use the highly valued skill of persuasion. Whether you're asking your roommate to help you clean the kitchen, seeking an extension on your term paper, or trying to convince the school board not to raise taxes, you too need the power to persuade.

In 333 B.C.E., Aristotle was among the first to write a comprehensive guide to persuasion. His work, *Rhetoric*, was used by other Greek and Roman writers who sought to summarize principles and strategies of persuasion. The chapter you are reading draws on some of that classic advice and updates it with contemporary research. We first define persuasion, noting how it is both similar to and different from informing others. We then explore how persuasion works by explaining how to motivate an audience. We also offer strategies for developing a persuasive speech; present ideas to help you organize your persuasive message; provide methods to help you move an audience with your credibility, logic, and emotional appeals; and help you adapt your message not only to receptive audiences but also to those who are neutral or unreceptive.

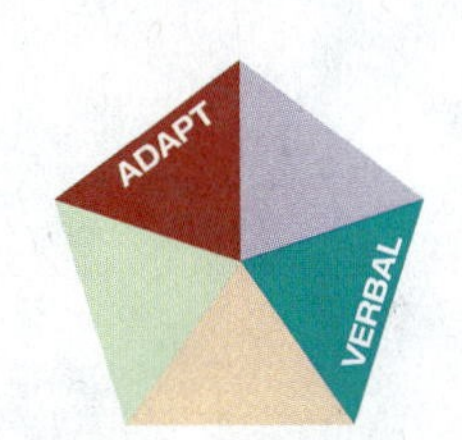

Understanding Persuasion

15.1 Define persuasion and describe five ways listeners may be motivated.

As we have already noted, since the time of Aristotle, people have been trying to understand and explain what persuasion is and how it works. In this section, we will examine some of the most influential ideas.

Persuasion Defined

persuasion
The process of attempting to change or reinforce a listener's attitudes, beliefs, values, or behavior.

coercion
The use of force to get another person to think or behave as you wish; coercion is unethical because it takes away free choice.

Persuasion is the process of attempting to change or reinforce attitudes, beliefs, values, or behavior. When we persuade, we are urging someone to modify or maintain the way he or she thinks, feels, or behaves.

Using force to achieve your goal is **coercion**, not persuasion. Weapons, threats, and other unethical strategies may momentarily achieve what you want, but it certainly is not appropriate or ethical to use such means. Efforts to persuade should be grounded in giving people options rather than forcing them to respond in a certain way.

Communication & ETHICS

Hidden Agendas

David is trying to get businesspeople to invest in the new Internet company he works for. He told a group of people at a Chamber of Commerce meeting that he wanted to inform them about some of the new and exciting ideas his company was developing. His real purpose, however, was to get people to invest in his company. Was it ethical of David not to tell his listeners that he really wanted them to become investors? Why or why not?

The Psychology of Persuasion

How does persuasion work? What makes you dial the phone to have a piping hot pepperoni pizza delivered to your door after you watch a television commercial for pizza? What motivates people to do things that they wouldn't do unless they were persuaded to do so? Let's look at five explanations of why people respond to efforts to persuade.

DISSONANCE When you are presented with information that is inconsistent with your current thinking or feelings, you experience a kind of mental discomfort called **cognitive dissonance**. For example, if you frequently drive when you are drowsy and then learn that driving when drowsy is a major contributor to traffic accidents, dissonance theory predicts that you will experience cognitive dissonance. The incompatibility between your customary behavior and your new knowledge will make you feel uncomfortable. Your discomfort may prompt you to change your thoughts, likes or dislikes, feelings, or behavior so that you can restore your comfort level or sense of balance. For example, you may decide to stop driving when drowsy.

Skilled persuasive speakers know that creating dissonance and then offering their listeners a way to restore balance is an effective persuasive strategy. For example, Sean wants to persuade his listeners to take greater safety precautions in preparing food. He begins by focusing on the health threat posed by bacteria in even the cleanest kitchens:

> Right now, as you sit and listen to me speak about kitchen bacteria, millions of them are probably reproducing in your kitchen, simply waiting for the perfect opportunity to join you for lunch.[1]

Sean is deliberately creating dissonance. He knows that his audience members value their health and that they have always assumed their kitchens to be relatively clean. His next task is to restore his listeners' sense of balance. He assures them that solutions exist and that "they are simple and you can start them as early as today." If the audience members implement such simple actions as washing their hands frequently, using paper towels, and washing sponges and dishcloths along with the dishes, they can resolve their dissonance and once again feel secure about their kitchen safety. The need to resolve dissonance provides one explanation of why people may respond to a speaker's attempts to persuade.

NEEDS Need is one of the best motivators. A shopper who just broke the heel off a shoe is much more likely to buy new shoes than is someone who is just browsing. When you are a speaker, the better you understand what your listeners need, the better you can adapt to them and the greater the chance that you can persuade them to change an attitude, belief, or value or get them to take some action.

The classic theory that outlines our basic needs was developed by Abraham Maslow.[2] If you've taken a psychology course, you have undoubtedly encountered this theory, which has important applications for persuasion. Maslow suggested

cognitive dissonance
The sense of mental disorganization or imbalance that may prompt a person to change when new information conflicts with previously organized thought patterns.

Figure 15.1 Maslow's Hierarchy of Needs

SOURCE: Maslow, Abraham (1954). *Motivation and Personality.* New York: HarperCollins.

hierarchy of needs
Abraham Maslow's classic theory that humans have five levels of needs and that lower-level needs must be met before people can be concerned about higher-level needs.

that a **hierarchy of needs**, illustrated in Figure 15.1, motivates the behavior of all people:

- *Physiological needs.* At the bottom of the hierarchy are basic physiological needs (such as needs for food, water, and air), which have to be satisfied before we can attend to any other concern.
- *Safety needs.* Once our physiological needs have been met, we think next about safety needs. We need to feel safe and be able to protect those we love.
- *Social needs.* Comfortable and secure, we attend next to social needs, including the need to be loved and the need to belong to a group.
- *Self-esteem needs.* The next level of need is for self-esteem, or to think well of ourselves.
- *Self-actualization needs.* Finally, if the first four levels of need have been satisfied, we may attend to the need for self-actualization, or achieving our highest potential.

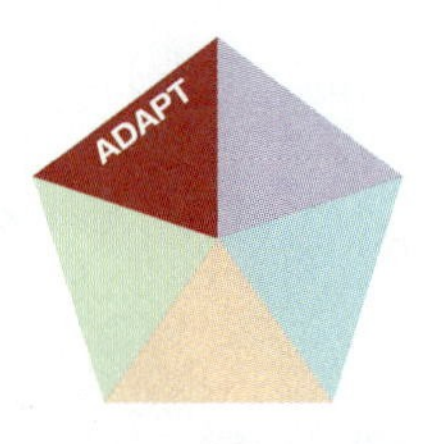

Understanding and applying the hierarchy of needs helps you adapt to your audience. One practical application is to do everything in your power to ensure that your audience's physiological needs are met. For example, if your listeners are sweating and fanning themselves, they are unlikely to be very interested in whether Bigfoot exists or whether the city should reopen River Park. If you can turn on the air conditioning or fans, you will stand a greater chance of persuading your audience than if you continue in that stifling atmosphere.

Another way you can apply the hierarchy of needs is by appealing to an audience's basic need for safety. For example, Mike knows that most of his audience members have young friends or family members who routinely ride school buses. As he begins to talk about the problem of safety hazards on school buses, he appeals to the audience's need to protect those they love.

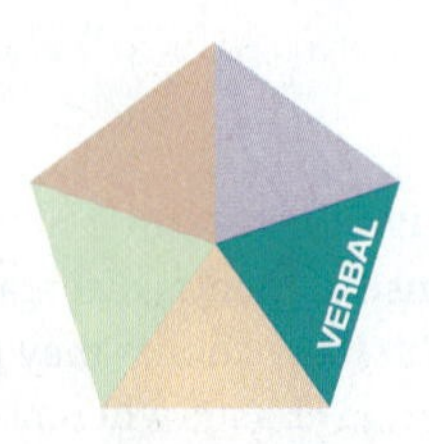

FEAR APPEALS One of the oldest ways to convince people to change their minds or their behavior is by scaring them into compliance. Fear works. The appeal to fear often takes the form of a verbal message—an "if–then" statement. *If* you do (or don't do) X, *then* something awful will happen to you. "If you don't get a flu shot, then you will probably catch the flu." "If you don't wear a seatbelt, then you are more likely to die in an automobile accident." "If you smoke cigarettes, you will get lung cancer." These statements are all examples of fear appeals. A variety of research studies support the principles outlined in Figure 15.2 for using fear as a motivator.[3]

Figure 15.2 Using Fear to Motivate Listeners

Make the threat applicable to listeners' loved ones.	*"If your parents don't have a smoke alarm in their house, they are ten times more likely to die in a house fire."*
Make the threat credible.	*"Doctors agree that lack of sleep poses a threat to students' health and academic performance."*
Make the threat imminent.	*"An overly fatty diet coupled with lack of exercise is the primary cause of heart disease in the United States. Eat less fat and get more exercise, or you may die prematurely."*
Make the threat strong.	*"After the category 5 hurricane comes ashore, most of the coastal area will remain uninhabitable for weeks if not months."*

The effectiveness of fear appeals is based on the theory of cognitive dissonance and Maslow's need theory. The fear aroused creates dissonance. Taking action reduces the fear and can meet a need, such as to live a long life, to be safe from harm, to have good friends, or to have a fulfilling career.

Of course, you have an ethical responsibility not to overstate your case or fabricate evidence when using a fear appeal. The persuader always has an ethical responsibility to be truthful when trying to arouse fear in the listener.

POSITIVE APPEALS A political candidate's TV ad declares: "Vote for me! You'll have lower taxes and higher wages, and your children will be better educated." Does this politician's promise sound familiar? It sounds like what most politicians offer: better days ahead if you'll vote for the person you see on your TV screen. Politicians, salespeople, and most other successful persuaders know that one way to change or reinforce your attitudes, beliefs, values, or behavior is to use a positive motivational appeal.

Positive motivational appeals are verbal messages promising that good things will happen if the speaker's advice is followed. The key to using positive motivational appeals is to know what your listeners value. Most Americans value a comfortable, prosperous life; stimulating, exciting activity; a sense of accomplishment; world, community, and personal peace; and overall happiness and contentment. In a persuasive speech, you can motivate your listeners to respond to your message by describing what will happen to them if they follow your advice.

THE ELABORATION LIKELIHOOD MODEL One of the newest frameworks for understanding persuasion is called the **elaboration likelihood model (ELM)**.[4] ELM theory, which focuses on how audience members interpret persuasive messages,

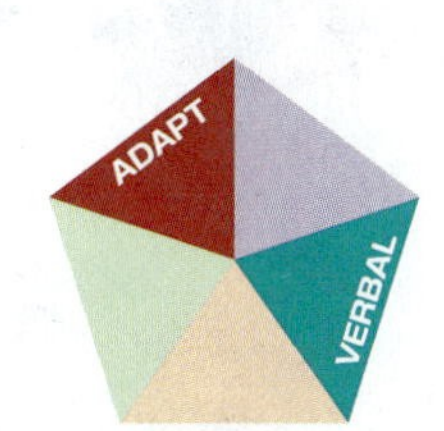

elaboration likelihood model (ELM)
A contemporary theory that people can be persuaded both directly and indirectly.

includes a category of factors that researchers call *indirect* or *peripheral*. If you respond to the catchy music, creative logo, or attractive spokesperson in an advertisement, you have been indirectly persuaded. When hearing a speech by one of your classmates, you may be influenced by the speaker's stylish outfit or jazzy PowerPoint template. If you can't identify exactly why you were persuaded, you were probably persuaded by peripheral factors.

Advertisers have long been aware of the effectiveness of indirect persuasion. One researcher points out,

> In current advertising practice, it is rare to find magazine ads that lead off with a direct verbal claim such as "[Brand X] gets clothes clean." Instead of straightforward claims that a brand possesses some attribute or delivers some benefit, one encounters pictures of . . . measuring cups full of blue sky.[5]

Because ELM theory is a more audience-centered model than other persuasive theories, it can be especially valuable in helping you understand how you have been persuaded. It also suggests that, as a speaker, you should be aware of and adapt the indirect factors—such as your delivery, appearance, and general impression of preparedness—that can influence your listeners.

According to the elaboration likelihood model, we are often persuaded by indirect factors that are not central to the product or message. What indirect factors do the advertisers of this product hope will persuade shoppers to buy it?
Vladimir Wrangel/Fotolia

Developing Your Audience-Centered Persuasive Speech

15.2 Explain how to select and narrow a persuasive topic, identify a persuasive purpose, and develop and support a persuasive proposition.

Now that you have an understanding of what persuasion is and isn't, you probably wonder how to develop a persuasive message. The audience-centered model of public speaking, introduced in Chapter 11 and shown again in Figure 15.3, can help you design and deliver a persuasive speech, just as it can an informative one. As Figure 15.3 shows, you start your preparation for a persuasive speech in the same way that you begin preparing for any speech: by considering the needs, interests, and background of your audience. Ethically adapting to listeners is important in any communication situation, but it is especially important in persuading others.

Narrowing Your Topic

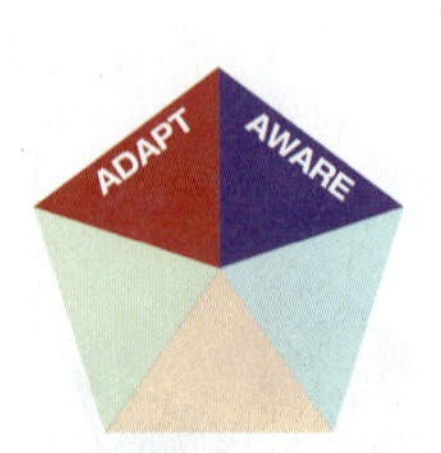

As with any speech, after you've thought about your audience, the next step is to select and narrow your topic. The best persuasive topic is one about which you feel strongly. If your listeners sense that you are committed to and excited about your topic, chances are that they will be interested and involved as well.

The principle of appropriately adapting messages to others can help guide your choice of persuasive topic. Know the local, state, national, and international issues that interest and affect your listeners:

- Should the city build a new power plant?
- Should convicted child molesters be permitted to live in any neighborhood they like?
- Should the United States drop economic sanctions against Cuba?

These and other significant controversial issues make excellent persuasive speech topics. Avoid frivolous topics, such as "why you should make your own potholders," when so many important issues challenge the world and your listeners.

Pay particular attention to electronic and print media so that you remain informed about important issues of the day. Blogs and Internet chat rooms or news sites can provide ideas for persuasive speeches. Other potential sources of persuasive topics include talk radio and daily newspapers. After you have chosen a topic for your persuasive message, keeping up with the latest information from media can help you narrow your topic and find interesting and appropriate supporting material for your speech.

Figure 15.3 Audience-Centered Model of the Public Speaking Process

Identifying Your Purpose

Attitudes, beliefs, and values, identified in Chapter 2 as components of a person's self-concept, are also integral to understanding how to persuade. When your general purpose is to persuade, your specific purpose will target your listeners' **attitudes, beliefs,** or **values**, or their behavior.

Figure 15.4 defines attitudes, beliefs, and values; provides examples of specific purpose statements that target each one; and illustrates that attitudes lie fairly close to the surface of our convictions, with values the most deeply ingrained in the center of the model.

Be aware of whether your specific purpose targets an attitude, a belief, a value, or a behavior, and be realistic in assessing what you will need to do in your speech to effect change. Recall, too, from our definition of *persuasion* that you can try to *reinforce*

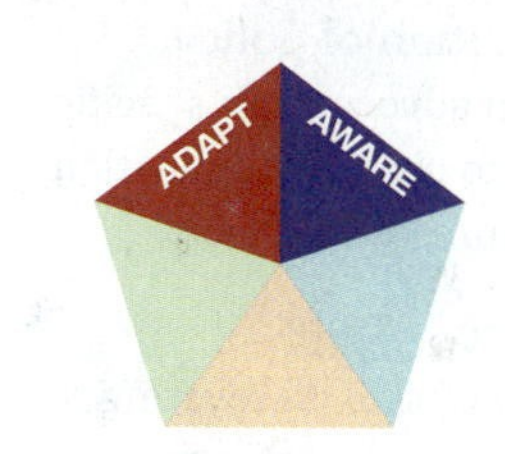

Figure 15.4 Comparing Attitudes, Beliefs, and Values

Attitudes—our likes and dislikes—are much more likely to change than are our beliefs or values. Our sense of what is right and wrong—our values—are least likely to change.

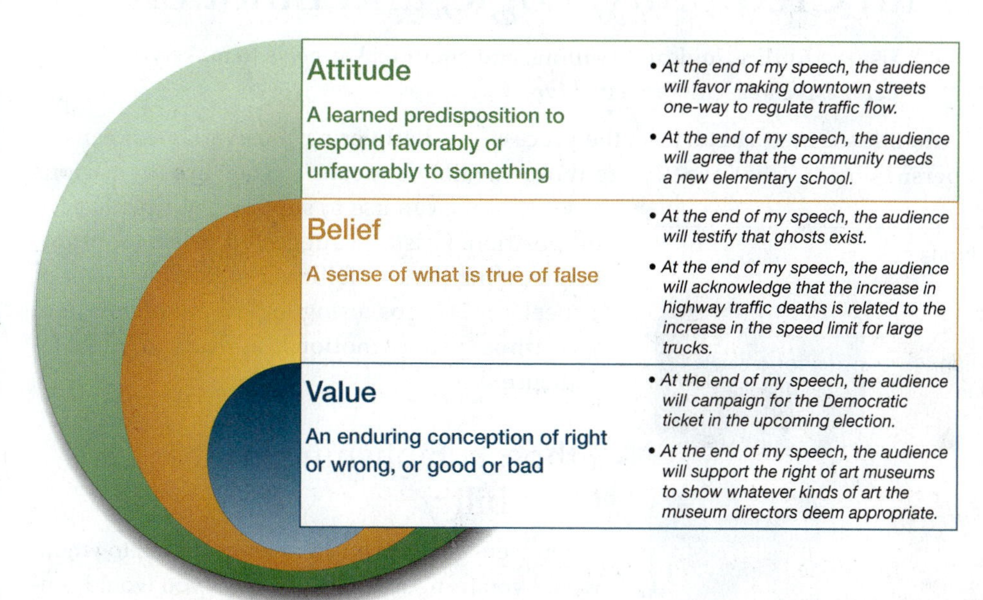

attitude
A learned predisposition to respond favorably or unfavorably to something; a like or dislike.

belief
A sense of what is true or false.

value
An enduring conception of right or wrong, or good or bad.

attitudes, beliefs, values, and behavior that audience members already hold, or you can try to *change* their attitudes, beliefs, values, or behavior. Reinforcing what listeners already know or think is relatively easy; it's more of a challenge to change their minds.

Developing Your Central Idea as a Persuasive Proposition

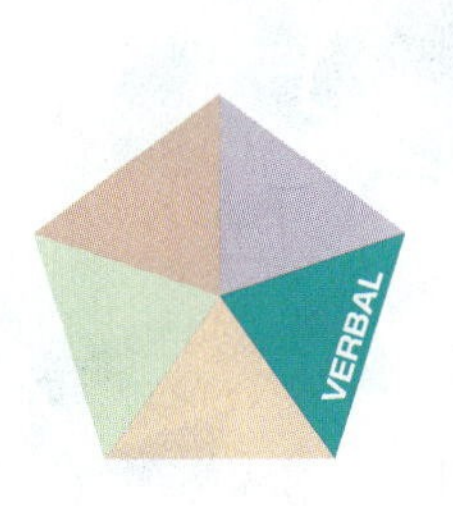

After clarifying their specific purpose, most persuasive speakers find it useful to cast their central idea as a **proposition**, a statement with which they want their audience to agree. A well-worded proposition is a verbal message that can help you fine-tune your persuasive objective and develop strategies for convincing your audience that your proposition is true. There are three categories of propositions: propositions of fact, propositions of value, and propositions of policy. Let's examine each type in more detail.

proposition
A claim with which you want your audience to agree.

proposition of fact
A claim that something is or is not the case or that something did or did not happen.

proposition of value
A claim that calls for the listener to judge the worth or importance of something.

proposition of policy
A claim advocating a specific action to change a regulation, procedure, or behavior.

rhetoric
The process of discovering the available means of persuasion.

ethos
The credibility or ethical character of a speaker.

logos
Logical arguments.

pathos
Emotional appeals.

PROPOSITIONS OF FACT A **proposition of fact** is a claim that something is or is not the case or that something did or did not happen. A speaker who uses a proposition of fact as the central idea of a persuasive speech focuses on changing or reinforcing the listeners' beliefs—what they think is true.

PROPOSITIONS OF VALUE As the word *value* suggests, a **proposition of value** calls for the listener to judge the worth or importance of something. A simple example is "Tattoos are beautiful." Other value propositions compare two ideas, things, or actions and suggest that one is better than the other.

PROPOSITIONS OF POLICY The third type of proposition, the proposition of policy, advocates a specific action, such as changing a regulation, procedure, or behavior. **Propositions of policy** include the word *should*.

Figure 15.5 provides an example of each of the three types of persuasive propositions.

With your specific purpose and central idea in hand, you are ready to move to the next stages in the public speaking process. In most cases, you can draw your main ideas from several reasons *why* the persuasive proposition is true. Then you will be ready to begin selecting supporting material.

Supporting Your Persuasive Message with Credibility, Logic, and Emotion

15.3 Use credibility, logical reasoning, and emotional appeals to make your persuasive speech more effective.

Aristotle defined **rhetoric** as the process of "discovering the available means of persuasion."[6] What exactly are those "available means"? They are the various strategies you can use to support your persuasive proposition. Aristotle suggested three: (1) **ethos**, emphasizing the credibility or ethical character of a speaker; (2) **logos**, using logical arguments; and (3) **pathos**, using emotional appeals to move an audience.

Figure 15.5 Persuasive Propositions

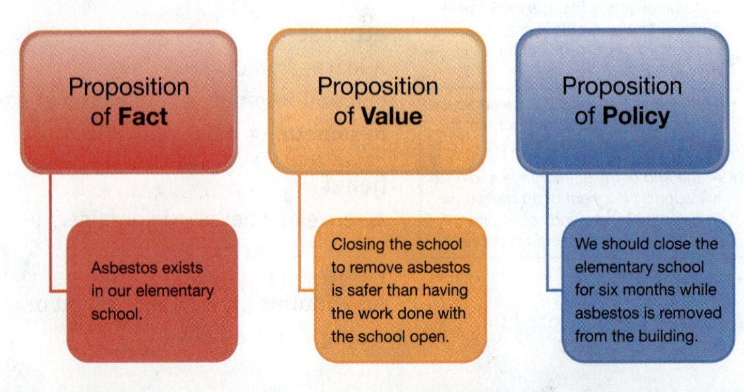

Ethos: Establishing Your Credibility

If you were going to buy a new computer, to whom would you turn for advice? Perhaps you would consult your brother, who is a computer geek, or your roommate, who is a computer science major? Alternatively, you could seek advice from *Consumer Reports*, a monthly publication of studies of various consumer products. You would turn to a source that you consider knowledgeable, competent, and trustworthy, or, in other words, credible.

Credibility is an audience's perception of a speaker's competence, trustworthiness, and dynamism. Your listeners, not you, determine whether you have credibility.

For centuries, teachers and researchers have sought to understand the factors that audiences consider in deciding whether a speaker is credible. Aristotle thought that a public speaker should be ethical, possess good character, display common sense, and be concerned for the well-being of his audience. Quintilian, a Roman teacher of public speaking, advised that a speaker should be "a good man speaking well." These ancient speculations about the elements that enhance a speaker's credibility are reflected in our modern understanding of credibility as a product of three factors: competence, trustworthiness, and dynamism.

credibility
An audience's perception of a speaker's competence, trustworthiness, and dynamism.

competence
An aspect of a speaker's credibility that reflects whether the speaker is perceived as informed, skilled, and knowledgeable.

trustworthiness
An aspect of a speaker's credibility that reflects whether the speaker is perceived as believable and honest.

COMPETENCE One clear factor in credibility is **competence**. A speaker should be informed, skilled, or knowledgeable about the subject he or she is discussing. You will be more persuasive if you can convince your listeners that you know something about your topic. How can you do that?

You can use verbal messages effectively by talking about relevant personal experience with the topic. If you have taken and enjoyed a cruise, for instance, you can tell your audience about the highlights of your trip. You can also cite evidence to support your ideas. Even if you have not taken a cruise yourself, you can be prepared with information about what a good value a cruise is—how much it costs and what is included—in comparison to how much the same trip would cost if one were to travel by air and stay and eat in hotels.

TRUSTWORTHINESS A second factor in credibility is **trustworthiness**. While delivering a speech, you need to convey honesty and sincerity to your audience. You can't do so simply by saying, "Trust me." You have to earn trust by demonstrating that you are interested in and experienced with your topic. Again, speaking from personal experience makes you seem to be a more trustworthy speaker. Conversely, having something to gain by persuading your listeners may make you suspect in

Audiences often perceive a dynamic, charismatic speaker, such as this one, as credible. What steps can you take to be more dynamic in your delivery, or to assure your audience of your competence or trustworthiness?
Stockbyte/Getty Images

Figure 15.6 Enhancing Your Credibility

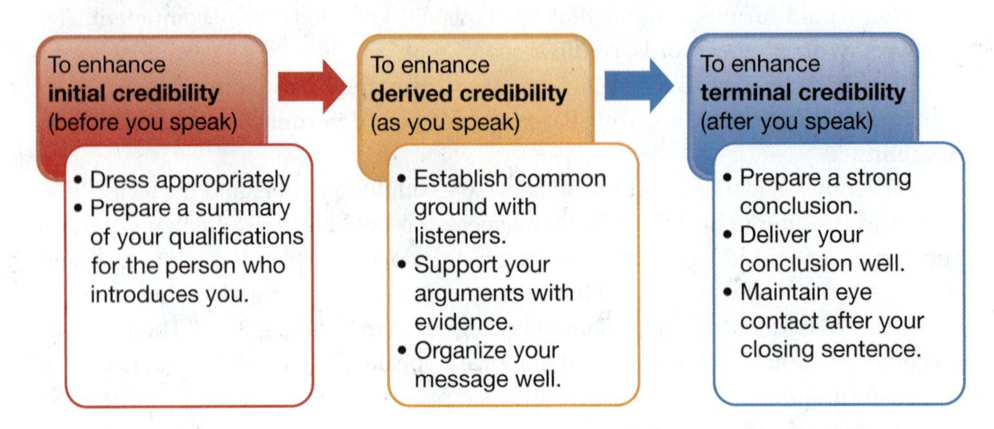

their eyes, which is why salespeople and politicians often lack credibility; if you do what they say, they will clearly benefit by earning sales commissions or being elected to public office.

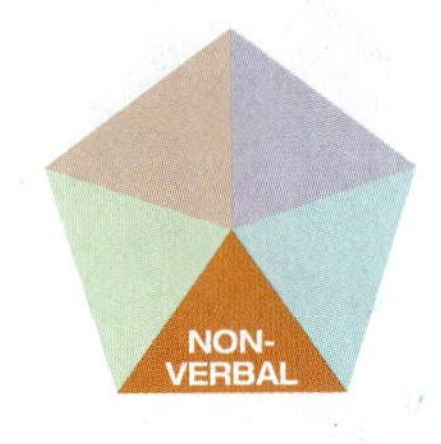

dynamism
An aspect of a speaker's credibility that reflects whether the speaker is perceived as energetic.

charisma
Talent, charm, and attractiveness.

initial credibility
The impression of a speaker's credibility that listeners have before the speaker begins to speak.

derived credibility
The impression of a speaker's credibility based on what the speaker says and does during the speech.

terminal credibility
The final impression listeners have of a speaker's credibility, after the speech has been concluded.

proof
Evidence plus reasoning.

evidence
The material used to support a point or premise.

reasoning
The process of drawing a conclusion from evidence.

inductive reasoning
Using specific instances or examples to reach a probable general conclusion.

DYNAMISM A third factor in credibility is a speaker's **dynamism**, or energy. Dynamism is often projected through delivery. If we apply the communication principle of using and understanding nonverbal messages effectively, a speaker who maintains eye contact, has enthusiastic vocal inflection, and moves and gestures purposefully is likely to be seen as dynamic. **Charisma** is a form of dynamism. A charismatic speaker possesses charm, talent, magnetism, and other qualities that make the person attractive and energetic. Many people considered President Franklin Roosevelt and Pope John Paul II charismatic speakers.

STAGES OF CREDIBILITY You have opportunities before, during, and after your speech to enhance your credibility. **Initial credibility** is the impression your listeners have of you before you even begin to speak. They grant you initial credibility on the basis of such factors as your appearance and your credentials. **Derived credibility** is the perception your listeners form as you deliver your speech. And **terminal credibility** is the perception of your credibility that your listeners have when you finish your speech. Figure 15.6 provides specific suggestions for enhancing your credibility at each of these three stages.

Logos: Using Evidence and Reasoning

In addition to being considered a credible speaker, you will gain influence with your audience if you can effectively use logically structured arguments supported with evidence. As we noted earlier, Aristotle called logical arguments *logos*, which, translated from Greek, means "the word." Using words effectively to communicate your arguments to your listeners is vital to persuading thoughtful and informed listeners.[7]

The goal is to provide logical proof for your arguments. **Proof** consists of both evidence and reasoning. **Evidence** is another word for the illustrations, definitions, statistics, and opinions that are your supporting material. **Reasoning** is the process of drawing conclusions from your evidence. There are three major ways to draw logical conclusions: inductively, deductively, and causally.

INDUCTIVE REASONING Reasoning that arrives at a general conclusion from specific instances or examples is known as **inductive reasoning**. You reason inductively when you claim that a conclusion is probably true because of specific evidence.

Reasoning by analogy is a special type of inductive reasoning. An analogy demonstrates how an unfamiliar idea, thing, or situation is similar to something the audience already understands. If you develop an original analogy, rather than quote one you find in a printed source, you are reasoning inductively. Here's an example of reasoning by analogy: Mandatory rear seatbelt laws that were enacted in Missouri saved lives; therefore, Kansas should also develop mandatory rear seatbelt laws. The key to arguing by analogy is to claim that the two things you are comparing (such as driving habits in Missouri and Kansas) are similar, so your argument is sound. Here's another example: England has a relaxed policy toward violence being shown on television and has experienced no major rise in violent crimes; therefore, the United States should relax its policy on showing violence on TV.

DEDUCTIVE REASONING Reasoning from a general statement or principle to reach a specific conclusion is called **deductive reasoning**. Deductive reasoning can be structured as a **syllogism**, a three-part argument that consists of a major premise, a minor premise, and a conclusion. In a message in which you are attempting to convince your audience to vote for an upcoming school bond issue, your syllogism might look like the following:

MAJOR PREMISE: Keeping schools in good repair extends the number of years that school buildings can be used.

MINOR PREMISE: The proposed school bond issue provides money for school repairs.

CONCLUSION: The proposed school bond issue will extend the number of years that we can use our current school buildings.

Contemporary logicians note that when you reason deductively, your conclusion is certain rather than probable. The certainty of the conclusion rests primarily on the validity of the major premise and secondarily on the truth of the minor premise. If you can prove that keeping schools in good repair extends the useful life of school buildings, and if it is true that the proposed bond issue provides money for school repairs, your conclusion will be certain.

CAUSAL REASONING You use **causal reasoning** when you relate two or more events in such a way as to conclude that one or more of the events probably caused the others. For example, you might argue that public inoculation programs during the twentieth century eradicated smallpox.

As we noted in Chapter 12 when we discussed cause and effect as an organizational strategy, there are two ways to structure a causal argument. One is by reasoning from cause to effect—that is, predicting a result from a known fact. For example, you know that it has rained more than an inch over the last few days, so you predict that the aquifer level will rise. The inch of rain is the cause, and the rising aquifer is the effect. The other way to structure a causal argument is by reasoning from a known effect to the cause. National Transportation Safety Board accident investigators reason from effect to cause when they reconstruct airplane wreckage to determine the cause of an air disaster.

The key to developing any causal argument is to be certain that a causal relationship actually exists between the two factors you are investigating. A few summers ago, a young science student took part in a project involving counting chimney swifts in a given area just before sunset. He counted the most chimney swifts on the Fourth of July. It would not have been valid, however, to argue that fireworks (or parades or hot dogs or anything else connected with the Fourth of July) caused an increase in the number of chimney swifts seen in the area. The Fourth of July holiday and the bird count were not related by cause and effect.

LOGICAL FALLACIES. Unfortunately, not all people who try to persuade you will use sound evidence and reasoning. Some will try to develop arguments in ways that are irrelevant or inappropriate. Such reasoning is called a **logical fallacy**. To be a

reasoning by analogy
A special kind of inductive reasoning that draws a comparison between two ideas, things, or situations that share some essential common feature.

deductive reasoning
Moving from a general statement or principle to reach a certain specific conclusion.

syllogism
A three-part argument, including a major premise, a minor premise, and a conclusion.

causal reasoning
Relating two or more events in such a way as to conclude that one or more of the events caused the others.

logical fallacy
False reasoning that occurs when someone attempts to persuade without adequate evidence or with arguments that are irrelevant or inappropriate.

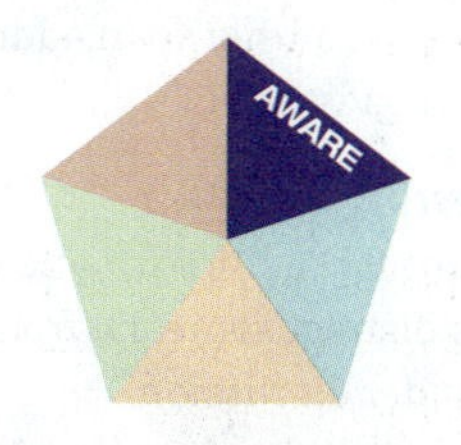

Communication & DIVERSITY

"Elementary Reasoning, My Dear Watson"

Although we frequently use the word *diversity* to refer to readily discernible differences in sex, race, culture, and age, diversity can also involve differences in perspective or point of view. As the following narrative shows, people may draw different conclusions from the same evidence.

Sherlock Holmes and Dr. Watson went on a camping trip. After a good meal and a bottle of wine, they lay down for the night and went to sleep. Some hours later, Holmes awoke and nudged his faithful friend.

"Watson, look up at the sky and tell me what you see."

Watson replied, "I see millions and millions of stars."

"What does that tell you?" inquired Holmes.

Watson pondered for a minute. "Astronomically, it tells me that there are millions of galaxies and potentially billions of planets. Astrologically, I observe that Saturn is in Leo. Horologically, I deduce that the time is approximately a quarter past three. Theologically, I can see that God is all powerful and that we are small and insignificant. Meteorologically, I suspect that we will have a beautiful day tomorrow. What does it tell you?"

Holmes was silent for a moment and then spoke. "Watson, you idiot! Someone has stolen our tent!"

better-informed consumer, as well as a more ethical persuasive speaker, you should be aware of some of the following common logical fallacies.

- *Causal fallacy.* Trying to link the Fourth of July with the chimney swift count would be an example of a **causal fallacy**, or, to use its Latin term, *post hoc, ergo propter hoc* ("after this; therefore, because of this"). Simply because one event follows another does not mean that the two are related.
- *Bandwagon fallacy.* "Jumping on the bandwagon" is a colloquial expression for thinking or doing something just because everybody else is. Someone who argues that "everybody thinks that, so you should too" is using the **bandwagon fallacy**. Speakers using the bandwagon fallacy often use the word *everybody:*

  Everybody knows that taxes are too high.

  Everybody agrees that the government should support a strong military.
- *Either–or fallacy.* "Either we support the bond issue, or we end up busing our students to another school district!" shouts Lupe in a moment of heated debate among the members of the school board. This **either–or fallacy** ignores the possibility of other solutions to the district's problem of dilapidated buildings (for example, purchasing portable classroom buildings or establishing new attendance zones within the district).
- *Hasty generalization.* A person who draws a conclusion from too little evidence or nonexistent evidence is making a **hasty generalization**. For example, one person's failing a math test does not necessarily mean that the test was too difficult or unfair.
- *Personal attack.* Using a **personal attack** as a substitute for a refutation of issues is also a logical fallacy. This approach is also known as an *ad hominem* argument, a Latin phrase that means "to the man." For example, "The HMO bill is a bad idea because it was proposed by that crazy senator" is a personal attack. Don't dismiss an idea solely because you have something against the person who presents it.
- *Red herring.* Someone who argues against an issue by bringing up irrelevant facts or arguments is using a **red herring**. This fallacy takes its name from the old trick of distracting dogs who are following a scent by dragging a smoked herring across a trail. Speakers use a red herring when they want to distract an audience from certain issues. A congressional representative, indicted for misuse of federal funds, would be using a red herring if he or she called a press conference and spent most of the time talking about a colleague's sexual indiscretions.

causal fallacy
Making a faulty cause and effect connection between two things or events.

bandwagon fallacy
Suggesting that because everyone believes something or does something, it must be valid, accurate, or effective.

either–or fallacy
Oversimplifying an issue as offering only two choices.

hasty generalization
Reaching a conclusion without adequate supporting evidence.

personal attack
Attacking irrelevant personal characteristics of someone connected with an idea, rather than addressing the idea itself.

red herring
Irrelevant facts or information used to distract someone from the issue under discussion.

RECAP

Inductive, Deductive, and Causal Reasoning

Type of Reasoning	Reasoning begins with . . .	Reasoning ends with . . .	Conclusion is . . .	Example
Inductive	specific examples	a general conclusion	probable or not probable	Dell, Gateway, and Asus computers are all reliable. Therefore, PCs are reliable.
Deductive	a general statement	a specific conclusion	certain or not certain	All professors at this college have advanced degrees. Tom Bryson is a professor at this college. Therefore, Tom Bryson has an advanced degree.
Causal	something known	a speculation about causes or effects of what is known	likely or not likely	The number of people with undergraduate degrees has risen steadily since 1960. This increasing number has caused a glut in the job market of people with degrees.

- *Appeal to misplaced authority.* When advertisers trot out baseball players to endorse breakfast cereal or movie stars to pitch credit cards, they are guilty of an **appeal to misplaced authority**. Although baseball players may know a great deal about the game of baseball, they are no more expert than most of us about breakfast cereal. Movie stars may be experts at acting, but they probably are not experts in the field of personal finance.

appeal to misplaced authority
Using someone without the appropriate credentials or expertise to endorse an idea or product.

non sequitur
Latin for "it does not follow"; presenting an idea or conclusion that does not logically follow the previous idea or conclusion.

- *Non sequitur.* If you argue that students should give blood because it is nearly time for final exams, you are guilty of using a **non sequitur** (Latin for "it does not follow") because your reason has nothing to do with your argument.

©Glenn and Gary McCoy/Distributed by Universal Uclick via CartoonStock.com

Glenn and Gary McCoy/CartoonStock

Persuasive speakers who provide logical proof (evidence and reasoning) for their arguments and who avoid logical fallacies heighten their chances for success with their audience. Good speakers also know that evidence and reasoning are not their only tools. Emotion is another powerful strategy for moving an audience to support a persuasive proposition.

Pathos: Using Emotion

People often make decisions based not on logic but on emotion. Advertisers know all about it; just think of soft-drink commercials. There is little rational reason for people to spend any part of their food budget on soft drinks that are "empty calories." So soft-drink advertisers turn instead to emotional appeals, striving to connect feelings of pleasure with their product. Smiling people, upbeat music, and good times are usually part of the formula for selling soft drinks.

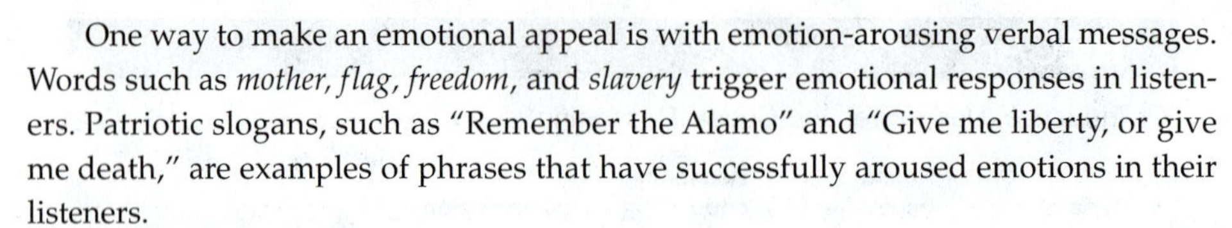

One way to make an emotional appeal is with emotion-arousing verbal messages. Words such as *mother, flag, freedom*, and *slavery* trigger emotional responses in listeners. Patriotic slogans, such as "Remember the Alamo" and "Give me liberty, or give me death," are examples of phrases that have successfully aroused emotions in their listeners.

Another way to appeal to emotions is to use concrete illustrations and descriptions. Although illustrations and descriptions are themselves types of evidence or supporting material, their effect is often emotional, as in the following example:

> Michelle Hutchinson carefully placed her three-year-old daughter into her child safety seat. She was certain that Dana was secure. Within minutes Michelle was involved in a minor accident, and the seat belt that was never designed to hold a child safety seat allowed the seat to lunge forward, crushing the three-year-old's skull on the dash. Dana died three days later.[8]

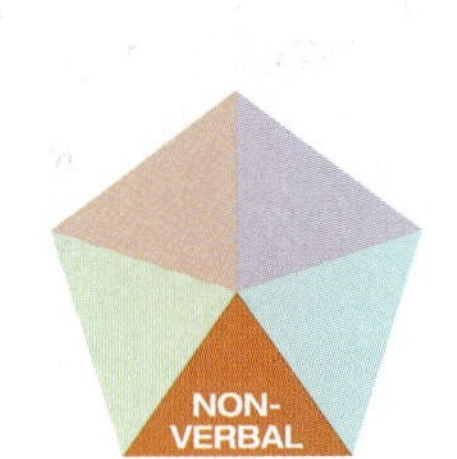

Effective use of nonverbal messages can also appeal to audience members' emotions. Visual aids—pictures, slides, or video—can provide emotion-arousing images. A photograph of a dirty, ragged child alone in a big city can evoke sadness and pain. A video clip of an airplane crash can arouse fear and horror. A picture of a smiling baby makes most of us smile, too. As a speaker, you can use visual aids to evoke both positive and negative emotions.

When you use emotional appeals, you have an obligation to be ethical and forthright. Making false claims, misusing evidence or images, or relying exclusively on emotion without any evidence or reasoning violates standards of ethical public speaking.

Organizing Your Persuasive Message

15.4 Organize your persuasive message.

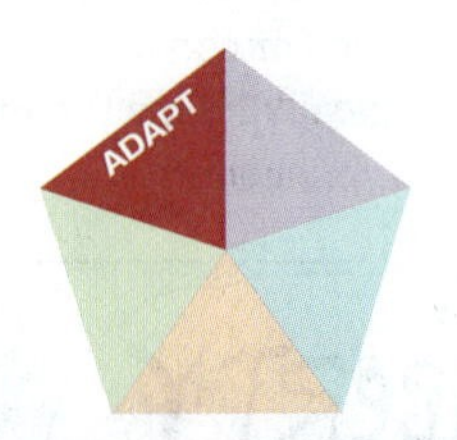

An audience-centered persuasive speaker adapts the organization of the speech to the audience's needs, attitudes, beliefs, behaviors, and background. Most persuasive speeches are organized according to one of four strategies: problem–solution, cause-and-effect, refutation, or the motivated sequence. The first two strategies were also discussed in Chapter 12; the last is a special variation of the problem–solution format.

RECAP

Tips for Using Emotion to Persuade

- Use emotion-arousing words.
- Use concrete illustrations and descriptions to create emotional images.
- Use visual aids to evoke both positive and negative emotions.
- Be ethical and forthright. Avoid making false claims, misusing evidence or images, or relying exclusively on emotion.

Problem–Solution

When you use a problem–solution organization for your persuasive message, apply the principle of appropriately adapting messages to others. If you are speaking to an apathetic audience or one that is not aware that a problem exists, emphasize the problem portion of the message. If your audience is already aware of the problem, emphasize the solution or solutions. In either case, your challenge will be to provide ample evidence that your perception of the problem is accurate and reasonable. You'll also need to convince your listeners that the solution or solutions you advocate are the most appropriate ones to solve the problem.

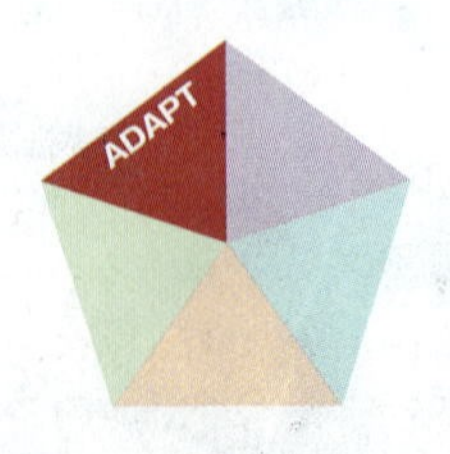

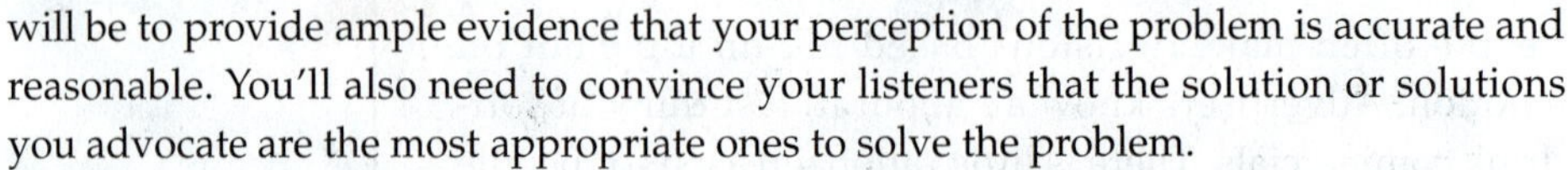

Notice how Nicholas organizes his speech "The Death of Reading" in a problem–solution pattern:[9]

I. PROBLEM: Reading is a dying activity.
   A. Each year more than 500 courts hear arguments to ban books.
   B. Since 1990, more than 2,000 libraries across America have closed.
   C. Leisure reading has decreased more than 50 percent since 1975.

II. SOLUTIONS:
   A. Teach children that reading as an activity has worth and beauty.
   B. Teach children that books in and of themselves only express ideas and should not be banned.
   C. Support programs such as "One City, One Book" that encourage community involvement and literary discussion.
   D. Give books as gifts.
   E. Allow others to see you read.

The persuasive speech at the end of this chapter is an example of a message organized by first stating the problem and then presenting some specific solutions.

Cause and Effect

If two or more situations are causally related, a cause-and-effect strategy can work well for a persuasive speech. Here is an example of a persuasive outline organized from cause to effect:[10]

I. CAUSE: The foster care system is in crisis.
   A. Since 1987, there has been a 90 percent increase in the number of children placed in foster care nationally.
   B. During that same time, there has been a 3 percent decrease in the number of licensed foster homes.

II. EFFECT: Children in foster care are at risk.
   A. Children in the foster care system are five times more likely to die as a result of abuse than children in the general population.
   B. 80 percent of federal prisoners spent time in the nation's foster care system as children.

An effect may have more than one cause. For example, standardized test scores may be low in your state both because of low per-pupil expenditures and because of a lack of parental involvement in the schools. To argue that only one of the two factors causes the low test scores would probably not be accurate.

It is also possible for two situations to coexist but not be causally related. Suppose that standardized test scores are indeed low in your state and that your state has a lottery. Both situations exist, but one does not cause the other.

This speaker uses a graph to persuade the audiences that a new marketing plan has affected profits. How would relating cause and effect help you to persuade your audience?
Thinkstock Images/Stockbyte/Getty Images

refutation
Organization according to objections your listeners may have to your ideas and arguments.

Refutation

A third way to organize your efforts to persuade an audience is especially useful when you are facing an unreceptive audience—one that does not agree with your point of view or your specific proposition. **Refutation** is an organizational strategy in which you identify likely objections to your proposition and then refute those objections with arguments and evidence.

You will be most likely to organize your persuasive message by refutation if you know your listeners' chief objections to your proposition. In fact, if you don't acknowledge such objections, the audience will probably think about them during your speech anyway. Credible facts and statistics will generally be more effective in supporting your points of refutation than will emotional arguments.

One speaker organized a persuasive speech on organ donation by providing the following refutations for four common misconceptions about the process:[11]

I. Anyone who decides to become a donor can reconsider that decision at any time.
II. Doctors will do everything to save the life of an organ donor that they would do for a non-donor.
III. No one who views the body of an organ donor will be able to tell that organs have been removed.
IV. Families of organ donors do not pay for any procedure related to the organ donation.

The Motivated Sequence

The **motivated sequence**, devised by Alan Monroe, is a five-step organizational plan that integrates the problem–solution method with principles that have been confirmed by research and practical experience.[12] The five steps are attention, need, satisfaction, visualization, and action.

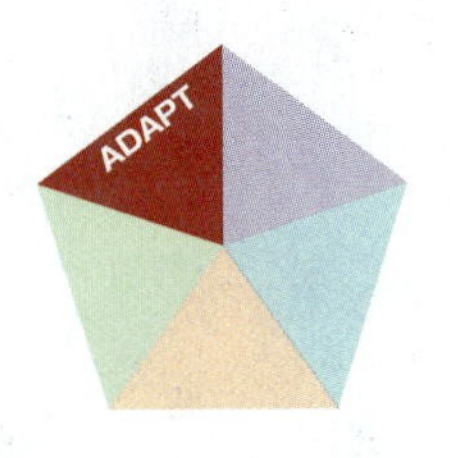

ATTENTION Your first task in applying the motivated sequence, as well as the first stage in appropriately adapting your message to others, is to get your listeners' attention. You already know attention-getting strategies for introductions: rhetorical questions, illustrations, startling facts or statistics, quotations, humorous stories, and references to historical or recent events. The attention step is, in essence, your application of one of these strategies.

Samin begins his persuasive speech about landmines with this attention-catching illustration:

> In Angola, little Tusnia became yet another one of the town's orphans. She was out in the field playing with her friends when she stumbled onto the ground and screamed. Her mother went running to see what happened, stepped in the wrong place, and was mutilated instantly. Parts from her body were found as far as 30 meters from the explosion site.[13]

NEED After getting your audience's attention, establish why your topic, problem, or issue should concern your listeners. Tell your audience about the problem. Adapt your message to them by convincing them that the problem affects them directly. Argue that there is a need for change. During the need step (which corresponds to the problem step in a problem–solution strategy), you should develop logical arguments backed by evidence. At this point, you create dissonance or use a credible fear appeal to motivate listeners to respond to your solution. Samin outlines his need step as follows:

> Citizens of countries with landmines face two major problems: risk of death or serious injury, and disruption of daily routines.

motivated sequence
Alan H. Monroe's five-step plan for organizing a persuasive message: attention, need, satisfaction, visualization, and action.

SATISFACTION After you explain and document a need or problem, identify your plan (or solution) and explain how it will satisfy the need. You need not go into painstaking detail. Present enough information for your listeners to gain a general understanding of how the problem may be solved. Samin recommends two solutions in his satisfaction step:

> One possible solution is to spread awareness. Luckily, this process has already been started by the United Nations Children Fund or UNICEF. . . . And a second solution is to teach successful de-mining technology to indigenous populations.

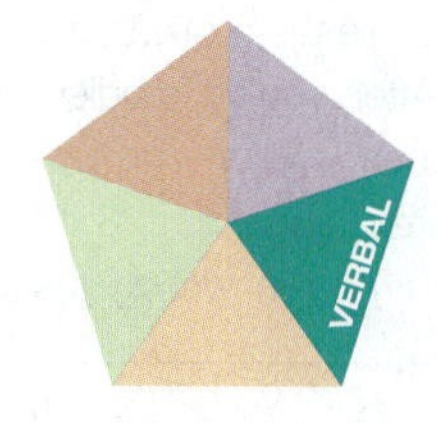

VISUALIZATION Now you need to give your audience a sense of what it would be like if your solution were adopted or, conversely, not adopted. **Visualization**—a word picture of the future—applies the fundamental principle of using and understanding verbal messages effectively. An appropriate presentation aid can also help your audience visualize the implications of your persuasive message. With a **positive visualization** approach, you paint a rosy picture of how wonderful the future will be if your satisfaction step is implemented. With a **negative visualization** approach, you paint a bleak picture of how terrible the future will be if nothing changes; you use a fear appeal to motivate your listeners to do what you suggest to avoid further problems. You might also combine the two approaches: The problem will be solved if your solution is adopted, but things will get increasingly worse if it is not. An ethical speaker makes sure that the positive or negative visualization message is accurate and not overstated. Samin offers positive visualization to communicate what can happen if his second solution is implemented:

visualization
A word picture of the future.

positive visualization
A word picture of how much better things will be if a solution is implemented.

negative visualization
A word picture of how much worse things will be if a solution is not implemented; a fear appeal.

> Perhaps in the future Tusnia can use this technology to start de-mining Angola so that the horrific atrocity that she faced will not happen to anyone else.

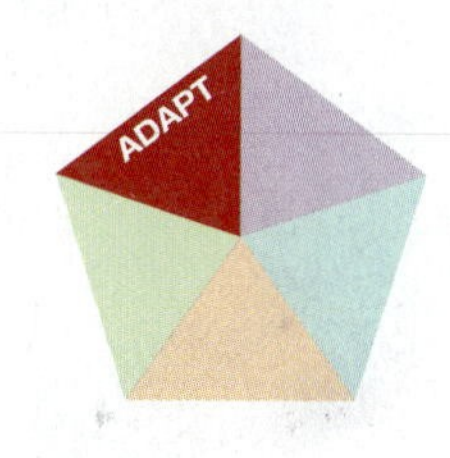

ACTION The final step of the motivated sequence requires you to adapt your solution to your audience. Offer your listeners some specific action they can take to solve the problem you have discussed. Identify exactly what you want them to do. Give them simple, clear, and easy-to-follow steps. At the end of your speech, provide a phone number to call for more information, an address to which they can write a letter of support, or a petition to sign. Samin suggests a specific action step his listeners can take to solve the problem of landmines:

> First, sign the People's Treaty to Support the Convention on Cluster Munitions, which is a de-mining effort. Second, Help the International Campaign to Ban Landmines by donating money to their cause.

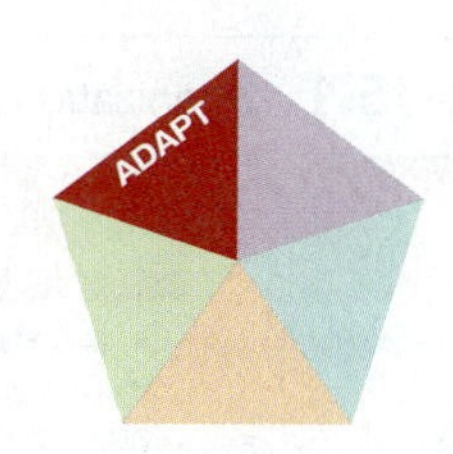

Figure 15.7 illustrates the steps in the motivated sequence. You can adapt the motivated sequence to both your topic and the needs of your audience. For example, if you are speaking to a knowledgeable, receptive audience, you do not need to spend a great deal of time on the need step. Your listeners already know that the need is serious. However, they may feel helpless to do anything about it. In this case, you would want to emphasize the satisfaction and action steps.

Figure 15.7 The Motivated Sequence

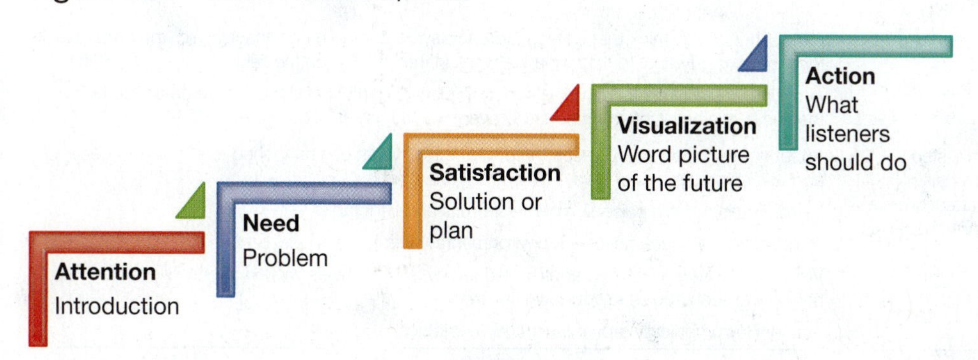

Communication & TECHNOLOGY

The Motivated Sequence in Television Advertising

Strategies for organizing persuasive messages are used not just by public speakers but also by advertisers. Many TV commercials use the motivated sequence, at least in part, to persuade.

After you've studied the description of the motivated sequence, search YouTube for a television commercial that is organized according to the motivated sequence. Analyze the ad, identifying in writing the target audience, and prepare a brief written explanation of how the video uses the motivated sequence. If you have an online class discussion board, post your written analysis and a link to the video.

Be sure to bookmark the video, as your instructor may also ask you to be prepared to show to your class the commercial you found, to discuss the target audience, and to present your outline of the motivated sequence.[14]

On the other hand, if you are speaking to neutral or apathetic audience members, you will need to spend time getting their attention and proving that a problem exists, is significant, and affects them personally. In this case, you will emphasize the attention, need, and visualization steps.

The organizational strategies for persuasive speeches are summarized in Table 15.1. Is there one best way to organize a persuasive message? The answer is no. The organizational strategy you select must depend on your audience, message, and desired objective. Just remember that your decision can have a major effect on your listeners' response to your message.

Adapting Ideas to People and People to Ideas

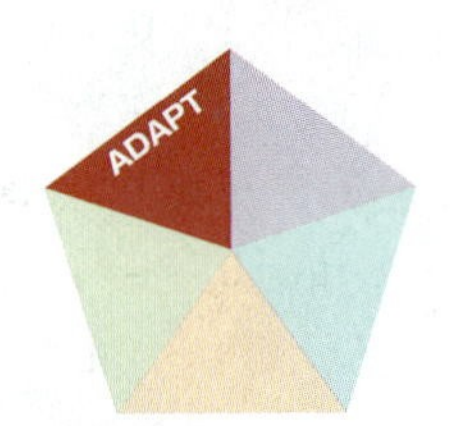

15.5 Provide specific suggestions for adapting to receptive audiences, neutral audiences, and unreceptive audiences.

Rhetoric scholar Donald C. Bryant's definition of rhetoric emphasizes the principle of appropriately adapting a message to an audience, which he calls the process of adjusting ideas to people and people to ideas.[15] With this thought, we've now come

Table 15.1 Organizational Patterns for Persuasive Speeches

Organizational Pattern	Definition	Example
Problem–Solution	Organization by discussing a problem and then its various solutions	I. Tooth decay threatens children's dental health. II. Inexpensive, easy-to-apply sealants make teeth resistant to decay.
Cause and Effect	Organization by discussing a situation and its causes, or a situation and its effects	I. Most HMOs refuse to pay for treatment they deem "experimental." II. Patients die who might have been saved by "experimental" treatment.
Refutation	Organization according to objections your listeners may have to your ideas and arguments	I. Although you may think that college football players get too much financial aid, they work hard for it, spending twenty to thirty hours a week in training and on the field. II. Although you may think that college football players don't spend much time on academics, they have two hours of enforced study every weeknight.
Motivated Sequence	Alan H. Monroe's five-step plan for organizing a persuasive message: attention, need, satisfaction, visualization, and action	I. Attention: "An apple a day keeps the doctor busy." What has happened to the old adage about keeping the doctor away? Why has it changed? II. Need: Pesticides are poisoning our fresh fruits and vegetables. III. Satisfaction: Growers must seek environmentally friendly alternatives to pesticides. IV. Visualization: Remember the apple poisoned by Snow White's wicked stepmother? You may be feeding such apples to your own children. V. Action: Buy organically grown fruits and vegetables.

full circle in the process of developing a persuasive message. As we have emphasized throughout our discussion of public speaking, analyzing your audience members and adapting to them is at the heart of the speech-making process; it's one of the fundamental Communication Principles for a Lifetime. In a persuasive speech, adapting begins with identifying your specific purpose and understanding whether you are trying to change or reinforce attitudes, beliefs, values, or behavior. It continues when you select an organizational strategy.

For example, if your audience members are unreceptive toward your ideas, you might organize your speech by refutation and address their objections directly. In addition, research studies and experienced speakers can offer other useful suggestions to help you adapt to your audience. Let's look at some specific strategies for persuading receptive, neutral, and unreceptive audiences.

The Receptive Audience

It is usually a pleasure to address an audience that already supports you and your message. In these situations, you can explore your ideas in depth and can be fairly certain of a successful appeal to action. The following suggestions can help you engage your receptive audience members:

- *Identify with your audience.* Emphasize your similarities and common interests. A good place to do so is often in the introduction of your message.
- *State your speaking objective overtly.* Tell your audience members exactly what you want them to do, and ask them for an immediate show of support. If your listeners are already receptive, you don't have to worry that being overt will antagonize them. Rather, it will give you more time to rouse them to passionate commitment and action.

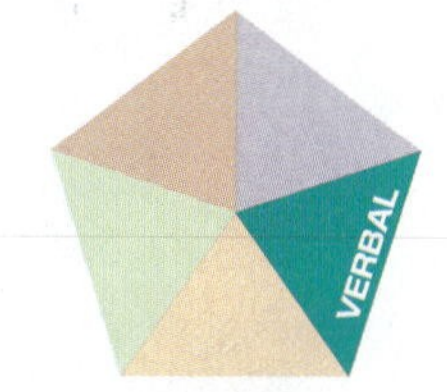

- *Use emotional appeals.* If your listeners already support your position, you can spend less time providing detailed evidence and instead focus on using strong emotional appeals to move them to action.

The Neutral Audience

Many audiences will fall somewhere between being wildly enthusiastic and being hostile and will simply be neutral. The listeners' neutrality may take the form of indifference: They know about the topic or issue, but they don't see how it affects them, or they can't make up their minds about it. Alternatively, their neutrality may take the form of ignorance: They just don't know much about the topic. Regardless of whether they are indifferent or ignorant, your challenge is to get them interested in your message. Otherwise, they may escape by sleeping through your speech or engaging in such self-distracting activities as texting on their cell phones or surfing the web on their laptops. The following suggestions can help you engage your neutral audience members:

- *Hook your neutral audience with an especially engaging introduction or attention step.* Brian provided such an introduction to his persuasive speech about the number of Americans who live with chronic pain:

> "I can't shower because the water feels like molten lava. Every time someone turns on a ceiling fan, it feels like razor blades are cutting through my legs. I'm dying." Meet David Bogan, financial advisor from Deptford, New Jersey; Porsche, boat, and homeowner; and a victim of a debilitating car accident that has not only rendered him two years of chronic leg pain, but a fall from the pinnacle of success. Bogan has nothing now. Life to him, life with searing pain, is a worthless tease of agony and distress.[16]

Most audiences will start out fairly neutral toward your persuasive goal. To persuade such an audience, you can establish common ground between their needs and your goals and appeal to their interests.
Digital Vision/Photodisc/Getty Images

- *Appeal to common ground.* Another strategy for persuading neutral audiences is to refer to universal beliefs or common concerns. For example, protecting the environment and having access to good health care might be common concerns.
- *Appeal to your listeners' interests.* Show how the topic affects not only them but also people they care about. For example, parents will be interested in issues and policies that affect their children.
- *Limit your persuasive purpose.* Be realistic about what you can accomplish. People who are neutral at the beginning of your speech are unlikely to change their opinion in just a few minutes. Persuasion is unlikely to occur all at once or after only one presentation of arguments and issues.

The Unreceptive Audience

As a speaker, you will find that one of your biggest challenges is to persuade audience members who are unreceptive toward you or your message. If they are unreceptive toward you personally, you need to find ways to enhance your credibility and persuade them to listen to you. If they are unreceptive toward your point of view, the following strategies may help:

- *Focus on universal beliefs and concerns.* Don't immediately announce your persuasive purpose. Explicitly telling your unreceptive listeners that you plan to change their minds can make them defensive. Instead, refer to areas of agreement, as you would with a neutral audience. Rather than saying, "I'm here this morning to convince you that we should raise city taxes," you might say, "I think we can agree that we have an important common goal: achieving the best quality of life possible here in our small community."
- *Following the principle of primacy, advance your strongest arguments first.* If you save your best argument for last (the recency principle), your audience may already have stopped listening.
- *Acknowledge the opposing points of view that audience members may hold.* Summarize the reasons they may oppose your point of view; then cite evidence and use

arguments to refute the opposition and support your conclusion. In speaking to students seeking to hold down tuition costs, a dean might say, "I am aware that many of you struggle to pay for your education. You work nights, take out loans, and live frugally." Then the dean could go on to identify how the university could provide additional financial assistance to students.

- *Be especially aware of, and effectively use, nonverbal messages.* One study suggests that unreceptive audiences may more negatively evaluate speakers who do not gesture than they do those who use gestures.[17]

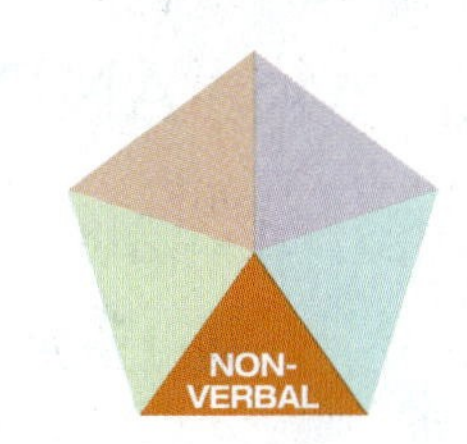

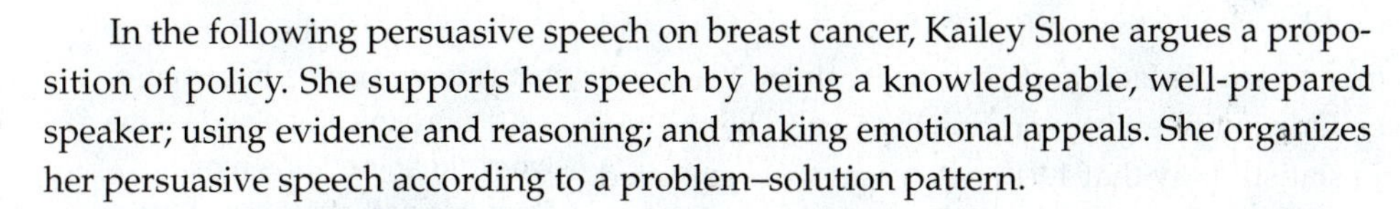

In the following persuasive speech on breast cancer, Kailey Slone argues a proposition of policy. She supports her speech by being a knowledgeable, well-prepared speaker; using evidence and reasoning; and making emotional appeals. She organizes her persuasive speech according to a problem–solution pattern.

RECAP

Adapting Ideas to People and People to Ideas

Persuading the Receptive Audience	Persuading the Neutral Audience	Persuading the Unreceptive Audience
• Identify with your audience.	• Gain and maintain your audience's attention.	• Don't tell listeners that you are going to try to convince them to support your position.
• Emphasize common interests.	• Refer to beliefs and concerns that are important to listeners.	• Present your strongest arguments first.
• Provide a clear objective; tell your listeners what you want them to do.	• Show how the topic affects people your listeners care about.	• Acknowledge opposing points of view.
• Appropriately use emotional appeals.	• Be realistic about what you can accomplish.	• Use appropriate gestures.

Sample Persuasive Speech

Real Men AND Women Wear Pink

Kailey Slone[18] *Texas State University*

Note: You can visit MyCommunicationLab to watch a video of Kailey delivering this speech.

Imagine yourself sitting in a cold, stale doctor's office, with sweaty palms and a racing heart. The doctor steps in, you see his face, and your heart sinks. You were just diagnosed with breast cancer. One out of eight women who live to be the age 85 will contract breast cancer. And statistics say that 1,910 new cases were expected to be found in men in the year 2009. These rising statistics show that breast cancer can and will hit close to home. My grandmother was recently diagnosed with and treated for breast cancer. Because I just went through treatment with her, I realize what a breast cancer patient goes through. Because breast cancer is a growing epidemic among men and women each year in the United States, and because a cure for breast cancer has yet to be found, I propose that you participate in the Susan G. Komen Race for the Cure to help contribute to breast cancer research. But before we talk about the solution, we must first understand breast cancer as a problem. The problem is that without a cure, breast cancer will continue to be on the rise in the United States.

Kailey captures the attention of her listeners with a hypothetical illustration, indicated by the word "Imagine." She moves from this soft evidence to statistics that include both men and women, communicating to her entire audience that "This issue concerns you."

According to the Susan G. Komen Foundation, since 1940, breast cancer cases in the United States have increased by 1% each year—which means that over the last seventy years, breast cancer cases have increased by 70%. That's shocking. In 2005, breast cancer cases were 122 in every 100,000 women and 1.2 per 100,000 men. Then, in a more recent study done by clinicians, titled "Cancer Statistics," 180,150 estimated new cases were added to the growing number. Now, college students, this is where breast cancer can affect people like you and me. In college, we are all faced with the opportunity to consume alcohol. (Stick with me here!) One analysis of a combination of fifty-three case studies found that every one alcoholic drink per day increases our chance as women 7%. Having two to three alcoholic drinks per day increases women's risk by 20%. Also, for women who have an immediate family member who has been diagnosed, treated, or affected by breast cancer, the chances for contracting breast cancer double in their lifetime.

Kailey provides statistics to support her argument that the incidence of breast cancer in the United States is rising.

She adds a fear appeal to convince her listeners that the threat of breast cancer is real and could directly affect them.

As you can see, breast cancer is affecting more and more people, year after year. Thus, it is necessary for us to become involved in the solution.

The solution that I propose is one that requires you and me to take action. It is one that requires us to *be* the change that we want to see in the future. I propose that you participate in the Susan G. Komen Race for the Cure. This solution will work because other foundation fundraisers have been proven to work. I say "proven to work" because research happens with funding, and a cure happens from research. For example, according to an article titled, "Relay for Life, Second Life," Relay for Life has raised 1.5 billion dollars for the American Cancer Society. Another foundation, titled Pink Hair for Hope, brought 375 hair salons together and raised one million dollars for breast cancer. In a study done in Michigan, a fundraiser for Crop Hunger and a walk with over 15,000 participants, sponsored by Church World Service, raised over $250,000 to help feed children in third-world countries.

Kailey urges her audience to take direct, specific action.

In conclusion, it should be obvious to us now that breast cancer is affecting more and more people every year in the United States. It should also be apparent

(continued)

Sample Persuasive Speech *(continued)*

that with these rising statistics, breast cancer will likely affect you and me in our future. Therefore, we must take action in making the dream of a cure become a reality. I am urging you to sign up for and participate in the Susan G. Komen Race for the Cure to continue cancer research. I was with my grandmother the day she got the news. I saw the fear in her eyes, and I saw the trembling in her hands. I don't wish this on anyone else. Thankfully, my grandmother today is a breast cancer survivor. As a survivor, she believes in Susan G. Komen's ability to contribute to a cure. And because she does, so should you. Register for a race—and remember that real men *and* women wear pink.

As Kailey summarizes her main points, she makes a final fear appeal by telling her listeners that "breast cancer will likely affect you and me in our future." Reminding them of her experience with her grandmother, she adds, "I don't wish this on anyone else."

STUDY GUIDE:
Review, Apply, and Assess Your Knowledge and Skill

Review Your Knowledge

Understanding Persuasion

15.1 Define persuasion and describe five ways listeners may be motivated.

Persuasion is the process of attempting to change or reinforce attitudes, beliefs, values, or behaviors. Several theories suggest how listeners may be motivated to respond to a persuasive message. Cognitive dissonance, a sense of mental disorganization or imbalance that arises when new information conflicts with previously organized thought patterns, may prompt a person to change attitudes, beliefs, values, or behavior. Maslow's classic hierarchy of needs attempts to explain why people may be motivated to respond to persuasive appeals to various levels of need. Both fear appeals and positive motivational appeals can prompt listeners to respond to a persuasive message. The elaboration likelihood model (ELM) explains how listeners may be motivated by such peripheral factors as the speaker's appearance.

Developing Your Audience-Centered Persuasive Speech

15.2 Explain how to select and narrow a persuasive topic, identify a persuasive purpose, and develop and support a persuasive proposition.

Your specific persuasive purpose targets your audience's attitudes, beliefs, values, or behavior. Attitudes are learned predispositions to respond favorably or unfavorably toward something. A belief is one's sense of what is true or false. Values are enduring conceptions of right or wrong or good or bad. Of the three, attitudes are most susceptible to change, and values are least likely to change. After clarifying your specific purpose, you can word your central idea as a proposition of fact, value, or policy.

Supporting Your Persuasive Message with Credibility, Logic, and Emotion

15.3 Use credibility, logical reasoning, and emotional appeals to make your persuasive speech more effective.

Support for your persuasive proposition can include credibility, logic, and emotion. Credibility is your audience's perception of your competence, trustworthiness, and dynamism. Enhancing your initial credibility before you speak, your derived credibility during your speech, and your terminal credibility after your speech will help you improve your overall credibility as a speaker. Reasoning, the process of drawing a conclusion from evidence, is integral to your persuasive process. The three primary types of reasoning are inductive, deductive, and causal. You can also reason by analogy. You can be a more effective and ethical persuader by avoiding such reasoning fallacies as the causal fallacy, bandwagon fallacy, either–or fallacy, hasty generalization, personal attack, red herring, appeal to misplaced authority, and non sequitur. In addition to persuading others because of who you are (ethos) or how well you reason (logos), you can move an audience to respond by using emotional appeals (pathos).

Organizing Your Persuasive Message

15.4 Organize your persuasive message.

Ways to organize your persuasive message include problem–solution, cause and effect, refutation, and the motivated sequence. The motivated sequence includes five steps: attention, need, satisfaction, visualization, and action.

Adapting Ideas to People and People to Ideas

15.5 Provide specific suggestions for adapting to receptive audiences, neutral audiences, and unreceptive audiences.

Be prepared to adapt your persuasive messages to receptive, neutral, and unreceptive audiences. If your listeners are receptive, identify with them, be overt in stating your speaking objective, and use emotional appeals. If they are neutral, hook them with your introduction, refer to universal beliefs and common concerns, show them how the topic affects them and those they care about, and be realistic about what you can accomplish. If your listeners are unreceptive, focus on areas of agreement rather than telling them that you are going to try to convince them to support your position, present your strongest arguments first, acknowledge opposing points of view, and use appropriate gestures.

Key Terms

Persuasion, p. 344
Coercion, p. 344
Cognitive Dissonance, p. 345
Hierarchy of Needs, p. 346
Elaboration Likelihood Model (ELM), p. 347
Attitude, p. 349
Belief, p. 349
Value, p. 349
Proposition, p. 350
Proposition of Fact, p. 350
Proposition of Value, p. 350
Proposition of Policy, p. 350
Rhetoric, p. 350
Ethos, p. 350
Logos, p. 350
Pathos, p. 350
Credibility, p. 351
Competence, p. 351
Trustworthiness, p. 351
Dynamism, p. 352
Charisma, p. 352
Initial Credibility, p. 352
Derived Credibility, p. 352
Terminal Credibility, p. 352
Proof, p. 352
Evidence, p. 352
Reasoning, p. 352
Inductive Reasoning, p. 352
Reasoning by Analogy, p. 353
Deductive Reasoning, p. 353
Syllogism, p. 353
Causal Reasoning, p. 353
Logical Fallacy, p. 353
Causal Fallacy, p. 354
Bandwagon Fallacy, p. 354
Either–Or Fallacy, p. 354
Hasty Generalization, p. 354
Personal Attack, p. 354
Red Herring, p. 354
Appeal to Misplaced Authority, p. 355
Non Sequitur, p. 355
Refutation, p. 357
Motivated Sequence, p. 358
Visualization, p. 359
Positive Visualization, p. 359
Negative Visualization, p. 359

The Principle Points

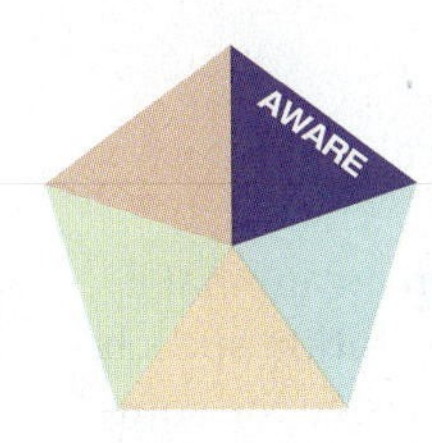

Principle One:

Be aware of your communication with yourself and others.

- Know whether the specific purpose of your persuasive speech is to change or reinforce an attitude, a belief, a value, or a behavior, and be realistic in assessing what you need to do to effect change.
- Relate personal experience to show that you are a competent and trustworthy speaker.
- To help enhance your initial credibility, have a brief summary of your qualifications and accomplishments ready for the person who will introduce you.
- To be a better informed consumer of persuasive messages, as well as a more ethical persuasive speaker, be aware of and avoid using common logical fallacies.

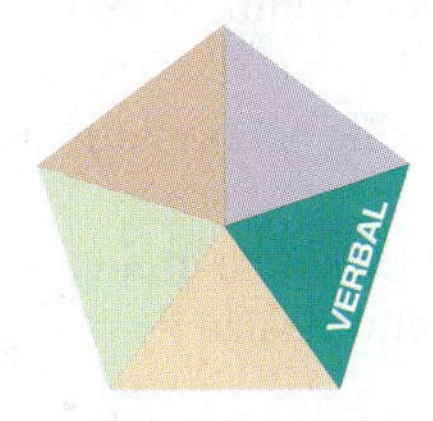

Principle Two:

Effectively use and interpret verbal messages.

- To create negative visualization, describe in detail how bleak or terrible the future will be if your solution is not implemented.
- To create positive visualization, describe in detail how wonderful the future will be if your solution is implemented.
- To select and narrow a topic for your persuasive speech, stay current on important issues of the day by paying attention to print and electronic media.
- Word your central idea as a proposition to help you fine-tune your speaking objective and develop strategies for persuading your listeners.
- To bolster your audience's opinion of your competence, cite evidence to support your ideas.
- To enhance your terminal credibility, prepare a thoughtful conclusion.
- Provide logical proof (evidence and reasoning) for your arguments and avoid logical fallacies to heighten your chances for success with your audience.
- Use emotion-arousing words and concrete illustrations and descriptions to appeal to an audience's emotions.

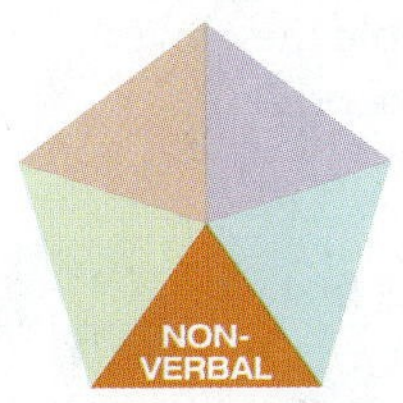

Principle Three:

Effectively use and interpret nonverbal messages.

- Maintain eye contact, use enthusiastic vocal inflection, and move and gesture purposefully to increase the likelihood that your audience will view you as dynamic.

- Dress appropriately to enhance your credibility.
- To enhance your terminal credibility, maintain eye contact through and even after your closing sentence.
- Use presentation aids to help evoke both positive and negative emotions as well as positive and negative visualization.
- Use gestures when speaking to an unreceptive audience.

Principle Four:

Listen and respond thoughtfully to others.

- As a speaker, the better you understand what your listeners need, the better you can adapt to them and the greater the chance that you can persuade them to change an attitude, belief, or value or get them to take some action.
- If your audience is receptive to your ideas, you can identify with them, state your speaking objective overtly, and use emotional appeals.
- If your audience is neutral, hook them with an engaging introduction, appeal to common ground and their interests, and limit your persuasive purpose.
- If your audience is unreceptive to your ideas, you might organize your speech by refutation and address their objections directly.

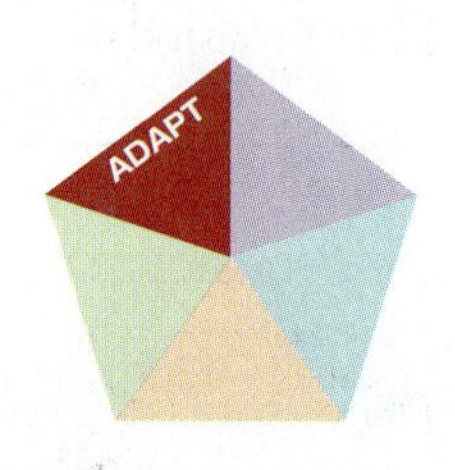

Principle Five:

Appropriately adapt messages to others.

- As you develop your persuasive purpose, consider the background and cultural expectations of your listeners.
- To motivate your listeners, appeal to their basic needs.
- Do everything possible to ensure that your audience's physiological and safety needs are met.
- If you are speaking to an apathetic audience or one that is not even aware that a problem exists, emphasize the problem portion of your problem–solution speech.
- If your audience is aware of the problem you are discussing, emphasize the solution or solutions in your problem–solution speech.
- Acknowledge and then refute the opposing points of view held by an unreceptive audience.
- In the need step of your motivated-sequence speech, establish why your topic, problem, or issue should concern your listeners. Convince audience members that the problem affects them directly.
- In the action step of the motivated-sequence speech, suggest a specific action your listeners can take to solve the problem you have discussed.
- If you are speaking to a knowledgeable, receptive audience, do not spend a great deal of time on the need step of the motivated sequence; instead, emphasize the satisfaction and action steps.
- If you are speaking to a neutral audience, emphasize the attention, need, and visualization steps of the motivated sequence.
- Establish common ground with your audience.
- Make the most of your opportunity to speak to a receptive audience by identifying with them.
- If your audience is receptive, state your speaking objective overtly, tell your listeners exactly what you want them to do, and ask them for an immediate show of support.
- Use emotional appeals with a receptive audience.
- To persuade a neutral audience, appeal to universal beliefs and concerns.
- Show a neutral audience how your topic affects them and the people they love.
- Be realistic about what you can accomplish with neutral and unreceptive audiences.
- With an unreceptive audience, focus on areas of agreement.
- If your audience is unreceptive, advance your strongest arguments first.

Apply Your Skill

Consider the following questions. Write your answers and/or share them with your classmates:

1. Describe a time you experienced cognitive dissonance, whether as a result of persuasive communication or not, and explain how you resolved the feeling.
2. State an attitude, a belief, and a value that you hold related to the topic of transportation. Use your attitude, belief, and value to develop a proposition of fact, a proposition of value, and a proposition of policy that could each be a central idea for a persuasive speech.
3. Imagine you are giving a speech to your classmates near the end of the term. What specific strategies can you use to enhance your credibility with this audience?
4. You want your listeners to support a local ordinance that will restrict noise after 10:00 P.M. in your community. Using the motivated sequence, identify a way to catch their attention, establish a need, identify a solution, visualize the benefits of this proposal, and present a specific action step they could take to help the ordinance pass.
5. You are hoping to persuade members of your communication class to buy snacks from the campus World Environment Club, whose members donate the profits to save South American rainforests. Most of your classmates don't even know or care much about rainforests half a world away and some have stereotyped the Environment Club as a bunch of useless hippies. What persuasive speaking strategies would be helpful in achieving your goal?
6. What are three topics that would make a good persuasive speech for an audience of your communication classmates?

Assess Your Skill

Checklist for a Persuasive Speech

Figure 13.5 at the end of Chapter 13 includes speech evaluation questions linked to the audience-centered model. You may also find it useful to refer to the following checklist specific to persuasive speaking.

Element	Criteria	Additional Comments
Audience	______ Adapted to needs, interests, and background of audience.	
	______ Evidence of analyzing and adapting to the receptive, neutral, or unreceptive audience.	
Topic	______ Appropriate to audience, occasion, and speaker.	
	______ Focused on an important issue.	
	______ Narrowed to fit the time limits.	
Purpose	______ Persuasive general purpose—to change or reinforce listeners' attitudes, beliefs, values, or behavior.	
	______ Audience-centered specific purpose.	
	______ General and specific purposes achieved.	
Central Idea	______ Clear one-sentence declarative summary of the speech.	
	______ A proposition of fact, value, or policy.	
Main Ideas	______ Related to central idea as natural divisions, reasons, or chronological steps.	
	______ Previewed in speech introduction.	
	______ Developed in body of speech.	

Element	Criteria	Additional Comments
	_______ Summarized in conclusion of speech.	
Supporting Material	_______ Ethos evident in speaker's appearance, credentials, preparation, and delivery.	
	_______ Logos evident in logically reasoned arguments supported by evidence.	
	_______ Pathos evident in emotion-arousing words and phrases, concrete illustrations and descriptions, and evocative presentation aids.	
Organization	_______ Introduction caught attention, established motive for audience to listen, stated central idea, and previewed main ideas.	
	_______ Body organized in a logical way—for example, according to problem–solution, cause and effect, refutation, or the motivated sequence.	
	_______ Conclusion restated central idea, summarized main ideas, and provided closure.	
Delivery	_______ Nonverbal reinforcement of key ideas.	
	_______ Eye contact with listeners.	
	_______ Appropriate volume and vocal inflection.	
	_______ Appropriate gestures, movement, and posture.	
	_______ Positive and negative emotions and visualization evoked by presentation aids, if any.	

Appendix A
Interviewing

Appendix Outline

- Types of Interviews
- Phases of an Interview
- How to Be Interviewed for a Job
- How to Be Interviewed in an Information-Gathering Interview
- The Responsibilities of the Interviewer
- Study Guide: Review, Apply, and Assess Your Knowledge and Skill

Appendix Objectives

After studying this appendix, you should be able to

A.1 Define what an interview is, and identify five different kinds of interviews.

A.2 Describe the three phases of a well-structured interview.

A.3 Identify and describe how to be interviewed for a job, including how to develop a well-worded resumé.

A.4 Identify and describe how to be interviewed in an information-gathering interview

A.5 Explain how to conduct an interview.

We imagine that you won't be as unwise as the job applicant who put on his resumé that his availability for work was limited because Friday, Saturday, and Sunday were "drinking time" or the one who tried to explain away an arrest found during a background check by admitting, "We stole a pig, but it was a really small pig." Nonetheless, you can still benefit from reading tips, strategies, and suggestions for polishing your interviewing skills.[1]

An **interview** is a form of oral interaction structured to achieve a goal; it often involves just two people who take turns speaking and listening, but it can include more than two people. An effective interview is not a random conversation; rather, the person conducting the interview has carefully framed the objectives of the interview and developed a structured plan for achieving the objectives. The person being interviewed should also prepare by considering the kinds of questions he or she may be asked and being ready to give appropriate responses.

In this introduction to interviewing, we'll discuss communication strategies that can enhance your job interview skills and offer tips about how to participate in an information-gathering interview. We'll conclude the appendix by identifying strategies that can help you polish your talents if you are the person interviewing others.

Whether you are a recent high school graduate or have been in the workforce for several years and have come back to school to finish your degree and pursue a new career, the Communication Principles for a Lifetime that we've emphasized in this book can help you enhance your interviewing skills.

Types of Interviews

A.1 Define what an interview is, and identify five different kinds of interviews.

The planned or structured nature of the interview sets it apart from other communication situations, yet interviews sometimes include elements of interpersonal, group, and presentational communication. Interviews embody interpersonal communication in that there are two or more people participating in the interview who must establish a relationship. If the goal of the interview is to find a solution to a vexing problem, the interview may resemble elements of a group discussion in which a problem is defined and analyzed and solutions are generated, evaluated, and then implemented. Preparing for a job interview is like a public speaking situation; you focus on your audience (the interviewer), keep your purpose in mind as you research the company you're interviewing with, organize your ideas, and even rehearse your responses to questions you think you may be asked.

When people think of the term *interview,* what most commonly comes to mind is a job interview. Yet interviews can also be means of gathering information, sharing job performance feedback, solving problems, and persuading others. Even though we are focusing primarily on employment and information-gathering interviews, the strategies we present can help you with *any* interview situation.

Information-Gathering Interview

Information-gathering interviews, just as the name suggests, are designed to seek information from the person being interviewed. *Public-opinion polls* are one type of information-gathering interview. When you leave an organization, you may be asked to participate in an *exit interview,* an interview designed to assess why you are leaving the company. A reporter for a blog, newspaper, radio, or TV station interviews people to gather information for a story.

The people who are most skilled at conducting information-gathering interviews do their homework before the interview. They come prepared with specific questions and have already conducted background research. In addition to preparing questions,

interview
A form of oral interaction structured to achieve a goal; it involves two or more people who take turns speaking and listening.

information-gathering interview
An interview, such as an opinion poll, whose purpose is to seek information from another person.

a skilled information-gathering interviewer listens and develops questions that stem from the information that is shared during the interview.

Appraisal Interview

An **appraisal interview**, sometimes called a performance review, occurs when a supervisor or employer shares information with you about your job performance. Such an interview enables you to see how others perceive your effectiveness and helps you determine whether you are likely to get a promotion or a layoff. During an appraisal interview, you can typically express your observations about the organization and your goals for the future. Usually, a supervisor prepares a written report summarizing your strengths and weaknesses and then meets with you to review it.

When you are receiving feedback from a supervisor, the best approach is to listen and gather as much information about the supervisor's perceptions as possible. In an evaluation situation, especially if the feedback is negative, it is easy to become defensive. Instead, you should try to manage your emotions and use the information to your benefit. If you disagree with your supervisor's evaluation, consider using the conflict management skills we discussed in Chapter 8. In addition, provide specific examples to support your position. Just saying that you don't like the review is likely to do more harm than good.

Problem-Solving Interview

A **problem-solving interview** is designed to resolve a problem that affects one or both parties involved in the interview. A disciplinary interview to consider corrective action toward an employee or students is one type of problem-solving interview. Grievance interviews are also problem-solving interviews; one person brings a grievance or complaint against another person, and solutions are sought to resolve the problem or conflict.

The strategies presented in Chapter 10 for structuring a problem-solving group discussion can also help you organize a problem-solving interview. Before seeking to solve or manage a problem, first define the issues; then analyze the causes, history, and symptoms of the problem. Rather than focusing on only one solution, brainstorm several possible solutions, and then evaluate the pros and the cons of the potential solutions before settling on a single solution.

appraisal interview
An interview during which a supervisor or employer shares information with an employee about his or her job performance.

problem-solving interview
An interview, such as a grievance or disciplinary interview, that is designed to solve a problem.

persuasion interview
An interview that attempts to change or reinforce attitudes, beliefs, values, or behavior, such as a sales interview.

job interview
A focused, structured conversation whose goal is to assess a person's credentials and skills for employment.

Persuasion Interview

During a **persuasion interview**, one person seeks to change or reinforce the attitudes, beliefs, values, or behavior of one or more other people. The sales interview is a classic example of an interview in which the goal is to persuade. A political campaign interview is another example of a persuasion interview.

Our discussion in Chapter 15 of the principles and strategies of persuading others can help you prepare for a persuasion interview. The advantage of trying to persuade someone during an interview rather than in a speech is the size of the audience; during a persuasive interview, you may have an audience of one. It is especially important to analyze and adapt to your listener when seeking to persuade.

Job Interview

A **job interview** is a focused, structured conversation whose goal is to assess a person's credentials and skills for employment. The job interview may involve elements of each of the types of interviews we've already discussed. Information is both gathered and shared, and a job interview will certainly solve a problem if you're the one looking for a job and you are hired. Elements of persuasion are also involved in a job interview. If you are seeking a job, you're trying to persuade the interviewer to hire you; if you are the interviewer and you're interviewing an exceptionally talented person, your job is to persuade the interviewee to join your organization.

Regardless of the purpose or format of the interview, the five Communication Principles for a Lifetime that we've used to organize our discussion of interpersonal, group and team, and presentational communication situations will serve you well when you participate in an interview. Whether you are the interviewer or the interviewee, it is important to be aware of how you are coming across to others. Using and interpreting verbal and nonverbal messages are critical to having a successful interview. In our definition of an interview, we noted that all individuals involved both talk and listen. Adapting to others is also essential. Effective interview participants listen, respond, and speak extemporaneously rather than delivering overly scripted, planned messages.

Phases of an Interview

A.2 Describe the three phases of a well-structured interview.

Just as a speech or term paper has a beginning, a middle, and an end, so does a well-structured interview. No matter what type, most interviews have three phases:

1. *The opening.* The interviewer puts the interviewee at ease and presents an overview of the interview agenda.
2. *The body.* During the longest part of an interview, the interviewer asks questions, and the interviewee listens and responds. The interviewee may also ask questions.
3. *The conclusion.* The interviewer summarizes what will happen next and usually gives the interviewee an opportunity to ask any final questions.

It is the responsibility of the interviewer, the person leading the interview, to develop a structure for the interview. But it's also helpful for the interviewee to understand the overall structure in advance to know what to expect both before and during the interview. So whether you're the interviewer or the interviewee, understanding the interview structure we discuss should be of value to you.

The Opening

The opening of any interview is crucial because it creates a climate for positive and open communication. When interviewing someone, you should strive to establish rapport and to clarify the goals of the interview.

To establish rapport, start the conversation with something that will put the interviewee at ease. The discussion could be about something as simple as the weather, recent events both of you attended, or other light topics. Make direct eye contact, smile appropriately, and offer a firm handshake to establish a warm atmosphere.

Besides making the interviewee comfortable, the interviewer should clarify the goals of the interview by explicitly stating the general purpose for the meeting. After the opening conversation, it may be helpful to provide a general overview of the nature and purpose of the interview and an estimate of how long the interview will last. Clarifying a meeting's purpose helps both parties get their bearings and check their understanding. A good interviewer makes sure that everyone is on the same wavelength before the actual questioning begins.

Both the interviewer and the interviewee should arrive a few minutes ahead of the scheduled hour of the interview. Be prepared, however, to wait patiently if necessary. If you are the interviewer and have decided to use a recording device, set it up. You may keep it out of sight once the interviewee has seen it, but *never* try to hide the fact that you are recording the interview—such a ploy is unethical and illegal. If you are going to take written notes, get out your paper and pen. Now you are ready to begin asking your prepared questions.

The Body: Asking Questions

Once the interviewee has been put at ease during the opening of the interview, the bulk of the interview will consist of the interviewer asking the interviewee questions. Even though both parties listen and speak, the interviewer has the primary responsibility for questioning. If the interviewer has done a good job of identifying and clarifying his or her objectives and gathering information, the key questions to be asked are usually fairly obvious.

QUESTION TYPES Interview questions fall into one of four categories: open, closed, probing, or hypothetical.[2] A typical interview usually includes some of each type.

Open Questions **Open questions** are broad and unstructured questions that allow interviewees considerable freedom to determine the amount and kind of information they will provide. Because they encourage the interviewee to share information almost without restriction, open questions are useful in determining opinions, values, and perspective. Such questions as "What are your long- and short-term career goals?" "Why do you seek employment here?" and "How do you feel about gun control?" prompt personal and wide-ranging responses.

Closed Questions **Closed questions** limit the range of possible responses. They may ask for a simple yes or no—"Do you enjoy working in teams?"—or they may allow interviewees to select responses from a number of specific alternatives: "How often do you go to the movies? (1) Less than once a month, (2) Once a month, (3) Twice a month, (4) Once a week." Closed questions enable the interviewer to gather specific information by restricting interviewees' freedom to express personal views or elaborate on responses. Closed questions are most often used when an interviewer is trying to obtain a maximum amount of information in a short period of time.

Probing Questions **Probing questions** encourage interviewees to clarify or elaborate on partial or superficial responses. Through the use of these questions, interviewers attempt to clarify or direct responses. Such questions as "Could you elaborate on your coursework in the area of communication?" "Do you mean to say that you already own three vacuum cleaners?" and "Will you tell me more about your relationship with your supervisor?" call for further information in a particular area. Often spontaneous, probing questions follow up on the key questions that interviewers have prepared in advance.

Hypothetical Questions Interviewers use **hypothetical questions** when they describe a set of conditions and ask interviewees what they would do if they were in that situation. Such questions are generally used either to gauge reactions to emotion-arousing or value-laden circumstances or to reveal on interviewee's likely responses to real situations. A police officer might ask an eyewitness to a murder, "What if I told you that the man you identified as the murderer in the line-up was the mayor?" During an exit interview, a personnel manager might ask, "If we promoted you to chief sanitary engineer and paid you $4 an hour more, would you consider staying with Bob's Landfill and Television Repair?"

open question
A question that is broad and unstructured and that allows the respondent considerable freedom to determine the amount and kind of information provided.

closed question
A question that limits the range of possible responses and requires a simple, direct, and brief answer.

probing question
A question that encourages the interviewee to clarify or elaborate on partial or superficial responses and that usually takes the discussion in a desired direction.

hypothetical question
A question used to gauge an interviewee's reaction to an emotion-arousing or value-laden situation or to reveal an interviewee's likely reactions to a real situation.

RECAP

Types of Interview Questions

	Uses	Example
Open Question	Prompts wide-ranging responses. Answers reveal interviewee's opinions, values, perspectives.	Tell me about your previous job duties. How would you describe your son's problems in school?
Closed Question	Requests simple yes or no response or forces interviewee to select a response from limited options.	Have you been skiing in the past month? Which one of the following drinks would you buy? a. Coke b. Pepsi c. 7-Up
Probing Question	Encourages clarification of or elaboration on previous responses. Leads response in a specific direction.	Would you tell me more about the pain in your side? We've talked about your mother. Can you describe how you felt about your father's long absences from home when you were a child?
Hypothetical Question	Gauges reactions to emotional or value-laden situations. Elicits response to a real or imaginary situation.	How would you support your opponent if she were elected chair of the board? What would you do if your secretary lost an important file?

Figure A.1 The Funnel Sequence

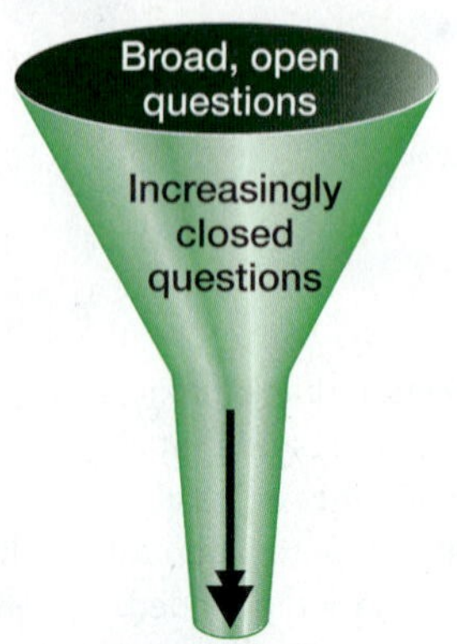

Getting at specific pieces of information through use of direct questioning

QUESTIONING SEQUENCES Open, closed, probing, and hypothetical questions may be used in any combination, as long as their sequence is thoughtfully planned. Depending on the purpose, these questions may be arranged into three basic sequences: funnel, inverted funnel, and tunnel.

The Funnel Sequence As Figure A.1 shows, the **funnel sequence** begins with broad, open questions and proceeds to more closed questions. The advantage of this format is that it allows an interviewee to express views and feelings without restriction, at least early in an interview. For example, it may be more useful to begin a grievance interview with the question "How would you describe your relationship with your supervisor?" than with "What makes you think that your supervisor treats you like an idiot?" The first question allows the free expression of feelings, whereas the second clearly reflects an interviewer's bias, immediately forcing the discussion in a negative direction. The following series of questions provides an example of a funnel sequence that might be used for an information-gathering interview.

1. Why do you find communication interesting?
2. What area of communication are you primarily interested in?
3. How long have you studied interpersonal communication?
4. Why do you think interpersonal attraction theory is useful?
5. What would you do to test interpersonal attraction theory?

Notice that the questions start by asking for general information and then focus on more specific ideas.

funnel sequence
A questioning sequence that begins with broad, open questions and proceeds toward more closed questions.

inverted funnel sequence
A questioning sequence that begins with closed questions and proceeds to more open questions, intended to encourage an interviewee to respond easily early in the interview.

tunnel sequence
A way of structuring interview questions so that parallel open or closed questions (or a combination of open and closed questions) are asked to gather a large amount of information in a short amount of time; no probing questions are asked.

The Inverted Funnel Sequence The opposite of the funnel sequence is the **inverted funnel sequence**, shown in Figure A.2, which begins with closed questions and proceeds to more open questions. An interview designed to gather information about a worker's grievance might be based on the inverted funnel and might include the following series of questions:

1. Do you believe that your supervisor wants to fire you?
2. What makes you think that you'll be fired soon?
3. What do you think has caused this problem between you and your supervisor?
4. How has this problem affected your work?
5. How would you describe the general working climate in your department?

The relatively closed questions that begin the inverted funnel sequence are intended to encourage an interviewee to respond easily, because they require only brief answers (yes or no, short lists, and the like). As the sequence progresses, the questions become more open and thus require more elaborate answers and greater disclosure.

The inverted funnel sequence is appropriate when an interviewer wants to direct the interview along specific lines and encourage an interviewee to respond with short, easily composed answers. An interviewer can follow up with more general questions to provide increasingly broad information—the "big picture."

Figure A.2 The Inverted Funnel Sequence

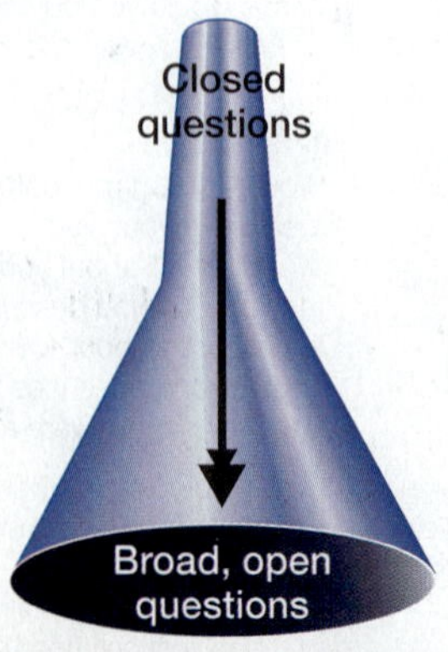

Building the "big picture" with repeated questioning, integrating previous responses

The Tunnel Sequence Finally, the **tunnel sequence** consists of a series of related open or closed questions or a combination of the two; the sequence is intended to gather a wide range of information. This sequence does not include probing questions; it goes into less depth than the other three sequences. An interviewer may use the tunnel sequence to gather information about attitudes and opinions without regard for the reasons behind an interviewee's answers or the intensity of the interviewee's feelings. The following is a typical tunnel sequence:

1. What are the three major issues in the presidential campaign this year?
2. Which candidate would you vote for if the election were held today?
3. For whom do you think you will vote in the race for U.S. senator?

4. Are you a registered voter in this state?
5. What do you think of the proposition to set up a nuclear waste dump in this state?

The tunnel sequence is most appropriate when an interviewer wants some general information on a variety of topics in a relatively short period of time.

Although these sequences have been discussed as if they were independent and easily distinguishable, good questioning strategy will probably combine one or more question sequences. The key to effective interviewing is to prepare a set of questions that will get the needed kinds and amount of information. An interviewer should remain flexible enough to add, subtract, and revise questions as a discussion proceeds. Such an approach ensures that the objectives of the interview will be accomplished.

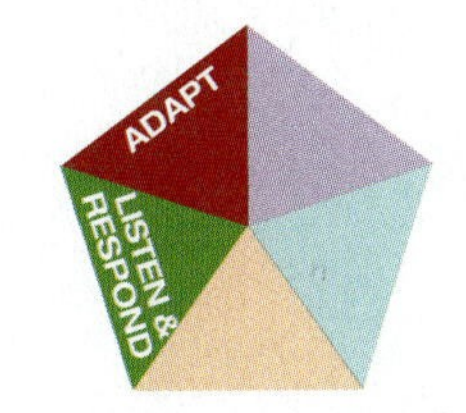

As you conduct the interview, use the questions you have prepared as a general guide but not a rigid schedule. If the person you are interviewing mentions an interesting angle you did not think of, don't be afraid to pursue the point. Listen carefully to the person's answers, and ask for clarification of any ideas you don't understand.

The Conclusion

Opinion polls, marketing surveys, and sales pitches often end rather abruptly with a "Thank you for taking the time to help me." Many other kinds of interviews require follow-up meetings or some form of future contact. For this reason, and for reasons of common courtesy, the conclusion of an interview is very important. Conclusions can summarize the interview and establish a basis for a continued relationship as well as bringing the meeting to a close.

SUMMARIZING A primary function of the conclusion is to summarize the proceedings. All parties should be aware of and agree on what happened during the meeting. To ensure understanding and agreement, an interviewer summarizes the highlights of the discussion, asking for and offering clarification if necessary.

CONTINUING THE RELATIONSHIP Another function of the conclusion is to encourage a continued, friendly relationship. The positive communication climate developed during the interview should be carried into the conclusion. The interviewer may need to establish interpersonal harmony if you asked questions that resulted in conflict or made the interviewee uncomfortable. Comments such as "I'm glad we had a chance to talk about this problem" or "Thank you for sharing and listening" enable both parties to feel that they have had a positive and productive encounter.

CLARIFYING EXPECTATIONS An interviewer can tell the interviewee when to expect further contact or action, if appropriate. A job applicant wants to know when to expect a phone call about a follow-up interview or a job offer. An expert, interviewed by a journalist, wants to know what will be done with his or her comments and when the story is likely to be published.

ENDING THE MEETING At the end of virtually any interview, good manners require both the interviewer and the interviewee to say, "Thank you." Because an interview is a mutual effort, both parties deserve recognition. One final suggestion: Do not prolong the interview beyond the time limits of your appointment.

RECAP

Organizing an Interview

Phase	Goals
Opening	Put the interviewee at ease. Review the purpose. Establish rapport. Provide an orientation.
Body	Use questions appropriate to the interview type and objective: • Use open questions to elicit wide-ranging responses. • Use closed questions to get specific responses. • Use probing questions to seek clarification or elaboration. • Use hypothetical questions to gauge a reaction to an imaginary situation. Design questioning sequences appropriate to the interview purpose: • Use the funnel sequence to elicit general comments first and specific information later. • Use the inverted funnel sequence to elicit specific information first and more general comments later. • Use the tunnel sequence to gather lots of information without probing too deeply.
Conclusion	Summarize the proceedings. Encourage friendly relations. Arrange further contact(s). Exchange thank-yous.

How to Be Interviewed for a Job

A.3 Identify and describe how to be interviewed for a job, including how to develop a well-worded resumé.

Woody Allen once said, "80 percent of success is showing up." We suggest that you do more than just show up for a job interview, however. Like giving an effective speech, having a successful job interview involves thoughtful preparation and careful planning. According to *CareerBuilder*, a popular website for job hunters, it takes an average of seventeen interviews to get one job offer.[3] To increase your odds of getting hired after an interview, we present research-based suggestions and strategies that can help you make your first impression your best impression when looking for employment.

Be Aware of Your Skills and Abilities

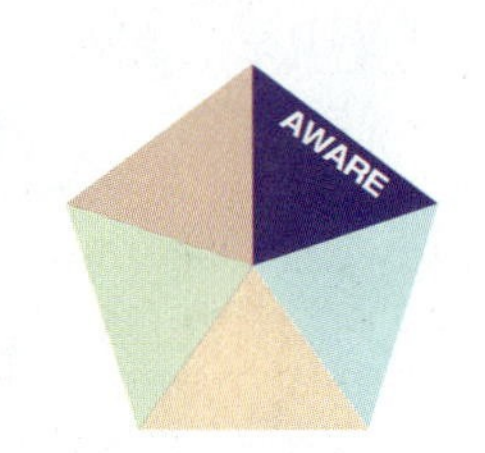

The first communication principle we introduced in this book is to be aware of your communication. Before you interview for a job, it is important to be aware not only of your communication as you interact with others, but also of your unique skills, talents, and abilities. Many people select a career because they think that they might like to *be* a lawyer, doctor, or teacher. But rather than thinking about what you want to be, we suggest considering what you like to *do*. Ask yourself these questions:

- What do I like to do in my free time?
- What are my best skills and talents?
- What education and training do I have?
- What experiences or previous jobs have I had?

In addition to answering these questions, write down responses to complete this statement: "I can . . . ." For example, you might respond, "I can cook, write, relate well to others." List as many answers as possible. Here's another statement to complete: "I have . . . ." You might answer, "I have traveled, worked on a farm, sold magazine subscriptions." Responding to the "I can" and "I have" statements will help you develop an awareness of your skills and experiences that will help you respond readily when you are asked about them during the interview. Reflecting on your interests can help you decide which career will best suit your talents; you will also be able to develop a resumé that reflects your best abilities.

Prepare Your Resumé

A **resumé** is a written, concise, well-organized description of your qualifications for a job. A resumé is essentially your professional story. And like a story, it has a main character (you), the story background (your credentials), and a plot (your professional work history). How long should a resumé be? Many employers don't expect a resumé to be longer than two printed pages; some will look only at a one-page resumé. (Resumés of experienced career professionals may be longer than two pages, however.)

Although your resumé is important in helping you land a job, its key function is to help you get an interview. How you perform in the interview is what will determine whether you get the job. Employers rarely hire someone only on the basis of on a resumé. Most employers spend less than a minute—and some only a few seconds—looking at each resumé, and as we describe in Communication & Technology, many resumés are never even read by a human being. Therefore, your resumé should be clear and easy to read and should focus on the essential information an employer seeks.

Most employers will be looking for standard information on your resumé. (Study the sample resumé that appears in this appendix.[4]) Be sure to include the following information on your resumé:

resumé
A written, concise, well-organized description of a person's qualifications for a job.

Communication & TECHNOLOGY

Maybe You Should Stop Fussing with the Formatting

Most resumés are sent electronically today, so it's important to use techniques to make sure your resumé is accurately transmitted and, once it gets to the employer, stands out in the e-crowd. Career-search expert Katherine Hansen has offered several useful tips for submitting your resumé online:[5]

- *Use your words—and theirs.* Many resumés are first "read" by a computer software program that scans your resumé for keywords, words that are mentioned in the job posting or are used frequently in your career field. To avoid having your resumé screened out or never even reach a human being, make liberal use of appropriate keywords as well as specific action verbs. As you word your resumé, remember the importance of staying truthful.
- *Keep it plain and simple.* Text formatting, such as boldfaced text, larger fonts in headings, or lines to divide sections, helps people find key information in your resumé more quickly. However, that same formatting can create problems when you submit your resumé electronically. Many larger employers have online applications that require you to paste your resumé into a blank area in a form, for example. You may also decide to paste all or part of your resumé in an e-mail submitted in response to a job board posting. For these purposes, you need a plain-text resumé, with no formatting.[6]
- *Be (a little) creative with plain text.* You can use bullets, asterisks (*), lower-case letter o's (o), and carets (>) to format lists of accomplishments in a plain-text resumé. It's also possible to create lines or boxes using text characters such as equal signs (======), plus signs (++++++), and tildes (~~~~~~~~), but don't overdo it.
- *Prepare to be published.* Smaller employers may not use electronic scanning, and larger employers who do use it may still print the resumés of those who make the "short list" of applicants. So in addition to your plain-text resumé, you may want to prepare a version of your resumé with formatting that looks good to the human eye as well as the electronic eye. You can submit your formatted resumé as an attachment to your e-mail or, often, upload it to an online application site. Numerous resumé guides available in books or on the Internet can provide formatting tips. No matter what format you choose, one task is essential: Before submitting your resumé to employers, review a printed copy yourself to spot and correct any errors that could cause you to be rejected.
- *Publish yourself.* In some career fields, employers expect you to establish your own website or social media profile where you provide your resumé in HTML format, along with a portfolio of work samples. Although the HTML format permits you to use more graphics, remember that unless you are a graphic designer, the purpose of any graphics should be to help tell your story simply and effectively, not to dazzle the reader with your graphic design talent.
- *Adapt.* Rather than preparing only one resumé and sending it to every job posting, follow our Communication Principle Five and customize your story for each audience. Appropriately adapt not only the content of your resumé but also the format to ensure that the resumé meets each prospective employer's requirements.

- *Personal information.* Employers will look for your name, address, phone numbers, e-mail address, and website address (if you have one). Provide phone numbers where you can be reached during both the day and the evening.
- *Career objective.* Many employers will want to see your career objective. Make it brief, clear, and focused. Customize your career objective for each different position you seek.
- *Education.* Include your major, your degree, your graduation date, and the institution you attended.
- *Experience.* Describe your relevant work experience, listing your most recent job first. Include the names of employers, dates when you worked, and a very brief description of your duties.
- *Honors and special accomplishments.* List any awards, honors, offices held, or other leadership responsibilities.
- *Optional information.* If you have volunteer experience, have traveled, or have computer skills or other pertinent experience, be sure to include it if it is relevant to your objective and the job.
- *References.* List the names, phone numbers, and e-mail addresses of people who can speak positively about your skills and abilities. Or you may indicate that your references are available on request.

Sample Resumé

MARIA SANCHEZ
3124 West Sixth Street
San Marcos, TX 78666
(512) 555-0102
(512) 555-0010
mariasanchez@emailprovider.com

PROFESSIONAL OBJECTIVE: Seeking a position in human resources as a training specialist.

EDUCATION:
Bachelor of Arts Degree
Major: Communication Studies
Minor: English
Texas State University
Graduation Date: May 20XX

PROFESSIONAL EXPERIENCE:

20XX–Present, Intern, GSD&M, Austin, Texas

- Assisted in creating a leadership training program
- Designed flyers and display ads using desktop publishing software
- Made cold calls to prospective clients

20XX–August 20XX, Intern, Target Market, Houston, Texas

- Developed sales training seminar
- Coordinated initial plan for writing advertising copy for Crest Inc.'s advertising campaign

20XX–20XX, Supervisor, S&B Associates, San Marcos, Texas

- Supervised three employees editing training materials

20XX–20XX, Advertising Sales and Reporter, *University Star*, San Marcos, Texas

- Sold ads for university paper and worked as social events reporter

OTHER EXPERIENCE:
20XX–20XX, Summer job at Target, San Marcos, Texas
20XX–20XX, Summer job at YMCA, Austin, Texas

SKILLS: Team Leadership, Photography, Computer Proficiency, Research and Analysis, Public Speaking, Customer Service

ACCOMPLISHMENTS & HONORS: Paid for majority of my college education while maintaining a 3.5 grade point average, Presidential Scholarship, Vice President of Texas State University Communication Club, Editor/Historian of MortarBoard, John Marshall High School Vice President of Junior Class, Yearbook Coordinator

PROFESSIONAL ORGANIZATIONS: Lambda Pi Eta, American Society for Training and Development, Communication Club, National Communication Association

INTERESTS: Photography, tennis, softball, theater

REFERENCES: Available at your request

When developing your resumé, be sure to use specific action verbs to describe your experience. Also use these action words during your interview. Rather than using a general verb such as "I *worked* on a project," use more descriptive action words that clarify the role you assumed. Consider using some of the following words when listing or describing your activities or accomplishments:

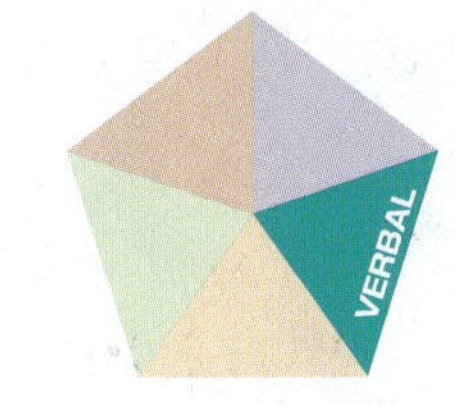

accelerated
accepted
accomplished
achieved
adapted
administered
analyzed
approved
built
completed
conceived
conducted
controlled
coordinated
created
delegated
demonstrated
designed
developed
directed
effected
eliminated
evaluated
expanded
expedited
facilitated
found
generated
guided
improved
increased
initiated
instructed
interpreted
maintained
managed
mastered
motivated
negotiated
operated
organized
originated
participated
planned
promoted
proposed
provided
recommended
reduced
researched
resulted in
reviewed
revised
selected
solved
stimulated
structured
supervised
tested
trained
translated
traveled
updated
utilized
won

Identify the Needs of Your Potential Employer

After you have analyzed your skills and abilities and have prepared a well-crafted resumé, you need to anticipate the needs and goals of your potential employer. A good interviewee adapts his or her message to the interviewer.

How do you find information about an organization that will help you adapt your message to fit its needs? In a word: research. Gather as much information as you can about not only the person who will interview you but also the needs and goals of the organization or company where you seek a job.

Explore information about the organization available on the Internet. As a starting point, virtually every organization these days has a web presence. Do more than just look at the organization's home page; click on the various links that help you learn about what the organization does.

Look and Communicate Your Best

The opportunity to assess your appearance and the way in which you express yourself nonverbally is one of the most important reasons an interviewer wants to meet you face to face.

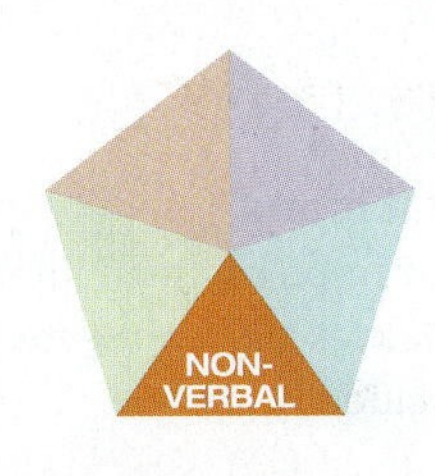

DRESS FOR SUCCESS As we discussed in Chapter 4, don't forget about the power of nonverbal messages in making a good impression. Dressing for success is

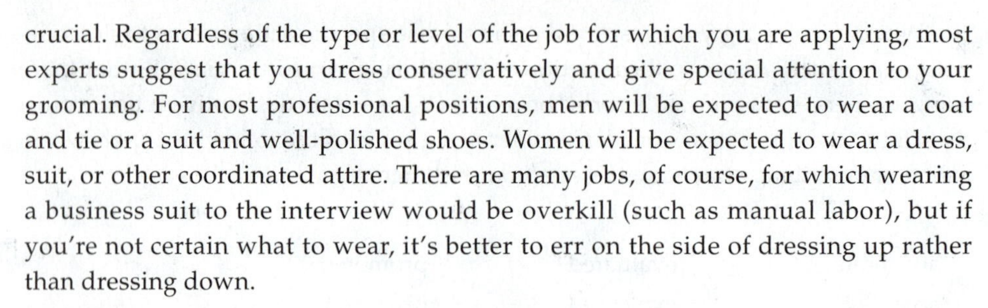

crucial. Regardless of the type or level of the job for which you are applying, most experts suggest that you dress conservatively and give special attention to your grooming. For most professional positions, men will be expected to wear a coat and tie or a suit and well-polished shoes. Women will be expected to wear a dress, suit, or other coordinated attire. There are many jobs, of course, for which wearing a business suit to the interview would be overkill (such as manual labor), but if you're not certain what to wear, it's better to err on the side of dressing up rather than dressing down.

COMMUNICATE YOUR BEST What determines whether you are hired for the job? In short, it's the way you communicate. By the time you get to an interview, your interviewer has already determined that you have at least the minimum qualifications for the job. Your ability to apply the Communication Principles for a Lifetime that we've reiterated throughout the book is key to making a good impression on your interviewer. In Chapter 1, when we discussed why it's important to learn about communication, we noted the key factors that employers look for in a job applicant, and the top three factors focus on your communication skill.[7] Your ability to listen, respond, and relate to your interviewer is one of the best predictors of whether you will be hired for a job. Among the areas an interviewer is trying to assess by observing your behavior are the following:

- *Self-expression.* Are you clear or are you vague when you respond to questions? Do you make effective eye contact? Do you talk too much or too little?
- *Maturity.* Are you likely to make good judgments and effective decisions?
- *Personality.* What's your overall style of relating to people? Are you outgoing, shy, quiet, overbearing, enthusiastic, warm, friendly?
- *Experience.* Can you do the job? Do you have a track record that suggests you can effectively do what needs to be done?
- *Enthusiasm.* Do you seem interested in this job and the organization? Do you seem to be genuine and authentic, or is your enthusiasm phony?
- *Goals.* Where are you heading in life? Are your short-term and long-term goals compatible with the needs of the organization?

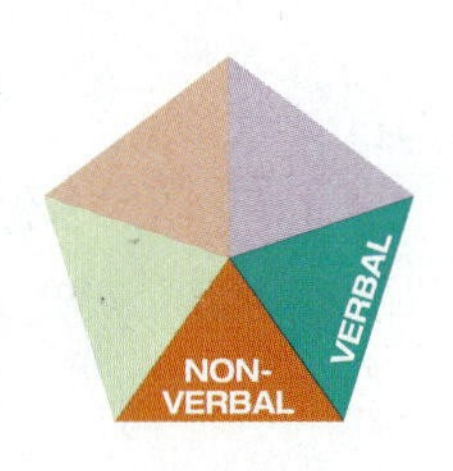

Marketing experts know the importance of developing a brand name (such as Coke, Kleenex, or Starbucks) to make a product memorable and distinctive. A **personal brand** works the same way. Your personal brand is the clear impression you leave when the interview has concluded. As career counselor Delores Dean notes, "The goal in branding is to leave behind an impression of you that will be remembered. You must stand out above the rest and be the best."[8] How do you develop yourself as a memorable brand? One way is to use both nonverbal and verbal messages effectively. Nonverbally, you can make sure that you are remembered through your appearance. Pay special attention to what you wear and how you interact nonverbally with the interviewer to leave a positive impression. Verbally, if you project a positive attitude when you speak, you can leave a lasting, positive impression. A memorable, appropriate, and well-told brief story in response to a question can also help you be remembered. The goal of the interview is not only to *make* a positive impression, but also to *leave* a positive impression that will be remembered when the interviewer sifts through the notes and memories of multiple interviews.

Polish Your Online Appearance

personal brand
The clear impression an interviewee leaves when the interview has concluded.

Journalist Andy Simmons noted, "Every American has, at some point, appeared naked, drunk, unconscious, rude, crude or felonious online. Okay, maybe not everyone, but surf the Net and that's the impression you'll get."[9] Simmons's point is that it's important to make sure your online impression is as presentable as your live-and-in-person appearance. If you have a Facebook or other social media profile, make sure that it contains no embarrassing photos or quotes that might damage your reputation, because employers are surfing the web to see whether applicants are as credible as their resumés or personal impressions suggest. According to *CareerBuilder*, when employers checked the facts on people's resumés by using the power of the Internet, here's what they found:

- 31 percent had lied about their qualifications.
- 24 percent had some link to criminal behavior.
- 19 percent had made negative comments about a past employer.
- 19 percent had bragged about drinking or using illegal drugs.
- 15 percent had shared confidential information about their former employers.
- 11 percent had posted unflattering or sexually explicit photos.
- 8 percent had used an obscene or unprofessional online screen name.

Monster.com reported that among the most common lies on a resumé include education, employment dates, job titles and technical skills.[10] Although you may think no one will check or know if you fudge on resumé information, it's easy for employers to double-check the accuracy of your resumé. Career counselor Liz Ryan cautioned, "People think that they can make up and embellish details about companies that have been sold or gone out of business. But LinkedIn, Facebook and our wide-ranging networks will put a quick stop to most efforts to change history in our favor."[11]

So always be truthful, and monitor your online presence. Don't think that no one will find out about something that you have fabricated on your resumé or a "friend" of yours has posted about you online. Increasingly, employers are using social networks such as Facebook to see whether your cyberpersonality is consistent with the well-scrubbed, polished appearance you presented in your interview and on your resumé.

Monitor the privacy settings for your Facebook and other social media accounts to make sure that only people you authorize can review any personal information. Better yet, purge your social network files of anything that is unflattering or embarrassing. What's to prevent someone who does have access to your information from sharing it with a wider audience? Keep a close eye on what is posted on the Internet about you. Also, make sure that the people who do have access to your e-pages don't post unflattering comments about your socializing habits. When you are in job-hunting mode, search for your name through Google or another search engine frequently to make sure that nothing negative about you is showing up online. By signing up for Google Alert, you'll find out when your name pops up on the Internet. One final tip: Avoid what you and your friends may think are cute or funny screen names, such as Imlazyandbored or hottotrot; a prospective employer is not likely to be amused and is not likely to hire you.

"We were ready to hire you until we saw the photo of you on Facebook sliding on the ice at Rockefeller Center wearing only bowling shoes and a viking helmet."

Listen, Respond, and Ask Appropriate Questions

Because an interview is a structured, planned discussion, it is important to demonstrate effective listening and responding skills. Stay focused on what your interviewer is asking you.

Remember to stop, look, and listen for both the details of the questions and the major points of the questions.

When you respond to questions, you should project genuine enthusiasm and competence. Don't put on an act: Be yourself while being professional. Be friendly and pleasant without being overly effusive or giddy. Communication researcher Mary Minto found that how you respond to an interviewer's questions could be even more important than what you say.[12] Your tone of voice, use of pauses and gestures, and posture are vital in expressing your personality and overall mood. Talking rapidly and nonstop without periodically pausing, for example, communicates that you are not sensitive to others.

One of the best ways to prepare for an interview is to anticipate the interviewer's questions. Table A.1 lists typical questions that may be asked during an interview.[13] We don't recommend that you memorize "canned" or overly rehearsed answers, but it may help to think about possible responses to these questions. Also be prepared to answer questions about your unique experiences, such as military service, vocational training, or membership on sports teams.

It is important to be sure to get a good night's sleep before the interview and to eat sensibly (don't skip breakfast; don't stuff yourself at lunch) so that you can stay alert. Long interviews can be physically demanding.

Consider the interview an opportunity to ask questions as well as to answer them; toward the end of an interview, most interviewers will give you an opportunity to ask whatever questions you'd like. Asking questions about an organization is a way to display enthusiasm for the job as well as a means of assessing whether you really want to join the organization. You will want to know the following:

- Will there be any job training for this position?
- What are the opportunities for advancement?
- What is the atmosphere like in the workplace? (You will also be able to observe the workplace during the interview.)
- What hours do people work?
- Is there flexibility in scheduling the work day?
- When do you anticipate making a decision about this position?

The very first question you ask should *not* be "How much does this job pay?" Usually, the interviewer will discuss salary and benefits with you during the interview. If it is a preliminary interview and there is a chance that you will be called back for another interview, you may want to defer questions about salary and benefits until you know that the organization is seriously considering you for the position.

During the interview, maintain eye contact and speak assertively. The goal in an interview is to project a positive attitude to the interviewer. As motivational speaker Zig Ziglar once noted, "Your attitude, not your aptitude, will determine your altitude."

Follow Up after the Interview

After the interview, it is wise to write a brief letter or e-mail to thank the interviewer and to provide any additional information that may have been requested. You may also want to send a thank-you note to others in the organization, such as a secretary or administrative assistant, for helping you arrange the interview. If the interviewer asked for references, make sure to let your reference providers know as soon as possible that they may be contacted. If you are asking them to send letters of recommendation to the organization, expedite the process by providing addressed, stamped envelopes or the appropriate e-mail addresses and a copy of your resumé so that they can personalize their letters with specific information.

Is it appropriate to call the person who interviewed you to ask when a decision will be made about hiring someone? Some employers abide by the philosophy "Don't call us, we'll call you," but many others would interpret your call as a sign of your

Table A.1 Typical Questions Asked during Job Interviews

I. Education

1. Why did you select your major area of study?
2. Why did you select your college/university?
3. If you were starting college again, what would you do differently? Why?
4. What subjects were most and least interesting? Useful? Why?
5. Other than the courses you studied, what is the most important thing you learned from your college experience?
6. How did you finance your college education?

II. Experience

7. What do you see as your strengths as an employee?
8. You say that a strength you have is _____. Give me some indication, perhaps an example, that illustrates this strength.
9. What special skills would you bring to this position?
10. Describe your last few work experiences. Why did you leave each one?
11. What were the best and worst aspects of your last job?
12. What were some of your achievements and disappointments in your last job?
13. Do you see yourself as a leader/manager of people? Why?
14. What kinds of work situations would you like to avoid? Why?
15. What frustrations have you encountered in your work experience? How have you handled these frustrations?
16. What do you look for in a boss?
17. Most employees and bosses have some disagreements. What are some things that you and your boss have disagreed about?

III. Position and Company

18. Why did you select this company?
19. Why did you decide to apply for this particular position?
20. How do you see yourself being qualified for this position?
21. Are you willing to relocate?

IV. Self-Evaluation

22. Tell me a little bit about yourself. Describe yourself.
23. What do you see as your personal strengths? Talents? How do you know that you possess these? Give examples of each.
24. What do you see as your weak points? Areas for improvement? Things you have difficulty doing? What have you done to deal with these weak areas?
25. Describe a specific work problem you had. Tell what you did to solve this problem.
26. What do you consider to be your greatest work achievement? Why?

V. Goals

27. Where do you see yourself being in your profession in five years? In ten years? How did you establish these goals? What will you need to do to achieve these goals?
28. What are your salary expectations for this position? Starting salary? Salary in five years?

interest in the position and a testament to your ability to follow through. You may want to take the direct approach and simply ask the interviewer toward the end of the interview, "Would it be all right if I called you in a few days to find out if you have made a decision or if you need additional information?" If the interviewer tells you that a decision will be made by a certain date and then that date passes by, it is probably okay to call and find out whether the job has been offered to someone else and to express your continued interest in the position if it hasn't been filled.

How to Be Interviewed in an Information-Gathering Interview

A.4 Identify and describe how to be interviewed in an information-gathering interview.

The bulk of the responsibility for an effective information-gathering interview falls on the person who is doing the interviewing. If you are the interviewer in an information-gathering interview, review the suggestions we offer in this appendix for structuring the interview. Most information-gathering interviews follow this general structure.

If you are the person being interviewed, however, your primary responsibilities are to be prepared, to listen carefully, and to respond appropriately to questions. In addition, a good interviewee knows what to expect in an information-gathering interview. You should prepare responses to anticipated questions, pay close attention to requests for specific information, and answer questions directly and accurately.

Prepare for the Interview

In most cases, interviewees have some advance knowledge of the purpose and objective of interviews, especially if someone is seeking specific information or advice. You can therefore anticipate probable topics of discussion. If you are uncertain what the interview is about, it is appropriate to ask the person who will interview you how best to prepare for the questions he or she plans to ask. Yes, sometimes news programs have an interviewer pop up in an office, thrust a microphone in an interviewee's face, and ask a pointed question. In most cases, however, NBC news anchor Brian Williams (or his equivalent) is not going to ambush you.

Depending on the nature of the interview, you might want to brush up on the facts you may be asked about. Jot down a few notes to remind you of names, dates, and places. In some cases, you may want to do some background reading on the topic of the interview.

Finally, think about not only what you will say in the interview but also how you will respond nonverbally. Be on time. Maintain an attitude of interest and attentiveness with eye contact, attentive body positions, alert facial expressions, and an appropriately firm handshake.

Listen Effectively

Interviewing situations require you to listen to determine the amount and depth of information desired. If your responses are to be appropriate and useful, you must know what is being requested. If questions are unclear, ask for clarification or elaboration. By doing so, you can respond more fully and relevantly.

Successful interviewees practice empathy. Interviewers are people, and interviewing situations are interpersonal encounters. Effective interviewees consider situations from interviewers' points of view, listen "between the lines" of what someone says to focus on underlying emotions, and watch for nonverbal cues. When interviewees listen to all facets of the communication, they can better adapt to the situation.

Respond Appropriately

Just as questioning is the primary responsibility of an interviewer, responding is the primary responsibility of an interviewee. Keep answers direct, honest, and appropriate in depth and relevance. For example, in response to the question "How would you describe the quality of your relationship with your family?" don't give a fifteen-minute speech about your problems with your ex-spouse, keeping the children in clothes, and finding dependable home care for your aging parents. To make sure that you give the best possible answer, listen carefully when a question is posed and, if necessary, take a few moments to think before you answer. A response that is well thought out, straightforward, and relevant will be much more appreciated than one that is hasty, evasive, and unrelated to the question.

Using language and vocabulary that are appropriate to the situation is also important. The use of too much slang or technical terminology in an attempt to impress an interviewer can easily backfire by distracting the interviewer or distorting communication. Direct and simple language promotes understanding.

Finally, be flexible and adapt to the needs of the interviewing situation. Some interviewers will ask questions to throw you off guard. If that happens to you, take a moment to think before you respond. Try to discover the reason for the question and respond to the best of your ability. Listen carefully for the content *and* intent of questions so that you provide the information requested, especially when the interviewer changes topics. Flexibility and adaptability depend on good listening, empathy, accurate reading and interpretation of nonverbal communication, and practice. Just remember: "Engage brain before opening mouth."

The Responsibilities of the Interviewer

A.5 Explain how to conduct an interview.

So far, we've emphasized how to behave when you are the person being interviewed. As you assume leadership positions in your profession and community, you will undoubtedly be called on to interview others. In addition to knowing how to structure the opening, body, and conclusion of an interview, which we discussed earlier, there are several other characteristics of effective interviewers, whether you are seeking a future employee or simply gathering information.

Be Aware of Biases and Prejudices

First and foremost, an interviewer must be aware of his or her own biases and prejudices. Each person has a set of experiences, beliefs, attitudes, and values that influence how that person receives, interprets, and evaluates incoming stimuli. If accurate and useful information is to be shared in an interview, an interviewer must be aware of his or her own perceptual processes so as to make accurate and objective interpretations. An otherwise qualified candidate for a job shouldn't be eliminated from consideration just because the interviewer has a bias against red-haired people, for example.

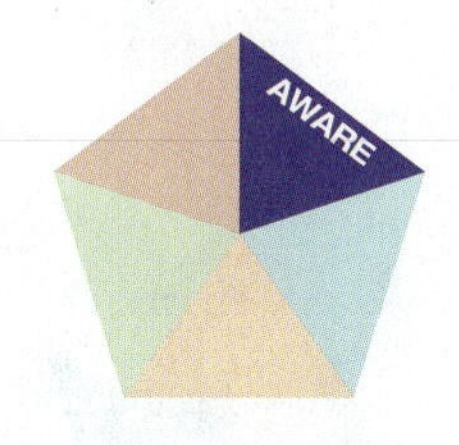

Adapt to an Interviewee's Behavior

Skilled interviewers observe, evaluate, and adapt to the communication behavior of their interviewees. Because no two interviews—and no two interviewees—are exactly alike, interviewers adapt their communication behavior accordingly. A flexible communication style is a necessity. Interviewers should have predetermined plans, but they should not be thrown off balance if an interviewee suddenly turns the tables and asks, "How much money do *you* make for *your* job?"

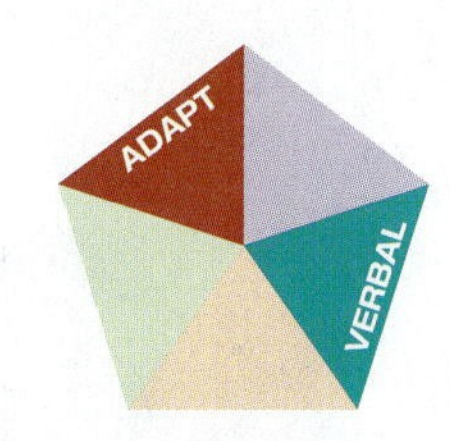

Adaptability also includes the use of appropriate language and vocabulary. You should consciously choose language and vocabulary that interviewees will understand. Little is gained by the use of technical, ambiguous, or vague terms. Words should be straightforward, simple, and specific but not so simple that interviewees feel "talked down" to. Empathy is important in determining the most appropriate language and vocabulary to use.

Deal Wisely with Sensitive Content

When planning questions for an interview, consider possible sensitive topics and topics to be avoided. A question in a grievance interview such as "Why were you fired from your last job?" will provoke a defensive reaction.

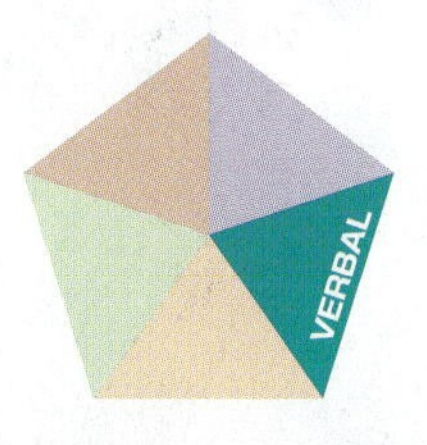

Good judgment and careful choice of words play crucial roles. One ill-chosen question can destroy the positive and open communication developed in an opening. Effective interviewers avoid potentially troublesome topics and attempt to put interviewees at ease. They discuss sensitive issues *if and only if* they are related to the purpose of the interviews. When a sensitive subject must be discussed, experienced interviewers choose their words carefully; for example, the question "Why were you fired?" might be rephrased as "How would you describe your relationship with your previous supervisor?"

Listen Effectively

The admonition to listen effectively has appeared frequently in this appendix. Effective listening is at the heart of any interview. No matter how well interviewers have prepared, the time will have been wasted if they are poor listeners. They need strong listening skills to make sure that they are receiving the kind and amount of information they need. They must be able to identify partial or irrelevant responses.

Highly developed listening skills also increase the ability to accurately perceive and interpret unintentional messages and beliefs, attitudes, and values. Interviewers learn a great deal from nonverbal as well as verbal communication.

Record Information

The information accumulated from an interview is useless if it is not recorded completely and accurately. A partial or inaccurate report can lead to poor decisions and mistaken actions. Take appropriate, legible, written notes. If you plan to record audio or video, ask the interviewee in advance for permission to do so.

Ask Appropriate Questions

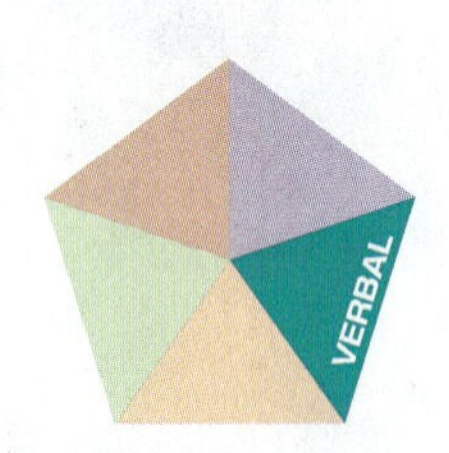

The success of most interviews will be determined by the quality of the questions asked during the conversation. Think of questions as "mental can openers" designed to reveal how the other person thinks and behaves. Earlier, we discussed question types (open, closed, probing, and hypothetical) and question sequences (funnel, inverted funnel, and tunnel). Some of your questions should be planned. Other questions may evolve from the discussion. The best questions during an interview emerge from simply listening to what the other person is saying and then probing or following up on information and ideas verbalized.

If you are interviewing a job applicant, be aware that there are certain questions that you should *not* ask. These questions are inappropriate because they ask for information that either laws or court interpretations of laws suggest could lead to illegal discrimination. Here's a list of topics you should not bring up during an employment interview when you're asking the questions:[14]

arrest records
less-than-honorable discharges
gender and marital status
maiden name
number of children
ages of children
number of preschool children
spouse's name
spouse's education
spouse's income
form of birth control
family plans
child care arrangements
car accidents
insurance claims
judgments
citizenship or national origin
mother's maiden name
place of birth
disabilities
handicap
illnesses or accidents
hospitalizations
current or prior medication/treatment
workers' compensation claims
weight
religion
church affiliation

- lawsuits
- legal complaints
- ownership of home
- rental status
- length of residence
- date of high school graduation
- age
- sexual orientation
- social organizations
- loans
- wage assignments or garnishments
- bankruptcy
- credit cards
- form of transportation
- ownership of car

STUDY GUIDE:
Review, Apply, and Assess Your Knowledge and Skill

Review Your Knowledge

Types of Interviews

A.1 Define what an interview is, and identify five different kinds of interviews.

An interview is a form of oral interaction that is structured to achieve a goal and that involves two or more people who take turns speaking and listening. We have identified five types of interview situations: the information-gathering interview, the appraisal interview, the problem-solving interview, the persuasion interview, and the job interview.

Phases of an Interview

A.2 Describe the three phases of a well-structured interview.

All interviews have an opening, in which the interviewee is put at ease; a body, during which questions are asked and answered; and a conclusion, which brings the interview to a comfortable close.

How to Be Interviewed for a Job

A.3 Identify and describe how to be interviewed for a job, including how to develop a well-worded resumé.

When you are seeking employment, start by becoming aware of your skills and abilities; then use your personal inventory to develop a well-written resumé. Focus on the needs of your prospective employer: Research the organization where you seek a job. During the interview, listen carefully to the questions asked by the interviewer and respond appropriately. After the interview, it may be appropriate to send a thank-you note to the interviewer.

How to Be Interviewed in an Information-Gathering Interview

A.4 Identify and describe how to be interviewed in an information-gathering interview

When you are preparing to be interviewed for an information-gathering interview, there are three primary tasks. First, prepare for the interview by reviewing information you think that the interviewer will ask you about. Second, listen closely to the questions you are being asked. Finally, respond appropriately by keeping answers direct and honest. Don't ramble. Observe the nonverbal responses of the interviewer to determine whether you are answering the questions appropriately.

Responsibilities of the Interviewer

A.5 Explain how to conduct an interview.

When you interview others, don't let your own biases and prejudices interfere with your job of listening and responding to the interviewee. Although it's useful to have a list of questions, be prepared to adapt to the interviewee's behavior. The best interviews have a spontaneous flow rather than a rigid structure. Don't ask illegal questions during a job interview, and handle sensitive questions with tact and diplomacy. Listening well is the hallmark of an effective interviewer. Develop a strategy to record the information you gather from the interview. Finally, the key to any interview is the quality of the questions asked. As the interviewer, you are responsible for asking clear, appropriate, and answerable questions.

Key Terms

The Principle Points

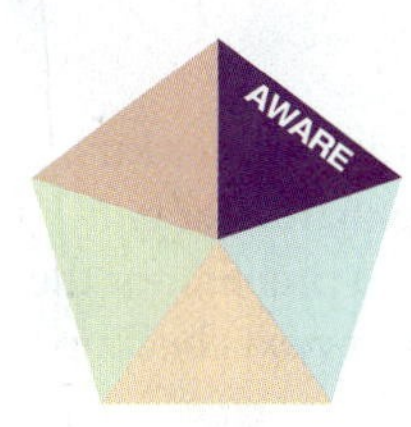

Principle One:

Be aware of your communication with yourself and others.

- Take inventory of your skills and abilities to help you determine the job opportunities and careers that are best for you.
- Use your analysis of your talents to help you develop your resumé.
- During an interview, monitor your messages to ensure that you are communicating clearly and effectively.

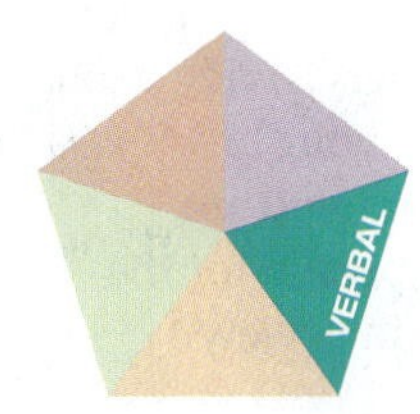

Principle Two:

Effectively use and interpret verbal messages.

- Speak clearly, and respond to each question you are asked during an interview.
- Use action-oriented words on your resumé and during an interview to describe your accomplishments.
- Organize your resumé to include key elements of your education, experience, and special qualifications.
- When conducting an employment interview, don't ask illegal or unethical questions.

Principle Three:

Effectively use and interpret nonverbal messages.

- Pay special attention to your appearance when you interview for a job; dress conservatively and appear neat and well groomed.
- Speak with confidence, use appropriate eye contact, and communicate interest and enthusiasm during the interview.
- When you interview someone, monitor your interviewee's nonverbal messages for clues about the individual's personality and ability to work with people.
- As an interviewer, observe, evaluate, and then appropriately adapt to the communication behavior of the interviewee.

Principle Four:

Listen and respond thoughtfully to others.

- When you are interviewed for a job, be sure to stop, look, and listen to the questions and comments of the interviewer.
- Listen for both the details of the message and the major points or key ideas.
- When interviewing others, consider listening among your most important tasks.

Principle Five:

Appropriately adapt messages to others.

- Learn as much as you can about any prospective employer so that you can describe how your abilities best fit with the needs of the organization to which you are applying.
- Appropriately adapt your communication behavior during an interview, whether you are the interviewer or the interviewee, on the basis of what you learn and observe during the interview.

Apply Your Skill

Consider the following questions. Write your answers and/or share them with your classmates:

1. It may seem as though most of the preparation for an appraisal interview is done by the supervisor, but what should an employee do to prepare before an appraisal interview?
2. Write a series of questions for a job interview for a social media blogger that follows either the funnel sequence or the inverted funnel sequence.
3. If you've been interviewed for a job, think back on the experience. On the basis of the information in this appendix, what did you do right in your interview? What could you have improved? If you've never been interviewed, what will the information in this chapter prevent you from doing wrong when you are?
4. A visit to your doctor or dentist for a regular checkup is, in part, an interview in which the practitioner gathers information from you. How can you prepare for the typical questions you'll be asked at your next checkup?
5. What are some ways you, as an interviewer, could adapt a planned list of questions to specific interviewees?
6. Imagine that you are an employer interviewing a job applicant. The applicant's answers to your first few questions have not impressed you, and you are growing fairly certain this is not the person for the job. How should you proceed in the interview?

Assess Your Skill

1. Resumé checklist. Before submitting your resumé to a prospective employer, use the following checklist to ensure that it meets the criteria of an effective resumé.

    ____ Name, address, and all contact numbers are accurate.
    ____ My career objective matches the advertised need of the employer.
    ____ My employment dates are accurate.
    ____ I've described the projects completed and skills I possess using action verbs and appropriate keywords.
    ____ My resumé is clearly formatted.
    ____ There are no spelling errors.
    ____ There are no grammar or punctuation errors.

2. Watch an information-gathering interview on *60 Minutes, Today, Good Morning America,* or another news or news magazine program. Identify the types of questions that the interviewer asks (open question, closed question, probing question, hypothetical question). On the basis of the information presented in this appendix, evaluate the effectiveness of both the interviewer and the interviewee.

Appendix B

Sample Speeches for Discussion and Evaluation

Informative Speech

The Ekocenter: Water Project or Corporation Cover-up?

Farrah Bara[1]

As a restaurant owner in Heidelberg, South Africa, Malehlohonolo Moleko has managed to cook herself an unconventional life, compared to other women in her town. She is a successful entrepreneur, has a college-educated son, and makes a killer beef stew. Moleko is a woman of many accomplishments, which is why, last August, she received the opportunity of a lifetime when the Coca-Cola Corporation asked her to run their first ever Ekocenter, a kiosk that provides food and clean water to villages.

The October 8, 2013, *International Business Times* explains that the Ekocenter is a 20-foot long shipping container that has been repurposed to provide electricity, Internet, refrigeration for vaccines, and bottles of Coca-Cola to the world's impoverished communities. Because when you and your family are dying of extreme poverty, clearly Coke is the solution you need.

But this is not your typical food truck. Instead the Ekocenter utilizes groundbreaking water and energy innovations to meet its consumers' needs. The September 30, 2013, *New York Times* adds that Coca-Cola hopes to place 1500 Ekocenters in twenty developing countries by the end of next year, meaning that in addition to providing resources to areas that desperately need them, the corporation is looking to market its product to the world's poorest regions for the first time.

The September 25, 2013, *Guardian* explains Coke is pioneering an "emotional innovation," gaining an advantage over other companies trying to operate in developing nations by offering the one product most do not—charity. Given that the *Guardian* of March 4, 2014, reports that 2.5 billion people—more than a third of the world's population—live without access to water or basic sanitation, let's gain a better understanding of this behemoth of a business model, by first, examining its economic developments; then, analyzing its focus on water; before finally, discussing some implications of the technology that the Coca-Cola Corporation calls a "downtown in a box" but critics have dubbed a glorified concession stand.

Coca-Cola and its partners from the Clinton Initiative first announced the Ekocenter at the 2013 Women in the World Conference. . . . The origin of the Ekocenter can be understood by examining its economic structure and interaction with local companies.

On a micro level, the September 24, 2013, *Financial Times* details that at the forefront of the Ekocenter are women, like Moleko, who are exclusively given the management roles. Hoping to empower five million female entrepreneurs, Coke is taking a leadership role in gender inequality. But the Middle Eastern Newspaper, *Zawya*, explains on February 23, 2014, that as much as the Ekocenter is a female-run charity, it is also a business opportunity. The Ekocenter provides money and training directly to women, creating a better economic environment, and a better economic environment in areas with Ekocenters means more Coca Cola sales.

But on a larger scale, Coca-Cola's Ekocenter changes the business dynamic for local economies. The September 25, 2013, *Drinks Business Review* explains that Coca-Cola is operating under the Golden Triangle Rule, by partnering with business, government, and non-profits. For example, The Clinton Initiative and the Inter-American Development Bank help fund the Ekocenter, IBM provides business consulting, DEKA supplies installation expertise, and UPS offers overpriced transportation. Coca-Cola is a multibillion-dollar corporation, with large-scale access to resources that make production efficient and the cost of owning an Ekocenter extremely cheap. The October 30, 2013, *Small Business Newswire* posits that as a result of widespread Ekocenters, local companies are being out-competed. For example, Malehlohonolo Moleko, whose Ekocenter has been thriving, watched her restaurant go out of business when she couldn't match the Ekocenter's prices.

As much as the Ekocenter is a business, most of Coca-Cola's focus is on water. To understand what makes the Ekocenter so different from other water aid programs, let's look at how the water is provided and then examine the reasoning behind Coca Cola's focus on water.

First, at the heart of the Ekocenter, and the resource most needed, is a water distiller. *Wired* explains on December 16, 2013, the Ekocenter uses a new kind of "vapor compression" system, a machine known as the Slingshot, which can turn any liquid into clean water. Dean Kamen—inventor of the Slingshot—explains that by boiling the liquid, collecting the water vapor, and recompressing vapor into water, the Slingshot can make water out of the most polluted liquids, which is how Kamen once shocked audiences by turning his own urine into water that he then drank. Additionally, the October 19, 2013, *World Industrial Reporter* notes that while purifying 300,000 liters of water a year, the hydropower also generated by the Slingshot fuels the electricity and refrigeration that the Ekocenter needs to run.

But interestingly, the innovative water structure and the pilot Ekocenter's location in Heidelberg was not an accident. A September 2013 press release by Coca Cola revealed that the location was less than a mile Coca-Cola's Valpre natural spring bottling plant—clearly an attempt by Coca-Cola to replenish the water it uses in production. The November 2014 publication of the book *Citizen Coke* illuminates how Coca-Cola may be the worst perpetrator when it comes to water shortages in third world countries, using an annual 79 billion gallons of water that it never replaces, dehydrating millions every day in countries like India, Guatemala, Mexico, and El Salvador. As much as the Ekocenter is a charity, the company hosting the Slingshot technology knows it has a bad rep when it comes to water pollution, meaning that Coca-Cola may be using the Ekocenter to conduct the largest self-admitted corporation cover-up of all time.

When CEO Muhtar Kent was asked whether the Ekocenter would allow for the sale of Pepsi, his response was, "What's the benefit of that?" In addition to not being able to say, "We're out of Coke, is Pepsi okay?" the Ekocenter brings us to two critical implications—a new form of imperialism and a growing global crisis.

Initially, the Ekocenter turns charity into imperialism. The Winter 2014 *Journal of Interdisciplinary History* explains that modern-day imperialism is humanitarian, not governmental. By controlling the aid that countries desperately need, the company is able to purchase control over the countries themselves. The Summer 2013 *Earth Island Journal* explains that Coca-Cola owns a technology—the Slingshot—that has the potential to save the world, unless the corporation actively chooses not to use it. The Ekocenter is in some ways a charitable act, but it also further establishes corporate imperialism.

On the flipside, the Ekocenter unveils problems in government responsiveness to water scarcity. The *Pakistan News International* of November 19, 2013, notes that the next ten years will be the most significant in determining global water policies, especially since 12 percent of the world's population consumes 85 percent of the world's fresh water. The subsequent shortages in developing countries have been so large that the *Gulf Daily News* of November 29, 2013, predicts that the next world war will be fought over water. But even then, the technology for Slingshot existed back in 2005 and was available to the United Nations, but the UN never financed it. Coca-Cola did, eight years later. In its most basic form, a corporation is motivated by a private endgame, but if the Ekocenter disappears, so too do all the health benefits it brings.

PepsiCo recently announced that they will construct the Mother Cellar Water Project, a series of water towers in Asia that also happen to be located near the site of one of their bottling plants. As much as companies have to compete with each other in a business realm, they also have to compete in philanthropy. After exploring the Ekocenter's economic and water focus and some implications, it remains unclear what the future holds for the Ekocenter. For now, it will provide water and food to those in need. But ultimately, the Ekocenter serves as a symbol of the divide between corporate interests and the needs of a community.

Persuasive Speech

The Epidemic of Sexual Assault on College Campuses

Brittany Shulman[2]

Jeanne Clery was raped and murdered in her Lehigh University dorm room when she was only 19 years old. After the conviction of Clery's attacker, her parents fought for groundbreaking legislation to protect students like Jeanne. In 1990, 14 years after Jeanne's death, George H.W. Bush finally signed the Jeanne Clery Act into law, requiring all colleges to keep a public crime log and issue safety warnings. And though the Jeanne Clery Act inspired future legislation, like the Victim's Bill of Rights and the Campus Sexual Violence Elimination Act, *The Chronicle of Higher Education* notes on May 23, 2013, that universities across the country are refusing to properly address rape on their campuses. From UC-Berkeley to Yale, colleges are ignoring legal requirements, belittling victims, and sweeping these crimes under the rug. In the first month of 2014 alone, the Department of Education's Office of Civil Rights received 16 complaints against universities violating the legislation put in place to protect students. *ThinkProgress* of September 24, 2013, suggests that anti-sexual assault legislation has been rendered useless by our universities because our administrations are more concerned with saving face than saving students.

A report from *Jezebel* of November 10, 2013, highlights the epidemic. One in four women and one in seven men will be raped during their time as an undergraduate. Because the threat of being sexually assaulted is heightened on the very campuses we all call home, it is crucial that we understand how university inaction is facilitating a culture of rape; next, examine the re-victimization that occurs as a result; before finally, crafting solutions—because I am the same age as Jeanne Clery. Discourse downplaying the severity of this issue is not conducive to a productive discussion. Forty years have passed since Jeanne Clery's brutal attack, yet I am no safer on my college campus than she was on hers.

UC-Berkeley junior Sofie Karasek was one of four women to report a serial rapist on her campus. After her formal complaint was ignored, the *Huffington Post* reported on February 26, 2014, a university official told her that it's better to keep the rapist on campus because if he assaults someone else, his friends can help him realize his wrongdoing. Our universities prioritize their own public image over justice for rape victims in two ways: by using autonomy to ignore legal obligation, and victim blaming.

First, colleges have utilized their ability to self-govern as a PR method. In the latest examination of the collegiate judicial system, *Time* of November 2011 found that most universities are solely responsible for enforcing legislation. But, as Landen Gambill was shocked to discover, justice for survivors of rape at institutions with judicial autonomy is not always top priority. *Think Progress* of July 8th, 2013, notes that when Gambill sought legal recourse outside The University of North Carolina at Chapel Hill, where officials found her rapist not guilty, UNC retaliated by threatening her with expulsion. By choosing not to refer cases involving rape to legitimate outlets, universities maintain their ability to act as the sole arbiter of the cases' outcome, ensuring that, if necessary, the interest of the institution is prioritized over justice for the survivor.

Second, there is a bias that insists rape is the fault of the victim or a figment of the imagination. Salon.com noted on August 16, 2013, that colleges have historically avoided using terminology like "rape," lessening the perceived severity of these offenses. In fact, rape is considered by some college administrations as simply "non-consensual sex" or "a bad hook-up." More telling, *Slate* argues on October 16, 2013, that when acknowledging that rape does exist, colleges like The University of Southern California actively shift the burden of the crime from the rapist to the raped by informing students that they should expect to get raped if they've been doing certain things, like drinking, according to *Alternet* on July 13th, 2013. Instead of acknowledging rape for the despicable violation of humanity that it is, college administrators have embarked on a campaign to trivialize and pin all responsibility on the shoulders of the survivor.

When Ari Mostov was raped at The University of Southern California and tried to report the crime to the campus police, *Washington Post* of July 26th, 2013, notes the police told her that since her rapist didn't orgasm, no crime was actually committed. The callous indifference toward instances of rape on our college campuses produces two effects: the widespread distribution of inaccurate rape data, and the re-victimization of rape survivors.

First, there is grossly inaccurate data on sexual assault. Because the Department of Education is lax when it comes to university oversight, colleges have been allowed to sweep mishandled matters of justice under the rug. Unsurprisingly, when the Center for Public Integrity conducted a nine-month study of 152 major college campuses that concluded in June 2013, only nine of them provided accurate crime reports, a provision required by the aforementioned Jeanne Clery Act. Because college campuses refuse to seriously address rape on campus, collection of data regarding rape on campus is compromised, and as such, the crimes and the victims are treated as statistical outliers.

Second, survivors of rape on campus are mistreated by their institution. Otterbein University's newspaper details on May 7, 2013, how administrators silence survivors through forced non-disclosure documents, which favors perpetrators, and is a blatant violation of the Clery Act. Students who do have the courage to speak out don't have it much better. *The Nation* of January 7, 2013, explains that Lizzy Seeberg was raped by a star Notre Dame football player and reported her crime to campus police. After being relentlessly harassed, her charges were dropped, and Lizzy committed suicide. Another Notre Dame rape survivor, who wishes to remain nameless, told previously cited *The Nation* that after seeing what Lizzy went through, she is not reporting her rape for fear of backlash. Survivors are victimized not just once by their attacker, but a second time by their university.

In January 2014, President Obama pledged to create sexual assault task forces on college campuses across the country. *Change.org* offers an initial step toward stopping the injustices. Visit the link I will provide and sign the petition to reform sexual assault policies. However, action solely on a federal level will not create the immediate protection that we need. Starting movements at our respective colleges is the most effective tool for change.

First, engage in a discussion of sexual violence on your campus. *PolicyMic* of February 24, 2013, emphasizes that bringing sexual violence into mainstream discourse refutes the idea that it is the survivor's, not society's problem. *Stanford Daily* of May 8, 2013, explains that many of Stanford's equality based groups banded together to initiate a campus-wide discussion about consent, rape culture, and legal options available for survivors. We need to learn the strengths and shortcomings of the resources available to us on our campuses. Creating a socially aware environment on campus will not only make survivors feel safer, but hold our institutions accountable.

Second, we must foster education that limits these types of crimes. On August 29, 2012, *Inside Higher Ed* published a report that the University of Montana has created a mandatory sexual assault awareness program. It's composed of a series of eight videos and a seven-question quiz. In order to register for second semester classes, students must receive a perfect score. While this is a small step, it's at least a step in the right direction. By educating students, we can keep these horrific crimes from occurring and, subsequently, from falling into the hands of our college administrations.

I have compiled a list of resources to help you implement these solutions. We have a long road in front of us; it will take a collective voice like ours to truly make a difference.

Jeanne, Sophie, Landen, and Ari have sparked a national discussion, which shouldn't end here. After examining our universities' inaction, the emotional trauma that results, and solutions . . . it becomes evident that our colleges must start protecting us. These stories of survival are powerful; we cannot allow the bureaucracy of our administrations to silence these survivors. Let's band together so all of our voices can be heard.

Notes

Chapter 1

1. R. Emanuel, J. Adams, K. Baker, E. K. Daufin, C. Ellington, E. Fitts, J. Himsel, L. Holladay, and D. Okeowo, "How College Students Spend Their Time Communicating," *International Journal of Listening* 22 (2008): 12–28; E. T. Klemmer and F. W. Snyder, "Measurement of Time Spent Communicating," *Journal of Communication* 20 (1972): 142.
2. We thank Tom Burkholder, University of Nevada, Las Vegas, for this idea.
3. J. C. Humes, *The Sir Winston Method: The Five Secrets of Speaking the Language of Leadership* (New York: William Morrow, 1991).
4. V. Marchant, "Listen Up!" *Time* (June 28, 1999): 72.
5. A. Vangelisti and J. Daly, "Correlates of Speaking Skills in the United States: A National Assessment," *Communication Education* 38 (1989): 132–143.
6. M. Cronin, ed., "The Need for Required Oral Communication Education in the Undergraduate General Education Curriculum," unpublished paper, 1993, available from the National Communication Association, Washington, DC.
7. J. Ayres and T. S. Hopf, "The Long-Term Effect of Visualization in the Classroom: A Brief Research Report," *Communication Education* 39 (1990): 75–78.
8. See J. C. McCroskey and M. Beatty, "The Communibiological Perspective: Implications for Communication in Instruction," *Communication Education* 49 (2000): 1; also see J. C. McCroskey, J. A. Daly, M. M. Martin, and M. J. Beatty, eds., *Communication and Personality: Trait Perspectives* (Cresskill, NJ: Hampton Press, 1998).
9. J. H. McConnell, *Are You Communicating? You Can't Manage without It* (New York: McGraw-Hill, 1995).
10. Value Investors Portal, "Warren Buffet on Communication Skills," *YouTube*, December 6. 2010, accessed May 14, 2013, www.youtube.com/watch?v=tpgcEYpLzP0.
11. J. L. Winsor, D. Curtis, and R. D. Stephens, "National Preferences in Business and Communication Education: A Survey Update," *Journal of the Association of Communication Administration* 3 (1997): 170–179. For a summary of the values and virtues of studying communication, see S. P. Morreale and J. C. Pearson, "Why Communication Education Is Important: The Centrality of the Discipline in the 21st Century," *Communication Education* 57.2 (2008): 224–240; also see S. P. Morreale, D. W. Worley, and B. Hugenberg, "The Basic Communication Course at Two- and Four-Year U.S. Colleges and Universities: Study VIII—The 40th Anniversary," *Communication Education* 59.4 (2010): 405–430; Hart Research Associates "Raising the Bar: Employers' Views on College Learning in the Wake of the Economic Downturn," Washington, DC, Association of American Colleges and Universities (January 10, 2010); D. Sellnow, "Integrated Composition and Communication: Addressing the Needs of the 21st Century," paper presented at the Rhetoric Society of America annual conference, Minneapolis, Minnesota (May 2010).
12. Career Services, "What Skills and Attributes Employers Seek When Hiring Students," *University of Wisconsin–River Falls*, accessed June 7, 2007, www.uwrf.edu/ccslskills/htm; C. Luckenbaugh and K. Gray, "Employers Describe Perfect Job Candidate," *Association of Colleges and Employers Survey*, accessed June 4, 2007, www.naceweb.org/press/display.asp?year=2003&prid=169; R. S. Hansen and K. Handson, "What Do Employers Really Want? Top Skills and Values Employers Seek from Job Seekers," *Quintessential Careers*, accessed June 4, 2007, www.quintcareers.com/job_skills_values.html. For evidence that communication skills can be developed, see R. F. Brown, C. L. Bylurd, J. A. Gueguen, C. Diamond, J. Eddington, and D. Kissane, "Developing Patient-Centered Communication Skills Training for Oncologists: Describing the Content and Efficacy of Training," *Communication Education* 59.3 (2010): 235–248; G. Sulcas and J. English, "A Case for Focus on Professional Communication Skills at Senior Undergraduate Level in Engineering and the Built Environment," *Southern African Linguistics & Applied Language Studies* 28.3 (2010): 219–226.
13. M. M. Robles, "Executive Perceptions of the Top 10 Soft Skills Needed in Today's Workplace," *Business Communication Quarterly* 75, no. 4 (2012): 453–465.
14. K. E. Davis and M. Todd, "Assessing Friendship: Prototypes, Paradigm Cases, and Relationship Description," in *Understanding Personal Relationships*, edited by S. W. Duck and D. Perlman (London: Sage, 1985); B. Wellman, "From Social Support to Social Network," in *Social Support: Theory, Research and Applications*, edited by I. G. Sarason and B. R. Sarason (Dordrecht, Netherlands: Nijhoff, 1985); R. Hopper, M. L. Knapp, and L. Scott, "Couples' Personal Idioms: Exploring Intimate Talk," *Journal of Communication* 31 (1981): 23–33.
15. M. Argyle and M. Hendershot, *The Anatomy of Relationships* (London: Penguin Books, 1985), 14.
16. D. Goleman, "Emotional Intelligence: Issues in Paradigm Building," in *The Emotionally Intelligent Workplace*, edited by C. Chemiss and D. Goleman (San Francisco: Jossey-Bass, 2001), 13.
17. V. Satir, *People Making* (Palo Alto, CA: Science and Behavior Books, 1972), 1.
18. M. Argyle, *The Psychology of Happiness* (London: Routledge, 2001).
19. J. Lynch, *The Broken Heart: The Medical Consequences of Loneliness* (New York: Basic Books, 1977).
20. D. P. Phillips, "Deathday and Birthday: An Unexpected Connection," in *Statistics: A Guide to the Unknown*, edited by J. M. Tanur (San Francisco: Holden-Day, 1972); also see F. Korbin and G. Hendershot, "Do Family Ties Reduce Mortality? Evidence from the United States 1968," *Journal of Marriage and the Family* 39 (1977): 737–746; K. Heller and K. S. Rook, "Distinguishing the Theoretical Functions of Social Ties: Implications of Support Interventions," in *Handbook of Personal Relationships* 2e, edited by S. W. Duck, K. Dindia, W. Ickes, R. Milardo, R. S. L. Mills, and B. R. Sarason (Chichester, UK: Wiley, 1997); B. R. Samson, L. G. Sarason, and R. A. R. Gurung, "Close Personal Relationships and Health Outcomes: A Key to the Role of Social Support, in *Handbook of Personal Relationships* 2e, edited by S. W. Duck, K. Dindia, W. Ickes, R. Milardo, R. S. L. Mills, and B. R. Sarason (Chichester, UK: Wiley, 1997); S. Duck, *Relating to Others* (Buckingham, UK: Open University Press, 1999), 1.
21. Pamela Paul, "Does Facebook Make Someone Social Offline?" *New York Times* (January 30, 2011): Style 8; also see S. Craig Watkins and H. Erin Lee, "Got Facebook? Investigating What's Social About Social Media," *University of Texas at Austin*, accessed January 31, 2011, www.thevoungandthedigital.com/wp-content/uploads/2010/11/watkins_lee_facebookstudy-nov-18.pdf.
22. F. E. X. Dance and C. Larson, *Speech Communication: Concepts and Behavior* (New York: Holt, Rinehart and Winston, 1972).
23. Dance and Larson, *Speech Communication.*
24. J. T. Masterson, S. A. Beebe, and N. H. Watson, *Invitation to Effective Speech Communication* (Glenview, IL: Scott, Foresman, 1989).
25. M. Gladwell, *Blink: The Power of Thinking without Thinking* (New York: Little, Brown, 2005).

26. L. Barker, R. Edwards, C. Gaines, K. Gladney, and F. Holley, "An Investigation of Proportional Time Spent in Various Communication Activities of College Students," *Journal of Applied Communication Research* 8 (1981): 101–109.
27. D. Barnlund, *Interpersonal Communication: Survey and Studies* (Boston: Houghton Mifflin, 1968).
28. See, for instance, C. R Berger and J. J. Bradac, *Language and Social Knowledge: Uncertainty in Interpersonal Relations* (London: Arnold, 1982).
29. O. Wiio, *Wiio's Laws—and Some Others* (Espoo, Finland: Welin-Goos, 1978).
30. T. Watzlawick, J. B. Bavelas, and D. Jackson, *The Pragmatics of Human Communication* (New York: W. W. Norton, 1967).
31. S. B. Shimanoff, *Communication Rules: Theory and Research* (Beverly Hills, CA: Sage, 1980).
32. H. Lasswell, "The Structure and Function of Communication in Society," in *The Communication of Ideas*, edited by L. Bryson (New York: Institute for Religious and Social Studies, 1948), 37.
33. See V. E. Cronen, W. B. Pearce, and L. M. Harris, "The Coordinated Management of Meaning: A Theory of Communication," in *Human Communication Theory: Comparative Essays*, edited by F. E. X. Dance (New York: Harper & Row, 1982), 61–89.
34. This section is based on Masterson, Beebe, and Watson, *Invitation to Effective Speech Communication*. We are especially indebted to J. T. Masterson for this discussion.
35. Adapted from W. Ham, *Man's Living Religions* (Independence, MO: Herald Publishing House, 1966), 39–40.
36. See R. P. Wolff, *About Philosophy* (Upper Saddle River, NJ: Prentice Hall, 2000), 308–335.
37. C. S. Lewis, *The Abolition of Man* (New York: Macmillan, 1947); also see A. M. Nicholi Jr., *The Question of God: C. S. Lewis and Sigmund Freud Debate God, Love, Sex, and the Meaning of Life* (New York: Free Press, 2002).
38. C. Christians and M. Traber, *Communication Ethics and Universal Values* (Beverly Hills, CA: Sage, 1997); also see S. Bok, *Common Values* (Columbia: University of Missouri Press, 2002).
39. Christians and Traber, *Communication Ethics and Universal Values*.
40. For additional discussion of the ethical values taught in the world's religions, see H. Smith, *The World's Religions* (San Francisco: HarperSanFrancisco, 1991).
41. "NCA Credo for Communication Ethics," *National Communication Association*, 1999, accessed June 27, 2001, www.natcom.org/conferences/Ethicslethicsconfcred099.htm.
42. N. S. Baron, *Always On: Language in an Online and Mobile World* (New York: Oxford University Press, 2008); also see D. Crystal, *txtng: The gr8 db8* (Oxford, UK: Oxford University Press, 2008); S. Turkle, *Alone Together: Why We Expect More from Technology and Less from Each Other* (New York: Basic Books, 2011); M. A. Dourin, "College Students' Text Messaging, Use of Textese, and Literacy Skills," *Journal of Assisted Learning* 27.1 (2011): 67.
43. A. Ramirez and K. Broneck, "'IM Me': Instant Messaging as Relational Maintenance and Everyday Communication," *Journal of Social and Personal Relationships*, 29 (2009): 292–314.
44. Watkins and Lee, "Got Facebook?"
45. Y. Amichai-Hamburger, *The Social Net: Human Behavior in Cyberspace* (Oxford, UK: Oxford University Press, 2005); K. Y. A. McKenna and J. A. Bargh, "Plan 9 from Cyberspace: The Implications of the Internet for Personality and Social Psychology," *Personality and Social Psychology Review* 4 (2000): 57–75.
46. S. Turkle, *Alone Together*, 1.
47. Ami Sedghi, "Facebook: 10 Years of Social Networking, in Numbers," *The Guardian*, February 4, 2014, accessed March 28, 2014, www.theguardian.com/news/datablog/2014/feb/04/facebook-in-numbers-statistics.
48. Watkins and Lee, "Got Facebook?"
49. A. Smith, "6 New Facts about Facebook," *Pew Research Center*, Accessed February 3, 2014, www.pewresearch.org/fact-tank.
50. C. Smith, "Facebook by the Numbers," *Digital Market Ramblings*, accessed March 28, 2014, expandedramblings.com/index.php/by-the-numbers-17-amazing-facebook-stats/#.UzWMY1xNw8M.
51. Smith, "Facebook by the Numbers."
52. Smith, "Facebook by the Numbers."
53. Watkins and Lee, "Got Facebook?"
54. Watkins and Lee, "Got Facebook?"
55. D. J. Saul, "3 Million Teens Leave Facebook in 3 Years: The 2014 Facebook Demographic Report," January 15, 2014, accessed March 28, 2014, istrategylabs.com/2014/01/3-million-teens-leave-facebook-in-3-years-the-2014-facebook-demographic-report/.
56. Watkins and Lee, "Got Facebook?"
57. A. Smith, "6 New Facts about Facebook.".
58. A. Smith, "6 New Facts about Facebook."
59. R. Kraut, M. Patterson, V. Lundmark, S. Kiesler, M. Tridas, and W. Scherlis, "Internet Paradox: A Social Technology That Reduces Social Involvement and Psychological Well-Being?" *American Psychologist* 53 (1998): 1017–1031.
60. R. Kraut, S. Kiesler, B. Boneva, J. Cummings, V. Helgeson, and A. Crawford, "Internet Paradox Revisited," *Journal of Social Issues* 58 (2002): 49–74; P. E. N. Howard, L. Raine, and S. Jones, "Days and Nights on the Internet: The Impact of a Diffusing Technology," *American Behavioral Scientist* 45 (2001): 383–404; M. A. Mazur and R. J. Bums, "Perceptions of Relational Interdependence in Online Relationships: The Effects of Communication Apprehension and Introversion," *Communication Research Reports* 17.4 (2000): 397–406.
61. B. Jin and J. F. Pena, "Mobile Communication in Romantic Relationships: Mobile Phone Use, Relational Uncertainty, Love, Commitment, and Attachment Styles," *Communication Reports* 23.1 (2010): 39–51.
62. 2014 Facebook Demographic Report.
63. We appreciate and acknowledge our friend and colleague M. Redmond for his contributions to our understanding of interpersonal communication. For more information, see S. A. Beebe, S. J. Beebe, and M. V. Redmond, *Interpersonal Communication: Relating to Others* 7e (Boston: Pearson, 2014).
64. For an excellent discussion of the power of dialogue to enrich the quality of communication, see D. Yankelovich, *The Magic of Dialogue: Transforming Conflict into Cooperation* (New York: Simon & Schuster, 1999).
65. S. A. Beebe and J. T. Masterson, *Communicating in Small Groups: Principles and Practices* 10e (Boston: Pearson, 2012).
66. M. S. Poole and I. Ahmed, "Group Decision Support Systems," in *21st Century Communication: A Reference Handbook*, edited by W. Eadie (Thousand Oaks, CA: Sage, 2010); also see M. C. Poole, "Collaboration, Integration, and Transformation: Directions for Research on Communication and Information Technologies," *Journal of Computer-Mediated Communication* 14 (2009): 753–763.
67. For an excellent review of intrapersonal communication theory and research, see D. Voate, *Intrapersonal Communication: Different Voices, Different Minds* (Hillsdale, NJ: Lawrence Erlbaum, 1994).
68. D. Quinn, *My Ishmael* (New York: Bantam Books, 1996).
69. B. Plester and C. Wood, "Exploring Relationships between Traditional and New Media Literacies: British Preteen Texters at School," *Journal of Computer-Mediated Communication* 14 (2009): 1108–1129.
70. Robert Fulghum, *All I Really Need to Know I Learned in Kindergarten* (New York: Ballantine Books, 1988).
71. Barker et al., "An Investigation of Proportional Time Spent in Various Communication Activities of College Students."

Chapter 2

1. S. R. Covey, *The Seven Habits of Highly Effective People*, anniversary ed. (New York: Simon & Schuster, 2013), 74.
2. D. W. Johnson, *Reaching Out: Interpersonal Effectiveness and Self-Actualization* 11e (Boston: Pearson, 2012), 51.

3. S. E. Wood, E. Green Wood, and D. Boyd, *Mastering the World of Psychology* 5e (Boston: Pearson, 2013), 115.
4. R. A. Baron and N. R. Branscombe, *Social Psychology* 13e (Boston: Pearson, 2011).
5. G. Bukobza, "The Epistemological Basis of Selfhood," *New Ideas in Psychology* 25 (2007): 37–65.
6. Bukobza, "The Epistemological Basis of Selfhood," 39.
7. For more information on self-concept and culture, see S. E. Cross and J. S. Gore, "Cultural Models of the Self," in *Handbook of Self and Identity* 2e, edited by M. R. Leary and J. Price Tangney (New York: Guilford, 2013), 587–614; C. Kanagawa, S. E. Cross, and H. R. Markus, "'Who Am I?' The Cultural Psychology of the Conceptual Self," *Personality and Social Psychology Bulletin* 27 (2001): 90–103; S. Kitayama, H. R. Markus, H. Matsumoto, and V. Norasakkunkit, "Individual and Collective Processes in the Construction of the Self: Self-Enhancement in the U.S. and Self-Criticism in Japan," *Journal of Personality and Social Psychology* 72 (1997): 1245–1267; D. Watkins et al., "Cultural Dimensions, Gender, and the Nature of Self-Concept: A 14-Country Study," *International Journal of Psychology* 33 (1998): 17–31.
8. K. Horney, *Neurosis and Human Growth* (New York: W. W. Norton, 1991), 17.
9. A. Elliott, *Concepts of the Self* 3e (Cambridge, UK: Polity Press, 2013); K. J. Gergen, *The Saturated Self: Dilemmas of Identity in Contemporary Life* (New York: Basic Books, 2000); B. Goss, *Processing Communication: Information Processing in Intrapersonal Communication* (Belmont, CA: Wadsworth, 1982), 72.
10. J. T. Masterson, S. A. Beebe, and N. H. Watson, *Invitation to Effective Speech Communication* (Glenview, IL: Scott, Foresman, 1989).
11. S. Harter, *The Construction of the Self* (New York: Guilford, 2012); D. O. Oyserman, K. E. Elmore, and G. S. Smith, "Self, Self-Concept, and Identity," in *Handbook of Self and Identity* 2e, edited by M. R. Leary and J. Price Tangney (New York: Guilford, 2013), 69–104.
12. W. James, *Principles of Psychology* (New York: Henry Holt, 1890).
13. J. Veldhuis, E. A. Konjin, and J. C. Seidell, "Counteracting Media's Thin-Body Ideal for Adolescent Girls: Informing Is More Effective Than Warning," *Media Psychology* 17 (2014): 154–184; M. Tiggemann, "The Status of Media Effects on Body Image Research: Commentary on Articles in the Thematic Issue on Body Image and Media," *Media Psychology* 17 (2014): 127–133; R. M. Puhl, J. Luedicke, and C. A. Heuer, "The Stigmatizing Effect of Visual Media Portrayals of Obese Persons on Public Attitudes: Does Race or Gender Matter?" *Journal of Health Communication* 18 (2013): 805–826; M. E. Shuttlesworth and D. Zotter, "Disordered Eating in African American and Caucasian Women: The Role of Ethnic Identity," *Journal of Black Studies* 42 (2011): 906–922; K. E. Van Vonderen and W. Kinnally, "Media Effects on Body Image: Examining Media Exposure in the Broader Context of Internal and Other Social Factors," *American Communication Journal* 14 (2012): 41–57; M. S. Richardson and J. S. Paxton, "An Evaluation of a Body Image Intervention Based on Risk Factors for Body Dissatisfaction: A Controlled Study with Adolescent Girls," *International Journal of Eating Disorders* 43 (2010): 112–122.
14. National Institute on Media and the Family, "Shocking Dieting Statistics," *Healthkicker*, May 19, 2010, www.healthkicker.com.
15. L. A. Ricciardelli and M. P. McCabe, "Body Image Development in Adolescent Boys," in *Body Image: A Handbook of Science, Practice, and Prevention* 2e, edited by T. F. Cash and L. Smolak (New York: Guilford, 2013), 85–92; S. Lee, R. Misra, and E. Kaster, "Active Intervention Program Using Dietary Education and Exercise Training for Reducing Obesity in Mexican American Male Children," *Health Educator* 14 (2012): 2–13; M. P. McCabe, L. A. Ricciardelli, and G. Karantzas, "Impact of a Healthy Body Image Program among Adolescent Boys on Body Image, Negative Affect, and Body Change Strategies," *Body Image: An International Journal of Research* 7 (2010): 117–123.
16. C. H. Cooley, *Human Nature and the Social Order* (New York: Scribner's, 1912).
17. G. H. Mead, *Mind, Self, and Society* (Chicago: University of Chicago Press, 1934).
18. R. M. Dailey, "Testing Components of Confirmation: How Acceptance and Challenge from Mothers, Fathers, and Siblings Are Related to Adolescent Self-Concept," *Communication Monographs* 77 (2010): 592–617.
19. J. Stewart, K. E. Zediker, and S. Witteborn, *Together: Communicating Interpersonally* 6e (Los Angeles: Roxbury, 2005).
20. M. L. Hecht, M. J. Collier, and S. A. Ribeau, *African American Communication: Ethnic Identity and Cultural Interpretation* (Newbury Park, CA: Sage, 1993).
21. A. Aron and N. Nardone, "Self and Close Relationships," in *The Handbook of Self and Identity* 2e, edited by M. R. Leary and J. Price Tangney (New York: Guilford, 2013), 520–541.
22. J. N. Martin and T. K. Nakayama, *Experiencing Intercultural Communication* 5e (New York: McGraw-Hill, 2013).
23. M. A. Hogg, "Social Identity and the Psychology of Groups," in *The Handbook of Self and Identity* 2e, edited by M. R. Leary and J. Price Tangney (New York: Guilford, 2013), 502–519.
24. D. K. Ivy, *GenderSpeak: Personal Effectiveness in Gender Communication* 5e (Boston: Pearson, 2012); A. Ayres-Brown, "McDonald's Gave Me the 'Girl's Toy' with My Happy Meal. So I Went to the CEO," *Slate*, April 21, 2014, www.slate.com; E. Grinberg, "When Kids Play Across Gender Lines," *CNN*, August 28, 2012, www.cnn.com/2012/08/27/living/harrods-gender-neutral-toys/; J. E. O. Blakemore and R. E. Centers, "Characteristics of Boys' and Girls' Toys," *Sex Roles* 53 (2005): 619–634; T. L. Kuther and E. McDonald, "Early Adolescents' Experiences with and Views of Barbie," *Adolescence* 39 (2004): 39–51; M. A. Messner, "Barbie Girls versus Sea Monsters: Children Constructing Gender," *Gender and Society* 14 (2000): 765–784.
25. J. E. Stake, "Gender Differences and Similarities in Self-Concept within Everyday Life Contexts," *Psychology of Women Quarterly* 16 (1992): 349–363.
26. S. Lamb, L. M. Brown, and M. Tappan, *Saving Our Sons from Superheroes, Slackers, and Other Media Stereotypes* (New York: St. Martin's, 2009); S. Lamb and L. M. Brown, *Packaging Girlhood: Rescuing Our Daughters from Marketers' Schemes* (New York: St. Martin's, 2006).
27. A. Elliott, *Concepts of the Self* 3e; A. Elliott and P. du Gay, *Identity in Question* (Thousand Oaks, CA: Sage, 2009); J. Jorgenson, "Reflexivity in Feminist Research Practice: Hearing the Unsaid," *Women & Language* 34 (2011): 115–118; C. E. Medved and L. H. Turner, "Qualitative Research: Practicing Reflexivity," *Women & Language* 34 (2011): 109–112.
28. G. Steinem, *Revolution from Within: A Book of Self-Esteem* (Boston: Little, Brown, 1993), 26.
29. J. D. Campbell, P. D. Trapnell, S. J. Heine, I. M. Katz, L. F. Lavallee, and D. R. Lehman, "Self-Concept Clarity: Measurement, Personality Correlates, and Cultural Boundaries," *Journal of Personality and Social Psychology* 70 (1996): 141–156.
30. For more information on self-concept clarity, see J. D. Campbell, "Self-Esteem and Clarity of the Self-Concept," *Journal of Personality and Social Psychology* 59 (1990): 538–549; K. P. McIntyre, B. A. Mattingly, G. W. Lewandowski, and A. Simpson, "Workplace Self-Expansion: Implications for Job Satisfaction, Commitment, Self-Concept Clarity, and Self-Esteem among the Employed and Unemployed," *Basic & Applied Social Psychology* 36 (2014): 59–69; G. W. Lewandowski and N. Nardone, "Self-Concept Clarity's Role in Self-Other Agreement and the Accuracy of Behavioral Prediction," *Self & Identity* 11 (2012): 71–89; M. Blazek and T. Besta, "Self-Concept Clarity and Religious Orientations: Prediction of Purpose in Life and Self-Esteem," *Journal of Religion & Health* 51 (2012): 947–960.
31. L. Rill, E. Baiocchi, M. Hopper, K. Denker, and L. N. Olson, "Exploration of the Relationship Between Self-Esteem, Commitment, and Verbal Aggressiveness in Romantic Dating Relationships," *Communication Reports* 22 (2009): 102–113; T. DeHart

and B. W. Pelham, "Fluctuations in State Implicit Self-Esteem in Response to Daily Negative Events," *Journal of Experimental Social Psychology* 43 (2007): 157–165.

32. A. J. Holmstrom, J. C. Russell, and D. D. Clare, "Esteem Support Messages Received during the Job Search: A Test of the CETESM," *Communication Monographs* 80 (2013): 220–242.
33. Ivy, *GenderSpeak*.
34. G. D. Webster, L. A. Kirkpatrick, J. B. Neziek, C. V. Smith, and E. L. Paddock, "Different Slopes for Different Folks: Self-Esteem Instability and Gender as Moderators of the Relationship between Self-Esteem and Attitudinal Aggression," *Self and Identity* 6 (2007): 74–94; B. W. Pelham, S. L. Koole, C. D. Hardin, J. J. Hetts, E. Seah, and T. DeHart, "Gender Moderates the Relation between Implicit and Explicit Self-Esteem," *Journal of Experimental Social Psychology* 41 (2005): 84–89; American Association of University Women, *Shortchanging Girls, Shortchanging America* (Washington, DC: AAUW Educational Foundation, 1991); M. Sadker and D. Sadker, *Failing at Fairness: How America's Schools Cheat Girls* (New York: Scribner's, 1994), 77.
35. K. Kay and C. Shipman, *The Confidence Code: The Science and Art of Self-Assurance—What Women Should Know* (New York: Harper Business, 2014); S. Sandberg, *Lean In: Women, Work, and the Will to Lead* (New York: Alfred A. Knopf, 2013); M. Brzezinski, *Knowing Your Value: Women, Money, and Getting What You're Worth* (New York: Weinstein Books, 2011).
36. E. Pila, A. Stamiris, A. Castonguay, and C. M. Sabiston, "Body-Related Envy: A Social Comparison Perspective in Sport and Exercise," *Journal of Sport & Exercise* 36 (2014): 93–106; V. Hoorens and C. Van Damme, "What Do People Infer from Social Comparisons? Bridges between Social Comparison and Person Perception," *Social & Personality Psychology Compass* 6 (2012): 607–618; B. Butzer and N. A. Kuiper, "Relationships between the Frequency of Social Comparisons and Self-Concept Clarity, Intolerance of Uncertainty, Anxiety, and Depression," *Personality and Individual Differences* 41 (2006): 167–176; L. Festinger, "A Theory of Social Comparison Processes," *Human Relations* 2 (1954): 117–140.
37. R. L. Nabi and L. Keblusek, "Inspired by Hope, Motivated by Envy: Comparing the Effects of Discrete Emotions in the Process of Social Comparison to Media Figures," *Media Psychology* 17 (2014): 208–234; A. Arroyo and J. Harwood, "Exploring the Causes and Consequences of Engaging in Fat Talk," *Journal of Applied Communication Research* 40 (2012): 167–181; D. Smeesters, T. Mussweiler, and N. Mandel, "The Effects of Thin and Heavy Media Images on Overweight and Underweight Consumers: Social Comparison Processes and Behavioral Implications," *Journal of Consumer Research* 36 (2010): 930–949; S. H. Sohn, "Sex Differences in Social Comparison and Comparison Motives in Body Image Process," *North American Journal of Psychology* 12 (2010): 481–500.
38. M. M. Martin and J. W. Gentry, "Stuck in the Model Trap," in *Taking Sides: Clashing Views on Controversial Issues in Mass Media and Society* 8e, edited by A. Alexander and J. Hanson (Dubuque, IA: McGraw-Hill/Dushkin, 2005), 52–61.
39. M. Duggan and A. Smith, "Social Media Update 2013," *Pew Research Internet Project*, December 30, 2013, www.pewinternet.org/2013/12/30/social-media-update-2013.
40. P. M. Valkenburg, J. Peter, and A. P. Schouten, "Friend Networking Sites and Their Relationship to Adolescents' Well-Being and Social Self-Esteem," *CyberPsychology & Behavior* 9 (2006): 484–490; A. L. Gonzales and J. T. Hancock, "Mirror, Mirror on My Facebook Wall: Effects of Exposure to Facebook on Self-Esteem," *CyberPsychology, Behavior, & Social Networking* 14 (2011): 79–83; N. B. Ellison, C. Steinfield, and C. Lampe, "The Benefits of Facebook 'Friends': Social Capital and College Students' Use of Online Social Networking Sites," *Journal of Computer-Mediated Communication* 12 (2007): 1143–1168.
41. N. Haferkamp and N. C. Kramer, "Social Comparison 2.0: Examining the Effects of Online Profiles on Social-Networking Sites," *CyberPsychology, Behavior, & Social Networking* 14 (2011): 309–314.
42. C. L. Toma, "Feeling Better But Doing Worse: Effects of Facebook Self-Presentation on Implicit Self-Esteem and Cognitive Task Performance," *Media Psychology* 16 (2013): 199–220.
43. S. Wurm, L. M. Warner, J. P. Ziegelmann, J. K. Wolff, and B. Schuz, "How Do Negative Self-Perceptions of Aging Become a Self-Fulfilling Prophecy?" *Psychology & Aging* 28 (2013): 1088–1097; S. Madon, J. Willard, M. Guyll, and K. C. Scherr, "Self-Fulfilling Prophecies: Mechanisms, Power, and Links to Social Problems," *Social & Personality Psychology Compass* 5 (2011): 578–590; L. Jussim and K. D. Harber, "Teacher Expectations and Self-Fulfilling Prophecies: Knowns and Unknowns, Resolved and Unresolved Controversies," *Personality and Social Psychology Review* 9 (2005): 131–155; L. Jussim, K. D. Harber, J. T. Crawford, T. R. Cain, and F. Cohen, "Social Reality Makes the Social Mind: Self-Fulfilling Prophecy, Stereotypes, Bias, and Accuracy," *Interaction Studies* 6 (2005): 85–102; S. Madon, M. Guyll, R. Spoth, and J. Willard, "Self-Fulfilling Prophecies," *Psychological Science* 15 (2004): 837–845.
44. J. M. Twenge, *Generation Me: Why Today's Young Americans Are More Confident, Assertive, Entitled—and More Miserable Than Ever Before* (New York: Free Press, 2006), 2; J. M. Twenge, "The Narcissism Epidemic: Narcissism Is on the Rise among Individuals and in American Culture," *Psychology Today*, August 12, 2013, retrieved June 15, 2014, www.psychologytoday.com; F. Rhodewalt, "Contemporary Perspectives on Narcissism and the Narcissistic Personality Type," in *Handbook of Self and Identity*, edited by M. R. Leary and J. Price Tangney (New York: Guilford, 2013), 571–586.
45. J. M. Twenge, S. Konrath, J. D. Foster, W. K. Campbell, and B. J. Bushman, "Egos Inflating over Time: A Cross-Temporal Meta-Analysis of the Narcissistic Personality Inventory," *Journal of Personality* 76 (2008): 875–901; S. Konrath, J. M. Twenge, W. K. Campbell, J. D. Foster, and B. J. Bushman, "This Generation Is More Special Than the Others: A Cross-Temporal Meta-Analysis of the Narcissistic Personality Inventory," paper presented at the conference on Educating the Next Generation of College Students, University of San Diego, February 27, 2007.
46. H. Cai, V. S. Y. Kwan, and C. Sedikides, "A Sociocultural Approach to Narcissism: The Case of Modern China," *European Journal of Personality* 26 (2012): 529–535; M. S. Wilson and C. G. Sibley, "'Narcissism Creep?' Evidence for Age-Related Differences in Narcissism in the New Zealand General Populations," *New Zealand Journal of Psychology* 40 (2011): 89–95.
47. S. Mehdizadeh, "Self-Presentation 2.0: Narcissism and Self-Esteem on Facebook," *CyberPsychology, Behavior, & Social Networking* 13 (2010): 357–364.
48. S. M. Bergman, M. E. Fearrington, S. W. Davenport, and J. Bergman, "Millennials, Narcissism, and Social Networking: What Narcissists Do on Social Networking Sites and Why," *Personality & Individual Differences* 50 (2011): 706–711; E. Y. Ong, R. P. Ang, J. Ho, J. C. Lim, D. H Goh, C. S. Lee, and A. Y. Chua, "Narcissism, Extraversion, and Adolescents' Self-Presentation on Facebook," *Journal of Personality and Social Psychology* 43 (2011): 838–852.
49. For other research as well as popular literature on narcissism and self-esteem, see J. M. Twenge and W. K. Campbell, *The Narcissism Epidemic: Living in the Age of Entitlement* (New York: Free Press, 2011); J. K. Bosson, C. E. Lakey, W. K. Campbell, V. Zeigler-Hill, C. H. Jordan, and M. H. Kernis, "Untangling the Links between Narcissism and Self-Esteem: A Theoretical and Empirical Review," *Social and Personality Psychology Compass* 2 (2008): 1415–1439; V. Zeigler-Hill, "Discrepancies between Implicit and Explicit Self-Esteem: Implications for Narcissism and Self-Esteem Instability," *Journal of Personality* 74 (2006): 119–144; E. Hoover, "Here's You Looking at You, Kid: Study Says Many Students Are Narcissists," *The Chronicle of Higher Education* (March 9, 2007); A. L. Ball, "The New and Improved Self-Esteem," *O: The Oprah Winfrey Magazine* (January 2008): 164–265; P. Marx, "Can You Have Too Much Self-Esteem?" *O: The Oprah Winfrey Magazine* (May 2004): 249; C. Sedikides, E. A. Rudich, A. P. Gregg, M. Kumashiro, and C. Rusbult, "Are Normal Narcissists Psychologically Healthy?

Self-Esteem Matters," *Journal of Personality and Social Psychology* 87 (2004): 400–416; R. F. Baumeister, B. J. Bushman, and W. K. Campbell, "Self-Esteem, Narcissism, and Aggression: Does Violence Result from Low Self-Esteem or from Threatened Egotism?" *Current Directions in Psychological Science* 9 (2000): 26–29.

50. U. Orth, K. H. Trzesniewski, and R. W. Robins, "Self-Esteem Development from Young Adulthood to Old Age: A Cohort-Sequential Longitudinal Study," *Journal of Personality and Social Psychology* 98 (2010): 645–658.
51. A. Eryilmaz and H. Atak, "Investigation of Starting Romantic Intimacy in Emerging Adulthood in Terms of Self-Esteem, Gender, and Gender Roles," *Educational Sciences: Theory & Practice* 11 (2011): 595–600; S. Zhang and L. Stafford, "Perceived Face Threat of Honest but Hurtful Evaluative Messages in Romantic Relationships," *Western Journal of Communication* 72 (2008): 19–39; M. H. Kernis, C. E. Lakey, and W. L. Heppner, "Secure versus Fragile High Self-Esteem as a Predictor of Verbal Defensiveness: Converging Findings across Three Different Markers," *Journal of Personality* 76 (2008): 477–512.
52. Goss, *Processing Communication*, 72.
53. E. J. Oliver, D. Marklan, and J. Hardy, "Interpretation of Self-Talk and Post-Lecture Affective States of Higher Education Students: A Self-Determination Theory Perspective," *British Journal of Educational Psychology* 80 (2010): 307–323; J. Hardy, R. Roberts, and L. Hardy, "Awareness and Motivation to Change Negative Self-Talk," *Sport Psychologist* 23 (2009): 435–450; L. C. Lederman, "The Impact of Gender on the Self and Self-Talk," in *Women and Men Communicating: Challenges and Changes* 2e, edited by L. P. Arliss and D. J. Borisoff (Prospect Heights, IL: Waveland, 2001), 78–89; J. R. Johnson, "The Role of Inner Speech in Human Communication," *Communication Education* 33 (1984): 211–222; J. Ayres, "The Power of Positive Thinking," *Communication Education* 37 (1988): 289–296.
54. A. T. Latinjak, M. Torregrosa, and J. Renom, "Combining Self Talk and Performance Feedback: Their Effectiveness with Adult Tennis Players," *Sport Psychologist* 25 (2011): 18–31; N. Zourbanos et al., "The Social Side of Self-Talk: Relationships between Perceptions of Support Received from the Coach and Athletes' Self-Talk," *Psychology of Sport & Exercise* 12 (2011): 407–414; A. V. Tovares, "Managing the Voices: Athlete Self-Talk as a Dialogic Process," *Journal of Language & Social Psychology* 29 (2010): 261–277.
55. B. R. Schlenkere, S. A. Wowra, R. M. Johnson, and M. L. Miller, "The Impact of Imagined Audiences on Self-Appraisals," *Personal Relationships* 15 (2008): 247–260; see J. Ayres and T. S. Hopf, "The Long-Term Effect of Visualization in the Classroom: A Brief Research Report," *Communication Education* 39 (1990): 75–78; J. Ayres and T. S. Hopf, "Visualization: Is It More Than Extra-Attention?" *Communication Education* 38 (1989): 1–5.
56. J. Ayres, T. S. Hopf, and D. M. Ayres, "An Examination of Whether Imaging Ability Enhances the Effectiveness of an Intervention Designed to Reduce Speech Anxiety," *Communication Education* 43 (1994): 252–258.
57. A concept related to bravado and confidence is *communication bravado*, introduced by K. Quintanilla and J. Mallard, "Understanding the Role of Communication Bravado: An Important Issue for Trainers/Educators," *Texas Speech Communication Journal* 33 (2008): 44–49.
58. R. J. Sidelinger and M. Booth-Butterfield, "Starting Off on the Wrong Foot: An Analysis of Mate Value, Commitment, and Partner 'Baggage' in Romantic Relationships," *Human Communication* 12 (2009): 403–419.
59. P. R. Hinton, *The Psychology of Interpersonal Perception* (New York: Routledge, 1993).
60. E. B. Goldstein, *Sensation and Perception* 9e (Belmont, CA: Cengage Learning/Wadsworth, 2013); A. S. Rancer, F. F. Jordan-Jackson, and D. A. Infante, "Observers' Perceptions of an Interpersonal Dispute as a Function of Mode of Presentation," *Communication Reports* 16 (2003): 35–48; D. A. Kenny, *Interpersonal Perception: A Social Relations Analysis* (New York: Guilford Press, 1994).
61. M. Merleau-Ponty, D. Landes, and T. Carman, *Phenomenology of Perception* (New York: Routledge, 2013); J. Kornfield, *The Wise Heart: A Guide to the Universal Teachings of Buddhist Psychology* (New York: Bantam Dell/Random House, 2008), excerpted in "The One-Minute Miracle," *O: The Oprah Winfrey Magazine* (June 2008): 140.
62. E. S. Byers, "Beyond the Birds and the Bees and Was It Good for You? Thirty Years of Research on Sexual Communication," *Canadian Psychology* 52 (2011): 20–28; B. Fink, P. J. Matts, S. Roder, R. Johnson, and M. Burquest, "Differences in Visual Perception of Age and Attractiveness of Female Facial and Body Skin," *International Journal of Cosmetic Science* 33 (2011): 126–131; S. F. O'Neil and M. A. Webster, "Adaptation and the Perception of Facial Age," *Visual Cognition* 19 (2011): 534–550.
63. C. M. Steele, *Whistling Vivaldi: How Stereotypes Affect Us and What We Can Do* (New York: W. W. Norton, 2011); L. C. Aguilar, *Ouch! That Stereotype Hurts . . . Communicating Respectfully in a Diverse World* (Bedford, TX: Walk the Talk Company, 2006); D. J. Schneider, A. H. Hastorf, and P. C. Ellsworth, *Person Perception* 2e (Reading, MA: Addison-Wesley, 1979).
64. M. L. Shier, M. E. Jones, and J. R. Graham, "Perspectives of Employed People Experiencing Homelessness of Self and Being Homeless: Challenging Socially Constructed Perceptions and Stereotypes," *Journal of Sociology & Social Welfare* 37 (2010): 13–37; A. J. Kosor and L. Kendal-Wilson, "Older Homeless Women: Reframing the Stereotype of the Bag Lady," *Affilia* 17 (2002): 354–370.
65. D. T. Kenrick, S. L. Neuberg, and R. B. Cialdini, *Social Psychology: Goals in Interaction* 5e (Boston: Pearson, 2009).
66. C. Spears Brown, *Parenting Beyond Pink and Blue: How to Raise Your Kids Free of Gender Stereotypes* (New York: Ten Speed Press, 2014); A. P. Smiler, *Challenging Casanova: Beyond the Stereotype of the Promiscuous Young Male* (San Francisco: Jossey-Bass, 2012); M. Salesses, *Different Racisms: On Stereotypes, the Individual, and Asian American Masculinity* (New York: Thought Catalog, 2013); M. Muchnik, "Gender Stereotypes in the Language of *Be My Knife* by David Grossman," *Text & Talk* 30 (2010): 553–570; D. L. Oswald, "Gender Stereotypes and Women's Reports of Liking and Ability in Traditionally Masculine and Feminine Occupations," *Psychology of Women Quarterly* 32 (2008): 196–203; C. Hoessler and A. L. Chasteen, "Does Aging Affect the Use of Shifting Standards?" *Experimental Aging Research* 34 (2008): 1–12.
67. C. N. Macrae, G. V. Bodenhausen, A. B. Milne, and J. Jetten, "Out of Mind but Back in Sight: Stereotypes on the Rebound," *Journal of Personality and Social Psychology* 67 (1994): 808–817.
68. This chapter benefited from the fine scholarship and work of M. V. Redmond, coauthor of *Interpersonal Communication: Relating to Others* 7e (Boston: Pearson, 2013).

Chapter 3

1. D. K. Ivy and S. T. Wahl, *Nonverbal Communication for a Lifetime* 2e (Dubuque, IA: Kendall Hunt, 2014); D. Powell and M. Dixon, "Does SMS Text Messaging Help or Harm Adults' Knowledge of Standard Spelling," *Journal of Computer Assisted Learning* 28 (2011): 58–66; L. D. Rosen, J. Chang, L. Erwin, L. M. Carrier, and N. A. Cheever, "The Relationship between 'Textisms' and Formal and Informal Writing Among Young Adults," *Communication Research* 37 (2010): 420; F.-Y. F. Wei and Y. K. Wang, "Students' Silent Messages: Can Teacher Verbal and Nonverbal Immediacy Moderate Student Use of Text Messaging in Class?" *Communication Education* 59 (2010): 475–496; A. Angster, M. Frank, and D. Lester, "An Exploratory Study of Students' Use of Cell Phones, Texting, and Social Networking Sites," *Psychological Reports* 107 (2010): 402–404.
2. K. H. Turner, "Flipping the Switch: Code-Switching from Text Speak to Standard English," *English Journal* 98 (2009): 60–65; L. Thompson and J. Cupples, "Seen and Not Heard? Text Messaging and Digital Sociality," *Social and Cultural Geography* 9 (2008): 95–108.

3. "2013 Employer Survey," *Association of American Colleges and Universities*, April 10, 2013, accessed June 16, 2014, www.aacu.org; "Hiring 2013 College Graduates Survey," *Society for Human Resources Management*, June 11, 2013, accessed June 16, 2014, www.shrm.org.
4. B. Spitzberg and J. P. Dillard, "Social Skills and Communication," in *Interpersonal Communication Research: Advances Through Meta-Analysis*, edited by M. Allen, R. W. Preiss, B. M. Gayle, and N. Burrell (Mahwah, NJ: Lawrence Erlbaum, 2002), 89–107.
5. B. L. Whorf, "Science and Linguistics," in *Language, Thought, and Reality*, edited by J. B. Carroll (Cambridge: Massachusetts Institute of Technology Press, 1956).
6. R. F. Verderber and K. S. Verderber, "Elements of Language," in *Making Connections: Readings in Relational Communication* 5e, edited by K. M. Galvin (New York: Oxford University Press, 2011), 51–60.
7. *Oxford Desk Dictionary and Thesaurus, American Edition* (New York: Oxford University Press, 2007).
8. S.-T. Kousta, G. Vigliocco, D. P. Vinson, M. Andrews, and E. Del Campo, "The Representation of Abstract Words: Why Emotion Matters," *Journal of Experimental Psychology* 140 (2011): 14–34; D. A. Stapel and G. R. Semin, "The Magic Spell of Language: Linguistics Categories and Their Perceptual Consequences," *Journal of Personality and Social Psychology* 93 (2007): 23–33; A. M. Glenberg, M. Sato, L. Cattaneo, L. Riggio, D. Palumbo, and G. Buccino, "Processing Abstract Language Modulates Motor System Activity," *Quarterly Journal of Experimental Psychology* 61 (2008): 905–919.
9. L. M. Bauer, E. L. Olheiser, and J. Altarriba, "Word Type Effects in False Recall: Concrete, Abstract, and Emotion Word Critical Lures," *American Journal of Psychology* 122 (2009): 469–481; A. Parker and N. Dagnall, "Concreteness Effects Revisited: The Influence of Dynamic Visual Noise on Memory for Concrete and Abstract Words," *Memory* 17 (2008): 397–410.
10. A. G. Smith, ed., *Communication and Culture* (New York: Holt, Rinehart and Winston, 1966).
11. D. K. Ivy, *GenderSpeak: Personal Effectiveness in Gender Communication* 5e (Boston: Pearson, 2012).
12. McArdle, "Ask McArdle: Why Is My Phone's Autocorrect Almost Always Wrong?" Canadian Business, April 25, 2014, accessed September 23, 2014, www.canadianbusiness.com.
13. *Damn You Autocorrect*, accessed June 16, 2014, www.damnyouautocorrect.com.
14. C. T. Carr and C. Stefaniak, "Sent from My iPhone: The Medium and Message as Cues of Sender Professionalism in Mobile Telephony," *Journal of Applied Communication Research* 40 (2012): 403–424.
15. K. Steinmetz, "The Linguist's Mother Lode: What Twitter Reveals about Slang, Gender and No-Nose Emoticons," *Time* (September 9, 2013): 56–57.
16. J. Close Conoley, "Sticks and Stones Can Break My Bones and Words Can Really Hurt Me," *School Psychology Review* 37 (2008): 217–220.
17. Y. Osward, *Every Word Has Power: Switch on Your Language and Turn on Your Life* (New York: Atria Books/Simon & Schuster, 2008); P. Denton, *The Power of Our Words: Teacher Language That Helps Children Learn* (Turners Falls, MA: Northwest Foundation for Children, 2007).
18. C. M. Frisby, "Sticks 'n' Stones May Break My Bones, but Words They Hurt Like Hell: Derogatory Words in Popular Songs," *Media Report to Women* 38 (2010): 12–18; H. A. Schroth, J. Bain-Chekal, and D. F. Caldwell, "Sticks and Stones May Break Bones and Words Can Hurt Me: Words and Phrases That Trigger Emotions in Negotiations and Their Effects," *International Journal of Conflict Management* 16 (2005): 102–127; A. Palayiwa, P. Sheeran, and A. Thompson, "'Words Will Never Hurt Me!': Implementation Intentions Regulate Attention to Stigmatizing Comments About Appearance," *Journal of Social and Clinical Psychology* 29 (2010): 575–598; A. Ellis, *A New Guide to Rational Living* (North Hollywood, CA: Wilshire Books, 1977).
19. C. Peterson, M. E. P. Seligman, and G. E. Vaillant, "Pessimistic Explanatory Style Is a Risk Factor for Physical Illness: A 35-Year Longitudinal Study," *Journal of Personality and Social Psychology* 55 (1988): 23–27.
20. A. Oldenburg, "Big '*Bachelorette*' Drama: Racism and Mimes," *USA Today*, June 17, 2014, accessed June 18, 2014, www.usatoday.com .
21. C. J. Gilbert and J. P. Rossing, "Trumping Tropes with Joke(r)s: *The Daily Show* 'Plays the Race Card,'" *Western Journal of Communication* 77 (2013): 92–111; T. M. Harris, "Flying Solo: Negotiating the Matrix of Racism and Sexism in Higher Education," *Women & Language* 35 (2012): 103–107; J. Hartigan, *What Can You Say? America's National Conversation on Race* (Stanford, CA: Stanford University Press, 2010); R. T. Schaefer, *Racial and Ethnic Groups, Census Update* 12e (Boston: Prentice Hall, 2010); B. J. Allen, *Differences Matter: Communicating Social Identity* 2e (Long Grove, IL: Waveland, 2010); D. J. Napoli and V. Lee-Schoenfeld, *Language Matters: A Guide to Everyday Questions About Language* 2e (New York: Oxford University Press, 2010); M. P. Orbe and T. M. Harris, *Interracial Communication: Theory into Practice* 3e (Thousand Oaks, CA: Sage, 2013); J. Perlmann and M. C. Waters, eds., *The New Race Question: How the Census Counts Multiracial Individuals* (New York: Russell Sage Foundation, 2005).
22. A. Taylor, M. J. Hardman, and C. Wright, *Making the Invisible Visible: Gender in Language* (Bloomington, IN: IUniverse LLC, 2013); E. Teso and L. Crolley, "Gender-Based Linguistic Reform in International Organisations," *Language Policy* 12 (2013): 139–158; R. K. Mallett and D. E. Wagner, "The Unexpectedly Positive Consequences of Confronting Sexism," *Journal of Experimental Social Psychology* 47 (2011): 215–220; G. He, "An Analysis of Sexism in English," *Journal of Language Teaching and Research* 1 (2010): 332–335; J. B. Parks and M. A. Roberton, "Generation Gaps in Attitudes toward Sexist/Nonsexist Language," *Journal of Language and Social Psychology* 27 (2008): 276–283; J. B. Parks and M. A. Roberton, "Explaining Age and Gender Effects on Attitudes toward Sexist Language," *Journal of Language and Social Psychology* 24 (2005): 401–411; E. L. Cralley and J. B. Ruscher, "Lady, Girl, or Woman: Sexism and Cognitive Busyness Predict Use of Gender-Biased Nouns," *Journal of Language and Social Psychology* 24 (2005): 300–314.
23. C. Kramarae, "Muted Group Theory and Communication: Asking Dangerous Questions," *Women & Language* 28 (2005): 55–61; S. Ardener, "Muted Groups: The Genesis of an Idea and Its Praxis," *Women & Language* 28 (2005): 50–54; J. K. Swim, R. Mallett, and C. Stangor, "Understanding Subtle Sexism: Detection and Use of Sexist Language," *Sex Roles* 51 (2004): 117–128; J. Briere and C. Lanktree, "Sex-Role Related Effects of Sex Bias in Language," *Sex Roles* 9 (1983): 625–632; L. Brooks, "Sexist Language in Occupational Information: Does It Make a Difference?" *Journal of Vocational Behavior* 23 (1983): 227–232.
24. H. S. O'Donnell, "Sexism in Language," *Elementary English* 50 (1973): 1067–1072, as cited by J. C. Pearson, L. Turner, and W. Todd Mancillas, *Gender and Communication* 3e (Dubuque, IA: William C. Brown, 1995).
25. B. D. Earp, "The Extinction of Masculine Generics," *Journal for Communication & Culture* 2 (2012): 4-19; J. Flanigan, "The Use and Evolution of Gender Neutral Language in an Intentional Community," *Women & Language* 36 (2013): 27–41.
26. P. Gygax, U. Gabriel, O. Sarrasin, J. Oakhill, and A. Garnham, "Some Grammatical Rules Are More Difficult Than Others: The Case of the Generic Interpretation of the Masculine," *European Journal of Psychology of Education* 24 (2009): 235–246; M. A. Clason, "Feminism, Generic 'He,' and the *TNIV* Bible Translation Debate," *Critical Discourse Studies* 3 (2006): 23–35; L. Conkright, D. Flannagan, and J. Dykes, "Effects of Pronoun Type and Gender Role Consistency on Children's Recall and Interpretation of Stories," *Sex Roles* 43 (2000): 481–499; J. L. Stinger and R. Hopper,

"Generic *He* in Conversation?" *Quarterly Journal of Speech* 84 (1998): 209–221; J. Gastil, "Generic Pronouns and Sexist Language: The Oxymoronic Character of Masculine Generics," *Sex Roles* 23 (1990): 629–641; D. K. Ivy, L. Bullis-Moore, K. Norvell, P. Backlund, and M. Javidi, "The Lawyer, the Babysitter, and the Student: Inclusive Language Usage and Instruction," *Women & Language* 18 (1994): 13–21; W. Martyna, "What Does 'He' Mean? Use of the Generic Masculine," *Journal of Communication* 28 (1978): 131–138.

27. "Supplemental Material: Writing Clearly and Concisely, General Guidelines for Reducing Bias," *Publication Manual of the American Psychological Association* 6e, 2009, accessed September 23, 2014, www.apastyle.org.
28. L. Madson and R. M. Hessling, "Does Alternating between Masculine and Feminine Pronouns Eliminate Perceived Gender Bias in a Text?" *Sex Roles* 41 (1999): 559–576; D. Kennedy, "Review Essay: She or He in Textbooks," *Women & Language* 15 (1992): 46–49.
29. L. Madson and J. Shoda, "Alternating between Masculine and Feminine Pronouns: Does Essay Topic Affect Readers' Perceptions?" *Sex Roles* 54 (2006): 275–285; T. Strahan, "'They' in Australian English: Non-Gender-Specific or Specifically Non-Gendered?" *Australian Journal of Linguistics* 28 (2008): 17–29.
30. R. Goldman, "Here's a List of 58 Gender Options for Facebook Users," *ABC News*, February 13, 2014, accessed February 17, 2014, abcnews.go.com; K. Steinmetz, "A Comprehensive Guide to Facebook's New Options for Gender Identity," February 14, 2014, *Time*, accessed February 18, 2014, techland.time.com.
31. "Trans 101: Cisgender," *Basic Rights Oregon*, October 9, 2011, accessed February 18, 2014, www.basicrights.org.
32. Our understanding of asexual identity was informed by a student panel organized by Dr. Maureen Keeley, Texas State University, as part of the annual Communication Week programming, March 2014. Other resources include J. S. Decker, "How to Tell If You Are Asexual," September 20, 2014, accessed June 18, 2014, time.com; *The Asexual Visibility and Education Network*, accessed June 19, 2014, www.asexuality.org.
33. Ivy, *GenderSpeak*.
34. Ivy, *GenderSpeak*.
35. P. Weber, "Confused by All the New Facebook Genders? Here's What They Mean," *Slate*, February 21, 2014, accessed March 14, 2014, www.slate.com/blogs/lexicon_valley/2014/02/21/gender_facebook_now_has_56_categories_to_choose_from_including_cisgender.html.
36. Ivy, *GenderSpeak*.
37. J. Hall and B. LaFrance, "'That's Gay': Sexual Prejudice, Gender Identity, Norms, and Homophobic Communication," *Communication Quarterly* 60 (2012): 35–58; M. R. Woodford, M. L. Howell, A. Kulick, and P. Silverschanz, "'That's So Gay': Heterosexual Male Undergraduates and the Perpetuation of Sexual Orientation Microaggressions," *Campus Journal of Interpersonal Violence* 28 (2013): 416–435; M. R. Woodford, M. L. Howell, P. Silverschanz, and L. Yu, "'That's So Gay': Examining the Covariates of Hearing This Expression among Gay, Lesbian, and Bisexual College Students," *Journal of American College Health* 60 (2012): 429–434; N. Updike, "That's So Gay!" *Salon*, September 14, 2000, salon.com; Associated Press, "'That's So Gay' Prompts a Lawsuit: Student Sent to Principal's Office Insists It Was Not a Homophobic Putdown," *MSNBC*, February 28, 2007, msnbc.com.
38. P. C. McCabe, E. A. Dragowski, and F. Rubinson, "What Is Homophobic Bias Anyway? Defining and Recognizing Microaggressions and Harassment of LGBTQ Youth," *Journal of School Violence* 12 (2013): 7–26; M. Kantor, *Homophobia: The State of Sexual Bigotry Today* 2e (Santa Barbara, CA: Praeger, 2009); G. Griffin, "Understanding Heterosexism: The Subtle Continuum of Homophobia," *Women & Language* 21 (1998): 33–39.
39. T. D. Nelson (Ed.), *Ageism: Stereotyping and Prejudice against Older Persons* (Cambridge: Massachusetts Institute of Technology Press, 2004); A. Williams and J. F. Nussbaum, *Intergenerational Communication across the Life Span* (Mahwah, NJ: Lawrence Erlbaum, 2000); E. O'Reilly, *Decoding the Cultural Stereotypes about Aging: New Perspectives on Aging Talk and Aging Issues* (New York: Routledge, 1997).
40. R. K. S. Macaulay, *Talk That Counts: Age, Gender, and Social Class Differences in Discourse* (New York: Oxford University Press, 2005); M. Argyle, *The Psychology of Social Class* (New York: Routledge, 1993).
41. J. S. Seiter, J. Larsen, and J. Skinner, "'Handicapped' or 'Handicapable'? The Effects of Language about Persons with Disabilities on Perceptions of Source Credibility and Persuasiveness," *Communication Reports* 11 (1998): 21–31.
42. J. R. Gibb, "Defensive Communication," *Journal of Communication* 11 (1961): 141–148. For other research on communication climate, see K. Czech and G. L. Forward, "Leader Communication: Faculty Perception of the Department Chair," *Communication Quarterly* 58 (2010): 431–457; J. M. Reagle, "'Be Nice': Wikipedia Norms for Supportive Communication," *New Review of Hypermedia & Multimedia* 16 (2010): 161–180; J. A. H. Becker, B. Ellevold, and G. H. Stamp, "The Creation of Defensiveness in Social Interaction II: A Model of Defensive Communication among Romantic Couples," *Communication Monographs* 75 (2008): 86–110; L. Cairns, "Reinforcement," in *The Handbook of Communication Skills* 3e, edited by O. Hargie (London: Routledge, 2006), 147–164; J. A. H. Becker, J. R. B. Halbesleben, and H. D. O'Hair, "Defensive Communication and Burnout in the Workplace: The Mediating Role of Leader-Member Exchange," *Communication Research Reports* 22 (2005): 143–150.
43. B. Clark, "50 Trigger Words and Phrases for Powerful Multimedia Content," *copyblogger*, April 20, 2009, www.copyblogger.com/trigger-words; E. T. Booth, "Assign This: Trigger Words," *Spectra* (Washington, DC: National Communication Association, June/July 2007).
44. L. V. Oceja, M. W. Heerdkink, E. L. Stocks, T. Ambrona, B. Lopez-Perez, and S. Salgado, "Empathy, Awareness of Others, and Action: How Feeling Empathy for One-Among-Others Motivates Helping the Others," *Basic & Applied Social Psychology* 36 (2014): 111–124; P. L. Lockwood, A. Seara-Cardoso, and E. Viding, "Emotion Regulation Moderates the Association between Empathy and Prosocial Behavior," *PloS one* 9.5 (2014): e96555; A. J. Clark, "Empathy and Sympathy: Therapeutic Distinctions in Counseling," *Journal of Mental Health Counseling* 32 (2010): 95–101; I. Devoldre, M. H. Davis, L. L. Verhofstadt, and A. Buysse, "Empathy and Social Support Provision in Couples: Social Support and the Need to Study the Underlying Processes," *Journal of Psychology* 144 (2010): 259–284; T. G. Cassels, S. Chan, W. Chung, and S. A. J. Birch, "The Role of Culture in Affective Empathy: Cultural and Bicultural Differences," *Journal of Cognition and Culture* 10 (2010): 309–326; J. D. Trout, *The Empathy Gap: Building Bridges to the Good Life and the Good Society* (New York: Viking, 2009); J. Hakansson and H. Montgomery, "Empathy as an Interpersonal Phenomenon," *Journal of Social and Personal Relationships* 20 (2003): 267–284; M. V. Redmond, "The Functions of Empathy (Decentering) in Human Relations," *Human Relations* 42 (1993): 593–606.
45. C. Levesque, M-F. Lafontaine, A. Caron, J. L. Flescha, and S. Bjornson, "Dyadic Empathy, Dyadic Coping, and Relationship Satisfaction: A Dyadic Model," *Europe's Journal of Psychology* 10 (2014): 118–134; D. Johnson, "Helpful Listening and Responding," in Galvin, *Making Connections*, 70–76; D. F. Barone, P. S. Hutchings, H. J. Kimmel, H. L. Traub, J. T. Cooper, and C. M. Marshall, "Increasing Empathic Accuracy through Practice and Feedback in a Clinical Interviewing Course," *Journal of Social and Clinical Psychology* 24 (2005): 156–171.
46. T. Challies, "The Art and Science of the Humblebrag," *Challies.com*, October 22, 2013, accessed June 19, 2014, www.challies.com; *The Rachel Maddow Show*, msnbc, June 23, 2012, Television.

Chapter 4

1. M. Kaneko and J. Mesch, "Eye Gaze in Creative Sign Language," *Sign Language Studies* 13 (2013): 372–400; M. Fox, *Talking Hands: What Sign Language Reveals About the Mind* (New York:

Simon & Schuster, 2008); R. B. Grossman and J. Kegl, "Moving Faces: Categorization of Dynamic Facial Expressions in American Sign Language by Deaf and Hearing Participants," *Journal of Nonverbal Behavior* 31 (2007): 23–38.

2. T. Banziger, S. Patel, & K. Scherer, "The Role of Perceived Voice and Speech Characteristics in Vocal Emotion Communication," *Journal of Nonverbal Behavior* 38 (2014): 31–52; A. Lo Coco, S. Ingoglia, and L.-O. Lundqvist, "The Assessment of Susceptibility to Emotional Contagion: A Contribution to the Italian Adaptation of the Emotional Contagion Scale," *Journal of Nonverbal Behavior* 38 (2014): 67–87.
3. A. Mehrabian, *Nonverbal Communication* (Chicago: Aldine-Atherton, 1972).
4. R. L. Birdwhistell, *Kinesics and Context* (Philadelphia: University of Pennsylvania Press, 1970).
5. R. Petrician, A. Todorov, and C. Grady, "Personality at Face Value: Facial Appearance Predicts Self and Other Personality Judgments among Strangers and Spouses," *Journal of Nonverbal Behavior* 38 (2014): 259–277.
6. D. K. Ivy and S. T. Wahl, *Nonverbal Communication for a Lifetime* 2e (Dubuque, IA: Kendall Hunt, 2014); E. Krumhuber, K. Likowski, and P. Weyers, "Facial Mimicry of Spontaneous and Deliberate Duchenne and Non-Duchenne Smiles," *Journal of Nonverbal Behavior* 38 (2014): 1–11; S. Farley, "Nonverbal Reactions to an Attractive Stranger: The Role of Mimicry in Communicating Preferred Social Distance," *Journal of Nonverbal Behavior* 38 (2014): 195–208; R. C. Schmidt, S. Morr, P. Fitzpatrick, and M. J. Richardson, "Measuring the Dynamics of Interactional Synchrony," *Journal of Nonverbal Behavior* 36 (2012): 263–279; D. Lakens and M. Stel, "If They Move in Sync, They Must Feel in Sync: Movement Synchrony Leads to Attributions of Rapport and Entitativity," *Social Cognition* 29 (2011): 1–14; K. Wilt, K. Funkhouser, and W. Revelle, "The Dynamic Relationships of Affective Synchrony to Perceptions of Situations," *Journal of Research in Personality* 45 (2011): 309–321; J. L. Lakin, V. W. Jefferis, C. M. Cheng, and T. L. Chartrand, "The Chameleon Effect as Social Glue: Evidence for the Evolutionary Significance of Nonconscious Mimicry," *Journal of Nonverbal Behavior* 27 (2003): 145–161; N. Guéguen, "The Mimicker Is a Mirror of Myself: Impact of Mimicking on Self-Consciousness and Social Anxiety," *Social Behavior and Personality* 39 (2011): 725–728; N. Guéguen, "The Effects of Incidental Similarity with a Stranger on Mimicry Behavior," *The Open Behavioral Science Journal* 6 (2012): 15–22; N. Guéguen, A. Martin, and S. Meineri, "Mimicry and Helping Behavior: An Evaluation of Mimicry on Explicit Helping Request," *The Journal of Social Psychology* 15 (2011): 1–4; J. Holler and J. Wilkin, "Co-Speech Gesture Mimicry in the Process of Collaborative Referring During Face-to-Face Interaction," *Journal of Nonverbal Behavior* 35 (2011): 133–153.
7. C. Rush, *The Mere Mortal's Guide to Fine Dining* (New York: Broadway Books, 2006).
8. N. O. Rule and N. Ambady, "She's Got the Look: Inferences from Female Chief Executive Officers' Faces Predict Their Success," *Sex Roles* 61 (2009): 644–652; L. P. Naumann, S. Vazire, P. J. Rentfrow, and S. D. Gosling, "Personality Judgments Based on Physical Appearance," *Personality and Social Psychology Bulletin* 35 (2009): 1661–1671.
9. W. E. Chaplin, J. B. Phillips, J. D. Brown, N. R. Clanton, and J. L. Stein, "Handshaking, Gender, Personality, and First Impressions," *Journal of Personality and Social Psychology* 79 (2000): 110–117.
10. G. L. Stewart, S. L. Dustin, M. R. Barrick, and T. C. Darnold, "Exploring the Handshake in Employment Interviews," *Journal of Applied Psychology* 93 (2008): 1139–1146.
11. M. Argyle, *Bodily Communication* (New York: Methuen, 1988).
12. D. Matsumoto and H. S. Hwang, "Cultural Influences on Nonverbal Behavior," in *Nonverbal Communication: Science and Applications*, edited by D. Matsumoto, M. G. Frank, and H. S. Hwang (Thousand Oaks, CA: Sage, 2013a), 97–120; P. A. Andersen, "Tactile Traditions: Cultural Differences and Similarities in Haptic Communication," in *The Handbook of Touch: Neuroscience, Behavioral, and Health Perspectives*, edited by M. J. Hertenstein and S. J. Weiss (New York: Springer, 2011), 351–371; M. Jung and H. N. Fouts, "Multiple Caregivers' Touch Interactions with Young Children among the Bofi Foragers in Central Africa," *International Journal of Psychology* 46 (2011): 24–32; P. Yang, "Nonverbal Gender Differences: Examining Gestures of University-Educated Mandarin Chinese Speakers," *Text & Talk* 30 (2010): 333–357; P. Szarota, "The Mystery of the European Smile: A Comparison Based on Individual Photographs Provided by Internet Users," *Journal of Nonverbal Behavior* 34 (2010): 249–256; D. Matsumoto, A. Olide, J. Schug, B. Willingham, and M. Callan, "Cross-Cultural Judgments of Spontaneous Facial Expressions of Emotion," *Journal of Nonverbal Behavior* 33 (2009): 213–238; H. A. Elfenbein, "Learning in Emotion Judgments: Training and the Cross-Cultural Understanding of Facial Expressions," *Journal of Nonverbal Behavior* 30 (2006): 21–36; R. E. Axtell, *Gestures: Do's and Taboos of Body Language around the World* (New York: Wiley, 1998).
13. D. Matsumoto and H. Hwang, "Cultural Similarities and Differences in Emblematic Gestures," *Journal of Nonverbal Behavior* 37 (2013b): 1–27; E. Vennekens-Kelly, *Subtle Differences, Big Faux Pas: Test Your Cultural Competence* (Scottsdale, AZ: Summertime, 2012); L. A. Samovar, R. E. Porter, and E. R. McDaniel, "Approaches to Intercultural Communication," in *Intercultural Communication: A Reader* 13e, edited by L. A. Samovar, R. E. Porter, and E. R. McDaniel (Belmont, CA: Wadsworth, 2011), 1–3.
14. See J. K. Burgoon and S. B. Jones, "Toward a Theory of Personal Space Expectations and Their Violations," *Human Communication Research* 2 (1976): 131–146. For discussions and applications of expectancy violations theory, see E. L. Cohen, "Expectancy Violations in Relationships with Friends and Media Figures," *Communication Research Reports* 27 (2010): 97–111; A. Ramirez Jr. and Z. Wang, "When Online Meets Offline: An Expectancy Violations Theory Perspective on Modality Switching," *Journal of Communication* 58 (2008): 20–39; J. K. Burgoon and N. E. Dunbar, "Nonverbal Expressions of Dominance and Power in Human Relationships," in *The SAGE Handbook of Nonverbal Communication*, edited by V. Manusov and M. L. Patterson (Thousand Oaks, CA: Sage, 2006), 279–297.
15. W. Langewiesche, "Beijing's Olympic Makeover," *Vanity Fair*, April 2008, accessed June 22, 2014, www.vanityfair.com.
16. N. Winfield, "Cultural Gaffes, Clashes Inevitable at World Event Like the Olympics," *Morning Sentinel*, July 28, 2012, accessed June 22, 2014, www.onlinesentinel.com, retrieved June 22, 2014.
17. "Sensitive Cross-Cultural Snafus Highlighted During 2012 Summer Olympic Games in London," *Culture Coach International*, August 5, 2012, accessed June 22, 2014, www.culturecoach.biz.
18. J. Fast, *Body Language* (New York: M. Evans, 1970).
19. "The Second Screen: A Growing Phenomenon in the Multimedia Industry," white paper, *Beenius*, accessed June 21, 2014, www.beenius.tv; J. Bercovici, "The Second-Screen Trend Is Bigger Than Twitter Vs. Facebook," *Forbes*, October 10, 2013, accessed June 21, 2014, www.forbes.com; HUB Research, "What's TV Worth?" April 11, 2013, accessed June 21, 2014, hubresearchllc.com/download-report/2013-whats-tv-worth.
20. P. Ekman and W. V. Friesen, "The Repertoire of Nonverbal Behavior: Categories, Origins, Usage, and Coding," *Semiotica* 1 (1969): 49–98.
21. American Society for Aesthetic Plastic Surgery, "Cosmetic Procedures Increase in 2012," March 2013, accessed November 7, 2013, www.surgery.org/media/newsreleases/cosmetic-procedures-increase-in-2012.
22. A. A. Poorani, "Who Determines the Ideal Body? A Summary of Research Findings on Body Image," *New Media & Mass*

Communication 2 (2012): 1–12; K. Bissell and A. Rask, "Real Women on Real Beauty: Self-Discrepancy, Internalization of the Thin Ideal, and Perceptions of Attractiveness and Thinness in Dove's Campaign for Real Beauty," *International Journal of Advertising* 29 (2010): 643–668; S. Darlow and M. Lobel, "Who Is Beholding My Beauty? Thinness Ideals, Weight, and Women's Responses to Appearance Evaluation," *Sex Roles* 63 (2010): 833–843; M. S. Richardson and J. S. Paxton, "An Evaluation of a Body Image Intervention Based on Risk Factors for Body Dissatisfaction: A Controlled Study with Adolescent Girls," *International Journal of Eating Disorders* 43 (2010): 112–122; M. Krcmar, S. Giles, and D. Helme, "Understanding the Process: How Mediated and Peer Norms Affect Young Women's Body Esteem," *Communication Quarterly* 56 (2008): 111–130; J. S. Wrench and J. L Knapp, "The Effects of Body Image Perceptions and Sociocommunicative Orientations on Self-Esteem, Depression, and Identification and Involvement in the Gay Community," *Journal of Homosexuality* 55 (2008): 471–503.

23. B. Verhulst, M. Lodge, and H. Lavine, "The Attractiveness Halo: Why Some Candidates Are Perceived More Favorably Than Others," *Journal of Nonverbal Behavior* 34 (2010): 111–117; L. P. Naumann, S. Vazire, P. J. Rentfrow, and S. D. Gosling, "Personality Judgments Based on Physical Appearance," *Personality & Social Psychology Bulletin* 35 (2009): 1661–1671; T. H. Feeley, "Evidence of Halo Effects in Student Evaluations of Communication Instruction," *Communication Education* 51 (2002): 225–236.
24. M. Parry, "Researchers Find Ratemyprofessors.com Useful, If Not Chili-Pepper Hot," *The Chronicle of Higher Education* (December 2, 2011): A4; R. Wilson, "Being Hot Leaves Some Professors Cold," *The Chronicle of Higher Education* (August 13, 2010): A1, A9; K. Soper, "RateMyProfessor'sAppearance.com," *The Chronicle of Higher Education* (September 17, 2010): B24; T. A. Moriarty, "They Love Me, They Love Me Not," *The Chronicle of Higher Education* (April 24, 2009): A27; R. Toor, "Can't We Be Smart and Look Good, Too?" *The Chronicle Review* (April 3, 2009): B4–B5; C. Edwards, A. Edwards, Q. Qing, and S. T. Wahl, "The Influence of Computer-Mediated Word-of-Mouth Communication on Student Perceptions of Instructors and Attitudes toward Learning Course Content," *Communication Education* 56 (2007): 255–277; A. Edwards and C. Edwards, "The Impact of Instructor Verbal and Nonverbal Immediacy on Student Perceptions of Attractiveness and Homophily," *Journal on Excellence in College Teaching* 12 (2001): 5–16; K. A. Rocca and J. C. McCroskey, "The Interrelationship of Student Ratings of Instructors' Immediacy, Verbal Aggressiveness, Homophily, and Interpersonal Attraction," *Communication Education* 48 (1999): 308–316; G. Montell, "Do Good Looks Equal Good Evaluations?" *The Chronicle of Higher Education: Career Network*, October 15, 2003, http://chronicle.com.
25. M. L. Knapp, J. A. Hall, and T. G. Horgan, *Nonverbal Communication in Human Interaction* 8e (Belmont, CA: Wadsworth/Cengage Learning, 2013); M. Aliakbari and K. Abdollahi, "Does It Matter What We Wear? A Sociolinguistic Study of Clothing and Human Values," *International Journal of Linguistics* 5 (2013): 34–45.
26. J. Rowsell, G. Kress, and B. Street, "Visual Optics: Interpreting Body Art, Three Ways," *Visual Communication* 12 (2013): 97–122; W. Lim, D. Ting, E. Leo, and C. Jayanthy, "Contemporary Perceptions of Body Modifications and Its Acceptability in the Asian Society: A Case of Tattoos and Body Piercings," *Asian Social Science* 9 (2013): 37–42; K. Doss and A. S. Ebesu Hubbard, "The Communicative Value of Tattoos: The Role of Public Self-Consciousness on Tattoo Visibility," *Communication Research Reports* 26 (2009): 62–74; T. Vinciguerra, "AMA Proposal: Lose Lab Coats," *Dallas Morning News* (July 26, 2009): 8A.
27. E. M. Lamberg and L. M. Muratori, "Cell Phones Change the Way We Walk," *Gait & Posture* 35 (2012): 688–690.
28. N. Armstrong and M. Wagner, *Field Guide to Gestures: How to Identify and Interpret Virtually Every Gesture Known to Man* (Philadelphia: Quirk Books, 2003).
29. D. D. Henningsen, F. Kartch, N. Orr, and A. Brown, "The Perceptions of Verbal and Nonverbal Flirting Cues in Cross-Sex Interactions," *Human Communication* 12 (2009): 371–381; L. K. Guerrero, P. A. Andersen, and W. A. Afifi, *Close Encounters: Communicating in Relationships* 5e (Los Angeles: Sage, 2011); D. D. Henningsen, M. Braz, and E. Davies, "Why Do We Flirt?" *Journal of Business Communication* 45 (2008): 483–502; N. Guégen, "The Effect of a Woman's Smile on Men's Courtship Behavior," *Social Behavior and Personality* 36 (2008): 1233–1236.
30. M. M. Moore, "Nonverbal Courtship Patterns in Women: Context and Consequences," *Ethology and Sociobiology* 6 (1985): 237–247.
31. H. H. LaFrance, D. D. Henningsen, A. Oates, and C. M. Shaw, "Social-Sexual Interactions? Meta-Analyses of Sex Differences in Perceptions of Flirtatiousness, Seductiveness, and Promiscuousness," *Communication Monographs* 76 (2009): 263–285; C. Farris, T. A. Treat, R. J. Viken, and R. M. McFall, "Perceptual Mechanisms That Characterize Gender Differences in Decoding Women's Sexual Intent," *Psychological Science* 19 (2008): 348–354; M. R. Trost and J. K. Alberts, "How Men and Women Communicate Attraction: An Evolutionary View," in *Sex Differences and Similarities in Communication*, edited by K. Dindia and D. J. Canary (Mahwah, NJ: Lawrence Erlbaum, 2006), 317–336; D. D. Henningsen, "Flirting with Meaning: An Examination of Miscommunication in Flirting Interactions," *Sex Roles* 50 (2004): 481–489; M. M. Moore, "Courtship Communication and Perception," *Perceptual and Motor Skills* 94 (2002): 97–105; E. Koukounas and N. M. Letch, "Psychological Correlates of Perception of Sexual Intent in Women," *Journal of Social Psychology* 141 (2001): 443–456; A. Abbey, "Sex Differences in Attributions for Friendly Behavior: Do Males Misperceive Females' Friendliness?" *Journal of Personality and Social Psychology* 42 (1982): 830–838; L. B. Koeppel, Y. Montagne, D. O'Hair, and M. J. Cody, "Friendly? Flirting? Wrong?" *The Nonverbal Communication Reader: Classic and Contemporary Reading* 2e, edited by L. K. Guerrero, J. DeVito, and M. L. Hecht (Prospect Heights, IL: Waveland, 1999), 290–297.
32. A. Abbey, T. Zawacki, and P. O. Buck, "The Effects of Past Sexual Assault Perpetration and Alcohol Consumption on Reactions to Women's Mixed Signals," *Journal of Social and Clinical Psychology* 24 (2005): 129–157; H. J. Delaney and B. A. Gluade, "Gender Differences in Perception of Attractiveness of Men and Women in Bars," *Journal of Personality and Social Psychology* 16 (1990): 378–391.
33. K. M. Quintanilla and S. T. Wahl, *Business and Professional Communication: Keys for Workplace Excellence* (Thousand Oaks, CA: Sage, 2013); S. Mann, A. Vrij, S. Leal, P. A. Granhag, L. Warmelink, and D. Forrester, "Windows to the Soul? Deliberate Eye Contact as a Cue to Deceit." *Journal of Nonverbal Behavior* 36 (2012): 205–215; T. Field, J. E. Malphurs, R. Yando, D. Bendell, K. Carraway, and R. Cohen, "Legal Interviewers Use Children's Affect and Eye Contact Cues to Assess Credibility of Their Testimony," *Early Child Development & Care* 180 (2010): 397–404; A. Vrij, S. Mann, S. Leal, and R. Fisher, "'Look into My Eyes': Can an Instruction to Maintain Eye Contact Facilitate Lie Detection?" *Psychology, Crime, & Law* 16 (2010): 327–348.
34. Knapp, Hall, and Horgan, *Nonverbal Communication in Human Interaction.*
35. S. A. Beebe, "Eye Contact: A Nonverbal Determinant of Speaker Credibility," *Speech Teacher* 23 (1974): 21–25.
36. P. Ekman and W. Friesen, *Unmasking the Face* (Englewood Cliffs, NJ: Prentice Hall, 1975); R. L. Birdwhistell, "The Language of the Body: The Natural Environment of Words," in *Human Communication: Theoretical Explorations*, edited by A. Silverstein (New York: Wiley, 1974), 203–220.
37. C. Darwin, *Expression of Emotions in Man and Animals* (London, UK: Appleton; reprinted University of Chicago Press, 1965).
38. S. Gunnery and J. Hall, "The Duchenne Smile and Persuasion," *Journal of Nonverbal Behavior* 38 (2014): 181–194; A. G. Halberstadt, P. A. Dennis, and U. Hess, "The Influence

of Family Expressiveness, Individuals' Own Emotionality, and Self-Expressiveness on Perceptions of Others' Facial Expressions," *Journal of Nonverbal Behavior* 35 (2011): 35–50; K. U. Likowski, P. Weyers, B. Seibt, C. Stohr, P. Pauli, and A. Muhlberger, "Sad and Lonely? Sad Mood Suppresses Facial Mimicry," *Journal of Nonverbal Behavior* 35 (2011): 101–117; M. Gagnon, P. Gosselin, I. Hudon-ven der Buhs, K. Larocque, and K. Milliard, "Children's Recognition and Discrimination of Fear and Disgust Facial Expressions," *Journal of Nonverbal Behavior* 34 (2010): 27–42; J. P. Forgas and R. East, "How Real Is That Smile? Mood Effects on Accepting or Rejecting the Veracity of Emotional Facial Expressions," *Journal of Nonverbal Behavior* 32 (2009): 157–170; D. Matsumoto and B. Willingham, "Attitudes and Social Cognition: Spontaneous Facial Expressions of Emotion of Congenitally and Noncongenitally Blind Individuals," *Journal of Personality and Social Psychology* 96 (2009): 1–10; J. Beavin Bavelas and N. Chovil, "Nonverbal and Verbal Communication: Hand Gestures and Facial Displays as Part of Language Use in Face-to-Face Dialogue," in *The SAGE Handbook of Nonverbal Communication*, edited by V. Manusov and M. L. Patterson (Thousand Oaks, CA: Sage, 2006), 97–115.

39. C. M. Hurley and M. G. Frank, "Executing Facial Control During Deception Situations," *Journal of Nonverbal Behavior* 35 (2011): 119–131; M. Mendolia, "Explicit Use of Categorical and Dimensional Strategies to Decode Facial Expressions of Emotion," *Journal of Nonverbal Behavior* 31 (2007): 57–75; A. P. Atkinson, J. Tipples, D. M. Burt, and A. W. Young, "Asymmetric Interference Between Sex and Emotion in Face Perception," *Perception and Psychophysics* 67 (2005): 1199–1213.
40. Ekman and Friesen, *Unmasking the Face*.
41. D. Shichuran, T. Yong, and A. M. Martinez, "Compound Facial Expressions of Emotion," *Proceedings of the National Academy of Sciences* 111 (2014): 1454–1462.
42. P. M. Cole, "Children's Spontaneous Control of Facial Expression," *Child Development* 57 (1986): 1309–1321.
43. J. Hart, "Healing Touch, Therapeutic Touch, and Reiki: Energy Medicine Advances in the Medical Community," *Alternative & Complementary Therapies* 18 (2012): 309–313; K. Bundgaard and K. B. Nielsen, "The Art of Holding Hands: A Fieldwork Study Outlining the Significance of Physical Touch in Facilities for Short-Term Stay," *International Journal for Human Caring* 15 (2011): 34–41; R. Feldman, "Maternal Touch and the Developing Infant," in *The Handbook of Touch: Neuroscience, Behavioral, and Health Perspectives*, edited by M. J. Hertenstein and S. J. Weiss (New York: Springer, 2011), 373–408; K. Floyd, P. M. Pauley, and C. Hesse, "State and Trait Affectionate Communication Buffer Adults' Stress Reactions," *Communication Monographs* 77 (2010): 618–636; T. Field, "Touch Deprivation and Aggression against Self Among Adolescents," in *Developmental Psychobiology of Aggression*, edited by D. M. Stoff and E. J. Susman (New York: Cambridge University Press, 2005), 117–140.
44. Ivy and Wahl, *Nonverbal Communication for a Lifetime*.
45. Andersen, "Tactile Traditions."
46. Matsumoto and Hwang, "Cultural Influences on Nonverbal Behavior"; R. DiBiase and J. Gunnoe, "Gender and Culture Differences in Touching Behavior," *Journal of Social Psychology* 144 (2004): 49–62; E. T. Hall, *The Hidden Dimension* (Garden City, NY: Anchor, 1990); E. T. Hall, *Beyond Culture* (New York: Doubleday, 1981); M. S. Remland, T. S. Jones, and H. Brinkman, "Interpersonal Distance, Body Orientation and Touch: Effect of Culture, Gender, and Age," *Journal of Social Psychology* 135 (1995): 281–295.
47. S. Hughes, J. Mogilski, and M. Harrison, "The Perception and Parameters of Intentional Voice Manipulation," *Journal of Nonverbal Behavior* 38 (2014): 107–127; M. G. Frank, A. Maroulis, and D. J. Griffin, "The Voice," in *Nonverbal Communication: Science and Application*, edited by D. Matsumoto, M. G. Frank, and H. S. Hwang (Thousand Oaks, CA: Sage, 2013), 53–74; T. Vlahovic, S. Roberts, and R. Dunbar, "Effects of Duration and Laughter on Subjunctive Happiness within Different Modes of Communication," *Journal of Computer-Mediated Communication* 17 (2012): 436–450; M. Imhof, "Listening to Voices and Judging People," *International Journal of Listening* 24 (2010): 19–33; S. Hughes, S. Farley, and B. Rhodes, "Vocal and Physiological Changes in Response to the Physical Attractiveness of Conversational Partners," *Journal of Nonverbal Behavior* 34 (2010): 155–167; A. Karpf, *The Human Voice: How This Extraordinary Instrument Reveals Essential Clues About Who We Are* (New York: Bloomsbury, 2006).
48. A. M. Goberman, S. Hughes, and T. Haydock, "Acoustic Characteristics of Public Speaking: Anxiety and Practice Effects," *Speech Communication* 53 (2011): 867–876; F. Roberts, A. L. Francis, and M. Morgan, "The Interaction of Inter-Turn Silence with Prosodic Cues in Listener Perceptions of 'Trouble' in Conversation," *Speech Communication* 48 (2006): 1079–1093; T. DeGroot and S. J. Motowidlo, "Why Visual and Vocal Interview Cues Can Affect Interviewers' Judgments and Predict Job Performance," *Journal of Applied Psychology* 84 (1999): 986–993; N. Christenfeld, "Does It Hurt to Say Um?" *Journal of Nonverbal Behavior* 19 (1995): 171–186.
49. M. Zuckerman and V. Sinicropi, "When Physical and Vocal Attractiveness Differ: Effects on Favorability of Interpersonal Impressions," *Journal of Nonverbal Behavior* 35 (2011): 75–86.
50. S. Cain, *Quiet: The Power of Introverts in a World That Can't Stop Talking* (New York: Crown, 2012); H. R. Bosker, A.-F. Pinget, H. Quene, T. Sanders, and N. H. deJong, "What Makes Speech Sound Fluent? The Contributions of Pauses, Speed, and Repairs," *Language Testing* 30 (2012): 159–175; C. Ruhlemann, A. Bagoutdinov, and M. B. O'Donnell, "Windows on the Mind: Pauses in Conversational Narrative," *International Journal of Corpus Linguistics* 16 (2011): 198–230; M. M. Reda, *Between Speaking and Silence: A Study of Quiet Students* (Albany, NY: SUNY Press, 2010); M. Ephratt, "The Functions of Silence," *Journal of Pragmatics* 40 (2008): 1909–1938; A. Georgakopoulos, "The Role of Silence and Avoidance in Interpersonal Conflict," *Peace and Conflict Studies* 11 (2004): 85–95; A. Jaworski, "The Power of Silence in Communication," in *The Nonverbal Communication Reader: Classic and Contemporary Readings* 2e, edited by L. K. Guerro, J. DeVito, and M. L. Hecht (Prospect Heights, IL: Waveland, 1999), 156–162.
51. S. J. Baker, "The Theory of Silence," *Journal of General Psychology* 53 (1955): 145–167.
52. M. Costa, "Territorial Behavior in Public Settings," *Environment & Behavior* 44 (2012): 713–721; T. Bringslimark, T. Hartig, and G. Grindal Patil, "Adaptation to Windowlessness: Do Office Workers Compensate for a Lack of Visual Access to the Outdoors?" *Environment & Behavior* 43 (2011): 469–487; F. U. J. Paul, M. K. Mandal, K. Ramachandran, and M. R. Panwar, "Interpersonal Behavior in an Isolated and Confined Environment," *Environment & Behavior* 42 (2010): 707–717; A. Vogler and J. Jorgensen, "Windows to the World, Doors to Space: The Psychology of Space Architecture," *Leonardo* 38 (2005): 390–399; P. Harris and D. Sachau, "Is Cleanliness Next to Godliness? The Role of Housekeeping in Impression Formation," *Environment & Behavior* 37 (2005): 81–99.
53. J. Kim and R. DeDear, "Workspace Satisfaction: The Privacy-Communication Trade-Off in Open-Plan Offices," *Journal of Environmental Psychology* (2013): 18–26; I. Vilnai-Yavetz, A. Rafaeli, and C. Schneider-Yaacov, "Instrumentality, Aesthetics, and Symbolism of Office Design," *Environment & Behavior* 37 (2005): 533–551; J. Sandberg, "Want to Know Someone's Job Status? Look at Desk Location," *Corpus Christi Caller Times* (March 2, 2003): D4.
54. L. Biemiller, "To College Employees, the Work Environment Is All-Important," *The Chronicle of Higher Education* (July 18, 2008): B12, B14, B17; S. D. Gosling, S. J. Ko, T. Mannarelli, and M. E. Morris, "A Room with a Cue: Personality Judgments Based on Offices and Bedrooms," *Journal of Personality and Social Psychology* 82 (2002): 379–398; A. Lohmann, X. B. Arriaga, and W. Goodfriend, "Close Relationships and Placemaking: Do Objects

in a Couple's Home Reflect Couplehood?" *Personal Relationships* 10 (2003): 437–449.

55. V. W. Kupritz and T. Hillsman, "The Impact of the Physical Environment on Supervisory Communication Skills Transfer," *Journal of Business Communication* 48 (2011): 148–185; T. R. Herzog, L. E. Gray, A. M. Dunville, A. M. Hicks, and E. A. Gilson, "Preference and Tranquility for Houses of Worship," *Environment & Behavior* 45 (2011): 504–525; F. U. J. Paul, M. K. Mandal, K. Ramachandran, and M. R. Panwar, "Interpersonal Behavior in an Isolated and Confined Environment," *Environment & Behavior* 42 (2010): 707–717; J. F. Sallis and J. Kerr, "Physical Activity and the Built Environment," in *The Nonverbal Communication Reader* 3e, edited by L. K. Guerrero and M. L. Hecht (Long Grove, IL: Waveland, 2008), 270–286.
56. P. Monaghan, "Design for Disability Will Become the Norm," *The Chronicle Review* (February 12, 2010): B6–B7; T. R. Vandenbark, "Tending a Wild Garden: Library Web Design for Persons with Disabilities," *Information Technology & Libraries* 29 (2010): 23–29; D. K. White et al., "Are Features of the Neighborhood Environment Associated with Disability in Older Adults?" *Disabilities & Retention* 32 (2010): 639–645.
57. For more information on design for people with disabilities, see G. Pullin, *Design Meets Disability* (Cambridge, MA: MIT Press, 2009).
58. Matsumoto and Hwang, "Cultural Influences on Nonverbal Behavior"; M. Pearce and R. Woodford-Smith, "The (Dis)location of Time and Space: Trans-Cultural Collaborations in Tokyo," *Journal of Media Practice* 13 (2012): 197–213.
59. Hall, *The Hidden Dimension*.
60. Farley, "Nonverbal Reactions to an Attractive Stranger"; S. Li and Y. Li, "How Far Is Far Enough? A Measure of Information Privacy in Terms of Interpersonal Distance," *Environment & Behavior* 39 (2007): 317–331; D. Matsumoto, "Culture and Nonverbal Behavior," in *The SAGE Handbook of Nonverbal Communication*, edited by V. Manusov and M. L. Patterson (Thousand Oaks, CA: Sage, 2006), 219–235; C. M. J. Beaulieu, "Intercultural Study of Personal Space: A Case Study," *Journal of Applied Social Psychology* 34 (2004): 794–805.
61. S. Canagarajah, "Agency and Power in Intercultural Communication: Negotiating English in Translocal Spaces," *Language & Intercultural Communication* 13 (2013): 202–224; T. T. Prabhu, "Proxemics: Some Challenges and Strategies in Nonverbal Communication," *IUP Journal of Soft Skills* 4 (2010): 7–14; L. Van Doorn, "Perception of Time and Space of (Formerly) Homeless People," *Journal of Human Behavior in the Social Environment* 20 (2010): 218–238; Burgoon and Dunbar, "Nonverbal Expressions of Dominance and Power in Human Relationships"; D. R. Carney, J. A. Hall, and L. Smith LeBeau, "Beliefs about the Nonverbal Expression of Social Power," *Journal of Nonverbal Behavior* 29 (2005): 105–123.
62. V. Santilli and A. N. Miller, "The Effects of Gender and Power Distance on Nonverbal Immediacy in Symmetrical and Asymmetrical Power Conditions: A Cross-Cultural Study of Classrooms and Friendships," *Journal of International and Intercultural Communication* 4 (2011): 3–22; M. Costa, "Interpersonal Distances in Group Walking," *Journal of Nonverbal Behavior* 34 (2010): 15–26; J. A. Hall, "Women's and Men's Nonverbal Communication: Similarities, Differences, Stereotypes, and Origins," in *The SAGE Handbook of Nonverbal Communication*, edited by V. Manusov and M. L. Patterson (Thousand Oaks, CA: Sage, 2006), 201–218.
63. G. Brown and S. L. Robinson, "Reactions to Territorial Infringement," *Organization Science* 22 (2011): 210–224; J. Koen and K. Durrheim, "A Naturalistic Observational Study of Informal Segregation: Seating Patterns in Lectures," *Environment & Behavior* 42 (2010): 448–468; N. Kaya and B. Burgess, "Territoriality: Seat Preferences in Different Types of Classrooms," *Environment & Behavior* 39 (2007): 859–876; S. M. Lyman and M. B. Scott, "Territoriality: A Neglected Sociological Dimension," in *The Nonverbal Communication Reader: Classic and Contemporary Reading* 2e, edited by L. K. Guerro, J. DeVito, and M. L. Hecht (Prospect Heights, IL: Waveland, 1999), 175–183.
64. N. M. Doering and S. Poeschl, "Nonverbal Cues in Mobile Phone Text Messages: The Effects of Chronemics and Proxemics," in *The Reconstruction of Space and Time: Mobile Communication Practices*, edited by R. Ling and S. Campbell (New Brunswick, NJ: Transaction Publishers, 2009); V. Cho and H. Hung, "The Effectiveness of Short Message Service for Communication with Concerns of Privacy Protection and Conflict Avoidance," *Journal of Computer-Mediated Communication* 16 (2011): 250–270; Ivy and Wahl, *Nonverbal Communication for a Lifetime*; Knapp, Hall, and Horgan, *Nonverbal Communication in Human Interaction*.
65. Mehrabian, *Nonverbal Communication*.
66. For applications of Mehrabian's immediacy principle, see Santilli and Miller, "The Effects of Gender and Power Distance on Nonverbal Immediacy in Symmetrical and Asymmetrical Power Conditions"; P. B. O'Sullivan, S. K. Hunt, and L. R. Lippert, "Mediated Immediacy: A Language of Affiliation in a Technological Age," *Journal of Language and Social Psychology* 23 (2004): 464–490; L. Martin and T. P. Mottet, "The Effect of Instructor Nonverbal Immediacy Behaviors and Feedback Sensitivity on Hispanic Students' Affective Learning Outcomes in Ninth-Grade Writing Conferences," *Communication Education* 60 (2011): 1–19; P. L. Witt and J. Kerssen-Griep, "Instructional Feedback I: The Interaction of Facework and Immediacy on Students' Perceptions of Instructor Credibility," *Communication Education* 60 (2011): 75–94; F-Y. F. Wei and Y. K. Wang, "Students' Silent Messages: Can Teacher Verbal and Nonverbal Immediacy Moderate Student Use of Text Messaging in Class?" *Communication Education* 59 (2010): 475–496.
67. Argyle, *Bodily Communication*.
68. P. A. Andersen, *Nonverbal Communication: Forms and Functions* 2e (Long Grove, IL: Waveland, 2008): 168.
69. Lakens Stel, "If They Move in Sync, They Must Feel in Sync"; Wilt, Funkhouser, and Revelle, "The Dynamic Relationships of Affective Synchrony to Perceptions of Situations"; K. McGinty, D. Knox, and M. E. Zusman, "Nonverbal and Verbal Communication in 'Involved' and 'Casual' Relationships among College Students," *College Student Journal* 37 (2003): 68–71; B. Le Poire, A. Duggan, C. Shepard, and J. Burgoon, "Relational Messages Associated with Nonverbal Involvement, Pleasantness, and Expressiveness in Romantic Couples," *Communication Research Reports* 19 (2002): 195–206.
70. Burgoon and Dunbar, "Nonverbal Expressions of Dominance and Power in Human Relationships"; D. R. Carney and L. Smith LeBeau, "Beliefs about the Nonverbal Expression of Social Power," *Journal of Nonverbal Behavior* 29 (2005): 105–123; M. Schmid Mast and J. A. Hall, "Who Is the Boss and Who Is Not? Accuracy of Judging Status," *Journal of Nonverbal Behavior* 28 (2004): 145–165; M. Helweg-Larsen, S. J. Cunningham, A. Carrico, and A. M. Pergram, "To Nod or Not to Nod: An Observational Study of Nonverbal Communication and Status in Female and Male College Students," *Psychology of Women Quarterly* 28 (2004): 358–361; L. Z. Tiedens and A. R. Fragale, "Power Moves: Complementarity in Dominant and Submissive Nonverbal Behavior," *Journal of Personality and Social Psychology* 84 (2003): 558–568; Mehrabian, *Nonverbal Communication*.

Chapter 5

1. R. Emanuel, J. Adams, K. Baker, E. K. Daufin, C. Ellington, F. Fits, J. Himsel, L. Holladay, and D. Okeowo, "How College Students Spend Their Time Communicating," *International Journal of Listening* 22 (2008): 13–28; also see L. Barker et al., "An Investigation of Proportional Time Spent in Various Communication Activities for College Students," *Journal of Applied Communication Research* 8 (1981): 101–109; also see K. Dindia and B. L. Kennedy, "Communication in Everyday Life: A Descriptive Study Using Mobile Electronic Data Collection," paper presented at the annual conference of the National Communication Association, Chicago (November 2004).

2. For an excellent review of listening research, see M. L. Beall, J. Gill-Rosier, J. Tate, and A. Matten, "State of the Context: Listening in Education," *International Journal of Listening* 22 (2008): 123–132; also see A. D. Wolvin, "Listening Engagement: Intersecting Theoretical Perspectives," in *Listening and Human Communication in the 21st Century*, edited by A. D. Wolvin (Oxford, UK: Wiley-Blackwell, 2010), 7–30.
3. One study found that only 5 percent of colleges and universities offered a course in listening. See K. G. Wacker and K. Hawkins, "Curricula Comparison for Classes in Listening," *International Journal of Listening* 9 (1995): 14–28.
4. For additional support for the importance of listening in interpersonal relationships, see L. Sparks, S. S. Travis, and S. R. Thompson, "Listening for the Communication Signals of Humor, Narratives, and Self-Disclosure in the Family Caregiver Interview," *Health & Social Work* 30.4 (2005): 340–343; S. Wright, "The Beauty of Silence: Deep Listening Is a Key Nursing Skill That Can Be Learned with Practice," *Nursing Standard* 20.50 (2006): 18–20; M. R. Jalongo, "Listening in Early Childhood: An Interdisciplinary Review of the Literature," *International Journal of Listening* 24.1 (2010): 1–18.
5. J. Hackenbracht and K. Gasper, "I'm All Ears: The Need to Belong Motivates Listening to Emotional Disclosure," *Journal of Experimental Social Psychology* 49 (2013): 915–921.
6. Jacobs and Coghlan, "Sound of Silence: On Listening in Organizational Learning," *Human Relations* 58.1 (2005): 115–138.
7. P. Skaldeman, "Converging or Diverging Views of Self and Other: Judgment of Relationship Quality in Married and Divorced Couples," *Journal of Divorce & Remarriage* 44 (2006): 145–160.
8. For a review of the role of listening in business contexts, see J. Flynn, T. R. Valikoski, and J. Grau, "Listening in the Business Context: Reviewing the State of Research," *International Journal of Listening* 22 (2008): 141–151.
9. For a review of literature documenting the importance of listening in the health professions, see D. L. Roter and J. A. Hall, *Doctors Talking with Patients/Patients Talking with Doctors: Improving Communication in Medical Visits* (Westport, CT: Praeger, 2006); J. Davis, C. R. Thompson, A. Foley, C. D. Bond, and J. DeWitt, "An Examination of Listening Concepts in the Healthcare Context: Differences Among Nurses, Physicians, and Administrators," *International Journal of Listening* 22 (2008): 152–167.
10. K. W. Hawkins and B. P. Fullion, "Perceived Communication Skill Needs for Work Groups," *Communication Research Reports* 16 (1999): 167–174.
11. J. Brownell, "Perceptions of Effective Listeners: A Management Study," *Journal of Business Communication* (Fall 1990): 401–415; D. A. Romig, *Side by Side Leadership* (Austin, TX: Bard, 2001).
12. J. Burnside-Lawry, "Listening and Participatory Communication: A Model to Assess Organizational Listening Competency," *The International Journal of Listening* 26 (2012): 102–121; C. Jacobs and D. Coghlan, "Sound of Silence."
13. R. Bommelje, J. M. Houston, and R. Smither, "Personality Characteristics of Effective Listeners: A Five Factor Perspective," *International Journal of Listening* 17 (2003): 32–46.
14. M. S. Conaway, "Listening: Learning Tool and Retention Agent," in *Improving Reading and Study Skills*, edited by A. S. Algier and K. W. Algier (San Francisco: Jossey-Bass, 1996), 51–63.
15. For a review of how listening is discussed in public speaking textbooks, see W. C. Adams and E. S. Cox, "The Teaching of Listening as an Integral Part of an Oral Activity: An Examination of Public-Speaking Texts," *International Journal of Listening* 24.2 (2010): 89–105.
16. Adapted from the International Listening Association's definition of *listening*, which may be found on its website, www.listen.org; for a theoretical explanation of the attending listening process, see L. A. Januskik, "Building Listening Theory: The Validation of the Conversational Listening Span," *Communication Studies* 5.2 (June 2007): 139; see also G. D. Bodie, K. St. Cyr, M. Pence, M. Rold, and J. Honeycutt, "Listening Competence in Initial Interactions I: Distinguishing Between What Listening Is and What Listeners Do," *The International Journal of Listening* 26 (2012): 1–28.
17. S. C. Bentley, "Listening in the 21st Century," *International Journal of Listening* 14 (2000): 129–142; also see A. D. Wolvin and C. G. Coakley, "Listening Education in the 21st Century," *International Journal of Listening* 14 (2001): 143–152. For an excellent literature review of definitions and perspectives on defining listening, see S. Bentley, "Benchmarking Listening Behaviors: Is Effective Listening What the Speaker Says It Is?" *International Journal of Listening* 11.1 (2008): 51–68.
18. D. Mount and A. Mattila, "Last Chance to Listen: Listening Behaviors and Their Effect on Call Center Satisfaction," *Journal of Hospitality & Tourism Research* 26.2 (2002): 124–137.
19. C. Gallo, *Talk Like TED: The 9 Public-Speaking Secrets of the World's Top Minds* (New York: St. Martin's Press, 2014).
20. A. Mulanx and W. G. Powers, "Listening Fidelity Development and Relationship to Receiver Apprehension and Locus of Control," *International Journal of Listening* 17 (2003): 69–78.
21. N. S. Baron, *Always On: Language in an Online and Mobile World* (New York: Oxford University Press, 2008); also see D. Crystal, *txtng: The gr8 db8* (Oxford, UK: Oxford University Press, 2008); S. Turkle, *Alone Together: Why We Expect More from Technology and Less from Each Other* (New York: Basic Books, 2011); M. A. Dourin, "College Students' Text Messaging, Use of Textese, and Literacy Skills," *Journal of Assisted Learning* 27.1 (2011): 67.
22. D. A. Schwartz, "Review Essay Listening Out of the Box: New Perspectives for the Workplace," *International Journal of Listening* 18 (2004): 47–55.
23. W. L. Randall, S. M. Prior, and M. Skarborn, "How Listeners Shape What Tellers Tell: Patterns of Interaction in Lifestory Interviews and Their Impact on Reminiscence by Elderly Interviewees," *Journal of Aging Studies* 20.4 (2006): 381–396.
24. A. Zohoori, "A Cross-Cultural Comparison of the HURIER Listening Profile Among Iranian and U. S. Students," *International Journal of Listening* 27 (2013): 50–60.
25. K. W. Watson, L. L. Barker, and J. B. Weaver, *The Listener Style Inventory* (New Orleans: Spectra, 1995).
26. D. Worthington, G. D. Bodie, and C. Gearhart, "The Listening Styles Profile Revised (LSP-R): A Scale Revision and Validation," paper presented at the Eastern Communication Association, Arlington, VA (2011); G. D. Bodie and D. L. Worthington, "Revisiting the Listening Styles Profile (LSP-16): A Confirmatory Factor Analytic Approach to Scale Validation and Reliability Estimation," *International Journal of Listening* 24.2 (2010): 69–88.
27. D. L. Worthington, "Exploring the Relationship between Listening Style Preference and Personality," *International Journal of Listening* 17 (2003): 68–87; D. L. Worthington, "Exploring Juror's Listening Processes: The Effect of Listening Style Preference on Juror Decision Making," *International Journal of Listening* 17 (2003): 20–37.
28. Worthington, "Exploring the Relationship between Listening Style Preference and Personality."
29. Worthington, "Exploring Juror's Listening Processes."
30. Worthington, "Exploring Juror's Listening Processes."
31. Worthington, "Exploring Juror's Listening Processes."
32. J. B. Weaver III and M. Kirtley, "Listening Styles and Empathy," *Southern Communication Journal* 2 (1995): 131–141.
33. S. L. Sargent and J. B. Weaver, "Correlates Between Communication Apprehension and Listening Style Preferences," *Communication Research Reports* 14 (1997): 74–78.
34. M. K. Johnston, J. B. Weaver, K. W. Watson, and L. L. Barker, "Listening Styles: Biological or Psychological Differences?" *International Journal of Listening* 14 (2000): 14–31.
35. See C. Kiewitz, J. B. Weaver III, B. Brosius, and G. Weimann, "Cultural Differences in Listening Style Preferences: A Comparison of Young Adults in Germany, Israel, and the United

States," *International Journal of Public Opinion Research* 9 (1997): 233–248; N. Dragon and J. C. Sherblom, "The Influence of Cultural Individualism and Collectivism on U.S. and Post Soviet Listening Styles," *Human Communication* 11 (2008): 177–192.

36. L. L. Barker and K. W. Watson, *Listen Up* (New York: St. Martin's Press, 2000); also see M. Imhof, "Who Are We as We Listen? Individual Listening Profiles in Varying Contexts," *International Journal of Listening* 18 (2004): 36–45.
37. Imhof, "Who Are We as We Listen?"
38. W. Winter, A. J. Ferreira, and N. Bowers, "Decision-Making in Married and Unrelated Couples," *Family Process* 12 (1973): 83–94.
39. R. Montgomery, *Listening Made Easy* (New York: Amacom, 1981); also see O. Hargie, C. Sanders, and D. Dickson, *Social Skills in Interpersonal Communication* (London, UK: Routledge, 1994); O. Hargie, ed., *The Handbook of Communication Skills* (London, UK: Routledge, 1997).
40. R. G. Owens, "Handling Strong Emotions," in *The Handbook of Communication Skills*, edited by O. Hargie (London: Croom Helm/New York University Press, 1986).
41. D. Goleman, *Emotional Intelligence: Why It Can Matter More Than IQ* (New York: Bantam Books, 1995); also see D. Goleman, "Emotional Intelligence: Issues in Paradigm Building," in *The Emotionally Intelligent Workplace*, edited by C. Cherniss and D. Goleman (San Francisco: Jossey-Bass, 2001), 13.
42. For an excellent review of emotional intelligence research, see D. Grewal and P. Salovey, "Feeling Smart: The Science of Emotional Intelligence," *American Scientist* 93 (2005): 330–339. Also see J. Keaton and L. Kelly, "Emotional Intelligence as a Mediator of Family Communication Patterns and Reticence," *Communication Reports* 21.2 (2008): 104–116; R. Pishghadam, "Emotional and Verbal Intelligences in Language Learning," *Iranian Journal of Language Studies* 3.1 (2009): 43–64.
43. Goleman, *Emotional Intelligence*; Grewal and Salovey, "Feeling Smart."
44. J. L. Gonzalez-Balado, ed., *Mother Teresa: In My Own Words* (New York: Gramercy Books, 1997).
45. R. G. Nichols, "Factors in Listening Comprehension," *Speech Monographs* 15 (1948): 154–163; G. M. Goldhaber and C. H. Weaver, "Listener Comprehension of Compressed Speech When the Difficulty, Rate of Presentation, and Sex of the Listener Are Varied," *Speech Monographs* 35 (1968): 20–25.
46. M. Fitch-Hauser, D. A. Barker, and A. Hughes, "Receiver Apprehension and Listening Comprehension: A Linear or Curvilinear Relationship?" *Southern Communication Journal* 56 (1988): 62–71; P. E. King and R. R. Behnke, "Patterns of State Anxiety in Listening Performance," *Southern Communication Journal* 70.1 (2004): 72–81.
47. Fitch-Hauser et al., "Receiver Apprehension and Listening Comprehension."
48. Fitch-Hauser et al., "Receiver Apprehension and Listening Comprehension."
49. K. J. Anderson and C. Leaper, "Meta-Analyses of Gender Effects on Conversational Interruption: Who, What, When, Where, and How," *Sex Roles* 39 (1998): 225–252.
50. For a review of the literature on gender, listening, and communication, see D. K. Ivy, *GenderSpeak* 5e (Boston: Pearson, 2012).
51. B. R. Burleson, L. K. Hanasono, G. D. Bodie, A. J. Holmstrom, J. D. McCullough, J. J. Rack, and J. Gill Rosier, "Are Gender Differences in Responses to Supportive Communication a Matter of Ability, Motivation, or Both? Reading Patterns of Situation Effects Through the Lens of a Dual-Process Theory," *Communication Quarterly* 59 (2011): 37–60.
52. S. L. Sargent and J. B. Weaver, "Listening Styles," *International Journal of Listening* 17 (2003): 5–18.
53. C. G. Pearce, I. W. Johnson, and R. T. Barker, "Assessment of the Listening Styles Inventory," *Journal of Business & Technical Communication* 17 (2003): 84–113.
54. Sargent and Weaver, "Listening Styles."
55. J. Silverman, "Attentional Styles and the Study of Sex Differences," in *Attention: Contemporary Theory and Analysis*, edited by D. I. Mostofsky (New York: Appleton-Century-Crofts, 1970), 61–79.
56. K. Watson, L. Barker, and J. Weaver, "The Listening Styles Profile (LPP16): Development and Validation of an Instrument to Assess Four Listening Styles," *Journal of International Listening Association* (1995), research cited on *20/20*, ABC television network, September 1998.
57. J. O. Yum, "The Impact of Confucianism on Interpersonal Relationships and Communication Patterns in East Asia," in *Intercultural Communication: A Reader*, edited by L. A. Samovar and R. E. Porter (Belmont, CA: Wadsworth, 2000), 86.
58. C. Y. Cheng, "Chinese Philosophy and Contemporary Communication Theory," in *Communication Theory: Eastern and Western Perspectives*, edited by D. L. Kincaid (New York: Academic Press, 1987).
59. T. S. Lebra, *Japanese Patterns of Behavior* (Honolulu: University Press of Hawaii, 1976).
60. A. Yugi (trans. N. Chung), *Ilbon-in ye usikkoo-jo (Japanese Thought Patterns)* (Seoul, Korea: Baik Yang [in Korean], 1984).
61. Imhof, "Who Are We as We Listen?"
62. Bodie et al., "Listening Competence in Initial Interactions I."
63. Bodie et al., "Listening Competence in Initial Interactions I."
64. A. Carruthers, "Listening, Hearing and Changing," *Business Communication* 5 (2004): 3.
65. K. K. Halone and L. L. Pecchioni, "Relational Listening: A Grounded Theoretical Model," *Communication Reports* 14 (2001): 59–71.
66. I. W. Johnson, C. G. Pearce, T. L. Tuten, and L. Sinclair, "Self-Imposed Silence and Perceived Listening Effectiveness," *Business Communication Quarterly* 66 (2003): 23–45.
67. M. V. Redmond, "The Functions of Empathy (Decentering) in Human Relations," *Human Relations* 42 (1993): 593–606.
68. A. Mehrabian, *Nonverbal Communication* (Chicago: Aldine Atherton, 1970); A. Mehrabian, *Silent Messages* (Belmont, CA: Wadsworth, 1981); also see D. Lapakko, "Three Cheers for Language: A Closer Examination of a Widely Cited Study of Nonverbal Communication," *Communication Education* 46 (1997): 63–67.
69. I. M. Imhof, "Listening to Voices and Judging People," *International Journal of Listening* 24.1 (2010): 19–33.
70. H. J. Ferguson and R. Breheny, "Listeners' Eyes Reveal Spontaneous Sensitivity to Others' Perspectives," *Journal of Experimental Social Psychology* 48 (2012): 257–263.
71. M. Argyle and M. Cook, *Gaze and Mutual Gaze* (Cambridge, UK: Cambridge University Press, 1976).
72. Hargie et al., *Social Skills in Interpersonal Communication;* Hargie, *The Handbook of Communication Skills.*
73. For an excellent review of listening skills and research supporting listening skill development, see J. Brownell, "The Skills of Listening-Centered Communication," in *Listening and Human Communication in the 21st Century*, edited by A. D. Wolvin (Oxford, UK: Wiley-Blackwell, 2010), 141–157.
74. A. D. Wolvin and S. D. Cohen, "An Inventory of Listening Competency Dimensions," *The International Journal of Listening* 26 (2012): 64–66.
75. For a review of literature about measuring empathy, see G. D. Bodie, "The Active Empathic Listening Scale (AELS): Conceptualization and Validity Evidence," *Communication Quarterly* 59 (2011): 277–295.
76. See R. G. Nichols and L. A. Stevens, "Listening to People," *Harvard Business Review* 35 (September–October 1957): 85–92.
77. K. McComb and F. M. Jablin, "Verbal Correlates of Interviewer Empathic Listening and Employment Interview Outcomes," *Communication Monographs* 51 (1984): 353–371.
78. A. Clark, "Communication Confidence and Listening Competence: An Investigation of the Relationships of Willingness to Communicate, Communication Apprehension, and Receiver

Apprehension to Comprehension of Content and Emotional Meaning in Spoken Messages," *Communication Education* 38 (1989): 237–248.

79. Halone and Pecchioni, "Relational Listening."
80. Pearce et al., "Assessment of the Listening Styles Inventory."
81. Pearce et al., "Assessment of the Listening Styles Inventory."
82. G. D. Bodie, "The Nature of Supportive Listening II: The Role of Verbal Person Centeredness and Nonverbal Immediacy," *Western Journal of Communication* 76 (2012): 250–269.
83. E-A. Doohan, "Listening Behaviors of Married Couples: An Exploration of Nonverbal Presentation to a Relational Insider," *International Journal of Listening* 21 (2007): 24–41.
84. W. R. Miller, K. E. Hedrick, and D. R. Orlofsky, "The Helpful Responses Questionnaire: A Procedure for Measuring Therapeutic Empathy," *Journal of Clinical Psychology* 47 (1991): 444–448; A. Paukert, B. Stagner, and K. Hope, "The Assessment of Active Listening Skills in Helpline Volunteers," *Stress, Trauma, and Crisis* 7 (2004): 61–76; D. H. Levitt, "Active Listening and Counselor Self-Efficacy: Emphasis on One Micro-Skill in Beginning Counselor Training," *Clinical Supervisor* 20 (2001): 101–115; V. B. Van Hasselt, M. T. Baker, S. J. Romano, K. M. Schlessinger, M. Zuker, R. Dragone, and A. L. Perera, "Crisis (Hostage) Negotiation Training: A Preliminary Evaluation of Program Efficacy," *Criminal Justice and Behavior* 33 (2006): 56–69; H. Weger Jr., G. R. Castle, and M. C. Emmett, "Active Listening in Peer Interviews: The Influence on Perceptions of Listening Skill," *International Journal of Listening* 24 (2010): 34–49.
85. Weger et al., "Active Listening in Peer Interviews; also see M. R. Wood, "What Makes for Successful Speaker-Listener Technique? Two Case Studies," *Family Journal* 18.1 (2010): 50–54.
86. For a classic discussion of empathy and interpretive listening, see J. Stewart, "Interpretive Listening: An Alternative to Empathy," *Communication Education* 32 (1983): 379–391; Bommelje et al., "Personality Characteristics of Effective Listeners"; J. Håkansson and H. Montgomery, "Empathy as an Interpersonal Phenomenon," *Journal of Social & Personal Relationships* 20 (2003): 267–284.
87. Goleman, *Emotional Intelligence.*
88. A. de Saint-Exupéry, as quoted in Goleman, *Emotional Intelligence.*
89. P. Toller, "Learning to Listen, Learning to Hear: A Training Approach," *Time to Listen to Children: Personal and Professional Communication,* edited by C. Birgit (Florence, KY: Taylor, Frances/Routledge, 1999), 48–61; T. Drollinger, L. B. Comer, and P. T. Warrington, "Development and Validation of the Active Empathetic Listening Scale," *Psychology & Marketing* 23.2 (2006): 161–180; S. L. Do and D. L. Schallert, "Emotions and Classroom Talk: Toward a Model of the Role of Affect in Students' Experiences of Classroom Discussions," *Journal of Educational Psychology* 96.4 (2004): 619–634.
90. H. J. M. Nouwen, "Listening as Spiritual Hospitality," in *Bread for the Journey* (New York: HarperCollins, 1997).
91. C. R. Rogers, "Empathic: An Unappreciated Way of Being," in *A Way of Being* (Boston: Houghton Mifflin, 1980), 137–163.
92. J. C. McCroskey and M. J. Beatty, "The Communibiological Perspective: Implications for Communication in Instruction," *Communication Education* 49 (2000): 1–6; M. J. Beatty and J. C. McCroskey, "Theory, Scientific Evidence and the Communibiological Paradigm: Reflections on Misguided Criticism," *Communication Education* 49 (2001): 36–44.
93. M. E. Pence and A. J. Vickery, "The Roles of Personality and Trait Emotion Intelligence in the Active-Empathic Listening Process: Evidence from Correlational and Regression Analyses," *The International Journal of Listening* 26 (2012): 159–174.
94. D. F. Barone, P. S. Hutchings, H. J. Kimmel, H. L. Traub, J. T. Cooper, and C. M. Marshall, "Increasing Empathic Accuracy through Practice and Feedback in a Clinical Interviewing Course," *Journal of Social and Clinical Psychology* 24 (2005): 156–171.
95. Weaver and Kirtley, "Listening Styles and Empathy."
96. Goleman, *Emotional Intelligence.*
97. Hargie et al., *Social Skills in Interpersonal Communication;* R. Boulton, *People Skills* (New York: 1981). We also acknowledge others who have presented excellent applications of listening and responding skills in interpersonal and group contexts: D. A. Romig and L. J. Romig, *Structured Teamwork* (D Guide) (Austin, TX: Performance Resources, 1990); S. Deep and L. Sussman, *Smart Moves* (Reading, MA: Addison-Wesley, 1990); P. R. Scholtes, *The Team Handbook* (Madison, WI: Joiner Associates, 1988); Hargie, *The Handbook of Communication Skills.*
98. A. M. Nicotera, J. Steele, A. Catalani, and N. Simpson, "Conceptualization and Test of an Aggression Competence Model," *Communication Research Reports* 29 (2012): 12–25.
99. S. M. Jones, "Supportive Listening," *The International Journal of Listening* 25 (2011): 85–103.
100. R. Lemieux and M. R. Tighe, "Attachment Styles and the Evaluation of Comforting Responses: A Receiver Perspective," *Communication Research Reports* 21 (2004): 144–153; also see W. Samter, "How Gender and Cognitive Complexity Influence the Provision of Emotional Support: A Study of Indirect Effects," *Communication Reports* 15 (2002): 5–16.
101. Our discussion of appropriate and inappropriate social support responses is taken from B. D. Burleson, "Emotional Support Skill," in *Handbook of Communication and Social Interaction Skills,* edited by O. Greene and B. R. Burleson (Mahwah, NJ: Lawrence Erlbaum, 2003), 566–568. See also G. D. Bodie, A. J. Vickery, and C. C Gearhart, "The Nature of Supportive Listening, I: Exploring the Relation between Supportive Listeners and Supportive People," *International Journal of Listening* 27 (1): 39–49.
102. L. B. Comer and T. Drollinger, "Active Empathic Listening and Selling Success: A Conceptual Framework," *Journal of Personal Selling & Sales Management* 19 (1999): 15–29; S. B. Castleberry, C. D. Shepherd, and R. Ridnour, "Effective Interpersonal Listening in the Personal Selling Environment: Conceptualization, Measurement, and Nomological Validity," *Journal of Marketing Theory and Practice* (Winter 1999): 30–38.
103. F. C. B. Hansen, H. Resnick, and J. Galea, "Better Listening: Paraphrasing and Perception Checking—A Study of the Effectiveness of a Multimedia Skills Training Program," *Journal of Technology in Human Services* 20 (2002): 317–331; D. Ifert Johnson and K. Long, "Evaluating the Effectiveness of Listening Instruction in Introductory Communication Courses," paper presented at the International Communication Association (2008).

Chapter 6

1. Research documents several culture-based differences in communication, including approaches to leadership, deception, and conflict management styles. See N. Ensari and S. E. Murphy, "Cross-Cultural Variations in Leadership Perceptions and Attribution of Charisma to the Leader," *Organizational Behavior and Human Decision Processes* 92 (2003): 52–66; M. K. Lapinski and T. R. Levine, "Culture and Information Manipulation Theory: The Effects of Self-Construal and Locus of Benefit on Information Manipulation," *Communication Studies* 5 (2000): 55–73; D. Cai and E. L. Fink, "Conflict Style Differences between Individualists and Collectivists," *Communication Monographs* 69 (2002): 67–87; M. S. Kim and A. S. Ebesu Hubbard, "Intercultural Communication in the Global Village: How to Understand 'The Other,'" *Journal of Intercultural Communication Research* 36.3 (2007): 223–235.
2. For a discussion of the role of self-awareness as a strategy for enhancing intercultural competence, see R. C. Weigl, "Intercultural Competence through Cultural Self-Study: A Strategy for Adult Learners," *International Journal of Intercultural Relations* 33 (2009): 346–360.
3. C. Darwin, *On the Origin of Species by Means of Natural Selection, or the Preservation of Favoured Races in the Struggle of Life* (London: John Murray, 1859).
4. For a review of research identifying the importance of adapting to cultural differences, see Y. Hu and W. Fan, "An

Exploratory Study on Intercultural Communication Research Contents and Methods: A Survey Based on the International and Domestic Journal Papers Published from 2001 to 2005," *International Journal of Intercultural Relations* 35 (2011): 554–566.
5. J. Gray, *Men Are from Mars, Women Are from Venus* (New York: HarperCollins, 1992).
6. D. K. Ivy, *GenderSpeak: Personal Effectiveness in Gender Communication* 5e (Boston: Pearson, 2012); D. J. Canary and T. R. Emmers Sommer, *Sex and Gender Differences in Personal Relationships* (New York: Guilford, 1997).
7. D. Tannen, *You Just Don't Understand* (New York: William Morrow, 1990).
8. S. D. Farley, A. M. Ashcraft, M. F. Stasson, and R. L. Nusbaum, "Nonverbal Reactions to Conversational Interruption: A Test of Complementarity Theory and the Status/Gender Parallel," *Journal of Nonverbal Behavior* 34.4 (2010): 193–206.
9. A. C. Selbe, *Are You from Another Planet or What?* Workshop presented at the Joint Service Family Readiness Matters Conference, Phoenix, AZ (July 1999).
10. R. B. Rubin, E. M. Perse, and C. A. Barbato, "Conceptualization and Measurement of Interpersonal Communication Motives," *Human Communication Research* 14 (1988): 602–628; D. Tannen, *That's Not What I Meant!* (London: Dent, 1986).
11. P. Weber, "Confused by All the New Facebook Genders? Here's What They Mean," *Slate*, February 21, 2014, accessed March 22, 2014, www.slate.com/blogs/lexicon_valley/2014/02/21/gender_facebook_now_has_56_categories_to_choose_from_including_cisgender.html.
12. "A Survey of LGBT Americans: Attitudes, Experiences and Values in Changing Times," *Pew Research Social & Demographic Trends*, June 13, 2013, accessed March 18, 2014, www.pewsocialtrends.org/2013/06/13/a-survey-of-lgbt-americans; T. Mottet, "The Role of Sexual Orientation in Predicting Outcome: Value and Anticipated Communication Behaviors," *Communication Quarterly* 43 (Summer 2000): 223–239; for an excellent review of literature summarizing attitudes toward gay men and lesbians, see J. Soliz, E. Ribarsky, M. M. Harrigan, and S. Tye-Williams, "Perceptions of Communication with Gay and Lesbian Family Members: Predictors of Relational Satisfaction and Implications for Outgroup Attitudes," *Communication Quarterly* 58.1 (2010): 77–95.
13. "A Survey of LGBT Americans."
14. G. M. Herek, "Heterosexuals' Attitudes Toward Lesbian and Gay Men: Correlates and Gender Differences," *Journal of Sex Research* 25 (1988): 451–477.
15. Herek, "Heterosexuals' Attitudes Toward Lesbian and Gay Men"; M. S. Weinberg and C. J. Williams, *Male Homosexuals: Their Problems and Adaptations* (New York: Free Press, 1974); Mottet, "The Role of Sexual Orientation in Predicting Outcome."
16. "A Survey of LGBT Americans."
17. J. Soliz, E. Ribarsky, M. M. Harrigan, and S. Tye-Williams, "Perceptions of Communication with Gay and Lesbian Family Members: Predictors of Relational Satisfaction and Implications for Outgroup Attitudes," *Communication Quarterly* 58.1 (2010): 77–95.
18. "Removing Bias in Language; Sexuality," *American Psychological Association*, accessed March 2006, www.apastyle.org/sexuality.html; J. W. Peters, "The Decline and Fall of the 'H' Word," *The New York Times*, Sunday Styles (March 23, 2014): 10.
19. A. Williams and P. Garrett, "Communication Evaluations across the Life Span: From Adolescent Storm and Stress to Elder Aches and 'Pains,'" *Journal of Language and Social Psychology* 21 (June 2002): 101–126; also see D. Cai, H. Giles, and K. Noels, "Elderly Perceptions of Communication with Older and Younger Adults in China: Implications for Mental Health," *Journal of Applied Communication Research* 26 (1998): 32–51.
20. J. Montepare, E. Koff, D. Zaitchik, and M. Albert, "The Use of Body Movements and Gestures as Cues to Emotions in Younger and Older Adults," *Journal of Nonverbal Behavior* 23 (1999): 133–152.
21. J. Harwood, E. B. Ryan, H. Giles, and S. Tysoski, "Evaluations of Patronizing Speech and Three Response Styles in a Non-Service-Providing Context," *Journal of Applied Communication Research* 25 (1997): 170–195.
22. T. C. Segrin, "Age Moderates the Relationship between Social Support and Psychosocial Problems," paper presented at the International Communication Association, San Diego, CA (May 2003).
23. N. Howe and W. Strauss, *Millennials Rising: The Next Great Generation* (New York: Vintage Books, 2000).
24. Howe and Strauss, *Millennials Rising*.
25. K. Meyers and K. Sadaghiani, "Millennials in the Workplace: A Communication Perspective on Millennials' Organizational Relationships and Performance," *Journal of Business & Psychology* 25.2 (2010): 225–238.
26. "Millennials in Adulthood: Detached from Institutions, Networked with Friends," *Pew Research Social & Demographic Trends*, March 7, 2014, accessed March 20, 2014, www.pewsocialtrends.org/2014/03/07/millennials-in-adulthood.
27. Information summarized from Howe and Strauss, *Millennials Rising*.
28. Our discussion of generational differences and communication is also based on J. Smith, "The Millennials Are Coming," workshop presented at Texas State University, San Marcos, TX (2006).
29. Howe and Strauss, *Millennials Rising*; H. Karp, C. Fuller, and D. Sirias, *Bridging the Boomer-Xer Gap: Creating Authentic Teams for High Performance at Work* (Palo Alto, CA: Davies-Black, 2002).
30. *Random House Webster's Unabridged Dictionary* (New York: Random House, 1998), 1590.
31. R. Lewontin, "The Apportionment of Human Diversity," *Evolutionary Biology* 6 (1973): 381–397.
32. S. Saulny, "Black? White? Asian? More Young Americans Choose All of the Above," *New York Times* (January 30, 2011): 1, 20–21.
33. D. Matsumoto and L. Juang, *Culture and Psychology* (Belmont, CA: Wadsworth/Thomson, 2004), 16; also see H. A. Yee, H. H. Fairchild, F. Weizmann, and E. G. Wyatt, "Addressing Psychology's Problems with Race," *American Psychologist* 48 (1994): 1132–1140.
34. B. J. Allen, *Differences Matter: Communicating Social Identity* (Long Grove, IL: Waveland Press, 2004).
35. Matsumoto and Juang, *Culture and Psychology*, 80–81.
36. S. Roberts, *Who We Are Now: The Changing Face of America in the Twenty-First Century* (New York: Henry Holt, 2004).
37. M. E. Ryan, "Another Way to Teach Migrant Students," *Los Angeles Times* (March 31, 1991): B20, as cited by M. W. Lustig and J. Koester, *Intercultural Competence: Interpersonal Communication across Cultures* (Boston: Allyn & Bacon, 2009), 11.
38. Roberts, *Who We Are Now*, 126.
39. "One in Three US Residents Member of a Minority Group," Marketing Charts, May 21, 2007, accessed September 25, 2014, www.marketingcharts.com/traditional/one-in-three-us-residents-a-member-of-a-minority-group-418.
40. Roberts, *Who We Are Now*, 122; A. Caldwell, "Census: More Than Half of Texans Are Minorities," *Austin American-Statesman* (August 11, 2005): lB.
41. L. A. Jacobsen, M. Kent, M. Lee, and M. Mather, "Population Bulletin: America's Aging Population," Population Reference Bureau, February 2011, 66(1), 4, www.prb.org/pdf11/aging-in-America.pdf.
42. S. Saulny, "Black? White? Asian?"
43. G. Chen and W. J. Starosta, "A Review of the Concept of Intercultural Sensitivity," *Human Communication* 1 (1997): 7.
44. "One Nation, One Language?" *U.S. News & World Report* (September 25, 1995): 40, as cited by Lustig and Koester, *Intercultural Competence*, 10.
45. "One in Three US Residents Member of a Minority Group."

46. S. Jaschik, "Women Lead in Doctorates," *Inside Higher Ed*, September 14, 2010. Accessed September 25, 2014, www.insidehighered.com/news/2010/09/14/doctorates.
47. "Gay and Lesbian Population: Los Angeles County and the City of Los Angeles. *Los Angeles Almanac*, accessed May 26, 2008, www.laalmanac.com/population/po55.htm.
48. Yankelovich, Inc., "Beyond the Boomers: Millennials and Generation X," *Ketchum.com*, accessed May 26, 2008, http://resources.ketchum.com/weblboomers.pdf.
49. T. Friedman, *The World Is Flat: A Brief History of the Twenty-First Century* (New York: Farrar, Straus and Giroux, 2005).
50. Adapted from *Information Please Almanac* (Boston: Houghton Mifflin, 1990) and *World Almanac and Book of Facts* (New York: World Almanac, 1991), as cited by Lustig and Koester, *Intercultural Competence*, 11.
51. A. G. Smith, ed., *Communication and Culture* (New York: Holt, Rinehart and Winston, 1966).
52. E. T. Hall, *Beyond Culture* (Garden City, NY: Doubleday, 1976).
53. For example, see A. V. Matveeve and P. E. Nelson, "Cross Cultural Competence and Multicultural Team Performance: Perceptions of American and Russian Managers," *International Journal of Cross Cultural Management* 4 (2004): 253–270.
54. G. Hofstede, *Culture's Consequences: International Differences in Work Related Values* (Beverly Hills, CA: Sage, 1980); G. Hofstede and G. J. Hofstede, *Cultures and Organizations: Software of the Mind* 3e (New York: McGraw-Hill, 2010).
55. H. J. Ladegaard, "Global Culture—Myth or Reality? Perceptions of 'National Cultures' in Global Corporation," *Journal of Intercultural Communication Research* 36.2 (2007): 139–163; also see T. R. Levine, H. S. Park, and R. K Kim, "Some Conceptual and Theoretical Challenges for Cross-Cultural Communication Research in the 21st Century," *Journal of Intercultural Communication Research* 36.3 (2007): 205–221.
56. E. R. Pedersen, C. Neighbors, M. E. Larimer, and C. M. Lee, "Measuring Sojourner Adjustment Amount American Students Studying Abroad," *International Journal of Intercultural Relations* 35 (2011): 881–889.
57. For an excellent overview of issues in teaching intercultural communication, see Levine et al., "Some Conceptual and Theoretical Challenges for Cross-Cultural Communication Research in the 21st Century."
58. C. Ward, S. Bochner, and A. Fumham, *The Psychology of Culture Shock* (Hove, UK: Routledge, 2001).
59. T. L. Sandel, "Oh, I'm Here!': Social Media's Impact on the Cross-cultural Adaptation of Students Studying Abroad," *Journal of Intercultural Communication Research*, 45(1) (2014): 1–29.
60. Peter Coy, "The Future of Work," *Business Week* (August 20 and 27, 2007): 43.
61. See J. B. Walther, "Interpersonal Effects in Computer-Mediated Interaction: A Relational Perspective," *Communication Research* 19 (1992): 52–90; J. B. Walther, "Relational Aspects of Computer-Mediated Communication: Experimental and Longitudinal Observations," *Organizational Science* 6 (1995): 186–203; J. B. Walther, J. F. Anderson, and D. Park, "Interpersonal Effects in Computer-Mediated Interaction: A Meta-Analysis of Social and Anti-Social Communication," *Communication Research* 21 (1994): 460–487.
62. M. E. Heilman, S. Caleo, and M. L. Halim, "Just the Thought of It!: Effects of Anticipating Computer-mediated Communication on Gender Stereotyping," *Journal of Experimental Social Psychology* 46.4 (2010): 672–675.
63. C. H. Dodd, *Dynamics of Intercultural Communication* (New York: McGraw-Hill, 1998).
64. Hall, *Beyond Culture*.
65. L. A. Samovar, R. E. Porter, and L. A. Stefani, *Communication between Cultures* (Belmont, CA: Wadsworth, 1998).
66. Hofstede, *Culture's Consequences*; Hofstede and Hofstede, *Cultures and Organizations* 3e.
67. S. Ting-Toomey, "Applying Dimensional Values in Understanding Intercultural Communication," *Communication Monographs* 77.2 (2010): 169–180.
68. For research about the effect of individualistic and collectivistic cultural values on communication and conflict management, see R. Kaushal and C. T. Kwantes, "The Role of Culture and Personality in Choice of Conflict Management Strategy," *International Journal of Intercultural Relations* 30 (2006): 579–603.
69. Hofstede and Hofstede, *Cultures and Organizations* 3e.
70. W. B. Gudykunst, *Bridging Differences: Effective Intergroup Communication* (Newbury Park, CA: Sage, 1998).
71. H. C. Triandis, "The Many Dimensions of Culture," *Academy of Management Executive* 18 (2004): 88–93.
72. M. Voronov and J. A. Singer, "The Myth of Individualism-Collectivism: A Critical Review," *Journal of Social Psychology* 142 (2002): 461–480.
73. For an excellent review of Hofstede's work, see J. W. Bing, "Hofstede's Consequences: The Impact of His Work on Consulting and Business Practices," *Academy of Management Executive* 18 (2004): 80–87.
74. Hofstede, *Culture's Consequence;* Hofstede and Hofstede, *Cultures and Organizations* 3e.
75. G. Hofstede, "Cultural Dimensions in Management and Planning," *Asia Pacific Journal of Management* (January 1984): 81–98; Hofstede and Hofstede, *Cultures and Organizations* 3e.
76. For a discussion of a nation's long- and short-term time orientation, see Hofstede and Hofstede, *Cultures and Organizations* 3e, 210–238.
77. Hofstede and Hofstede, *Cultures and Organizations* 3e.
78. J. W. Neuliep, "Assessing the Reliability and Validity of the Generalized Ethnocentrism Scale," *Journal of Intercultural Communication Research* 31 (2002): 201–215. For additional research on the role of ethnocentrism in communication, see Y. Lin, A. Rancer, and A. Sunhee Lim, "Ethnocentrism and Intercultural Willingness to Communicate: A Cross-Cultural Comparison Between Korean and American College Students," *Journal of Intercultural Communication Research* 32 (2003): 117–128.
79. See Ensari and Murphy, "Cross-Cultural Variations in Leadership Perceptions and Attribution of Charisma to the Leader"; Lapinski and Levine, "Culture and Information Manipulation Theory"; Cai and Fink, "Conflict Style Differences between Individualists and Collectivists."
80. C. Kluckhohn and S. Murray, 1953, as quoted by J. S. Caputo, H. C. Hazel, and C. McMahon, *Interpersonal Communication* (Boston: Allyn & Bacon, 1994), 304.
81. Y. Kashima, E. S. Kashima, U. Kim, and M. Gelfand, "Describing the Social World: How Is a Person, a Group, and a Relationship Described in the East and in the West?" *Journal of Experimental Social Psychology* 42 (2006): 388–396.
82. D. E. Brown, "Human Universals and Their Implications," in *Being Humans: Anthropological Universality and Particularity in Transdisciplinary Perspectives,* edited by N. Roughley (New York: Walter de Gruyter, 2000, 156–174). For an applied discussion of these universals, see S. Pinker, *The Blank Slate: The Modern Denial of Human Nature* (London: Penguin Books, 2002).
83. D. W. Kale, "Ethics in Intercultural Communication," in *Intercultural Communication: A Reader* 6e, edited by L. A. Samovar and R. E. Porter (Belmont, CA: Wadsworth, 1991).
84. L. A. Samovar and R. E. Porter, *Communication between Cultures* (Stamford, CT: Wadsworth and Thomson Learning, 2001), 29.
85. C. S. Lewis, *The Abolition of Man* (New York: Macmillan, 1944).
86. M. Gladwell, *Blink: The Power of Thinking without Thinking* (New York: Little, Brown, 2005).
87. S. Kamekar, M. B. Kolsawalla, and T. Mazareth, "Occupational Prestige as a Function of Occupant's Gender," *Journal of Applied Social Psychology* 19 (1988): 681–688.
88. E. Roosevelt, as cited by Lustig and Koester, *Intercultural Competence*.

89. S. Ting-Toomey, "Intercultural Conflict Training: Theory-Practice Approaches and Research Challenges," *Journal of Intercultural Communication Research* 36.3 (2007): 255–271.
90. J. G. DeJaeghere and Y. Cao, "Developing U. S. Teachers' Intercultural Competence: Does Professional Development Matter?" *International Journal of Intercultural Relations* 33 (2009): 437–447.
91. P. Holmes and G. O'Neill, "Developing and Evaluating Intercultural Competence: Ethnographies of Intercultural Encounters," *International Journal of Intercultural Relations* 36 (2012): 707–718.
92. For a discussion of how intercultural competence has been applied to educational context, see P. Bayless, *Assessing the Intercultural Sensitivity of Elementary Teachers in Bilingual Schools in a Texas School District,* doctoral dissertation, University of Minnesota, Minneapolis (2009).
93. M. R. Hammer, M. J. Bennett, and R. Wiseman, "Measuring Intercultural Sensitivity: The Intercultural Development Inventory," *International Journal of Intercultural Relations* 27 (2003): 422.
94. Hammer, et al., "Measuring Intercultural Sensitivity," 421–443.
95. For additional research about the validity of measuring intercultural adaptation, see J. F. Greenholtz, "Does Intercultural Sensitivity Cross Cultures? Validity Issues in Porting Instruments across Languages and Cultures," *International Journal of Intercultural Relations* 29 (2005): 73–89.
96. R. Vollhardt, "Enhanced External and Culturally Sensitive Attributions after Extended Intercultural Contact," *British Journal of Social Psychology* 49.2 (2010): 363–383.
97. A. N. Miller and J. A. Samp, "Planning Intercultural Interaction: Extending Anxiety Uncertainty Management Theory," *Communication Research Reports* 24.2 (2007): 87–95.
98. Taking initiative when interacting with others from another culture can enhance intercultural competence. See E. S. Yakunina, I. K. Weigold, A. Weigold, S. Hercegovac, and N. Elsayed, "The Multicultural Personality: Does It Predict International Students' Openness to Diversity and Adjustment?," *International Journal of Intercultural Relations* 36 (2010): 533–540.
99. W. B. Gudykunst and Y. Kim, *Communicating with Strangers* (New York: Random House, 1984); Gudykunst, *Bridging Differences.*
100. Miller and Samp, "Planning Intercultural Interaction."
101. B. J. Lough, "International Volunteers' Perceptions of Intercultural Competence," *International Journal of Intercultural Relations* 35 (2011): 452–464.
102. For a classic discussion of egocentrism and ethnocentrism, see T. W. Adorno, E. Frenkel-Brunswik, D. J. Levinson, and R. N. Sanford, *The Authoritarian Personality* (New York: Harper & Brothers, 1950).
103. Neuliep, "Assessing the Reliability and Validity of the Generalized Ethnocentrism Scale"; Lin et al., "Ethnocentrism and Intercultural Willingness to Communicate."
104. M. V. Redmond, "The Functions of Empathy (Decentering) in Human Relations," *Human Relations* 42 (1993): 593–606; also see M. V. Redmond, "A Multidimensional Theory and Measure of Social Decentering," *Journal of Research in Personality* 1 (1995): 35–88; for an excellent discussion of the role of emotions in establishing empathy, see D. Goleman, *Emotional Intelligence* (New York: Bantam, 1995).
105. See B. J. Broome, "Building Shared Meaning: Implications of a Relational Approach to Empathy for Teaching Intercultural Communication," *Communication Education* 40 (1991): 235–249. Much of this discussion is based on the treatment of social decentering and empathy in S. A. Beebe, S. J. Beebe, and M. V. Redmond, *Interpersonal Communication: Relating to Others* 6e (Boston: Pearson, 2011).
106. F. Walter, M. S. Cole, and R. H. Humphrey, "Emotional Intelligence: *Sine Qua Non* of Leadership or Folderol?," *Academy of Management Perspectives* (2011): 45–59; Y. C. Lin, A. S. Y. Chen, and Y. C. Song, "Does Your Intelligence Help to Survive in a Foreign Jungle? The Effects of Cultural Intelligence and Emotional Intelligence on Cross-Cultural Adjustment," *International Journal of Intercultural Relations* 36 (2012): 541–552.
107. For an excellent discussion of empathy as it relates to intercultural communication, see D. W. Augsburger, *Pastoral Counseling across Cultures* (Philadelphia: Westminster Press, 1986), 28–30.
108. H. J. M. Nouwen, *Bread for the Journey* (New York: HarperCollins, 1997).
109. J. R. C. Kuntz, J. R. Kuntz, D. Elenkov, and A. Nabirukhina, "Characterizing Ethical Cases: A Cross-Cultural Investigation of Individual Differences, Organizational Climate, and Leadership on Ethical Decision-Making," *Journal of Business Ethics* (2013): 317–331.
110. R. H. Farrell, ed., *Off the Record: The Private Papers of Harry S. Truman* (New York: Harper & Row, 1980), 310.
111. S. M. Fowler, "Training across Cultures: What Intercultural Trainers Bring to Diversity Training," *International Journal of Intercultural Relations* 30 (2006): 401–411.
112. See, for example, A. Molinsky, "Cross-Cultural Code-Switching: The Psychological Challenges of Adapting Behavior in Foreign Cultural Interactions," *Academy of Management Review* (2007): 622–640.
113. L. J. Carrell, "Diversity in the Communication Curriculum: Impact on Student Empathy," *Communication Education* 46 (1997): 234–244.
114. Ting-Toomey, "Intercultural Conflict Training"; D. F. Barone, P. S. Hutchings, H. J. Kimmel, H. L. Traub, J. T. Cooper, and C. M. Marshall, "Increasing Empathic Accuracy through Practice and Feedback in a Clinical Interviewing Course," *Journal of Social and Clinical Psychology* 24 (2005): 156–171; J. Hamilton and R. Woodward-Kron, "Developing Cultural Awareness and Intercultural Communication through Multimedia: A Case Study from Medicine and Health Sciences," *System* 38.4 (2010): 560–568.

Chapter 7

1. B. D. Grill, "From Telex to Twitter: Relational Communication Skills for a Wireless World," in *Making Connections: Readings in Relational Communication* 5e, edited by K. M. Galvin (New York: Oxford University Press, 2011), 89–96; J. B. Walther and A. Ramirez Jr., "New Technologies and New Directions in Online Relating," in *New Directions in Interpersonal Communication Research,* edited by S. W. Smith and S. R. Wilson (Los Angeles: Sage, 2010), 264–284; E. A. Konijn, S. Utz, M. Tanis, and S. B. Barnes, *Mediated Interpersonal Communication* (New York: Routledge, 2008); S. B. Barnes, *Computer-Mediated Communication: Human-to-Human Communication Across the Internet* (Boston: Pearson, 2003); L. C. Tidwell and J. B. Walther, "Computer-Mediated Communication Effects on Disclosure, Impressions, and Interpersonal Evaluations: Getting to Know One Another a Bit at a Time," *Human Communication Research* 28 (2002): 317–348.
2. K. M. Galvin and C. A. Wilkinson, "The Communication Process: Impersonal and Interpersonal," in *Making Connections: Readings in Relational Communication* 5e, edited by K. M. Galvin (New York: Oxford University Press, 2011), 5–12.
3. E. Berscheid, "Interpersonal Attraction," in *The Handbook of Social Psychology,* edited by G. Lindzey and E. Aronson (New York: Random House, 1985), 413–484, as reported in J. A. Simpson and B. A. Harris, "Interpersonal Attraction," in *Perspectives on Close Relationships,* edited by A. L. Weber and J. H. Harvey (Boston: Allyn & Bacon, 1994), 45–66; W. G. Graziano and J. W. Bruce, "Attraction and the Initiation of Relationships: A Review of the Empirical Literature," in *Handbook of Relationship Initiation,* edited by S. Sprecher, A. Wenzel, and J. Harvey (New York: Psychology Press, 2008), 269–295; S. Sprecher and D. Felmlee, "Insider Perspectives on Attraction," in *Handbook of Relationship Initiation,* edited by S. Sprecher, A. Wenzel, and J. Harvey (New York: Psychology Press, 2008), 297–313.
4. D. K. Ivy and S. T. Wahl, *Nonverbal Communication for a Lifetime* 2e (Dubuque, IA: Kendall Hunt, 2014); L. K. Guerrero and K. Floyd, *Nonverbal Communication in Close Relationships* (Mahwah, NJ: Lawrence Erlbaum, 2006); J. H. Harvey and A. L. Weber,

Odyssey of the Heart: Close Relationships in the 21st Century 2e (Mahwah, NJ: Lawrence Erlbaum, 2002).

5. D. K. Ivy, *Genderspeak: Personal Effectiveness in Gender Communication* 5e (Boston: Pearson, 2012); F. Gaiba, "Straight Women and Gay Men Friends: A Qualitative Study," *Dissertation Abstracts International: Section A. Humanities and Social Sciences* 69 (2008): 262; L. M. Tillmann-Healy, *Between Gay and Straight: Understanding Friendship across Sexual Orientation* (Walnut Creek, CA: AltaMira Press, 2001); R. Hopcke and L. Rafaty, *Straight Women, Gay Men: Absolutely Fabulous Friendships* 2e (Berkeley, CA: Wildcat Canyon Press, 2001); R. Hopcke and L. Rafaty, *A Couple of Friends: The Remarkable Friendship between Straight Women and Gay Men* (Berkeley, CA: Wildcat Canyon Press, 1999).
6. N. H. Bartlett, H. M. Patterson, D. P. VanderLaan, and P. L. Vasey, "The Relation between Women's Body Esteem and Friendships with Gay Men," *Body Image* 6 (2009): 235–241.
7. M. Boler, "Hypes, Hopes, and Actualities: New Digital Cartesianism and Bodies in Cyberspace," in *The New Media and Cybercultures Anthology*, edited by P. K. Nayar (Malden, MA: Wiley-Blackwell, 2010), 185–208; D. Currier, "Assembling Bodies in Cyberspace: Technologies, Bodies, and Sexual Difference," in *The New Media and Cybercultures Anthology*, 254–267; J. A. McCown, D. Fisher, R. Page, and M. Homant, "Internet Relationships: People Who Meet People," *Cyberpsychology & Behavior* 4 (2001): 593–596; A. Cooper and L. Sportolari, "Romance in Cyberspace: Understanding Online Attraction," *Journal of Sex Education and Therapy* 22 (1997): 7–14; K. Y. A. McKenna, A. S. Green, and M. E. J. Gleason, "Relationship Formation on the Internet: What's the Big Attraction?" Journal of Social Issues 58 (2002): 9–31.
8. A. Cooper, I. P. McLoughlin, and K. M. Campbell, "Sexuality in Cyberspace: Update for the 21st Century," *Cyberpsychology & Behavior* 32 (2000): 521–536.
9. L. K. Guerrero, P. A. Andersen, and W. A. Afifi, *Close Encounters: Communicating in Relationships* 4e (Los Angeles: Sage, 2013), 54.
10. S. W. Duck, *Personal Relationships and Personal Constructs: A Study of Friendship Formation* (New York: Wiley, 1973).
11. S. A. Takeuchi, "On the Matching Phenomenon in Courtship: A Probability Matching Theory of Mate Selection," *Marriage and Family Review* 40 (2006): 25–51; G. B. Forbes, L. E. Adams-Curtis, B. Rade, and P. Jaberg, "Body Dissatisfaction in Women and Men: The Role of Gender-Typing and Self-Esteem," *Sex Roles* 44 (2001): 461–484; D. Bar-Tal and L. Saxe, "Perceptions of Similarity and Dissimilarity of Attractive Couples and Individuals," *Journal of Personality and Social Psychology* 33 (1976): 772–781.
12. D. M. Amodio and C. J. Showers, "'Similarity Breeds Liking' Revisited: The Moderating Role of Commitment," *Journal of Social and Personal Relationships* 22 (2005): 817–836.
13. S. Sprecher, "Effects of Actual (Manipulated) and Perceived Similarity on Liking in Get-Acquainted Interactions: The Role of Communication," *Communication Monographs* 81 (2014): 4–27; A. Bleske-Recheck, M. W. Remiker, and J. P. Baker, "Similar from the Start: Assortment in Young Adult Dating Couples and Its Link to Relationship Stability over Time," *Individual Differences Research* 7 (2009): 142–158; R. M. Montoya, R. S. Horton, and J. Kirchner, "Is Actual Similarity Necessary for Attraction? A Meta-Analysis of Actual and Perceived Similarity," *Journal of Social and Personal Relationships* 25 (2008): 889–922; B. Fehr, "Friendship Formation," in *Handbook of Relationship Initiation*, 29–54; Guerrero et al., *Close Encounters*.
14. P. M. Sias, H. Pedersen, E. B. Gallagher, and I. Kopaneva, "Workplace Friendship in the Electronically Connected Organization," *Human Communication Research* 38 (2012): 253–279; A. C. High and D. H. Solomon, "Locating Computer-Mediated Social Support within Online Communication Environments," in *Computer-Mediated Communication in Personal Relationships*, edited by K. B. Wright and L. M. Webb (New York: Peter Lang, 2010), 119–136; A. Kappas and N. C. Kramer (Eds.), *Face-to-Face Communication over the Internet: Emotions in a Web of Culture, Language, and Technology* (Cambridge, UK: Cambridge University Press, 2011); McKenna et al., "Relationship Formation on the Internet."
15. M. T. Whitty and J. K. Gavin, "Age/Sex/Location: Uncovering the Social Cues in the Development of On-Line Relationships," *Cyberpsychology and Behavior* 4 (2001): 623–630.
16. Fehr, "Friendship Formation"; Ivy and Wahl, *Nonverbal Communication for a Lifetime* 2e.
17. M. Prensky, "Digital Natives, Digital Immigrants," *On the Horizon* 9 (2001); *Digital Native*, accessed July 6, 2011, www.digitalnative.org/wiki.
18. P. B. Brandtzaeg, "Social Networking Sites: Their Users and Social Implications—A Longitudinal Study," *Journal of Computer-Mediated Communication* 17 (2012): 467–488; D. Ballard-Reisch, B. Rozzell, L. Heldman, and D. Kamerer, "Microchannels and CMC: Short Paths to Developing, Maintaining, and Dissolving Relationships," in *Computer-Mediated Communication in Personal Relationships*, edited by K. B. Wright and L. M. Webb (New York: Peter Lang, 2010), 56–78; K. Shonbeck, "Communicating in a Connected World," in *Making Connections: Readings in Relational Communication* 5e, edited by K. M. Galvin (New York: Oxford University Press, 2011), 393–400.
19. P. M. Markey and C. N. Markey, "Romantic Ideals, Romantic Obtainment, and Relationship Experiences: The Complementarity of Interpersonal Traits among Romantic Partners," *Journal of Social and Personal Relationships* 24 (2007): 517–533; Guerrero et al., *Close Encounters*.
20. H. Fisher, "The First Three Minutes," *O: The Oprah Winfrey Magazine* (November 2009): 140.
21. A. Mehrabian, *Nonverbal Communication* (Chicago: Aldine-Atherton, 1972).
22. J. Deyo, P. Walt, and L. Davis, "Rapidly Recognizing Relationships: Observing Speed Dating in the South," *Qualitative Research Reports in Communication* 12 (2011): 71–78; M. L. Houser, S. M. Horan, and L. A. Furler, "Dating in the Fast Lane: How Communication Predicts Speed-Dating Success," *Journal of Social and Personal Relationships* 25 (2008): 749–768; P. W. Eastwick and E. J. Finkel, "Speed-Dating: A Powerful and Flexible Paradigm for Studying Romantic Relationship Initiation," in *Handbook of Relationship Initiation*, edited by S. Sprecher, A. Wenzel, and J. Harvey (New York: Psychology Press, 2008), 297–313.
23. P. Collett, *The Book of Tells* (London: Bantam, 2004); J. A. Daly, E. Hogg, D. Sacks, M. Smith, and L. Zimring, "Sex and Relationship Affect Social Self-Grooming," in *The Nonverbal Communication Reader: Classic and Contemporary Readings* 2e, edited by L. K. Guerrero, J. DeVito, and M. L. Hecht (Prospect Heights, IL: Waveland, 1999), 56–61.
24. M. T. Whitty, "Cyber-Flirting: An Examination of Men's and Women's Flirting Behaviour Both Offline and on the Internet," *Behaviour Change* 21 (2004): 115–126. For more information on flirting and conveying attraction, see D. D. Henningsen, M. L. M. Henningsen, E. McWorthy, C. McWorthy, and L. McWorthy, "Exploring the Effects of Sex and Mode of Presentation in Perceptions of Dating Goals in Video-Dating," *Journal of Communication* 61 (2011): 641–658; D. D. Henningsen, F. Kartch, N. Orr, and A. Brown, "The Perceptions of Verbal and Nonverbal Flirting Cues in Cross-Sex Interactions," *Human Communication* 12 (2009): 371–381; J. M. Albright, "How Do I Love Thee and Thee and Thee: Self-Presentation, Deception, and Multiple Relationships Online," in *Online M@tchmaking*, edited by M. T. Whitty, A. Baker, and J. A. Inman (New York: Palgrave Macmillan, 2007), 81–93; D. D. Henningsen, M. Braz, and E. Davies, "Why Do We Flirt?" *Journal of Business Communication* 45 (2008): 483–502; M. T. Whitty and A. N. Carr, "Cyberspace as Potential Space: Considering the Web as a Playground to Cyber-Flirt," *Human Relations* 56 (2003): 869–891.
25. L. Stafford and J. D. Hillyer, "Information and Communication Technologies in Personal Relationships," *Review of*

Communication 12 (2012): 290–213; M. Lipinski-Harten and R. W. Tafarodi, "A Comparison of Conversational Quality in Online and Face-to-Face First Encounters," *Journal of Language and Social Psychology* 31 (2012): 331–341; J. P. Caughlin and L. L. Sharabi, "A Communicative Interdependence Perspective of Close Relationships: The Connections between Mediated and Unmediated Interactions Matter," *Journal of Communication* 63 (2013): 873–893.

26. D. Menaker, *A Good Talk: The Story and Skill of Conversation* (New York: Twelve Publishers, 2011); D. Menaker, "How to Break the Ice," *O: The Oprah Winfrey Magazine* (January 2010): 121; D. Pillet-Shore, "Doing Introductions: The Work Involved in Meeting Someone New," *Communication Monographs* 78 (2011): 73–95.
27. S. Sprecher and S. Metts, "Logging on, Hooking up: The Changing Nature of Romantic Relationship Initiation and Romantic Relating," in *Human Bonding: The Science of Affectional Ties*, edited by C. Hazan and M. I. Campa (New York: Guilford, 2013), 197–225; A. L. Vangelisti, "Interpersonal Processes in Romantic Relationships," in *The SAGE Handbook of Interpersonal Communication* 4e, edited by M. L. Knapp and J. A. Daly (Thousand Oaks, CA: Sage, 2011), 597–632; J. B. Walther, "Theories of Computer-Mediated Communication and Interpersonal Relations," in *The SAGE Handbook of Interpersonal Communication* 4e, 443–480.
28. M. Sunnafrank and A. Ramirez, "At First Sight: Persistent Relational Effects of Get-Acquainted Conversations," *Journal of Social and Personal Relationships* 21 (2004): 361–379.
29. C. R. Berger and R. J. Calabrese, "Some Explorations in Initial Interaction and Beyond: Toward a Developmental Theory of Interpersonal Communication," *Human Communication Research* 1 (1975): 99–112; C. R. Berger and J. J. Bradac, *Language and Social Knowledge: Uncertainty in Interpersonal Relations* (Baltimore: Edward Arnold, 1982).
30. For more research on relational uncertainty, a topic related to uncertainty reduction theory, we refer you to the work of Leanne Knobloch; see L. K. Knobloch, A. T. Ebata, P. C. McGlaughlin, and J. A. Theiss, "Generalized Anxiety and Relational Uncertainty as Predictors of Topic Avoidance During Reintegration Following Military Deployment," *Communication Monographs* 80 (2013): 452–477; L. K. Knobloch and J. A. Theiss, "Relational Uncertainty and Relationship Talk within Courtship: A Longitudinal Actor-Partner Interdependence Model," *Communication Monographs* 78 (2011): 3–26; L. K. Knobloch, "Relational Uncertainty and Interpersonal Communication," in *New Directions in Interpersonal Communication Research*, edited by S. W. Smith and S. R. Wilson (Los Angeles: Sage, 2010), 69–93; L. K. Knobloch, "Uncertainty Reduction Theory: Communicating under Conditions of Ambiguity," in *Engaging Theories in Interpersonal Communication: Multiple Perspectives*, edited by L. A. Baxter and D. O. Braithwaite (Los Angeles: Sage, 2008), 133–144.
31. N. B. Ellison, J. T. Hancock, and C. L Toma, "Profile as Promise: A Framework for Conceptualizing Veracity in Online Dating Self-Presentations," *New Media & Society* 14 (2012): 45–62; R. E. Guadagno, B. M. Okdie, and S. A. Kruse, "Dating Deception: Gender, Online Dating, and Exaggerated Self-Presentation," *Computers in Human Behavior* 28 (2012): 642–647; J. A. Hall, N. Park, S. Hayeon, and J. C. Michael, "Strategic Misrepresentation in Online Dating: The Effects of Gender, Self-Monitoring, and Personality Traits," *Journal of Social & Personal Relationships* 27 (2010): 117–135; J. T. Hancock and C. L. Toma, "Putting Your Best Face Forward: The Accuracy of Online Dating Photographs," *Journal of Communication* 59 (2009): 367–386; C. L. Toma and J. T. Hancock, "A New Twist on Love's Labor: Self-Presentation in Online Dating Profiles," in *Computer-Mediated Communication in Personal Relationships*, edited by K. B. Wright and L. M. Webb (New York: Peter Lang, 2010), 41–55.
32. C. L. Kleinke, F. B. Meeker, and R. A. Staneski, "Preference for Opening Lines: Comparing Ratings by Men and Women," *Sex Roles* 15 (1986): 585–600; E. Weber, *How to Pick Up Girls!* (New York: Bantam Books, 1970).
33. C. Senko and V. Fyffe, "An Evolutionary Perspective on Effective vs. Ineffective Pick-up Lines," *Journal of Social Psychology* 150 (2010): 648–667.
34. D. Dickson and O. Hargie, "Questioning," in *The Handbook of Communication Skills* 3e, edited by O. Hargie (London: Routledge, 2006), 121–145.
35. A. L. Vangelisti, M. L. Knapp, and J. A. Daly, "Conversational Narcissism," *Communication Monographs* 57 (1990): 251–274; J. M. Twenge, S. Konrath, J. D. Foster, W. K. Campbell, and B. J. Bushman, "Egos Inflating over Time: A Cross-Temporal Meta-Analysis of the Narcissistic Personality Inventory," *Journal of Personality* 76 (2008): 875–901; J. M. Twenge, *Generation Me: Why Today's Young Americans Are More Confident, Assertive, Entitled—and More Miserable Than Ever Before* (New York: Free Press, 2006); J. M. Twenge and W. K. Campbell, *The Narcissism Epidemic: Living in the Age of Entitlement* (New York: Free Press, 2011); J. M. Twenge, "The Narcissism Epidemic: Narcissism Is on the Rise among Individuals and in American Culture," August 12, 2013, accessed June 15, 2014, www.psychtoday.com; F. Rhodewalt, "Contemporary Perspectives on Narcissism and the Narcissistic Personality Type," in *Handbook of Self and Identity*, edited by M. R. Leary and J. Price Tangney (New York: Guilford, 2013), 571–586.
36. C. Derber, *The Pursuit of Attention: Power and Ego in Everyday Life* (New York: Oxford University Press, 2000).
37. J. Holmes, "Complimenting—A Positive Politeness Strategy," in *Language and Gender: A Reader*, edited by J. Coates (Malden, MA: Blackwell, 1998), 100–120.
38. M. Strobel, *The Compliment Quotient: Boost Your Spirits, Spark Your Relationships, and Uplift the World* (New York: Wise Roads Press, 2011); C. Matheson, *The Art of the Compliment: Using Kind Words with Grace and Style* (New York: Skyhorse Publishing, 2009); D. C. Marigold, J. G. Holmes, and M. Ross, "More Than Words: Compliments from Romantic Partners Foster Security in Low Self-Esteem Individuals," *Journal of Personality and Social Psychology* 92 (2007): 232–248; E. M. Doohan and V. Manusov, "The Communication of Compliments in Romantic Relationships: An Investigation of Relational Satisfaction and Sex Differences and Similarities in Compliment Behavior," *Western Journal of Communication* 68 (2004): 170–194; C. Parisi and P. Wogan, "Compliment Topics and Gender," *Women & Language* 29 (2006): 21–28.
39. M. Beck, "Why It's Harder to Receive Than to Give," *O: The Oprah Winfrey Magazine* (September 2006): 81–83.
40. "The Health Benefits of Strong Relationships," *Harvard Women's Health Watch* 18 (December 2010): 1.
41. K. C. Maguire, D. Heinemann-LaFave, and E. Sahlstein, "'To Be Connected, yet Not at All': Relational Presence, Absence, and Maintenance in the Context of a Wartime Deployment," *Western Journal of Communication* 77 (2013): 249–271; K. C. Maguire and T. A. Kinney, "When Distance Is Problematic: Communication, Coping, and Relational Satisfaction in Female College Students' Long-Distance Dating Relationships," *Journal of Applied Communication Research* 38 (2010): 27–46; L. Stafford, "Geographic Distance and Communication During Courtship," *Communication Research* 37 (2010): 275–297.
42. Harvey and Weber, *Odyssey of the Heart*, 105–106.
43. S. Jourard, *The Transparent Self* (Princeton, NJ: Van Nostrand, 1971).
44. D. W. Johnson, *Reaching Out: Interpersonal Effectiveness and Self-Actualization* 11e (Boston: Pearson, 2012), 48–49.
45. J. Kim and K. Dindia, "Online Self-Disclosure: A Review of Research," in *Computer-Mediated Communication in Personal Relationships*, edited by K. B. Wright and L. M. Webb (New York: Peter Lang, 2010), 156–180; C. M. H. Bane, M. Cornish, N. Erspamer, and L. Kampman, "Self-Disclosure through Weblogs and Perceptions of Online and 'Real-Life' Friendships among

Female Bloggers," *Cyberpsychology, Behavior, & Social Networking* 13 (2010): 131–139; R. West and L. H. Turner, "Technology and Interpersonal Communication," in *Making Connections: Readings in Relational Communication* 5e, edited by K. M. Galvin (New York: Oxford University Press, 2011), 379–386.

46. K. Shonbeck, "Thoughts on CMC by an E-mailer, IMer, Blog Reader, and Facebooker," in *Making Connections: Readings in Relational Communication* 4e, edited by K. M. Galvin and P. Cooper (Los Angeles: Roxbury, 2006), 372–378.
47. V. J. Derlega, B. Winstead, A. Mathews, and A. L. Braitman, "Why Does Someone Reveal Highly Personal Information? Attributions for and against Self-Disclosure in Close Relationships," *Communication Research Reports* 25 (2008): 115–130.
48. Sandra Petronio's body of work on communication privacy management (CPM theory) is our most significant source of information on this topic; see S. Petronio, *Boundaries of Privacy: Dialectics of Disclosure* (Albany: SUNY Press, 2002); S. Petronio, "Brief Status Report on Communication Privacy Management Theory," *Journal of Family Communication* 13 (2013): 6–14; J. T. Child and S. Petronio, "Unpacking the Paradoxes of Privacy in CMC Relationships: The Challenges of Blogging and Relational Communication on the Internet," in *Computer-Mediated Communication in Personal Relationships*, edited by K. B. Wright and L. M. Webb (New York: Peter Lang, 2010), 21–40; A. M. Hosek and J. Thompson, "Communication Privacy Management and College Instruction: Exploring the Rules and Boundaries That Frame Instructor Private Disclosures," *Communication Education* 58 (2009), 327–349; S. Petronio and W. T. Durham, "Communication Privacy Management Theory," in *Exploring Theories in Interpersonal Communication*, edited by L. A. Baxter and D. O. Braithwaite (Los Angeles: Sage, 2008), 309–322; S. Petronio, "Translational Research Endeavors and the Practices of Communication Privacy Management," *Journal of Applied Communication Research* 35 (2007): 218–222; S. Petronio, "The Boundaries of Privacy: Praxis of Everyday Life," in *Balancing Secrets of Private Disclosure*, edited by S. Petronio (Mahwah, NJ: Lawrence Erlbaum, 2000), 37–49; L. B. Rosenfeld, "Overview of the Ways Privacy, Secrecy, and Disclosure Are Balanced in Today's Society," in *Balancing Secrets of Private Disclosure*, edited by S. Petronio (Mahwah, NJ: Lawrence Erlbaum, 2000), 3–17. For other research on CPM, see the entire volume 13, year 2013, of the *Journal of Family Communication*, including the introductory piece: M. C. Morr Serewicz, "Introducing the Special Issue on Communication Privacy Management Theory and Family Privacy Regulation," *Journal of Family Communication* 13 (2013): 1–5. For related research on privacy and disclosure, see S.-A. A. Jin, "Peeling Back the Multiple Layers of Twitter's Private Disclosure Onion: The Roles of Virtual Identity Discrepancy and Personality Traits in Communication Privacy Management on Twitter," *New Media & Society* 15 (2013): 813–833; V. Cho and H. Hung, "The Effectiveness of Short Message Service for Communication with Concerns of Privacy Protection and Conflict Avoidance," *Journal of Computer-Mediated Communication* 16 (2011): 250–270; E. Butler, E. McCann, and J. Thomas, "Privacy Setting Awareness on Facebook and Its Effect on User-Posted Content," *Human Communication* 14 (2011): 39–55; T. Afifi and K. Steuber, "The Revelation Risk Model (RRM): Factors That Predict the Revelation of Secrets and the Strategies Used to Reveal Them," *Communication Monographs* 76 (2009): 144–176.
49. K. B. Carnelley, E. G. Hepper, C. Hicks, and W. Turner, "Perceived Parental Reactions to Coming Out, Attachment, and Romantic Relationship Views," *Attachment and Human Development* 13 (2011): 217–236; M. Vaughan and C. Waehler, "Coming Out Growth: Conceptualizing and Measuring Stress-Related Growth Associated with Coming Out to Others as a Sexual Minority," *Journal of Adult Development* 17 (2010): 94–109; L. Heatherington and J. A. Lavner, "Coming to Terms with Coming Out: Review and Recommendations for Family Systems-Focused Research," *Journal of Family Psychology* 22 (2008): 329–343; M. L. Rasmussen, "The Problem of Coming Out," *Theory into Practice* 43 (2004): 144–151.
50. I. Altman and D. Taylor, *Social Penetration: The Development of Relationships* (New York: Holt, Rinehart and Winston, 1973).
51. "Frequently Asked Questions," *Invisible Girlfriend,* accessed September 16, 2014, invisiblegirlfriend.com/home/faq.
52. B. Feldt, "How to Get Paid Being an 'Invisible Girlfriend,'" *The Business Journals*, July 1, 2014, retrieved July 2, 2014, www.bizjournals.com; P. Szoldra, "'Invisible Girlfriend' Startup Provides Fake Love for a Price," *Business Insider*, November 23, 2013, retrieved July 2, 2014, www.businessinsider.com; R. Zarrell, "'Invisible Girlfriend' App Aims to Make Your Friends and Family Think Your Life Is Slightly Less Depressing," *BuzzFeed*, November 20, 2013, retrieved July 2, 2014, www.buzzfeed.com.
53. J. Luft, *Group Process: An Introduction to Group Dynamics* (Palo Alto, CA: Mayfield, 1970).
54. P. D. Bolls, "Understanding Emotion from a Superordinate Dimensional Perspective: A Productive Way Forward for Communication Processes and Effects Studies," *Communication Monographs* 77 (2010): 146–152.
55. S. Metts and S. Planalp, "Emotional Experience and Expression: Current Trends and Future Directions in Interpersonal Relationship Research," in Knapp and Daly, *The SAGE Handbook of Interpersonal Communication*, 283–316; E. L. MacGeorge, B. Feng, and B. R. Burleson, "Supportive Communication," in Knapp and Daly, *The SAGE Handbook of Interpersonal Communication*, 317–354.
56. D. Hample, A. S. Richards, and C. Skubisz, "Blurting," *Communication Monographs* 80 (2013): 503.
57. Hample et al., "Blurting," 507.
58. Y. Kimura, "Expressing Emotions in Teaching: Inducement, Suppression, and Disclosure as Caring Profession," *Educational Studies in Japan: International Yearbook* 5 (2010): 63–78; M.-S. Kim and A. S. Ebesu Hubbard, "Intercultural Communication in the Global Village: How to Understand 'The Other,'" *Journal of Intercultural Communication Research* 36 (2007): 223–235; A. Molinsky, "Cross-Cultural Code-Switching: The Psychological Challenges of Adapting Behavior in Foreign Cultural Interactions," *Academy of Management Review* 32 (2007): 622–640; S. Glazer, "Social Support across Cultures," *International Journal of Intercultural Relations* 30 (2006): 605–622.
59. P. A. Andersen, "The Basis of Cultural Differences in Nonverbal Communication," in *Intercultural Communication: A Reader* 13e, edited by L. A. Samovar, R. E. Porter, and E. R. McDaniel (Belmont, CA: Wadsworth/Cengage Learning, 2011), 293–312.
60. U. Hess, R. B. Adams Jr., K. Grammer, and R. E. Kleck, "Face Gender and Emotion Expression: Are Angry Women More Like Men?" *Journal of Vision* 9 (2009): 1–8; A. Campbell and S. Muncer, "Intent to Harm or Injure? Gender and the Expression of Anger," *Aggressive Behavior* 34 (2008): 282–293; T. B. Kashdan, A. Mishra, W. E. Breen, and J. J. Froh, "Gender Differences in Gratitude: Examining Appraisals, Narratives, the Willingness to Express Emotions, and Changes in Psychological Needs," *Journal of Personality* 77 (2009): 1–40; R. W. Simon and L. E. Nath, "Gender and Emotion in the United States: Do Men and Women Differ in Self-Reports of Feelings and Expressive Behavior?" *American Journal of Sociology* 109 (2004): 1137–1176.
61. Jourard, *The Transparent Self.*
62. B. B. Burleson, "Introduction to the Special Issue: Psychological Mediators of Sex Differences in Emotional Support," *Communication Reports* 15 (2002), 1–4; W. Pollack, *Real Boys: Rescuing Our Sons from the Myths of Boyhood* (New York: Owl Books, 1999); O. Silverstein and B. Rashbaum, *The Courage to Raise Good Men* (New York: Penguin, 1995).
63. C. Hesse and E. A. Rauscher, "Privacy Tendencies and Revealing/Concealing: The Moderating Role of Emotional Competence," *Communication Quarterly* 61 (2013): 91–112.

Chapter 8

1. N. L. Galambos and L. A. Kotylak, "Transformations in Parent-Child Relationships from Adolescence to Adulthood," in *Relationship Pathways: From Adolescence to Young Adulthood*, edited by B. P. Laursen and W. A. Collins (Thousand Oaks, CA: Sage, 2011), 23–42; W. K. Rawlins, *The Compass of Friendship: Narratives, Identities, and Dialogues* (Los Angeles: Sage, 2009); M. Monsour, *Women and Men as Friends: Relationships across the Life Span in the 21st Century* (Mahwah, NJ: Lawrence Erlbaum, 2002); M. Paul, *The Friendship Crisis: Finding, Making, and Keeping Friends When You're Not a Kid Anymore* (New York: Rodale Books, 2004).
2. N. Way, *Deep Secrets: Boys' Friendships and the Crisis of Connection* (Cambridge, MA: Harvard University Press, 2011); R. Blieszner, "Close Relationships over Time," as reported in J. A. Simpson and B. A. Harris, "Interpersonal Attraction," in *Perspectives on Close Relationships*, edited by A. L. Weber and J. H. Harvey (Boston: Allyn & Bacon, 1994), 1–18.
3. C. A. Hafen, B. Laursen, and D. DeLay, "Transformations in Friend Relationships across the Transition into Adolescence," in B. P. Laursen and W. A. Collins, Eds., *Relationship Pathways: From Adolescence to Young Adulthood*, 69–90.
4. C. M. Chow, H. Roelse, D. Buhrmeister, and M. K. Underwood, "Transformations in Friend Relationships across the Transition into Adulthood," in B. P. Laursen and W. A. Collins, Eds., *Relationship Pathways: From Adolescence to Young Adulthood*, 91–112; J. Yager, *Friendshifts: The Power of Friendship and How It Shapes Our Lives* (Stamford, CT: Hannacrois Creek Books, 1999); W. Rawlins, "Being There for Friends," in *Making Connections: Readings in Relational Communication* 4e, edited by K. M. Galvin and P. Cooper (Los Angeles: Roxbury, 2006), 329–332.
5. B. McEwan and L. K. Guerrero, "Freshmen Engagement through Communication: Predicting Friendship Formation Strategies and Perceived Availability of Network Resources from Communication Skills," *Communication Studies* 61 (2010): 445–463; B. Fehr, "Friendship Formation," in *Handbook of Relationship Initiation*, edited by S. Sprecher, A. Wenzel, and J. Harvey (New York: Psychology Press, 2008), 29–54; G. Foster, "Making Friends: A Nonexperimental Analysis of Social Pair Formation," *Human Relations* 58 (2005): 1443–1465; A. J. Johnson, E. Wittenberg, M. M. Villagran, M. Mazur, and P. Villagran, "Relational Progression as a Dialectic: Examining Turning Points in Communication among Friends," *Communication Monographs* 70 (2003): 230–249.
6. "Work and Family Facts & Statistics," *AFL-CIO*, accessed July 4, 2014, www.aflcio.org; M. J. Fay and S. L. Kline, "Coworker Relationships and Informal Communication in High-Intensity Telecommuting," *Journal of Applied Communication Research* 39 (2011): 144–163; P. M. Sias and D. J. Cahill, "From Coworkers to Friends: The Development of Peer Friendships in the Workplace," *Western Journal of Communication* 62 (1998): 273–299; G. A. Fine, "Friendships in the Workplace," in K. M. Galvin and P. Cooper, Eds., *Making Connections* 4e, 270–277.
7. J. Harwood, *Understanding Communication and Aging* (Los Angeles: Sage, 2007); L. Gee, *Friends: Why Men and Women Are from the Same Planet* (New York: Bloomsbury, 2004); Monsour, *Women and Men as Friends*.
8. L. H. Turner and R. West, "The Challenge of Defining 'Family,'" in *The SAGE Handbook of Family Communication*, edited by L. H. Turner and R. West (Thousand Oaks, CA: Sage, 2014), 10–25; E. A. Suter, L. A. Baxter, L. M. Seurer, and L. J. Thomas, "Discursive Constructions of the Meaning of 'Family' in Online Narratives of Foster Adoptive Parents," *Communication Monographs* 81 (2014): 59–78; "A Woman's Nation Changes Everything," in *The Shriver Report* (Washington, DC: Center for American Progress, 2009), accessed October 29, 2009, awomansnation .com; "Women in America: Indicators of Social and Economic Well-Being," *White House*, March 1, 2011, accessed March 13, 2011, www.whitehouse.gov; K. Galvin and C. Bylund, "First Marriage Families: Gender and Communication," in *Women and Men Communicating: Challenges and Changes* 2e, edited by L. P. Arliss and D. J. Borisoff (Prospect Heights, IL: Waveland, 2001), 132–148; V. Satir, "The Rules You Live By," in *Making Connections* 4e, 168–174; R. S. Miller, *Intimate Relationships* 6e (New York: McGraw-Hill, 2011).
9. *Miami Herald* (July 9, 1982): 12A.
10. "Stepfamily Statistics," *The Stepfamily Foundation*, retrieved July 4, 2014, www.stepfamily.org; P. Schrodt, J. Soliz, and D. O. Braithwaite, "A Social Relations Model of Everyday Talk and Relational Satisfaction in Stepfamilies," *Communication Monographs* 75 (2008): 190–217; K. Floyd and M. T. Morman, *Widening the Family Circle* 2e (Thousand Oaks, CA: Sage, 2013); D. O. Braithwaite, P. W. Toller, K. L. Daas, W. T. Durham, and A. C. Jones, "Centered but Not Caught in the Middle: Stepchildren's Perceptions of Dialectical Contradictions in the Communication of Co-Parents," *Journal of Applied Communication Research* 36 (2008): 33–55.
11. E. A. Suter, "Communication in Lesbian and Gay Families," in L. H. Turner and R. West, Eds., *SAGE Handbook of Family Communication* 4e, 235–247; J. Dixon and D. S. Dougherty, "A Language Convergence/Meaning Divergence Analysis Exploring How LGBTQ and Single Employees Manage Traditional Family Expectations in the Workplace," *Journal of Applied Communication Research* 42 (2014): 1–19; J. Koenig Kellas and E. A. Suter, "Accounting for Lesbian-Headed Families: Lesbian Mothers' Responses to Discursive Challenges," *Communication Monographs* 79 (2012): 475–498.
12. V. Satir, *The New Peoplemaking* (Mountain View, CA: Science & Behavior Books, 1988), 4.
13. D. M. Keating, J. C. Russell, J. Cornacchione, and S. W. Smith, "Family Communication Patterns and Difficult Family Conversations," *Journal of Applied Communication Research* 41 (2013): 160–180; J. P. Caughlin, A. F. Koerner, P. Schrodt, and M. A. Fitzpatrick, "Interpersonal Communication in Family Relationships," in *The SAGE Handbook of Interpersonal Communication* 4e, edited by M. L. Knapp and J. A. Daly (Thousand Oaks, CA: Sage, 2011), 679–714.
14. P. Schrodt, P. L. Witt, and A. S. Messersmith, "A Meta-Analytical Review of Family Communication Patterns and Their Associations with Information Processing, Behavioral, and Psychosocial Outcomes," *Communication Monographs* 75 (2008): 248–269.
15. L. K. Knobloch, A. T. Ebata, P. C. McGlaughlin, and J. A. Theiss, "Generalized Anxiety and Relational Uncertainty as Predictors of Topic Avoidance During Reintegration Following Military Deployment," *Communication Monographs* 80 (2013): 452–477; L. K. Knobloch and S. R. Wilson, "Communication in Military Families across the Deployment Cycle," in L. H. Turner and R. West, Eds., *SAGE Handbook of Family Communication* 4e, 370–385.
16. S. Jana, A. Pande, A. Chan, and P. Mohapatra, "Mobile Video Chat: Issues and Challenges," *IEEE Communications Magazine* 51 (2013): 144–151.
17. S. Yarosh and G. D. Abowd, "Mediated Parent-Child Contact in Work-Separated Families," *Proceedings of the SIGCHI Conference on Human Factors in Computing Systems* (2011): 1185–1194.
18. J. A. Laser and P. M. Stephens, "Working with Military Families through Deployment and Beyond," *Clinical Social Work Journal* 39 (2011): 28–38.
19. J. M. Gottman, J. S. Gottman, and C. L. Atkins, "The Comprehensive Soldier Fitness Program: Family Skills Components," *American Psychologist* 66 (2011): 52–57.
20. A. L. Joseph and T. D. Afifi, "Military Wives' Stressful Disclosures to Their Deployed Husbands: The Role of Protective Buffering," *Journal of Applied Communication Research* 38 (2010): 412–434.
21. "Work and Family Facts & Statistics," *Contexts: A Publication of the American Sociological Association* 3, 2004, www.contexts .org.
22. "Job Outlook 2014," *National Association of Colleges and Employers*, www.jobweb.com.

23. P. M. Sias, H. Pedersen, E. B. Gallagher, and I. Kopaneva, "Workplace Friendship in the Electronically Connected Organization," *Human Communication Research* 38 (2012): 253–279.
24. K. K. Myers, D. R. Seibold, and H. S. Park, "Interpersonal Communication in the Workplace," in Knapp and Daly, Eds., *SAGE Handbook of Interpersonal Communication* 4e, 527–562; R. B. Adler, J. M. Elmhorst, and K. Lucas, *Communication at Work* 11e (New York: McGraw-Hill, 2012); D. O'Hair, G. W. Friedrich, and L. A. Dixon, *Strategic Communication in Business and the Professions* 7e (Boston: Pearson, 2010).
25. M. L. Knapp and A. Vangelisti, "Relationship Stages: A Communication Perspective," in K. M. Galvin and P. Cooper, Eds., *Making Connections* 4e, 132–139; M. L. Knapp, A. L. Vangelisti, and J. P. Caughlin, *Interpersonal Communication and Human Relationships* 7e (Boston: Pearson, 2013); K. N. Dunleavy and M. Booth-Butterfield, "Idiomatic Communication in the Stages of Coming Together and Falling Apart," *Communication Quarterly* 57 (2009): 416–432; P. A. Mongeau and M. L. Miller Henningsen, "Stage Theories of Relationship Development: Charting the Course of Interpersonal Communication," in *Engaging Theories in Interpersonal Communication: Multiple Perspectives*, edited by L. A. Baxter and D. O. Braithwaite (Los Angeles: Sage, 2008), 363–375; L. K. Guerrero, P. A. Andersen, and W. A. Afifi, *Close Encounters: Communication in Relationships* 4e (Thousand Oaks, CA: Sage, 2013).
26. D. Hauani Solomon, K. M. Weber, and K. R. Steuber, "Turbulence in Relational Transitions," in *New Directions in Interpersonal Communication Research*, edited by S. W. Smith and S. R. Wilson (Los Angeles: Sage, 2010), 115–134; R. M. Dailey, A. D. Hampel, and J. B. Roberts, "Relational Maintenance in On-Again/Off-Again Relationships: An Assessment of How Relational Maintenance, Uncertainty, and Commitment Vary by Relationship Type and Status," *Communication Monographs* 77 (2010): 75–101; R. M. Dailey, K. Rossetto, R. A. Pfiester, and C. A. Surra, "A Qualitative Analysis of On-Again/Off-Again Romantic Relationships: 'It's Up and Down, All Around,'" *Journal of Social and Personal Relationships* 26 (2009): 443–466; R. M. Dailey, R. A. Pfiester, B. Jin, G. Beck, and G. Clark, "On-Again/Off-Again Dating Relationships: How Are They Different from Other Dating Relationships?" *Personal Relationships* 16 (2009): 23–47.
27. Knapp and Vangelisti, "Relationship Stages"; Knapp et al., *Interpersonal Communication and Human Relationships*.
28. S. W. Duck, "A Topography of Relationship Disengagement and Dissolution," in *Personal Relationships 4: Dissolving Relationships*, edited by S. W. Duck (New York: Academic Press, 1982); Guerrero et al., *Close Encounters*.
29. V. S. Millner, "Internet Infidelity: A Case of Intimacy with Detachment," *Family Journal* 16 (2008): 78–82; B. H. Henline, L. K. Lamke, and M. D. Howard, "Exploring Perceptions of Online Infidelity," *Personal Relationships* 14 (2007): 113–128; B. L. Avila Mileham, "Online Infidelity in Internet Chat Rooms: An Ethnographic Exploration," *Computers in Human Behavior* 23 (2007): 11–31; K. M. Hertlein and F. P. Piercy, "Internet Infidelity: A Critical Review of the Literature," *Family Journal* 14 (2006): 366–371.
30. M. Rabbitt, "Is Infidelity Obsolete?" *Women's Health* (July/August 2010): 144.
31. I. Tsapelas, H. E. Fisher, and A. Aron, "Infidelity: When, Where, Why," in *The Dark Side of Close Relationships II*, edited by W. R. Cupach and B. H. Spitzberg (New York: Routledge, 2011), 175–196; E. Nersesian-Solé, "What He's Hiding from You," *Women's Health* (November 2010): 98–100; J. A. Samp and J. L. Monahan, "Alcohol-Influenced Nonverbal Behaviors During Discussions about a Relationship Problem," *Journal of Nonverbal Behavior* 33 (2009): 193–211; F. S. Christopher and S. Sprecher, "Sexuality in Marriage, Dating, and Other Relationships: A Decade Review," in *Speaking of Sexuality: Interdisciplinary Readings*, edited by J. K. Davidson Sr. and N. B. Moore (Los Angeles: Roxbury, 2005): 54–71.
32. M. L. Hans, B. D. Selvidge, K. A. Tinker, and L. M. Webb, "Online Performances of Gender: Blogs, Gender-Bending, and Cybersex as Relational Examples," in *Computer-Mediated Communication in Personal Relationships*, edited by K. B. Wright and L. M. Webb (New York: Peter Lang, 2010), 302–323.
33. K. Y. A. McKenna, A. S. Green, and P. K. Smith, "Demarginalizing the Sexual Self," *Journal of Sex Research* 38 (2001): 302–316; A. Cooper, I. P. McLoughlin, and K. M. Campbell, "Sexuality in Cyberspace: Update for the 21st Century," *Cyberpsychology & Behavior* 3 (2000): 521–536.
34. Duck, "A Topography of Relationship Disengagement and Dissolution."
35. K. Blackburn, N. Brody, and L. LeFebvre, "The I's, We's, and She/He's of Breakups: Public and Private Pronoun Usage in Relationship Dissolution Accounts," *Journal of Language & Social Psychology* 33 (2014): 202–213; L. A. Lee and D. A. Sbarra, "The Predictors and Consequences of Relationship Dissolution: Breaking Down Silos," in *Human Bonding: The Science of Affectional Ties*, edited by C. Hazan and M. I. Campa (New York: Guilford, 2013), 308–342.
36. K. Ramirez, "'Baby, WTF? Where Are You?!?' The Act of 'Ghosting' Explained," *Island Waves* (April 18, 2013), 5; A. Syrtash, "Are You Guilty of Ghosting?," *Yahoo*, September 9, 2012, accessed April 20, 2013, shine.yahoo.com.
37. T. Levine and S. L. Fitzpatrick, "You Know Why; The Question Is How? Relationships between Reasons and Methods in Romantic Breakups," paper presented at the meeting of the International Communication Association (May 2005), New York City, New York.
38. Knapp et al., *Interpersonal Communication and Human Relationships*; M. L. Knapp and A. L. Vangelisti, "Relational Decline," K. M. Galvin and P. Cooper, Eds., *Making Connections* 4e, 269–273; W. R. Cupach, "Dialectical Process in the Disengagement of Interpersonal Relationships," *Making Connections* 4e, 274–280; M. Pelaez, T. Field, M. Diego, O. Deeds, and J. Delgado, "Insecurity, Control, and Disinterest Behaviors Are Related to Breakup Distress in University Students," *College Student Journal* 45 (2010): 333–340; D. Davis, P. R. Shaver, and M. L. Vernon, "Physical, Emotional, and Behavioral Reactions to Breaking Up: The Roles of Gender, Age, Emotional Involvement, and Attachment Style," *Personality and Social Psychology Bulletin* 29 (2003): 871–884.
39. L. Locker Jr., W. D. McIntosh, A. A. Hackney, J. H. Wilson, and K. E. Wiegand, "The Breakup of Romantic Relationships: Situational Predictors of Perception of Recovery," *North American Journal of Psychology* 12 (2010): 565–578; D. Cullingson, *Breaking Up Blues: A Guide to Survival* (New York: Routledge, 2008); S. P. Banks, D. M. Altendorf, J. O. Greene, and M. Cody, "An Examination of Relationship Disengagement: Perceptions, Breakup Strategies, and Outcomes," *Western Journal of Speech Communication* 51 (1987): 19–41.
40. K. Matthews, "The Dear John Talk and Other Dreaded Conversations: Eight Ways to Make Them Easier, Kinder, Gentler," *O: The Oprah Winfrey Magazine* (August 2007): 144, 146.
41. D. K. Ivy, *GenderSpeak: Personal Effectiveness in Gender Communication* 5e (Boston: Pearson, 2012).
42. R. M. Dailey, K. R. Rossetto, A. A. McCracken, B. Jin, and E. W. Green, "Negotiating Breakups and Renewals in On-Again/Off-Again Dating Relationships: Traversing the Transitions," *Communication Quarterly* 60 (2012): 165–189; R. M. Dailey, B. Jin, A. Pfiester, and G. Beck, "On-Again/Off-Again Dating Relationships: What Keeps Partners Coming Back?" *Journal of Social Psychology* 151 (2011): 417–440; R. M. Dailey, A. V. Middleton, and E. W. Green, "Perceived Relational Stability in On-Again/Off-Again Relationships," *Journal of Social & Personal Relationships* 28 (2011): 1–25; Dailey et al., "Relational Maintenance in On-Again/Off-Again Relationships"; Dailey et al., "On-Again/Off-Again Dating Relationships"; Dailey et

al., "A Qualitative Analysis of On-Again/Off-Again Romantic Relationships."

43. R. M. Dailey, A. A. McCracken, B. Jin, K. R. Rossetto, and E. W. Green, "Negotiating Breakups and Renewals: Types of On-Again/Off-Again Dating Relationships," *Western Journal of Communication* 77 (2013): 382–410; S. A. Robbins and A. F. Merrill, "Understanding Posttransgressional Relationship Closeness: The Roles of Perceived Severity, Rumination, and Communication Competence," *Communication Research Reports* 31 (2014): 23–32.
44. P. J. Lannutti and K. A. Cameron, "Beyond the Breakup: Heterosexual and Homosexual Post-Dissolutional Relationships," *Communication Quarterly* 50 (2002): 153–170.
45. K. Koenig Kellas and S. Sato, "'The Worst Part Is, We Don't Even Talk Anymore': Post-Dissolutional Communication in Break Up Stories," in *Making Connections: Readings in Relational Communication* 5e, edited by K. M. Galvin (New York: Oxford University Press, 2011), 297–309; A. N. Lambert and P. C. Hughes, "The Influence of Goodwill, Secure Attachment, and Positively Toned Disengagement Strategy on Reports of Communication Satisfaction in Nonmarital Post-Dissolution Relationships," *Communication Research Reports* 27 (2010): 171–183; J. Koenig Kellas, D. Bean, C. Cunningham, and K. Y. Cheng, "The Ex-Files: Trajectories, Turning Points, and Adjustment in the Development of Post-Dissolutional Relationships," *Journal of Social and Personal Relationships* 25 (2008): 23–50.
46. L. A. Baxter and D. O. Braithwaite, "Relational Dialectics Theory, Applied," in S. W. Smith and S. R. Wilson, Eds., *New Directions in Interpersonal Communication Research*, 48–66; L. A. Baxter and D. O. Braithwaite, "Relational Dialectics Theory: Crafting Meaning from Competing Discourses," in L. A. Baxter and D. O. Braithwaite, Eds., *Engaging Theories in Interpersonal Communication*, 349–361; L. A. Baxter and B. M. Montgomery, *Relating: Dialogues and Dialectics* (New York: Guilford, 1996); L. A. Baxter and B. M. Montgomery, "Rethinking Communication in Personal Relationships from a Dialectical Perspective," in *Communication and Personal Relationships*, edited by K. Dindia and S. Duck (New York: Wiley, 2000), 31–53.
47. For recent research as well as extensions and applications of relational dialectics theory, see C. K. Rudick and K. B. Golsan, "Revisiting the Relational Communication Perspective: Drawing upon Relational Dialectics Theory to Map an Expanded Research Agenda for Communication and Instruction Scholarship," *Western Journal of Communication* 78 (2014): 255–273; R. Amati and A. G. Hannawa, "Relational Dialectics Theory: Disentangling Physician-Perceived Tensions of End-of-Life Communication," *Health Communication* 29 (2014): 962–973; N. O'Boyle, "Front Row Friendships: Relational Dialectics and Identity Negotiations by Mature Students at University," *Communication Education* 63 (2014): 169–191; J. Simmons, R. Lowery-Hart, S. T. Wahl, and M. C. McBride, "Understanding the African-American Student Experience in Higher Education through a Relational Dialectics Perspective," *Communication Education* 62 (2013): 376–394; E. Sahlstein, K. C. Maguire, and L. Timmerman, "Contradictions and Praxis Contextualized by Wartime Deployment: Wives' Perspectives Revealed through Relational Dialectics," *Communication Monographs* 76 (2009): 421–442.
48. E. Sahlstein and T. Dun, "'I Wanted Time to Myself and He Wanted to Be Together All the Time': Constructing Breakups as Managing Autonomy-Connection," *Qualitative Research Reports in Communication* 9 (2008): 37–45.
49. R. L. Duran, L. Kelly, and T. Rotaru, "Mobile Phones in Romantic Relationships and the Dialectic of Autonomy Versus Connection," *Communication Quarterly* 59 (2011): 19–36.
50. C. Prentice, "Relational Dialectics among In-Laws," *Journal of Family Communication* 9 (2009): 67–89.
51. T. A. Coffelt, "Is Sexual Communication Challenging between Mothers and Daughters?" *Journal of Family Communication* 10 (2010): 116–130; P. W. Toller and D. O. Braithwaite, "Grieving Together and Apart: Bereaved Parents' Contradictions of Marital Interaction," *Journal of Applied Communication Research* 37 (2009): 257–277; Sahlstein and Maguire, "Contradictions and Praxis Conceptualized by Wartime Deployment"; A. F. Hermann, "How Did We Get This Far Apart? Disengagement, Relational Dialectics, and Narrative Control," *Qualitative Inquiry* 13 (2007): 989–1007.
52. W. A. Donohue and D. A. Cai, "Interpersonal Conflict: An Overview," in *Managing Interpersonal Conflict: Advances through Meta-Analysis*, edited by N. A. Burrell, M. Allen, B. M. Gayle, and R. W. Preiss (New York: Routledge, 2014), 22–41; S. Ting-Toomey and J. G. Oetzel, "Introduction to Interpersonal Conflict," in *The SAGE Handbook of Conflict Communication: Integrating Theory, Research, and Practice* 2e, edited by J. G. Oetzel and S. Ting-Toomey (Thousand Oaks, CA: Sage, 2013), 99–104.
53. M. Deutsch, "Cooperation and Competition," in *The Handbook of Conflict Resolution: Theory and Practice*, edited by M. Deutsch, P. T. Coleman, and E. C. Marcus (New York: Jossey-Bass, 2006), 23–42.
54. Deutsch, "Cooperation and Competition."
55. W. W. Wilmot and J. L. Hocker, *Interpersonal Conflict* 9e (New York: McGraw-Hill, 2013).
56. G. R. Miller and M. Steinberg, *Between People: A New Analysis of Interpersonal Communication* (Chicago: Science Research Associates, 1975).
57. M. R. Roloff and K. L. Johnson, "Serial Arguing over the Relational Life Course: Antecedents and Consequences," in *Stability and Change in Relationships* (Cambridge, UK: Cambridge University Press, 2002), 107–128, as cited in M. R. Roloff and R. M. Reznik, "Communication During Serial Arguments," in *Studies in Applied Interpersonal Communication*, edited by M. T. Motley (Thousand Oaks, CA: Sage, 2008), 97; M. R. Roloff, "Conflict and Communication: A Roadmap through the Literature," *Managing Interpersonal Conflict*, 42–58.
58. S. Ting-Toomey and L. Chung, *Understanding Intercultural Communication* 2e (New York: Oxford University Press, 2011); S. Ting-Toomey and J. G. Oetzel, "Introduction to Intercultural/International Conflict," in J. G. Oetzel adn S. Ting-Toomey, Eds., *The SAGE Handbook of Conflict Communication* 2e, 635–638; S. Ting-Toomey and J. G. Oetzel, "Culture-Based Situational Conflict Model: An Update and Expansion," in J. G. Oetzel adn S. Ting-Toomey, Eds., *The SAGE Handbook of Conflict Communication* 2e, 763–790; M. D. Hazen and R. Shi, "Harmony, Conflict, and the Process of Argument in Chinese Societies," in *Intercultural Communication: A Reader* 13e, edited by L. A. Samovar and R. E. Porter (Belmont, CA: Wadsworth/Cengage Learning, 2011), 445–456; S. E. Quasha and F. Tsukada, "International Marriages in Japan: Cultural Conflict and Harmony," *Intercultural Communication*, 126–143; P. R. Kimmel, "Culture and Conflict," *The Handbook of Conflict Resolution*, 625–648; P. Pederson, "Multicultural Conflict Resolution," in M. Deutsch, P. T. Coleman, and E. C. Marcus, Eds., *The Handbook of Conflict Resolution*, 649–670; D. Tjosvold, K. Leung, and D. W. Johnson, "Cooperative and Competitive Conflict in China," *The Handbook of Conflict Resolution*, 671–692.
59. P. T. Coleman, "Intractable Conflict," *The Handbook of Conflict Resolution*, 533–559; C. Waite Miller, "Irresolvable Interpersonal Conflicts: Students' Perceptions of Common Topics, Possible Reasons for Persistence, and Communication Patterns," *Making Connections* 5e, 240–247.
60. N. A. Burrell and J. D. Shields, "An Overview of Interpersonal Conflict Management Issues in Personal, Intimate, and Social Contexts," *Managing Interpersonal Conflict*, 251–254; C. Segrin, A. Hanzal, and T. J. Domschke, "Accuracy and Bias in Newlywed Couples' Perceptions of Conflict Styles and the Association with Marital Satisfaction," *Communication Monographs* 76 (2009): 207–233; J. Benjamin, "Sex + Love: Learn to Fight Right," *Women's Health* (April 2010): 91–93; H. Chen, P. Cohen, S. Kasen, J. G. Johnson, M. Ehrensaft, and K. Gordon, "Predicting Conflict within Romantic Relationships During the Transition to Adulthood," *Personal Relationships* 13 (2006):

411–427; R. Domingue and D. Mollen, "Attachment and Conflict Communication in Adult Romantic Relationships," *Journal of Social and Personal Relationships* 26 (2009): 678–696.

61. P. T. Coleman, "Power and Conflict," *The Handbook of Conflict Resolution*, 120–143.
62. C. R. Berger, "Social Power and Interpersonal Communication," in *Explorations in Interpersonal Communication*, edited by G. R. Miller (Newbury Park, CA: Sage, 1976).
63. R. Miller, *Intimate Relationships* 7e (New York: McGraw-Hill, 2014).
64. M. Schuessler Harper, *Keeping Quiet: Self-Silencing and Its Association with Relational and Individual Functioning among Adolescent Romantic Couples*, unpublished doctoral dissertation, University of Tennessee, Knoxville, 2004; "Unhealthy for Women Not to Speak Up During Marital Spats," *Harvard Women's Health Watch* (January 2008): 6–7; T. Parker-Pope, "Marital Spats, Taken to Heart," *New York Times*, October 7, 2007, nytimes.com.
65. O. Hargie, *Skilled Interpersonal Communication: Research, Theory, and Practice* 5e (London: Routledge, 2010); A. Buchanan, "How to Make the Big Ask," *Women's Health* (March 2010): 104–105; E. Tien, "Just Say What You Want, Dammit!" *O: The Oprah Winfrey Magazine* (September 2008): 245–249.
66. A. S. Rancer and T. A. Avtgis, *Argumentative and Aggressive Communication: Theory, Research, and Application* 2e (Thousand Oaks, CA: Sage, 2014); A. S. Rancer, "Argumentativeness, Verbal Aggressiveness, and Persuasion," in *Perspectives on Persuasion, Social Influence, and Compliance-Gaining*, edited by J. S. Seiter and R. H. Gass (Boston: Allyn & Bacon, 2004), 113–131; D. A. Infante, A. S. Rancer, and D. F. Womack, *Building Communication Theory* 4e (Prospect Heights, IL: Waveland, 2003). For more research on verbal aggression, see P. Schrodt and A. N. Finn, "Students' Perceived Understanding: An Alternative Measure and Its Associations with Perceived Teacher Confirmation, Verbal Aggressiveness, and Credibility," *Communication Education* 60 (2011): 231–254; C. M. Anderson and M. Banerjee, "Aggressive Communication and Conflict in Small Groups," in *Arguments, Aggression, and Conflict*, edited by T. Avtgis and A. S. Rancer (New York: Routledge, 2010), 305–317; C. D. Kennedy-Lightsey and S. A. Myers, "College Students' Use of Behavioral Alteration Techniques as a Function of Aggressive Communication," *Communication Education* 58 (2009): 54–73; M. S. McCloskey, R. Lee, M. E. Berman, K. L. Noblett, and E. F. Coccaro, "The Relationship between Impulsive Verbal Aggression and Intermittent Explosive Disorder," *Aggressive Behavior* 34 (2008): 51–60; J. M. Lang, "Anger Management," *The Chronicle of Higher Education* (October 24, 2008): A39; D. A. Infante and A. S. Rancer, "Argumentativeness and Verbal Aggressiveness: A Review of Recent Theory and Research," *Communication Yearbook* 19 (1996): 319–351; P. Yelsma, "Couples' Affective Orientations and Their Verbal Aggressiveness," *Communication Quarterly* 43 (1995): 100–114.
67. P. Schrodt, P. L. Witt, and J. R. Shimkowski, "A Meta-Analytical Review of the Demand/Withdraw Pattern of Interaction and Its Associations with Individual, Relational, and Communicative Outcomes," *Communication Monographs* 81 (2014): 28–58; Satir, *The New Peoplemaking;* Wilmot and Hocker, *Interpersonal Conflict* 9e.
68. L. L. Putnam and C. E. Wilson, "Communicative Strategies in Organizational Conflicts: Reliability and Validity of a Measurement Scale," in *Communication Yearbook* 6, edited by M. Burgoon (Beverly Hills, CA: Sage, 1982).
69. C-C. Cheng and C. Tardy, "A Cross-Cultural Study of Silence in Marital Conflict," *Media Report Overseas* 6 (2010): 95–105; D. Cloven and M. E. Roloff, "The Chilling Effect of Aggressive Potential on the Expression of Complaints in Intimate Relationships," *Communication Monographs* 60 (1993): 199–219; M. L. Gunlicks-Stoessel, "Romantic Partners' Coping Strategies and Patterns of Cortisol Reactivity and Recovery in Response to Relationship Conflict," *Journal of Social and Clinical Psychology* 28 (2009): 630–649; J. Oduor-Frimpong, "Semiotic Silence: Its Uses as a Conflict Management Strategy in Intimate Relationships," *Semiotica* 167 (2007): 283–308; M. Hojjat, "Sex Differences and Perceptions of Conflict in Romantic Relationships," *Journal of Social and Personal Relationships* 17 (2000): 598–617; D. J. Canary and S. Lakey, *Strategic Conflict* (New York: Routledge, 2012); B. A. Budjac Corvette, *Conflict Management: A Practical Guide to Developing Negotiation Strategies* (New York: Prentice Hall, 2006); Deutsch et al., *The Handbook of Conflict Resolution.*
70. M. A. Gross, L. K. Guerrero, and J. K. Alberts, "Perceptions of Conflict Strategies and Communication Competence in Task-Oriented Dyads," *Journal of Applied Communication Research* 32 (2004): 249–270.
71. Deutsch, "Cooperation and Competition"; R. Fisher, W. Ury, and B. Patton, *Getting to Yes: Negotiating Agreement without Giving In* 2e (New York: Penguin Books, 1991).
72. This information is based on several excellent discussions of conflict management skills. We acknowledge W. R. Cupach, D. J. Canary, and B. H. Spitzberg, *Competence in Interpersonal Conflict* 2e (Long Grove, IL: Waveland, 2009); D. Borisoff and D. A. Victor, *Conflict Management: A Communication Skills Approach* 2e (Boston: Allyn & Bacon, 1999); D. Yankelovich, *The Magic of Dialogue: Transforming Conflict into Cooperation* (New York: Touchstone, 2001); Wilmot and Hocker, *Interpersonal Conflict* 9e; O. Hargie, *Skilled Interpersonal Communication*; O. Hargie, ed., *The Handbook of Communication Skills* 3e (London: Routledge, 2006); O. Hargie, C. Saunders, and D. Dickson, *Social Skills in Interpersonal Communication* 3e (London: Routledge, 1994); W. A. Donohue, with R. Holt, *Managing Interpersonal Conflict* (Newbury Park, CA: Sage, 1992); D. A. Romig and L. J. Romig, *Structured Teamwork© Guide* (Austin, TX: Performance Resources, 1990); S. Deep and L. Sussman, *Smart Moves* (Reading, MA: Addison-Wesley, 1990); Fisher et al., *Getting to Yes* 2e; M. D. Davis, E. L. Eshelman, and M. McKay, *The Relaxation and Stress Reduction Workbook* (Oakland, CA: New Harbinger, 1982); R. Boulton, *People Skills* (New York: Simon & Schuster, 1979).
73. B. M. Gayle and R. W. Preiss, "Language Intensity Plus: A Methodological Approach to Validate Emotions in Conflicts," *Communication Reports* 12 (1999): 43–50; Wilmot and Hocker, *Interpersonal Conflict* 9e.
74. A. S. Ebesu Hubbard, B. Hendrickson, K. S. Fehrenbach, and J. Sur, "Effects of Timing and Sincerity of Apology on Satisfaction and Changes in Negative Feelings During Conflicts," *Western Journal of Communication* 77 (2013): 305–322; Z. Qin and M. Andreychik, "Relational Closeness in Conflict: Effects on Interpersonal Goals, Emotion, and Conflict Styles," *Journal of International Communication* 19 (2013): 107–116; L. K. Guerrero, "Emotion and Communication in Conflict Interaction," in J. G. Oetzel and S. Ting-Toomey, Eds., *The SAGE Handbook of Conflict Communication* 2e, 105–131; E. G. Lindner, "Emotion and Conflict: Why It Is Impossible to Understand How Emotions Affect Conflict and How Conflict Affects Emotions," *The Handbook of Conflict Resolution*, 268–293; C. R. Knee, C. Lonsbary, A. Canevello, and H. Patrick, "Self-Determination and Conflict in Romantic Relationships," *Journal of Personality and Social Psychology* 89 (2005): 997–1009.
75. A. Ellis, *A New Guide to Rational Living* (North Hollywood, CA: Wilshire Books, 1977).
76. L. C. Lederman, "The Impact of Gender on the Self and Self-Talk," in L. P. Arliss and D. J. Borisoff, Eds., *Women and Men Communicating: Challenges and Changes* 2e, 78–89; Ellis, *A New Guide to Rational Living.*
77. Fisher, *Getting to Yes* 2e.

Chapter 9

1. For a comprehensive review of group process research, see G. Randsley de Moura, T. Leader, J. Pelletier, and D. Abrams, "Prospects for Group Processes and Intergroup Relations Research: A Review of 70 Years' Progress," *Group Processes & Intergroup Relations* 11 (2008): 575–596.

2. R. K. Mosvick and R. B. Nelson, *We've Got to Start Meeting Like This!* (Glenview, IL: Scott, Foresman, 1987).
3. Mosvick and Nelson, *We've Got to Start Meeting Like This!*
4. D. C. Strubler and K. M. York, "An Exploratory Study of the Team Characteristics Model Using Organizational Teams," *Small Group Research* 38 (2007): 670–695.
5. K. W. Hawkins and B. P. Fillion, "Perceived Communication Skill Needs for Work Groups," *Communication Research Reports* 16 (1999): 167–174; also see S. Burkhalter, J. Gastil, and T. Kelshaw, "A Conceptual Definition and Theoretical Model of Public Deliberation in Small Face-to-Face Groups," *Communication Theory* 12 (2002): 398–422.
6. S. A. Beebe and J. T. Masterson, *Communicating in Small Groups: Principles and Practices* 11e (Boston: Pearson, 2015).
7. J. S. Mueller, "Why Individuals in Larger Teams Perform Worse," *Organizational Behavior and Human Decision Processes* 117 (2012): 111–124.
8. B. Bell and S. W. J. Kozlowski, "A Typology of Virtual Teams: Implications for Effective Leadership," *Group & Organizational Management* 27 (2002): 14–49; A. Thatcher, "Small Group Decision-Making in Face-to-Face and Computer-Mediated Environments: The Role of Personality," *Behavior & Information Technology* 22 (2003): 203–218; D. R. Lemus, D. R. Seibold, A. J. Flanagin, and M. J. Metzger, "Argument and Decision Making in Computer Mediated Groups," *Journal of Communication* 54 (2004): 302–320; E. V. Hobman, P. Bordia, B. Irmer, and A. Chang, "The Expression of Conflict in Computer-Mediated and Face-to-Face Groups," *Small Group Research* 33 (2002): 439–464; R. Benbunan-Fich, S. R. Hiltz, and M. Turoff, "A Comparative Content Analysis of Face-to-Face vs. Asynchronous Group Decision Making," *Decision Support Systems* 34 (2002): 457–469; D. S. Staples and J. Webster, "Exploring Traditional and Virtual Team Members' 'Best Practices': A Social Cognitive Theory Perspective," *Small Group Research* 38 (2007): 60–97; S. Z. Schiller and M. Mandviwalla, "Virtual Team Research: An Analysis of Theory Use and a Framework for Theory Appropriation," *Small Group Research* 38 (2007): 12–59; J. T. Polzer, C. B. Crisp, S. L. Jarvenpaa, and J. W. Kim, "Extending the Faultline Model to Geographically Dispersed Teams: How Colocated Subgroups Can Impair Group Functioning," *Academy of Management Journal* 4 (2006): 679–692; also see C. Garon and K. Wegryn, *Managing Without Walls: Maximize Success with Virtual, Global and Cross-Cultural Teams* (Lewisville, TX: MC Press, 2006); T. Brake, *Where in the World Is My Team? Making Success of Your Virtual Global Workplace* (San Francisco: Jossey-Bass, 2008); D. Derosa and R. Lepsinger, *Virtual Team Success: A Practical Guide for Working and Leading from a Distance* (San Francisco: Jossey-Bass, 2010).
9. J. M. Wilson, S. G. Straus, and B. McEvily, "All in Due Time: The Development of Trust in Computer-Mediated and Face-to-Face Teams," *Organizational Behavior and Human Decision Processes* 99 (2006): 16–33; also see C. A. Nystrom and V. Asproth, "Virtual Teams—Support for Technical Communication?," *Journal of Organisational Transformation & Social Change* 10 (2013): 64–80; M. del C. Triana, B. L. Kirkman, and M. F. Wagstaff, "Does the Order of Fact-to-Face and Computer-Mediated Communication Matter in Diverse Project Teams? An Investigation of Communication Order Effects on Minority Inclusion and Participation," *Journal of Business Psychology* 27 (2013): 57–70.
10. Wilson et al., "All in Due Time."
11. N. N. Bazarova and Y. C. Yuan, "Expertise Recognition and Influence in Intercultural Groups: Differences between Fact-to-Face and Computer-Mediated Communication," *Journal of Computer-Mediated Communication* 18 (2013): 437–453.
12. C. E. Timmerman and C. R. Scott, "Virtually Working: Communicative and Structural Predictors of Media Use and Key Outcomes in Virtual Work Teams," *Communication Monographs* 73 (2006): 108–136.
13. N. Katz and G. Koenig, "Sports Teams as a Model for Workplace Teams: Lessons and Liabilities," *Academy of Management Executive* 15 (2001): 56–67; L. G. Snyder, "Teaching Teams about Teamwork: Preparation, Practice, and Performance Review," *Business Communication Quarterly* (2009): 74–79.
14. Our discussion of teams and teamwork is from Beebe and Masterson, *Communicating in Small Groups;* for an excellent review of teamwork theoretical models, see V. Rousseau, C. Aube, and A. Savoie, "Teamwork Behaviors: A Review and an Integration of Frameworks," *Small Group Research* 27 (2006): 540–570.
15. T. D. Fletcher and D. A. Major, "The Effects of Communication Modality on Performance and Self-Ratings of Teamwork Components," *Journal of Computer Mediated Communication* 11 (2006): 557–576.
16. A. G. Sheard and A. P. Kakabadse, "From Loose Groups to Effective Teams: The Nine Key Factors of the Team Landscape," *Journal of Management Development* 21 (2002): 133–151; also see R. A. Meyers and D. R. Seibold, "Making Foundational Assumptions Transparent: Framing the Discussion About Group Communication and Influence," *Human Communication Research* 35 (2009): 286–295.
17. See F. C. Broadbeck and T. Breitermeyer, "Effects of Individual versus Mixed Individual and Group Experience in Rule Induction on Group Member Learning and Group Performance," *Journal of Experimental Social Psychology* 36 (2002): 621–648.
18. S. B. Shimanoff, *Communication Rules: Theory and Research* (Beverly Hills, CA: Sage, 1980).
19. M. Hoegl, "Goal Setting and Team Performance in Innovative Projects: On the Moderating Role of Teamwork Quality," *Small Group Research* 34 (2003): 3–19; A. W. Woolley, M. E. Gerbasi, C. F. Chabris, S. M. Kosslyn, and J. R. Hackman, "Bringing in the Experts: How Team Composition and Collaborative Planning Jointly Shape Analytic Effectiveness," *Small Group Research* 39 (2008): 352–371; H. Van Mierlo and A. Kleingeld, "Goals, Strategies, and Group Performance: Some Limits of Goal Setting in Groups," *Small Group Research* 41 (2010): 524–555.
20. R. Rico, M. Sanchez-Manzanares, F. Gil, and C. Gibson, "Team Impact Coordination Processes: A Team Knowledge-Based Approach," *Academy of Management Review* 33 (2008): 163–184.
21. Beebe and Masterson, *Communicating in Small Groups.*
22. For a comprehensive discussion of bona fide groups, see L. L. Putnam, "Rethinking the Nature of Groups: A Bona Fide Group Perspective," in *Small Group Communication Theory and Practice: An Anthology,* edited by R. Y. Hirokawa, R. S. Cathcart, L. A. Samovar, and L. D. Hennman (Los Angeles: Roxbury, 2003).
23. M. Priesemuth, A. Arnuad, and M. Schminke, "Bad Behavior in Groups: The Impact of Overall Justice Climate and Functional Dependence on Counterproductive Work Behavior in Work Units," *Group & Organization Management* 38 (2013): 230–257.
24. C. Savelsbergh, J. M. P. Gevers, B. I. J. M. van der Heijden, and R. F. Poell, "Team Role Stress: Relationships with Team Learning and Performance in Project Teams," *Group & Organization Management* 37 (2012): 67–100.
25. K. D. Benne and P. Sheats, "Functional Roles of Group Members," *Journal of Social Issues* 4 (1948): 41–49; for a good review of role development in groups, see A. P. Hare, "Types of Roles in Small Groups: A Bit of History and a Current Perspective," *Small Group Research* 28 (1994): 433–438; A. J. Salazar, "An Analysis of the Development and Evolution of Roles in the Small Group," *Small Group Research* 27 (1996): 475–503.
26. T. Halfhill, E. Sundstrom, J. Lahner, W. Calderone, and T. M. Nielsen, "Group Personality Composition and Group Effectiveness: An Integrative Review of Empirical Research," *Small Group Research* 36 (2005): 83–105.
27. G. M. Wittenbaum, H. C. Shulman, and M. E. Braz, "Social Ostracism in Task Groups: The Effects of Group Composition," *Small Group Research* 41 (2010): 330–353.
28. R. F. Bales, *Interaction Process Analysis* (Chicago: University of Chicago Press, 1976).
29. Shimanoff, *Communication Rules.*

30. M. E. Scott, "'Communicate through the Roof': A Case Study Analysis of the Communicative Rules and Resources of an Effective Global Virtual Team," *Communication Quarterly* 61 (2013): 301–318.
31. For a discussion of monochronic and polychronic time, see E. T. Hall, *The Silent Language* (New York: Doubleday, 1959).
32. M. J. Waller, M. E. Zellmer-Bruhn, and R. C. Giambatista, "Watching the Clock: Group Pacing Behavior under Dynamic Deadlines," *Academy of Management Journal* 45 (2002): 1046–1055.
33. Hall, *The Silent Language*.
34. M. Shaw, *Group Dynamics: The Psychology of Small Group Behavior* (New York: McGraw-Hill, 1981), 281.
35. J. I. Hurwitz, A. F. Zander, and B. Hymovitch, "Some Effects of Power on the Relations among Group Members," in *Group Dynamics: Research and Theory*, edited by D. Cartwright and A. Zander (New York: Harper & Row, 1953), 483–492; D. C. Barnlund and C. Harland, "Propinquity and Prestige as Determinants of Communication Networks," *Sociometry* 26 (1963): 467–479; G. C. Homans, *The Human Group* (New York: Harcourt Brace and World, 1992); H. H. Kelly, "Communication in Experimentally Created Hierarchies," *Human Relations* 4 (1951): 36–56.
36. C. Anderson, J. S. Beer, J. Chatman, S. Srivastava, and S. E. Spataro, "Knowing Your Place: Self-Perceptions of Status in Face-to-Face Groups," *Journal of Personality and Social Psychology* 91 (2006): 1094–1110.
37. M. R. Singer, *Intercultural Communication: A Perceptual Approach* (Englewood Cliffs, NJ: Prentice Hall, 1987), 118.
38. J. R. P. French and B. H. Raven, "The Bases of Social Power," in *Group Dynamics: Research and Theory*, edited by D. Cartwright and A. Zander (New York: Harper & Row, 1953), 607–623.
39. A. V. Carron and L. R. Brawley, "Cohesion: Conceptual and Measurement Issues," *Small Group Research* 43 (2012): 726–743.
40. D. Neumann, "Small Group Cohesion and Frequency of Idiom Use," paper presented at the annual meeting of the National Communication Association, Chicago, November 2004.
41. C. R. Evans and K. L. Dion, "Group Cohesion and Performance: A Meta-Analysis," *Small Group Research* 43 (2012): 690–701; S. M. Gully, D. J. Devine, and D. J. Whitney, "A Meta-Analysis of Cohesion and Performance: Effects of Level of Analysis and Task Interdependence," *Small Group Research* 43 (2012): 702–725.
42. M. R. Barrick, B. H. Bradley, A. L. Kristof-Brown, and A. E. Colbert, "The Moderating Role of Top Management Team Interdependence: Implications for Real Teams and Working Groups," *Academy of Management Journal* 50 (2007): 544–557.
43. Adapted from E. G. Bormann and N. C. Bormann, *Effective Small Group Communication* (Minneapolis: Burgess, 1980), 70–72.
44. S. Wheelan, B. Davidson, and F. Tilin, "Group Development across Time: Reality or Illusion?" *Small Group Research* 34 (2003): 223–245; S. Furst, M. Reeves, B. Rosen, and R. S. Blackburn, "Managing the Life Cycle of Virtual Teams," *Academy of Management Executive* 18 (2004): 6–22; P. A. Hare, "Theories of Group Development and Categories for Interaction Analysis," *Small Group Research* 41 (2010): 106–140.
45. B. A. Fisher, "Decision Emergence: Phases in Group Decision Making," *Speech Monographs* 37 (1970): 60.
46. For a discussion of primary tension and group phases, see E. Bormann, *Discussion and Group Methods* (New York: Harper & Row, 1975).
47. P. J. Boyle, D. Hanlon, and J. E. Russo, "The Value of Task Conflict to Group Decisions," *Journal of Behavioral Decision Making* 25 (2012): 217–227; F. R. C. de Wit, K. A. Jehn, and D. Scheepers, "Task Conflict, Information Processing, and Decision-Making: The Damaging Effect of Relationship Conflict," *Organizational Behavior and Human Decision Processes* 122 (2013): 177–189.
48. For an examination of the practical role of conflict in jury deliberations, see M. S. Poole and M. Dobosh, "Exploring Conflict Management Processes in Jury Deliberations through Interaction Analysis," *Small Group Research* 41 (2010): 408–426.
49. M. A. Von Glinow, D. Shapiro, and J. Brett, "Can We Talk, and Should We? Managing Emotional Conflict in Multicultural Teams," *Academy of Management Review* 29 (2004): 578–592.
50. M. Janssens and J. M. Brett, "Cultural Intelligence in Global Teams: A Fusion Model of Collaboration," *Group & Organization Management* 31 (2006): 124–153.
51. G. Hofstede, *Culture's Consequences: International Differences in Work Related Values* (Beverly Hills, CA: Sage, 1980); G. Hofstede, *Cultures and Organizations: Software of the Mind* (London: McGraw-Hill, 1991).
52. Adapted from J. Mole, *Mind Your Manners: Managing Business Cultures in Europe* (New York: Nicholas Brealey, 1995).
53. S. A. Wheelan and T. Williams, "Mapping Dynamic Interaction Patterns in Work Groups," *Small Group Research* 34 (2003): 433–467; Wheelan et al., "Group Development across Time."
54. M. S. Poole, "Decision Development in Small Groups: A Multiple Sequence Model of Group Decision Development," *Communication Monographs* 50 (1983): 321–341; also see C. Pavitt and K. Kline Johnson, "Scheidel and Crowell Revisited: A Descriptive Study of Group Proposal Sequencing," *Communication Monographs* 69 (2002): 19–32.

Chapter 10

1. See N. R. F. Maier, "Assets and Liabilities in Group Problem Solving: The Need for an Integrative Function," *Psychological Review* 74 (1967): 239–249; M. Argyle, *Cooperation: The Basis of Sociability* (London: Routledge, 1991); H. A. M. Wilke and R. W. Meertens, *Group Performance* (London: Routledge, 1994).
2. Maier, "Assets and Liabilities in Group Problem Solving"; Argyle, *Cooperation*; Wilke and Meertens, *Group Performance*.
3. D. F. Crown, "The Use of Group and Groupcentric Individual Goals for Culturally Heterogeneous and Homogeneous Task Groups: An Assessment of European Work Teams," *Small Group Research* 38 (2007): 489–508.
4. C. E. Larson and F. M. J. LaFasto, *Teamwork: What Must Go Right/What Can Go Wrong* (Beverly Hills, CA: Sage, 1989); also see D. D. Chrislip and C. E. Larson, *Collaborative Leadership* (San Francisco: Jossey-Bass, 1994); D. A. Romig, *Breakthrough Teamwork: Outstanding Results Using Structured Teamwork* (Chicago: Irwin, 1996); M. A. Marks, J. E. Mathieu, and S. J. Zaccaro, "A Temporally Based Framework and Taxonomy of Team Processes," *Academy of Management Review* 26 (2001): 356–376; N. Katz, "Sports Teams as a Model for Workplace Teams: Lessons and Liabilities," *Academy of Management Executive* 15 (2001): 56–67.
5. Larson and LaFasto, *Teamwork*; Chrislip and Larson, *Collaborative Leadership*; Romig, *Breakthrough Teamwork*; Y. Gong, T.-Y. Kim, D.-R. Lee, and J. Zhu, "A Multilevel Model of Team Goal Orientation, Information Exchange, and Creativity," *Academy of Management Journal* 56 (2013): 827–851; A. N. Pieterse, D. van Knippenberg, and D. van Knippenberg, "Cultural Diversity and Team Performance: The Role of Team Member Goal Orientation," *Academy of Management Journal* 56 (2013): 782–804.
6. L. A. DeChurch and C. D. Haas, "Examining Team Planning through an Episodic Lens: Effects of Deliberate, Contingency, and Reactive Planning on Team Effectiveness," *Small Group Research* 39 (2008): 542–568.
7. Larson and LaFasto, *Teamwork*.
8. C. M. J. H. Savelsbergh, B. I. J. M. van der Heijden, and R. F. Poell, "The Development and Empirical Validation of a Multidimensional Measurement Instrument for Team Learning Behaviors," *Small Group Research* 40 (2009): 578–607.
9. J. R. Mesmer-Magnus, L. A. DeChurch, M. Jimenez-Rodriguez, and J. Wildman. "A Meta-Analytic Investigation of Virtuality and Information Sharing in Teams." *Organizational Behavior and Human Decision Processes* 115 (2011): 214–225.
10. T. Reimer, A. Reimer, and V. B. Hinsz, "Naive Groups Can Solve the Hidden-Profile Problem," *Human Communication Research* 36 (2010): 443–467.

11. For a review of research about the importance of sharing information to reach a high-quality decision or solution, see J. A. Bonito, M. H. DeCamp, and E. K. Ruppel, "The Process of Information Sharing in Small Groups: Application of a Local Model," *Communication Monographs* 75 (2008): 136–157; W. P. van Ginkel and D. van Knippenberg, "Group Information Elaboration and Group Decision Making: The Role of Shared Task Representations," *Organizational Behavior and Human Decision Processes* 105 (2008): 82–97; T. Reimer, S. Kuendig, U. Hoffrage, E. Park, and V. Hinsz, "Effects of Information Environment on Group Discussions and Decisions in the Hidden-Profile Paradigm," *Communication Monographs* 74 (2007): 1–28; W. P. van Ginkel and D. van Knippenberg, "Knowledge about the Distribution of Information and Group Decision Making: When and Why Does It Work?" *Organizational Behavior and Human Decision Processes* 108 (2009): 218–229.
12. O. S. Chernyshenko, A. G. Miner, M. R. Baumann, and J. A. Sniezek, "The Impact of Information Distribution, Ownership, and Discussion on Group Member Judgment: The Differential Cue Weighting Model," *Organizational Behavior and Human Decision Processes* 91 (2003): 12–25.
13. D. D. Henningsen and M. L. M. Henningsen, "Do Groups Know What They Don't Know? Dealing with Missing Information in Decision-Making Groups," *Communication Research* 34 (2007): 507–525.
14. D. R. Seibold and R. A. Meyers, "Group Argument: A Structuration Perspective and Research Program," *Small Group Research* 38 (2007): 312–336.
15. S. Y. Sung and J. N. Choi, "Effects of Team Knowledge Management on the Creativity and Financial Performance of Organizational Teams," *Organizational Behavior and Human Decision Processes* 118 (2012): 4–13.
16. M. Orlirtzky and R. Y. Hirokawa, "To Err Is Human, to Correct for It Divine: A Meta-Analysis of Research Testing the Functional Theory of Group Decision-Making Effectiveness." *Small Group Research* 32.3 (2001): 313–341.
17. Orlitzky and Hirokawa, "To Err Is Human, to Correct for It Divine"; B. L. Smith, "Interpersonal Behaviors That Damage the Productivity of Creative Problem Solving Groups," *Journal of Creative Behavior* 27 (1993): 171–187.
18. H. Ding and X. Ding, "Project Management, Critical Praxis, and Process-Oriented Approach to Teamwork," *Business Communication Quarterly* 71 (2008): 456–471.
19. A. B. Henley and K. H. Price, "Want a Better Team? Foster a Climate of Fairness," *Academy of Management Executive* 16 (2002): 153–155.
20. J. L. Thompson, "Building Collective Communication Competence in Interdisciplinary Research Teams," *Journal of Applied Communication Research* 37 (2009): 278–297.
21. P. K. Kim, C. D. Cooper, K. T. Dirks, and D. L. Ferrin, "Repairing Trust with Individuals versus Groups," *Organizational Behavior and Human Decision Processes* 120 (2013): 1–14.
22. A. T. Pescosolido, "Group Efficacy over Time on Group Performance and Development," *Small Group Research* 34 (2003): 20–43.
23. J. S. Prichard and M. J. Ashleigh, "The Effects of Team-Skills Training on Transactive Memory and Performance," *Small Group Research* 38 (2007): 696–726; T. L. Rapp and J. E. Mathieu, "Evaluating an Individually Self-Administered Generic Teamwork Skills Training Program across Time and Levels," *Small Group Communication* 38 (2007): 532–555.
24. S. A. Beebe and J. T. Masterson, *Communicating in Small Groups: Principles and Practices* 11e (Boston: Pearson, 2015); A. B. VanGundy, *Techniques of Structured Problem Solving* 2e. (New York: Van Nostrand Reinhold, 1988).
25. J. K. Brilhart and L. M. Jochem, "Effects of Different Patterns on Outcomes of Problem-Solving Discussion," *Journal of Applied Psychology* 48 (1964): 174–179; W. E. Jurma, "Effects of Leader Structuring Style and Task Orientation Characteristics of Group Members," *Communication Monographs* 49 (1979): 282–295; S. Jarboe, "A Comparison of Input-Output, Process-Output, and Input-Process-Output Models of Small Group Problem-Solving Effectiveness," *Communication Monographs* 55 (1988): 121–142; VanGundy, *Techniques of Structured Problem Solving*.
26. D. M. Berg, "A Descriptive Analysis of the Distribution and Duration of Themes Discussed by Task-Oriented Small Groups," *Speech Monographs* 34 (1967): 172–175; E. G. Bormann and N. C. Bormann, *Effective Small Group Communication* 2e (Minneapolis: Burgess, 1976), 132; M. S. Poole, "Decision Development in Small Groups III: A Multiple Sequence Model of Group Decision Development," *Communication Monographs* 50 (1983): 321–341.
27. For an excellent summary of the literature documenting these problems, see Sunwolf and D. R. Seibold, "The Impact of Formal Procedures on Group Processes, Members, and Task Outcomes," in *The Handbook of Group Communication Theory and Research*, edited by L. Frey (Thousand Oaks, CA: Sage, 1999), 395–431.
28. J. Dewey, *How We Think* (Boston: D.C. Heath, 1910).
29. This explanation of the journalists' six questions method is based on a discussion by J. E. Eitington, *The Winning Trainer* (Houston: Gulf Publishing, 1989), 157.
30. Based on the research of K. Lewin, "Frontiers in Group Dynamics," *Human Relations* 1 (1947): 5–42.
31. M. C. Schilpzand, D. M. Herold, and C. E. Shalley, "Members' Openness to Experience and Teams' Creative Performance," *Small Group Research* 42 (2011): 55–76; S. J. Shin, T.-Y. Kim, J.-Y. Lee, and L. Bian, "Cognitive Team Diversity and Individual Team Member Creativity: A Cross-Level Interaction," *Academy of Management Journal* 55 (2012): 197–212.
32. M. Gladwell, *Blink: The Power of Thinking without Thinking* (New York: Little, Brown, 2005).
33. See S. Taggar, "Individual Creativity and Group Ability to Utilize Individual Creative Resources: A Multilevel Model," *Academy of Management Journal* 45 (2002): 315–330; C. E. Johnson and M. A. Hackman, *Creative Communication: Principles and Applications* (Prospect Heights, IL: Waveland, 1995).
34. A. F. Osborn, *Applied Imagination* (New York: Scribner's, 1962).
35. A. L. Delberg, A. H. Van de Ven, and D. H. Gustason, *Group Techniques for Program Planning: A Guide to Nominal Group and Delphi Processes* (Glenview, IL: Scott, Foresman, 1975), 7–16.
36. D. Straker, *Rapid Problem Solving with Post-it Notes* (Tucson: Fisher Books, 1997).
37. Adapted from Beebe and Masterson, *Communicating in Small Groups*.
38. M. A. Roberto, "Strategic Decision-Making Processes: Beyond the Efficiency-Consensus Trade-Off," *Group & Organizational Management* 29 (2004): 625–658.
39. J. S. Rijnbout and B. M. McKimmie, "Deviance in Organizational Group Decision-Making: The Role of Information Processing, Confidence, and Elaboration," *Group Processes & Intergroup Relations* 15 (2012): 813–828.
40. R. Y. Hirokawa, D. S. Gouran, and A. Martz, "Understanding the Sources of Faulty Group Decision Making: A Lesson from the *Challenger* Disaster," *Small Group Behavior* 19 (1988): 411–433.
41. R. K. M. Haurwitz, "Faculty Doubted Bonfire's Stability," *Austin American-Statesman* (December 10, 1999): A1, A2.
42. D. Jehl, "Panel Unanimous: 'Groupthink' Backed Prewar Assumptions, Report Concludes," *New York Times* (July 10, 2004), 1; also see *The 9/11 Commission Report: Final Report of the National Commission on Terrorist Attacks upon the United States* (Washington, DC: National Commission on Terrorist Attacks, 2004).
43. J. F. Veiga, "The Frequency of Self-Limiting Behavior in Groups: A Measure and an Explanation," *Human Relationships* 44 (1991): 877–895.
44. I. L. Janis, *Victims of Groupthink* (Boston: Houghton Mifflin, 1973).
45. R. Y. Hirokawa and D. R. Scheerhorn, "Communication and Faulty Group Decision-Making," in *Communication and Group*

Decision-Making, edited by R. Y. Hirokawa, S. Poole, and M. S. Poole (Beverly Hills, CA: Sage, 1996), 63–80.

46. C. M. Mason and M. R. Griffin, "Group Task Satisfaction: The Group's Attitude to Its Task and Work Environment," *Group & Organizational Management* 30 (2005): 625–652.
47. M. S. Limon and B. H. La France, "Communication Traits and Leadership Emergence: Examining the Impact of Argumentativeness, Communication Apprehension, and Verbal Aggressiveness in Work Groups," *Southern Communication Journal* 70 (2005): 123–133; also see A. M. L. Raes, U. Glunk, M. G. Heijltjes, and R. A. Roe, "Top Management Team and Middle Managers: Making Sense of Leadership," *Small Group Research* 38 (2007): 360–386.
48. See B. M. Bass, *Stodgill's Handbook of Leadership* (New York: Free Press, 1981).
49. A. Srivastava, K. M. Bartol, and E. A. Locke, "Empowering Leadership in Management Teams: Effects of Knowledge Sharing, Efficacy, and Performance," *Academy of Management Journal* 49 (2006): 1239–1251.
50. G. J. Calanes, "In Their Own Words: An Exploratory Study of Bona Fide Group Leaders," *Small Group Research* 34 (2003): 741–770.
51. P. Balkundi and D. Harrison, "Ties, Leaders, and Time in Teams: Strong Inference about Network Structure's Effects on Team Viability and Performance," *Academy of Management Journal* 49 (2006): 49–68.
52. R. White and R. Lippitt, "Leader Behavior and Member Reaction in Three Social Climates," in *Group Dynamics* 3e, edited by D. Cartwright and A. Zander (New York: Harper & Row, 1968), 319.
53. M. Van Vugt, S. F. Jepson, C. M. Hart, and D. De Cremer, "Autocratic Leadership in Social Dilemmas: A Threat to Group Stability," *Journal of Experimental and Social Psychology* 40 (2004): 1–13.
54. S. Halverson, S. E. Murphy, and R. E. Riggio, "Charismatic Leadership in Crisis Situations: A Laboratory Investigation of Stress and Crisis," *Small Group Research* 35 (2004): 495–514.
55. D. S. DeRue, C. M. Barnes, and F. P. Morgeson, "Understanding the Motivational Contingencies of Team Leadership," *Small Group Research* 41 (2010): 621–651.
56. S. S. K. Lam, X. P. Chen, and J. Schaubroeck, "Participative Decision Making and Employee Performance in Different Cultures: The Moderating Effects of Allocentrism/Idiocentrism and Efficacy," *Academy of Management Journal* 45 (2002): 905–914.
57. D. C. Korten, "Situational Determinants of Leadership Structure," *Journal of Conflict Resolution* 6 (1962): 222–235.
58. P. Hersey, K. Blanchard, and D. Johnson, *Management of Organizational Behavior: Utilizing Human Resources* 9e (Englewood Cliffs, NJ: Prentice–Hall, 2007).
59. See K. W. Phillips, G. B. Northcraft, and M. A. Neale, "Surface-Level Diversity Collide: The Effects on Dissenting Group Members," *Organizational Behavior and Human Decision Processes* 9 (2006): 143–160; J. R. Larson, "Deep Diversity and Strong Synergy: Modeling the Impact of Variability in Members' Problem-Solving Strategies on Group Problem-Solving Performance," *Small Group Research* 3 (2007): 413–436.
60. R. Rodriguez, "Challenging Demographic Reductionism: A Pilot Study Investigating Diversity in Group Composition," *Small Group Research* 26 (1998): 744–759.
61. Phillips et al., "Surface-Level Diversity Collide."
62. For an excellent discussion of transformational leadership applied to teams, see S. D. Dionne, F. J. Yammarino, L. E. Atwater, and W. D. Spangler, "Transformational Leadership and Team Performance," *Journal of Organizational Change Management* 17 (2004): 177–193.
63. R. F. Fiedler, *A Theory of Leadership Effectiveness* (New York: McGraw-Hill, 1967), 144.
64. B. M. Bass and M. J. Avolio, "Transformational Leadership and Organizational Culture," *International Journal of Public Administration* 17 (1994): 541–554; also see F. J. Yammarino and A. J. Dubinsky, "Transformational Leadership Theory: Using Levels of Analysis to Determine Boundary Conditions," *Personnel Psychology* 47 (1994): 787–809.
65. For additional research about the efficacy of transformational leadership, see J. McCann, P. Langford, and R. M. Rawlings, "Testing Behling and McFillen's Syncretical Model of Charismatic Transformational Leadership," *Group & Organization Management* 31 (2006): 237–263; R. F. Piccolo and J. Colquitt, "Transformational Leadership and Job Behaviors: The Mediating Role of Core Job Characteristics," *Academy of Management Journal* 49 (2006): 327–340; R. S. Rubin, D. C. Muniz, and W. H. Bommer, "Leading from Within: The Effects of Emotion Recognition and Personality on Transformational Leadership Behavior," *Academy of Management Journal* 48 (2005): 845–858; A. Ergeneli, R. Gohar, and Z. Temirbekova, "Transformational Leadership: Its Relationship to Culture Value Dimensions," *International Journal of Intercultural Relations* 31 (2007): 703–724; B. J. Hoffman, B. H. Bynum, R. F. Piccolo, and A. W. Sutton, "Person-Organization Value Congruence: How Transformational Leaders Influence Work Group Effectiveness," *Academy of Management Journal* 54 (2011): 779–796; J.-W. Huang, "The Effects of Transformational Leadership on the Distinct Aspects Development of Social Identity," *Group Processes & Intergroup Relations* 16 (2013): 87–104; P. Wang, J. C. Rode, K. Shi, Z. Luo, and W. Chen, "A Workgroup Climate Perspective on the Relationships Among Transformational Leadership, Workgroup Diversity, and Employee Creativity," *Group & Organizational Management* 38 (2013): 334–360; P. Wang, J. C. Rode, K. Shi, Z. Luo, and W. Chen, "A Workgroup Climate Perspective on the Relationships Among Transformational Leadership, Workgroup Diversity, and Employee Creativity," *Group & Organizational Management* 38 (2013): 334–360.
66. P. M. Senge, "The Leader's New Role: Building Learning Organizations," *Sloan Management Review* 32 (1990).
67. D. I. Jung and J. J. Sosik, "Transformational Leadership in Work Groups: The Role of Empowerment, Cohesiveness, and Collective Efficacy on Perceived Group Performance," *Small Group Research* 33 (2002): 313–336; also see T. Dvir, D. Eden, B. J. Avolio, and B. Shamir, "Impact of Transformational Leadership on Follower Development and Performance: A Field Experiment," *Academy of Management Journal* 45 (2002): 735–744; C. L. Hoyt and J. Blascovich, "Transformational and Transactional Leadership in Virtual and Physical Environments," *Small Group Research* 34 (2003): 678–715; S. S. Kahai, R. Huang, and R. J. Jestice, "Interaction Effect of Leadership and Communication Media on Feedback Positivity in Virtual Teams," *Group & Organizational Management* 37 (2012): 716–751.
68. V. U. Druskar and J. V. Wheeler, "Managing from the Boundary: The Effective Leadership of Self-Managing Work Teams," *Academy of Management Journal* 46 (2003): 435–457.
69. M. Zellmer-Bruhn and C. Gibson, "Multinational Organization Context: Implications for Team Learning and Performance," *Academy of Management Journal* 49 (2006): 501–518.
70. J. A. Raelin, "Don't Bother Putting Leadership into People," *Academy of Management Executive* 18 (2004): 131–135; M. W. McCall, "Leadership Development through Experience," *Academy of Management Executive* 18 (2004): 127–130; J. Conger, "Developing Leadership Capability: What's Inside the Black Box?" *Academy of Management Executive* 18 (2004): 136–139; D. Vera and M. Crossan, "Strategic Leadership and Organizational Learning," *Academy of Management Review* 29 (2004): 222–239.
71. D. Barry, *Dave Barry Turns 50* (New York: Ballantine, 1998), 182.
72. T. A. O'Neill and N. J. Allen, "Team Meeting Attitudes: Conceptualization and Investigation of a New Construct," *Small Group Research* 43 (2012): 186–210.
73. S. Kauffeld and N. Lehmann-Willenbrock, "Meetings Matter: Effects of Team Meetings on Team and Organizational Success," *Small Group Research* 43 (2012): 130–158; S. Boerner, M. Schaffner, and D. Gebert, "The Complementarity of Team Meetings

and Cross-Functional Communication: Empirical Evidence from New Services Development Teams," *Journal of Leadership & Organizational Studies* 19 (2012): 256–266.

74. R. K. Mosvick and R. B. Nelson, *We've Got to Start Meeting Like This!* (Glenview, IL: Scott, Foresman, 1987).
75. Suggestions about organizing meeting agendas are based on M. Doyle and D. Straus, *How to Make Meetings Work* (New York: Playboy Press, 1976); Mosvick and Nelson, *We've Got to Start Meeting Like This!*; G. Lumsden and D. Lumsden, *Communicating in Groups and Teams: Sharing Leadership* (Belmont, CA: Wadsworth, 1993); D. B. Curtis, J. J. Floyd, and J. L. Winsor, *Business and Professional Communication* (New York: HarperCollins, 1992); Romig, *Breakthrough Teamwork*; T. A. Kayser, *Mining Group Gold* (El Segundo, CA: Serif, 1990); J. E. Tropman and G. Clark Morningstar, *Meetings: How to Make Them Work for You* (New York: Van Nostrand Reinhold, 1985), 56; Beebe and Masterson, *Communicating in Small Groups*.
76. J. E. Tropman, *Making Meetings Work* (Thousand Oaks, CA: Sage, 1996).
77. J. R. Mesmer-Magnus, L. A. DeChurch, M. Jimenez-Rodriguez, and J. Wildman, "A Meta-Analytic Investigation of Virtuality and Information Sharing in Teams," *Organizational Behavior and Human Decision Processes* 115 (2011): 214–225.
78. J. B. Walther and U. Bunz, "The Rules of Virtual Groups: Trust, Liking, and Performance in Computer-Mediated Communication," *Journal of Communication* (December 2005): 828–846.
79. Several suggestions adapted from *Leading Virtual Teams* (Boston: Harvard Business Press, 2010).
80. *Leading Virtual Teams.*
81. D. S. Staples and J. Webster, "Exploring Traditional and Virtual Team Members' 'Best Practices': A Social Cognitive Theory Perspective," *Small Group Research* 38 (2007): 60–97.
82. See J. A. Bonito, "A Longitudinal Social Relations Analysis of Participation in Small Groups," *Human Communication Research* 32 (2006): 302–321; M. W. Kramer, P. J. Benoit, M. A. Dixon, and J. Benoit-Bryan, "Group Processes in a Teaching Renewal Retreat: Communication Function and Dialectal Tensions," *Southern Communication Journal* 72 (2007): 145–168; J. A. Bonito, M. H. DeCamp, and E. K. Ruppel, "The Process of Information Sharing in Small Groups: Application of a Local Model," *Communication Monographs* 75 (2008): 136–157.
83. See D. S. Gouran, "Variables Related to Consensus in Group Discussions of Questions of Policy," *Speech Monographs* 36 (1969): 385–391; T. J. Knutsun, "An Experimental Study of the Effects of Orientation Behavior on Small Group Consensus," *Speech Monographs* 39 (1972): 159–165; A. Kline, "Orientation and Group Consensus," *Central States Speech Journal* 23 (1972): 44–47.
84. J. Wildman and W. L. Bedwell, "Practicing What We Preach: Teaching Teams Using Validated Team Science," *Small Group Research* 44 (2013): 381–394.
85. S. A. Beebe and J. K. Barge, "Evaluating Group Discussion," in *Small Group Communication: Theory & Practice*, edited by R. Y. Hirokawa, R. S. Cathcart, L. A. Samovar, and L. D. Henman (Los Angeles: Roxbury, 2003).

Chapter 11

1. G. Bodie, "A Racing Heart, Rattling Knees, and Ruminative Thoughts: Defining, Explaining, and Treating Public Speaking Anxiety," *Communication Education* 59 (2010): 70–105.
2. M. Beatty, J. McCroskey, and A. D. Heisel, "Communication Apprehension as Temperamental Expression: A Communibiological Paradigm," *Communication Monographs* 65 (1998): 197–219. D. Infante, A. Rancer, and T. Avtgis, *Contemporary Communication Theory* (Dubuque, IA: Kendall Hunt, 2010) 178.
3. S. Booth-Butterfield, "Instructional Interventions for Reducing Situational Anxiety and Avoidance," *Communication Education* 37 (1988): 214–223.
4. K. Dwyer and M. Davidson, "Is Public Speaking Really More Feared Than Death?" *Communication Research Reports* 29 (April-June 2012): 99–107; survey conducted by R. H. Bruskin and Associates, *Spectra* 9 (December 1973): 4.
5. S. Campbell and J. Larson, "Public Speaking Anxiety: Comparing Face-to-Face and Web-Based Speeches," *Journal of Instructional Pedagogies* 10 (April 2013): 1–12.
6. The sample speech referenced in this chapter is adapted from L. Albarran, "Poverty and the Brain," prepared for Individual Events/Informative Speaking competition, The University of Texas, Spring 2014.
7. A. Goberman, S. Hughes, and T. Haydock, "Acoustic Characteristics of Public Speaking: Anxiety and Practice Effects," *Speech Communication* 53 (2011): 875; K. Savitsky and T. Gilovich, "The Illusion of Transparency and the Alleviation of Speech Anxiety," *Journal of Experimental Social Psychology* 39 (2003): 618–625.
8. K. Dwyer and D. Fus, "Perceptions of Communication Competence, Self-Efficacy, and Trait Communication Apprehension: Is There an Impact on Basic Course Success?" *Communication Research Reports* 19 (2002): 29–37.
9. C. Berger, "Speechlessness: Causal Attributions, Emotional Features, and Social Consequences," *Journal of Language and Social Psychology* 23 (2004): 147–179; M. Booth-Butterfield, "Stifle or Stimulate? The Effects of Communication Task Structure on Apprehensive and Non-Apprehensive Students," *Communication Education* 35 (1986): 337–348.
10. J. Ayres, "Speech Preparation Processes and Speech Apprehension," *Communication Education* 45 (July 1996): 228–235.
11. N. Greengold and E. Grodziak, "Making Smart Use of Smart Phones to Improve Public Speaking," *Journal of Technology Integration in the Classroom* 5 (Spring 2013): 14.
12. P. Addison, E. Clay, S. Xie, C. R. Sawyer, and R. R. Behnke, "Worry as a Function of Public Speaking State Anxiety Type," *Communication Research Reports* 16 (2003): 125–131.
13. A. Brooks, "Get Excited: Reappraising Pre-performance Anxiety as Excitement," *Journal of Experimental Psychology* 143 (June 2014): 1144–1158.
14. S. C. McCullough, S. G. Russell, R. R. Behnke, C. R. Sawyer, and P. L. Witt, "Anticipatory Public Speaking State Anxiety as a Function of Body Sensations and State of Mind," *Communication Quarterly* 54 (2006): 101–109; P. L. Witt, K. C. Brown, J. B. Roberts, J. Weisel, C. R. Sawyer, and R. R. Behnke, "Somatic Anxiety Patterns before, during, and after Giving a Public Speech," *Southern Communication Journal* 71 (2006): 87–100.
15. K. Macklin, "Speak Easier," *Yoga Journal* 245 (March 2012): 28.
16. Addison et al., "Worry as a Function of Public Speaking State Anxiety Type."
17. L. Tracy, "Taming Hostile Audiences," *Vital Speeches of the Day* 71.10 (2005).
18. J. Humphrey, "Taking the Stage: How Women Can Achieve a Leadership Presence," *Vital Speeches of the Day* 67.14 (2001).
19. Data provided by Center for Defense Information, "Chronology of Major Terrorist Attacks against U.S. Targets," *CDI Terrorism Project*, June 27, 2002, www.cdi.org/terrorism/chronology-pr.html; "September 11 Fatalities Make 2001 the Worst Year," *Airwise News*, January 4, 2002, news.airwise.com/stories/2002/01/1010177858.html.
20. Ramin Setoodeh, "My Favorite Mistake" (Interview with Ann Curry), *Newsweek* (June 5, 2011).
21. These criteria for evaluating web resources are adapted from E. Kirk, "Practical Steps in Evaluating Internet Resources," *Johns Hopkins University*, 2010, http://guides.library.hhu.edu. See also M. Tate and J. Alexander, *Web Wisdom: How to Evaluate and Create Information Quality on the Web* (Mahwah, NJ: Lawrence Erlbaum, 1999).
22. G. W. Bush, State of the Union address, January 28, 2008, *Vital Speeches of the Day* 74.3 (March 2008).
23. M. Sanchez, "Diplomatic Immunity Unjustified," in *Winning Orations 1996* (Mankato, MN: Interstate Oratorical Association, 1996), 66.

24. M. Limon and D. Kazoleas, "A Comparison of Exemplar and Statistical Evidence in Reducing Counter-Arguments and Responses to a Message," *Communication Research Reports* 21 (2004): 291–298.
25. D. Lessing, "On Not Winning the Nobel Prize," *Vital Speeches of the Day* 74.2 (2008).
26. J. Davidson, "Managing the Pace with Grace," *Vital Speeches of the Day* 76.6 (2010).
27. S. Horton, "How Hollywood Learned to Stop Worrying and Love the (Ticking) Bomb," *Vital Speeches of the Day* 74.4 (2008).
28. K. Gunderson, "Following Fiscal Footsteps: Can European Tax Trends Work for America?" *Winning Orations 2006* (Mankato, MN: Interstate Oratorical Association, 2006), 28.
29. R. Pausch, "Really Achieving Your Childhood Dreams," lecture given at Carnegie Mellon University, *Randy Pausch's Web Page, Carnegie Mellon University*, September 18, 2007, download.srv.cs.cmu.edu/~pausch/.
30. J. Celoria, "The Counterfeiting of Airline Safety: An Examination of the Dangers of Bogus Airline Parts," *Winning Orations 1997* (Mankato, MN: Interstate Oratorical Association, 1997), 79.
31. J. Sweeney, "Fairness and Economic Equality," *Vital Speeches of the Day* 74.5 (2008).
32. C. Liu, "The Tarahumarans," prepared for Individual Events/Informative Speaking competition, University of Texas, Spring 2011.
33. W. McRaven, commencement address, The University of Texas, 17 May 2014, www.utexas.edu/news/2014/05/16/admiral-mcraven-commencement-speech/.
34. J. Pruitt, "College Credit Card Crisis," *Winning Orations 1996* (Mankato, MN: Interstate Oratorical Association, 1996), 26.
35. R. Brown, "Seven Ways of Looking at a Crisis," *Vital Speeches of the Day* 76.6 (2010).
36. See D. A. Lieberman, *Public Speaking in the Multicultural Environment* 2e (Boston: Allyn & Bacon, 1997).
37. J. T. Masterson and N. Watson, "The Effects of Culture on Preferred Speaking Style," paper presented at the meeting of the Speech Communication Association, November 1979.
38. F. Bara, "Domestic Violence," prepared for Individual Events/Persuasive Speaking competition, The University of Texas, Spring 2014.

Chapter 12

1. J. Pearson, J. Child, and D. Kahl Jr., "Preparation Meeting Opportunity: How Do College Students Prepare for Public Speeches?" *Communication Quarterly* 54 (August 2006): 351–366.
2. P. Steiger, "A Closer Look: Three Golden Ages of Journalism?" *Vital Speeches of the Day* 80.4 (2014): 111–114.
3. D. A. Lieberman, *Public Speaking in the Multicultural Environment* 2e (Boston: Allyn & Bacon, 1997), 23.
4. Lieberman, *Public Speaking in the Multicultural Environment*.
5. K. Aristilde, "Ignorance and Poverty," *Winning Orations 2006* (Mankato, MN: Interstate Oratorical Association, 2006), 33.
6. S. Agha, "The International Landmine Crisis," prepared for the Interstate Oratorical Association competition, Texas State University, Spring 2011.
7. K. Chiu, "Persuasive Speech on Abusing the FBI National Security Letter Program," prepared for Individual Events/Persuasive Speaking competition, University of Texas, Spring 2011.
8. M. Erikson, "See Jane, See Jane's Dilemma," *Winning Orations 1997* (Mankato, MN: Interstate Oratorical Association, 1997), 63.
9. G. Hildebrand, "Cinderella," Texas State University student speech, 2013.
10. S. Hamilton, "Cruise Ship Violence," *Winning Orations 2000* (Mankato, MN: Interstate Oratorical Association, 2000), 95.
11. B. Ruet, "Sudan's Forgotten War," *Winning Orations 2006* (Mankato, MN: Interstate Oratorical Association, 2006), 49.
12. C. O'Brien, Dartmouth College commencement address, June 12, 2011, *Dartmouth College*, www.dartmouth.edu.
13. K. Black, "Healthcare Tsunami: An Aging Population's Cognitive Decline," *Vital Speeches of the Day* 80.5 (2014): 151.
14. C. Reed, "Decreasing Red Meat in Your Diet," speech delivered at Texas State University, 2005.
15. A. Watson, "Post-Traumatic Stress Disorder: Our Soldiers' Next War," *Winning Orations 2007* (Mankato, MN: Interstate Oratorical Association, 2007), 81.
16. Watson, "Post-Traumatic Stress Disorder."
17. A. Lincoln, "Gettysburg Address," delivered at Gettysburg, PA, November 19, 1863, *Douglass Archives of American Public Address*, August 19, 1998, douglass.speech.nwu.edu/linc_b33.htm.
18. D. MacArthur, "Farewell to the Cadets," address delivered at West Point, May 12, 1962, in *Contemporary American Speeches* 7e, edited by R. L. Johannesen, R. R. Allen, and W. A. Linkugel (Dubuque, IA: Kendall/Hunt, 1992), 393.
19. T. Kirchhefer, "The Deprived," *Winning Orations 2000* (Mankato, MN: Interstate Oratorical Association, 2000), 151.
20. S. Brunner, "Advanced Technology: Solving the DUI Dilemma," *Winning Orations 2007* (Mankato, MN: Interstate Oratorical Association, 2007), 78.
21. The preparation outline and speaking notes in this chapter are adapted from a speech by L. Albarran, "Poverty and the Brain," prepared for Individual Events/Informative Speaking competition, The University of Texas, Spring 2014.

Chapter 13

1. P. Heinbert, "Relationship of Content and Delivery to General Effectiveness," *Speech Monographs* 30 (1963): 105–107.
2. A. Mehrabian, *Nonverbal Communication* (Hawthorne, NY: Aldine, 1972).
3. J. Detz, "Delivery plus Content Equals Successful Presentation," *Communication World* 15 (1998): 34.
4. Adapted from R. Ailes, *You Are the Message* (New York: Doubleday, 1989), 37–38.
5. P. Begala, "Flying Solo," PBS, *The Clinton Years: Anecdotes*, 2000, http://www.pbs.org.
6. J. Wareham, "Doing It Off-the-Cuff," *Across the Board* 35 (1998): 49–50.
7. Wareham, "Doing It Off-the-Cuff," 49–50.
8. L. White and L. Messer, "An Analysis of Interstate Speeches: Are They Structurally Different?" *National Forensic Journal* 21.2 (2003): 15.
9. D. Hersman, "I Saw a Woman Today," *Vital Speeches of the Day* 80.5 (2014): 151.
10. G. Orwell, "Politics and the English Language," in *About Language*, edited by W. H. Roberts and G. Turgeson (Boston: Houghton Mifflin, 1986), 282.
11. M. Klepper, *I'd Rather Die Than Give a Speech* (New York: Carol Publishing Group, 1994), 45.
12. W. Safire, "Faithful, Even in Death," *New York Times Magazine* (April 18, 1999): 72–74. Quotes from Vest's speech are from the text reprinted in this article.
13. B. Moyers, "What Adam Said to Eve," prepared remarks for the annual conference of the Association for Education in Journalism and Mass Communication, Washington, DC, *PBS*, August 8, 2007, www.pbs.org.
14. J. F. Kennedy, inaugural address, January 20, 1961, in *Speeches in English*, edited by B. Aly and L. F. Aly (New York: Random House, 1968), 272.
15. B. Obama, "We, the People" (second inaugural address), *Vital Speeches of the Day* 79 (March 2013): 60.
16. C. Christie, "In This Hour of Choice," *Vital Speeches of the Day* 80.3 (2014): 85.
17. J. Biden, remarks commemorating the fiftieth anniversary of Kennedy's "Moon Shot" Speech, delivered at the John F. Kennedy Library and Museum, Boston, MA, *White House*, May 25, 2011, www.whitehouse.gov.
18. N. Giovanni, convocation address at Virginia Tech, *Virginia Tech*, April 17, 2007, www.vt.edu.
19. B. Obama, address to commemorate the 70th anniversary of D-Day, *CNN*, June 6, 2014, www.cnn.com.

20. S. A. Beebe, "Eye Contact: A Nonverbal Determinant of Speaker Credibility," *Speech Teacher* 23 (1974): 21–25; S. A. Beebe, "Effects of Eye Contact, Posture and Vocal Inflection upon Credibility and Comprehension," *Australian Scan Journal of Nonverbal Communication* 7–8 (1979–1980): 57–70; M. Cobin, "Response to Eye Contact," *Quarterly Journal of Speech* 48 (1963): 415–419.
21. Beebe, "Eye Contact."
22. S. Campbell and J. Larson, "Public Speaking Anxiety: Comparing Face-to-Face and Web-Based Speeches," *Journal of Instructional Pedagogies* 10 (April 2013): 4.
23. E. Adler, "Gestures May Give You a Hand with Speaking," *Austin American-Statesman* (November 25, 1998): E6.
24. J. C. McCroskey, V. P. Richmond, A. Sallinen, J. M. Fayer, and R. A. Barraclough, "A Cross-Cultural and Multi-Behavioral Analysis of the Relationship between Nonverbal Immediacy and Teacher Evaluation," *Communication Education* 44 (1995): 281–290.
25. M. J. Beatty, "Some Effects of Posture on Speaker Credibility," library paper, Central Missouri State University, Warrensburg, MO, 1973.
26. R. Schmid, "Study: Posture Able to Communicate Fear," *Yahoo! News*, November 16, 2004, news.yahoo.com.
27. P. Ekman, W. V. Friesen, and S. S. Tomkins, "Facial Affect Scoring Technique: A First Validity Study," *Semiotica* 3 (1971): 37–58.
28. P. Ekman and W. Friesen, *Unmasking the Face* (Englewood Cliffs, NJ: Prentice Hall, 1975).
29. M. M. Gill, "Accents and Stereotypes: Their Effect on Perceptions of Teachers and Lecture Comprehension," *Journal of Applied Communication Research* 22 (1994): 348–361.
30. E. Bohn and D. Jabusch, "The Effect of Four Methods of Instruction on the Use of Visual Aids in Speeches," *Western Journal of Speech Communication* 46 (1982): 253–265.
31. A. Wilson, "In Defense of Rhetoric," *The Toastmaster* 70.2 (2004): 11.
32. American Council on Education, *From Soldier to Student II: Assessing Campus Programs for Veterans and Service Members, July 2012* (Washington, DC: U.S. Government Printing Office, 2013).
33. J. Orlando, "Improve Your PowerPoint Design with One Simple Rule," November 11, 2013, *Faculty Focus*, www.facultyfocus.com/articles/teaching-with-technology-articles/improve-your-powerpoint-design-with-one-simple-rule.
34. Adapted from D. Cavanaugh, *Preparing Visual Aids for Presentation* (Boston: Allyn & Bacon/Longman, 2001).
35. Detz, "Delivery plus Content Equals Successful Presentation."
36. Susan Cain, "10 Public Speaking Tips for Introverts: Introverts Can Seize the Microphone—and Bring the House Down," *Psychology Today*, 25 July 2011, www.psychologytoday.com.
37. T. Smith and A. B. Frymier, "Get 'Real': Does Practicing Speeches before an Audience Improve Performance?" *Communication Quarterly* 54 (2006): 111–125.
38. "Presidential Seal Falls Off Podium as Obama Speaks," *Washington Times*, October 6, 2010, www.washingtontimes.com.
39. J. Masterson, S. Beebe, and N. Watson, *Invitation to Effective Speech Communication* (Glenview, IL: Scott, Foresman, 1989), 4.

Chapter 14

1. J. R. Johnson and N. Szczupakiewicz, "The Public Speaking Course: Is It Preparing Students with Work-Related Public Speaking Skills?" *Communication Education 36* (1987): 131–137.
2. L. Lefever, *The Art of Explanation* (New Jersey: John Wiley & Sons, 2013), 10.
3. For an excellent discussion of teaching someone to perform a skill, especially a social skill, see M. Argyle, *The Psychology of Interpersonal Behavior* (London: Penguin, 1990).
4. G. K. Chesterton, "On Mr. Rudyard Kipling and Making the World Small," *Heretics*, 1905, *Project Gutenberg*, http://www.gutenberg.org/files/470/470-h/470-h.htm#chap03.
5. For an excellent discussion of strategies for informing others, see K. E. Rowan, "A New Pedagogy for Explanatory Public Speaking: Why Arrangement Should Not Substitute for Invention," *Communication Education 44* (1995): 236–250.
6. J. Chesebro, "Effects of Teacher Clarity and Nonverbal Immediacy on Student Learning, Receiver Apprehension, and Affect," *Communication Education* 52 (Apr. 2003): 135–147.
7. This suggestion is based on an excellent review of the literature found in Rowan, "A New Pedagogy for Explanatory Public Speaking."
8. M. Groover, "Learning to Communicate: The Importance of Speech Education in Public Schools," *in Winning Orations 1984* (Mankato, MN: Interstate Oratorical Association, 1984), 7.
9. See, for example, L. Rehling, "Teaching in a High-Tech Conference Room: Academic Adaptations and Workplace Simulations," *Journal of Business and Technical Communication* 19 (2005): 98–113; M. Patterson et al., "Effects of Communication Aids and Strategies on Cooperative Teaching," *Journal of Educational Psychology* 84 (1992): 453–461.
10. M. Klepper and R. Gunther, *I'd Rather Die Than Give a Speech* (New York: Carol Publishing Group, 1995).
11. Our discussion of using humor is adapted from Klepper and Gunther, *I'd Rather Die Than Give a Speech.*
12. J. Meyer, "Humor as a Double-Edged Sword: Four Functions of Humor in Communication," *Communication Theory* 10 (2000): 311.
13. Klepper and Gunther, *I'd Rather Die Than Give a Speech.*
14. John Macks, *How to Be Funny* (New York: Simon & Schuster, 2003).
15. S. Beebe, T. Mottet, and K.D. Roach, *Training and Development: Communicating for Success* (Boston: Pearson, 2013); M. Knowles, *The Adult Learner: A Neglected Species* 3e (Houston: Gulf Publishing, 1990).
16. Angelitta Armijo, "Elvis," Texas State University student speech, 2013.

Chapter 15

1. S. McLaughlin, "The Dirty Truth about Your Kitchen: Using Common Sense to Prevent Food Poisoning," in *Winning Orations 1996* (Mankato, MN: Interstate Oratorical Association, 1996), 73.
2. A. Maslow, "A Theory of Human Motivation," in *Motivation and Personality* (New York: Harper & Row, 1954), Chapter 5.
3. See K. L. Higbee, "Fifteen Years of Fear Arousal: Research on Threat Appeals, 1953–1968," *Psychological Bulletin 72* (1969): 426–444; I. L. Janis and S. Feshback, "Effects of Fear Arousing Communications," *Journal of Abnormal and Social Psychology 48* (1953): 78–92; P. A. Mongeau, "Another Look at Fear-Arousing Persuasive Appeals," in *Persuasion: Advances through Meta-Analysis*, edited by M. Allen and R. W. Preiss (Cresskill, NJ: Hampton Press, 1998), 65; F. A. Powell and G. R. Miller, "Social Approval and Disapproval Cues in Anxiety Arousing Situations," *Speech Monographs 34* (1967): 152–159.
4. R. Petty and D. Wegener, "The Elaboration Likelihood Model: Current Status and Controversies," in *Dual Process Theories in Social Psychology*, edited by S. Chaiken and Y. Trope (New York: Guilford, 1999), 41–72; see also R. Petty and J. T. Cacioppo, *Communication and Persuasion: Central and Peripheral Routes to Attitude Change* (New York: Springer-Verlag, 1986).
5. E. McQuarrie and B. Phillips, "Indirect Persuasion in Advertising: How Consumers Process Metaphors Presented in Pictures and Words," *Journal of Advertising* 34.2 (Summer 2005): 7–20.
6. Aristotle, *Rhetoric*, translated by L. Cooper (New York: Appleton-Century-Crofts, 1960).
7. For a discussion of the effects of both verbal and nonverbal messages on the persuasiveness of a speech, see N. Jackob et al., "The Effects of Verbal and Nonverbal Elements in Persuasive Communication: Findings from Two Multi-Method Experiments," *Communications: The European Journal of Communication Research* 36 (2011): 245–271.

8. A. Bogeajis, "The Danger of Child Safety Seats: Why Aren't They Safe?" in *Winning Orations 1996 (Mankato, MN: Interstate Oratorical Association, 1996)*, 10.
9. N. Barton, "The Death of Reading," in *Winning Orations 2004* (Mankato, MN: Interstate Oratorical Association, 2004), 33–35.
10. S. Groom, "Hope for Foster Care," in *Winning Orations 2004*, 60–62.
11. Adapted from L. Ford and S. Smith, "Memorability and Persuasiveness of Organ Donation Message Strategies," *American Behavioral Scientist* 34 (1991): 695.
12. D. Ehninger, B. Gronbeck, R. McKerrow, and A. Monroe, *Principles and Types of Speech Communication* (Glenview, IL: Scott, Foresman, 1986), 15.
13. The illustrations for the steps of the motivated sequence are adapted from S. Agha, "The International Landmine Crisis," prepared for the Interstate Oratorical Association competition, Texas State University, Spring 2011.
14. A. Quagliata, "Move Your Audience to Action: Using YouTube to Teach Persuasion," *Communication Teacher*, 28 (April 2014): 183–187.
15. D. C. Bryant, "Rhetoric: Its Functions and Its Scope," *Quarterly Journal of Speech 39* (1953): 26.
16. B. Sosnowchick, "The Cries of American Ailments," in *Winning Orations 2000* (Mankato, MN: Interstate Oratorical Association, 2000), 114.
17. G. Ficca, et al. "Effects of Different Types of Hand Gestures in Persuasive Speech on Receivers' Evaluations," *Language and Cognitive Processes* 24 (2009): 239–266.
18. K. Slone, "Real Men *AND* Women Wear Pink," *Communication 1310: Student Speeches for Texas State University* (CD). Boston: Pearson Learning, 2010.

Appendix A

1. Examples from *CareerBuilder*, as cited by *Reader's Digest* (May 2008): 34.
2. Our discussion of interview questions is based on J. T. Masterson, S. A. Beebe, and N. Watson, *An Invitation to Effective Speech Communication* (Glenview, IL: Scott, Foresman, 1989). We especially acknowledge the contributions of Norm Watson to this discussion.
3. *CareerBuilder*, accessed March 21, 2008, www.CareerBuilder.com.
4. This resumé and our suggestions for developing a resumé are based on the 2011 *Texas State University Career Services Manual* (San Marcos, TX: Office of Career Services, 2011).
5. These tips and suggestions are adapted from K. Hansen, "Top 10 Things Job-Seekers Need to Know about Submitting and Posting Your Resume Online," *Quintessential Careers*, accessed September 10, 2014, www.quintcareers.com/e-resumes.html. Also see K. Hansen, "Your E-Resume's File Format Aligns with Its Delivery Method," *Quintessential Careers*, accessed March 30, 2011, www.quintcareers.com/e-resume_format.html.
6. "What Everyone Should Know about Electronic Resumes (E-Resumes)," *CareerPerfect*, accessed September 11, 2014, www.careerperfect.com/tips/archives/electronic-e-resumes.
7. J. L. Winsor, D. B. Curtis, and R. D. Stephens, "National Preferences in Business and Communication Education: A Survey Update," *Journal of the Association for Communication Administration* 3 (1997): 174.
8. D. Dean, "How to Get an On-Site Interview," *Black Collegian*, Second Semester Super Issue (2010): 54.
9. *CareerBuilder*, retrieved March 21, 2008, www.CareerBuilder.com. Suggestions for managing your online persona were taken from A. Simmons, "How to Click and Clean," Reader's Digest (April 2008): 154–159.
10. C. Purdy, "The Biggest Lies Job Seekers Tell on Their Resumes—and How They Get Caught," *Monster*, accessed March 31, 2013, career-advice.monster.com/resumes-cover-letters/resume-writing-tips/the-truth-about-resume-lies-hot-jobs/article.aspx.
11. Purdy, "The Biggest Lies Job Seekers Tell on Their Resumes."
12. M. Minto, "The Relative Effects of Content and Vocal Delivery during a Simulated Employment Interview," *Communication Research Reports* 13 (1996): 225–238.
13. Adapted from M. S. Hanna and G. Wilson, *Communicating in Business and Professional Settings* (New York: McGraw-Hill, 1991), 263–265.
14. *Texas State University Career Services Manual.*

Appendix B

1. F. Bara, "The Ekocenter: Water Project or Corporation Cover-up?" prepared for Individual Events/Informative Speaking competition, The University of Texas, Spring 2014.
2. B. Shulman, "The Epidemic of Sexual Assault on College Campuses," prepared for Individual Events/Persuasive Speaking competition, The University of Texas, Spring 2014.

Credits

Chapter 1 Page 1: Michel de Montaigne, "Of Vanity," in *The Essays of Michel de Montaigne*. Translated by Charles Cotton, Edited by William Carew Hazlitt. 1877. http://www.gutenberg.org/files/3600/3600-h/3600-h.htm. Page 3: J. C. Humes, *The Sir Winston Method: The Five Secrets of Speaking the Language of Leadership* (New York: William Morrow, 1991). J. H. McConnell, *Are You Communicating? You Can't Manage without It* (New York: McGraw-Hill, 1995). *Value investors portal.* "Warren Buffet on Communication Skills." YouTube. 6 December 2010. Web. http://www.youtube.com/watch?v=tpgcEYpLzP0 Accessed May 14, 2013. Page 4: V. Satir, *People Making* (Palo Alto, CA: Science and Behavior Books, 1972), 1. Page 5: J. T. Masterson, S. A. Beebe, and N. H. Watson, *Invitation to Effective Speech Communication* (Glenview, IL: Scott, Foresman, 1989). Page 8: O. Wiio, *Wiio's Laws—and Some Others* (Espoo, Finland: Welin-Goos, 1978). Pages 8–9: S. B. Shimanoff, *Communication Rules: Theory and Research* (Beverly Hills, CA: Sage, 1980). 1.2: Page 9: Figure 1.2: © Pearson Education, Inc. Based on C.E. Shannon and W. Weaver, *The Mathematical Theory of Communication.* (Urbana, IL: University of Illinois Press, 1949). Page 11: Figure 1.3: © Pearson Education, Inc. Page 12: Figure 1.4 © Pearson Education, Inc. Page 13: Based on Masterson, Beebe, and Watson, *Invitation to Effective Speech Communication.* Page 14: C. Christians and M. Traber, *Communication Ethics and Universal Values* (Beverly Hills, CA: Sage, 1997). National Communication Association, "NCA Credo for Communication Ethics," 1999 (Accessed June 27, 2001), http://www.natcom.org/conferences/Ethicslethicsconfcred099.htm. Page 16: S. Turkle, *Alone Together: Why We Expect More from Technology and Less from Each Other* (New York: Basic Books, 2011), 1. Page 20: Figure 1.5: © Pearson Education, Inc. Page 22: D. Quinn, *My Ishmael* (New York: Bantam Books, 1996). Robert Fulghum, *All I Really Need to Know I Learned in Kindergarten* (New York: Ballantine Books, 1988). Pages 27–28: Richmond, Virginia P.; McCroskey, James C., *Communication: Apprehension, Avoidance, and Effectiveness* 5th Ed., © 1998. Reprinted and Electronically reproduced by permission of Pearson Education, Inc., Upper Saddle River, New Jersey.

Chapter 2 Page 29: Mabel A. Keenan quoted in Leta W. Clark, ed., *Women Women Women* (1977). Page 30: S. R. Covey, *The Seven Habits of Highly Effective People*, anniversary ed. (New York: Simon & Schuster, 2013), 74. D. W. Johnson, *Reaching Out: Interpersonal Effectiveness and Self-Actualization* 11e (Boston: Pearson, 2012), 51. Figure 2.1: © Pearson Education, Inc. Page 31: S. E. Wood, E. Green Wood, and D. Boyd, *Mastering the World of Psychology* 5e (Boston: Pearson, 2013), 115. Page 32: G. Bukobza, "The Epistemological Basis of Selfhood," *New Ideas in Psychology* 25 (2007): 37–65. Page 33: Phil McGraw, in *Life Strategies* (2002). K. Horney, *Neurosis and Human Growth* (New York: W. W. Norton, 1991), 17. Page 36: G. Steinem, *Revolution from Within: A Book of Self-Esteem* (Boston: Little, Brown, 1993), 26. Page 47: D. T. Kenrick, S. L. Neuberg, and R. B. Cialdini, *Social Psychology: Goals in Interaction* 5e (Boston: Pearson, 2009). Page 45: Figure 2.2: © Pearson Education, Inc. Pages 51–52: M. Rosenberg, *Society and the Adolescent Self-Image* rev. ed. (Middletown, CT: Wesleyan University Press, 1989). Reprinted with permission; retrieved from http:www.bsos.umd.edu.

Chapter 3 Page 53: N. Hawthorne as quoted in Sophia Hawthorne, "Passages from Hawthorne's Note-Books," *Atlantic Monthly* 18(110), Dec 1866 http://www.gutenberg.org/files/17217/17217-8.txt. Page 54: Figure 3.1: © Pearson Education, Inc. Page 58: *Oxford Desk Dictionary and Thesaurus*, American Edition (New York: Oxford University Press, 2007). D. K. Ivy, *GenderSpeak: Personal Effectiveness in Gender Communication* 5e (Boston: Pearson, 2012). Page 66: T. D. Nelson (Ed.), *Ageism: Stereotyping and Prejudice Against Older Persons* (Cambridge: Massachusetts Institute of Technology Press, 2004). Page 67: President George W. Bush, Address to a Joint Session of Congress and the American People, September 11, 2001, speech to Congress.

Chapter 4 Page 74: *Selected writings of Edward Sapir in Language, Culture and Personality* by SAPIR, EDWARD Reproduced with permission of UNIVERSITY OF CALIFORNIA PRESS in the format Republish in a book via Copyright Clearance Center. Page 75: Figure 4.1: © Pearson Education, Inc. Page 85: Table 4.1: © Pearson Education, Inc. Based on Knapp, Hall, and Horgan, *Nonverbal Communication in Human Interaction.* Page 86: D. Shichuran, T. Yong, and A. M. Martinez, "Compound Facial Expressions of Emotion," *Proceedings of the National Academy of Sciences* 111 (2014): 1454–1462. Page 87: John F. Kennedy's Inaugural Address, January 20, 1961. S. J. Baker, "The Theory of Silence," *Journal of General Psychology* 53 (1955): 145–167. Page 88: Figure 4.2: © Pearson Education, Inc. Based on E. T. Hall, *The Hidden Dimension* (Garden City, NY: Anchor, 1990). Page 90: P. A. Andersen, *Nonverbal Communication: Forms and Functions* 2e (Long Grove, IL: Waveland, 2008): 168.

Chapter 5 Page 94: Dr. Joyce Brothers as quoted in *Wisdom for the Soul: Five Millennia of Prescriptions for Spiritual Healing* (2006) by Larry Chang, p. 469. Page 95: Figure 5.1: © Pearson Education, Inc. Page 96: Figure 5.2: © Pearson Education, Inc. Page 97: D. Mount and A. Mattila, "Last Chance to Listen: Listening Behaviors and Their Effect on Call Center Satisfaction," *Journal of Hospitality & Tourism Research* 26.2 (2002): 124–137. Page 103: J. L. Gonzalez-Balado, ed., *Mother Teresa: In My Own Words* (New York: Gramercy Books, 1997). Page 114: A. De Saint-Exupery, as quoted in D. Goleman, *Emotional Intelligence: Why It Can Matter More Than IQ* (New York: Bantam Books, 1995). Page 114: H. J. M. Nouwen, "Listening as Spiritual Hospitality," in *Bread for the Journey* (New York: HarperCollins, 1997). Page 116: List of paraphrasing situations: O. Hargie, C. Sanders, and D. Dickson, *Social Skills in Interpersonal Communication* (London: Routledge, 1994); R. Boulton, *People Skills* (New York: 1981). We also acknowledge others who have presented excellent applications of listening and responding skills in interpersonal and group contexts: D. A. Romig and L. J. Romig, *Structured Teamwork* (D Guide) (Austin, TX: Performance Resources, 1990); S. Deep and L. Sussman, *Smart Moves* (Reading, MA: Addison-Wesley, 1990); P. R. Scholtes, *The Team Handbook* (Madison, WI: Joiner Associates, 1988); Hargie, *The Handbook of Communication Skills.* Table 5.1: © Pearson Education, Inc. Page 117: Table 5.2: © Pearson Education, Inc. Pages 117–118: Anonymous. Page 121: These scales are based on the work of Debra Worthington, Graham D. Bodie, and Christopher Gearhart, "The Listening Styles Profile Revised (LSP-R): A Scale Revision and Validation," paper presented at the Eastern Communication Association, Arlington, VA (April 2011).

Chapter 6 Page 123: C. S. Lewis, from *The Weight of Glory*, 1949. Page 124: Figure 6.1: © Pearson Education, Inc. Page 125: C. Darwin, *On the Origin of Species by Means of Natural Selection, or the Preservation of Favoured Races in the Struggle of Life* (London: John Murray, 1859). Page 127: A. C. Selbe, *Are You from Another Planet or What?* Workshop presented at the Joint Service Family Readiness Matters Conference, Phoenix, AZ (July 1999). Page 129: Table 6.1: Information summarized from N. Howe and W. Strauss, *Millennials Rising: The Next Great Generation* (New York: Vintage Books, 2000). Page 130: N. Howe and W. Strauss, *Millennials Rising: The Next Great Generation* (New York: Vintage Books, 2000). Page 132: Robert Bernstein, press release, Public Information Office, U.S. Census Bureau, http://www.census.gov/Press-Release/www/releases/archives/population/010048.html . Page 133: For an excellent overview of issues in teaching intercultural communication, see T. R. Levine, H. S. Park, and R. K Kim, "Some Conceptual and Theoretical Challenges for Cross-Cultural Communication Research in the 21st Century," *Journal of Intercultural Communication Research* 36.3 (2007): 205–221. Page 134: C. H. Dodd, *Dynamics of Intercultural Communication* (New York: McGraw-Hill, 1998). Page 135: Figure 6.2: © Pearson Education, Inc. Page 136: G. Hofstede and G. J. Hofstede, *Cultures and Organizations: Software of the Mind* 2e (New York: McGraw-Hill, 2005). W. B. Gudykunst, *Bridging Differences: Effective Intergroup Communication* (Newbury Park, CA: Sage, 1998). Page 142: Mark Twain quoted in Albert Bigelow Paine, *Mark Twain, A Biography: The Personal and Literary Life of Samuel Langhorne Clemens*, Volume 3 (Harper & Brothers, 1912). E. Roosevelt, as cited by M.W. Lustig and J. Koester, *Intercultural Competence: Interpersonal Communication across Cultures* (Boston: Allyn & Bacon, 2009), 11. Page 144: Philosopher André Gide quoted in *The Journals of André Gide*, 1889–1949: 1889–1924 (Northwestern University Press, 1987). Page 147: H. J. M. Nouwen, *Bread for the Journey* (New York: HarperCollins, 1997). Page 148 : R. H. Farrell, ed., *Off the Record: The Private Papers of Harry S. Truman* (New York: Harper & Row, 1980), 310.

Chapter 7 Page 154: Ralph Waldo Emerson, *The Conduct of Life* (J. R. Osgood, 1873). Page 155: Figure 7.1: © Pearson Education, Inc. Page 158: A. Cooper, I. P. McLoughlin, and K. M. Campbell, "Sexuality in Cyberspace: Update for the 21st Century," *Cyberpsychology & Behavior* 32 (2000): 521–536. L. K. Guerrero, P. A. Andersen, and W. A. Afifi, *Close Encounters: Communicating in Relationships* 4e (Los Angeles: Sage, 2013), 54. Page 164: J. Holmes, "Complimenting—A Positive Politeness Strategy," in *Language and Gender: A Reader*, edited by J. Coates (Malden, MA: Blackwell, 1998), 100–120. Page 165: J. H. Harvey and A. L. Weber, *Odyssey of the Heart: Close Relationships in the 21st Century* 2e (Mahwah, NJ: Lawrence Erlbaum, 2002), 105–106. Page 167: Figure 7.2: © Pearson Education, Inc. Based on I. Altman and D. Taylor, *Social Penetration: The Development of Relationships* (New York: Holt, Rinehart and Winston, 1973). Page 168: Figure 7.3: © Pearson Education, Inc. Quotation: P. D. Bolls, "Understanding Emotion from a Superordinate Dimensional Perspective: A Productive Way Forward for Communication Processes and Effects Studies," *Communication Monographs* 77 (2010): 146. Page 169: D. Hample, A. S. Richards, and C. Skubisz, "Blurting," *Communication Monographs* 80 (2013): 503-532, p. 503.

Chapter 8 Page 174: Franklin D. Roosevelt, undelivered Address Prepared for Jefferson Day, April 13, 1945. Page 177: *Miami Herald* (July 9, 1982): 12A. Page 182: M. Rabbitt, "Is Infidelity Obsolete?" *Women's Health* (July/August 2010): 144. Page 184: P. J. Lannutti and K. A. Cameron, "Beyond the Breakup: Heterosexual and Homosexual Post-Dissolutional Relationships," *Communication Quarterly* 50 (2002): 153–170. Page 187: W. W. Wilmot and J. L. Hocker, *Interpersonal Conflict* 9e (New York: McGraw-Hill, 2013). G. R. Miller and M. Steinberg, *Between People: A New Analysis of Interpersonal Communication* (Chicago: Science Research Associates, 1975). M. R. Roloff and K. L. Johnson, "Serial Arguing over the Relational Life Course: Antecedents and Consequences," in *Stability and Change in Relationships* (Cambridge, UK: Cambridge University Press, 2002), 107–128, as cited in M. R. Roloff and R. M. Reznik, "Communication during Serial Arguments," in *Studies in Applied Interpersonal Communication*, edited by M. T. Motley (Thousand Oaks, CA: Sage, 2008), 97. Page 190: R. Fisher, W. Ury, and B. Patton, *Getting to Yes: Negotiating Agreement without Giving In* 2e (New York: Penguin Books, 1991).

Chapter 9 Page 198: Andrew Carnegie. Margaret Mead quoted in Frank G. Sommers, Tana Dineen (1984) *Curing Nuclear Madness*. p. 158. Page 204: S. A. Beebe and J. T. Masterson, *Communicating in Small Groups: Principles and Practices* 10e (Boston: Pearson, 2012). Pages 205–207: Table 9.1: © Pearson Education, Inc. Page 212: Table 9.2: Based on E. G. Bormann and N. C. Bormann, *Effective Small Group Communication* (Minneapolis: Burgess, 1980), 70–72. Page 213: Figures 9.1, 9.2, and 9.3: © Pearson Education, Inc. Page 214: Walter Lippmann quoted in Roger Lajoie, *Greatest. Day. Ever.: How to Make Every Day Your Greatest* (Balboa Press, 2014). Page 215: M. A. Von Glinow, D. Shapiro, and J. Brett, "Can We Talk, and Should We? Managing Emotional Conflict in Multicultural Teams," *Academy of Management Review* 29 (2004): 578–592.

Chapter 10 Page 221: Margaret Mead quoted in Frank G. Sommers, Tana Dineen (1984) *Curing Nuclear Madness*. p. 158. Page 227: Table 10.1: © Pearson Education, Inc. Page 228: Figure 10.1: © Pearson Education, Inc. Page 233: Table 10.2: © Pearson Education, Inc. Based on Beebe and Masterson, *Communicating in Small Groups*. Page 234: Based on J. F. Veiga, "The Frequency of Self-Limiting Behavior in Groups: A Measure and an Explanation," *Human Relationships* 44 (1991): 877–895. Pages 238–239: Table 10.3: © Pearson Education, Inc. Based on R. White and R. Lippitt, "Leader Behavior and Member Reaction in Three Social Climates," in *Group Dynamics* 3e, edited by D. Cartwright and A. Zander (New York: Harper & Row, 1968), 319. Page 239: D. C. Korten, "Situational Determinants of Leadership Structure," *Journal of Conflict Resolution* 6 (1962): 222–235. Page 241: Lao Tsu, from the *Tao Te Ching*, 1963:77. D. Barry, *Dave Berry Turns 50* (New York: Ballantine, 1998), 182. Page 242: Table 10.4: © Pearson Education, Inc. Page 244: D. S. Gouran, "Variables Related to Consensus in Group Discussions of Questions of Policy," *Speech Monographs* 36 (1969): 385–391. Pages 248–249: S. A. Beebe and J. K. Barge, "Evaluating Group Discussion," in *Small Group Communication: Theory & Practice*, edited by R. Y. Hirokawa, R. S. Cathcart, L. A. Samovar, and L. D. Henman (Los Angeles: Roxbury, 2003).

Chapter 11 Page 252: Franklin D. Roosevelt: "Campaign Address at Cleveland, Ohio.," November 2, 1940. Online by Gerhard Peters and John T. Woolley, *The American Presidency Project*. http://www.presidency.ucsb.edu/ws/?pid=15893. Page 254: Figure 11.1: © Pearson Education, Inc. Page 256: A. Brooks, "Get Excited: Reappraising Pre-performance Anxiety as Excitement," *Journal of Experimental Psychology* 143 (June 2014): 1144–58. Page 258: Figure 11.2: © Pearson Education, Inc. Page 260: Figure 11.3: © Pearson Education, Inc. Page 261: Table 11.1: © Pearson Education, Inc. Page 263: J. Humphrey, "Taking the Stage: How Women Can Achieve a Leadership Presence," *Vital Speeches of the Day* 67.14 (2001). Page 267: Ramin Setoodeh, "My Favorite Mistake" (Interview with Ann Curry), *Newsweek* (June 5, 2011). Page 268: Table 11.2: These criteria for evaluating web resources are adapted from E. Kirk, "Practical Steps in Evaluating Internet Resources," Johns Hopkins University, 2010, http://guides.library.hhu.edu. Page 269: G. W. Bush, State of the Union address, January 28, 2008, *Vital Speeches of the Day* 74.3 (March 2008). Page 270: M. Sanchez, "Diplomatic Immunity Unjustified," in *Winning Orations 1996* (Mankato, MN: Interstate Oratorical Association, 1996), 66. D. Lessing, "On Not Winning the Nobel Prize," *Vital Speeches of the Day* 74.2 (2008). J. Davidson, "Managing the Pace with Grace," *Vital Speeches of the Day* 76.6 (2010). Page 271: S. Horton, "How Hollywood Learned to Stop Worrying and Love the (Ticking) Bomb," *Vital Speeches of the Day* 74.4 (2008). K. Gunderson, "Following Fiscal Footsteps: Can European Tax Trends Work for America?" *Winning Orations 2006* (Mankato, MN: Interstate Oratorical Association, 2006), 28. R. Pausch, "Really Achieving Your Childhood Dreams," lecture given at Carnegie Mellon University, September 18, 2007, download.srv.cs.cmu.edu/~pausch/. J. Celoria, "The Counterfeiting of Airline Safety: An Examination of the Dangers of Bogus Airline Parts," *Winning Orations 1997* (Mankato, MN: Interstate Oratorical Association, 1997), 79. Page 272: J. Sweeney, "Fairness and Economic Equality," *Vital Speeches of the Day* 74.5 (2008). C. Liu, "The Tarahumarans," prepared for Individual Events/Informative Speaking competition, University of Texas, Spring 2011. W. McRaven, commencement address, The University of Texas, 17 May 2014. www.utexas.edu/news/2014/05/16/admiral-mcraven-commencement-speech/. J. Pruitt, "College Credit Card Crisis," *Winning Orations 1996* (Mankato, MN: Interstate Oratorical Association, 1996), 26. Page 273: R. Brown, "Seven Ways of Looking at a Crisis," *Vital Speeches of the Day* 76.6 (2010). Page 274: F. Bara, "Domestic Violence," prepared for Individual Events/Persuasive Speaking competition, The University of Texas, Spring 2014. Pages 277–278: J. McCroskey, "Measures of Communication-Bound Anxiety," *Speech Monographs* 37 (1970): 269–77.

Chapter 12 Page 279: Florynce R. Kennedy (b. 1916), U.S. lawyer, civil rights activist. "The Verbal Karate of Florynce R. Kennedy, Esq." Quoted by Gloria Steinem, in *Ms* (New York, March 1973). Page 284: K. Aristilde, "Ignorance and Poverty," *Winning Orations 2006* (Mankato, MN: 2006), 33. Page 284: S. Agha, "The International Landmine Crisis," prepared for the Interstate Oratorical Association competition, Texas State University, Spring 2011. Page 285: K. Chiu, "Persuasive Speech on Abusing the FBI National Security Letter Program," prepared for Individual Events/Persuasive Speaking competition, University of Texas, Spring 2011. M. Erikson, "See Jane, See Jane's Dilemma," *Winning Orations 1997* (Mankato, MN: Interstate Oratorical Association, 1997), 63. Page 286: G. Hildebrand, "Cinderella," Texas State University student speech, 2013. S. Hamilton, "Cruise Ship Violence," *Winning Orations 2000* (Mankato, MN: Interstate Oratorical Association, 2000), 95. Page 287: B. Ruet, "Sudan's Forgotten War," *Winning Orations 2006* (Mankato, MN: Interstate Oratorical Association, 2006), 49. C. O'Brien, Dartmouth College commencement address, June 12, 2011, www.dartmouth.edu. K. Black, "Healthcare Tsunami: An Aging Population's Cognitive Decline, *Vital Speeches of the Day* 80.5 (2014): 151. Page 288: C. Reed, "Decreasing Red Meat in Your Diet," speech delivered at Texas State University, 2005. A. Lincoln, "Gettysburg Address," delivered at Gettysburg, PA, November 19, 1863, *Douglass Archives of American Public Address*, August 19, 1998, douglass.speech.nwu.edu/linc_b33.htm. D. MacArthur, "Farewell to the Cadets," address delivered at West Point, May 12, 1962, in *Contemporary American Speeches* 7e, edited by R. L. Johannesen, R. R. Allen, and W. A. Linkugel (Dubuque, IA: Kendall/Hunt, 1992), 393. A. Watson, "Post-Traumatic Stress Disorder: Our Soldiers' Next War," *Winning Orations 2007* (Mankato, MN: Interstate Oratorical Association, 2007), 81. Page 289: S. Brunner, "Advanced Technology: Solving the DUI Dilemma," *Winning Orations 2007* (Mankato, MN: Interstate Oratorical Association, 2007), 78. T. Kirchhefer, "The Deprived," *Winning Orations 2000* (Mankato, MN: Interstate Oratorical Association, 2000), 151. Page 294: Figure 12.2 © Pearson Education, Inc.

Chapter 13 Page 298: Walt Whitman (1819–1892), U.S. poet. "Calamus: A Song of Joys," *Leaves of Grass* (1855). Page 299: J. Detz, "Delivery plus Content Equals Successful Presentation," *Communication World* 15 (1998): 34. Page 300: Table 13.1: Based on R. Ailes, *You Are the Message* (New York: Doubleday, 1989), 37–38. Page 301: Table 13.2: © Pearson Education, Inc. Quotation: P. Begala, "Flying Solo," PBS, *The Clinton Years: Anecdotes*, 2000, http://www.pbs.org. Table 13.3: © Pearson Education, Inc. Includes information from J. Wareham, "Doing It Off-the-Cuff," *Across the Board* 35 (1998): 49–50. Page 302: Table 13.4: © Pearson Education, Inc. Quotation: L. White and L. Messer, "An Analysis of Interstate Speeches: Are They Structurally Different?" *National Forensic Journal* 21.2 (2003): 15. Page 303: Quotation: D. Hersman, "I Saw a Woman Today," *Vital Speeches of the Day* 80.5 (2014): 151. Figure 3.1: © Pearson Education, Inc. Quotation: G. Orwell, "Politics and the English Language," in *About Language*, edited by W. H. Roberts and G. Turgeson (Boston: Houghton Mifflin, 1986), 282. Page 304: M. Klepper, *I'd Rather Die Than Give a Speech* (New York: Carol Publishing Group, 1994), 45. B. Moyers, "What Adam Said to Eve," prepared remarks for the annual conference of the Association for Education in Journalism and Mass Communication, Washington, DC, August 8, 2007, www.pbs.org. J. F. Kennedy, inaugural address, January 20, 1961, in *Speeches in English*, edited by B. Aly and L. F. Aly (New York: Random House, 1968), 272. B. Obama, "We, the People" (second inaugural address), *Vital Speeches of the Day* 79 (March 2013): 60. C. Christie, "In This Hour of Choice," *Vital Speeches of the Day* 80.3 (2014): 85. Page 305: J. Biden, remarks commemorating the fiftieth anniversary of Kennedy's "Moon Shot" Speech, delivered at the John F. Kennedy Library and Museum, Boston, MA, May 25, 2011, www.whitehouse.gov. N. Giovanni, convocation address at Virginia Tech, April 17, 2007, www.vt.edu. B. Obama, address to commemorate the 70th anniversary of D-Day, June 6, 2014, www.cnn.com. Page 312: A. Wilson, "In Defense of Rhetoric," *The Toastmaster* 70.2 (2004): 11. Page 313: Figures 13.2 and 13.3: © Pearson Education, Inc. Based on data from American Council on Education, *Soldier to Student II: Assessing Campus Programs for Veterans and Service Members*, July 2012 (Washington, DC: U.S. Government Printing Office, 2013). Page 315: Figure 13.4: © Pearson Education, Inc. Quotation: J. Orlando, "Improve Your PowerPoint Design with One Simple Rule," *Faculty Focus* (11 November 2013), www.facultyfocus.com/articles/teaching-with-technology-articles/improve-your-powerpoint-design-with-one-simple-rule/. List of tips: Based on D. Cavanaugh, *Preparing Visual Aids for Presentation* (Boston: Allyn & Bacon/Longman, 2001). Page 316: J. Detz, "Delivery plus Content Equals Successful Presentation," *Communication World* 15 (1998): 34. Page 317: Susan Cain, "10 Public Speaking Tips for Introverts: Introverts Can Seize the Microphone—and Bring the House Down," *Psychology Today* (25 July 2011), www.psychologytoday.com. Page 319: "Presidential Seal Falls Off Podium as Obama Speaks," *The Washington Times* (October 6, 2010), www.washingtontimes.com.

Chapter 14 Page 324: P. B. de La Bruère, *Twenty-First Report of the Dairymen's Association of the Province of Quebec* (Quebec: Printed by Charles Pageau), 1903. Page 325: L. Lefever, *The Art of Explanation* (New Jersey: John Wiley & Sons, 2013), 10. Page 326: Figure 14.1: © Pearson Education, Inc. Based on information from M. Argyle, *The Psychology of Interpersonal Behavior* (London: Penguin, 1990). Page 328: G. K. Chesterton, "On Mr. Rudyard Kipling and Making the World Small," *Heretics*, 1905, Project Gutenberg, http://www.gutenberg.org/files/470/470-h/470-h.htm#chap03. Page 330: Table 14.1: © Pearson Education, Inc. Page 334: M. Groover, "Learning to Communicate: The Importance of Speech Education in Public Schools," in *Winning Orations 1984* (Mankato, MN: Interstate Oratorical Association, 1984), 7. M. Klepper and R. Gunther, *I'd Rather Die than Give a Speech* (New York: Carol Publishing Group, 1995). J. Meyer, "Humor as a Double-Edged Sword: Four Functions of Humor in Communication," *Communication Theory* 10 (2000): 311. Pages 334–335: M. Klepper and R. Gunther, *I'd Rather Die than Give a Speech* (New York: Carol Publishing Group, 1995). Pages 338-339: Angelitta Armijo, "Elvis," Texas State University student speech, 2013.

Chapter 15 Page 343: Joseph Conrad, *A Personal Record*, 1912. Page 345: S. McLaughlin, "The Dirty Truth About Your Kitchen: Using Common Sense to Prevent Food Poisoning," in *Winning Orations 1996* (Mankato, MN: Interstate Oratorical Association, 1996), 73. Page 347: Figure 15.2: © Pearson Education, Inc. Created based on information from K. L. Higbee, "Fifteen Years of Fear Arousal: Research on Threat Appeals, 1953–1968," *Psychological Bulletin* 72 (1969): 426–444; I. L. Janis and S. Feshback, "Effects of Fear Arousing Communications," *Journal of Abnormal and Social Psychology* 48 (1953): 78–92; P. A. Mongeau, "Another Look at Fear-Arousing Persuasive Appeals," in *Persuasion: Advances Through MetaAnalysis*, edited by M. Allen and R. W. Preiss (Cresskill, NJ: Hampton Press, 1998), 65; F. A. Powell and G. R. Miller, "Social Approval and Disapproval Cues in Anxiety Arousing Situations," *Speech Monographs* 34 (1967): 152–159. Page 348: E. McQuarrie and B. Phillips, "Indirect Persuasion in Advertising: How Consumers Process Metaphors Presented in Pictures and Words," *Journal of Advertising* 34.2 (Summer 2005): 7–20. Page 349: Figures 15.3 and 15.4: © Pearson Education, Inc. Page 350: Figure 15.5: © Pearson Education, Inc. Quotation: Aristotle, *Rhetoric*, translated by L. Cooper (New York: Appleton-Century-Crofts, 1960). Page 352: Figure 15.6: © Pearson Education, Inc. Page 356: A. Bogeajis, "The Danger of Child Safety Seats: Why Aren't They Safe?" in *Winning Orations 1996* (Mankato, MN: Interstate Oratorical Association, 1996), 10. Pages 356-357: N. Barton, "The Death of Reading," in *Winning Orations 2004* (Mankato, MN: Interstate Oratorical Association, 2004), 33–35. Page 357: Based on L. Ford and S. Smith, "Memorability and Persuasiveness of Organ Donation Message Strategies," *American Behavioral Scientist* 34 (1991): 695. S. Groom, "Hope for Foster Care," in *Winning Orations 2004*, 60–62. Pages 358-359: S. Agha, "The International

Landmine Crisis," prepared for the Interstate Oratorical Association competition, Texas State University, Spring 2011. Page 359: Figure 15.7: © Pearson Education, Inc. Page 360: Table 15.1: © Pearson Education, Inc. Page 361: B. Sosnowchick, "The Cries of American Ailments," in *Winning Orations 2000* (Mankato, MN: Interstate Oratorical Association, 2000), 114. Pages 364–365: Based on K. Slone, "Real Men AND Women Wear Pink," Communication 1310: *Student Speeches for Texas State University* (CD). Pearson Learning, 2010.

Appendix A Page 372: Examples from *CareerBuilder*, as cited by *Reader's Digest* (May 2008): 34. Page 376: Figures A.1 and A.2: © Pearson Education, Inc. Page 378: Woody Allen, as quoted in William Safire, "On Language; The Elision Fields", *The New York Times*, August 13, 1989. Page 382: D. Dean, "How to Get an On-Site Interview," *Black Collegian*, Second Semester Super Issue (2010): 54. Page 382: www.CareerBuilder.com >, retrieved March 21, 2008. Suggestions for managing your online persona were taken from A. Simmons, "How to Click and Clean," *Reader's Digest* (April 2008): 154–159. Page 383: C. Purdy, "The Biggest Lies Job Seekers Tell on Their Resumes—and How They Get Caught," *Monster* http://career-advice.monster.com/resumes-cover-letters/resume-writing-tips/the-truth-about-resume-lies-hot-jobs/article.aspx. Accessed March 31, 2013. Page 384: Zig-Ziglar quoted in Jennifer Beckham, *Get Over Yourself!* (Destiny Image Publishers, 2011). Page 385: Table A.1: Based on M. S. Hanna and G. Wilson, *Communicating in Business and Professional Settings* (New York: McGraw-Hill, 1991), 263–265.

Appendix B Page 393–395: F. Bara, "The Ekocenter: Water Project or Corporation Cover-up?" prepared for Individual Events/Informative Speaking competition, The University of Texas, Spring 2014. Page 395–397: B. Shulman, "The Epidemic of Sexual Assault on College Campuses," prepared for Individual Events/Persuasive Speaking competition, The University of Texas, Spring 2014.

Index

D

Q

R

S

T

U

V

W